EILEEN HACKMAN

WITHDRAWN

#14691955

Developmental/Adapted Physical Education

Making Ability Count

SECOND EDITION

Carl B. Eichstaedt
ILLINOIS STATE UNIVERSITY
NORMAL, ILLINOIS

Leonard H. Kalakian
MANKATO STATE UNIVERSITY
MANKATO, MINNESOTA

MACMILLAN PUBLISHING COMPANY
New York
COLLIER MACMILLAN PUBLISHERS
London

Development editor: Anne E. Heller
Assistant development editor: Charlene J. Brown
Copy editor: Betsey I. Rhame
Production editor: Jean R. Starr
Cover design: Terry Dugan
Cover photographs: Taken by Leonard H. Kalakian at Camp Courage, a service of Courage Center, Golden Valley, MN.

Macmillan Publishing Company
866 Third Avenue, New York, New York 10022
Collier Macmillan Canada, Inc.

Library of Congress Cataloging in Publication Data

Eichstaedt, Carl B.
    Developmental/adapted physical education.

    Kalakian's name appears first on the earlier ed.
    Includes bibliographies and index.
    1. Physical education for handicapped children—
United States.   2. Mainstreaming in education—United
States.   I. Kalakian, Leonard H.   II. Title.
GV445.K34   1987   371.9′044   86-28449
ISBN 0-02-331710-8

Printing: 1 2 3 4 5 6 7 8 Year: 7 8 9 0 1 2 3 4 5

ISBN 0-02-331710-8

Contents

iii

Skip

Skip

Preface

We intend *DEVELOPMENTAL/ADAPTED PHYSICAL EDUCATION: MAKING ABILITY COUNT* to serve not only as the title of this book but also as its underlying statement of philosophy. This Second Edition was undertaken to provide a reliable and updated source of detailed information regarding the ever-expanding area of adapted physical education. Since 1980, extensive changes have occurred in methodology and teaching techniques used for individuals with handicapping conditions. These changes have evolved from both empirical and experimental research.

All human beings climb a universal developmental ladder. The climb up this ladder is characterized by an orderly, sequential achievement of developmental milestones. The universality of human development is founded in the fact that relative ability or disability does *not* have a material impact on the sequence of developmental achievements. Relative ability or disability can, however, materially affect both the rate of developmental achievement and the potential for ultimate achievement.

Knowledge of human motor development as a basis for understanding developmental delays is incumbent on the physical educator. When circumstances impede one's climb up the developmental ladder, the educator must seek approaches to education that accommodate the learner's unique developmental needs. The curriculum thus becomes adapted. The goal of adapting curriculum is to minimize and, if possible, eliminate the gap between developmental status and developmental potential.

Throughout this text, the guiding principle is that adaptations are made only to the extent necessary to accommodate the learner's unique developmental needs. Too often, the learner with a disability who requires special attention is perceived in a negative context of what *cannot* be done. The negative context then breeds negative expectations, and challenges set before the learner are based on *no* expectations. In a negative context, the learner is perceived more as a disabled person than as a person first who *happens* to have a disability. In contrast, the idea of "making ability count" places the person *before* the disability and shifts the emphasis to what the learner *can* do. This approach accentuates the positive.

In the physical domain, we are convinced that all students, handicapped and non-handicapped, should be taught using the developmental approach. We also believe that these methods are the foundation of all good physical education curricula. In revising the text, we assumed that for the great majority of undergraduate and graduate physical education majors and minors, basic concepts of teaching developmental physical education have already been learned. It would be inappropriate, therefore, to repeat in this text the extensive developmental process of how to catch and throw a ball. We do review many basic skills in brief, but we acknowledge that other physical education and motor learning textbooks are written for this specific purpose.

We receive questions continually from physical education teachers, special education teachers, and elementary classroom teachers on *how* certain activities should be taught and *which* activities should be taught to students with disabilities. Additionally, other questions include: What can I do to help, and what is contraindicated for these youngsters? What is acceptable and what is dangerous? What are the limitations?

Today's physical educator must be able to teach all children, including those with impairments. In addition, the educator must know how to perform valid and reliable assessment, how to select appropriate programming, how to make proper placement, and how to use various teaching methods and evaluation procedures. The Second Edition attempts to meet these needs.

A wide gap presently exists between the medical profession and many public school physical education programs. Too often, physicians do not believe that physical educators are able to administer appropriate programs of a developmental or rehabilitative nature. The physical educator of today must be able to converse intelligently with physicians about the special fitness and motor needs of youngsters with handicapping conditions.

To address this issue, all chapters in the Second Edition have been expanded or revised. We have contacted national and state organizations that deal with different handicapping conditions to ensure that we have included the latest terminology, the most recent research, new trends in rehabilitation, and exemplary teaching methods.

Special mention should be made regarding the chapters on allergy and asthma, diabetes, and obesity and overweight. In the past, individuals with these conditions did not fit easily into traditional physical education classes, nor were they readily assignable to adapted physical education sections because they usually were not considered legally handicapped. Students with these conditions generally have not been offered *appropriate* programs. One hypothesis as to why weak programs occur is that physical education instructors have not been given adequate explanations and programming information to address the special needs of individuals with such common conditions as asthma, diabetes, and obesity. We have therefore developed an entirely new chapter on obesity and overweight. We believe that the Second Edition identifies and presents graphically the state of the art in these areas.

The multidisciplinary team approach is continually emphasized, and we include methods of incorporating special educators, physicians, administrators, therapists, and parents into a smoothly functioning unit. The physical educator must be able to use the vocabulary of the other professionals on the team. Without a thorough background in and understanding of handicapping conditions, the educator risks being excluded (overtly or covertly) from this all-important multidisciplinary group. In an attempt to bridge this gap, we have added a new and comprehensive glossary to provide quick reference to important words and terms.

Finally, adapted physical education instructors must never lose sight of the overall role that they play in the total development of each child who comes under their guidance. The emotional, social, and cognitive benefits that accrue from positive experiences in an exciting physical education program should never be underestimated. No youngster should ever be excluded from participation in physical education for any reason! The Second Edition of *DEVELOPMENTAL/ADAPTED PHYSICAL EDUCATION: MAKING ABILITY COUNT* was written with these basic tenets continually in mind.

This edition could not have been written without the new insight gained from my (CBE) association with the residents, administrators, and teachers at Lincoln Developmental Center, Lincoln, Illinois. I am indebted to the many retarded children and adults with whom I was privileged to consult and whom I tried to assist through a variety of motor and physical education programs. The in-depth information gained from working closely with individual retarded persons cannot be replaced by research or reading. The unique flexibility and adaptiveness of such individuals, as well as the frustrating problems they present, can be fully appreciated only from intense, hands-on personal experiences. I remember especially Louise, Jane, Bobby, Joe, and Patty Anne.

I also am indebted to the many teachers of these very special people who did not allow me to pigeonhole the severe, profound, and multihandicapped, but made me reach out to each individual. These teachers and leaders who shared with me their hopes, frustrations, ideas, and experiences have given me a new perspective on life and teaching. Quite often, the individual who is involved most intimately with a particular handicapped child knows more about that person and understands the individual better than any "professional" does.

Special recognition is given to one youngster as he embarks on his road in life. His birth announcement reads: "Jeffery Daniel Jones was born at 5:41 p.m. on November 26, 1984. Shortly after his birth he developed complications which left him a very sick baby. The serious nature of the problems indicate that Jeff will require special care for his entire life. We are nervous and excited about the prospect of providing the love and care necessary for his life to be as full as it possibly can be."

We wish to acknowledge gratefully the detailed comments, suggestions, and criticisms given by reviewers of this manuscript. Special thanks go to Lew Sarff, Garth Tymeson, Barry Lavay, and Julian Stein for their particularly outstanding contributions. Dr. Stein has, through persistency, finally removed "normal" from my (CBE) vocabulary.

Finally, I (CBE) acknowledge especially the primary forces behind my desire to create something very special—my wife Donna, my daughters Annie and Susie, and my grandsons Gabe and Cory. To them I dedicate this book.

CHAPTER 1

But First I Have Some Questions, Professor

This chapter focuses on questions that physical education students often ask as they start their adapted physical education experience. When confronted by a new and challenging situation, we need to know where that situation may ultimately lead.

We are more inclined to ask questions when a new situation seems relatively removed from previous experiences. Often, a new situation brings us in contact with persons whose life and educational needs differ from the norm. Particular concern arises when physical educators become responsible for developing and implementing programs for persons with special needs.

Let us consider some important initial questions. As concerns arise, questions should be encouraged, for there is far less risk in asking a question than in allowing a possibly harmful situation to develop as the result of an unasked question.

Who Are the Handicapped?

They include, among others, those who are mentally retarded, orthopedically handicapped, deaf or hard of hearing, blind or partially sighted, and speech impaired. **Handicap** is, however, a relative term. Some mentally handicapped persons are trained to assemble complex electronic components. Max Clelend, a triple amputee, is physically active and earned acclaim as chief administrator for veteran's affairs during the Carter administration. A respected stunt woman in the international film and television industry is totally deaf. Country music entertainer Mel Tillis stutters. Each of these people is in some way handicapped, yet in other important ways each is not at all handicapped.

You are very probably handicapped in some fashion. Indeed, given the broad spectrum of human attributes and potentials, people are *not* created equal. There are few, if any, "plain vanilla" people (i.e., an average person, born of average parents, from an average neighborhood in an average community). Rather, each person is an individual with an array of capabilities and limitations. Each may, or may not, be capable of becoming a track star, a Bruce Jenner, or an Albert Schweitzer. Each faces life's challenges with a unique combination of aptitudes that may be assets or deficits.

When limitations occur in those areas of life that draw attention, they may become handicaps. Everyone has limitations, but the handicapped person's limitations may be of sufficient magnitude to affect achievement negatively in terms of society's expectations.

Some handicaps may go virtually unnoticed, except under trying circumstances, while others may be so extreme that lifetime custodial care is required. Everyone is handicapped to some degree. The question is: to what degree and in which area of human performance?

General Characteristics of a Handicapping Condition

How and when does an individual become handicapped? Some persons become handicapped during prenatal development or during birth. Deformation or partial formation of a limb usually occurs during prenatal development. Brain damage may result from a compressed umbilical cord during birth. All handicapping conditions that develop during prenatal growth or during birth are **congenital.**

All handicaps that are not congenital are **acquired** and are incurred anytime after birth, usually as a result of illness or injury. Mental retardation resulting from meningitis is an example of a handicap due to illness. Seizures that become symptomatic following a severe head injury are an accident-caused handicap.

Do handicaps last forever? Not necessarily. Some handicapping conditions are **acute** and may cause significant disability for a few weeks or months. A fractured collar bone is an example of an acute handicap, a temporarily disabling condition from which complete recovery is possible.

Some handicapping conditions are **chronic** (long-term, but not necessarily lifelong) and may persist for many years. Juvenile rheumatoid arthritis is a chronic handicap that typically persists for years, yet when the disease is in complete remission, there is usually no residual joint damage and no handicap remains.

Some handicapping conditions are **permanent** and remain throughout life. Down syndrome, a frequent cause of mental retardation, is permanent.

Does the handicap become worse? Not necessarily. Many permanently handicapping conditions are **nonprogressive.** They do not increase in extent or severity. Cerebral palsy is a permanent but nonprogressive handicapping condition.

Some handicaps do increase in extent or severity and are considered **progressive.** A condition may be progressively debilitating but may not necessarily be terminal. For example, certain arthritic conditions are chronically and progressively debilitating, but are not fatal. Other handicaps are relentlessly progressive and may end in death. Among school-age children, muscular dystrophy (Duchenne type) is presently the most devastating example of a fatal progressive handicap for which there is no known cure.

Do handicapped people have special needs? The answer often expected is an unqualified "yes," but the more correct answer is "yes and no." For example, a deaf child may have special needs during a square dance unit but not during a gymnastics unit. Special needs vary for persons with different handicapping conditions, and needs vary among persons with the same type of handicap depending on the severity of the condition.

Generally, the handicapped person tends to be more like, rather than different from, the nonhandicapped. The handicapped person usually has some limitations and special needs, but not in every area and not even in most areas. Whenever the handicapped individual is capable of participation on an equal basis with the nonhandicapped, he is for the moment truly not handicapped and has no special needs.

Education of the Handicapped: A Brief History

How have children with special needs been accommodated in education? Historically, the appropriateness of any school program for the child with a handicapping condition has been determined by whether or not the child could reasonably be expected to experience safe and successful participation. The safe and successful participation philosophy is a decisive basis for judging program appropriateness. In reality, however, interpretation of these criteria has often been inadequate. Until recently, safe and successful participation in many school programs, including physical education, has been left to local interpretation, which sometimes meant no participation at all for the handicapped. In other instances, it has meant meaningful commitment sometimes backed by law. Most educators have struggled to make the most of often inadequate resources, both human and material, to meet the special needs of the handicapped.

Until recently, some handicapped children were not merely isolated from a school program, but were excluded from school entirely. Parents of the handicapped became accustomed to "sorry, but" excuses for a child's ineligibility for public education: "Sorry, but . . . your child has too serious a behavior problem . . . we are not able to provide special services for children who are moderately retarded . . . your child does not hear well enough . . . the facilities in our district were not designed for nonambulatory children." Until recently, parents had no alternative but to accept such explanations without recourse.

When handicapped children were afforded public learning opportunities, they were often grouped categorically (segregated) according to handicap. Although generally well-intentioned, such efforts denied the individuality of chidren with special needs. Categorical grouping by handicap created an atmosphere in which the individual child was overshadowed and obscured by the disability. Teachers, parents, and society often failed to perceive the total child. When the child's participation in such programs complied with the safe and successful participation criterion, little effort generally was made to determine *appropriateness* of the program in meeting the child's unique needs.

Categorical approaches tend to focus on the negative—on the handicap—which emphasizes what the child cannot do. When concerns about individual needs arise, they then occur within the negative context of the general category, which fosters such categorical questions as: "What are the educational needs of cerebral palsied children?" This general question ignores the individual child who happens to have cerebral palsy. The appropriate question is asked in a different context, which emphasizes the individual: "Here is a child who happens to have cerebral palsy. What are the unique educational needs of this child?"

Growing dissatisfaction with categorical approaches, owing to their insensitivity to individual needs, has provided the basis for opposition. As opposition gathered momentum, changes in the law occurred, which meant profound, positive changes in the education of persons with special needs.

What is behind the current change in education of the handicapped? On 29 November 1975, Congress enacted Public Law 94-142, the Education for All Handicapped Children Act. The profound effects that this law is having and will have on the kind and quality of education for persons with special needs is discussed here briefly so that we can compare the past with the emerging concept of adapted physical education. The full significance of P.L. 94-142 in meeting the handicapped child's special needs in physical education is analyzed in Chapter 2.

Through guarantees provided by P.L. 94-142, children with special needs have been granted for the first time the right to receive a "free, appropriate public education in the least restrictive environment" (*Federal Register* 23 August 1977, p. 42488). **Free** means that a local education agency is now legally obligated to accept and educate a child with special needs without cost to the parent or guardian. **Appropriate** means that, by valid assessment and evaluation, education will be individualized to meet the child's unique needs. **Least restrictive environment** means that the child cannot be removed arbitrarily from the regular mainstream educational environment. The child is placed in a modified educational setting only when the results of individualized assessment and evaluation justify such placement. Above all, P.L. 94-142 guarantees that the child's individual needs, rather than a categorical handicap grouping, must determine appropriate education of the child.

In what major ways is P.L. 94-142 changing how teachers perceive the educational needs of handicapped children? The repudiation of categorical approaches in favor of needs-based individualized education has created an awareness that *all* children follow similar developmental patterns characterized by order and sequence. Their accomplishments may be likened to achieving successive rungs on a developmental ladder. Emphasis on the word *all* implies that, regardless of abilities and disabilities, the ladder of human development is universal. Each individual has unique attributes and is faced with personalized, individual challenges. Those who are relatively nonhandicapped tend to climb life's developmental ladder with comparative ease. Those who are relatively handicapped tend to experience greater difficulty.

A philosophy focused on the need to reach rungs of a universal developmental ladder encourages the educator to identify the child's developmental achievement level, and to determine how the child might best reach each successive stage (rung). Knowledge about the child's handicap becomes one consideration, but not the major consideration in determining how the child's education should proceed.

For the adapted physical educator, this means that all handicapped children cannot be grouped arbitrarily in one physical education class, nor can children exhibiting the same categorical handicap be grouped arbitrarily. Rather, physical education requirements must now be determined through valid assessment and evaluation. The child is then placed in a regular or adapted physical education setting based on results of the assessment process.

P.L. 94-142 sounds comprehensive. Is it? The law is comprehensive and specific, but it poses particular concerns for physical educators. P.L. 94-142 is first and foremost a **special education act,** and physical education is included as part of special education. Writers of the Education for All Handicapped Children Act were not physical educators. They perceived physical education as purely an education of the physical phenomenon (i.e., physical and motor fitness; fundamental motor skills and patterns; skills in aquatics, dance, and individual group games and sports, including intramural and lifetime sports). The law does not recognize the role of physical education in facilitating nonphysical outcomes of physical education experiences. Most physical educators include the elevation of self-esteem and social development as two important nonphysical outcomes. Difficulties associated with the objective measurement of such nonphysical outcomes are acknowledged as the reason for their exclusion from the law. Their significance, however, warrants their inclusion as part of the physical education experience of all children.

Everyone has a self-concept. The esteem in which one holds that concept becomes one's level of self-esteem. Self-satisfaction is determined, at least in part, by how a person perceives that she is like others and is likable. Children who realize success and recognition through movement-centered experiences may enjoy a concomitant elevation of self-esteem. Particularly important is the child's perception of having achieved something significant in the eyes of others.

Helping a child to achieve a higher level of self-esteem through successful participation in physical education is not one of the school's P.L. 94-142 physical education-related *legal* obligations. The law makes no mention of the role of physical education in striving for nonphysical outcomes. Despite the law, however, achieving greater self-

FIGURE 1.1.   Social development, an outgrowth of group-centered experiences.

esteem can be important to the child who, as a result of heightened self-esteem, spends more time actively pursuing communication with others.

Physical education experiences are thought to enhance social development, because the setting offers the child opportunities to gain experience and proficiency in functioning as a group member (Figure 1.1). With teacher guidance, the child forms concepts in the activity setting about cooperation, competition, giving and taking, leading and following, taking turns, abiding by rules, playing fair, and working together to achieve a common goal.

Physical education provides a basis for developing positive social traits, because competition and cooperation and give and take occur as teacher-guided experiences. Many school experiences outside the physical education setting are solitary, independent situations in which few opportunities exist for students to practice and learn social amenities under teacher guidance. The handicapped child often has relatively few opportunities for social development under any circumstances. Physical education, with its emphasis on individual-to-group relationships, seems to facilitate the socialization process of the child with special needs.

While the law does not recognize social development as an outcome of the handicapped child's physical education, most physical educators do. To the extent that success in activities enhances self-esteem and activity experiences foster socialization, the child becomes educated through the physical. One noted adapted physical educator rejects the concept of education through the physical, indicating that such a concept tends to dichotomize the human being falsely into separate mind and body entities. We reject this notion, for movement is simply one of many educational media through which a child gains experience.

FIGURE 1.2. Positive physical education experiences can foster socialization.

P.L. 94-142 falls short in yet another way. It fails to recognize many children who have movement-centered special needs. For example, among such children are certain obese, underdeveloped, awkward, clumsy, and temporarily (acutely) handicapped youngsters. Physical educators are obligated professionally, if not legally, to ensure that such children, who may be truly handicapped, receive a physical education tailored to meet their unique needs.

Many physical educators would consider the Education for All Handicapped Children Act to be significantly more complete if it addressed the special physical education needs of all children and if certain nonmovement-centered outcomes had been included. The law, however, does represent a giant step forward in the education of children with special needs, and this progress will undoubtedly be followed by subsequent steps on behalf of these children. As guarantees of a quality education for handicapped children continue to evolve, the physical educator's voice should be assertive, articulate, and ever present when future curricula are proposed and legislation is drafted. If the educator does not assume this responsibility actively, who will?

How can I develop confidence and become comfortable working with handicapped children? A mystique seems to surround working with persons who have handicaps. Teachers' basic insecurities often increase when they learn that they will be responsible for handicapped youngsters as well. Veteran teachers are not immune. Most teachers who have little or no previous background in working with the handicapped will experience apprehension when teaching children with special needs for the first time. Such apprehensions are consistent with human nature and are to be expected.

No magic formula exists for overcoming such apprehensions, but the in-depth theoretical and practical information in this text will help the reader to better understand people with special needs who, as individuals, sometimes have special needs in physical education. Even with this information, however, the preparation to teach adapted physical education is incomplete until one has had supervised, hands-on experience working with persons who have special needs. The major goals of this text are to complement the professor's expertise in preparing the teacher or future teacher for initial hands-on adapted physical education experiences and to serve as a future reference.

Summary

Students who are new to developmental/adapted physical education commonly ask the questions answered in this chapter. The term *handicapped* is defined broadly as any mental, emotional, or physical disadvantage that makes achievement unusually difficult. Being "handicapped" is often an attitude imposed on individuals with disabilities by those who are nonhandicapped, including teachers. Physical education instructors must become familiar with the origin, duration, and severity of many handicapping conditions, but even more importantly, they must learn to look beyond the disability and to develop appropriate and exciting physical education programs that help students maximize their performance potential. The most common reason for exclusion of youngsters with impairments from traditional physical education programs is the teacher's inability to understand that students with disabilities have the same physical and motor needs as their nonhandicapped peers.

P.L. 94-142 emphasizes as its goal that every handicapped child be provided a free, appropriate education in the least restrictive environment. This law includes physical education in its definition of special education, and designates physical education as required for all handicapped children.

P.L. 94-142 guarantees that the handicapped student will receive needed special education services and will be educated in a setting as close to the mainstream as possible.

This law is explicit in its definition of handicapping conditions that make the student eligible for special services, including physical education, but is limited in its definition of physical education. Nonphysical outcomes (e.g., social and self-esteem development) are not considered a part of physical education. Many students perceived by physical educators as having special needs (e.g., perceptual handicap, low fitness, obesity, poor motor skills) are not defined as handicapped under the law. Such children are deemed handicapped and thus eligible for P.L. 94-142 services only if the disability is *organically based*. Despite these limitations, P.L. 94-142 is acknowledged as a significant step forward in providing quality education for children with special needs.

Reference

Federal Register. Final Regulations of Education of Handicapped Children, Implementation of Part B of the Education of the Handicapped Act. Department of Health, Education, and Welfare, Office of Education, 42(163), Part II, 23 August 1977, Section 121a301 (b) Free Appropriate Public Education—Methods and Payments, p. 42488.

CHAPTER 2

Education for All Handicapped Children: The Laws

During the 19th century, federal laws concerning the handicapped were designed primarily to meet the needs of groups with specific disability problems such as deafness or blindness. Not until the 1920s were laws enacted to provide services for all handicapped persons. This was achieved through vocational rehabilitation legislation that was drafted to assist the many people disabled during World War I or injured while working in the rapidly growing industrial society. Legislation for the handicapped over the next 35 years focused mainly, although not exclusively, on services and programs for the blind. These early laws did little for the handicapped child in the public schools.

Education of the Handicapped—1954 to 1973: A Precedent Is Set

The increasing national concern for the needs of handicapped children is of relatively recent origin. The initial impetus for establishing the right of the handicapped child to an equal educational opportunity came in the historic 1954 Supreme

Court school desegregation case, *Brown v. Board of Education.* The rationale behind this court decision was stated as follows: "In these days it is doubtful that any child may reasonably be expected to succeed in life if he is denied the opportunity for an education. Such an opportunity, where the state has undertaken to provide it, is a right which must be made available to all on equal terms."

Relying on the legal principles of the Brown decision, parents of handicapped children demanded the child's constitutional rights to a free and appropriate education. The first major breakthrough in the form of direct congressional support came in 1965 with Title VI of the Elementary and Secondary Education Act (Public Law 89-750). This law, signed by President Lyndon Johnson, authorized grants to the states to initiate, expand, and improve educational programs for handicapped children, and created a Bureau of Education for the Handicapped.

Although P.L. 89-750 was designed to provide educational opportunities for handicapped children, many schools circumvented its directives. At this point, the courts exerted even more pressure. What was to become a national phenomenon began in 1971 when the Pennsylvania Association for Retarded Children filed suit (*P.A.R.C. v. Commonwealth of Pennsylvania*) on behalf of 13 retarded children in that state. Citing guarantees in the U.S. Constitution of due process and equal protection under the laws, the suit argued that these children's access to public education should be equal to that afforded other children. In a consent agreement, the court ruled in favor of the handicapped children.

One year later (1972), the federal court in the District of Columbia made a similar ruling involving not only children with mental retardation but also the full range of handicapping conditions. All children, said U.S. District Judge Joseph Waddy (*Mills v. Board of Education*) have a right to suitable publicly supported education, regardless of the degree of the child's mental, physical, or emotional disability or impairment. In response to arguments that this position would impose an intolerable financial burden on the community, Judge Waddy added the following: "If sufficient funds are not available to finance all of the services and programs needed and desirable in the system, then the available funds must be expended equitably in such a manner that no child is entirely excluded from a publicly supported education."

During the next few years, an avalanche of suits followed as concerned groups in other jurisdictions asked the courts to enforce the constitutional rights of handicapped children. Today, more than 40 suits are still in litigation, and of completed cases, not one decision has gone against the plaintiff. The impact of these rulings has not only opened school doors but also has stimulated states to improve the quality and comprehensiveness of education offered to the handicapped.

Section 504 of the Rehabilitation Act of 1973 (P.L. 93-112)

In September 1973, Congress passed a law that prohibits those agencies that receive federal funding from discrimination on the basis of handicapping conditions. Section 504 states that "no otherwise qualified handicapped individual in the United States . . .

shall, solely by reason of his handicap, be excluded from the participation in, be denied the benefits of, or be subjected to discrimination under any program or activity receiving Federal financial assistance."

In April 1977, the U.S. Department of Health, Education, and Welfare issued the final Section 504 rules and regulations governing all recipients of federal funds, which included all elementary and secondary public schools. This law affects many facts of life in the United States and has a direct bearing on all individuals with handicaps. Joseph A. Califano, Jr., former secretary of HEW, is quoted in the *Federal Register* (23 April 1977) as stating:

> Today I am issuing a regulation, pursuant to Section 504 of the Rehabilitation Act of 1973, that will open a new world of equal opportunity for more than 35 million handicapped Americans—the blind, the deaf, persons confined to wheelchairs, the mentally ill or retarded, and those with other handicaps. . . . The 504 Regulation attacks the discrimination, the demeaning practices and the injustices that have afflicted the nation's handicapped citizens. It reflects the recognition of Congress that most handicapped persons can lead proud and productive lives. It will usher in a new era of equality for handicapped individuals in which unfair barriers . . . will begin to fall before the force of law (p. 32101).

This law provides that programs must be accessible to handicapped persons. It does not require that every building or part of a building be accessible, but that the whole program must be directly available. Structural changes must be undertaken only if alternatives, such as reassignment of classes or rooms, are not possible. Institutions were given 3 years to complete structural changes in their physical plants.

All buildings for which clearance was begun after 3 June 1977 must have been designed and constructed to be accessible to handicapped persons. Design standards of the American National Standards Institute determine minimal requirements for accessibility (Figure 2.1).

The implications of Section 504 for physical education become exceedingly clear, since emphasis is given to guarantee that no individual shall be excluded from, denied benefits of, or discriminated against in any program sponsored by recipients of federal funds. This is further emphasized in the rules and regulations, and although not specifically stated, includes all aspects of physical education instruction, intramurals, and interscholastic sports (Auxter et al. 1980).

Programmatic concerns emphasize that all people must have activities and learning experiences conducted in the least restrictive and most integrated setting feasible. In 1978, the Brockport Invitational Task Force, chaired by Joseph P. Winnick, defined appropriate physical education in relation to Section 504. Two restrictions were identified to avoid in conducting programs: (1) Do not separate categorically individuals with handicapping conditions from individuals without such conditions, and (2) do not indiscriminately place individuals with handicapping conditions in special or segregated programs and activities or both (Auxter et al. 1980, p. 8).

Compliance with these suggestions is mandated by law, and when a handicapped student is denied the opportunity to participate, that individual has the legal right to

FIGURE 2.1. The international symbol of access.

sue the school for discrimination. If any public agency does not comply with Section 504, it jeopardizes its federal funds.

In a 1984 legal case (Pittsburgh, Pa.), five physically handicapped students, whose disabilities included hemophilia and spina bifida, were not receiving appropriate physical education opportunities. The case was brought to the U.S. Office of Civil Rights (OCR). The OCR determined that the students were receiving appropriate physical education, but were being denied other opportunities as defined in Section 504. After investigation, the OCR concluded that the students did qualify as handicapped persons because each had a physical impairment that substantially limited one or more major life activities. The most critical point made was that the youngsters had undergone no preassessment, as required in P.L. 94-142, to determine their physical and motor needs. The students were not listed as "handicapped children" on the local school district's roster. The OCR and the school district reached an agreement establishing that these students be listed officially as "legally handicapped" students per P.L. 94-142. The students would thus fall under the requirements of *both* P.L. 94-142 and Section 504, and would be eligible for all benefits. In other words, P.L. 94-142 mandates physical education for all legally handicapped students between the ages of 3 and 21. Section 504 does not list physical education as being specifically required, but the law does state that no program or activity can be denied to any handicapped person (National Consortium on Physical Education and Recreation for the Handicapped 1985).

On 22 February 1984, P.L. 98-221 was passed to revise and extend the Rehabilitation Act of 1973. This new law was entitled the Rehabilitation Act Amendments of 1984. It calls specifically for continuation of the Architectural and Transportation Barriers Compliance Board. The board will continue to review complaints concerning accessibility to buildings. All other major phases of the 1973 law, including access to programs, remain intact (Programs for the Handicapped 1985).

Education Amendments of 1974 (P.L. 93-380)

This landmark law authorized giving higher levels of educational monetary aid to the states. P.L. 93-380 identifies particularly the principle of placing children in the least restrictive educational environment commensurate with their needs, and requires the state not only to establish a goal of providing full educational services to handicapped children but also to develop a plan that indicates how and when the state expects to achieve that goal.

Education for All Handicapped Children Act of 1975 (P.L. 94-142)

In 1975, P.L. 93-380 was broadened by enactment of an even more significant measure, the Education for All Handicapped Children Act, P.L. 94-142. Some positions established in the bill are significant. First, unlike other federal education laws, P.L. 94-142 has no expiration date and is regarded as a permanent instrument. Second, the act is not simply another expression of federal interest in special education programming; it also provides a specific commitment to all handicapped children. Third, P.L. 94-142 sets forth as national policy the proposition that education must be extended as a fundamental right to individuals with handicapping conditions.

A full commitment by the local school district must be recognized as the handicapped person's right. Moreover, that right cannot be abridged, even on such grounds as unavailability of necessary funds. Handicapped children should be provided with an exciting, stimulating, and meaningful educational experience that is geared to their individual needs and aspirations.

Since its enactment on 19 November 1975, P.L. 94-142 has received tremendous attention, both positive and negative, from all branches of the educational community. Whatever one may think about the law, its provisions clearly will have far-reaching effects on every handicapped child.

Most provisions in the law are not new. The following key components were first identified in P.L. 93-380 and incorporated subsequently into P.L. 94-142: (1) **Child find** means that *all* children in the state, regardless of handicap severity, who need special education and related services must be located, identified, and evaluated. The importance of this provision extends to the moral and logical commitment that all children can learn if given appropriate educational opportunity, and that society can no longer use as an excuse that old cliche: "We didn't know they were there." Handicapped youngsters, often ignored before, must be brought out of the closet and accounted for by local school districts. (2) A **least restrictive environment** is considered to be that place where each handicapped child is assigned educationally, and also must be the most beneficial teaching and learning environment for the child. To the maximum extent possible, all handicapped children should be given opportunities to be mainstreamed with nonhandicapped children. (Mainstreaming and its frequently confused interpretation are discussed and analyzed in Chapter 3.) Least restrictive environment emphasizes identifying the specific child's needs. Recognizing those needs before considering the most appropriate placement or placements is of utmost importance. These placements (note the plural) can be at different sites, but all must be identified and listed as necessary to meet adequately the child's individual needs.

Additional P.L. 94-142 regulations that govern major service areas required under the law ensure that the statutory requirement is met of making available to all handicapped persons ages 3 to 21 a free and appropriate public education (Figure 2.2). Regulations also incorporate identical components from Section 504 guidelines:

> If placement in a public or private residential program is necessary to provide special education and related services to a handicapped child, the program, including non-medical care and room and board, must be at no cost to the parents of the child. . . . Nothing in these regulations . . . relieves an insurer or similar party [i.e., local school district] from an otherwise valid obligation to provide or pay for services provided to a handicapped child (*Federal Register* 23 April 1977, p. 42488).

With reference to residential programs, the courts and hearing examiners have concluded that residential programming is required when (1) more than 6 hours of

FIGURE 2.2. No individual shall be denied an education because of handicap. (Photograph courtesy of Gary Geiger)

instruction is necessary to meet the child's educational needs, (2) the severity of the child's language deficiency precludes meaningful benefit from pregroup learning and interaction with nonhandicapped children in the mainstream setting, and (3) social and emotional adjustment are poor in the mainstream setting (Silverstein 1985).

Note that part B of P.L. 94-142 also requires that **physical education be made available to every handicapped child who is receiving a free appropriate public education.** The child must participate either in the regular physical education program or, if necessary, in a specially designed physical education program.

The goal of offering *full educational opportunities* to children with handicaps is a key point of the law, and two top priority groups that must be served are identified. The first priority group is children who are not presently receiving any formal education, and the second is children with severe handicaps who are receiving a partial but inadequate or incomplete education. These children must "move to the head of the class" so they, too, will benefit from meaningful educational techniques. A major misunderstanding of a child's needs often stems from not looking specifically at each individual child's immediate needs—physical, emotional, social, and intellectual. Existing levels of ability and performance will almost always differ from child to child, and the individualized educational program should reflect these differences.

To meet the handicapped child's individual needs, P.L. 94-142 mandates and outlines a method for educators to follow. The **individualized educational program (IEP)** is defined as a written document that must be developed by a team of professionals who are associated directly with the child. This written program must include five general components: (1) present level of educational performance, (2) annual goals and short-term objectives, (3) specific educational services to be provided for the child and the extent to which the child can participate in regular educational activities, (4) starting date and duration of services, and (5) evaluative criteria and procedures for determining whether the program objectives have been achieved. (Chapter 8 discusses development of the physical education component of an IEP.)

P.L. 98-199, Education of the Handicapped Act Amendments of 1983, was signed on 2 December 1983 to revise and extend the Education of the Handicapped Act. The major purposes of the law were to (1) set a yearly spending ceiling for the state grants program, a permanently authorized program (budgeted for $1.32 billion for fiscal year 1985), (2) change the age range (at the state's discretion) of children eligible to receive special education and related services to include birth to age 3 years, and (3) establish grant authority for projects to help handicapped youth make a successful transition from the public school system to adult life (Programs for the Handicapped 1985). This new law retains *all* major components of P.L. 94-142.

Physical Education for the Handicapped Child

P.L. 94-142 requires that all handicapped children be provided with a physical education program designed to meet individual and specific motor needs. The law clearly attempts to identify the importance of physical education in the total education of the handicapped child. As stated in the *Federal Register,* a government publication containing rules and regulations of the law, "Physical education services, specially designed if necessary, must be made available to every handicapped child receiving a free appropriate public education" (1977, p. 42489). This requirement is emphasized in section 121a14, which reads: "The term special education means specifically designed instruction, at no cost to the parent, to meet the unique needs of a handicapped child including . . . instruction in physical education" (1977, p. 42480).

In the same section, **physical education** is defined as follows:

(i) . . . the development of: (A) physical and motor fitness; (B) fundamental motor skills and patterns; and (C) skills in aquatics, dance, individual and group games, and sports (including intramural and lifetime sports). (ii) The term includes special physical education, adapted physical education, movement education, and motor development (1977, p. 42480).

The student's placement and involvement in classes with nonhandicapped children are also emphasized in describing physical education. Support for this concept is reiterated in the law by the committee that formulated the bill:

Special education as set forth in the Committee bill includes instruction in physical education, which is provided as a matter of course to all nonhandicapped children enrolled in public elementary and secondary schools. The Committee is concerned that although these services are available to and required of all children in our schools, they are often viewed as a luxury for handicapped children. The Committee expects the Commissioner of Education to take whatever action is necessary to assure that physical education services are available to all handicapped children and has specifically included physical education within the definition of special education to make clear that the Committee expects such service, especially designed where necessary, to be provided as an integral part of the educational program of every handicapped child (1977, p. 42489).

In 1978, the Steering Committee on Adapted Physical Education of the Illinois Office of Education (p. 3) interpreted the law to mean that (1) all handicapped children will participate in some type of physical education program as an integral part of their total education program, (2) handicapped children must be afforded the opportunity to participate in educational programs and activities with their nonhandicapped peers as much as is appropriate, and (3) if participation in the regular physical education class is not appropriate for the student's needs, a specially designed physical education program to meet her needs must be provided.

Reinforcement of P.L. 94-142 is again found in the Vocational Rehabilitation Act of 1973, Section 504, and is explained in the *Federal Register* (4 May 1977, p. 22682) as follows:

A recipient[1] may offer to handicapped students physical education and athletic activities that are separate or different from those offered to non-handicapped students only

---

1. As used here, the *recipient* is any agency, facility, or organization that receives federal funding.

if separation or differentiation is consistent with the requirements of section 84.34 and only if no qualified handicapped student is denied the opportunity to compete for teams or to participate in courses that are not separated or different.

Section 84.34 sanctions the participation of handicapped students in separate academic, extracurricular, or nonacademic programs or activities, and the use of private or alternate facilities provided that (1) the education of the child in the regular environment with the use of supplementary aids and services cannot be achieved satisfactorily, (2) the student has the opportunity to participate with nonhandicapped peers as much as is appropriate, (3) placement in an alternate or private facility is considered with regard to its proximity to the student's home, and (4) programs and services offered in the private or alternate facility are comparable to other facilities, services, and activities being offered by the recipient.

Although individual interpretations may vary to include certain vested interests, the law is clear when it states that any separate educational program in any curricular or extracurricular area may be provided to handicapped students as long as they are also given the opportunity to participate in the regular programs, including organized and team sports, as appropriate. When participation in the regular programs is not appropriate, their participation in a comparable adapted program is allowable. Again, the key to appropriate placement begins with a thorough knowledge of the handicapped child's needs. Only then can the child be placed in an appropriate setting in which he learns efficiently and effectively.

With physical education instruction mandated as a part of special education under the Education for All Handicapped Children Act of 1975 and with further support from the civil rights legislation of the Vocational Rehabilitation Act of 1973, adapted physical education programs are now viewed by the law as an appropriate and nondiscriminatory means of meeting requirements to provide opportunities in a least restrictive environment. Failure to provide physical education to all students of the public school population is no longer justifiable.

Where does the money come from for these added services mandated by P.L. 94-142? Provisions between the state and local agencies have increased to a permanent 75 percent of appropriated money. This indicates a total and ongoing commitment by the federal government to support the law. The local school district must ensure and be able to prove that handicapped children are being given an appropriate free public education. Furthermore, the local agency is expected to support educational services for handicapped children to the same extent that it supports services for the nonhandicapped. All children, handicapped and nonhandicapped, will receive identical monies for education. Beyond these monies, additional allotments will then be given to subsidize programs to meet the special needs of the handicapped.

P.L. 94-142 funds cannot be used solely to initiate new programs or services for the handicapped. These experiences are assumed to be necessary components of an appropriate education, and as such should be initiated, regardless of cost, by local agencies. A lack of local school funds is not an acceptable reason for failure to meet the special educational needs of children (AAHPERD, February 1978).

Figure 2.3 summarizes the possible placement alternatives for handicapped children, ranging from complete integration (mainstreaming) to complete individualization.

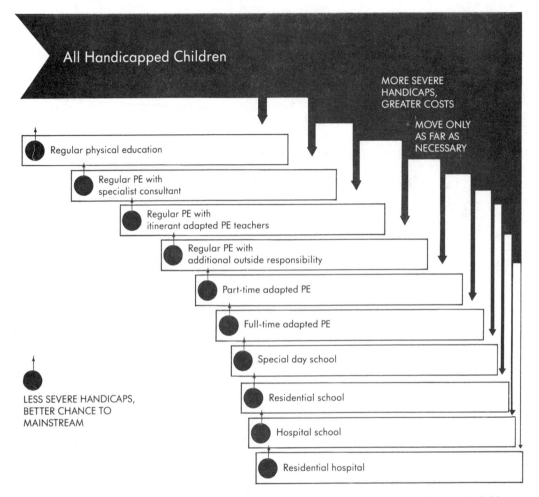

FIGURE 2.3. Possible placement alternatives in physical education for handicapped children. If, for whatever reason, a child must be transferred from a less restrictive to a more restrictive setting, the goal should be to return the student as soon as is feasible to the less restrictive environment.

Problems and Solutions—The Law and Physical Education for the Handicapped

Laws, in their written form, can be confusing. Too often, teachers and school administrators have a distorted view of the law's true intent. Realistic and meaningful questions arise as to possible effects of the law on existing programs, curricula, faculty, finances, facilities, equipment, and most important, on the children.

Update, the monthly newsletter of the American Alliance for Health, Physical Education, Recreation and Dance (AAHPERD),[2] served as a clearing house for specific questions and answers concerning P.L. 94-142 and Section 504 of the Rehabilitation act. The AAHPERD unit on *Programs for the Handicapped* (1985) provided information about implementation of federal legislation affecting school physical education programs for handicapped children. The following questions and responses were drawn from *Update* but are modified to clarify and highlight important points.

[handwritten: WHAT IF SOME STATES DO NOT REQUIRE P.E. FOR ALL STUDENT]

Question: Some state education agencies and state boards of education have asserted that physical education is not required for children with handicapping conditions if it is not required for nonhandicapped students. This conflicts with other interpretations of P.L. 94-142.

Response: All handicapped children must be assessed to determine whether the individual has special physical or motor needs or both. Specific physical education areas defined in the rules and regulations of P.L. 94-142 include development of physical and motor fitness, fundamental motor skills and patterns, and skills in aquatics, dance, individual and group games, and sports, including lifetime sports. The child with no special physical or motor needs is governed by the same requirements as those used for other students at the same grade level. If, after appropriate assessment procedures, an individual is identified as having special physical or motor needs, then that child must be given an individualized program, regardless of whether or not able-bodied students are required to take physical education. This is consistent with the provisions of the law, intent of Congress, and further interpretations regarding needed services. Whether those services are currently available or not, or whether such services are provided to able-bodied students does not affect the individualized program content (AAHPERD, July/August 1979, p. 9).

Question: If a handicapped child is placed in a regular physical education class, must an IEP be developed for that child?

Response: No. A total IEP evolves from the initial assessment of the child. The recommendations of the multidisciplinary team (authors of the IEP) would indicate that the child does not need a specially designed adapted physical education program beyond the program provided for nonhandicapped peers. The child therefore need only participate in the regular and comprehensive physical education program. That physical education program will meet all of the child's psychomotor needs, and will thus include positive reinforcement in the emotional, social, and intellectual domains (AAHPERD, June 1978, p. 6; January 1978, p. 6). If, for example, a moderately mentally handicapped child tests at average or above average levels in a general motor ability

---

2. This organization was formerly termed the American Alliance for Health, Physical Education and Recreation (AAHPER). In 1980, the name was changed to reflect a growing involvement in dance. In this text, the abbreviation AAHPERD will be used for all references to the organization, regardless of the actual organization name at the time.

test battery and in a physical fitness test battery, then placement in a regular physical education class would seem appropriate.

Question: Must children be placed in regular physical education classes if their needs can be more effectively met in a separated setting such as an adapted physical education class?

Response: The fact that children are not mainstreamed in the regular program indicates that they have certain physical or motor needs or both that require a specially designed adapted physical education program. Placement decisions are based on previous physical fitness and on general motor ability assessment. Scheduling flexibility is of extreme importance in such situations. Learning opportunities are maximized when children are placed in different classes to meet weekly or daily needs. For example, the asthmatic child who is allergic to swimming pool chemicals could be transferred temporarily to another activity that has similar basic strength and fitness components (arm, shoulder, and leg strength and cardiorespiratory endurance). The rules and regulations of P.L. 94-142 deal specifically with alternative placements in regular classes, special classes, home instruction, and even in hospitals and institutions (AAHPERD, November 1977, p. 13; June 1978, p. 6). Individuals with low motor skill ability often need short-term placement in a separate adapted physical education class where they can receive intensive and exacting instruction. The student's needs dictate placement. The adapted class is therefore *less* restrictive in this instance than the regular class would be. Both the setting and the time involved must be considered when applying the least restrictive environment mandate. Children identified as handicapped who have been receiving special education services do not automatically need an adapted physical education program. As with any specially designed program, adapted physical education must be prescribed in the child's IEP. Before P.L.94-142, a child with special needs was often labeled, placed, and *then* programmed. Now the process moves from assessment, to programming, and then to appropriate placement. No longer can placement be a function of organizational pattern or administrative inflexibility of the school system or the teacher. If a child cannot learn in one way, then the teacher must teach in another way that enables the child to learn (AAHPERD, January 1978, p. 5).

Question: Should a special education class consisting entirely of students who are grouped homogeneously according to specific handicapping conditions (e.g., all moderately mentally retarded) be sent as a group to physical education class?

Response: Emphatically no! One of the main reasons for drafting P.L. 94-142 was to stop such indiscriminate placement and to force educators to look specifically at each child's unique needs. Each child must be placed according to individual, not group, needs. Grouping children categorically by handicapping condition is not appropriate in terms of either the intent or letter of the law. Once a child has been assessed and found to possess physical and motor abilities consistent with those of nonhandicapped children, then the school district should follow the same processes and procedures that govern all nonhandicapped children in its jurisdiction (AAHPERD, November 1978, p. 7). A blind child, for example, should not be placed automatically in an adapted physical education swimming class if her potential to learn swimming techniques is similar to that of nonhandicapped children. Decisions regarding programs and placement must be based on present ability level (i.e., beginning swimmer, intermediate swimmer). Teachers and leaders must strive to identify children with special physical and motor needs that require attention, determine specific goals and objectives, and alter teaching methods to include appropriate activities, adaptations, and modifications. For example, a teaching technique modified for the blind child might involve moving the youngster's arms, rather than saying, "Watch me do this."

Question: What type of adapted physical education program can be provided without a special facility?

Response: When a handicapped child's needs cannot be met in the regular class setting, then the adapted physical education placement becomes the least restrictive environment. Special program needs must be justified on the basis of IEP planning. Legal, legislative, philosophical, and programmatic trends are away from segregated facilities and special programs, except in cases in which a productive educational experience is not possible in the regular classroom (AAHPERD, January 1978, p. 5). For example, a 16-year-old spastic cerebral palsied youngster might have great difficulty trying to participate in regular class units on volleyball and basketball. Extreme rule modification of either game would so restrict the participation of nonhandicapped children that the game would not fulfill their needs. That would be a violation of the goals of P.L. 94-142 and Section 504. Assuming that playing volleyball and basketball is essential for the motor development (i.e., agility, balance, explosive leg power, and eye-hand coordination) of all individuals, then these sports should be offered also to the handicapped child in a form commensurate with individual ability. The adapted physical educator will have to modify specific activities to allow for improvement and success for the handicapped individual. In this example, it is questionable if the regular program could span such extreme ability differences.

Placement in an adapted physical education class must ensure that the new program is as good or better than the regular class would be for the student. In the past, too many handicapped children were given nonchallenging, irrelevant, and inappropriate activities. The adapted physical education program must *not* consist of handing out towels, keeping score, or maintaining equipment, nor will a watered-down activity program of checkers, chess, pingpong, shuffleboard, or table games satisfy the mandates of P.L. 94-142.

Question: If a child is so disruptive that he makes it difficult for others to learn or function effectively, must he be kept in a given educational setting?

Response: No. The laws emphasize that when a handicapped child impairs the learning opportunity of another child, then placement is not considered appropriate (AAHPERD, January 1978, p. 5), and additional assessment is necessary. Assignment must be made to an alternative least restrictive setting (e.g., an adapted physical education class could afford a lower teacher-pupil ratio and thus provide a more individualized program).

Question: My 13-year-old autistic daughter is not getting physical education, which I requested during the IEP conference. I was told that gross motor activities are part of the classroom program. I asked for physical education in the gym or outdoors, not in the regular classroom. Doesn't my child have the right to participate in a program defined specifically as "physical education"?

Response: Physical education is the only curricular area in the definition of special education (P.L. 94-142). As such, physical and motor needs must be considered by every IEP planning committee. If, based on appropriate assessment, a child is found to have no special physical or motor needs, then nothing more need be done at the committee meeting. Ideally, the IEP form should indicate this and specify that the child is therefore subject to the same rules, regulations, and requirements as other students. A child with special physical and motor needs must be IEP-processed and programmed. It is important to distinguish between children with special needs who have specific goals and those who require adaptive devices, curricular adjustments, and method adaptations. In the latter case, a modification of rules may be all that is necessary to allow a child to remain in the regular class.

The purpose of physical activity must be considered. P.L. 94-142, its rules and regulations, and official interpretations all state clearly that physical education must be included. Physical and motor activities used for social or emotional purposes do not meet the intent or letter of the law, which insists on provision of a physical education. Indeed, physical activities should be encouraged for many reasons, including the academic and social, but these activities must be in addition to and not in place of activities designed to meet physical and motor needs.

A local education agency is therefore not fulfilling the mandates of either P.L. 94-142 or Section 504 if (1) no consideration is given to a child's physical and motor needs during the IEP committee meeting and in the IEP itself, or if (2) the child is being denied categorically the participation in physical education programs or activities comparable to those provided to nonhandicapped children (AAHPERD, May 1979, p. 3).

Question: If a regular or special education classroom teacher uses motor, physical, or recreational activities that reach certain students, has the physical education requirement been satisfied?

Response: No. To satisfy the requirements of P.L. 94-142, a certified physical education instructor must make a clear-cut effort to meet the handicapped child's motor needs. While classroom teachers should be encouraged to provide additional physical and developmental activities, these opportunities are in addition to, and not in place of, instruction by a professional physical educator. Free play, recess, or recreational activities do not meet the intent of physical education for the IEP (AAHPERD, October 1978, p. 11; November 1977, p. 13).

Having trained physical educators is just as important as having trained driver education teachers. While almost everyone can learn to drive a car without the aid of a trained educator, the student's safety and meaningful progression are left to chance.

Question: Do the same provisions that apply to handicapped children also apply to students who are obese or malnourished, or who possess low levels of physical fitness or have poor motor development?

Response: Students not legally identified as handicapped may also need an adapted physical education program to meet their needs effectively. Despite the need, however, there are no legal or binding statements requiring development of an IEP for these children. Additional P.L. 94-142 money is not available to support programs for such students. The rationale for hiring an adapted physical education specialist can be supported strongly when both handicapped and nonhandicapped students require highly individualized instruction. Obese children may exhibit needs that cannot be met if they are always included in regular programs. The structured activities of specific units (i.e., gymnastics and tumbling) will not provide proper exertion to stimulate the cardiovascular system. A flexible physical education curriculum can result in a better program for all students. The assumption that a regular curriculum will meet the individual needs of all chidren is outdated. Physical education programs should include regular and adapted classes to provide a range of activities to meet the fluctuating and individual motor fitness needs of all children (AAHPERD, January 1978, p. 6).

Question: What can be done for students who are excused completely from physical education because no adapted physical education program exists?

Response: According to both P.L. 94-142 and Section 504, which mandate a free appropriate education for every handicapped child, no child should be excused from physical education. Both laws require that each child's special needs be met through individualized programs. P.L. 94-142 requires that this be done through a written IEP, which must include annual goals, short-term instructional objectives, a statement of specific special education and related services to be provided, dates for initiation of services and anticipated duration of services, and criteria and procedures by which achievement can be evaluated. Congressional intent is to provide every handicapped child with an appropriate physical education program. Interpretations of both laws indicate clearly that no justification exists for not meeting the identified needs of any child. Because a local education agency or school does not have a particular service is not an acceptable justification. This position was clarified by Dr. Edwin Martin, Deputy Commissioner of the Bureau of Education for the Handicapped, in a November 1978 letter to all chief state school officers. Needed services are to be provided whether they are currently available or not; this is the responsibility of the local education agency. The interpretation includes adapted physical education (AAHPERD, January 1979, p. 5).

Question: How many persons (age 3 to 21) are considered to be legally handicapped and eligible for P.L. 94-142 and Section 504 services?

Response: The numbers of handicapped children served in the United

NUMBER OF CHILDREN (THOUSANDS)^a

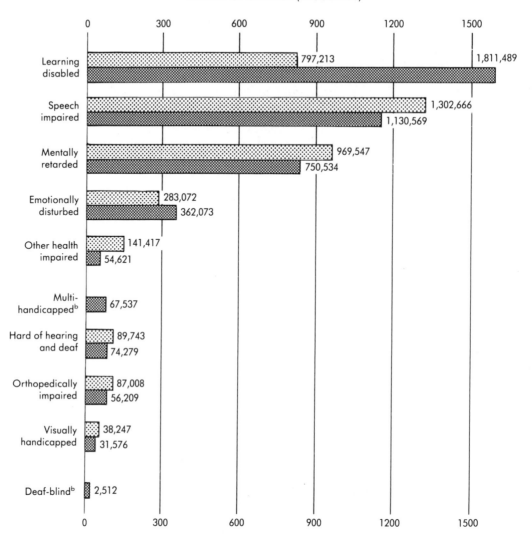

Total:
1976–1977   3,708,913
1983–1984   4,341,399

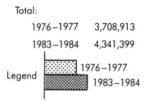

Legend
1976–1977
1983–1984

^aThe figure represents children 3 to 21 years old served
under P.L. 94-142 and children 0 to 20 years old served under P.L. 89-313.

^bData not available for 1976–1977.

FIGURE 2.4. Distribution of children served under P.L. 89-313 and P.L. 94-142 by
handicapping condition for school years 1976–1977 and 1983–1984. (From U.S. Department
of Education, *Seventh Annual Report to Congress on the Implementation of the Education of the
Handicapped Children Act,* 1985, p. 5.)

TABLE 2.1

PERCENTAGE OF SCHOOL ENROLLMENT SERVED AS HANDICAPPED, BY HANDICAPPING CONDITION, DURING 1976–1977, 1982–1983, AND 1983–1984 FOR THE 50 STATES AND THE DISTRICT OF COLUMBIA[a]

Handicapping Condition	1976–77 (%)	1982–83 (%)	1983–84 (%)
Learning disabled	1.79	4.40	4.57
Speech impaired	2.84	2.86	2.86
Mentally retarded	2.16	1.92	1.84
Emotionally disturbed	0.64	0.89	0.91
Other health impaired	0.32	0.13	0.13
Multihandicapped[b]	—	0.07	0.07
Hard of hearing/deaf	0.20	0.18	0.18
Orthopedically impaired	0.20	0.14	0.14
Visually handicapped	0.09	0.07	0.07
Deaf-blind[b]	—	0.01	0.01
Total	8.33	10.76	10.89

[a]Percentages are based on school enrollment for preschool through twelfth-grade youngsters and handicapped enrollment for individuals age 3 through 21.
[b]Data for these categories were not collected for 1976–1977.
SOURCE: U.S. Department of Education. To Assure the Free Appropriate Public Education of All Handicapped Children. *Seventh Annual Report to Congress on the Implementation of the Education of the Handicapped Children Act.* Washington D.C.: 1985, p. 2.

States in 1983–1984 as compared with 1976–1977 are shown in Figure 2.4. Among all school-age children in the United States, the percentage of handicapped children attending the public schools and in institutions is just under 11 percent (10.89 percent) for the 1983–1984 school year. Comparisons are shown in Table 2.1.

Summary

On 23 August 1977, the *Federal Register* printed the final regulations of the U.S. Office of Education concerning the Education for All Handicapped Children Act of 1975 (P.L. 94-142). These regulations agree closely with the nondiscrimination requirements set forth in Section 504 of the Rehabilitation Act of 1973. Both laws require that: (1) handicapped persons be provided a free and appropriate public education, (2) handicapped students be educated with nonhandicapped students as appropriate, (3) education agencies identify and locate all unserved handicapped children, (4) evaluation procedures be adopted to ensure appropriate classification and educational services, and (5) procedural safeguards be established. The penalties for noncompliance are severe and include severance of all federal financial assistance.

Specific legal implications surround the provision of special education, which is defined as specially designed instruction, to be offered at no cost to parents and tailored to meet the unique needs, including physical education, of the handicapped child. Physical education is the only curricular area included in the defined elements of special education.

Physical education encompasses special physical education, adapted physical education, and motor development. A physical education program should provide for the development of physical and motor fitness, fundamental motor skills and patterns, body mechanics, individual and group games, and sport skills, which include intramural and lifetime sports, aquatics, dance, and movement education. Physical education must be made available to every handicapped child receiving a public education, and when necessary, must be provided for in the IEP. Technically, each handicapped child must have the opportunity to participate in the regular physical education program available to nonhandicapped children. Only after appropriate assessment can students be placed in a special class.

"The goals of P.L. 94-142 are being achieved," stated Madeleine Will, Assistant Secretary for Special Education and Rehabilitative Services, on submission of the *Sixth Annual Report to Congress on the Implementation of Public Law 94-142: The Education for All Handicapped Children Act.* She continued, "The data contained in this report show steady improvement in the provision of educational services to handicapped children. At the same time, there are areas where further improvement is needed. There are needs to expand and improve services to young handicapped children in the least restrictive environment with maximum appropriate integration, and to improve preparation for the transition of adolescents from school to work, with increased coordination among the agencies involved. The federal government will continue its efforts to assist the states in passage of the Education of the Handicapped Act and to improve the effectiveness of special education programs to assist all children in realizing their full potential" (1984, p. 111).

References

AAHPERD. Questions and Answers: P.L. 94-142 and Section 504. *Update,* November 1977.
――――. *Update,* January 1978.
――――. *Update,* February 1978.
――――. *Update,* June 1978.
――――. *Update,* October 1978.
――――. *Update,* November 1978.
――――. *Update,* January 1979.
――――. *Update,* May 1979.
――――. *Update,* July/August 1979.
Auxter, D., Jansma, P., Sculli, J., Stein, J., Weiss, R. A., and Winnick, J. P. Implications of Section 504 of the Rehabilitation Act as Related to Physical Education Instruction, Personnel Preparation, Intramural, and Interscholastic/Intercollegiate Sports Programs. *Practical Pointers* 3(11):8, 1980. Reston, Va.: AAHPERD.

Brown v. Board of Education. 347 U.S. 483, 74 Ct. 686, 98 L. Ed. 873, 1954.

Federal Register. Final Regulations of Education of Handicapped Children, Implementation of Part B of the Education of the Handicapped Act. Department of Health, Education, and Welfare, Office of Education, 42(163), Part II, 23 April 1977, Section 121a302 Residential Placement, p. 42488.

———. Section 121a301 (b) Free Appropriate Public Education—Methods and Payments, p. 42488.

———. Section 121a307 Physical Education, p. 42489.

———. Section 121a14 Special Education, p. 42480.

———. Rules and Regulations—Section 504. Department of Health, Education, and Welfare, Office of Education, 42(65), 4 May 1977, Section 84.34 Participation of Students, p. 22682.

Illinois Office of Education, Department of Specialized Educational Services. *Adapted Physical Education: Related Legislation, IEP Development and Programmatic Considerations for Illinois.* Springfield, Ill., 1978.

Mills v. Board of Education of the District of Columbia. 348 F. Supp. 866 (D.D.C., 1972).

National Consortium on Physical Education and Recreation for the Handicapped. #504 Applies to Physically Handicapped Not in Special Education. *NCPERH Newsletter* 13(III): Spring 1985, p. 1.

PARC v. Commonwealth of Pennsylvania. 334 F. Supp. 1257 (E.D. Pa., 1971) and F. Supp. 279 (E.D. Pa., 1972).

Programs for the Handicapped. Clearinghouse on the Handicapped. Washington, D.C.: Department of Education/Office of Specialized Educational Services and Rehabilitation, Office of Information and Research for the Handicapped. January/February 1985, p. 12.

Public Law 93-112. *Rehabilitation Act of 1973,* Section 504, Title V, 23 April 1977.

Public Law 93-380. *Education Amendments of 1974.* 93rd Congress, 21 August 1974.

Public Law 94-142, *Education for All Handicapped Children Act of 1975.* 94th Congress, S.6 (20 USC 1401), 29 November 1975.

Public Law 98-199. *Education of the Handicapped Act Amendments of 1983.* 98th Congress, 2 December 1983.

Silverstein, R. The Legal Necessity for Residential Schools Serving Deaf, Blind, and Multiply Impaired Children. *Journal of Visual Impairment & Blindness* 81(3):145–149, April 1985.

U.S. Department of Education. To Assure the Free Appropriate Public Education of All Handicapped Children. *Seventh Annual Report to Congress on the Implementation of the Education of the Handicapped Children Act.* Washington, D.C.: 1985.

Will, M. To Assure the Free Appropriate Public Education of All Handicapped Children. *Sixth Annual Report to Congress on the Implementation of Public Law 94-142: The Education for All Handicapped Children Act.* U.S. Department of Education. Washington, D.C.: 1984.

CHAPTER 3

Mainstreaming and the Least Restrictive Environment

Current federal and state legislation uses the term **least restrictive environment** to suggest that the regular class offers less restriction of opportunities for learning (Meyen 1982). **Mainstreaming,** often used synonymously with the phrase least restrictive environment, is the practice of providing handicapped persons with the best education possible in an integrated setting with their nonhandicapped peers (Gearheart 1980). This means that individuals, regardless of type or severity of handicapping condition, should participate in activities with nonhandicapped students whenever possible. Mainstreaming is the movement of handicapped children out of segregated special education classes and into classes with nonhandicapped youngsters (Figure 3.1).

An assessment of the least restrictive environment (LRE) provisions of Public Law 94-142 requires an examination of the settings in which handicapped children are served, the options available to children with various handicapping conditions, and the decision-making processes used to place children in appropriate settings. During the 1982–1983 school year, large numbers of handicapped stu-

FIGURE 3.1. Adapted physical education teachers soon learn that handicapped students are a lot like nonhandicapped kids.

dents were served in relatively less restrictive settings. Almost 68 percent of all handicapped children received most of their education in regular classes. Another 25 percent received services in separate classes within a regular education building (Figure 3.2). Together, these settings accounted for 4,298,327 children who received special education services. Fewer than 7 percent of all handicapped children were educated in separate schools or in other environments (i.e., home, hospitals, institutions). Furthermore, most handicapped children were educated in public rather than in private settings (U.S. Department of Education 1985).

Research and Mainstreaming

In recent years, the growing interest in mainstreaming has produced controversy. Many special educators and investigators still believe that traditional, self-contained, segregated classrooms remain the most appropriate placement for children with special

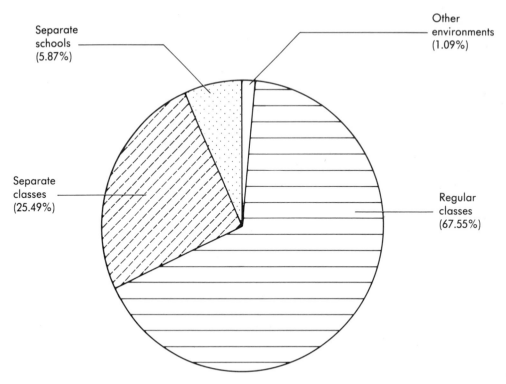

FIGURE 3.2. Percent of handicapped persons served (age 3 to 21) in four educational environments for school year 1982–1983. (From U.S. Department of Education, *Seventh Annual Report to Congress on the Implementation of the Education of the Handicapped Children Act,* 1985, p. 39.)

needs (Warner, Thrapp, and Walsh 1973). On the other hand, criticism of traditional methods often centers on the possible negative effects of segregation on the child's self-image and social relationships (Meyerowitz 1962, Rapier et al. 1972). Birch (1974) states that mainstream education is a valid alternative to self-contained classrooms, while Cantrell and Cantrell (1976) indicate that children with borderline retardation might be maintained in the regular classroom if trained support staff are available.

Although mainstreaming has received much philosophical, emotional, and legal support, little empirical research regarding its effectiveness has been conducted. Budoff and Gottlieb (1974) report that educable mentally retarded (EMR) children integrated in a regular education program showed more positive attitudes toward school and more positive perceptions of self than a control group of self-contained EMR children. Gottlieb, Gambel, and Budoff (1975) report that integrated EMR children showed more prosocial behavior than segregated children (same samples studied by Budoff and Gottlieb). Macy and Carter (1978) found that mainstream education for a selected group of EMR, trainable mentally retarded (TMR), and emotionally disturbed (ED) children was as effective as the regular segregated special education program.

A new thrust has emerged in relation to the more severely handicapped and their integration in regular public school settings. Brinker and Thorpe (1984) used 13 school districts ($N = 245$) and found that over and above functional level, the degree of integration (measured by interaction with nonhandicapped students) was a significant predictor ($p > .025$) of educational progress as measured by the proportion of individualized educational program (IEP) objectives met. They consider integration an important aspect of the curriculum for severely handicapped students (age 3–22 years).

In the 1970s, severely handicapped children were usually the responsibility of private schools or institutions. The idea of mainstreaming had, however, gained wide acceptance by the late 1970s, but cautions were being voiced. MacMillan and Becker (1977, p. 209) state:

> It is assumed that the regular classroom teacher can deal with a wide range of individual differences, and that either the curriculum accommodates a diversity of needs and interests or can be adapted readily to do so. It is interesting to note that in the past these children failed in the regular classroom, and now they are being required to return to the same setting. We question whether regular education has changed sufficiently to warrant the apparent optimism regarding the educational plight of the handicapped learner. One cannot lose sight of the fact that traditionally these have been 'hard to teach' children, and to delabel and mainstream does nothing to alter the fact.

Abramson (1980) found little support for mainstreaming as a means of improving the social acceptability or academic performance of exceptional children. While few would argue against the need for mainstreaming in principle, implementation of the mainstreaming concept is no easy matter. Hallahan and Kauffman (1982) suggest that the mere establishment of special classes does not bring about miracle cures for exceptional children, nor does the abolition of these classes.

Research focused on mainstreaming in physical education has been widely accepted over the past few years. Initially, concern was expressed regarding the effectiveness of physical educators with traditional teaching styles and their ability or desire to teach students with handicapping conditions (Morreau and Eichstaedt 1983). Full integration is unquestionably desirable, but many physical educators have difficulty when they attempt to mainstream the majority of disabled students. Mizen and Linton (in DePaepe and Lavay 1985, p. 44) state: "By the very nature of their program physical education teachers are constantly reminded that teaching children with handicaps in a mainstreaming program can be frustrating and disappointing." Although this statement seems foreboding, they conclude their comments by saying: "The time has come to meet the challenge" (1983, p. 63). Marston and Leslie (1983) determined that a strong correlation exists between positive teacher attitudes toward the disabled and direct teacher involvement with handicapped students. Those not directly teaching students with handicaps retained their negative attitudes. Jansma and Schultz (1982) suggest the use of a mainstreaming attitude inventory to evaluate the attitudes of those physical educators who may teach students with disabilities.

There is strong evidence that attitudes of both nonhandicapped and handicapped youngsters improve when they are placed together in a physical education setting (Karper and Martinek 1982; Morreau and Eichstaedt 1983).

The Physical Education Opportunity Program for Exceptional Learners (PEOPEL) program, developed in 1974 in Phoenix, Arizona, is an innovative approach to mainstreaming, or integrating the nonhandicapped and the handicapped. PEOPEL uses the concept and practice of peer teaching, which enables students who may have a handicap to benefit from peer instruction in physical education. Peer teachers, called PEOPEL student aides, provide a 1:1 instruction ratio with handicapped students in a daily, coeducational class of 30 students, including 15 exceptional learners and up to 15 student aides.

The Law and Mainstreaming

Mainstreaming represents one level in the continuum of services required by the least restrictive environment mandate in P.L. 94-142, the Education for All Handicapped Children Act, and P.L. 93-112, Section 504 of the Rehabilitation Act. The rules and regulations of P.L. 94-142 require that each public agency ensure a continuum of alternative placements to meet the needs of handicapped children for special education and related services. Instruction in regular classes, in special classes, and in special schools, home instruction, and instruction in hospitals and institutions are all on this continuum. These requirements are consistent with Section 504 provisions that mandate program accessibility and appropriate accommodations so handicapped individuals can participate to the maximum degree possible with nonhandicapped peers.

Most states have included mainstreaming in their school codes. The following statements are typical: (1) The child shall be placed in an appropriate educational program that is least restrictive for interaction with nonhandicapped children. (2) Students receiving special education services must attend school in the same buildings as nonhandicapped students. Special classes and separate schooling are permitted only when the nature or severity of the child's handicap prohibits education in regular classes. (3) When a child is removed from a special education program and placed in a regular classroom, the local school district must help to make the transition successful.

The Illinois Office of Education (1976, p. ii) addresses the subject as follows: "The principle of least restrictive placement, 'mainstreaming'—placing exceptional children with all kinds of students—shall be followed whenever feasible." Since this 1976 statement, the Illinois State Board of Education has taken a strong stand on deletion of the term *least restrictive environment*, because the Board believes that the term is unnecessary and counterproductive. The 1981 *Special Education Mandates: A Preliminary Report* contains this statement: "Conflicting evidence exists about the value of this concept [least restrictive environment]. Further, a compelling State interest is not served by the mandate. The mandate for IEP, diagnosis and evaluation, placement, and due process can assure, in the absence of a least restrictive environment mandate, that the individual needs of the child are being met. Therefore, it is recommended that the least restrictive environment mandate be removed" (p. 45).

Mainstreaming has three basic thrusts: (1) removal of labels, (2) desegregation, and (3) more effective programming. Although all three concerns are being addressed by public school physical educators, the main thrust of mainstreaming thus far has been class placement. Educators are examining specifically how much time the handicapped child is spending in the regular class environment.

Social or Physical Development?

Often, the primary goal in placing handicapped children in a regular physical education class is not the attainment of physical fitness or enhancement of motor development, but rather to promote acceptable social behavior by exposure to appropriate peer models or to provide competitive situations that the child must ultimately experience. While these are meaningful goals for a handicapped child, they should be recognized for what they are: social and not physical education goals. Miller and Switzky (1978, p. 126) emphasize this point: "In implementation, a least restrictive environment might be best considered at the individual level where it is based primarily on meeting the target students' identified needs." An evaluation of mainstreamed education must therefore begin with a clear statement as to whether placing the handicapped child in a regular class will go beyond social opportunities to actually promote the student's physical improvement.

Is Mainstreaming Appropriate for All Handicapped?

Controversy exists within educational circles regarding implementation of mainstreaming. The key questions are: (1) who is to be mainstreamed, and (2) is mainstreaming the most appropriate placement for all children? Teachers are concerned that handicapped children may be "dumped" in regular classes. Although this practice is completely contrary to the intent of the laws, some administrators are misinterpreting the laws and are requiring all handicapped children to remain in regular physical education classes. Gorton (1977, p. 28) expresses his concerns regarding improper mainstreaming as follows: "I continuously hear teachers complain that children have been precipitously and indiscriminately mainstreamed. The children have been placed back into the very environment in which they failed" (Figure 3.3).

It is unrealistic to expect *all* handicapped children to benefit from placement in a regular physical education class for *all* activities. Most comprehensive physical education curricula contain activities to meet the total psychomotor needs of a particular age group, but the individualized needs of the handicapped are not always considered in initial program planning. Many activities are compatible with the needs of the handicapped child, while others require modification. For example, a trainable mentally retarded student may experience difficulty playing a version of basketball in which team strategy is important.

WHEN WOULD IT NOT BE APPROPRIATE?

FIGURE 3.3. Frustration from constant failing must be avoided. (Photograph courtesy of Gary Geiger and the Illinois Special Olympics)

Handicapped children should be placed in activities in which they can participate actively (Figure 3.4). Exclusion from or severe modification of an activity may indicate that the child's ability has not been considered properly and that the placement is inappropriate.

Zneimer (1976) cautions against the assumption that mainstreaming will cure all problems that existed in segregated programs. The total child must be the key to placement; integration is not an end in itself.

Gardner (1978, p. 128) emphasizes that continued and consistent failure does not develop positive attitudes. He states: "An emotionally disturbed, mentally retarded, or learning disabled child cannot learn achievement orientation, to be relaxed, satisfied, friendly, or to be free of anxiety, and related defensive behavior patterns in an environment that promotes excessive failure. A child with severe visual or auditory problems cannot learn to like himself, to relate warmly to others, or to accept his own sensory limitations realistically if he experiences a preponderance of failure."

FIGURE 3.4.   Rewards gained through active participation will have a lasting result. (Photograph courtesy of Gary Geiger and the Illinois Special Olympics)

Mainstreaming handicapped students into public school physical education programs is feasible and in certain instances desirable if personnel have a positive attitude and if appropriate, flexible program planning and activity modifications are made when necessary (Information and Research Utilization Center 1977).

Random, inappropriate, and hasty placement can be physically, socially, and emotionally detrimental to the handicapped child. When, however, handicapped children can participate safely, successfully, and with personal satisfaction, then, and only then, should they be placed in the regular program.

The Least Restrictive Environment

A *least restrictive environment* provides the best match between a child and a specific learning program. An ideal combination should promote maximum development and functioning in the physical education curriculum. Movement experiences

FIGURE 3.5. The effective adapted physical education teacher must identify a handicapped child's motor needs. This child shows a marked weakness of the upper body for which specific upper body exercises have been prescribed.

may occur through large group instruction (mass techniques with everyone doing similar tasks), through individualized experiences within the regular class (in-class grouping), or through a highly individualized small class setting designed especially for a particular child (Figure 3.5). In the small class, such as an adapted physical education section, the individual child and his immediate psychomotor and fitness needs take precedence (Information and Research Utilization Center 1975). In other words, the least restrictive environment must be interpreted as that place where the child learns best.

A *most restrictive environment* is that place where the handicapped child is assigned unnecessarily, a place that is distinctly different and physically separate from the setting in which nonhandicapped students are being taught. Although an institution may be the most appropriate (and least restrictive) environment for a relatively small number of severely and profoundly handicapped persons, an institution is the most restrictive environment for most handicapped individuals (Special Olympics 1982).

As Madeleine Will, Assistant Secretary for Special Education and Rehabilitative Services, states: "Education in the least restrictive environment (LRE), or the elimination of obstacles to the least restrictive environment, is what I envision as the last barrier to full implementation of P.L. 94-142. This concept is becoming the cornerstone upon which federal special education policy is being built" (1985, p. 1).

Placement Alternatives

Any decision regarding the most appropriate placement should not be considered a simple choice between regular and adapted physical education programs. Neither should placement be considered final once a decision is made. Rather, practitioners should examine continually those placement alternatives, which, when implemented, will produce a least restrictive environment that enables the child to learn effectively and completely. For example, a mentally handicapped girl with normal levels of physical fitness may be successful in regular activities that involve strength, speed, and endurance but may perform poorly in activities that require striking with a racket (e.g., badminton, tennis). Her motor performance could be almost two standard deviations below that of an average child. Instead of instruction in racket sports, she should be taught more basic activities involving eye-hand coordination. Her performance indicates that she is not yet ready to use an implement but should learn first to hit an object with her hands. An adapted physical education class can provide meaningful activities at her ability level. When a child's needs call for a more effective learning environment, the regular program may provide some activities and an adapted class the others.

Stein (1976) explains that while mainstreaming can produce positive results, it is not the only alternative. He states: "Some activities lend themselves more readily to mainstreaming than others. For example, exploratory activities, tumbling, gymnastics . . . are excellent for this process, since success or failure does not depend on the performance or ability of others" (Figure 3.6).

Placement in the Regular Program

For a handicapped child to receive maximum benefits from a regular class, two conditions must be satisfied. First, the handicapped child's physical needs must be compatible with the instruction level that is offered to the nonhandicapped children. Incompatibility, for example, is evident when a handicapped child is assigned to play shuffleboard while classmates are engaged in volleyball. The basic skills developed by playing volleyball (i.e., eye-hand coordination, explosive leg power, agility) are not acquired by playing shuffleboard. Alternative activities should help the student to develop similar skills (Table 3.1).

Second, the teacher must be able to modify regular class instructional practices to accommodate the child with abilities that are quite different from those of other students. Such modifications may not be appropriate when extreme differences of ability exist between the handicapped child and the others. For example, placing a child in a wheelchair in a regular volleyball class is usually inappropriate. In-class grouping by ability levels may provide a viable alternative, but the extremely handicapped should

FIGURE 3.6. Many gymnastics activities accommodate a wide range of abilities.

be placed in an adapted physical education class where a better opportunity for success exists, and where the obvious frustration of a watered-down activity is not experienced (Eichstaedt 1976).

The Illinois Office of Education's Department of Specialized Educational Services (1978) has developed a model that supports flexible placement with a continuum of alternatives. Based on assessment data, placement alternatives should be considered and the individual assigned to the regular or adapted physical education class as each student's needs dictate. Suggested transitional placement should occur as follows: (1) The child should remain in a regular physical education class with supplementary adapted programming available when modifications in activities, equipment, facilities, or in the performer's role are impractical or not possible. For example, a student with perceptual motor disability may need adapted programming when regular program activities require well developed visual-motor skills, as in badminton or tennis. In yet another example, a student with a hearing impairment may need adapted programming when the regular program activities require an acute sense of balance, as in tumbling and gymnastics. (2) The child should be placed in an adapted physical education class

TABLE 3.1
ALTERNATIVE ACTIVITIES FOR VOLLEYBALL

Basic Fundamental Skill	Alternative Activities
Eye-hand coordination	Wall volley Sidewalk tennis 4-Square Balloon volley Tether ball
Explosive leg power	Line jump Vertical wall jump Hopscotch Hopping relays Hop tag
Agility	Belly-back-stand Line jump Shuttle run Obstacle run Boomerang

with supplementary regular programming when modifications in the regular program activities, equipment, facilities, or in the performer's role are possible. For example, a student with visual impairment can use a handrail or guide rope to participate in bowling with normal vision students, or a student with cerebral palsy can use flotation devices to participate in the regular swimming program.

These proposed transitional placements allow the child with special needs to participate in a least restrictive physical education environment.

Organization and Administration of a Flexible Curriculum

Many handicapped children have unfortunately been placed in learning environments because of their handicapping label (e.g., only EMR children in the class). This practice does not consider each child's individual motor differences or each child's diverse physical needs. For example, although mental ability is below normal range, the child's motor ability may be quite adequate and he might participate successfully in a traditional physical education program.

The identification and placement of handicapped children are two major obstacles for school administrators. Performance levels, and not diagnostic group labels, should determine organization and administration of appropriate physical education experiences. Hobbs (1975, p. 197) summarizes this position:

> In schools that are most responsive to individual differences in abilities, interests, and learning styles of children, the mainstream is actually many streams, sometimes as many streams as there are individual children, sometimes several streams as groups are formed for special purposes, sometimes one stream only as concerns of all converge. We see no advantage in dumping exceptional children into an undifferentiated mainstream; but we see great advantage to all children, exceptional children included, in an educational program modulated to the needs of individual children, singly, in small groups, or all together. Such a flexible arrangement may well result in functional separations of exceptional children from time to time, but the governing principle would apply to all chidren: school programs should be responsive to the learning requirements of individual children, and groupings should serve this end.

Mainstreaming is not intended to change the special child so that she fits into the regular classroom, but rather to change the nature of the regular classroom so it becomes more accommodating to all children.

The Teacher's Responsibility

Once a handicapped child is retained in the regular class for a specific purpose (e.g., tumbling to develop agility, balance, and kinesthetic awareness), the logical question is whether the ongoing lessons will meet the stated goals of the IEP. What steps can the teacher take to accomplish goals that were established for the child?

The question has no simple answer, because the material offered to a handicapped child, or to any child, depends largely on the teaching strategies of the instructor. The teacher may develop a learning environment that enables students to progress at their own rate or that provides all students with identical opportunities. (The teaching approach of "what's good for one is good for all" is usually not conducive to meeting individual needs.)

The National Information Center for Handicapped Children and Youth (1983, p. 1) cautions: "Placing students with handicaps into the 'mainstream,' or regular class, does not guarantee that they will be liked, or chosen as friends by their nonhandicapped peers. Without careful attention by sensitive teachers, such a placement could even be a harmful experience."

Miller and Sabatino (1978) identify two major problem areas regarding mainstreaming of the handicapped: (1) the teacher's attitude toward the child, and (2) the teacher's ability to teach the child. Awareness sessions, including actual contact with handicapped individuals, are necessary if teachers are to overcome their natural fears and misconceptions about the handicapped. All undergraduate physical education majors should participate in awarenes sessions. This also must be a priority for in-service and retraining experiences for already certified physical educators.

Research shows that the majority of teachers believe that they are not equipped to deal with handicapped youngsters. Gickling and Theobold (1975) found that 85 percent of teachers polled believed that they lacked the necessary skills to teach exceptional children. Two separate studies (Agard 1975; Shotel, Iano, and McGettigan 1972) indicate that teachers harbor generally negative attitudes toward handicapped children whose ability levels and needs are different from those of most students. It is therefore extremely important that the physical education teacher become knowledgeable about handicapped children. A close working relationship should be established with the special educator who has been trained and will be able to answer questions about most handicapping conditions (e.g., What causes Down syndrome? Is it a disease? Will the child become progressively worse? Will the child have difficulty understanding instructions?). The special educator should act as a consultant when specific information about a child is required (e.g., Is Susie cooperative? Is she shy? Does she have many friends? What makes her happy?).

Teaching Techniques for Successful Mainstreaming

One central impediment to mainstreaming—competition—is deeply ingrained in our educational system. Many classroom procedures, management programs, and curricular materials emphasize the selection and sorting functions of the schools, that is, schools, both officially and tacitly, sort out the able from the less able and rank students according to specific criteria. Physical educators should truly question the validity of grading students by their performance levels. This process inevitably leads to failure for a significant number of individuals when they are compared with the norm. Although these same individuals may try their best, their skills do not permit them to reach acceptable levels. If the basic goal of physical educators is to develop positive attitudes toward physical activity, then everything possible must be done to motivate the less skilled and the handicapped child. The concept of zero-fail should be an integral component of all physical education programs (Figure 3.7) (Eichstaedt 1976).

Successful mainstreaming begins with a total picture of an individual's present level of physical fitness and general motor ability. These ability levels, determined by using appropriate testing instruments, indicate the child's proper placement. Werder and Kalakian (1985) believe that assessment in adapted physical education should focus on identifying the needs of students with motor difficulties and on measuring the progress of students who cannot safely or successfully participate in the traditional mainstream physical education program. Certain individuals will be difficult to assess because of their emotional and social skill levels. The questions asked in Figure 3.8 can assist in placement.

A large class size, often typical of the regular program, may necessitate the use of alternate teaching methods to integrate the handicapped child. Alternate methods might include: (1) circuit or station organizational patterns, (2) a buddy system that

A

B

C

D

FIGURE 3.7.   Success and self-image go hand in hand. (A) "I can make it—let me try!" (B) "Up and over." (C) "I may have some problems but . . ." (D) "I told you I could do it!" (Photographs courtesy of Photo Associates Limited)

TO: PHYSICAL EDUCATION INSTRUCTORS
FROM: ADAPTED PHYSICAL EDUCATION INSTRUCTOR
RE: POSSIBLE CANDIDATES FOR ADAPTED PHYSICAL EDUCATION PROGRAMMING

STUDENT _____ GRADE LEVEL _____

COUNSELOR _____ PE INSTRUCTOR _____

PLEASE ANSWER THE FOLLOWING QUESTIONS PERTAINING TO THE STUDENT

YES NO SOMETIMES 1. Is this student rejected by classmates because of ability?

YES NO SOMETIMES 2. Does this student avoid competive games and activities?

YES NO SOMETIMES 3. Does this student continually finish toward the bottom of the class on skill tests and/or physical fitness tests?

YES NO SOMETIMES 4. Does this student have difficulty when playing ball games?

YES NO SOMETIMES 5. Does this student seem sincerely happy to be in physical education class? (Does the student outwardly enjoy most activities? Is it difficult to determine the individual's true feelings?)

YES NO SOMETIMES 6. Does this student make negative comments about physical education?

SPECIFIC REASONS FOR REFERRAL

_____ Excessive overweight

_____ Excessive underweight

_____ Lacks coordination

_____ Lacks strength

_____ Poor posture

_____ Poor physical fitness

_____ Class adjustment (In your opinion, would he/she benefit from a more individualized program?)

FIGURE 3.8.   Answers to these questions will aid in identification of the student's adapted physical education needs.

pairs a handicapped child with an able-bodied partner for specific activities, (3) peer tutoring, (4) contract techniques using problem solving, exploratory, and movement education activities, (5) use of paraprofessionals, aides, volunteers, parents, and older students, (6) elective programs in which students select activities or units according to their interests and abilities.

Summary

Mainstreaming, now a top priority in public schools, provides an exciting opportunity for handicapped youngsters if cautiously administered. It does not mean simply including all handicapped children in the regular physical education program. Mainstreaming should be a carefully executed process by which the physical needs of the handicapped child are identified and met. Moderate and severe degrees of motor disability may require a flexible combination of several alternatives with each one contributing to the child's education. The indiscriminate placement of handicapped individuals in regular classes for which they are not ready is as inappropriate as the exclusion from regular classes of those handicapped students who are ready for the challenge of physical activity with nonhandicapped peers.

Jones et al. (1978) stress that the effectiveness of any mainstream program for handicapped children can be measured only by *what* is being taught, which is far more important than *where* the students are being taught.

Students should not be shuffled between rigid, narrowly conceived experiences, which ensure that a certain percentage of children will fail. The concept of "zero-reject," or "zero-fail," must be practiced by all physical educators. Ideally, mainstreaming will become the impetus for examining and redesigning special education and many other aspects of our school system.

References

Abramson, M. Implications of Mainstreaming: A Challenge for Special Education. In *The Fourth Review of Special Education,* edited by L. Mann and D. A. Sabatino. New York: Grune and Stratton, 1980.

Agard, J. A. The Classroom Ecological Structure: An Approach to the Specification of the Treatment Problem. Paper presented at annual meeting of American Educational Research Association, Washington, D.C., 1975.

Birch, J. W. *Mainstreaming: Educable Mentally Retarded Children in Regular Classes.* Minneapolis: University of Minnesota Leadership Training Institute/Special Education, 1974.

Brinker, R. P., and Thorpe, M. E. Integration of Severely Handicapped Students and the Proportion of IEP Objectives Achieved. *Exceptional Children* 51(2):168–175, 1984.

Budoff, M., and Gottlieb, J. S. A Comparison of EMR Children in Special Classes With EMR Children Who Have Been Reintegrated Into Regular Classes. *Studies in Learning Potential* 3:50, 1974.

Cantrell, R. P., and Cantrell, M. L. Preventive Mainstreaming: Impact of a Supportive Services Program on Pupils. *Exceptional Children* 42:381–386, 1976.

DePaepe, J. L., and Lavay, B. W. A Bibliography of Mainstreaming in Physical Education. *The Physical Educator* 42(1):41–45, 1985.

Eichstaedt, C. B. Can Low Motor Skilled Students Achieve Success in Public School Physical Education? *Illinois Journal of Health, Physical Education and Recreation* 2:11–12, 1976.

Gardner, W. I. *Learning and Behavior Characteristics of Exceptional Children and Youth,* 2nd ed. Boston: Allyn and Bacon, 1978.

Gearheart, B. R. *Special Education for the 80's.* St. Louis: C. V. Mosby, 1980.

Gickling, E. E., and Theobold, J. T. Mainstreaming: Affect or Effect. *Journal of Special Education* 9:317–328, 1975.

Gorton, C. E. The Mainstream—Both Wide and Deep. *Mainstreaming in Health, Physical Education, Recreation, and Dance: Proceedings of National Conference.* Denton: Texas Woman's University, 22–23 April 1977, p. 28.

Gottlieb, J. A., Gambel, D. H., and Budoff, M. Classroom Behavior of Retarded Children Before and After Integration Into Regular Classes. *Journal of Special Education* 9:307–315, 1975.

Hallahan, D. P., and Kauffman, J. M. *Exceptional Children: Introduction to Special Education.* Englewood Cliffs, N.J.: Prentice-Hall, 1982.

Hobbs, L. *The Future of Children.* San Francisco: Jossey-Bass, 1975.

Illinois Office of Education. *Illinois State Rules and Regulations to Govern the Administration and Operation of Special Education.* Springfield, Ill.: 1976.

Illinois Office of Education, Department of Specialized Educational Services. *Adapted Physical Education: Related Legislation, IEP Development and Programmatic Considerations for Illinois.* Springfield, Ill.: 1978.

Illinois State Board of Education. *Special Education Mandates: A Preliminary Report.* Springfield, Ill.: The Board, 21 November 1981.

Information and Research Utilization Center (IRUC) in Physical Education and Recreation for the Handicapped. *Physical Education and Recreation for Impaired, Disabled, and Handicapped Individuals—Past, Present, and Future.* Reston, Va.: AAHPERD, 1975.

———. *Integrating Persons With Handicapping Conditions Into Regular Physical Education and Recreation Programs.* Reston, Va.: AAHPERD, 1977.

Jansma, P., and Schultz, B. Validation and Use of a Mainstreaming Attitude Inventory With Physical Educators. *American Corrective Therapy Journal* 36:150–158, 1982.

Jones, R. L., Gottlieb, J., Guskin, S., and Yoshida, R. K. Evaluating Mainstreaming Programs: Models, Caveats, Considerations, and Guidelines. *Exceptional Children* 44(8):588–601, 1978.

Karper, W. B., and Martinek, T. J. Differential Influences of Various Instructional Factors on Self-Concepts of Handicapped and Non-Handicapped Children in Mainstreamed Physical Education Classes. *Perceptual and Motor Skills* 54:831–835, 1982.

MacMillan, D. L., and Becker, L. D. Mainstreaming the Mildly Handicapped Learner. In *Changing Perspectives in Special Education,* edited by R. D. Kneedler and S. G. Tarver. Columbus, Ohio: Charles E. Merrill, 1977.

Macy, D. J., and Carter, J. L. Comparison of a Mainstream and Self-Contained Special Education Program. *Journal of Special Education* 12(3):303–313, 1978.

Marston, R., and Leslie, D. Teacher Perceptions From Mainstreamed Versus Non-Mainstreamed Handicapped and Non-Handicapped Teaching Environments. *The Physical Educator* 40:8–15, 1983.

Meyen, E. L. *Exceptional Children and Youth: An Introduction*, 2nd. ed. Denver: Love Publishing, 1982.

Meyerowitz, J. Self Derogation in Young Retardates and Special Class Placement. *Child Development* 33:443–451, 1962.

Miller, T. L., and Sabatino, D. A. An Evaluation of the Teacher Consultant Model as an Approach to Mainstreaming. *Exceptional Children* 45(2):86–91, 1978.

Miller, T. L., and Switzky, H. N. The Least Restrictive Alternative: Implications for Service Providers. *Journal of Special Education* 12(2):123–131, 1978.

Mizen, D. W., and Linton, N. Guess Who's Coming to PE: Six Steps to More Effective Mainstreaming. *JOPERD* 54:63–65, 1983.

Morreau, L. E., and Eichstaedt, C. B. Least Restrictive Programming and Placement in Physical Education. *American Corrective Therapy Journal* 37(1):7–17, 1983.

National Information Center for Handicapped Children and Youth. *Attitudes*. Washington, D.C.: The Center, 1983.

Public Law 94-142, *Education for All Handicapped Children Act of 1975*. 94th Congress, S.6 (20 USC 1401), 29 November 1975.

Rapier, J., Adelson, R., Carey, R., and Croke, K. Changes in Children's Attitudes Toward Physically Handicapped. *Exceptional Children* 39:219–224, 1972.

Shotel, J. R., Iano, R. P., and McGettigan, J. F. Teacher Attitudes Associated With Integration of Handicapped Children. *Exceptional Children* 38:677–683, 1972.

Special Olympics. *P.L. 94-142: It's the Law. Physical Education and Recreation for the Handicapped*. Washington, D.C.: U.S. Office of Education, 1982, p. 23.

Stein, J. U. Sense and Nonsense About Mainstreaming. *JOPER* 47(1):43, 1976.

U.S. Department of Education. To Assure the Free Appropriate Public Education of All Handicapped Children. *Seventh Annual Report to Congress on the Implementation of the Education of the Handicapped Children Act*. Washington, D.C., 1985.

Warner, F., Thrapp, R., and Walsh, S. Attitudes of Children Toward Their Special Class Placement. *Exceptional Children* 40:37–38, 1973.

Werder, J. K., and Kalakian, L. H. *Assessment in Adapted Physical Education*. Minneapolis: Burgess Publishing, 1985.

Will, M. "Least Restrictive Environment." Speech given at Topical Conference on Least Restrictive Environment, Washington, D.C., 8 January 1985.

Zneimer, L. Mainstreaming: A Fad or a Reality? *Journal for Special Educators of the Mentally Retarded* 12(2):95–101, 1976.

CHAPTER 4

Psychosocial Aspects of Disability

I am America's child, a spastic slogging on demented limbs drooling I'll trade my PhD for a telephone voice.

(Bart Lanier Safford III, *An Obscured Radiance*)

This chapter investigates some psychosocial variables that influence the adjustment of handicapped persons. Sometimes greater degrees of handicap are associated with greater adjustment problems, but this generalization is an oversimplification. Any study of psychosocial variables must be tempered by respect for the person's individuality and the handicap's significance to that person. As Levine (1959) states:

The extent of the [disability's] impact experienced by each individual is related to the significance which the disability possesses for him. This, in turn, will depend on the pattern of events in his life that have contributed to the values he holds, the way he perceives himself in relation to the rest of the world, and the form which his reactions to stress take.

Self-Concept

Self-concept is an important psychosocial variable that influences the disability's impact on the individual. Just as each person formulates attitudes about others, so each person also formulates attitudes about himself, which become his self-concept. Research in social psychology indicates consistently that arousal levels, motivation to achieve, and quality of interpersonal relationships are closely related to strength of self-concept (Fig. 4.1). Researchers also assert that the strength of one's self-concept is governed by one's understanding of how she is perceived by others. This implies that if a feeling of self-worth is not shared by important others, it is of little value. Simply stated, "What I think about me depends largely on what I think you think about me."

FIGURE 4.1.   Meeting challenges in physical education can be good for self-concept.

Self-concept is a dynamic phenomenon. Among adults, self-concept is relatively stable; among young people, it is in a state of flux. A self-concept that is not improving may well be depreciating.

Self-concept is also a psychophysical phenomenon. No dichotomy exists between the mind and the body in a person's evaluation of self-worth. The handicapped individual who perceives his entire person as undesirable is unable to formulate a valid concept of self-worth. Bigge and O'Donnell (1976, p. 80) states:

> Growing up in a family with fixed attitudes toward disability, and living in a society which treats persons with disability as a disfavored minority, the person with the disabling condition is faced with preconceived, distorted perceptions of his state. . . . The fact that a disabled person may be different in appearance, behavior, or habits often suggests to others (and eventually to the person) that there is something deviant about him.

Distorted perceptions of self-worth and of deviance become, for some persons with handicaps, the basis for a distorted, negative self-concept.

Bigge and O'Donnell state further that "if a disabled person can be perceived as 'a person with a disability' rather than as 'a disabled person,' there will be greater emphasis placed upon the person than upon the disability" (p. 80). When we focus primarily on the person and secondarily on the disability as only one of the person's numerous traits, we realize that many persons with a handicap are not disabled at all times. Important others who perceive the individual's disability in a true context play a significant role in facilitating the individual's realistic, positive self-concept.

Dealing with the individual first and with the disability second does not avoid or ignore the disability. Treating the disability as if it were nonexistent does not allow the individual to accept limitations, to make an accurate appraisal of strengths and abilities, or to apply concerted effort toward achievable ends (Bigge and O'Donnell 1976).

Defense Mechanisms

Realistic attitudes about one's handicap avoid self-defeating behavior and inordinate reliance on defense mechanisms. Everyone relies on defense mechanisms to deal with stress. When a person relies consistently on defense mechanisms as an escape, however, that individual is perhaps unconsciously avoiding the source of stress. Reliance on the following defense mechanisms is common:

- **Regression**—The person, confronted by a threatening situation, returns to an earlier level of maturity or adjustment.
- **Repression**—The person purposefully, but unconsciously, forgets (obliterates from memory) events with which she is unable to cope.
- **Denial**—The person refuses to acknowledge the existence of real situations and circumstances. In repression, the person obliterates stressful situations

and circumstances from his thoughts. In denial, the person may acknowledge stressful situations and circumstances, but he denies that they have consequence or significance.

- **Rationalization**—The person creates "acceptable" reasons for events or circumstances because the true reasons are emotionally unacceptable.
- **Resignation**—The person gives up when confronted by seemingly insurmountable circumstances.
- **Becoming Dependent, Demanding**—The person requires unnecessary assistance to ensure that she gets attention, affection, and care from important others.

During stress, all persons rely to some extent on defense mechanisms. An over-reliance is, however, incompatible with healthy, adaptive attitudes toward the source of stress. Achieving healthy, adaptive attitudes facilitates one's ability to progress toward achievable ends. The adage that developing new habits is less difficult than breaking old ones merits consideration.

Body Image

The image of one's own body and the value of that image are significant in formulating self-concept. The body is the hub of one's identity. The individual's somatic limitations and strengths are variables that may alienate the individual from his environment. Among the physically disabled, difficulty may arise in integrating positively a bodily disability into a healthy self-concept. Goldberg (1974) confirms that social adjustment correlates negatively with self-concept when the handicap is visible. The more visible the handicap, the greater the difficulty in adjusting socially and developing a positive self-concept.

Striving for Acceptance Often Extracts Its Price

Virtually all persons strive to be accepted by others and to count positively in another's life. Persons with or without handicaps can become trapped in their efforts to develop a false front that might be more acceptable to others. This behavior is self-defeating for the handicapped person, particularly if a false front is used to cover up certain traits. Wright (1960, p. 24) states:

> The price of trying above all to hide and forget is high. It is high because the effort is futile. A person cannot forget when reality requires him to take his disability into account time and again. The vigilance required for covering up leads to strain, not only physically but also in interpersonal relations, for one must maintain a certain distance (social as well as physical) in order to fend off the frightening topic of the disability. . . . Trying to forget is the best way of remembering.

Wright (1960, pp. 36–37) points out that "acting like a normal person" is not the same as "feeling like a normal person" (i.e., a worthy human being). She concludes that "all too often, one pays a price for the apparent success when the motivation (to act like a normal person) is to prove that one is 'as good as anybody else.'" Any attempt to hide, forget, or cover up traits considered unacceptable will have a negative impact on a person's self-concept. Horney (1937) states that a person wishing to obscure a handicap often finds himself without associates. On the one hand, the person may resist association with other similarly handicapped persons for fear of drawing attention to his handicap. On the other hand, the person may avoid association with nonhandicapped persons for fear of differences being even more obvious. The person threatened by contact will avoid contact with either group. Given the need to feel "at home" with oneself, such a person is virtually homeless.

Severity of Handicap, Adjustment, and Self-Concept

Empirical evidence suggests that severe disability does not necessarily go hand in hand with maladjustment. Conversely, mild disability offers no guarantee of positive adjustment. Wright (1960) reasons that a person with mild disability, because he is relatively normal, may recognize greater potential for hiding his disability. She asserts that the hiding process prompts denial and thwarts adjustment, because the person hiding a trait judged to be undesirable has already engaged in self-devaluation. Self-devaluation, in turn, affects negatively the self-concept. Persons with severe undeniable disabilities may have little recourse but to accept themselves as persons with a disability.

In either case, the person who does adjust may need to cling temporarily to the "normal ideal." Wright believes that it may be necessary to embrace that ideal before one can truly give it up and find satisfaction in being oneself.

The foregoing discussion is not intended to deny the significance of adjustment problems that confront the severely handicapped person. An investigation by Bansavage (1968) found that persons with severe congenital handicaps experience the least status in the social community. Persons with severe acquired handicaps experience a higher social status. Bansavage hypothesizes that a severe congenital handicap, because it is omnipresent from birth, greatly limits experiences that ensure status in the community.

Siller et al. (1967) report that most able-bodied persons accept persons with disabilities in school or work settings, but reject disabled persons in personal relationships. Richardson and Emerson (1970) reinforce Bansavage and Siller et al.'s findings, which suggest that disability, particularly physical disability, may overshadow even racial discrimination as a force in social preference.

The degree and type of handicap confronting the individual thus play a significant role in adjustment and self-concept development. Each person's unique individuality is, however, also significant in the adjustment and self-concept development process.

Empathy Versus Sympathy

Empathy and sympathy are similar in sound only. Recognizing the difference in the meaning of these words and the different concepts that they embody is critical for those who teach or otherwise function in a professional or personal relationship with persons who have handicaps.

Empathy is the mature, genuine understanding of another's situation and circumstances. A saying in Native American lore speaks eloquently to the issue of empathy when the speaker admonishes, "Make no judgments about me until you have walked a mile in my moccasins." Empathy is the ability to understand another's thoughts or state of mind without actually having experienced her circumstances. Inability to empathize with another diminishes the teacher's potential to influence positively the learner's development. The ability to empathize goes beyond establishing rapport; it fosters insight, which creates an effective working relationship.

Sympathy is feeling sorry for another. It connotes, "Oh, you poor unfortunate fellow!" Sympathy is synonymous with pity; pity devalues worth, and devalued worth causes additional suffering. People want understanding, not pity.

Stories about outstanding achievements by persons with handicaps often unwittingly provoke sympathy and pity. The story of Pete Gray provides a case in point. Gray, who at age 6 lost an arm in a truck accident, became a major league baseball player. One newspaper account (cited in Rusk and Taylor 1946, p. 140) of Gray's achievement read:

> Gray is an inspiration. . . . The mere fact that a one-armed ball player has crashed the big league opens up new and electrifying vistas for each of them [similarly handicapped persons]. If one can overcome his handicap in such fashion, there is hope for them all.

Reference to "them" effectively, though unwittingly, promotes the we-they dichotomy, which, based on disability alone, sets the disabled person apart from able-bodied persons. The last phrase, "there is hope for them all," drives home the stigma: Poor fellow. But don't worry. Even for people like you there is hope.

Inspirational messages should not be eliminated, but should be tempered with empathy and an understanding that undertones can devalue the self-worth of the persons for whom the message is intended.

Handling of Death in Our Society

Life's ultimate reality is death, yet death remains a reality with which many persons are unable to cope. Anxieties surrounding the imminent death of a terminally ill child are perplexing for everyone. People accept the death of older persons, but a child's death assaults reason. Human beings need to search philosophically for some purpose surrounding a child's death, yet an obsessive search disallows dealing with death's reality.

Some decades ago, most people in the United States were born and died at home. Three generations (children, parents, and grandparents) often lived together in a single dwelling, and the entire family was witness to birth, life, and death. Today, birth and death have been effectively obscured from human experience, because people are born and die in hospitals. Once, death was part of life's experiences; today death has become taboo because of its removal from view. While death in the home was not a welcome event, those who witnessed death were somewhat better prepared to accept its consequences as life's natural culmination.

Terminal Illness in Children

The dying child, if mature enough to grasp death's significance, and those affected by the child's death, experience changes in attitude as death approaches. If adjustment time is sufficient, people can accept death as inevitable and imminent. The dying person often takes comfort in the closeness and presence of loved ones.

Attitudinal changes that lead to acceptance include anger, denial, bargaining (most often with God), and depression. Kübler-Ross (1964) states that each stage, given sufficient time, is "worked through," with the person ultimately accepting death's arrival and reality. This working through is experienced by the dying person and by those affected.

Kübler-Ross says that the dying child often will single out one adult with whom to communicate feelings about death. That person is often not a parent but a teacher or therapist. Parents are not chosen because the child, sensitive to the parents' grief, does not wish to compound that grief. The selected person must be willing to accept the child's feelings, or the child will experience profound loneliness.

Teacher's Roles

The teacher's roles are complex, for the teacher must communicate personally and sensitively with the child, the child's parents, and the child's friends. The teacher must recognize that his primary role is that of teacher to the dying child and teacher to the child's classmates. Responsibility is not only to the terminally ill child but also to the children who remain.

In coping with this situation, teachers must first work through their own thoughts and concepts about death. Bigge and O'Donnell's work (1976) on the psychological aspects of physical disability, particularly implications of terminal illness, should be read. They suggest strategies and attitudes helpful to parents and professionals who work with terminally ill children:

- Treat all children the same. If children with cerebral palsy are disciplined, also discipline those with terminal illness.
- Be objective in goal setting, building toward attainable goals.
- Maintain mental health. Be available to those who are dying and to those who remain after the classmate's death.
- Develop an understanding of the Kübler-Ross stages of coping with death and how children, parents, and professionals may use them. Recognize that everyone does not progress at the same pace, and allow for individual differences in coping.
- Define your role as an educator, remembering that your role and responsibility are to teach. Included in that role is a responsibility as a human being to meet the personal needs of students. Your primary role, however, remains that of teacher.
- Respond to, and accept, your own feelings of anxiety, anger, guilt, and sorrow, and share these, when appropriate, with the children.
- Recognize the teacher as a catalyst for hope, but do not be foolishly optimistic.
- Prepare to answer the child's questions, such as "Am I going to die?" Such questions must be answered carefully and honestly in response to individual needs.
- Prepare yourself to deal with the behavior of youngsters who cannot act out physically, and thus may rebel verbally against the world.
- Establish rapport with professionals in medicine and mental health who can be valuable resources.
- Deal with yourself.

The Helping Relationship

In a helping relationship, the person being helped is often assumed to be unable to help herself. The act of helping another can be easily interpreted as helplessness on the part of the person receiving assistance. The judgment of helplessness can be made by the helper, by the person being helped, or by persons observing the assistance. Because helping suggests a one-sided relationship, value judgments are made about the person receiving aid. The person who receives help consistently may be judged inferior to others who seem self-reliant and independent.

Virtually everyone needs help sometimes, and one's sensitivity to receiving help is a highly individual reaction. Most persons respond positively to assistance if it is genuinely needed and is not offered primarily to satisfy the helper's ego.

A person with a disability usually desires minimum assistance and only when necessary. Before helping, always obtain the consent of the person involved. Do not assume that help is needed or wanted. Assistance, particularly unsolicited assistance, may be interpreted as denial of the person's independence. If a person desires help but uncertainty exists about what exactly is needed, the helper should simply ask. Assistance should be focused on the task, not on the relationship. Fuss and emotional display by the helper suggest ego feeding at the expense of the person receiving assistance.

Helping has psychological as well as physical impact on the recipient. The helper who understands clearly his own motivations will probably offer specific assistance only when needed, which is appreciated and which acknowledges the recipient's self-respect.

This chapter opened with five lines of poetry by Bart Lanier Safford III. We close this chapter with another of Safford's poems. Safford, who has cerebral palsy, has earned three degrees in higher education. In the opening excerpt, however, he placed his academic achievements in perspective in fewer than 20 words. For Safford and for those to whom he speaks, disability in psychosocial perspective is not pristine, abstract theory but an enduring fact of life. Safford, whose gift with words enables him to say more in a few words than others say in volumes, has written the following poem, which might well have been directed to physical education teachers or to those who coach persons with disabilities. His poem is entitled "The Baseball Manager and the Warm-up Jacket":

> In high school in Brooklyn
> I was the baseball manager,
> proud as I could be
> I chased baseballs,
> gathered thrown bats,
> handed out the towels
> It was very important work
> for a small spastic kid,
> but I was a team member
> When the team got
> their warm-up jackets
> I didn't get one
> Only the regular team
> got these jackets, and
> surely not a manager
> Eventually, I bought my own
> but it was dark blue while
> the official ones were green
> Nobody ever said anything
> to me about my blue jacket;
> the guys were my friends
> Yet it hurt me all year
> to wear that blue jacket
> among all those green ones
> Even now, forty years after,
> I still recall that jacket
> and the memory goes on hurting.
>
>   Bart Lanier Safford III
>   from *An Obscured Radiance* (1978, p. 2)

Summary

The psychosocial implications of disability can extend further than the direct impact of the disability itself. Disabilities of great proportion do not, however, always precipitate greater problems of psychosocial adjustment. The impact that any disability has on psychosocial well-being is largely an individual phenomenon.

When difficulties in adjustment are apparent, defense mechanisms may be used. These include regression, repression, denial, rationalization, resignation, and becoming dependent or demanding.

Teachers should strive to empathize with the disabled person. Sympathy denies the self-worth of the individual at whom it is directed and has a devaluing effect on the recipient's self-esteem. The person whose level of self-esteem waivers will find pity particularly devastating. Conversely, empathy reflects a mature effort to understand the circumstances and challenges confronting an individual. Sympathy is synonymous with pity, empathy with understanding.

The adapted physical educator may encounter students with terminal illness. In these circumstances, the teacher should be prepared to provide appropriate support to the dying child and to the child's peers. Both the dying child and the child's peers may rely heavily on the teacher. The educator must understand her own responses to death and must be prepared to deal with the children's responses.

In the adapted physical education setting, the teacher becomes involved in helping relationships. These relationships must preserve the recipient's self-esteem. Help should be offered only when needed and desired. Offering help too quickly in specific situations may deny the opportunity to achieve independence. In many instances, the teacher, uncertain of how much help is needed, should simply ask the student.

All persons, irrespective of disability or nondisability, have psychosocial needs. Whether or not these needs are met determines the individual's adjustment to personal circumstances. Just as all able-bodied persons do not manifest positive psychosocial adjustment, so all persons with disability do not exhibit problematic adjustment. In facilitating all psychosocial adjustments, the individual's integrity must be preserved.

References

Bansavage, J. Social Acceptance in a Group of Orthopedically Impaired Adolescents. *APA Proceedings* 28:647–648, 1968.

Bigge, J. L., and O'Donnell, P. A. *Teaching Individuals With Physical and Multiple Disabilities.* Columbus, Ohio: Charles E. Merrill, 1976.

Goldberg, R. T. Adjustment of Children With Visible and Invisible Handicaps. *Journal of Counseling Psychology* 21:428–432, 1974.

Horney, K. *The Neurotic Personality of Our Time.* New York: W. W. Norton, 1937.

Kübler-Ross, A. O. *The Exceptional Child in the Family.* Orlando, Fla.: Grune & Stratton, 1964.

Levine, L. S. (as cited by Bigge). *The Impact of Disability.* Address to Oklahoma Rehabilitation Association Convention, Oklahoma City, October 1959.

Richardson, S., and Emerson, P. Race and Physical Handicap in Children's Preference for Other Children. *Human Relations* 23:31–36, 1970.

Rusk, H. A., and Taylor, E. J. *New Hope for the Handicapped.* New York: Harper & Row, 1946.

Safford, Bart Lanier, III. The Baseball Manager and the Warm-up Jacket. *Disabled USA* 2:2, 1978.

———. *An Obscured Radiance.* El Paso, Tex.: Endeavors of Humanity Press, n.d.

Siller, J., Jordan, T. A., Brown, F., and Thompson, C. A. *Studies in Attitudes Toward Disability,* vol. XI. *Attitudes of the Non-Disabled Toward the Disabled.* New York: New York University Press, 1967.

Wright, B. A. *Physical Disability—A Psychological Approach.* New York: Harper & Row, 1960.

CHAPTER 5

Basic Physical and Motor Proficiency: Component Parts and Their Assessment

All living organisms must survive in an environment surrounded by energy. Radiant, mechanical, and thermal energies are primary stimuli sources with which the organism must contend. Survival in such an energy surround is contingent on movement. If movement cannot be initiated independently, the organism is at the mercy of energy forces or is dependent on others for survival (Barsch 1965, p. 5).

Much of survival depends on movement. Independent living implies the ability to initiate movement independently to fulfill life's basic needs. Those who do not move efficiently or who must rely on others for their mobility are relatively dependent on others for survival.

Basic physical and motor proficiency are the basis of movement independence. Development of these proficiencies is *not* founded on the belief that all persons can achieve total movement independence, but rather on the belief that all persons must be afforded full opportunity to progress toward the *goal* of total movement independence.

To enable all persons to achieve movement independence commensurate with their unique potential, the educator must be able to (1) delineate the components of basic physical and motor proficiency, (2) measure proficiency by component, and (3) suggest activities to develop component proficiency.

Dissecting Physical and Motor Fitness

The term **physical and motor fitness** is global and can be described as having three major components. One component is **physical fitness proficiency.** Another component involves **motor proficiency.** The remaining component is part motor proficiency and part organic proficiency. This component is called **power,** or **explosive strength,** and is a combination of speed and strength (Figure 5.1).

Differentiating Physical Fitness and Motor Proficiency

Organic performance depends primarily on the functional integrity of the circulatory, respiratory, and muscular systems. Development of organic performance is not

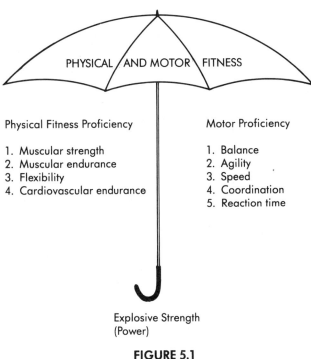

PHYSICAL /AND MOTOR\ FITNESS

Physical Fitness Proficiency

1. Muscular strength
2. Muscular endurance
3. Flexibility
4. Cardiovascular endurance

Motor Proficiency

1. Balance
2. Agility
3. Speed
4. Coordination
5. Reaction time

Explosive Strength
(Power)

FIGURE 5.1

directly associated with development of any specific motor skill. There are, however, indirect relationships. Persons who have good motor skills tend to have an active life-style, which stimulates organic fitness. Organic fitness cannot be learned as a motor skill. Rather, it is attained through physical exercise or training.

Motor performance fitness is identified closely with motor skill development. For example, balance is a motor performance component of fitness, and by developing appropriate motor skills, one might improve balance. Likewise, agility, which requires rapid direction change, is improved by developing skills that promote prompt, efficient direction change. Motor performance fitness components therefore differ from their organic counterparts in that the latter tend to be enhanced as the person's motor skill repertoire expands, while the former tend to improve primarily through physical exercise or training.

Specificity in Fitness

Because the term *physical fitness* has many specific components, it is misleading to speak in general terms about a person's degree of physical fitness. Greater accuracy is attained by considering a person's "fitness for a given task."

The components of fitness tend to represent different performance attributes that support fitness specificity and fitness for a given task. In practical terms, possessing good balance does not necessarily predict or guarantee strength, good agility does not necessarily predict or guarantee speed, explosive strength does not necessarily guarantee agility, and so forth. As a rule, a person is "fit for a given (specific) task" if that task is executed with a reasonable degree of skill, without undue fatigue, and with rapid recovery from exertion.

Developing Fitness and the Overload Principle

The overload principle implies that a body system or function can develop (i.e., increase capacity to function) only if work loads in excess of normal demands are experienced.

These practical observations indicate that overload is occurring:

1. Elevated breathing
2. Perspiration
3. Noticeably diminished performance
4. Strained facial expression
5. Flushed face
6. Elevated pulse rate

Overload is a highly individual phenomenon, so different levels of exercise stress will affect individuals differently. In establishing overload levels for handicapped persons, it is important that the task demand be beyond, yet still within, the person's grasp. The handicapped person who has not had successful experiences does not need to fail at yet another task demand, in this case one that is fitness oriented. Remember also that many disabled students do not possess average levels of strength or endurance. Overload for them should be at a relatively low level of intensity. A good rule to follow is: A little more today than yesterday.

Winnick and Short (1985) believe that to increase strength, including strength of those with physically handicapping conditions, overloading the muscles is necessary. Auxter and Pyfer (1985, p. 369) list five ways to achieve muscle overload: (1) increase number of repetitions or sets, (2) increase distance covered, (3) increase speed at which the exercise is performed, (4) increase number of minutes of continuous effort, and (5) decrease rest interval between activity sessions.

To determine the appropriate exercise or activity stress level for persons with special needs (i.e., heart valve defect, cystic fibrosis, juvenile rheumatoid arthritis, Duchenne muscular dystrophy), the opinion of the person's physician should be sought. The physician can assist in ascertaining activity levels that bring the person to, but not past, the threshold of overload stress tolerance.

Organic Performance Components of Fitness

Strength—maximal or near maximal muscular exertion of relatively brief duration. The duration is necessarily brief because intense, concentrated muscular effort is required. Pushing a stalled automobile is an example of an activity requiring strength. Another example would be lifting oneself from the ground into a wheelchair. Virtually any activity that meets the criteria of brief duration and maximal or near maximal exertion will develop muscular strength. Repetitive (i.e., dynamic) exercise tends to develop strength when the resistance encountered permits only ten or fewer repetitions.

Strength development is important for all persons regardless of disability, because a certain amount of strength is required to do virtually everything. Indeed, minimal levels of strength must be achieved before minimal skill levels can be developed. For example, one cannot become proficient at working with crutches until minimal levels of grip and arm and shoulder girdle strength have been achieved. Without sufficient strength, even simple activities are difficult (Figures 5.2 and 5.3).

Flexibility—the ability of body segments to move through normal ranges of motion. Like strength, flexibility can be a major determinant of success in many physical and motor activities. Virtually all require a minimum degree of flexibility before the activity can be executed comfortably, correctly, and with minimum risk of muscle strain.

Unexpected muscle stretching beyond normal motion range may cause strain on a continuum from mild to strain so severe that surgical repair is needed. The range of motion through which a body can move comfortably is largely a function of the muscle

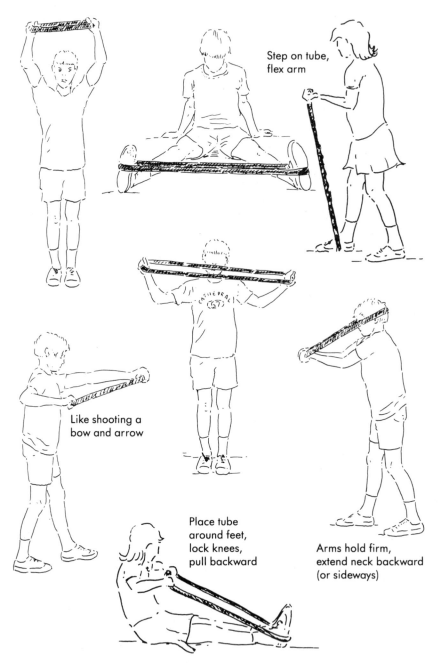

Step on tube, flex arm

Like shooting a bow and arrow

Place tube around feet, lock knees, pull backward

Arms hold firm, extend neck backward (or sideways)

FIGURE 5.2.   Strength development using inner tube strips. (Reprinted from Moran and Kalakian 1977, p. 42.)

FIGURE 5.3. Flexed arm hang requires strength and endurance. Here, an upper extremity amputee receives assistance from her instructor.

stretching that an individual is accustomed to experiencing. Relative inactivity may precipitate loss of flexibility. Maintenance of flexibility in persons with handicaps is particularly important to the extent that such persons may tend to have a sedentary life-style.

Flexibility maintenance is a lifelong need. Without flexibility, one's capacity to enjoy movement is reduced. Reduced enjoyment then fosters activity avoidance, reduced activity fosters further flexibility loss, and the cycle continues. Significant flexibility loss with advancing age is often due more to progressive inactivity than to advancing age.

To foster flexibility through activity and exercise, it is important that muscles be stretched to, but not through, the discomfort threshold (Figure 5.4). Without discomfort, sufficient stretching does not occur to enhance flexibility (remember the overload principle). When one stretches beyond the initial discomfort sensation, however, muscles can be overextended to the point of injury.

Muscular endurance—submaximal muscular effort that continues for a relatively long period of time. Unlike strength activities, muscular endurance activities do not involve brief, all-out exertions. Rather, they require persistent, submaximal effort.

FIGURE 5.4. Flexibility development.

Many activities in industry, workshops, domestic upkeep, and physical education require muscular endurance. Lifting medium-heavy weights or meeting medium-heavy resistance over an extended period involves muscular endurance.

Muscular endurance and muscular strength may be thought of as opposite extremes of a continuum. Most activities require relative strength or relative endurance, and fall somewhere between the two extremes. Many activities that enhance strength can, with modest alteration, be used to develop muscular endurance. In strength-building activities, the resistance encountered must be sufficient to require immediate, near maximal exertion. Because of the intensity of a strength activity, its duration is necessarily brief. A similar activity can be used to develop muscular endurance by simultaneously reducing the resistance and increasing the duration. Muscles then fatigue gradually and the body's response is to increase muscular capacity for submaximal, protracted effort.

Cardiovascular endurance—ability of the heart and circulatory system to adapt to the demands of prolonged, total body physical exertion. This fitness component is perhaps the most important of all, for it involves the functional integrity of vital organs. Since cardiovascular disease is the leading cause of death in the United States and is the very antithesis of a healthy and active life, the teacher of handicapped persons must stress development and maintenance of cardiovascular fitness.

Any activity that is sufficiently taxing to elevate significantly an individual's heart rate for more than 5 min is considered cardiovascular activity. To achieve noticeable results, the activity must be performed a minimum of 3 days per week. Typical cardiovascular activities include prolonged walking, swimming, jogging, cycling, or crutch- or wheelchair-assisted ambulation. Locomotor rhythm activities and dance are equally appropriate ways to stimulate cardiovascular development. Cardiovascular activities may be particularly taxing for some persons with paraplegia, because flaccid (flax' sid) paralysis (in this case, in the lower extremities) prevents the "milking" action of muscles, which returns venous blood to the heart. This relative inability of lower extremity muscles to contract and relax may cause inordinate pooling of venous blood in the lower extremities. To put this condition in a broader context, consider the fact that an increasing number of highly conditioned wheelchair athletes consistently demonstrate the ability to "run" full marathons in times that are equal to or better than those of nondisabled runners in the same race.

Training studies and other research have demonstrated that mentally retarded youngsters, when offered appropriate programs, are able to achieve levels of physical fitness equal to fitness levels of nonretarded peers. Thomas (1984) found that mentally retarded children could perform qualitatively as well as their chronological age counterparts when *taught* or *motivated* to do so. She states: "MR individuals can be both cued to attend and forced to rehearse, and exhibit normal retention. With more time (or trials), MR students can reach and maintain mastery" (p. 182).

Motor Performance Components of Fitness

Balance—ability to maintain a proper relationship between one's points of support (i.e., hands, feet) and one's center of gravity.   Balance may be either static or dynamic. **Static balance** involves balance in a stationary position. **Dynamic balance** involves balance with the body in motion. Either static or dynamic balance may occur on moving surfaces. All types of balancing are required in everyday life and can be replicated and practiced in physical education settings.

Some controversy exists as to whether balance is a general trait in the physical and motor performance area. Some believe that balance is highly specific to the task being executed (Ulrich and Ulrich 1985). Others suggest that the balance trait is, indeed, general, and that general balance activities improve balance in the broad spectrum of motor performance (Williams 1983). The issue of balance specificity has not been fully resolved. Pending resolution of the controversy, general balance activities are cautiously recommended (Figure 5.5).

Agility—ability to rapidly and effectively change direction.   Agility is an important fitness component, especially in activities requiring sudden, unexpected direction change. Agility is also an important means of side-stepping unexpected danger (e.g., jumping from the path of an oncoming car). In sports, agility is important when one must guard or "shadow" an opponent. Teachers can promote agility through a variety

FIGURE 5.5. Examples of balance activities. (Reprinted from Moran and Kalakian 1977, p. 47.)

of low-organized games, tag games, and relays. Students can be told to mirror the random, rapid direction changes of another person. Any activity that requires rapid movement coupled with frequent direction change develops agility.

Speed—ability to traverse straight, short distances rapidly. While speed is generally associated almost exclusively with running, Safrit (1973) notes that speed is observed whenever the individual demonstrates any rapid, successive movement. Most fitness tests, however, rely on running as the primary means of assessing speed.

For purposes of assessing or enhancing speed, distance should not exceed 50 yd. This is considered a long enough distance to attain maximum speed while minimizing the influence of reaction time, and a short enough distance to avoid involvement of the variable of cardiovascular endurance.

In assessing speed among persons with motor involvement, including bipedal, crutch-assisted, and wheelchair-assisted ambulation, distances may be modified as individual needs dictate.

Coordination—harmonious interaction of individual muscles and muscle groups to produce skilled movement patterns. It involves the ability of muscles to contract with proper intensity at the opportune moment and in proper sequence. Coordination is a twofold function, resulting from effective instruction, of practice and properly directed effort. Specific skills such as catching or hitting a ball are examples of the eye-hand type of coordination.

Reaction time—elapsed time between activation of a stimulus and the organism's response. The stimulus may be auditory (buzzer), visual (hand signal), or tactile (touch). This component is the least modifiable, and for that reason is often not emphasized.

Explosive strength (power)—a combination of speed and strength produced by the force and rapidity with which muscles are able to contract. This fitness component does not fall exclusively in either the organic or motor category, but incorporates speed from motor performance fitness and strength from organic performance fitness. Power is used for throwing, kicking, running (start), striking, or self-propelling as in a jump, hop, or leap.

Assessing Basic Physical and Motor Proficiency

Assessment items, test batteries, and parts of batteries are available for the adapted physical educator. Identifying the specific component of physical and motor performance to be assessed and the characteristics of the person to be assessed are essential for selection of the proper item or battery.

Assessment tools are available for certain special populations and for the nonhandicapped population. In some instances, items or batteries designed for the nonhandicapped can be used appropriately to assess the handicapped.

Some batteries are general and are used for screening. Others are more comprehensive and serve as diagnostic tools.

Different Ways of Reporting and Interpreting Test Scores

Some tests are designed so the individual's score is compared with the scores of others. In such instances, the individual's score is compared with established norms. These tests are called **norm referenced.** When using norm-referenced tests, the evaluator must be certain that the norms are derived from a group representative of the person to whom the norms are being applied. For example, extreme caution must be exercised when applying fitness norms for nonhandicapped persons to the performance of a moderately retarded person. In contrast, if the instructor is attempting to determine if a handicapped student can participate successfully in traditional, unrestricted physical education classes, then the teacher should use the test battery and norms designed for nonhandicapped students. For example, to determine if a mildly mentally handicapped boy can be integrated successfully in the regular physical education program, he should be given the *AAHPERD Youth Fitness Test* battery, which is used for nonhandicapped youngsters. Raw scores and appropriate norm references would provide the information necessary for appropriate placement.

Some tests are **criterion referenced.** In these tests, a performance criterion is stated as a behavioral objective, and the person's performance is assessed with respect to conformance to the criterion. Both norm- and criterion-referenced instruments measuring fitness are discussed later in this chapter.

Assessment Must Not Discriminate Unfairly

When administering tests and other evaluations to a child with impaired sensory, manual, or speaking skills, care must be taken to ensure that the test results reflect accurately the child's aptitude, achievement level, or whatever other factors the test purports to measure, rather than reflecting the child's impairment (unless specific skill impairment is the factor that the test measures) (AAHPERD 1977).

When the physical or motor performance items are not appropriate to the specific capabilities or characteristics of the individual, then the instrument is worthless in that given situation. For example, sit-ups, used as a measure of muscular endurance, could discriminate unfairly against a person whose paralysis limits abdominal or hip flexor function. Instead, pull-ups, flexed arm hang, hang time, or parallel bar dips might be more appropriate endurance tests. For blind or partially sighted persons, the shuttle run as a measure of agility should be replaced by the less discriminatory squat thrust (burpee). In assessing the physical and motor performance of mentally retarded persons, test results should reflect actual physical or motor ability, not the individual's limited comprehension of task demands. In evaluating persons with special needs, the adapted physical educator must be sure that the results truly reflect what the test purports specifically to measure.

Assessment Instruments

We do not offer an exhaustive delineation of physical and motor proficiency assessment tools in this text. Rather, we present selected tools as exemplary of the available instruments. Each is intended for a specific population and may provide an initial reference in the search for additional and perhaps more appropriate instruments.

Some instruments function as *screening devices* but do not purport to be thoroughly diagnostic. Rather, they identify persons whose physical and motor performance fitness levels are less than adequate for safe, successful participation in a mainstream program. While the definition of *adequacy* may vary, passing a screening test does not necessarily mean high or even moderate fitness. Passing may mean simply that the person has achieved the bare minimum.

Bruininks-Oseretsky Test of Motor Proficiency

One screening test for basic motor proficiency is the short form of the *Bruininks-Oseretsky Test of Motor Proficiency* (Bruininks 1978). The form includes 14 of the 46 items that appear on the Bruininks-Oseretsky long form. The long form is more comprehensive and is recommended as a motor proficiency diagnostic instrument. The short form may serve as an initial screening device when many children must be assessed in a short time. The instrument is designed for persons age 4½ to 14½ years. The short form yields both stanine and percentile rank scores and measures proficiency in the following components of motor behavior: running speed and agility, balance, bilateral coordination, upper limb coordination, strength,[1] lower limb coordination, response speed, visual-motor control,[1] and upper limb speed and dexterity.

AAHPERD Youth Fitness Test (AAHPERD 1976a)

Perhaps the best known test that purports to measure physical and motor fitness is the *AAHPERD Youth Fitness Test* offered by the American Alliance for Health, Physical Education, Recreation and Dance (AAHPERD 1976a). The test has existed since 1958 and has undergone revisions. In its present form, it includes national norms and assesses physical fitness of youngsters age 9 to 17+ years. Items in the current revision include the following:

1. Flexed arm hang (girls) (Figure 5.6) and pull-up (boys) (Figure 5.7) (shoulder girdle muscular strength or muscular endurance, depending on student's fitness level at time of testing)
2. Flexed knee sit-up (Figure 5.8) (timed: number completed in 1 min) (abdominal

---

1. Physical fitness literature from the physical education profession typically does not include these items as measures of *motor* proficiency. Strength generally is considered organic fitness, while visual-motor control generally appears in batteries that assess perceptual-motor competence.

FIGURE 5.6.   Flexed arm hang. (Reprinted from Moran and Kalakian 1977, p. 51.)

and hip flexor strength or muscular endurance, depending on student's fitness level at time of testing)

3. Shuttle run (Figure 5.9) (agility)
4. Standing long jump (Figure 5.10) (explosive strength)
5. 50 yard dash (running speed)
6. 600 yard run (optional 1 mi or 9 min run for ages 10 to 12, or 1½ mi or 12 min run for ages 13 or older) (cardiovascular endurance)

AAHPERD (1980) published the *Health Related Physical Fitness Test*. This test is alleged to focus solely on items known to correlate with health. Items believed to be more directly related to the acquisition of motor skills are not on the test. Health-related physical fitness items include the following:

1. Triceps, subscapular, and abdominal skin fold (subcutaneous body fat)
2. Sit-ups (abdominal strength and endurance)
3. Sit and reach (flexibility)
4. One mi or 9 min run for ages 10 to 12, 1½ mi or 12 min run for ages 13 or older (cardiovascular endurance)

Peabody Developmental Motor Scales

The *Peabody Developmental Motor Scales* (1983) are designed to identify gross and fine motor skills of children between the ages of birth and 7 years. The test battery gathers knowledge about the skills that the children have mastered, those skills that

FIGURE 5.7. Palms away pull-up. (Reprinted from Moran and Kalakian 1977, p. 50.)

they are currently developing, and those not yet developed. Over 200 specific gross motor skills and 130 fine motor skills are listed through the 7-year developmental sequence. Suggested activities for improving and strengthening needed skills are also included.

Ohio State University Scale of Intra-Gross Motor Assessment (O.S.U. SIGMA)

This test battery was developed by Drs. Mike Loovis and Walt Ersing (1980). It is designed to assess the efficiency and maturity of children from preschool age through 14 years. Eleven gross motor skills were selected: walking, running, hopping, jumping, catching, throwing, stair climbing, ladder climbing, kicking, skipping, and striking.

Brigance Diagnostic Inventories

This series includes three different test batteries, but the *Diagnostic Inventory of Early Development* (Brigance, 1978) contains a strong component of motor skill assessment. The test battery is designed for use with individuals who have developmental ages of less than 7 years. It is criterion referenced, and also has norm referencing included. The following areas are identified: (1) 4 preambulatory motor sequences (i.e., supine, prone, sitting, and standing positions), (2) 13 gross motor sequences (e.g., walking, catching, rhythm), and (3) 9 fine motor sequences (e.g., eye-finger-hand manipulations, painting).

Hands behind head

FIGURE 5.8. Flexed knee sit-up. (Reprinted from Moran and Kalakian 1977, p. 52.)

Other Commonly Encountered Measures of Fitness by Component

Strength

1. Push-ups (ranging from most difficult to easiest) (Figures 5.11 and 5.12)
2. Parallel bar dips
3. Grip-strength dynamometer (Figure 5.13)

Muscular Endurance

Items that measure muscular strength will also measure endurance for students who are able to continue execution over an extended period. Generally, strength is

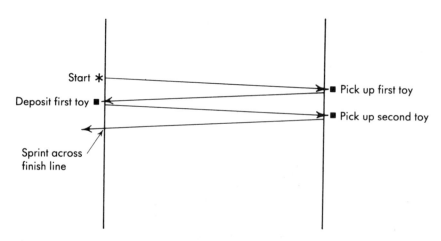

Start ✳

Deposit first toy ■

Pick up first toy

Pick up second toy

Sprint across finish line

FIGURE 5.9. Agility run configuration. (Reprinted from Moran and Kalakian 1977, p. 56.)

FIGURE 5.10. Standing long jump.

FIGURE 5.11. Straight back push-up (most difficult).

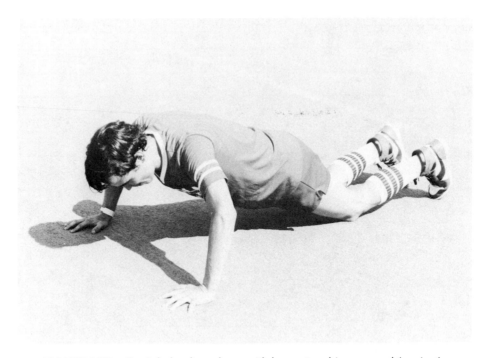

FIGURE 5.12. Straight back push-up with knees touching ground (easiest).

FIGURE 5.13. Grip strength.

measured when maximum repetitions fall below ten. Muscular endurance is measured as the student repeats executions beyond ten.

Flexibility

1. Back lifts (Figure 5.14). Measure height from floor while in maximum extension.
2. Front and side splits (Figure 5.15). Measure distance from crotch to floor.
3. Shoulder rotation. Grasp the rope with both hands positioned shoulder width apart and with the rope passing in front of the body. Keeping arms straight, the student should rotate her arms up, over her head, and back until the rope rests against the buttocks. The rope should slide through her hands only to the extent necessary to execute the action correctly. A score is derived by subtracting shoulder width from the rope length required to execute shoulder rotation.

Cardiovascular Endurance

Measures heavily relied on include 300 (Figure 5.16) and 600 yard runs, 1 and 1½ mi runs, and 9 and 12 min runs. These are found in the *AAHPERD Youth Fitness Test Manual* (AAHPERD 1976a) and in AAHPERD manuals modified for use with special

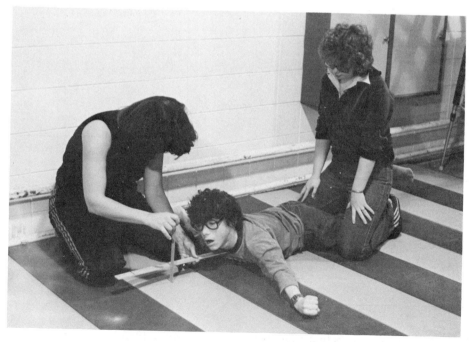

FIGURE 5.14.   Back lifts measure flexibility.

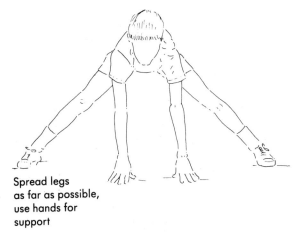

Spread legs
as far as possible,
use hands for
support

FIGURE 5.15. Side split (straddle) flexibility. (Reprinted from Moran and Kalakian 1977, p. 44.)

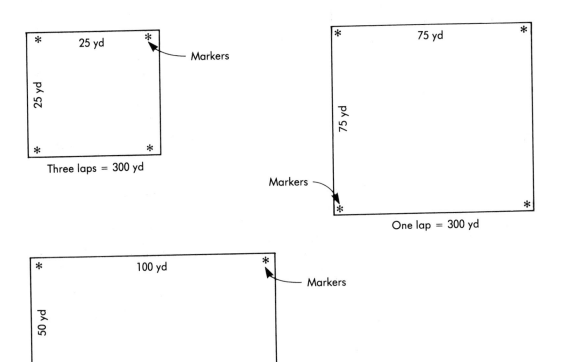

FIGURE 5.16. Suggested configurations for 300 yard run-walk. (Reprinted from Moran and Kalakian 1977, p. 54.)

populations (blind and partially sighted, mildly and moderately retarded) (Buell 1973; AAHPERD 1975, 1976b). (See page 179 for a comparison of these test batteries.)

Balance

1. Stork stand (Figure 5.17). Stand on ball of preferred foot (on flat foot if necessary), hands on hips, with opposite foot touching inside of support knee. Score is number of seconds that the student is able to maintain the correct stork-stand position. Ten sec maximum.
2. Bass stick (crosswise) (Bass 1956). Stand on ball of preferred foot crosswise on a 1 × 1 × 12 in. stick. Six 60-sec trials are given (three trials per foot). Score is the total time from six trials during which the student remains in the correctly balanced position.
3. Bass stick (lengthwise) (Bass 1956). Same as no. 2 except for direction change of stick.
4. Beam walking forward, backward, and sideward (observe both left foot lead and right foot lead in the sideward item). Take six steps in each of the four directions and receive a separate evaluation for each performance. During each of the four separate trials, each step on the beam scores one point, a step off the beam scores zero. Maximum score is six points per trial. Beam height and width must be standardized when comparisons between trials or between students are made. Among low ability students, a stripe on the floor may replace the beam.

Coordination

1. Throw ball for accuracy.
2. Throw ball in air and catch (ball should rise a distance approximately equal to the person's height). Ball must be thrown directly overhead, must be caught before it bounces, and must not require locomotion for catching. Ten trials are required, and one point is scored for each correct effort.
3. Alternate foot tap and hand clap. Person, while seated, alternately and rhythmically taps left and right foot. With rhythm established, person claps hands simultaneously with each tap. Each properly timed hand clap scores one point. Thirty sec maximum.

Speed

Speed generally is measured in dashes not to exceed 50 yd. Given Safrit's (1973, p. 142) observation that speed "is observed whenever the individual demonstrates rapid successive movements of the same kind," a number of alternatives exist to measure speed. Examples are:

Tiptoe,
hands on hips

Flat foot,
hands on hips

FIGURE 5.17.   Stork stand. (Reprinted from Moran and Kalakian 1977, p. 55.)

1. Pencil tap with preferred hand. (Note in 30 sec number of dots the student makes on a piece of paper.)
2. Note in 30 sec number of hand claps the student executes.
3. Note in 30 sec number of foot taps made with the preferred foot.
4. Measure distance run during specific time period (e.g., 6 sec dash). Flying start may be incorporated to reduce influence of explosive strength or reaction time.

Agility

1. Time zigzag run, crutch-assisted ambulation, or chair wheeling (Figure 5.18) through obstacle course.
2. During finite period of time, observe number of cones in zigzag run that the student maneuvers successfully.
3. Use shuttle run in the *AAHPERD Youth Fitness Test*, but eliminate block handling to limit influence of eye-hand coordination on student's score.
4. Use the two-count burpee (stand, squat) when the relatively more complicated measures of agility might inadvertently measure intelligence.

Explosive Strength

1. Throw ball for distance from stationary position. (Stationary position reduces influence of throwing skill on performance.) Record score to nearest foot.
2. Throw medicine ball for distance (administer same as no. 1).
3. Throw for velocity at a wall target. Use a stopwatch to record elapsed time

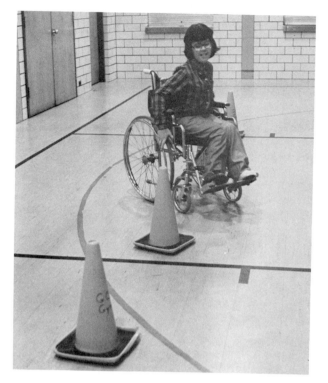

FIGURE 5.18. Wheelchair agility.

from release to impact for a designated distance. Consider only instances when ball strikes target. Impact within target area ensures that distance remains constant between trials and students. Record time to nearest tenth of second.

Selected Assessment Batteries for Special Populations

In discussing fitness assessment thus far, we have focused primarily on batteries and items not intended for any special population. The preceding items and batteries may, in many instances, be used appropriately for persons with certain disabilities. For example, a partially sighted or blind, or hearing impaired or deaf person could be tested by using some of the regular *AAHPERD Youth Fitness Test* items and norms. Items might include sit-ups, flexed arm pull-ups, and one of the various endurance runs. (For the endurance run, a blind child can run with a sighted partner who has a bell or similar noise-emitting device fixed to wrist or ankle.) The deaf person should take the entire *AAHPERD Youth Fitness Test* designed for the nonhandicapped. The most significant modification required when using the regular *AAHPERD Youth Fitness* battery with a deaf or hearing impaired person involves visual cues in timed events.

When one must rely on batteries intended specifically for a special population, the following instruments should be considered:

Blind and Partially Sighted

Buell Test (CA² 8–18) (Buell 1973)

Includes pull-ups (pull-ups for boys, flexed arm-hang pull-ups for girls), sit-ups, 50 yard dash, 600 yard run-walk, and standing long jump. All items except 50 yard dash and 600 yard run-walk incorporate regular *AAHPERD Youth Fitness Test* norms.

Mentally Retarded

Special Fitness Test for the Mildly Mentally Retarded (CA 8–18) (AAHPERD 1976b)

Includes flexed arm hang, sit-ups (bent knee, straight leg but no longer recommended), shuttle run, 50 yard dash, 300 yard run-walk, standing long jump for distance, and softball throw for distance. (See Chapter 9 on mental retardation for additional discussion of this battery.)

Motor Fitness Test for the Moderately Mentally Retarded (CA 6–21) (AAHPERD 1975)

Includes flexed arm hang, sit-ups (bent knee in 30 sec), 50 yard dash, 300 yard run-walk, standing long jump for distance, softball throw for distance, recording of height and weight, sitting bob and reach, hopping, skipping, and tumbling progression. This battery is discussed further in Chapter 9, Mental Retardation.

Physical Fitness and Health Related Fitness Norms for Mild, Moderate, and Down Syndrome Mentally Handicapped Students in Illinois (CA 6–21) (Polacek, Wang, and Eichstaedt 1985)

Includes 12 test items taken from the *AAHPERD Youth Fitness Test* battery (1976a) and from the *AAHPERD Health Related Physical Fitness Test* battery (1980). Norm-referenced tables are included for all test items for the three mental handicap classifications and for both males and females.

---

2. CA = chronological age.

Physically Handicapping Conditions

Winnick and Short (Project UNIQUE 1985) have developed national physical fitness and motor proficiency norms for persons with sensory and orthopedic impairments (CA 10–17). The following disabilities are included: blind and visually impaired, deaf and hard of hearing, orthopedic amputee, congenital defects, spinal cord defects and injuries, and cerebral palsy.

Project UNIQUE normative data were collected nationwide as to type of disability, extent of disability, and whether the person was receiving education in a regular setting or an institution.

Many items in the UNIQUE battery are from the *AAHPERD Youth Fitness Test* for the nonhandicapped and from the recent *AAHPERD Health-Related Physical Fitness Test*. The type and extent of the disability will provide the basis for determining whether the item is appropriate or requires modification to ensure suitability.

Another test that can be used to assess a physically handicapped child was adapted from the work of Bobath and Bobath by the California Department of Public Health (1964). The battery (see Chapter 17, Figure 17.5) measures basic motor control of persons with cerebral palsy by assessing various positions and postures and culminating in the skill of walking.

Fitness Games and Activities

Once the teacher understands the basic components of physical and motor proficiency, she can select activities that enhance specific proficiencies, particularly of students with low fitness. There is not room here to list or explain the many activity alternatives for persons with different abilities, special needs, and varying potentials. We can, however, cite activities that are valuable for specific fitness development.

In selecting activities to enhance fitness, the teacher should use a "means to an end" philosophy. The activity is the "means," and the fitness component is the "end." By knowing which activities and experiences promote each component of physical fitness, the teacher can develop a file of "means to an end" activities categorized according to fitness value. The following activities were selected for their specific fitness value.

Straddle Bowling
Component of fitness: Body coordination.

Students participate in groups of three. One student stands in straddle position. Student in wheelchair may substitute by placing foot rests in the "up" position. One student bowls. One student retrieves. After each roll of the ball, students rotate. Bowler tries to roll ball between

FIGURE 5.19.   Straddle bowling.

the other student's straddled legs. A ball between the legs scores 2 points; a ball that touches one leg but deflects outside the straddle scores 1 point. Distance rolled and scoring may be modified to suit each situation (Figure 5.19).

Squirrels in Trees
Components of fitness: Agility resulting from rapid change of direction in search of an unoccupied "tree"; explosive strength resulting from forcefully thrusting oneself into motion from a stationary start.

Students are designated as either squirrels or trees. Trees face each other and clasp hands with arms extended. One squirrel is permitted inside each tree. Squirrels without trees are interspersed in the midst of the activity area. When the teacher calls out "squirrels change," trees raise arms on one side, and all squirrels ambulate to get into a tree. (Those squirrels in trees must leave and seek a new tree.) Only one squirrel is allowed per tree, leaving some squirrels always in the midst of the group. The object is not to get caught without a tree. The teacher should change designations often so all students have an opportunity to be active (Figure 5.20).

Circle Hook-on
Components of fitness: Cardiovascular endurance and agility.

Three students form a circle. A fourth student remains outside the circle. One student, a member of the circle, is designated to be tagged by the student outside the circle. Circle players may maneuver in any way they wish so the pursuing child (tagger) cannot tag the designated circle member. Tagger cannot enter the circle. In avoiding the tagger, circle students cannot release clasped hands. If the designated child is tagged or if the circle players release their hand clasp, the tagger becomes part of the circle and one of the circle members then becomes the new tagger.

Jump the Shot
Components of fitness: Dynamic balance resulting from taking off and landing, explosive strength resulting from jumping, and cardiovascular endurance if activity is prolonged.

Students form a circle. A student in the center swings a weighted rope while moving within the circle. A dampened towel wadded up and tied to a rope end functions as a safe yet sufficiently heavy weight. The student in the center gradually lengthens the rope until students forming the circle must jump over the shot. The shot should be swung midway between the ankle and knee. A child who entangles the rope by failing to jump takes the student's place in the center and swings the shot until another child misses.

For some children, the weighted rope swings much too rapidly, and repeated failure should be limited. For such students, a long fiberglass rod (which may be ordered from an equipment catalog or fashioned from a defunct spinning rod or long CB whip antenna) may replace the weighted rope. Using the rod, the student (or teacher) in the center can move the rod on the floor at a speed slow enough to be compatible with a child's jumping and balance capabilities. For some children, the rod might be stopped completely before the child jumps. As the child is momentarily airborne, the rod may be slid under his feet, thereby building success into the activity (Figure 5.21).

FIGURE 5.20. Squirrels in trees. (Reprinted from Moran and Kalakian 1977, p. 64.)

FIGURE 5.21. Jump the shot. (Reprinted from Moran and Kalakian 1977, p. 65.)

Inch Worm
Components of fitness: Hop extensor flexibility, muscular strength or endurance depending on individual's level of fitness and body coordination.

The student assumes push-up position. Hands remain stationary, and feet step forward toward stationary hands. When the student is in as tight a pike as possible, the feet become stationary, and the hands walk forward until the starting push-up position is again assumed. Repeat (Figure 5.22).

Hot Potato Relay and Tag
Component of fitness: Speed.

Speed is generally considered a phenomenon of running. Actually, speed is involved whenever any body segment moves rapidly. In the hot potato relay, two circles are formed. A beanbag is the hot potato. At the signal, students pass the "hot potato" around the circle as rapidly as

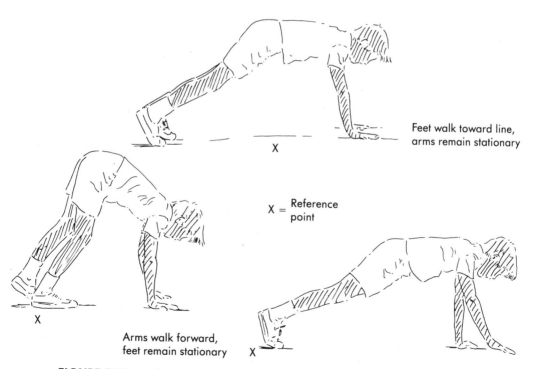

Feet walk toward line, arms remain stationary

X = Reference point

Arms walk forward, feet remain stationary

FIGURE 5.22.   Inch worm. (Reprinted from Moran and Kalakian 1977, p. 65.)

possible. In this game, all students can be seated so crutch and wheelchair ambulators are not at a disadvantage. The group that first passes the hot potato around the entire circle for a specified number of times is the winner. Circles should be kept small so activity is intense. For purposes of skill development only, introducing competition may be of little value. In such situations, students can pass the hot potato as rapidly as possible with no need to win.

Tag activities requiring running or rapid ambulation appropriate to the child also develop speed. Tag games that involve running must have physical boundaries to confine the activity, thereby increasing the activity level. Boundaries should never be hazardous. Trees, building walls, and fences are unsafe boundaries. Lime markings on a field, plastic bleach bottles, or the edge of a building shadow are appropriate, safe boundary markers.

Summary

Basic physical and motor proficiencies provide the foundation for efficient movement, and should include ten specific components. Nine of these tend to function as independent phenomena; proficiency in one component does not ensure proficiency in any other. The remaining component, power or explosive strength, is comprised of muscular strength and speed, which function together.

Tests that measure fitness may be either norm or criterion referenced. Norms compare one person's performance with that of another (i.e., one may achieve some percentile for performance on a test item). Criterion referencing compares one person's performance with a preestablished, behaviorally stated performance criterion (i.e., if the performance criterion for overarm distance throwing is 20 ft, the student's actual throwing distance is compared with that criterion). Criterion-referenced instruments are particularly useful in testing special populations for which applicable norms have not been developed.

Tests of fitness can serve initially to screen persons who may need more thorough assessment. Assessment batteries that are more thorough are considered diagnostic. Diagnostic tests of physical and motor proficiency detect only the extent and focus of developmental delay. Such tests do not identify the specific reason or reasons underlying the deficient performance level.

Whenever fitness assessment is done for special populations, the tester must be sure that the administered test item does not discriminate on the basis of handicap. For example, among persons with mental retardation, agility run times tend to correlate positively with IQ. The evaluator must therefore question whether the score is a valid measure of agility or is inaccurate because of the participant's limited understanding of the task. Student performance scores from test batteries must provide meaningful information if the adapted physical educator is to plan appropriate motor and fitness activities based on the instrument findings. Making subjective assumptions about performance levels is *not* desirable, particularly when many test batteries are now available to the physical educator.

When evaluating students, the instructor must include all dimensions of the psychomotor domain. For example, if a test battery assesses only physical fitness components, then the instructor must search out additional test items (from another test battery) that include motor skill performance (e.g., balance and eye-hand coordination).

Only after a total motor and fitness picture has been developed can appropriate activities be selected and included in the student's individualized physical education program. Posttesting also should be included in every individualized educational program to evaluate whether the selected activities had the desired effect on the child's development.

References

AAHPERD. *Motor Fitness Testing Manual for the Moderately Mentally Retarded.* Reston, Va.: AAHPERD, 1975.

———. *AAHPERD Youth Fitness Test Manual.* Reston, Va.: AAHPERD, 1976a.

———. *Special Fitness Test Manual for Mildly Mentally Retarded Persons.* Reston, Va.: AAHPERD, 1976b.

———. *Practical Pointers* 1(6):10. Reston, Va.: AAHPERD, 1977.

———. *AAHPERD Health Related Physical Fitness Test Manual.* Reston, Va.: AAHPERD, 1980.

Auxter, D., and Pyfer, J. *Principles and Methods of Adapted Physical Education and Recreation,* 5th ed. St. Louis: Times Mirror/Mosby College Publishing, 1985.

Barsch, R. *A Movegenic Curriculum.* Madison, Wis.: Bureau for Handicapped Children, 1965.

Bass, R. An Analysis of the Components of Tests of Semi-Circular Canal Function and of Static and Dynamic Balance. *Research Quarterly* 27:261, 1956.

Brigance, A. *Diagnostic Inventory of Early Development.* North Billerica, Mass.: Curriculum Associates, 1978.

Bruininks, R. H. *Bruininks-Oseretsky Test of Motor Proficiency: Examiner's Manual.* Circle Pines, Minn.: American Guidance Service, 1978.

Buell, C. *Physical Education and Recreation for the Visually Handicapped.* Reston, Va.: AAHPERD, 1973.

California Department of Public Health, Bureau of Crippled Children Services. *Cerebral Palsy Assessment Chart—Basic Motor Control.* Sacramento, Calif.: The Department, 1964.

Loovis, M. E., and Ersing, W. F. *Assessing and Programming Gross Motor Development for Children.* Loudonville, Ohio: Mohican Publishing, 1980.

Moran, J. M., and Kalakian, L. H. *Movement Experiences for the Mentally Retarded or Emotionally Disturbed Child,* 2nd ed. Minneapolis: Burgess Publishing, 1977.

Peabody Developmental Motor Scales. Nashville, Tenn.: George Peabody College, 1983.

Polacek, J. J., Wang, P. Y., and Eichstaedt, C. B. *A Study of Physical and Health Related Fitness Levels of Mild, Moderate, and Down Syndrome Students in Illinois.* Normal, Ill.: Illinois State University Press, 1985.

Safrit, M. J. *Evaluation in Physical Education.* Englewood Cliffs, N.J.: Prentice-Hall, 1973.

Thomas, K. T. Applying Knowledge of Motor Development to Mentally Retarded Children. In *Motor Development During Childhood and Adolescence,* edited by J. R. Thomas. Minneapolis: Burgess Publishing, 1984.

Ulrich, B. D., and Ulrich, D. A. The Role of Balancing Ability in Performance of Fundamental Motor Skills in 3-, 4-, and 5-Year-Old Children. In *Motor Development—Current Selected Research*, Vol. I, edited by J. E. Clark and J. H. Humphrey. Princeton, N. J.: Princeton Book Co., 1985.

Williams, H. *Perceptual and Motor Development*. Englewood Cliffs, N.J.: Prentice-Hall, 1983.

Winnick, J. P., and Short, F. X. *Physical Fitness Testing of the Disabled—Project UNIQUE*. Champaign, Ill.: Human Kinetics Publishers, 1985.

CHAPTER 6

Fundamental Motor Skills

> *In about the third grade, I could neither catch nor throw a ball with the proficiency that would enhance my self-concept. By the time I finished third grade, I had come to detest that ball, because it was the source of all those feelings of inadequacy which, at the time, mattered most. One day, after an eternity of missed catches, inaccurate throws, strikeouts, and being chosen last (or being told by the team captain to play in the outfield because the ball seldom got that far), I managed to get that damned ball when nobody was looking. Intent upon punishing that ball for all it had done to me, I took it to the farthest corner of the playground and literally buried it. For a while, I felt good, because I knew my spheroid enemy, in its final resting place, couldn't hurt me any more. Unfortunately, our class soon got a new ball.*
>
> Len Kalakian

Movement behavior in humans is as indigenous to the pursuit of happiness as to survival itself. In fact, many motor behaviors are part of our biological heritage and enhance human survival potential. They emerge quite naturally without formal modeling or instruction.

Vocabulary

All species have their respective repertoire of phylogenetic behaviors. Among birds, an obvious phylogenetic behavior is flying; among fish, swimming; among humans, walking. In each instance, each animal's survival would be threatened without the instinctive and timely appearance of its respective phylogenetic skills.

Because many phylogenetic skills are motor skills, movement is, indeed, indigenous to survival. This fact suggests, perhaps, why we admire skilled movement and those who move well.

Children recognize the significance of movement early in life and learn that movement competence often means recognition, acceptance, and friendship. This is unfortunately a two-edged sword. Just as those with good motor skill tend to gain positive attention, so those who are unskilled go unrecognized, or worse, are ridiculed. By making positive value judgments about people who possess desirable attributes, we consciously or unconsciously make negative value judgments about those who do not possess such attributes. As a result, possessors of positive attributes tend to perceive themselves as being valuable, while those without such attributes tend to perceive themselves as having lesser value. Self-worth becomes largely a reflection of how individuals perceive that they are valued by others.

Just as important as the psychosocial significance of skilled movement is the physiological significance. Normal amounts of activity on a regular basis are essential to normal growth and development. Furthermore, virtually all components of basic physical and motor proficiency essential for continued well-being require movement for maintenance. While skill in movement is not essential for fitness, skill is often the necessary ingredient that motivates the individual to remain active and fit.

Causative Factors of Low Motor Skills

Known causes underlying low motor skills can be categorized as follows: (1) attitudinal and environmental influences, (2) delayed development of the central nervous system (CNS), and (3) minimal neurological dysfunction. Gallahue (1982) suggests that low motor skill efficiency can also occur if students have inadequate instruction or too few opportunities to practice. In many instances, low motor skills cannot be attributed to known causes.

Delineating three causes of this complex problem risks oversimplification. In many instances, low motor skills are the result of combined influences. For example, low motor skills originating from delayed CNS development may precipitate an attitude that causes conscious avoidance of activity and skill development. Long after the CNS has matured, a negative attitude may remain and influence activity involvement and skill development. A child whose low motor skills are founded in minimal neurological dysfunction (e.g., mild cerebral palsy) might become the focus of well-meaning but misdirected efforts to remediate a problem for which there is no cure. This child should have opportunities for skill development in accordance with potential. A realistic intervention program must be sensitive to limitations owing to a single cause. Unrealistic expectations result in the child's becoming a nonachiever for reasons that the child cannot control. Understanding the cause of low motor skill development focuses remedial efforts on the problem's source, rather than on the symptoms.

Intervention for Children With Low Motor Skills Owing to Attitudinal and Environmental Influences

Poor attitudes resulting in low motor skills often can be modified. Sometimes the child's attitudes toward physical education and motor skill development are a reflection of parental attitudes. In an apropos study, Zeller (1968) used the Wear Attitude Scale (Wear 1955) to determine parental attitudes toward physical education. Children of parents responding to the Wear Scale were administered a six-category motor proficiency test including agility, balance, ball handling, and body image items. Results indicated that parents with positive attitudes tended to have children whose motor skills were high. Conversely, negative parental attitudes coincided with low motor skills among those children. Further analyses indicated that the parents' degree of activity participation also influenced their children's performance. Children with low motor skills tended to have parents who did not participate in activity.

These limited data do not prove conclusively that parental attitudes directly affect children's attitudes and participation patterns. They do, however, indicate that some attitude sharing between parents and children may occur. These results suggest that intervention programs for some children with low motor skills might also include efforts to modify parental attitudes toward physical education.

An "I can't" attitude among children with low motor skills tends to reinforce low achievement and often is the product of peer attitudes toward the nonachiever. The low achiever who is ridiculed and ostracized for awkwardness will avoid negative attention, which means avoiding physical education. This is the beginning of a physical education dropout. Every reasonable effort should be made to ensure that children with low motor skills do not become objects of verbal abuse. Such children are in need of significant psychosocial support to counteract the association between low motor skills and fragile or negative self-concept.

Pagenoff (1984) found that a 14-year-old, spastic cerebral palsied student was exceptionally self-conscious of others' observations of her physical appearance being different from her peers. Fearing failure, the youngster refused to perform many activities both in treatment and extracurricularly. Her development of self-esteem and of performance skills was therefore limited. The girl in Pagenoff's study was quoted as saying, "I'm deformed, no one wants me around. I can't do what my friends can." A 2-day-a-week program, which continued for 8 weeks, was planned for the girl. To ensure optimum performance, the immediate area surrounding the pool was off limits to anyone else during the treatment sessions. (The student had refused to perform swimming activities when her mother or outside observers were present.) After the girl completed the planned progressive program, Pagenoff found both positive physiological and motor skill improvement, and found in addition that "The most significant changes were noted in self-image" (p. 472).

Even in an empathetic environment, children may not progress. In this case, they deserve a program tailored to meet their unique needs. Enlist peer teaching, a teacher aide, or an adapted physical education resource teacher. When special needs are more pronounced, consider placement, at least part-time, in a special class.

For these children, it is particularly important that special programming be challenging but not frustrating. Challenges should be reasonable, with progress often measured in inches rather than feet. The child should be prodded gently by sincere and regular encouragement. Progress, no matter how modest, should be recognized as an important accomplishment (Figure 6.1).

Fortunately, young people's attitudes toward skill development and physical education are often malleable. It is difficult, however, to determine whether attitudes improve because motor skills have improved or vice versa. In all likelihood, improved motor skills promote an improved attitude toward the activity, and the improved attitude in turn fosters a desire to improve motor skills further.

Attitudes, like habits, are often more easily formed than changed. This suggests that prevention is the best cure, and that intervention, when necessary, should begin as early as possible.

FIGURE 6.1. The child should be prodded gently by sincere and regular encouragement.

Intervention for Children With Low Motor Skills Owing to Delayed CNS Development

Needs to catch up.

The child whose CNS develops more slowly than the norm will demonstrate motor proficiencies commensurate with the developmental status of the CNS. When attitudinal influences on the child are positive and one finds no reason to suspect neurological dysfunction, then delayed CNS development is the probable cause of low motor skills. In most instances, minor developmental delays reflect the normal range of CNS maturation at any age. At the normal CNS growth rate, maturation does not occur until age 8 or 9 (Rarick and Dobbins 1975). While an apparent developmental delay is not sufficient cause for alarm over CNS well-being, examination by a pediatrician or pediatric neurologist should be considered. Continuing delays or continued negative response to remediation indicate the need for medical evaluation.

Once the cause of low motor skills is attributed to delayed CNS development within normal parameters, intervention can follow one of two courses depending on individual circumstances. If delayed development has been accompanied by a history of low achievement in regular physical education, the child may need remediation to achieve present motor potential. This child needs to catch up! When the child's developmental delay is identified early, remediation to "catch up" will not be as necessary if a program is sensitive to the child's developmental pace and level. Such a child, by virtue of early diagnosis and prescription, may have little or no catching up to do. While the latter child may be behind his chronological age peers, he is not lagging in achievement according to potential. The developmental tasks confronting the former child may well be more formidable than those confronting the latter. Again, prevention is the best cure.

Intervention for Children With Low Skills Owing to Minimal Brain Dysfunction

The emergence and refinement of certain motor behaviors are indicators of CNS well-being. While delays in neurological development that are within normal parameters may delay certain motor behaviors, differentiating between these maturation delays and delays owing to minimal neurological dysfunction is important. In the former instance, time and sensitive instruction should diminish the problem gradually. In the latter case, neither time nor remediation offers complete resolution. Intervention efforts should focus on raising the child's skill level to present potential. Subsequent intervention efforts should focus on meeting the child's motor skill needs according to developmental status. It is important to recognize that an underlying neurological dysfunction is causing motor difficulties and will ultimately limit motor development potential.

When a child's low motor skills are founded in minimal neurological dysfunction, teachers, parents, and others must not make categorical judgments about what the child cannot do. Objectives for such a child must be realistic, and realistic objectives focus on ability rather than disability. Sparling et al. (1984) found a significant change occurring ($p < 0.01$) in the gross motor skill ability of neurologically impaired preschoolers when a planned program of "play" was provided for a 7-week period.

Screening, Diagnosis, and Activity Prescription

The adapted physical educator is not expected to diagnose specific causative factors that underlie low motor skills, but the educator should be able to diagnose delays in specific motor proficiency areas and the extent of the delay.

Teacher or parent observation often identifies the rate of motor skill development as problematic. A screening device can be administered to confirm or allay suspicions. Possible screening tests for younger children include gross motor development scales that appear in the *Denver Developmental Screening Test* (Frankenburg et al. 1975). This screening device was developed to measure motor proficiencies of youngsters age 1 month to 6 years. Werder and Kalakian (1985) warn that the validity and reliability of this test battery are questionable and that the battery should be used only with children between the ages of 4 and 6. For children who chronologically and developmentally are beyond 6 years, the short form of the *Bruininks-Oseretsky Test of Motor Proficiency* (Bruininks 1978) is appropriate.

Should screening indicate the need for further evaluation of children chronologically or developmentally from 6 months to 6 years, the *Learning Accomplishment Profile—Diagnostic Edition* (Sanford 1974) may be considered. This consists of 89 developmental milestones arranged chronologically according to expected order of appearance. Scale items are divided into two general categories—body management and object control. Among older children (CA 4½ to 14½), the Bruininks-Oseretsky identifies specific areas of motor function and dysfunction (static balance, performance balance, speed and agility, response speed, and bilateral coordination). It is diagnostic in that it identifies general performance areas in which deficits exist. Once areas of performance deficit, including suspected causes, have been identified, specific activities can be prescribed to improve proficiency in those areas.

The Ohio State University SIGMA (*Scale of Intra-Gross Motor Assessment*) by Loovis and Ersing (1980) is a criterion-referenced assessment battery. It offers flexibility in assessing basic motor skill development of the nonhandicapped, mentally handicapped, and developmentally delayed children of preschool or elementary school age. The test battery includes 11 test items: walking, stair climbing, running, throwing, catching, jumping, hopping, skipping, striking, kicking, and ladder climbing.

Learning and Performance

Physical educators must be knowledgeable about the basics of motor learning to teach in ways compatible with the child's learning capabilities. Sound teaching practices are particularly vital when teaching children who demonstrate poor achievement in physical education.

By definition, a motor performance is skilled when a minimum amount of extraneous movement occurs. Newell (1984) uses Guthrie's definition of **skill** as the ability to bring about a predetermined outcome with maximum certainty and minimum outlay of time and energy.

When teaching motor skills, the teacher must recognize the difference between learning and performance (Figure 6.2). Although students may have learned what they must do to execute a skill properly, they may not have developed the motor responses to transform their knowledge into action. When evaluating skill levels, particularly among low achievers, the teacher may find merit in reporting not only what can be performed, but also what has been learned.

Massed Versus Distributed Practice

In **massed practice**, the learner practices a skill or skills over an extended period. In **distributed practice**, total practice time may be the same, but practice periods are relatively brief and occur in greater number. For example, given the choice, the teacher should determine whether more learning will occur in four 30-min practice periods or in eight 15-min practice periods. While total instruction time may remain the same, the amount of learning may not be the same. Students with relatively high skill levels often learn best in massed practice settings. When a high skill level is accompanied by high motivation, the student may persist in practice for an extended time. Children

FIGURE 6.2. In evaluating the student with spastic cerebral palsy, the disparity between learning and performance must be considered.

with a relatively short attention span and low skill levels often have low motivation and poor frustration tolerance as well. They learn best in distributed practice settings because the short practice periods accommodate their briefer concentration span. The teacher can use inherently satisfying movement experiences to hold the child's attention while changing from distributed to massed practice situations. In so doing, the child may learn not only the desired skills but may also acquire an increased attention span.

There are no absolutes in selecting massed or distributed time blocks. Because children exhibit different learning characteristics, massed and distributed learning experiences should be prescribed on a child-by-child basis.

Specificity

Learning a motor skill tends to be a specific phenomenon. We learn only the skills that we practice, with little carry-over to other skills. The principle of specificity has many implications. It means that learning to throw a large ball first is *not* a prerequisite to learning to throw a small ball; the child probably should throw a small ball in the first place.

Breaking down a skill unnecessarily into what appear to be its component parts (i.e., beyond the developmental sequence for any given skill) may promote proficiency only in the component parts practiced. Specificity suggests that using gimmicks to teach motor skills may teach only proficiency in executing the gimmick. For example, telling students to position a tennis racket as if to scratch their back may teach back scratching with a tennis racket rather than serving. Specificity in practice suggests that the student should be directed to practice the whole skill. A guiding principle should be that, whenever possible, the ultimate skill to be learned should be practiced.

Cephalocaudal and Proximodistal Progressions

A child's ability to learn any motor skill depends largely on the nervous system's maturational status. A skill presented prior to nervous system readiness for the task will not be learned.

The child's nervous system progresses in two directions. In the cephalocaudal progression, the nervous system matures first in the upper part of the body. Control then is achieved successively over the lower body parts. One example of cephalocaudal progression is demonstrated in the stages of learning to throw overarm. The first stage is characterized by arm action only. Successive stages extend to lower body segments, including body rotation, then weight shifts accompanied by leg and foot movements.

In the proximodistal progression, control first is achieved at the body midline, then gradually progresses distally to the arms, forearms, hands, and fingers. This progression

FIGURE 6.3. Balance on lower extremities may be problematic in cases of delayed cephalocaudal progression.

is observed in learning to catch. Initial efforts are characterized primarily by the arms coming together in front of the body. Purposeful elbow, hand, or finger action is not present. The second stage is characterized by a "scooping" response. Action occurs at the shoulders and elbows in an attempt to trap, or scoop, the ball into the chest. Finally, hand and finger actions are integrated with shoulder and arm actions.

Recognizing these progressions has practical significance for the physical educator, because complex skills requiring precise functions of lower extremities or distal members of upper extremities may be inappropriate for some children (Figure 6.3). Such children may be those whose low motor skills are founded in delayed CNS development.

Gross and Fine Motor Control

Children tend to acquire and achieve control over gross motor skills before acquiring and achieving control over fine motor skills. This suggests that as children become older, they become progressively more capable of executing precise, fine motor movements. Children with low motor skills may not yet be neurologically able to develop precise, fine motor coordinations.

Summarizing the Skill Acquisition Process

Our effort to shed light on certain aspects of the skill acquisition process has been brief. In this text, only a few of the more significant factors influencing motor skill acquisition can be covered. Teachers in the adapted physical education area, who regularly encounter children with special needs, should undertake further study of motor learning theory. In this way, they can apply their knowledge of motor learning theory selectively to individual students.

Developing Fundamental Motor Skills

Children with low motor skills often experience difficulties in achieving even basic skill performance levels, yet acquisition of basic skills is essential. Such skills are the foundation of efficient movement.

Gallahue (1982, p. 180) explains the goals of fundamental locomotor activities: "The child must be able to: (1) use any one of a number of types of movements to reach the goal; (2) shift from one type of movement to another when the situation demands it; and (3) alter each movement as the conditions of the environment change."

Keogh and Sugden (1985) have developed an interesting concept regarding motor development. They state:

> One problem in studying development is that we come to think of age as being development, that age becomes an agent of change, perhaps even the agent of change. It is easy to look at a graph of improved performance across age and think that age determines or influences change. We must remember that time itself is not causal and that age merely marks the passage of time or a period of time. Agents of change, such as biological processes or social interactions, function during the passage of time to determine or influence change. This means that we must consider what is happening during a given period of time rather than view age as an agent of change. To reiterate, age is merely time, and our problem is to identify and understand the changes in movement development across time (1985, p. 20).

Concern about motor development is well founded, for effortless locomotor patterns are the basis of an active life-style and of success in play, games, and sports. The basic motor skills are often identified as problematic in persons exhibiting poor motor patterns (Figure 6.4).

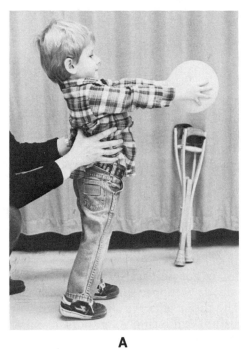

A

B

C

FIGURE 6.4. Developmental stages in catching. (A) Shoulder action only—immature response. (B) Shoulder and elbow action—scooping response. (C) Shoulder, elbow, wrist, and finger action—mature response.

Walking

Walking is the most used basic locomotor skill. It is incorporated in daily living to such an extent that one's walk is taken for granted. Physically and mechanically, walking is the least demanding of the upright locomotor skills; it is the first of the bipedal locomotor skills to appear in young children. If the walking skill is never mastered, the child may not be able to develop subsequent bipedal skills such as running, jumping, and skipping.

Mechanically correct walking begins with good posture, which requires an alignment of body segments resulting in minimum fatigue. Good posture is an individual matter. Body alignment that constitutes good posture for one person may not be the same for another. There are, however, key body alignment characteristics that imply effective posture in most individuals. (See Chapter 14 on postural deviations.)

Good posture, whether standing or walking, is not necessarily characterized by ramrod straightness. Rather, spinal curves (thoracic, or upper spine, and lumbar, or lower spine) should be present but moderate. The thoracic curve should not create a forward protrusion of the head and neck. In posture exhibiting good thoracic curve, the ear is aligned directly above the shoulder. In posture exhibiting good lumbar curve, the individual should be able to stand with back, hips, and heels against the wall and *snugly* fit a hand (palm flat against the wall) between the lumbar region and the wall. If the hand fits loosely, the lumbar curve may be excessive.

An excessive lumbar curve often produces an excessive thoracic curve and vice versa. These excessive curves place undue stress on the posture muscles and ligaments that maintain the spinal column in an erect position. In addition, undue stress may also be placed on the last lumber vertebra, which articulates with the pelvis. An excessive lumbar curve is often accompanied by a sagging abdomen, because the forward tilt of the pelvis forces the stomach muscles to stretch. An excessive thoracic curve is often accompanied by a sunken chest, which, if sufficiently sunken, may create some breathing blockage.

In good posture, the feet should be pointed forward, which ensures an advantageous position to bear weight and facilitate locomotion.

Deviations from good posture should be assessed by a physical educator, physician, pediatrician, orthopedist, or physical therapist. Assessment will determine whether the child's posture problems are remediable. If they are, appropriate activities and exercises can be suggested (see Chapter 14 on postural deviations).

Good posture characteristics are important to efficient walking. When walking, the child's arms should swing opposite from the legs. In mature walking, weight is transferred from the toe of the trailing foot to the heel of the lead foot. Arm, leg, and foot movement should be in the direction of the walk.

Running

Running is the most rapid form of bipedal locomotion and is an integral part of many physical education and recreation activities. The child who learns to run well can enjoy success in many games and sports. In contrast, an inability to run well virtually ensures failure in many activities. Such failure can in turn result in avoidance of activities that could otherwise bring years of enjoyment and enhance health and fitness.

Skilled running implies the ability to run in a straight line. Any other direction than straight is counterproductive to speed. To visualize correct foot placement, a straight line should be drawn on the running surface. The line, approximately 2 in. wide and extending the full running distance, enables the child to observe proper foot placement as it occurs. To avoid failure for children whose feet seldom hit the line, lanes can be provided to direct proper foot contact. The lane should be 12 in. wide and should be narrowed gradually as the child's running skill improves.

In running, the feet should be pointed straight ahead or should be slightly pigeon-toed. This placement maximizes foot leverage and thrust. Proper foot placement can be seen when the child runs a straight line in loose dirt. The placement should be parallel to and preferably superimposed on the line. The most common error in foot placement is the toes-out position, which greatly reduces leverage, thrust, and therefore speed. If the child is running on a hard surface, powdered chalk dusted on the shoe soles will indicate foot placement.

In running, the arms should swing opposite to the feet. Arm swing should be in a forward-backward plane, the direction of thrust. The head should remain stable and be pointed in the intended direction of travel. Left or right head rotation while running can be uncomfortable and makes staying on course difficult. Any rotation of the head back and forth is evident when children endeavor to run very fast.

Running requires forward lean to maintain forward momentum. Generally, the faster one runs, the greater the forward lean. When jogging comfortably, forward lean may be barely discernible. When sprinting forward, lean may be pronounced.

The student should endeavor to relax when running. Relaxation assists coordination and minimizes fatigue resulting from extraneous effort. Relaxation is indicated when jaw, hands, and fingers wobble loosely while running.

There are occasions in physical education or recreation activities when running backward may be required. This warrants some development of backward running abilities.

Hopping

Hopping is rising and landing on the same foot. A student should be able to hop on either foot and in any direction. The nonhopping leg is off the floor, bent at the knee. Arms and the nonhopping leg aid in body balance. The arms, if not used for balance, aid in lifting the body for hopping. Using 3-, 4-, and 5-year-old children, Ulrich and Ulrich (1985) found that the level of hopping skill was directly related to the existing level of balance skill. In addition, significant positive correlations were found between balance and jumping.

Hopping is an important basic motor skill for safety. When a student is pushed or falls off balance in any direction other than directly forward or backward, hopping regains balance. The push or fall transfers weight onto one foot. Before balance is completely lost, the weighted foot and leg thrust the body momentarily into the air. While the body is airborne, the same leg is aligned with the direction of travel, and on landing, balance is regained.

Hopping is the most demanding of basic locomotor skills in terms of strength, because it requires total body weight to be carried on one leg. For this reason, hopping is also most demanding in terms of balance.

Children should be encouraged to hop in hopscotch-type games or in relays. Colorful marks or footprints can be drawn randomly on the playing surface, and the children told to hop from mark to mark. In the initial stages, marks on the playing surface should be placed close together. As hopping skill improves, marks should be placed farther apart in varying directions.

Children who fear losing their balance and falling may be timid about hopping from spot to spot. If the student cannot hop from mark to mark, have the child hop vertically on the same mark. Hold the child's hand to inspire confidence. Should difficulty persist, an assistant can hold the child's other hand. The child should, however, be supported only enough to ensure success. This enables the youngster to gain a feel for the skill much sooner.

When children hop, they hop naturally forward on the preferred foot. To ensure that hopping becomes a truly versatile skill, provide opportunities that encourage the child to hop on either foot in different directions.

Skipping

Skipping is the most complex of all basic locomotor skills. It involves alternation of the feet and a combination of one walking step followed by an immediate hop on the same foot.

The pattern for skipping is: left foot—step, hop; right foot—step, hop. In fact, the verbal command "step-hop, step-hop, step-hop" provides a cue and the correct rhythm.

The arm swing for skipping is similar to the alternate arm swing used in walking and running. The arms maintain body balance and assist in obtaining height. To produce the desirable springy, joyful, carefree quality in skipping, movements should be performed on the balls of the feet.

Because skipping is a relatively complex motor skill, the teacher may need to employ more concrete modes of instruction. One mode involves the use of a full-length mirror. Teacher and student hold hands and stand side-by-side 15 ft from and facing the mirror. The child is instructed to step-hop simultaneously with the teacher. The teacher can cue the child verbally with "step-hop, step-hop." The mirror image and the verbal cues facilitate learning this skill. As the child progresses, the mirror can be eliminated. Teacher and student may continue to hold hands and skip to the verbal cue. Eventually, the verbal cue is sufficient for the child to skip alone. Finally, the child can skip alone without the cue.

Sliding

Sliding is the most effective locomotor skill for rapid lateral movement. It permits quick movement to one side, and facilitates a rapid stop and a return slide.

Many games and activities require sliding as an appropriate motor skill. Such games involve situations in which one child is "it" and another child attempts to run past the tagger to reach a goal or safety zone. As the runner begins to switch direction in an effort to get past, "it" shadows the runner by sliding from side to side. If the tagger breaks prematurely into a run, thus committing herself to one direction, the runner can take off easily in the opposite direction and reach the goal.

Sliding is also important when catching a ball hit to one side of the fielder. If the ball is hit obviously to one side, the child may run to catch the ball. If the child is nearer to the ball, however, one or two slide steps are the quickest way to place the fielder in position to catch the ball.

The movement pattern for the slide is step-close-step. In sliding to the left, the left foot steps to the side followed by an immediate slide of the right foot next to the left. This sequence continues as long as a slide to the left is the objective. In sliding to the right, the right foot steps sideways, followed by a slide of the left foot next to the right.

Sliding can be taught easily if teacher and student face each other and hold hands. Instruct the child to imitate the teacher. The teacher should begin slowly to step-close-step sideways. As the child moves with the teacher, the tempo can be increased, and as the child's skill improves, teacher and student can work parallel but need not hold hands. Sliding can also be taught by using a full-length mirror; teacher and student then perform side-by-side.

Galloping

Galloping is a modification of sliding. It involves the same step-close-step foot pattern, but is used in straight forward-backward or diagonal planes. Children can gallop in situations similar to those described for sliding. Whether one slides or gallops depends solely on movement direction. Step-close-step sideways or laterally is a slide. Step-close-step in any other direction becomes a gallop.

When galloping diagonally to the right, the right leg leads the step-close-step pattern. When galloping to the left, the left leg leads. When galloping forward or backward, either foot can lead.

Galloping is taught easily by using a full-length mirror. The child, beside the teacher, is instructed to imitate the teacher's movements. Another way to learn galloping is by walking with a limp. As the child begins limping, the tempo is increased gradually. A rapid limp using the step-close-step foot sequence is identical to the gallop.

To ensure versatility, provide galloping experiences in all directions. Ability to slide in either direction sideways and to gallop in all other directions enables the child to move quickly in all directions without having to commit to any one direction. When a specific direction is necessary, the child ceases to gallop or slide and breaks into a run.

Leaping

Leaping is similar to running and is used often in conjunction with running. Running accentuates forward motion; leaping accentuates upward motion. In leaping, as in running, the child takes off on one foot and lands on the other foot. Although there is no set rule, a run becomes a leap when more effort is expended going upward than forward.

During takeoff and landing, weight should be concentrated on the ball of the foot. This provides maximum spring on takeoff and maximum cushion on landing. The knee bearing the weight on landing should be flexed slightly to avoid jarring on impact.

A leap can be used to surmount small obstacles such as a puddle or fallen log. Leaping can also be used to surmount greater obstacles or to catch a ball in flight.

In teaching children to leap, encourage the use of both left and right foot for takeoff. If the child can leap easily with either foot, the skill becomes more versatile.

Lengths of rope can be used to teach children to leap. Two ropes are stretched parallel. The distance between the ropes can be varied depending on the child's physical size and capability. The area between the ropes might be called "the river," and the child's objective is to leap across the river. Initially, the child should leap from a stationary position. As skill improves, the leap can be preceded by a walk or run. To make the obstacle more challenging as skill increases, the ropes can be placed farther apart or raised off the ground. If ropes are held above the ground, be sure that they can be released easily should a child trip.

Colorful marks on the floor can also be used to practice leaping. Random placement of the marks stimulates the children to leap for height and distance and in various directions.

Jumping

Jumping is defined as taking off on either or both feet, but landing on two feet. Jumping can occur from a stationary position or from a run. Although a jump can be in any direction, most jumping is vertical, straight ahead, or almost straight ahead.

The power necessary for a successful jump results from vigorous extension of the hips, knees, and plantar flexion of the feet. The arms assist in lifting the body by swinging upward or forward in the desired direction. When landing, the body should be relaxed. The balls of the feet contact the ground first, while the knees and ankles bend to absorb the landing force. The arms may assist in balancing the body as the legs are extended and the jumper returns to standing position.

In teaching children to jump vertically, arrange a piece of rope to form a circle on the ground. The child should stand in the circle, jump vertically, and land inside the circle. To motivate children to jump straight up, suspend a brightly colored ball or familiar toy directly above the circle. Suspend it with elastic to prevent detachment when caught. The height of the ball or toy can be varied according to each child's vertical jumping capability.

In teaching children to jump forward, place two lengths of rope parallel, as when teaching youngsters to leap. In jumping across the two ropes, the child can take off using one foot or both feet. If the takeoff is on one foot, it can be preceded by a walking or running start.

Holding the child's hand as he jumps off a low step can also develop jumping skill. Variety and motivation can be added by painting colorful circles on the floor to use as landing targets and by increasing the number of step risers from which to jump. When jumping from steps above the first riser, the child should jump to the side rather than forward over lower risers.

Activities to improve general locomotor ability are illustrated in Figure 6.5.

Kicking

Kicking is a somewhat different motor skill. All skills discussed thus far are body projection skills. Each bipedal locomotor skill represents a means of projecting or moving one's body through space. Conversely, kicking is an object projection skill. The purpose of any object projection skill is to impart velocity to a projectile (e.g., a ball). Although one may project one's body through space in the execution of an object projection skill, the basic purpose is to control the projectile's velocity and accuracy.

Kicking requires eye-foot coordination. In the United States, most children seldom realize their full eye-foot coordination potential because kicking activities are emphasized less in our physical education classes and in recreation.

A ball can be kicked from a walk, run, or stationary position. In any instance, it can be rolling or stationary. In all kicking, the eye must be kept on the ball to maintain contact, hence the use of eye-foot coordination.

The ankle of the kicking foot can be turned outward so contact is made on the inside of the foot, or the ankle can be turned inward so contact is made on the outside or top of the foot. The foot also can point straight ahead so toe contact is made.

Controlling the ball is most difficult when toe contact is used. The small contact surface of the pointed toe makes the ball's direction unpredictable when the kicker is unskilled or only marginally skilled.

The height of the kicked ball is determined by placement of the nonkicking (supporting) foot. When the supporting foot is placed beside the ball, it will soar upward as well as forward. This occurs because the supporting foot is placed in such a way that the kicking foot can get well under (and scoop up) the ball. When the supporting foot is placed behind the ball, the ball will follow a low trajectory. This occurs because the position of the supporting foot does not permit the kicking foot to get too far under the ball.

In teaching children to kick, a wall can be used so the ball rebounds. In this way, little time is lost retrieving the ball. The direction of rebound tells the child immedi-

FIGURE 6.5. Activities to improve locomotor skills.

ately whether or not the ball was kicked in the intended direction. The children also can walk or run to kick an oncoming ball that has been rolled by the teacher, or they can form a circle and kick the ball back and forth. In either activity, the ball can be kicked while it is moving, or stopped (trapped) and kicked from a stationary position.

Dribbling

A series of short kicks to move the ball from one play area to another is a form of dribbling. In dribbling with the feet, the primary concern is to keep the ball close to the feet and under control at all times. Dribbling is first performed while walking and then while running.

Dribbling can be taught by having children maneuver the ball to a point and back again. This activity can become a relay when children acquire more advanced dribbling skills.

Children should learn to kick with either foot; the child who kicks well with either foot is naturally more versatile. In teaching children with low motor skills to kick with a specific foot, tie a ribbon or similar colorful object to the kicking foot. This helps the child remember which foot to use. It also enables the teacher to determine at a glance whether or not the child is using the intended foot.

Modified kicking can be done by crutch walkers and wheelchair ambulators. For the former, a striking implement or surface is affixed to the crutch. For the latter, a plywood striking surface is affixed to the chair's footrests. Both modifications facilitate learning and enjoyment of games such as modified soccer in which many types of ambulators participating together can be accommodated.

Striking

Striking, like kicking, is an object projection skill. It involves the hand or some hand-held striking implement (e.g., bat, racket, club) to impart velocity to an object (e.g., ball, shuttlecock). Striking requires eye-hand coordination and, like kicking, requires keeping an eye on the object.

Initial striking experiences are most successful if the object is bright in color and stationary (e.g., ball against contrasting background placed on a batting tee). Such an arrangement minimizes the impact that visual tracking, spatial awareness, and figure-ground discrimination have on success. Although the child may need eventually to strike moving objects, striking stationary objects ensures success and continued interest in learning striking skills. When the child progresses to striking moving objects, the learner can begin by striking (volleying) a balloon or a slow-moving object that permits time for body movement and positioning.

Children who are blind or visually impaired can develop striking skills by using balls that jingle or beep electronically. A child with upper extremity orthopedic impairment, which affects grasp, can use rackets and paddles taped securely to the preferred extremity.

To learn striking skills, children should be given implements of proper size and weight. A small child should not have an adult-sized implement. An implement that is too heavy for the user ensures failure. Striking surfaces can be enlarged to enhance success, but care must be taken that the implement remains easy to grasp and move.

Throwing

The underarm throw (toss) is the first throw observed in children. In the least mature underarm throwing attempts, only arm action is noted. Later, a follow-through with the right foot (right-handed thrower) accompanies arm action. Finally, the left foot steps forward in preparation as the throwing arm swings backward. As the throwing arm swings forward, the right foot moves forward in follow-through fashion. Common variations of throwing include bowling, serving a volleyball, and pitching horseshoes.

Of all throwing patterns, the overarm throw is the most effective in terms of velocity and distance. It is therefore the pattern most often used in throwing-related activities. An extensive study of overarm throwing skill development was made by Wild (1938) who found that four phases of overarm throwing are closely associated with chronological age. In children with low motor skills, these phases are also associated with chronological age, but the age at which each phase appears is later than that of normally progressing youngsters. Wild identified four throwing phases as follows:

Phase one (CA 2–3 years). Throw involves the arm only. There appears to be no shift in body weight or rotation of the trunk. Both feet remain planted firmly on the ground.
Phase two (CA 3½–5 years). Throw differs from phase one in that body rotation has been added, which increases ball velocity. There is still no foot movement or weight shift.
Phase three (CA 5–6 years). Throw involves body rotation but adds a step forward with the right foot (right-handed thrower).
Phase four (CA 6½ years and older). Left foot steps forward as the ball is being delivered. Weight then is transferred from the right to left foot so the right foot can step forward in follow-through motion as the ball is released.

Wild observed that many girls never progressed beyond phase three. Note, however, that Wild's observations occurred at a time when girls were not reinforced socially for effective throwing skills. A replication of Wild's studies today would be interesting to determine how far beyond the third phase most girls have progressed. His observation would probably no longer hold true.

Data indicate that throwing distance decreases as children are given larger balls to throw. Factors besides weight difference contribute to this phenomenon. When an excessively large ball is used, the child usually modifies her throwing pattern to accommodate the ball size. In fact, the theory of specificity suggests that learning to throw a large ball first may actually retard the skill acquisition process of throwing a small ball with mature overhand delivery. When the child switches from a large ball to a small ball, he must unlearn many large ball throwing skills before learning skills related to throwing a small ball. Two considerations are appropriate in teaching the child to throw: (1) the ball must accommodate the child's hand size, and (2) the ball should be the size that the child will throw most frequently. Teach the child to throw a large ball only if throwing a large ball is the objective.

Ball Bouncing

Ball bouncing, or dribbling with the hands, plays a major role in many physical education and recreational activities. It requires concentration, visual tracking, and eye-hand coordination. While bouncing the ball, the child can stand still, walk, run, slide, or gallop.

In bouncing the ball, children should be instructed to tap, not slap it. A slapped ball bounces out of control. As the child becomes more highly skilled, she should be taught to bounce the ball with the thumb and fingertips, which affords greatest control.

Recordings with a heavily emphasized beat can be used to teach children to dribble. First, practice with the record to be sure that the tempo is neither too fast nor too slow. With the record on, demonstrate by bouncing the ball to the tempo in full view of the children. The teacher's participation plus the accentuated beat will give the children visual and auditory cues, which facilitate understanding the rhythmic pattern that underlies dribbling.

In the initial stages of dribbling, the child may use both hands simultaneously to thrust the ball toward the ground and then catch it with both hands. As the child progresses, he may soon be capable of dribbling with one hand. At this stage, the child should be taught to dribble with either hand to make the skill as versatile as possible (Figure 6.6).

Catching

Developmentally, catching (see Figure 6.4) is more complex than throwing and is perfected only after throwing skills are learned. Catching challenges should conform to the child's developmental status. A rolled ball is easiest to catch (Figure 6.7). Following this, intercepting a ball bounced on the ground is relatively easy, particularly if the child has placed the ball in motion. Self-initiation of ball action eliminates many uncertainties associated with catching a ball that another has thrown (Figure 6.8). Finally, the child is ready to catch a ball thrown by another.

A common error in teaching children to catch is throwing the ball too slowly. When learning to catch, many children cue on the thrower, not on the ball. Throwing the ball initiates a catching response in the child. If the ball is thrown inordinately slowly, the catching response may occur before the ball has come within reach. When this occurs, the thrower should try to determine the time lapse between the throw and response initiation. The thrower should then adjust the velocity of the ball so it comes within reach at the precise time when the catching response is initiated. Should the

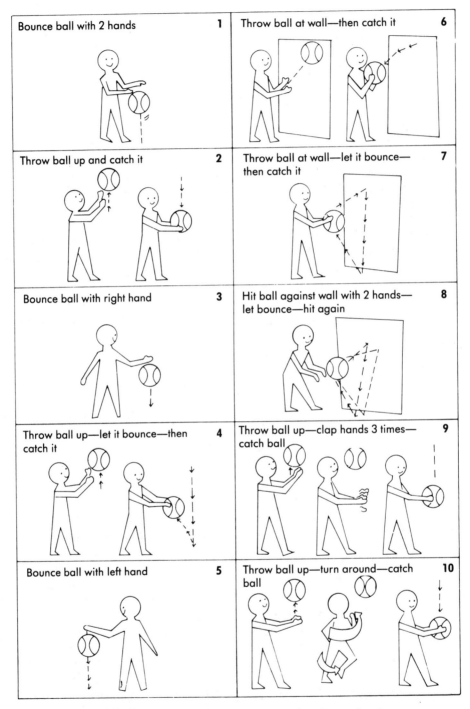

FIGURE 6.6. Activities to improve eye-hand coordination.

The following text appears within the figure panels:

1. Bounce ball with 2 hands
2. Throw ball up and catch it
3. Bounce ball with right hand
4. Throw ball up—let it bounce—then catch it
5. Bounce ball with left hand
6. Throw ball at wall—then catch it
7. Throw ball at wall—let it bounce—then catch it
8. Hit ball against wall with 2 hands—let bounce—hit again
9. Throw ball up—clap hands 3 times—catch ball
10. Throw ball up—turn around—catch ball

FIGURE 6.7. A rolled ball is easiest to catch.

FIGURE 6.8. The easiest airborne ball to catch is the one you bounce.

ball arrive consistently before the catching response, the ball's velocity can be reduced. Should the ball's velocity need to be reduced excessively, a balloon can be used.

Data indicate that ball size is significant when learning to catch. Du Randt (1985) found that a smaller ball size (e.g., the size of a tennis ball) stimulates the occurrence of a more mature catching response in 6- and 8-year-olds, but not in 4-year-olds. She states: "It is therefore recommended that 8- and 6-year-olds be encouraged to play with a small ball as often as possible, whereas 4-year-olds need not be confronted formally with a small ball until they are relatively proficient with a larger ball" (p. 42). Cratty (1979) reports reasonable success with 5-year-olds attempting to catch an 8-in. diameter ball. He cites little success with 5-year-olds catching a tennis ball. In each case, the ball was bounced to the child. The balls were, however, bounced from different distances, and the same children were not observed in each instance. Nevertheless, the data suggest that the larger ball is easier for 5-year-olds to catch because it provides a more substantial visual stimulus and offers greater surface area for catching.

Children learning to catch should be given balls with a rough surface. The roughness creates friction for hand contact.

For learners with limited manipulative ability, mittens and Velcro-covered balls can build success in catching activities. Velcro should also cover the mitten grasping surfaces. When a Velcro-covered nerf, cloth, or whiffle ball contacts the mitten surfaces, it then sticks. The child thus experiences successful catching without demonstrating a prerequisite grasp.

Inflatable balls are easier to catch if partially deflated. A partially deflated ball is easier to grasp and does not hurt when missed. The child who is hurt by the ball while trying to learn to catch may soon concentrate more on avoiding than on catching the ball. Beanbags also serve to teach catching.

Pushing, Pulling, Lifting, and Carrying

When pushing, the body moves forward, near forward, or sideward against resistance. Body lean should be toward the object being pushed. One leg should be placed almost fully extended behind the object. This leg is a major force contributor during the push. The opposite leg is flexed to a somewhat greater degree and is placed ahead of the fully extended driving leg. It assists in the push but also facilitates balance.

During the push, the body should form a nearly straight line from point of force application (foot to ground) to point of force application (hand to object). The straight body configuration pits bone against bone during the push, thus increasing efficiency of energy expenditure. In effective pushing, hip-knee extension is a major force contributor.

Objects with a high center of gravity and a small support base often topple over when pushed (or pulled). When pushing such objects, force should be applied near the base to avoid tipping.

In pulling activities, the body generally leans in the opposite direction, and grip strength is important. When pulling, one leg should be almost fully extended and relatively near the object. The opposite leg assumes a greater degree of flexion to assist in force application and in balance. As in pushing, hip-knee extension is a major force contributor. Additional pulling force results from simultaneous arm and shoulder action.

During pulling, the body should form a nearly straight line from point of force application (driving foot against the ground) to point of force application (one's grip on the object). Often, heavy or cumbersome objects can be pulled with greater efficiency if a rope is attached to the object. A top-heavy object should be pulled near the base to avoid toppling.

Lifting is a potentially dangerous activity, especially if the object to be lifted is heavy or cumbersome. Improper lifting techniques will result in lower back strain.

When an object is to be lifted, knowing the object's approximate weight is important. In preparing to lift, the child should be as near to the object as possible. Knees and hips should be flexed and held perpendicular or nearly perpendicular to the back. The major force should come from hip-knee extension and not from the back. With the back erect and with the lifting force coming from hip-knee extension, the possibility of back injury is minimized. In lowering an object, the lifting procedure is simply reversed. The weight should be carried by the lower extremities (i.e., hip-knee flexion).

Once lifted, an object can be carried in many ways, depending on its physical characteristics and weight. Objects with handles (e.g., suitcases) may require only one arm. Relatively small, lightweight objects can be carried under the arm. Larger, heavier objects may require both hands with the object resting against the front of the body. Heavy or cumbersome objects can be carried on one shoulder with the hands used to balance the object.

Whenever an object is too heavy or cumbersome for one person to manage, two or more persons should assist. Lifting and carrying principles remain the same for each individual, even though several individuals may be involved simultaneously. When more than one person participates in lifting or carrying, coordinating efforts is important. Signals should inform each helper when to lift, carry, and lower the object. Such a procedure minimizes wasted or misdirected effort and reduces the possibility of injury.

Evaluating Progress

Performance can be evaluated through anecdotal records, norm-referenced tests, and criterion-referenced tests.

Anecdotal records are valuable for recording improvements to which standardized tests are not sensitive. For example, anecdotal records can note increases in willingness to participate during class and to engage in active play with others during free time.

Norm-referenced tests (e.g., Bruininks-Oseretsky) are valuable in determining the extent to which a child's motor proficiencies continue to depart from the norm. Norm-referenced tests are of interest to parents who want to know "how my child is doing." Caution should be exercised, however, when using norm-referenced test results. Children with low motor skills may know that they are performing below the norm. Continued comparison with others, which is the basis of norm-referenced test interpretation, can serve only to embarrass the child.

Criterion-referenced tests measure progress according to developmentally sequenced performance criteria. Criterion-referenced instruments do not compare the child's performance with that of others, as do norm-referenced tests. Rather, the child's performance is evaluated in terms of improved performance measured against a behaviorally stated performance criteria. In effect, children become their own norm and thus do not experience unwanted or unnecessary comparisons. Two criterion-referenced instruments that measure motor proficiency and that are appropriate for children with low motor skills are the criterion-referenced modification of the Project A.C.T.I.V.E. (Vodola 1974) and *I CAN* (Wessel 1976).

Summary

Movement and acquisition of motor skills are fundamental elements of human behavior. Many fundamental motor skills that children and youth acquire under normal circumstances actually require little formal instruction. The major concern should be that opportunities exist for such skills to emerge and be perfected. For children with special motor development needs, these basic skills sometimes do not emerge naturally. The possible reasons for this include lack of opportunity for skill practice and developmental interruption owing to the nature and extent of a disability. Whenever such situations arise, special attention in physical education is indicated.

Motor skill acquisition has both physiological and psychosocial significance. Sufficient movement opportunities are essential for normal growth and development. Skilled movement is also significant as a means of communicating and establishing rapport with others.

Children with disabilities tend to manifest low motor skills disproportionately in comparison with the nonhandicapped population. Fundamental motor skills, often problematic among children with special needs, include body and object projection skills.

The physical educator must become familiar with the various skill categories, including a thorough understanding of each skill's significance and the developmental stages necessary for skill acquisition. Only then can the educator arrive at effective methods for facilitating skill acquisition and for modifying instruction to accommodate the learning characteristics of children with specific disabilities.

References

Bruininks, R. H. *Bruininks-Oseretsky Test of Motor Proficiency: Examiner's Manual.* Circle Pines, Minn.: American Guidance Service, 1978.

Cratty, B. J. *Perceptual and Motor Development in Infants and Children.* Englewood Cliffs, N.J.: Prentice-Hall, 1979.

Du Randt, R. Ball-Catching Proficiency Among 4-, 6-, and 8-Year-Old Girls. In *Motor Development Current Selected Research,* Vol. I, edited by J. E. Clark and J. H. Humphrey. Princeton, N.J.: Princeton Book Company, 1985.

Frankenburg, W. K., Goldstein, A., and Camp, B. *Denver Developmental Screening Test, Reference Manual,* revised 1975 ed. Denver: LADOCA Project Publishing Foundation, 1975.

Gallahue, D. L. *Understanding Motor Development in Children.* New York: John Wiley and Sons, 1982.

Keogh, J., and Sugden, D. *Movement Skill Development.* New York: Macmillan, 1985.

Loovis, M. E., and Ersing, W. F. *Assessing and Programming Gross Motor Development for Children.* Loudonville, Ohio: Mohican Publishing, 1980.

Newell, K. M. Physical Constraints to Development of Motor Skills. In *Motor Development During Childhood and Adolescence,* edited by J. R. Thomas. Minneapolis: Burgess Publishing, 1984.

Pagenoff, S. A. The Use of Aquatics With Cerebral Palsied Adolescents. *The American Journal of Occupational Therapy* 38(7):469–473, July 1984.

Rarick, G. L., and Dobbins, D. A. Basic Components in the Motor Performance of Children Six to Nine Years of Age. *Medicine and Science in Sports* 7:105–110, 1975.

Sanford, A. *Learning Accomplishment Profile (Diagnostic Edition).* Winston-Salem, N.C.: Kaplan Press, 1974.

Sparling, J. W., Walker, D. F., and Singdahlsen, J. Play Techniques With Neurologically Impaired Preschoolers. *The American Journal of Occupational Therapy* 38(9):603–612, September 1984.

Ulrich, B. D., and Ulrich, D. A. The Role of Balancing Ability in Performance of Fundamental Motor Skills in 3-, 4-, and 5-Year-Old Children. In *Motor Development-Current Selected Research,* Vol. I, edited by J. E. Clark and J. H. Humphrey. Princeton, N.J.: Princeton Book Company, 1985.

Vodola, T. M. *A.C.T.I.V.E.—All Children Totally Involved Exercising.* Oakhurst, N.J.: Township of Ocean School District, 1974.

Wear, C. L. Construction of Equivalent Forms of an Attitude Scale. *Research Quarterly* 26:113–119, 1955.

Werder, J. K., and Kalakian, L. H. *Assessment in Adapted Physical Education.* Minneapolis: Burgess Publishing, 1985.

Wessel, J. A. *I CAN: Primary Skills.* Northbrook, Ill.: Hubbard Scientific Co., 1976.

Wild, M. The Behavior Patterns of Throwing and Some Observations Concerning Its Course of Development. *Research Quarterly* 9:20–24, 1938.

Zeller, J. (as cited by Cratty). The Relationship Between Parental Attitude Toward Physical Education and Physical Performance of the Child. Master's thesis, University of California, Los Angeles, 1968.

CHAPTER 7

Perceptual-Motor Development

Danielle is a 7-year-old who seems lost in space. Even though her movements appear thoughtful and pensive, she often stumbles or bumps into objects. When she walks down the school halls, she bumps into other children. In the classroom, her achievements fall noticeably below those of her peers. Although she is in the second grade, she continues to reverse *p*s and *q*s, and *b*s and *d*s, and she has difficulty with reading comprehension. When asked to draw a person, she omits body parts, and draws other parts out of proportion. She is awkward in executing gross motor movements, and perhaps for this reason, avoids other children (and is avoided by other children) in active play. Her pediatrician and a pediatric neurologist concur that her developmental difficulties have no obvious medical explanation.

Tommy is a 9-year-old with a marginal (35 decibel) conductive hearing loss. A hearing aid has been helpful in overcoming Tommy's amplification problem. Although his vestibular apparatus has not been affected by his hearing impairment, Tommy has poor balance when executing many motor skills. Both gross and fine motor coordinations are noticeably immature when compared with others. He seldom initiates active play, and those activities that he does select are solitary and sedentary. His achievements in school are below average, and his teacher states that he is not achieving in accordance with his potential.

Children like Danielle and Tommy are far from unique. Danielle's developmental delays seem particularly perplexing because nothing is apparently "wrong." Tommy's developmental delays are less baffling, but are disproportionate to his hearing loss, much of which has been restored.

What plausible explanations might shed light on the whys of such developmental delays? One possible, though controversial explanation is suggested, at least in part, by perceptual-motor theory. Although perceptual-motor theorists vary, a common theme is that perceptual competence evolves initially through movement, and in large measure determines readiness to undertake subsequent, more complex learning challenges.

Perceptual-motor theory is just that—theory. Its advocates and critics are equally vociferous. One perceptual-motor theorist, the late Newell C. Kephart, proposed that all learning has its basis in movement. One critic, Bryant J. Cratty (1986), criticizes proponents like Kephart as "movement messiahs."

We have developed this chapter with an awareness that a controversy does indeed exist concerning the merits of perceptual-motor theory and practice. Some programs are based on this theory, however, and are likely to continue. This requires that perceptual-motor development theory be scrutinized.

Definitions and Rationale

Perception is the interpretation of information (sensory stimuli) monitored by the nervous system. Gallahue (1982, p. 14) defines the term **perceptual-motor** in the following way: "In its broadest sense a perceptual-motor act is any voluntary movement that relies on sensory data to process information used in the performance of that act. In other words, all voluntary movement may be viewed as perceptual-motor in nature."

Perceptual-motor efficiency is the ability to interpret sensory stimuli resulting from movement. Perceptual-motor efficiency may involve perceiving through movement (e.g., the interpretation of a tactile sensation as roughness) or making appropriate motor responses to sensory input (e.g., placing the hands in proper position to catch a ball).

The key word in the definition of perceptual-motor efficiency is **interpretation.** Interpretation is important because sensory experiences alone have no meaning. They are merely electrical impulses traveling from sensory input mechanisms (e.g., the eyes) along nerve pathways to the brain. The ability to discriminate among countless sensory experiences is interpretation, hence perception.

Perception and translating perception into concept is how an individual organizes and systematizes his environment. When perceptions and concepts are adequate, the individual can communicate with the environment. When precepts and concepts are inadequate, one's ability to communicate with the environment is inadequate. This inadequacy in communicating with the environment is thought to result from an inability to derive meaning from sensory information.

Dummer (1985) believes that to succeed at a motor task, the individual must (1) recognize the current task to be either like or unlike previously learned skills, (2) retrieve from memory examples of past similar movements and sensory consequences, (3) decide on a motor plan for the current task by interpolating new response specifications from past response specifications and movement outcomes, (4) execute the motor plan, (5) correct the movement in progress by updating the motor plan (if the movement is more than one reaction time in duration), (6) evaluate the completed movement in terms of both actual outcome and sensory consequences, and (7) update and revise the motor schema.

In perceptual-motor theory, perception is thought to arise from action connoting movement. Movement is thought to be the primary means by which the child encounters sensory experiences in early learning. The child who does not move ably experiences some sensory deprivation. Since perception evolves out of sensory experiences, movement that produces sensory experiences is considered an important component of early learning.

An experienced observer will note that an infant's interactions with her surroundings are almost exclusively motor. The child gathers perceptual information about the world primarily through motor experiences. As the child moves, sensory experiences are encountered, and perception through motion gives meaning and order to a world characterized by sensory chaos.

Development of perceptual competence through movement may be likened to the scaffold required to build a house. Movement is the scaffold and perceptual competence is the house. The scaffold is necessary to build the house. Once the house is built, however, the scaffold is no longer needed. While movement is important to achieve many other objectives, it has fulfilled its purpose as a scaffold to build perceptual competence. Without the scaffold (movement) the house (perceptual competence) might never become functional.

In reference to perceptual-motor learning, a quotation from Kerr (1985, pp. 45–46) provides an interesting comparison. He states:

> The term "motor capacity" is an intuitively relevant concept which eludes definition. To use a computer analogy, one can enhance the performance of a computer by changing either the hardware or the software. One can increase the computer's memory storage—the capacity of the system—or one can write more programs which can function within the existing capacity of the system. Thus, improvement in the motor performance of a child could reflect changes in motor capacity—for example, the ability to store or process larger amounts of motor information—or it could reflect the adoption of new strategies which would allow the child to process information at a faster rate or would require the processing of less information due to an improved selection or sampling process.

Thomas (1984, p. 92) agrees with Kerr and states that "if memory is compared to a computer, then the size of the computer does not change; however, the programming becomes better, and more knowledge and programs are available."

Perceptual-motor inadequacies can be observed in a child whose sensory mechanisms are intact (e.g., an able-bodied child with normal eyesight whose immature visual perceptual-motor development prevents successful catching) or in a child whose sensory mechanisms are partially or totally nonfunctioning (e.g., a partially sighted or blind child whose handicap prevents successful catching).

In the former child's case, perceptual-motor inadequacies may be the result of inadequate sensory experiences. Kephart (1960) suggests that as society becomes more civilized, it restricts its children's freedom of movement. He states that restrictions result in perceptual inadequacies owing to deprivation of movement-centered sensory experiences. In the handicapped child's case, impairment may prevent initial motor-based environmental exploration, which in turn delays acquisition of perceptual-motor and cognitive skills. The child, however, may still learn depending on the site, extent, and severity of the handicap, although an optimum level of skill may not be attainable.

Considerable evidence exists that memory plays an important part in the motor learning process. In particular, encoding, rehearsal, and organization are all memory functions that younger children use less effectively than older children, and older children use these processes less efficiently than adults. Thomas (1984, p. 101) states:

> Experience is in large part the knowledge base in LTS [long term storage]. In general, children have less knowledge than do adults, but research shows that when children have a larger knowledge base than do adults, children's performance is better. Thus, enriching the knowledge base through varied movement experiences should be a major objective of teachers and coaches. Remember that the base of knowledge about movement not only includes movement patterns themselves but also how, why, and when to use these movements. Thus, cognition is a vital and important part of the effective acquisition and performance of motor skills: The correlation between memory, understanding, cognition, and motor learning may be a major reason why mentally handicapped children have difficulty when attempting to learn motor skills.

What Does the Literature Say?

The literature suggests associations between motor experiences and perceptual, motor, and intellectual capabilities. In recent years, acceptance of the perceptual-motor rationale and allegiance to perceptual-motor theorists and practitioners have increased. For some educators and parents of children with special needs, the perceptual-motor rationale has become a panacea. Rather than indict or deny validity of perceptual-motor theory, we need to explore and evaluate the issues with scholarly scrutiny.

Itard

Jean-Marc Itard (1801), a French physician, was perhaps the first person to try effecting positive changes in human behavior by training of the senses. His work was undertaken early in the 19th century when he was responsible for a 12-year-old boy captured in the forests of Aveyron. The boy, named Victor, had been diagnosed by a physician as being severely retarded. Itard endeavored to work with the boy by using intensive, systematic sensory and motor training. Although this training resulted in marked changes in the boy's behavior, Victor never learned to speak or live independently in Parisian society. Itard viewed his efforts as a failure, but his work with Victor marks the first scientific attempt to teach a child with special needs through particular sensory and movement-centered experiences.

Seguin

Edovard Seguin (a student of Itard's) and his contemporaries who followed Itard's teachings were called **sensationalists** or **environmentalists.** They believed that an environment, enriched with sensory experiences, would effect positive behavioral changes in persons with special needs (i.e., the mentally retarded). Seguin emphasized sensory experiences and the maturing of sensory perception through movement-centered experiences. He also espoused education through perception development rather than through abstract reasoning, because he believed that perceptions evolved through sensory experiences that result from muscular activity. As Seguin (1907) stated his theory: "The physiological education of the senses must precede the psychological education of the mind. . . . The physiological education of the senses is the royal road to education of the intellect."

Montessori

Deteressa Maria Montessori was an early proponent of movement experiences as a means of acquainting the child with his environment. She believed that the child must become proficient in walking, balancing, and coordinating movements through motor activities. The Montessori approach to education (1912) emphasizes sensory training and contends that a child's intellectual development is founded in observing, comparing, and judging environmental phenomena. Sensory experience, which occurs through movement, is purported to acquaint the child with the environment and to develop intelligence.

Piaget

Jean Piaget is perhaps the most renowned scholar to have studied the nature of learning. Piaget, in observing his own children, became convinced that their intellect developed initially not through coping with abstractions, but from thoughts spawned by movement-centered experiences. According to Piaget (1936), such movement-centered experiences comprise the first of four developmental periods through which the child passes to achieve intellectual potential. The first period, the *sensorimotor* period, is concerned principally with the sequence of interrelated sensorimotor experiences believed to be the foundation of perceptual and symbolic fluency development. Initially, movement is random. Soon, thoughts spring from movements (i.e., mind follows hand). Eventually, movements spring from thoughts (i.e., mind leads hand). Piaget believes that adequate development during the sensorimotor period is prerequisite to more complex forms of cognitive development.

Barsch

Ray H. Barsch, a special educator, theorizes that perceptual development is the basis of intellect. He believes that perceptual fluency owes its functional integrity to efficient movement patterns.

Earlier work by Barsch culminated in his *movigenic theory*. This theory correlates learning ability with movement efficiency. The movigenic theory involves the study of movement patterns, their origins and development, and how they relate and contribute to learning.

Movigenic theory speculates that movement efficiency is the primary principle underlying the human organism, which learns first to move so it can move to learn. As the organism moves, it matures, and symbolic fluency (i.e., ability to deal with abstractions) replaces motor-based modes of experience and comprehension. Major tenets of Barsch's movigenic theory (1965, p. 15) are stated in part as follows:

> All living organisms must survive in an energy surround. Radiant mechanical and thermal energies represent the primary sources with which the organism must contend. . . . Survival in such an energy surround is contingent upon movement. The organism must move to survive. If movement cannot occur from independent initiation, the organism is at the mercy of the energy forces or dependently reliant upon others for survival. . . . The pull of gravity represents the major force to be resolved by the human organism in developing patterns of movements to promote survival. . . . Building an adequate repertoire of movement patterns for survival in a variable uncertain energy surround requires walking, crawling, hopping, running, squatting, rolling, etc. . . . . The terrain of movement is space. Each individual must organize a visual space volume, an auditory space and a kinesthetic space volume. Failure to organize each spatial volume results in some constricting penalty to the survival efficiency of the organism. . . . Efficient patterns of movement then become crucial to communicative proficiency.

To develop movement efficiency and thereby perceptual awareness, Barsch prescribes activities in 12 categories: (1) muscular strength, (2) dynamic balance, (3) spatial awareness, (4) body awareness, (5) visual dynamics, (6) auditory dynamics, (7) kinesthesia, (8) tactile dynamics, (9) bilaterality, (10) rhythm, (11) flexibility, and (12) motor planning.

Vernon

M. D. Vernon (1962) alleges that perception primarily influences development of knowledge about and phenomena identification in the environment. He believes that initial perception results from motor experiences. Motor contact provides the child's initial experiences of similarities and differences in environment.

Taylor

J. G. Taylor (1962) suggests that spatial orientation (awareness of one's body in space in relation to other objects) depends largely on organism mobility. He contends that movement enables one to experience concretely the relationships between distances and sizes of objects. He believes that, until the child experiences the environment from many vantage points, her perceptual perspectives remain immature.

Kephart

Newell C. Kephart, a special educator, believes that well-integrated patterns of motor behavior are prerequisite to environmental exploration and learning. In his view, motor proficiency is therefore essential to development of perceptual integrity, including laterality, directionality, postural flexibility, body image, and ocular control. Kephart contends that inadequate development of motor proficiencies inhibits the child's later development of ability to perform more sophisticated tasks. His belief is based on the assumption that acquisition of learning tools is a hierarchical process and that advanced learning depends on fundamental, motor-based experiences.

In Kephart's opinion, separation of perceptual experiences from motor experiences is probably not possible. He stresses combining perceptual and motor experiences so the child can match perceptual and motor information. Perceptual inefficiency is alleged to correlate with academic failure.

He believes that a child engages in more complex motor activity to develop increasingly more complex perceptual competencies. Kephart alleges that activity and resultant perceptual competence become increasingly complex in the following hierarchical order:

Posture and Balance. Kephart, like Barsch, believes that achieving control over the force of gravity represents the most basic conflict that confronts the human organism. Kephart surmises that without posture and balance, the child is not ready for efficient movement. Children with poor posture and balance are incapable of the most rudimentary forms of movement, and therefore are not ready to learn through movement. Kephart believes that the child with poor balance, who should be learning through movement-centered experiences, is instead distracted by poor balance. Efficient posture and balance set the stage for locomotion.

Locomotion. Through locomotion skills, children can explore their environment. They are no longer limited to those sensory experiences within reach. The child with efficient locomotion moves freely in quest of sensory experiences; organizing and systematizing those experiences gives meaning to the child's world. Inefficient locomotion limits movement and requires concentration on the mastery of locomotor skills. The child's attention is drawn away from the productive encounter with sensory experiences.

Contact. Although contact experiences often occur before locomotion, they are limited in quantity and quality by immobility. Once the child has achieved proficiency in locomotion, contact (manipulative) experiences increase and enable the child to understand objects.

Receipt and Propulsion. Following contact (manipulative) experiences, the child propels objects by throwing, kicking, and striking, and receives objects by catching. Through these activities, Kephart believes that the child acquires an understanding of size, velocity, direction, and distance.

The goal of perceptual-motor experience, according to Kephart, is for the child to make *motor generalizations*, which involve the ability to apply learned perceptual competence to other life situations. To Kephart the skills are not as important as the ability to generalize precepts and concepts derived from those skills.

Ayres

A. J. Ayres (1960, 1972, 1977) believes that the integrity of higher brain centers (i.e., cortex) is dependent on the supporting integrity of lower brain centers. Ayres points out that kinesthetic, vestibular, and tactile stimulation activities affect the brain stem and produce improved cortical functions. She contends that both motor and academic tasks are cortical functions that can be improved through her activity-centered programs. Her procedures are appropriate only for children with learning difficulties and sensorimotor deficits. According to Ayres, the child with learning difficulties who exhibits sound sensorimotor behavior should respond positively to other treatment (she does not specify).

Ayres is associated with "sensory integration," a phrase implying that a person's motor responses are appropriate to the sensory input. Through improved sensorimotor integration, the individual's central nervous system (CNS) supposedly achieves a higher degree of functional sophistication, which results in improved motor and academic performance.

In questioning the validity of Ayres' premises, Cratty (1980) notes that Ayres' research indicates that academic learning, including auditory perception and reading proficiency, appears to function *independently* of sensory integration proficiencies. In effect, Ayres found that kinesthetic, tactile, and vestibular proficiencies are *not* predictive of auditory perception or language and reading proficiencies. For this reason, Cratty questions Ayres' allegations that improvements in kinesthetic, tactile, and vestibular functions will result in improved academic performance.

Ayres' approach to treating learning disorders through movement-centered experiences is similar to that of Kephart and Barsch. Although specifics differ, each believes that perceptual and academic functions will respond positively to sensorimotor experiences.

Getman

G. N. Getman suggests that children who do not develop minimal levels of coordination or neuromuscular control will experience difficulty or failure when confronted with formal academic tasks. Getman, an optometrist, is concerned with the role that movement plays in a child's visual readiness skills. Getman and Kane (1964, p. 1) believe that cognitive development is preceded by "physiological readiness" to learn:

> Remedial instruction assumes (or ignores) physiological readiness to profit from instruction. Apparently the remedy seems to be not to keep working on the second story of the house of learning, but to repair the foundations so that they can support greater learning weights above. Physiological readiness cannot be skipped over any more than a second story of a house can rest on a shaky, inadequate foundation.

Doman and Delacato

Doman and Delacato (Delacato 1959) have developed a motor therapy program called *neurological organization*. Although the authors of this theory are not proponents of perceptual-motor development, they believe that their program of "patterning" improves the learning abilities of brain-injured and environmentally deprived children. The Doman-Delacato theory states that failure to learn may be the result of inadequate neurological organization of the central nervous system, diagnosed by the absence of specific motor patterns. Delacato purports to determine inadequate neurological organization through motor testing, and to remedy that inadequacy with a strictly supervised program of motor activity.

According to these authors, brain hemisphere dominance results from concentration on activities that stimulate the dominant side. A primary concern in achieving neurological organization is hemispheric dominance. Conversely, they recommend avoidance of activities that stimulate the nondominant hemisphere, because such activities might interfere with establishment of cerebral dominance.

The program espoused by Delacato is the most controversial of motor therapies. Research and thought in the professional community do not support his neurological organization theory and practice. Support is substantial, however, in the lay community, particularly among parents who believe that Delacato's methods have influenced positively their children with special needs.

Questioning the Validity of Perceptual-Motor Theory and Practice

Perceptual-motor practice as a tool for learning is supported more by theoretical musings that seem logical than by scientific evidence. Indeed, when carefully controlled studies are reviewed, one finds cause to question the claims made by prominent perceptual-motor advocates.

Cratty (1969) has been relentless in his efforts to determine the efficacy of perceptual-motor theories and practices. He concludes that perceptual-motor advocates have oversimplified or misunderstood the child's developmental process. He recognizes, however, that behavioral attributes are often affected positively by perceptual-motor experiences. He suggests that the child may improve performance simply as a result of such factors as receiving attention (social stimulation), developing a longer attention span, or developing coordination that improves handwriting.

Stein (1973) agrees with Cratty that positive results from perceptual-motor experiences can be explained in other ways. Stein states: "Despite the many contributions that perceptual-motor programs make, we cannot overlook the possibility that the major contributions may be psychological and emotional."

Heightened perceptual awareness, as espoused by perceptual-motor advocates, may not necessarily contribute to the desired results. The desired outcomes may result instead from social development, improved self-concept, and increased attention span.

The literature indicates that motor experiences may be a catalyst that stimulates functional development. The fact that many children who encounter learning difficulties also exhibit perceptual-motor deficits is sufficient reason to consider perceptual-motor programming for some children with special needs.

Components of Perceptual-Motor Efficiency

Perceptual-motor efficiency, like physical fitness, is a general term that covers a broad spectrum of perceptual attributes. Unlike the components of physical and motor fitness, however, the components of perceptual-motor efficiency seem closely interrelated. For example, locomotor awareness is dependent on visual perception, posture is related to balance, tactile perception to body awareness, and so on. Components of perceptual-motor efficiency are discussed separately to ensure that the total picture does not obscure individual components. When, therefore, a balance activity is suggested, that activity should produce tactile perception, body awareness, visual perception, and kinesthetic experiences simultaneously. This will hold true for almost any activity that fosters perceptual-motor efficiency.

Components of perceptual-motor efficiency include balance, postural and locomotor awareness, visual perception (including localization, tracking, and spatial awareness), auditory perception, kinesthetic perception, tactile perception, body awareness, laterality, and directionality.

Balance

Balance is important because the ability to control one's center of gravity is critical to development of skilled movement patterns. A person has good balance when an

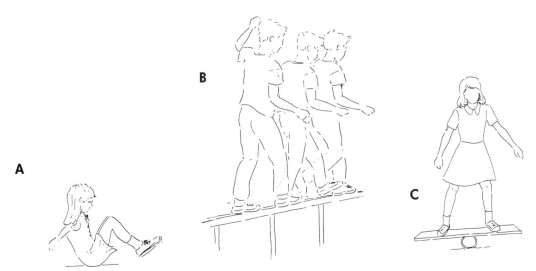

FIGURE 7.1.   Three types of balance. (A) Static balance. (B) Dynamic balance. (C) Balance with the medium moving. (Reprinted from Moran and Kalakian 1977, pp. 47, 418.)

effective working relationship can be maintained between points of support and center of gravity. Three types of balance (Figure 7.1) are static balance (e.g., standing on one foot), dynamic balance (e.g., walking the balance beam), and balance with the medium moving (e.g., walking on a bus in motion). Perceptual-motor advocates generally allege that persons with good balance can focus attention on more important tasks and keep their balance. These theorists believe that good balance often indicates functional integrity of the nervous system.

Most tests of physical and motor ability include balance in the test battery, but controversy exists as to whether general balance is a motor performance factor. Critics suggest that balance is highly specific, and that any specific balance assessment item measures only the *specific* motor skill being observed. Balance activities are presented here despite this controversy, because the possibility of achieving a number of desirable results transcends the controversy.

The following activities are recommended:

1. Have the child assume and maintain various body configurations on a static surface.
2. Have the child attempt to maintain various body configurations while on a moving surface (tilt board or lazy Susan).
3. Have the child maintain balance by contacting the surface with any three body parts (e.g., both knees and one hand).
4. Have the child tuck-sit with feet and buttocks touching the floor, with buttocks only touching the floor, and V-sit and pass a ball under the legs.

5. Have the child straddle a large padded barrel and maintain balance as the barrel is rolled to the left and right.
6. Have the child sit on a T-stool. Engage in progressively more distracting activities (i.e., manipulative activities) as balance improves.
7. Have the child assume the stork stand position (left foot, then right foot). Variations include eyes closed, on tiptoe, hands on hips, hands over head, hand free to aid in balancing.
8. Have the child assume a pike from the back lying position (V-sit).
9. Have the child assume a swan position (left leg, then right leg).
10. Have the child assume a knee swan position.
11. Have the child sit (or stand on one or both feet) while holding a moderately heavy object in one or both hands. Have the child move the object around the body (this constantly shifts one's center of gravity).
12. Have the child sit back-to-back with a partner, partners' arms interlocked, feet drawn in toward the buttocks. At a given signal, both partners rise simultaneously and carefully to a back-to-back standing position.

Postural and Locomotor Awareness

The human organism possesses ability, need, and desire to move. Almost all human functions exhibit some movement component. In turn, movement is the primary medium through which humans find purpose and achieve objectives. Barsch (1965) suggests that locomotion is entwined inseparably with human survival potential. When an individual experiences movement deficits, Barsch suggests that that individual then becomes dependent on others for survival.

Because perception occurs through movement, ability to select and control movement (i.e., postural and locomotor awareness) becomes significant when teaching children. Postural and locomotor awareness activities assist the individual in realizing movement potential. The more effectively one can move, the more one is able to make direct contact with and take control of (rather than being controlled by) the environment. Postural and locomotor awareness, a facilitator of effective movement, precipitates comfortable feelings as one moves through the environment. Secure, threat-free movement minimizes stress. Easy movement also minimizes distractions, thus maximizing perceptual fluency.

Postural and locomotor awareness in children is developed by ensuring that movement opportunities exist. For a variety of reasons ranging from overprotection, to misdirected effort, to ignorance of the child's needs, movement experiences are sometimes not available to children with special needs.

As previously pointed out, postural awareness involves the ability to cope effectively with the force of gravity. Control of gravitational force manifests itself in the child's ability to assume and maintain appropriate postural attitudes. Postural awareness among children with special needs and particularly among orthopedically handicapped children is highly individual. Postural skills are the foundation for locomotion and may have to be developed using a brace, crutch, prosthesis, or wheelchair-assisted ambulation. The goal is not a predesignated postural model, but is, rather, an individualized goal that considers the person's anatomical and physiological strengths.

Development of locomotor awareness is also highly individual among children with special needs. The gait, locomotor skills, and needs of a child with cerebral palsy differ from those of a child with spina bifida who walks using braces and crutches. Persons in wheelchairs require different skills from those who walk with an above-knee prosthesis. All ambulation is not walking, and all walking is not bipedal. Effective ambulation for any child must be determined within the context of the child's anatomical, physiological, and, sometimes, psychological needs. Some persons capable of brace- and crutch-assisted walking opt for wheelchair ambulation because it is physically less taxing or because they believe that sitting ambulation appears more normal to others than dragging paralyzed limbs behind crutches.

In perceptual-motor development, ambulation is important because it allows exploration of the environment. Exploration leads in turn to stimulation of the senses and thus to perceptual development.

The following activities are suggested for development of postural and locomotor awareness.

1. Children may participate in rolling (e.g., log roll), crawling, creeping, walking, hopping (using both left and right feet), galloping (in all directions and leading with both left and right foot), sliding, jumping, leaping, running, and skipping activities. These skills can be taught directly or experienced in almost all activities. Movement versatility and experimentation should be encouraged.
2. Wheelchair ambulators may move to predesignated stations. Circular, straight, zigzag, and random direction patterns should be used. Such activities are equally applicable for nonwheelchair ambulators.
3. Include changes in direction and pace (e.g., fast-slow, stop-start, left-right, backward-forward) in all activities.
4. Ask all ambulators to respond to the teacher's movements. Alternate between characteristic ambulation, use of crutches, and a wheelchair.
5. Have children walk, hop, leap, or jump between designated spots (Figure 7.2).
6. Roll a ball toward but out of reach of the child. Ask the child to intercept the ball before the ball stops (i.e., stop the ball with chair wheel, crutch, foot, or hands). Encourage the child to get to the ball as soon as possible.
7. Have the child demonstrate several different ways to move from point *A* to point *B*.
8. Have children crawl through tunnels and mazes.
9. Have children bounce on a bounce board, trampoline, or other device. Those unable to bounce may experience bouncing by sitting or lying (whichever is appropriate) on the trampoline bed, and by being bounced gently by the teacher.
10. Have children walk on sinking tires (i.e., automobile tires without rims).
11. Pair children with like (or dissimilarly) handicapped individuals. Designate one as the leader who makes some purposeful motion. The other imitates the purposeful motion (if handicaps are similar) or makes an alternate motion to accomplish the same objective (if handicaps are dissimilar).

FIGURE 7.2.   Footprints on floor designate where to step.

12. Have children ambulate on level and uneven terrain. Help each child discover the skills of ambulation appropriate to her unique needs.

Visual Perception

Visual perception is more than seeing; it involves making value judgments and interpreting what one sees. Because persons rely heavily on the sensory modality (sight), the ability to derive meaning from visual perception is of utmost importance.

The development of visual perception is considered to be dependent on a broad base of motor experiences. Visual perceptual-motor experiences occur when one simultaneously sees and manipulates an object. Manipulation, the motor component, is important because there is concreteness in the physical manipulation of objects. The relative concreteness of physically manipulating an object coupled with the simultaneous visual experience develops a visual impression about that object. These simultaneous impressions and judgments provide the basis for visual perceptual-motor efficiency.

As visual perception becomes more acute and visual impressions are firmly established, physical manipulation becomes less crucial. Repeated visual perceptual-motor experiences eventually render the motor component unnecessary or less necessary. For example, a child who manipulates a stuffed toy also concentrates visually on the toy. The visual information about the toy is reinforced and augmented by the tactual sensations. Eventually, visual information alone provides sufficient sensory input to make an accurate visual judgment (perception).

When objects start to move in the environment, youngsters encounter more visual problems to solve. The child must *detect* motion and *track* moving objects, as well as *predict* their future locations. Keogh and Sugden (1985) state: "When an object is moving they [the children] also must use all of the visual skills needed when the environment is stationary and do so more continuously. The object is no longer a static picture of a moment in time; it is constantly changing and thus requires continuous perceptual reorganization, for example, we must be able to know that other persons are walking, must be able to keep them in sight, and must be able to know where they will be in another few steps" (p. 289).

Movement experiences are vital when developing **visual tracking and fixating** capabilities. Visual tracking involves willful direction and focusing of one's eyes from one visual stimulus to another (e.g., reading from left to right across a page). The visual tracking experience actually is *not* uninterrupted eye movement, but is in fact composed of minute, sequential fixations as the eyes pursue a visual stimulus. In the tracking process, the most meaningful visual information comes during the points of fixation. Another form of visual tracking involves directing and focusing one's eyes on a single moving stimulus such as a moving automobile or a thrown ball. Either experience may be further complicated by the individual's moving simultaneously. Yet another form of visual tracking occurs when one's eyes are directed and focused on a stationary object while the viewer is moving. Physical education and recreation movement experiences provide many opportunities for enhancing visual-motor coordination, visual tracking, and visual fixating capabilities.

Visual spatial awareness facilitates making judgments about distances between objects and between oneself and the objects. Spatial awareness evolves as a result of experiencing distances while moving. Having experienced distances as a concomitant outcome of movement, the individual eventually understands distances without actually having to travel them.

Visual spatial awareness allows correct interpretation of perceptual distortions. Perception of any phenomenon changes as one's vantage point changes. For example, a ball at the far end of the gymnasium appears extremely small, yet may be identical in size to a larger appearing ball in the foreground. Visual spatial awareness not only facilitates a judgment of the distant ball's characteristics, but also of one's distance from the ball. Physical education and recreation skills that encourage movement through and exploration of the environment are conducive to the development of visual spatial awareness.

Figure-ground discrimination is the ability to focus and concentrate visually on a specific stimulus when many stimuli are being received simultaneously. A figure-ground discrimination problem involves focusing on one ball against a cluttered background. A baseball catcher might experience difficulty seeing a ball thrown from the outfield against a background of variously colored signs or against the outfield fence.

The ball (the figure) and the multicolored signs (the ground) are the components in the figure-ground problem.

Children rely heavily on visual perception to learn, and their learning environment, both formal and informal, is replete with figure-ground challenges. Movement-centered experiences in which the teacher controls figure-ground relationships can improve significantly the child's figure-ground discrimination. Through gradually increased background complexity (or decrease in the object's stimulus value), the child can achieve greater figure-ground awareness.

The following activities are suggested to develop visual perception and its components:

1. Provide opportunity for children to play with numerous objects. Whenever possible, children should be permitted to sort through, see, and simultaneously manipulate objects in the environment.
2. Have the child ambulate across a room and visually spot a brightly colored picture on the wall. The picture can be of the child's own making, which is a visual perceptual-motor experience.
3. Ask the child to finger-trace dittos prepared by the teacher. Forms to be traced might include straight lines followed by geometric forms. Place a picture of an automobile on one side of a page with a garage on the other side. Draw parallel lines approximately 1 in. apart to connect the automobile with the garage. Ask the child to trace the path of the car into the garage. Create similar additional examples.
4. Place large numbers, letters, or geometric forms on the play surface. Ask the child to walk heel to toe on the lines that form the figures.
5. Have the child stand at varying distances from a wall and roll, throw, or bounce a brightly colored ball at the wall. Have the child retrieve the ball. Emphasize visual concentration on the ball. Vary the background to control the figure-ground relationship between ball and wall.
6. Place a ladder horizontally on the ground or a few inches above the ground. Ask the child to walk the length of the ladder stepping between, but not touching, the rungs, or have the child step *on* the rungs.
7. Hold a broomstick at different heights, depending on capability and characteristics of the child, and have the child duck under, step over, or slip around but not touch the stick (Figure 7.3).
8. Tie the ends of a 10-ft rope together so the rope forms a circle. Place the rope circle on the ground. Pretend that the circle is a mud puddle, and have the children leap or jump across (but not into) the puddle.
9. Have assistants hold two tightly stretched, parallel ropes at approximately elbow height and slightly more than shoulder width apart. Have the child ambulate forward (backward, sideways) between the ropes but not touch either rope.
10. Have children push a small ball as they creep around the playing surface.
11. Have the child throw two different-colored objects simultaneously. One or both hands may be used. Have the child determine, without traversing the

FIGURE 7.3. Student stepping over wand.

distance, which object went the farthest. Use reference cues in the form of lines perpendicular to the object's trajectory to assist the child in making distance judgments. To judge distance initially, the child may actually have to traverse the distances traveled by the objects.

12. Have each child place one shoe (or mitten) in a pile. Stir the pile. Have the children compare and visually identify their own clothing article. Have each child retrieve his article and put it on.

Auditory Perception

Auditory perception is more than hearing. It is the ability to translate what one hears into meaningful information. The ability to understand sound develops, in some measure, from the ability to move. Movement produces sound and sets the stage for auditory perception development. From movement experiences, a child observes that different movements cause different sounds and she comes to understand the cause-effect relationship between movement and the sounds created.

The child also realizes similarities and differences in sounds that emanate from different objects. The mass and consistency of objects create different sounds when the objects are manipulated, but the objects remain mute until accidentally or purposefully contacted and manipulated.

Initially, the individual encounters through movement many auditory sensations that stimulate auditory perception. This sound perception, linked inseparably with motor experiences, becomes auditory perceptual-motor awareness.

Repeated auditory perceptual-motor experiences enable the individual to comprehend sounds caused by someone or something else. Having learned through motor experience that circumstances result in sound emissions, the individual does not need to create sound nor to be in its immediate vicinity to make a value judgment about the sound. The motor component in auditory perception becomes less crucial, and the individual's repertoire of sound and auditory perception experiences provides understanding of sound concepts merely by hearing them.

Auditory spatial awareness is related closely to and depends on movement experiences. Precepts and concepts of up-down, near-far, left-right, behind-in front develop as movement capabilities allow exploration of a sound-filled environment. The individual, through movement, soon understands that sounds emanate from different directions and that sounds change over distances as one moves nearer-farther from a sound source (i.e., the sound seems to become progressively louder-quieter). Soon, the child, having perceived sound from many vantage points, becomes adept at judging the distance, direction, direction of travel, and characteristics of the sound.

The following activities are suggested to develop auditory perceptual-motor efficiency and its components:

1. Rhythm band activities that promote auditory perceptual-motor awareness, because rhythm instruments demonstrate cause-effect relationships between movement and sound.
2. Rhythm and dance activities that require movement toward, away from, and around sound sources and provide auditory spatial orientation.
3. Exercises in which the child keeps time with an audible cadence.
4. Creative motor responses to recorded sounds of various animals.
5. Activities in which the child makes an appropriate quantity of motor responses on hearing a number of sounds (e.g., the child may be asked to execute as many hops as there are drumbeats).
6. Activities in which the child is asked to make appropriate responses to sounds (e.g., Walk when you hear the bell; stop when you hear the whistle).
7. Activity that involves analyzing the origin of a sound. Show the child two small, clean paint cans. Place two marbles in one can and seal the lid. Place one marble in the other can and seal the lid. Now mix up the cans so the child does not know which can is which. Have her shake and manipulate each can and then guess how many marbles are in each.
8. Activities in which children play with balls that have sound producers inside. As the ball is manipulated, cause-effect relationships are fostered between movement and sound. Sound emissions from the ball as it is rolled and thrown allow children to track the sound. Tracking the movement of sound develops auditory spatial awareness.
9. Auditory experiences in which sounds range in intensity from quiet to loud. Have children become as small as possible when sounds are quiet; have them

become progressively larger as sound becomes more intense. Use recorded music and control the volume, or sounds of a drum, tom-tom, or tambourine can be altered by varying striking strength (Figure 7.4).

10. Auditory experiences in which the pitch ranges from low to high. Have children become as small as possible when pitch is low and as large as possible when pitch is high. Notes or chords from a piano are appropriate.

11. Activities in which blindfolded children are asked to turn toward (ambulate toward) a sound.

12. Activities in which children play with balls of various weights and materials. The child should realize that construction materials, weight, and size contribute to the sounds that things make. Such play might involve different playing surfaces (e.g., turf, wood, rubber, asphalt, concrete) to help the child realize that dissimilar surfaces also affect sound. These activities help the child learn to discriminate among sounds and to judge an object by the sounds it makes.

Kinesthetic Perception

Kinesthetic perception is an awareness of one's body position in space. It enables one to conceptualize configurations that the body assumes and the body's relationship to its immediate environment. Kinesthetic perception is involved in judgments such as whether or not one is moving, and if moving, how rapidly. It provides awareness of the body's form whether moving or standing still. If moving, kinesthetic perception helps determine whether one is moving forward, backward, sideways, at an angle, in an arc, or in any combination. If the individual is airborne, it enables determination of speed, trajectory, and distance from the surface. In these situations, kinesthetic perception is an important safety skill.

Kinesthetic perception is an extension of the previously discussed perceptual-motor attribute of postural and locomotor awareness. Postural maintenance and locomotion require competence in kinesthetic perception. Postural and locomotor awareness are, however, extremely basic and cannot be the sole stimulant for development of kinesthetic perception.

Almost any activity that requires an awareness and control of body position in space stimulates kinesthetic perception. Sage (1984) warns that participation in general activities may not always provoke kinesthetic development. He states: "Practice in a wide variety of motor activities will presumably result in some improved body positional control, balance, and movement control, but large general improvements in kinesthesis probably do not occur" (p. 184). The instructor should remember that if a student has a static balance weakness, then the prescribed activities should relate specifically to static balance.

Activities that enhance kinesthetic perception should be challenging yet not frustrating to the children. The following are examples of motor activities and equipment typically used to enhance kinesthetic perception:

FIGURE 7.4. (A) Ask children to become tall when the music is loud. (B) Have them become small when the music is quiet.

1. Almost all motor activities that provide sensations of movement.
2. Activities requiring changes in body or body segment direction, starting and stopping, or fast-slow movement.
3. Playground equipment, including slides, swings, spring-mounted rocking horses, and jungle gyms.
4. Activities in which the child tries to stand on one foot with eyes closed and not lose balance. Children exhibiting low levels of kinesthetic perception may have to do this skill with eyes open. Another variation for more highly skilled children involves standing on the tiptoe of the supporting leg. Eyes may be open or closed, depending on the child's performance level.
5. Activities that provide opportunity to crawl and creep through improvised tunnels. Children should not touch the top or sides of the tunnel. More highly skilled children may be able to crawl and creep backward through the tunnel.
6. Activities in which the child holds a 24-in. rope in her hands. The rope should hang in front of the body like a jump rope, with the lower part of the rope at approximately knee height. Have the child jump forward over the rope so that, on completion of the jump, the child's body is in front of the rope.
7. Activities in which the child walks a circle marked on the playing surface. After several trials, have the child walk the circle without looking at the line. As necessary, suggest that the child look at the line for reorientation.
8. Activities in which the child lies on a safety mat with a line drawn down its center. Have the child lie flat on the mat with arms at sides and body extended. Have the child logroll down the length of the mat, straight to the end rather than off to the side. Have the child roll to the left and right.
9. Activities with scooter boards that enable the child to propel across the playing surface, preferably a smooth floor. The child may sit or lie on the scooter board and propel in any direction (Figures 7.5 and 7.6).
10. Activities with balancing devices including beams, balance (vestibular) boards, bounce boards, and lazy Susans.

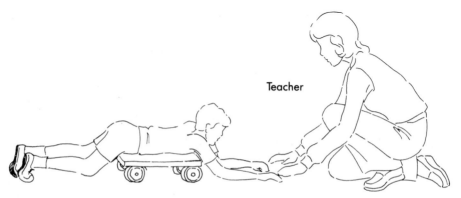

Teacher

FIGURE 7.5.   Scooter activity with teacher assistance. (Reprinted from Moran and Kalakian 1977, p. 73.)

FIGURE 7.6. Scooter activity without assistance.

11. Activities in which the child ambulates through a zigzag obstacle course, trying not to touch any object marking the course.
12. Activities in which the child leans in different directions, one direction at a time, trying not to lose balance. The children can stand, kneel, or assume an all-fours position. Coincidentally, the children form concepts about the body position that is most stable.

Tactile Perception

Tactile perception is the ability to interpret sensations of touch. Touching, feeling, and manipulating objects are dependent on movement to experience tactual sensations. Certainly tactile sensations are experienced by passive as well as active persons, but tactile experiences are more numerous when actively pursued.

Tactile awareness is important for learners who, regardless of chronological age, are in the early stages of coping with abstractions. Tactile experiences tend to be concrete. To experience tactually, one touches, feels, holds, or manipulates. Such actual physical contact provides concrete knowledge of the world.

Tactile perception is important in developing manual dexterity and fine motor skill. Tactual perception is the primary informant when determining how an object has been grasped. It is also the primary informant when one formulates judgments about objects that cannot be seen but can be touched.

Tactile perception serves as an adjunct to visual perception. Simultaneously seeing and feeling are often more informative than a single perception from either sensory modality.

Because tactile perception is prompted by action, it is facilitated by movement experiences that emphasize the sensation of touch. The following activities exemplify tactile perception through motor experience:

1. Place several familiar objects in a paper bag. Have the child identify objects by feel before pulling them from the bag.
2. Fill two pans with water, one warm and one cool. Have the child immerse her hands in one pan and then in the other. Have her determine which pan of water is warmer. Repeat this activity using foot and elbow contacts.
3. Have the child touch objects with his feet, and without visual or other sensory input, identify the things touched.
4. Permit the child to walk barefoot over different surfaces—smooth, rough, warm, cool, damp, or dry.
5. Have children roll, crawl, and creep over different textured surfaces (e.g., tile floor, lawn, safety mats, gymnasium floor, carpet). If possible, have them roll, crawl, and creep over many varied surfaces during a relatively short time. This experience enables a child to perceive tactile sensations with the entire body, rather than just hands or feet.
6. Place a length of tape in a straight line on the floor. Permit the child to walk barefoot, and without looking for the tape, feel the tape with his feet.
7. Place a piece of tape approximately 2 in. square on the flat surface of a 1 × 12 × 12-in. board. Place the board in the child's lap, tape side down. Have the child feel the tape side of the board with her fingers and tell her to stop feeling as soon as she locates the tape. Have her hold that spot and turn the board over to see if she did in fact locate the tape.
8. Have the child play with several different shaped and textured toys. Encourage the child to simultaneously manipulate and look. Tactual sensations supplement and enhance visual perception and vice versa.
9. Have the child string beads. For children whose manual dexterity and tactile perceptions are somewhat lacking, use bolts or blocks of wood with large holes. As manual dexterity and tactual awareness improve, substitute smaller objects and lighter rope or string.
10. Place three square blocks (or balls) of different sizes (same texture) inside a bag. Have the child (without looking) feel each object, and pull the largest object from the bag. The child should then empty the bag to see if the choice was correct.
11. Encourage children to engage in sand play for tactile stimulation (Figure 7.7).
12. Touch the child's back or other body parts with one or more fingers. Without access to the experience, have the child identify how many fingers are pressing against her body. Other sensations involving tactile discrimination without aid of visual cues might include warm-cool, wet-dry, rough-smooth, or soft-firm.

FIGURE 7.7. Sand play provides tactile stimulation.

Body Awareness

Body awareness, sometimes called body image, refers to an awareness of body parts and segments. It encompasses the ability to name body parts and an awareness of one's body parts as one moves.

Body awareness is an important initial step in becoming aware of one's environment. Essentially, one must know oneself before organizing and systematizing the external world. This suggests that body awareness must be established before establishing the components to be discussed next—laterality and directionality.

Body awareness activities focus attention on body segments and parts. Such activities help the individual to understand that the body has two sides that work together, in opposition, or individually. Body awareness activities also focus attention on capabilities and limitations of body parts and segments. The following are examples of motor activities used to develop body awareness:

1. Swimming activities promote body awareness through the sensation of movement through water.
2. Have the child identify ears, eyes, hips, nose, arms, knees, elbows, toes, ankles, and shoulders.
3. Place a bright-colored ribbon or loose elastic band on a body part or segment to draw attention to it as the child moves about.

4. Attach a jingle bell to various body parts and segments. The bell's jingle calls attention to that body part or segment. This activity is most successful when working with one child or with a small group of children. With larger groups, the noise is a distraction.
5. Have the child execute several elementary motor skills while watching his image in a mirror.
6. Have the child pose or move before a mirror, then have her attempt to draw a picture of her movement.
7. Have children stand facing the teacher. Provide adequate space between children so movements can be made freely. Tell them to "Do as I do." Move your arms and legs in various combinations. Movements may be unilateral, bilateral, and cross-lateral (e.g., left arm only, right arm and left arm simultaneously, left arm and right leg simultaneously).
8. Have the child lie on his back and move one or more body parts by sliding them along the floor. Point to (do not touch) the body parts to be moved, so the child does not get tactual cues. Have the child make unilateral, bilateral, and cross-lateral movements. Movement patterns in this activity resemble patterns experienced when playing angels in the snow.
9. Secure a weighted belt to a body segment while the child participates in several motor experiences. The weight should be heavy enough to create an awareness of that segment but not so heavy that it inhibits movements. The belt may be moved from segment to segment.
10. Have the children stand facing a wall or screen with their back to an overhead projector. Turn on the projector so they see their body image shadowed against the wall or screen. Have them move in a variety of ways for an immediate cause-effect feedback, which develops body awareness (Figure 7.8).
11. Introduce and play games or activities like hokey pokey, which requires the child to activate one body part at a time.
12. Have the children engage in activities before a large window fan (or outdoors on a breezy day). Air movement, like water resistance, enables children to feel various body segments as they move.

Laterality and Directionality

Laterality is an internal awareness that the body has a left and right side. **Directionality** is the extension of laterality into the external world. Directionality is thought to develop largely as a result of movement experience. In the hierarchy of perceptual-motor development, body image or body awareness emerges first, followed by laterality. Laterality development is thought to be the foundation of the subsequent emergence of directionality.

Establishing lateral preference is believed to be important to development of laterality. Well-established lateral preference enables the individual to distinguish between left and right. Certain learning difficulties are thought to result in part from a lack of lateral preference or from a mixed preference. A common problem associated with

FIGURE 7.8. Observing one's shadow develops body awareness.

laterality inadequacies is reversals. Common reversals include substitution of a *p* for a *q* and vice versa, or substitution of a *b* for a *d* and vice versa. A child who does not have well-established left-right orientation may perceive little or no difference between these letters.

Another theory regarding reversals supports the view that development of body awareness is sequential—first laterality, then directionality. Until he is cognizant of body parts and segments (body image), the child cannot become fully aware that the body has sides (laterality). Until laterality enables the child to deal with the concept of sidedness in internal space (the body), he is unready to deal with the complex concepts of sidedness and direction in external space (the environment). The child who has not fully conceptualized sidedness and direction in external space may, for example, view *b*s and *d*s or *p*s and *q*s as simply undifferentiated circles with lines attached. He may unwittingly write "bog" instead of "dog." The child who unknowingly holds a picture book upside down does not understand sidedness, including "up" and "down."

Directionality is also thought to give dimension to space. A child with good directionality development may be capable of conceptualizing right-left, above-below, in front-behind, and various combinations.

Directionality and spatial orientation or awareness are closely related perceptual attributes. Each gives dimension to space and enables the child to determine where he is in relation to other phenomena in the environment. Motor experiences that enhance development of laterality and directionality include the following:

1. Provide a variety of throwing and kicking experiences that encourage selection and use of the dominant or preferred side of the body.
2. Have the child participate in rhythm and dance activities that require movement in many directions.
3. Encourage movement activities in all conceivable directions, using each of the basic locomotor skills.
4. Have the child wad up a 10 ft segment of rope and throw it high in the air. When the rope lands on the playing surface, have the child walk heel to toe from one end of the rope to the other.
5. Draw or tape geometric figures, letters, numbers, and words on the playing surface. Have the child walk heel to toe along the full length of the lines that comprise each figure.
6. Have the child walk forward and backward on a balance beam. The child may perform before a full-length mirror to help conceptualize direction changes.
7. Have the child walk in both directions sideways on the balance beam. Be sure that she walks with the left foot as the lead foot and then with the right foot as the lead foot.
8. Place safety mats on the playing surface, and have children roll from one end of the mat to the other, rolling both to left and right.
9. Draw a straight line or lane on the playing surface. Provide an old tire or hula hoop and have the child roll the tire or hoop straight down the line or between the lines that form the lane. The child may walk sideways, forward, or backward in performing this activity.
10. Place brightly colored circles randomly on the floor. Have the child leap, hop, or jump in any order he chooses from one circle to another. Encourage movement in all directions if the child does not do so spontaneously.
11. Have the child respond similarly to the teacher or a peer who is making rapid, sequential direction changes (i.e., forward-backward, right-left, forward diagonal left-right, backward diagonal left-right).
12. Have the child respond to large flash cards that have arrows pointing in different directions.

Evaluating Perceptual-Motor Efficiency

All motor activities possess some perceptual-motor component, some activities more than others. Success with any activity in the motor performance domain depends on the person's level of perceptual-motor competence.

Perceptual-motor assessment typically serves one of several purposes. In some cases, the perceptual-motor skills of an entire class of students are assessed in an effort to identify those having perceptual-motor difficulties. Appropriate physical education training programs can then be developed to prevent further learning difficulties. Students who perform poorly on these tests are said to demonstrate perceptual-motor problems, which are thought to contribute negatively to academic learning capabilities. In other cases, youngsters having academic problems are assessed in an effort to identify the extent to which perceptual-motor difficulties may be causing lack of academic success (Salvia and Ysseldyke 1981). Finally, identification of perceptual-motor disabilities is imperative so the adapted physical educator can begin immediate remediation activities for the "clumsy, awkward" child. A lack of smooth and efficient body movement has left many youngsters with tremendous feelings of inferiority. For these children, who so often experience failure in physical education class, the future looks grim unless appropriate programming is initiated immediately! The negative carryover must not be underestimated. Some professionals believe that a major part of an individual's personality is affected adversely if the youngster is forced continually to take part in frustrating motor activities at which she always fails (Taylor 1985, Lohmann 1985).

While assessment identifies physical and motor deficiencies, it does not generate labels or identify causes of deficiency. For example, deficiencies may be symptoms of deeper underlying causes. Werder and Kalakian (1985, p. 17) list the following possible reasons for poor performance: "(1) attitudinal or environmental influences, (2) emotional or behavioral disturbances, (3) minimal neurological dysfunction (i.e., mild ataxia), (4) delayed development of the central nervous system, (5) muscular weakness, and (6) structural abnormalities." The instructor must consider using the team approach, that is, calling on allied professionals including therapists, the special educator, the school nurse, and the child's pediatrician.

Tests and surveys of perceptual-motor efficiency vary in sophistication. Authorities agree that more definitive perceptual-motor assessment tools are needed. Those currently in existence are primarily screening devices and evaluation guides for perceptual-motor assessment and programming.

The *Purdue Perceptual-Motor Survey* (Roach and Kephart 1966) has been used most heavily. Owing to vagueness in scoring criteria and because more than one perceptual component is present in many of the survey's 22 items, interpretations of results should be made with caution. All survey items are rated on a 4-point scale. Subtests of the survey focus on posture and balance, body image and differentiation, perceptual-motor integration, ocular control, and form perception.

The following items are laden with perceptual-motor components and are suggested as screening tools in the initial identification of children with deficits (Taylor 1984). As noted before, perceptual-motor activities often do not isolate a single perceptual-motor component. Although some items can be measured objectively (i.e., number of seconds the child remains balanced), others call for subjective judgments that are only as good as the teacher's judgmental consistency and powers of observation. The following items are suggested for consideration in perceptual-motor assessment:

Balance

Item	Performance Criteria
Stork stand (10 sec maximum).	Number of seconds child remains balanced. Removal of hands from hips, nonsupporting foot from side of supporting leg, or hopping is considered loss of balance.
Sitting tuck balance (10 sec maximum).	Number of seconds child can hold this position without touching feet to floor or rolling onto back (Figure 7.9).
Vertical stick balance on index finger of preferred hand from sitting position (10 sec maximum).	Number of seconds child can maintain stick in upright position.
Teeter board (10 sec maximum).	Record number of times edges of teeter board touch the floor. Fewer touches are interpreted as better performance (Figure 7.10).
Child stands motionless with eyes closed (10 sec maximum).	Note excessive swaying in an effort to remain balanced. Note flexion in knees, hips, and ankles (need to maintain

FIGURE 7.9. Sitting tuck balance.

FIGURE 7.10. Teeter board balance. (Reprinted from Moran and Kalakian 1977, p. 429.)

balance by lowering center of gravity), removal of hands from sides, facial expressions signaling difficulty, need to take a step, and opened eyes.

Postural and Locomotor Awareness

Item	**Performance Criteria**
Child walks heel-to-toe (forward and backward) along 1-in. wide line 10 ft in length (minimum of ten heel-to-toe contacts required).	Note any movements that appear excessive or extraneous. Note number of missed heel-to-toe contacts. Note number of steps totally missing the line (Figure 7.11).
Child crawls (total body in contact with floor). Child creeps (hands and knees position).	In either case, note preference for homolateral pattern (arm and leg on same side move simultaneously) or for cross-lateral pattern (arm and opposite leg move simultaneously). Note any deviations in simultaneous arm-leg movement (e.g., arm movement, delay, then leg movement). Evaluate ability to move in a straight line. Note any extraneous or abortive movements (Figure 7.12).

FIGURE 7.11. Heel-toe walking on a 1-in. wide line.

Bipedal locomotion.

Walking, hopping (preferred and nonpreferred foot), jumping, leaping, galloping (right and left foot lead, forward and backward), sliding (left and right), running, skipping.

Rolling (right and left) (maximum of five complete rolls in each direction).

Place two parallel lines on the floor approximately 1 ft wider apart than the child is tall. Ask the child to roll in log-roll fashion parallel to and between the lines. Note ability to roll without touching either line. Note extraneous or abortive movements.

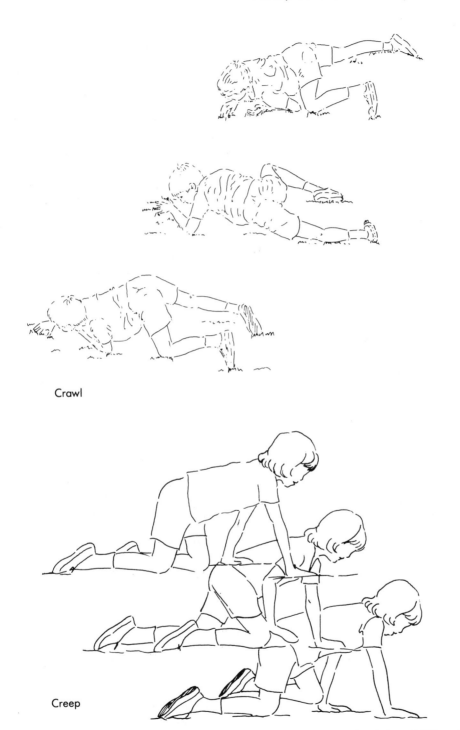

Crawl

Creep

FIGURE 7.12. Crawling and creeping. (Reprinted from Moran and Kalakian 1977, p. 74.)

Crossover walking (forward and backward) along 1-in. wide line 10 ft in length (maximum of five contacts with each foot in each direction).

Child stands on left side of line. Child steps diagonally with right foot, placing it on left side of line. Child now steps diagonally with left foot, placing it on right side of line. Note number of foot contacts by both left and right foot, in both forward and backward directions, that cross completely over the line.

Visual

Item	**Performance Criteria**
Pendulum ball suspended on 2-ft string (three trials maximum).	Place ball in lateral motion (approximately 180-degree arc). Child must intercept ball with index finger before ball completes three cycles.
Horizontal ladder fashioned from tagboard, contrasting background (ten rungs).	Note child's ability to step between, but not on, rungs.
Horizontal ladder fashioned from tagboard, blending background (ten rungs).	Note child's ability to step between, but not on, rungs.
Child catches rolled ball (five trials).	Child seated in straddle position must successfully grasp the ball, which has been rolled from a distance of 10 ft, with both hands. Note number of successful catches.
Child catches thrown ball (five trials).	Child in standing position must successfully grasp ball with both hands. Catching by trapping ball between arms and chest should be noted as a relatively less sophisticated response. Ball should be thrown from approximately 6 to 8 ft and should arrive at chest height. Record number of successful catches.

Auditory

Item	**Performance Criteria**
Child shakes cans.	In each of two cans of the same size, place one and three marbles, respectively. Replace lids on cans. Ask child to shake each can and to designate which has the greater number of noisemaking objects inside.

Child walks to drum or metronome cadence (20 beats maximum, 10 beats per foot).

Child must walk in a straight line in time to the beat. Establish beat and let child move to get in time with the beat before counting begins. Note number of foot contacts that strike the surface simultaneously with the drum or metronome cadence.

Child faces sound source (five trials).

Tape a circle 15 ft in diameter on the floor. Add 12 radials from the axis (e.g., one o'clock, two o'clock). Child, blindfolded, stands on circle axis. Teacher at edge of circle shakes a rattle. Child must turn toward sound source. Sound should emanate from a different spot on the circle's periphery for each of the five trials. For each trial, record, to the nearest radial, the discrepancy between direction that the child faces and direction from which the sound has come. Discrepancies for five trials are totaled. Lower score is interpreted as better performance.

Tactile

Item	**Performance Criteria**
Grab bag (six trials).	Place three similarly textured but differently shaped objects familiar to the child in a bag. Identify specifically shaped object to be retrieved from the bag. Child reaches into the bag without looking, and tries to retrieve the specific object requested. Object is replaced in bag. Ask for another object. Ask randomly for each object twice. Note number of correct responses.
Rough-smooth (three trials).	Two objects, one rough, one smooth (e.g., sandpaper, typing paper) are placed out of child's view. Child is asked to manipulate each object and to identify which is smoother. Two out of three correct trials scores a pass.
Pennies in a cup (20 sec).	Using preferred hand, child picks up pennies one at a time and places as many pennies as possible into a cup in the allotted time.

Large-small (three trials).

Two objects similar in every way but size are placed out of the child's view. Child is asked to manipulate and identify the larger of the two objects. Two out of three correct trials scores a pass (Figure 7.13).

Soft-hard (three trials).

Same as large-small item, except objects are dissimilar only in consistency (e.g., hard and soft or spongy ball). Two out of three correct trials scores a pass.

Kinesthetic

Item	Performance Criteria
Heel click (three trials).	Child jumps vertically into air and clicks heels as many times as possible before landing. Record best of three trials.

FIGURE 7.13. "Which ball is larger?"

Jump and knee touch (three trials).

Child jumps vertically and touches knees once before landing. Two out of three successful trials scores a pass.

Jog in place, heel touch (maximum ten foot contacts for each foot).

Child jogs in place and attempts to touch right hand to right heel (left hand to left heel) each time the heel rises from the jogging surface. Seven out of ten (for each foot) scores a pass.

Bounce board (maximum ten bounces).

Circumscribe 12-in. circle on center of bounce board surface. Note child's ability to bounce rhythmically in place. Record number of contacts in which rhythm is not broken and at least part of both feet simultaneously contact some portion of the circle.

Straddle jump and arm raise (10 sec maximum).

Child begins rhythmic straddle jumping (feet out to side, feet together). As feet assume straddle position, straight arms parallel to each other are raised forward to shoulder height. When feet come together, arms lower to starting position. Allow child to get rhythm going before commencing 10-sec count. Count number of correct cycles demonstrated during 10-sec period.

Body Awareness

Item	**Performance Criteria**
Identification of body parts (simple).	Have child touch nose, hips, stomach, knees, feet, elbows, ankles, ears, shoulders, eyes, and mouth. Note any incorrect or uncertain responses.
Identification of body parts (complex).	At the same time, touch your nose and knee (e.g., left hand to nose, right hand to right knee), hip and knee, eye and ear, stomach and foot. Note any incorrect or uncertain responses (Figures 7.14 and 7.15).
Angels in the snow.	Ask child, lying on back with feet together and arms at sides, to move body segments as requested;

       Right arm only (lateral)
       Left arm only (lateral)

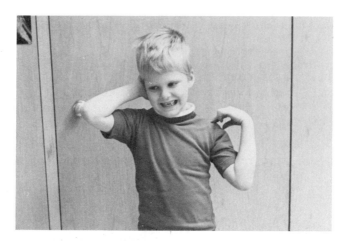

FIGURE 7.14. "Touch your shoulder and your ear."

FIGURE 7.15. "Touch your ear and your eye."

Both arms simultaneously
(bilateral)
Right leg only (lateral)
Left leg only (lateral)
Both legs simultaneously (bilateral)
Right arm, left leg simultaneously
(cross-lateral)
Left arm, right leg simultaneously
(cross-lateral)

Note incorrect responses, extraneous movement of other segments, unsure or abortive movements.

Fist I.

Have child make fist with preferred hand. Point randomly to (but do not touch) each of the five fingers one at a time and ask child to point that finger only. Note any pointing of incorrect finger, opening of hand, or pointing of more than one finger. Record number of correct responses.

Fist II.

Have child make fist. Ask child to open fist sequentially, one finger at a time, until hand is entirely open, starting with the thumb. Note number of fingers opened in proper sequence only.

Laterality and Directionality

Item	Performance Criteria
Establishment of lateral preference.	Note informally the child's preference or lack of preference for a given hand or foot. Try to differentiate between children who might show mixed preference but have already established a strong lateral preference and those whose mixed preference more truly reflects relatively less mature lateral preference development. Suggested activities to observe include writing, drawing, eating, throwing, catching, kicking, striking, pushing, pulling, hopping, galloping, and sliding.
Follow me (stationary).	Stand before the child and assume different stationary body poses (e.g., hands over head, hands to sides, hands to front, one arm up-other arm down, hands on hips and bend to left-right-front-back). Feet straddled-feet together, half straddle left foot only-right foot only, forward straddle one foot forward-one foot back. Note whether child parallels exactly or mirrors teacher's pose. Parallel responses show relatively

more sophisticated response. Mirrored response is thought to be of little concern provided mirroring is constant over entire observation period. Note particularly any unsure responses or any combination of responses that sometimes are parallel and other times are mirrored.

Follow me (locomotor).

Circumscribe two squares approximately 8 ft on a side in a side-by-side position on the floor. Stand in one square and have child stand in other. Move to various parts of the square with child endeavoring to imitate precisely your movements. Stand in each of the square's corners randomly and on each of the lines midway between each of the corners. Note child's ability to replicate your movements. Score a point for each correct response.

When using any perceptual-motor test battery, accuracy becomes of major importance. Objective-based assessments (i.e., how far, how many, how fast) are valuable tools for the adapted physical educator. Reuschlein and Vogel state: "The qualitative standards . . . are generalizable to children . . . since they are elements of performance that define skilled or unskilled performance. As such, they form the basis for systematic and quantitative performance at a level that is consistent with the innate ability levels of individual children" (1985, p. 151).

Summary

Perceptual-motor theory and practice reflect the premise that perceptual competence is achieved initially largely through the medium of movement. Although the specific interpretations of various perceptual-motor theorists and practitioners cited here may differ, the basic tenet remains constant.

Some degree of controversy arises over whether development of perceptual competence through movement automatically translates into heightened readiness for academic challenges. Logical persuasions can be offered to support such a premise, but such persuasions remain to be proved through research. While achievement of desirable outcomes is acknowledged, caution is urged in making outcome claims that cannot be substantiated objectively.

Unlike the components of physical and motor fitness, the various components that comprise perceptual-motor efficiency are closely interrelated. Nevertheless, the physical educator can create activities that focus on development of proficiency in each component.

Methods of assessing perceptual-motor efficiency vary in sophistication, and more definitive tools are needed. At the present time, the *Purdue Perceptual-Motor Survey* is the most frequently used instrument.

As an adjunct to existing instruments, teachers are encouraged to design their own assessments using selections from the assessment items and performance criteria in this chapter as a starting point. Three to five ways of measuring proficiency for each perceptual component are recommended.

References

Ayres, A. J. Occupational Therapy for Motor Disorders of the Central Nervous System. *Rehabilitation Literature* 21:302–310, 1960.

———. Types of Sensory Integrative Dysfunction Among Disabled Learners. *American Journal of Occupational Therapy* 26:13–18, 1972.

———. Cluster Analyses of Measures of Sensory Integration. *American Journal of Occupational Therapy* 31:362–366, 1977.

Barsch, R. H. *A Movegenic Curriculum.* Madison, Wis.: Bureau for Handicapped Children, 1965.

Cratty, B. J. *Motor Activity in the Education of Retardates.* Philadelphia: Lea and Febiger, 1969.

———. *Adapted Physical Education for Handicapped Children and Youth.* Denver: Love Publishing, 1980.

———. *Perceptual and Motor Development in Infants and Children*, 3rd ed. Englewood Cliffs, N.J.: Prentice-Hall, 1986.

Delacato, C. *The Treatment and Prevention of Reading Problems.* Springfield, Ill.: Charles C Thomas, 1959.

Dummer, G. M. Developmental Differences in Motor Schema Formation. In *Motor-Development—Current Selected Research*, Vol. I, edited by J. E. Clark and J. H. Humphrey. Princeton, N.J.: Princeton Book Company, 1985.

Gallahue, D. L. *Understanding Motor Development in Children.* New York: John Wiley & Sons, 1982.

Getman, G. N., and Kane, E. R. *The Physiology of Readiness.* Minneapolis: Program to Accelerate School Readiness, 1964.

Itard, J. M. *The Wild Boy of Aveyron.* New York: Appleton-Century-Crofts, 1801.

Keogh, J., and Sugden, D. *Movement Skill Development.* New York: Macmillan, 1985.

Kephart, N. C. *The Slow Learner in the Classroom.* Columbus, Ohio: Charles E. Merrill, 1960.

Kerr, R. Fitts' Law and Motor Control in Children. In *Motor Development—Current Selected Research*, Vol. I, edited by J. E. Clark and J. H. Humphrey. Princeton, N.J.: Princeton Book Company, 1985.

Lohmann, J. P. Personal correspondence, 1985.

Montessori, D. M. *The Montessori Method.* New York: Frederick A. Stokes, 1912.

Moran, J. M., and Kalakian, L. H. *Movement Experiences for the Mentally Retarded or Emotionally Disturbed Child*, 2nd ed. Minneapolis: Burgess Publishing, 1977.

Piaget, J. *The Origin of Intelligence in Children.* New York: New York University Press, 1936.

Reuschlein, P. L., and Vogel, P. G. Motor Performance and Physical Fitness Status of Regular and Special Education Students. In *Motor Development—Current Selected Research*, Vol. I, edited by J. E. Clark and J. H. Humphrey. Princeton, N.J.: Princeton Book Company, 1985.

Roach, E., and Kephart, N. *The Purdue-Perceptual Motor Survey.* Columbus, Ohio: Charles E. Merrill, 1966.

Sage, G. H. *Motor Learning and Control—A Neuropsychological Approach.* Dubuque, Iowa: Wm. C. Brown, 1984.

Salvia, J., and Ysseldyke, J. E. *Assessment in Special and Remedial Education*, 2nd ed. Boston: Houghton Mifflin, 1981.

Seguin, E. *Idiocy, Its Treatment by the Physiological Method.* New York: Columbia University Press, 1907.

Stein, J. U. Perceptual-Motor Development of Handicapped Children: Thoughts, Observations and Questions. *Foundations and Practices in Perceptual-Motor Learning.* Reston, Va.: AAHPERD, 1973.

Taylor, C. Personal correspondence, 1985.

Taylor, J. G. *The Behavioral Basis for Perception.* New Haven, Conn.: Yale University Press, 1962.

Taylor, R. L. *Assessment of Exceptional Students: Educational and Psychological Procedures.* Englewood Cliffs, N.J.: Prentice-Hall, 1984.

Thomas, J. R. *Motor Development During Childhood and Adolescence.* Minneapolis: Burgess Publishing, 1984.

Vernon, M. D. The Psychology of Perception. Baltimore: Penguin Books, 1962.

Werder, J. K., and Kalakian, L. H. *Assessment in Adapted Physical Education.* Minneapolis: Burgess Publishing, 1985.

CHAPTER 8

Individualized Educational Programming: The Process and the Product

An **individualized educational program (IEP)** is a detailed, written plan to meet the educational needs of a handicapped child. It should contain all dimensions of a total education, including specific information regarding the intellectual, social, emotional, and physical programs for each child (Figure 8.1).

The underlying concept of the IEP is that students must have their most important and immediate needs identified if they are to receive the best education possible. This planning, therefore, is essential and must be completed before any programming, placement, or teaching can begin.

Individualized teaching and learning have proved to be highly effective with both handicapped and nonhandicapped students. In fact, many states (more than half) were requiring IEPs for handicapped children even before Public Law 94-142 became law (Hayes and Higgins 1978).

MIDSTATE SPECIAL EDUCATION
INDIVIDUALIZED EDUCATIONAL PROGRAM

White—Building
Yellow—Parent
Goldenrod—Midstate
Pink—Regional Supervisor

_____ 19 _____ to _____ 19 _____

Student's name _____ Birthdate _____

Resident district _____ Building _____

Placement _____ Building _____

Type of Sp. Ed. Program _____

Date of initial placement _____

Date of IEP _____ Date of review _____

THE FOLLOWING PERSONS ATTENDED

IEP staffing/review:

Reg. Ed. Admin. _____

Standard Teacher _____

Special Teacher _____

Parent(s) _____

Student _____

Other (Title) _____

IEP Manager _____

Sp. Ed. Admin. _____

Psychologist _____

PE Teacher _____

SERVICES TO BE PROVIDED

Type	Start	Teacher or Itinerant	No. of Min. Per Week	No. of Weeks

Transportation:

Physical education:

Extent of time in standard program:

Vocational/Career Educ.

FIGURE 8.1.   Example of the individualized educational program planning form.

Overview of the IEP and Legal Requirements

P.L. 94-142 requires that an IEP be developed for all handicapped students between the ages of 3 and 21 years. All local school districts receiving federal funds must write an annual IEP for each handicapped child. If a child is sent outside the school district, the IEP, its implementation, and total financial cost of education are still the responsibility of the local school board. For example, meeting the needs of a severely multihandicapped child within the local school district may not be possible. The school district and the parents should decide if the child will receive more effective educational opportunities in a state-operated developmental center. If the answer is *yes*, the total cost of educating this child must be paid by the local school district.

Some states have attempted to relieve the local school districts of financial responsibility for severely handicapped students who reside in state-operated developmental centers. These states have passed legislation to assume the entire cost of meeting the mandates of P.L. 94-142.

Illinois is experiencing positive results from special funding entitled The Orphanage Act (Illinois 14-7.03). At Lincoln Developmental Center, Lincoln, Illinois, 86 severely and profoundly handicapped students are being educated effectively in classroom settings with a maximum of eight students. One certified teacher and two teacher aides are assigned to each group. Daily physical education is provided by a certified adapted physical education teacher who is assisted by a certified therapeutic recreation specialist (Landis 1985).

The Written Document

The IEP describes the educational plan and how education and related services will be provided. It must contain the following elements:

1. A statement of the child's present levels of educational performance.
2. A statement of long-term educational performance goals to be achieved by the child at year end.
3. A statement of short-term instructional objectives for each annual goal, which represent measurable intermediate steps between the child's present level of performance and the desired level.
4. A statement of special education and related services to be provided, including the type of physical education program in which the child will participate and any special media or materials required to implement the child's IEP.
5. Initiation date and anticipated duration of special education and related services.
6. Description of extent to which the child will participate in regular education programs.
7. Justification for the child's educational placement.

8. Objective criteria, evaluation procedures, and schedules for determining on an annual basis whether short-term instructional objectives have been achieved.

While the total IEP should stress improving intellectual abilities, it must also provide specific details regarding the student's physical and motor program. Physical educators, because of their psychomotor expertise, thus become the appropriate professionals to define the status of a child's present motor and fitness ability.

The components and depth or detail of an IEP may be more extensive than the general class planning that physical educators are currently using, and some terminology may be new, but the actual development of an IEP simply represents sound physical education planning. What the educator has always done for a large group of students must now be done for an individual child. Basically, the law asks educators, including physical educators, to provide the following: (1) a clear statement of the child's current levels of ability, (2) precise identification of the most important skills to be learned, (3) specific programming suggestions, (4) placement recommendation for the most effective program, and (5) how the child's progress will be evaluated.

Do All Handicapped Children Need an IEP in Physical Education?

Many handicapped children can remain in the regular physical education class because they do not need a specially designed adapted program. For example, after assessing a 10-year-old educable mentally handicapped girl, her levels of general motor ability and physical fitness were found to be comparable to those of her nonhandicapped peers. Presumably, therefore, she could learn physical skills as effectively as those youngsters in the mainstream, so she was placed into the regular program. In this child's case, the regular physical education curriculum was assumed to provide appropriate developmental sequences to meet the overall needs of all children her age. Consequently, because of her placement, an IEP was not needed for her physical education experience. In most cases, the IEP form will contain a specific section that identifies whether the student is to be placed in regular or adapted physical education (see Figure 8.1).

Conversely, when a child is found to possess unusually low levels of motor ability or fitness, it is necessary to write an IEP (Figure 8.2). In this case, performance dictates the need for special programming. The IEP will specify present levels of ability at which the most effective learning can occur, and will list specific goals and objectives. For example, after testing, a hearing impaired boy was found to possess an extremely low level of perceptual motor ability, including catching and striking problems and deficiencies in static and dynamic balance. Because of these particular skill problems, one assumes that he cannot participate successfully and competitively with his normal age group (Figure 8.3). The most appropriate placement for this boy is an adapted physical education class that has a more concentrated program to improve performance in perceptual motor tasks.

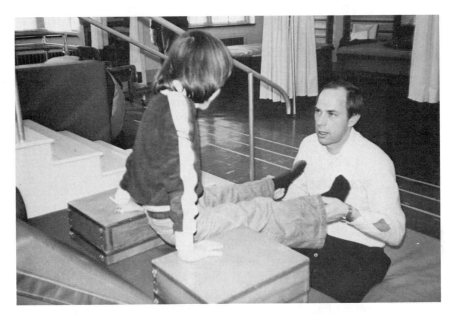

FIGURE 8.2.   Individualized assessment determines individual need.

FIGURE 8.3.   Static balance is often lacking in handicapped children.

These examples are at the extremes of full-time placement in either regular or adapted physical education. Most handicapped individuals can perform or learn many activities in a regular physical education class with nonhandicapped peers. The hearing impaired boy could be placed for part of the time in the regular program, particularly when planned activities involve strength and cardiorespiratory improvement. Weight training activities and endurance running would also provide opportunities for him to return to the mainstream. The IEP should identify those activities for which the boy can remain in the regular program (see Figure 8.1).

The Multidisciplinary Team

An IEP should be planned and written by those individuals most closely involved with the child's education. These professionals—teachers, school administrators, and support personnel—become the multidisciplinary team. Support personnel often includes physicians, therapists, psychologists, and social workers. The team works in cooperation and agreement with the child's parents, and when appropriate, with the child. For instance, it is appropriate for a 17-year-old blind boy to participate in planning his educational program, whereas a 4-year-old Down syndrome child cannot provide meaningful input. This yearly face-to-face exchange of ideas and information serves as the basis for the child's complete educational program.

Preplanning by the local school district is necessary so school personnel can discuss the following issues with the child's parents at the multidisciplinary staff conference: (1) child's eligibility, (2) present levels of educational performance, (3) annual goals, (4) supportive services, and (5) placement. Individuals responsible for implementing the child's IEP must also be identified and should attend the multidisciplinary staff conference.

The purpose of preplanning is to assure parents that the school has reviewed the child's case study evaluation, examined the child's needs, identified potential goals for the child, and considered placement and service options. By engaging in some preplanning, the multidisciplinary staff conference can be used to present program options to the child's parents and to discuss goals and needed services for the child.

The IEP planning process requires systematic organization so the educational program is individualized and student-oriented. The IEP provides a comprehensive plan for meeting the needs of the child.

Thomas and Marshall (1977) outline an approach for developing and coordinating the IEP. They state that successful adaptation, both physical and social, is the primary goal of the process. Specifically, the process involves information gathering, data pooling, initial programming, periodic reassessment, and program modification. They emphasize total communication among child, family, and public school personnel. Adaptability and flexibility on the part of all involved personnel are necessary to facilitate efforts to meet each child's unique needs.

Williamson (1978) identifies three goals that should influence the exchange of knowledge and function among multidisciplinary team members: (1) Consider the whole child. "Splintering" of the child along disciplinary lines must be avoided, that is, the old saying "the arms and legs to the physical educator, the joints to the physical therapist, and the brain to the teacher" is no longer appropriate. (2) Increased communication among team members should be a constant goal. (3) Maintain a positive attitude toward increased services to children regardless of fiscal constraint (i.e., when budgetary restrictions limit the number of full-time personnel, some disciplines may provide assistance on a consulting basis). These considerations do not imply that one individual or discipline must assume total responsibility for a child's program, but rather that team members share their information, and when appropriate, their skills to ensure consistency in the child's program.

Cooperation and better understanding among professionals is illustrated in the following examples:

Case 1: A physician mistakenly diagnosed a severely involved cerebral palsied child as mentally retarded because he could not elicit any communication from the child. The classroom teacher, on the other hand, saw the child every day, and was able to provide significant insights on reevaluation. The teacher knew that the child, who was quite intelligent, was terribly frightened by fear of failing. The child therefore gave the doctor a totally inaccurate picture during diagnostic examination.

Case 2: A physical educator augmented regular classroom instruction by incorporating simple group movement experiences. The classroom teacher supplied information to the physical educator regarding the social, emotional, and intellectual abilities of two new students. The physical educator also learned that the teacher wanted to develop geometric design concepts (squares, triangles, circles). For several weeks, the physical educator therefore included movement activities and games that involved geometric figures.

Lavay and French (1985) emphasize the extreme importance of communication among representatives of all disciplines. In fact, they stress the need for the adapted physical educator to become a driving force—the individual who takes responsibility for articulating the effort required in the motor and fitness areas. They make reference to a new term, "transdisciplinary approach." In their view, an ongoing dialogue must be maintained among physical educators, medical personnel, regular and special educators, and psychologists.

Parents and professionals can assist in the development of IEPs by collecting written data that provide information related to their discipline or to involvement with the handicapped child. Some specific areas that warrant attention are: (1) priorities for the IEP, (2) evaluation criteria, (3) suggested strategies for change, (4) the child's strengths and limitations, (5) the child's special attitudes, (6) performance potential, (7) psychosocial development, (8) specific problems encountered by the student, (9) specific suggestions as to what others can do to facilitate skill development, and (10) recommendations for other support programs (Table 8.1).

All individuals involved in the conference should be able to state specific needs and objectives clearly to facilitate better understanding. The formal staff conference should result in: (1) identification of educational program priorities, (2) identification of persons who will provide necessary instruction, (3) understanding of the child's placement for most effective learning, and (4) choices of evaluation methods.

TABLE 8.1

SPECIFIC QUESTIONS TO BE CONSIDERED WHEN COLLECTING INFORMATION FOR AN INDIVIDUALIZED EDUCATIONAL PROGRAM (IEP)

Specific Questions	Examples of Information Given for a Boy With Duchenne Muscular Dystrophy
1. Priorities of IEP	a. Maintain upper-body strength and endurance. b. Increase joint range of motion. c. Reduce joint contractures. d. Increase recreational skills.
2. Evaluation criteria	a. Use hand dynamometer for strength evaluation. b. Use goniometer for joint range of motion. c. Use cupcake pan and tennis ball for eye-hand coordination. Time with stopwatch.
3. Suggested strategies for change	a. Include progressive exercises, allowing for ample rest periods. b. Involve in activities that use the hands. c. Modify games for play in wheelchair.
4. Child's strengths and limitations	a. Nonambulatory; must remain in wheelchair. b. Close supervision in swimming pool is a must. He cannot support himself in standing position.
5. Child's special aptitudes	a. Positive mental attitude and enjoys physical education class.
6. Performance potential	a. Decreasing strength levels will be developing due to the disease. b. Fatigue will set in after shorter periods of time.
7. Psychosocial evaluation	a. Very cooperative with peers and teachers. b. Eager to be involved in team activities.
8. Specific problems encountered by the student	a. Severe contractures of ankles and feet. b. Legs cannot be lifted by student.
9. Specific suggestions for what others can do to facilitate skill development	a. Allow student to wheel own wheelchair. b. Allow student to use arms and hands in all activities to maintain strength levels.
10. Recommendations for other support programs	a. Physical therapist should conduct additional exercises for reduction of contractures. b. The Business Education Department should begin training student to use typewriter and calculator.

Parents' Approval of the IEP

The IEP is deemed complete only after the parents sign the IEP approval sheet. This final step is usually a mere formality if the parents have been involved and informed during the initial phases of IEP development. If the parents are not pleased and do not agree with any aspect of the document, they are not required to sign the approval form. They have the right, ensured in P.L. 94-142, to challenge the school's decisions or the quality of services provided. This right is referred to as **due process provisions of the law.**

Specific examples of why some parents have disapproved of an IEP include the following:

- Evaluation was not appropriate.
- Parents' opinions concerning their child's education were not considered or addressed in planning conferences.
- IEP is deemed inappropriate based on evaluation.

The parent or parents also have the right to question whether the IEP is being followed carefully. According to a Special Olympics publication discussing implementation of P.L. 94-142 (1980), parental concerns often stem from one of the following:

- The school is not using special education services as specified in the IEP.
- The child is not showing any progress in the areas targeted for remediation.
- The school is delaying implementation of a service specified in the IEP.
- Racial, cultural, or disability biases have led to development of an inappropriate IEP.

All involved in writing an IEP must understand the legal steps that parents can take to challenge the school's IEP. Possible legal actions include: (1) appeal to the local school district administration, (2) request for independent evaluation, (3) request for a hearing before an independent and neutral officer, (4) filing an administrative appeal, (5) filing a complaint to the Federal Office for Civil Rights, and (6) filing a lawsuit. Every attempt should be made to resolve disagreements and misunderstandings early so the child's program can be implemented quickly. It is always preferable to try to settle issues by working with local officials before proceeding to other action (Ekstrand and Edmister 1984).

The Physical Educator's Role on the Multidisciplinary Team

The psychomotor area is an integral component of the child's IEP. All handicapped children therefore must be assessed to determine (1) physical and motor fitness, (2) fundamental motor skills and patterns, and (3) skills in aquatics, dance, individual and group games, and lifetime sports. Since physical education instruction is a defined part of special education, the committee should review motor and physical fitness needs of each child to determine if a need exists for specially designed physical education programs. Too often, such assessment is completed by professionals other than the physical educator (e.g., the special educator or the physical therapist). Certified physical educators have been trained to assess, program, teach, and evaluate within all of these parameters; they must be involved at the beginning of the evaluation process, particularly if a motor problem exists. Figure 8.4 illustrates how a physical educator should participate in the initial phases of the IEP.

Physical educators must take the initiative to become actively involved in the development of each handicapped child's IEP. Stein (1977, pp. 8–9) lists ten suggestions for physical educators to follow when working with the multidisciplinary team:

1. Ensure that physical education is included in each child's IEP when necessary and appropriate.
2. Volunteer information about the child's physical and motor development, and about social, emotional, and personal characteristics to the team for preparation of the IEP.
3. Be available to participate in planning conferences and show a personal interest in contributing actively to this process.
4. Make sure that children who need a specially designed physical education program receive such programs and are not inappropriately placed in regular programs.
5. Make sure that children are not programmed for specially designed physical education when their needs can be adequately and appropriately met in regular programs.
6. Remind the committee that every handicapped child does not need, want, or require specially designed physical education.
7. Remind the committee that certain specially designed physical education programs can be accomplished in regular classes, some with additional support and others without any supplementary assistance.
8. Primarily, remember and remind the committee of the specific nature of physical education as IEPs are planned and implemented.
9. See that placement flexibility is maintained so the child participates in regular physical education activities whenever possible and in specially designed programs as necessary.
10. Remember that individualized education and one-to-one relationships are not synonymous.

Therapist's Role in Developing the IEP

P.L. 94-142 clearly identifies physical and occupational therapies as **related services.** This means that therapists and their services cannot replace required physical

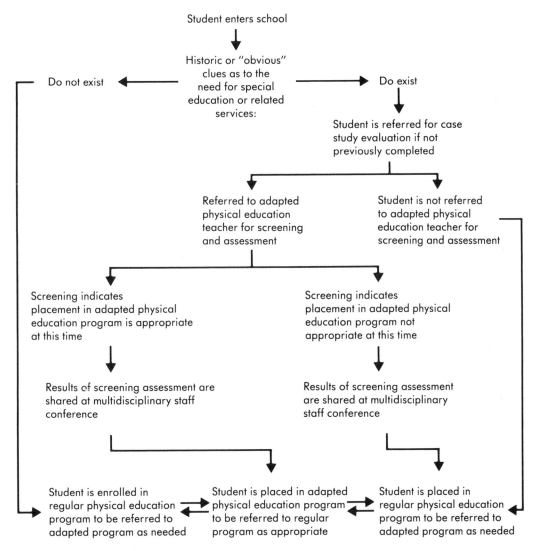

Student enters school

Historic or "obvious" clues as to the need for special education or related services:

Do not exist

Do exist

Student is referred for case study evaluation if not previously completed

Referred to adapted physical education teacher for screening and assessment

Student is not referred to adapted physical education teacher for screening and assessment

Screening indicates placement in adapted physical education program is appropriate at this time

Screening indicates placement in adapted physical education program not appropriate at this time

Results of screening assessment are shared at multidisciplinary staff conference

Results of screening assessment are shared at multidisciplinary staff conference

Student is enrolled in regular physical education program to be referred to adapted program as needed

Student is placed in adapted physical education program to be referred to regular program as appropriate

Student is placed in regular physical education program to be referred to adapted program as needed

(At this level of the process, program success depends on ease with which students can transfer from the regular program into the adapted program and vice versa. Although most participants in the adapted program will be students with permanent handicaps, from time to time students with temporary handicaps, such as physical injuries or overweight and obesity, who might benefit from limited participation will be placed in the adapted program. To receive the greatest impact and benefit from the adapted physical education program, smooth transition between regular and adapted classes is essential.)

FIGURE 8.4. Model showing appropriate involvement of physical educator in IEP development.

education programming. Any prescribed therapy should be given *in addition to* the physical education class. If the specialized services of a therapist are identified as necessary in the child's IEP, then both physical education and therapy must be given.

Drawing clear lines between the roles of the adapted physical educator and the therapist is difficult, for similar responsibilities are often within the professional expertise of both. When the multidisciplinary team requests specific motor performance data, the physical educator is the committee member who should provide this information. The majority of handicapped children can be tested effectively by the adapted or regular physical education teacher. When the severity or complexity of a handicapping condition is beyond the physical educator's expertise, then the child's motor assessment should be done by a therapist. Table 8.2 provides a partial list of major handicapping conditions and suggests areas of responsibility for the physical educator and therapist.

Some motor abilities can be evaluated by both teacher and therapist, but testing duplication of the same skill should be avoided. Through cooperation and sharing of information, the child will receive a more complete and effective evaluation. Skills to be assessed are shown in Table 8.3.

A well-coordinated schedule, including a cooperatively planned program, will provide for optimum growth and development. Each related service and teaching experience should contribute important and necessary motor experiences to the handicapped child's education.

Specific Assessment Techniques Used by Therapists

One distinctive technique used by therapists includes **muscle testing,** which is the subjective strength evaluation of specific muscles and muscle groups. The ratings usually are categorized as normal, good, fair, poor, trace, and zero. Muscle testing is designed to assess the extent and degree of weakness occurring from disorders that involve contractile muscles, myoneural junction, and lower motor neuron (Daniels and Worthingham 1972).

Analysis of a handicapped child's range of motion is also a specialty of the therapist. Children with restricted movement (i.e., children with cerebral palsy, muscular dystrophy, and postoperative conditions) can be measured with specific instruments. The goniometer measures joint angles and permits a fairly accurate comparison of joint angle before remediation with joint angle during rehabilitation. Many physical educators are trained to use the goniometer and to administer range-of-motion tests.

Evaluation of an individual's gait pattern (and teaching of gait) is also done by the therapist. Many children with permanent physical handicaps can learn or improve their walking pattern. These initial progressions are usually highly structured and demand a one-on-one teaching situation, often using orthotics (braces) or specialized parallel-bar walking equipment or both. The therapist has usually received special training to work in these areas.

TABLE 8.2
PARTIAL LIST OF HANDICAPPING CONDITIONS AND AREAS OF ASSESSMENT
RESPONSIBILITIES FOR PHYSICAL EDUCATORS AND THERAPISTS

Adapted Physical Educator	Therapist
Blind and visually impaired	Cerebral palsy (severely involved)[a]
Deaf and hearing impaired	Muscular dystrophy (Duchenne)[a]
Mentally handicapped (EMH, TMH, and Down Syndrome[a])	Severe birth defects[a]
	Mentally handicapped (severe and profound, nonambulatory)[a]
Behavior disorders	
Learning disabilities	Postoperative (extreme low levels of strength, endurance, and range of motion)[a]
Obese/overweight/underweight	

[a]Conditions that necessitate a physician's written prescription.

TABLE 8.3
COMPARATIVE AREAS OF EXPERTISE BETWEEN THERAPIST AND PHYSICAL EDUCATOR

Therapist	Physical Educator
Basic biological efficiency 　Strength 　Endurance 　Range of motion 　Flexibility 　Gross motor coordination	**Advanced locomotor skills, including degree of performance (How fast? How far? How many?)** 　Dynamic balance 　Jumping 　Hopping 　Running 　Galloping 　Skipping 　Leaping
Basic perceptual-motor skills 　Infant reflexes 　Sensory stimulation 　Conditioned reflexes 　Static balance 　Figure-ground relationships 　Spatial relationships 　Kinesthesis	**Advanced biological efficiency** 　Muscular strength 　Cardiovascular efficiency 　Gross motor coordination 　Agility 　Speed 　Reaction time
Basic locomotor skills 　Rolling 　Crawling 　Creeping 　Walking	**Eye-hand coordination skills** 　Throwing 　Catching 　Kicking 　Striking

A therapist's rehabilitation program can be conducted only with a physician's written approval. This written prescription consists of medical guidelines from which the therapist develops a plan of action. The physician may include statements such as, "Quad setting exercises for the rehabilitation of the right knee." This prescription allows the therapist (or adapted physical education teacher) to begin a progressive program with the student. Some prescriptions will be more detailed and specifically designate the rehabilitation program. If the doctor's prescription is too vague, the therapist should contact the physician before any program is initiated. Figure 8.5 provides a specific example of a written prescription. Figures 8.6 and 8.7 show how the IEP includes the services of the therapist.

Three types of therapist are commonly associated with physical development and rehabilitation: the certified corrective therapist (CCT), the registered physical therapist (RPT), and the registered occupational therapist (OTR).

The **corrective therapist** must possess an undergraduate degree in physical education to be eligible for corrective therapy certification and is quite often a certified physical education teacher as well. In many cases, this individual has an unusually strong background in both rehabilitation and physical education of the handicapped student. Specifically, the corrective therapist, in cooperation with a physician, applies principles, tools, techniques, and psychology of medically oriented physical education to assist individuals with special physical and mental conditions. The therapist's ultimate goal is to accomplish prescribed treatment objectives in a rehabilitation or habilitation program. More recently, corrective therapists have also become involved in adapted physical education and perceptual-motor and related programs for children with special needs.

FROM THE DESK OF:

DONALD R. BROWN, M.D.
C. M. PETERSON,   M.D.
ROBERT F. SMITH,   M.D.

TELEPHONE 445-2120

Susan March

Spastic quadriplegia-cerebral palsy

Reduction of contractures and range of motion exercises for all extremeties

Place specific emphasis on extension activities

Robert F. Smith   9/10/88
PHYSICIAN   DATE

FIGURE 8.5. Example of a written prescription from a physician for a student with cerebral palsy.

INDIVIDUALIZED EDUCATIONAL PROGRAM
Sample Form

Student's Name: Fred Brown

IEP Manager's Name:

Initial Planning Conference Date:

Date for Review/Revision:

PRESENT LEVELS OF PERFORMANCE

Academics:
Not applicable

Speech/Language:
Says own name, Mommy, Daddy, go, baby;
uses jargon otherwise

Motor:
Nonambulatory
Pincher grasps, palmar group

Social Behavior:
Parallel play
Follows directions to sit, lie down, etc.

Prevocational/Vocational:

Self-Help:
No dressing skills, cooperates, only
finger feeds

Extent of Participation in Regular Education:
Possible lunch, Bus — may be in feeding
program, may ride adapted bus

SERVICES TO BE PROVIDED FOR CURRENT YEAR

Type	Initiation Date	No. Minutes Per Week	No. Weeks
Physical therapy	9/3/87	150	40
Speech/Language Therapy	9/3/87	120	40

Placement:
Self-contained primary classroom for severely
handicapped (below trainable)

Justification for Placement:
Needs low ratio, special attention, special equipment

FIGURE 8.6.   The related services of the physical therapist are identified in a typical IEP.

IEP
Sample Form

Instructional Area: Mobility

Goal Statement: Transfer from wheelchair

Student's Name: Fred Brown

Implementer's Name:

SHORT-TERM INSTRUCTIONAL OBJECTIVES

Condition	Behavior	Criteria	Special Media and Materials	Evaluation/Schedule	Date Objective Mastered
1. With student sitting in wheelchair	1. Student transfers from wheelchair to floor	5 out of 5 trials for 5 consecutive days		Weekly	
2. With student sitting in wheelchair	2. Student transfers from wheelchair to chair	5 out of 5 trials for 5 consecutive days			
3. With student sitting in wheelchair	3. Student transfers to toilet	5 out of 5 trials for 5 consecutive days			
4. With student on the floor	4. Student climbs into wheelchair	5 out of 5 trials for 5 consecutive days			
5. With student sitting in a chair	5. Student transfers to wheelchair	5 out of 5 trials for 5 consecutive days			
6. With student sitting on toilet	6. Student transfers to wheelchair	5 out of 5 trials for 5 consecutive days			

FIGURE 8.7. The physical therapist has developed an individualized program of mobility for a severely handicapped child.

The **physical therapist** plans, implements, and evaluates treatment programs under physician supervision. Such programs typically include (1) exercises for increasing strength, endurance, coordination, and range of motion, (2) activities to facilitate motor capacity and learning, (3) instruction in use of assistive devices and activities relevant to daily living, and (4) application of physical agents such as heat or cold, ultrasound, or water to relieve pain or alter physiological status.

An **occupational therapist** evaluates clients, decides on treatment needs, develops treatment programs, and supervises the evaluation process—all under direct physician supervision.

Assessment

Central to the IEP are the child's present levels of physical and motor performance: what the child can and cannot do. Since program planning, development, placement, teaching, and evaluation begin with assessment, testing must be valid, reliable and easily administered, and the test results must be accurately interpreted. In planning the assessment, two basic questions must be asked:

1. *What information is needed to write an effective physical education program for a handicapped student?* The information needed to write the program will contain evaluation of such basic components as the child's strength, endurance, agility, flexibility, speed, eye-hand coordination, and balance.
2. *How will this information be collected?* Specific tests or test batteries must be selected to evaluate accurately the student's total motor performance. The results of these tests will contain specific data such as how many, how fast, how far.

A number of objective measures are desirable in the assessment process. Students, parents, teachers, and administrators understand objective test scores readily. The physical education teacher will be better able to describe and justify program recommendations in everyday language if objective scores are available.

Basic Principles of Assessment

The student's placement in, and the direction and intensity of, the child's individualized physical education program are based on the student's present levels of ability. Placement in the least restrictive environment depends on the analysis of test scores and on observations. Important considerations involving the collection of data are as follows:

1. The test results should describe a specific component of the physical education program (e.g., balance, agility, strength).

2. Consider employing a variety of test batteries to assess more than one area (e.g., physical fitness tests, general motor ability tests, sport skill tests).
3. A competent professional should administer and interpret the tests.
4. Results must reflect the student's "true" achievement level. For example, a mentally handicapped student may not understand the concept of "run as fast as you can," and therefore does not perform at maximum level. The test score would be misleading, and an inaccurate picture might develop.

Assessment of performance and achievement must be included as part of every physical education curriculum. Testing becomes crucial in diagnosing students' strengths and weaknesses. Each student's needs and the benefits of a specific physical education experience can be effectively evaluated only through a planned testing method.

Different assessment techniques are considered useful by physical educators. The AAHPERD publication *Testing for Impaired, Disabled, and Handicapped Individuals* (1975, p. 11) describes the following techniques and measures:

- **Informal techniques**—observation of student performance, self-testing activities, exploration activities; discussions with students, professionals, and volunteers who work with students; use of rating scales, checklists, inventories, questionnaires, and screening activities.
- **Formal techniques**—tests for perceptual-motor functions, coordination, gross motor ability, physical fitness, cardiorespiratory function, anthropometric characteristics, and specific sport skills.
- **Developmental measures**—tests for intelligence, learning ability, academic achievement, social-emotional behavior, speech, perception, adaptive behavior.
- **Tests, examinations, and assessments by experts**—results of evaluations and assessments made by specialists, available to physical education teachers.
- **Individual records**—data about each child organized for physical education program personnel. Time should be allotted for specialists who have evaluated youngsters to meet with teachers to discuss appropriate activities and approaches that will meet each student's needs.

To comply with P.L. 94-142 and to develop an effective and appropriate IEP, physical education instructors need to understand a variety of assessment methods. Although the administration of tests to handicapped children is often considered difficult, most children with handicaps are able to be tested and can perform on the identical tests given to the nonhandicapped. To illustrate: Mentally handicapped children are often considered physically unable to function in regular physical education activities. This impression is not supported by fact, since most (89%) of the mentally handicapped are classified as mildly retarded. This means that of the mentally handicapped population, nine out of ten will be able to complete the same motor tests as the nonhandicapped (Broadhead and Rarick 1978).

Polacek, Wang, and Eichstaedt (1985) conducted a study of 1298 mildly to moderately mentally handicapped and Down syndrome males and females between the ages of 6 and 21. The *AAHPERD Youth Fitness Test* battery (1976) and the *AAHPERD*

Health Related Physical Fitness Test battery (1980) were administered to all subjects. The researchers found that both test batteries were appropriate for use with these mentally handicapped populations.

Inadequate Testing Can Be Misleading

Too often, a physical education department administers only one standardized test battery and expects the results to provide complete psychomotor information regarding the student. The inadequacy of such an assessment is further compounded if the tests are given only once a year. For example, at Average High School, U.S.A., the *AAHPERD Youth Fitness Test* (1976) is administered only in late spring. The scores provide information about student levels of performance involving abdominal and upper body strength and endurance, explosive leg power, speed, agility, and running endurance. While this information is important, other areas covered in a comprehensive physical education program are missing (eye-hand coordination, balance, game and sport skills). This illustrates incomplete testing procedures because all areas of general motor ability are not included. A well-planned curriculum must be based on complete assessment data. Program effectiveness (i.e., Does the curriculum meet the immediate needs of the students?) can be evaluated only if initial performance levels are determined and compared with final achievement. The school in this example should include additional tests.

A testing program can be effective only when the persons responsible for the overall curriculum understand the importance (and limitations) of test results. The authors of *Testing for Impaired, Disabled, and Handicapped Individuals* (AAHPERD 1975, p. 9) make an important point: "Too many educators in every sphere of every discipline fail to realize that a test in itself is not important—how it is used is all that really counts. It does no good and makes no sense to administer a physical fitness test, perceptual-motor scale, or developmental profile and then stick results in a drawer until the next year or until the test is administered again."

One often-asked question regarding the assessment of handicapped children is: "Which test battery should I use for my youngsters?" The answer becomes mindboggling because physical educators often look for a single approach, but in most instances, no one test battery measures effectively all dimensions of physical education.

When identifying common components of general motor ability tests, strength, endurance, balance, speed, agility, and eye-hand coordination are most often listed. Although other components are also considered important, when accurately tested in those areas mentioned, children with poor motor skills and fitness can be identified.

Researchers agree that strength is the single most important element contributing to success in motor activity performance. Because of this, strength tests should be used. Most commonly identified areas of assessment are grip strength, upper body strength, abdominal strength, and explosive leg power.

Balance, both static and dynamic, is considered necessary in movement and skilled performance, such as running, throwing, jumping, and striking objects. Balance is also an integral component of test batteries and research as cited by Rarick, Dobbins, and Broadhead (1976), Bruininks (1978), Cratty (1979), Keogh and Sugden (1985), and Werder and Kalakian (1985).

Speed and agility, together, are essential elements of psychomotor ability and are necessary for successful performance in play and sports. Specific reference is made to this in the research of Bruininks (1978), Cratty (1979), and Rarick, Dobbins, and Broadhead (1976).

Perceptual-motor ability (eye-hand and eye-foot coordination) is an extremely important component of general motor ability.

Visual tracking of arm, hand, and foot movements is necessary for successful catching, throwing, striking, and kicking. Gallahue (1982) and Sage (1984) stress the necessity to identify these abilities specifically when developing a complete motor picture of the individual.

A Short General Motor Ability Test Battery

The test battery shown in Table 8.4 is a composite and modification of many test components designed to identify minimal levels of proficiency. A student who scores low becomes a potential candidate for adapted physical education programming.

Standardized or Norm-Referenced Tests

The standardized test, often called the norm-referenced test, is considered an exacting evaluation technique. These tests are the basis for comparative research and practice in the psychomotor area. This method of measuring performance enables physical educators to make comparisons between individuals with similar characteristics (i.e., age, sex, height, weight, handicapping condition). The most recent example of extensive research conducted to establish norm-referenced instruments is *Project UNIQUE*, reported by Winnick and Short (1985). They collected data from 23 states and the District of Columbia. The subjects tested were 3914 children and youth ages 10 to 17. Nonhandicapped youngsters and youngsters with visual, auditory, and orthopedic impairments were included in the study. Percentile norms were established for physical fitness measures.

This type of test is valuable because it provides a better understanding of how to evaluate objectively a student's performance. The following items are commonly observed to identify specific levels of ability: (1) *Time* (using a stopwatch) for: agility run, endurance run, dash, skipping a given distance, holding a balance position. (2) *Distance* (using a tape measure): walked on a balance beam, ball is thrown, jumped, run in a given time. (3) *Number* of times (watching and counting): a ball is bounced; sit-ups, pull-ups, or squat thrusts are performed; objects are picked up in a given time.

Standardized tests are extremely useful for preliminary classification of students into homogeneous groups, for diagnosis of weaknesses in specific areas of motor and physical performance, and for testing physical achievement (Johnson and Nelson 1986).

TABLE 8.4
MINIMAL LEVELS OF PERFORMANCE WHEN DETERMINING PLACEMENT OF STUDENTS FOR ADAPTED PHYSICAL EDUCATION

Age	Upper Body Strength (Flexed Arm Hang) (seconds)		Explosive Leg Power (Standing Long Jump) (total inches)		Speed and Agility (Shuttle Run) (seconds)[a]		Balance (Stork Stand, Eyes Open) (seconds)		Eye-Hand Coordination (Basketball Wall Pass)[b]	
	Female	Male	Female	Male	Female	Male	Female	Male	Female	Male
6	1	1	32	35	17.4	16.4	4.0	4.5	5	5
7	1	2	36	39	16.8	15.8	5.5	5.5	5	6
8	2	4	39	42	16.3	15.3	5.5	5.0	6	8
9	3	4	41	45	12.5	14.8	6.5	5.5	9	11
10	3	5	44	49	12.5	13.9	6.0	5.5	11	13
11	3	6	46	52	12.1	12.8	6.5	5.5	12	15
12	3	6	49	55	12.0	12.5	5.0	5.5	12	15
13	3	5	50	57	12.0	12.0	6.0	5.5	13	16
14	3	7	52	60	11.8	12.0	6.0	5.0	13	16
15	4	6	53	68	12.0	12.0	6.5	6.0	12	16
16	3	9	52	69	12.0	12.2	6.5	6.0	12	16
17	3	10	54	72	12.0	11.4	7.0	6.5	12	16
18	4	15	56	74	12.1	11.5	8.0	6.5	12	16
19	4	16	58	76	12.2	11.5	8.0	7.0	12	16
20	4	17	60	78	12.3	11.4	9.0	8.0	12	16

[a]30 ft by four trips.
[b]Total bounces completed in 15 sec from 4 ft away.

The most common way to present standardized test results is by using percentiles. The results of many tests for handicapped children are described in terms of percentile scores, which compare the student's performance with that of peers. For example, a percentile score of 35 means that 35 percent of the people taking the test had lower scores and 65 percent had higher scores.

When children score in the 25th percentile or lower, they may be strong candidates for individualized instruction or an adapted physical education program. Sherrill (1981) suggests that most students scoring one standard deviation below the norm (at approximately the 16th percentile) could benefit from specialized instruction. Keogh and Sugden (1985) suggest that approximately 3 out of every 40 students in a regular physical education class will possess extreme levels of awkwardness. This number includes approximately 7.5 percent of every class. The use of objective test scores and percentiles thus provides valuable clues when one is trying to develop a total picture of a child's motor ability. This information is absolutely necessary when writing the IEP.

Standardized Physical Fitness Test Batteries

The *Special Fitness Test Manual for Mildly Mentally Retarded Persons* (AAHPERD 1976) and the *Motor Fitness Testing Manual for the Moderately Mentally Retarded* (AAHPERD 1975) are standardized test batteries that use percentile scores. Scoring tables for both test batteries are found in these manuals. Table 8.5 describes these tests and includes also the *AAHPERD Youth Fitness Test* battery (1976) for nonhandicapped students.

Instructors must be certain that standardized testing is not the only assessment used. The standardized test will provide initial (pretest) and final (posttest) levels of achievement, but is of little help when analyzing specific causes for success or failure.

For example, a 10-year-old moderately mentally handicapped student can throw a softball 15 ft. This performance places the student in the 20th percentile as determined by the *Motor Fitness Testing Manual for the Moderately Mentally Retarded* (AAHPERD 1975). Percentile ranking, by itself, does not provide enough information for future educational planning or IEP development. In this instance, it indicates only that the child definitely needs to improve this skill.

A youngster who has difficulty kicking a rolling ball (e.g., kick baseball) could have any one or all three of the following problems: (1) inability to balance for that fraction of a second that it takes to swing one's leg once the ball is rolling (i.e., inability to kick may stem from balance deficiency), (2) inability to judge speed and position of the ball and inability to coordinate perceptually the kicking action (i.e., swinging the leg too soon or too late), or (3) inability, when contact is made, to kick the ball very far because leg strength may be well below average.

In this situation, we see that more objective testing is necessary to determine specific levels of performance. The following tests might be administered: static and dynamic balance test (e.g., stork stand and balance beam walk), perceptual-motor tests (e.g., bounce a ball, catch a ball, kick a ball), and a leg strength test (e.g., standing long jump or Sargent jump test).

TABLE 8.5
YOUTH PHYSICAL FITNESS TEST BATTERIES, WITH SELECTED COMPONENTS OF PHYSICAL FITNESS

Measured Component of Physical Fitness	Youth Fitness Test[a]	Special Fitness Test[b] for Mildly Mentally Retarded	Motor Fitness Test[c] for Moderately Mentally Retarded
Shoulder girdle muscular endurance	Pull-ups (boys) Flexed arm hang (girls)	Flexed arm hang	Flexed arm hang
Abdominal muscular endurance	Sit-ups (bent knee in 1 min)	Sit-ups (straight leg in 1 min)	Sit-ups (bent leg in 30 sec)
Agility	Shuttle run	Shuttle run	. . . .
Speed	50 yard dash	50 yard dash	50 yard dash
Cardiorespiratory endurance	600 yard run-walk or 9 or 12 min run or 1 or 1½ mi run	300 yard run-walk	300 yard run-walk
Leg power	Standing long jump for distance	Standing long jump for distance	Standing long jump for distance
Coordination and explosive power of arm and shoulder girdle	. . . .	Softball throw for distance	Softball throw for distance
			Height, weight, sitting bob and reach, hopping, skipping, and a tumbling progression are also included

SOURCE: Reprinted with permission from AAHPERD. Individualized Education Programs: Assessment and Evaluation in Physical Education. *Practical Pointers* 1(9):12, 1978.
[a]*AAHPERD Youth Fitness Test Manual,* 1976 ($4.25) (#0-88314-214-7).
[b]*Special Fitness Test Manual for Mildly Mentally Retarded Persons,* 1976 ($4.95) (#0-88314-172-8).
[c]*Motor Fitness Testing Manual for the Moderately Mentally Retarded,* 1975 ($6.80) (#0-88314-135-3).
These publications are available from American Alliance Publications, P.O. Box 704, Waldorf, MD 20601.

Criterion-Referenced Assessment

Criterion-referenced assessment can help to determine an individual's performance level on many tasks that lead to a major or terminal skill. These assessments identify exactly what a student can and cannot do in a given skill. Consider students participating in "jungle relays." All students perform each of the following tasks for a distance of 20 ft: bear walk, bunny hop, frog leap, crab walk, snake wiggle, and lame dog walk. Children unable to support themselves with their arms for the entire distance (i.e., they stop or collapse) apparently possess low levels of hand, wrist, arm, and shoulder strength or low endurance level or both in comparison with other children who can perform the tasks. Ability to observe this weakness becomes the basis for criterion-referenced programming.

The instructor must become familiar with specific aspects or terms that are essential to an understanding of the criterion-referenced process. Writing a criterion-referenced program is similar in format to writing an IEP.

A **skill** can be compared to an annual goal. Ability to learn a skill will result in the child's being able to perform that skill in more advanced activities. Examples of skills are the mature skipping pattern, the mature run, and the mature overhand throw. After having learned the mature overhand throw, the student will be able to use this skill in games such as softball. All skills can be broken down into smaller components that are also observable and measurable.

The criterion-referenced approach requires the teacher to select appropriate short-term objectives (a list of specific activities) for the student. These objectives consist of three parts: (1) a **behavior** is the specific observable skill, such as skipping, (2) a **condition** states how and where the behavior should occur (e.g., with bare feet on a tumbling mat), and (3) a **criterion** establishes a certain standard of performance (e.g., for 5 m).

The advantage of this type of assessment is that it can be used to observe children actively at play. Each child can be closely watched and evaluated while performing different activities and games. For example, assessment could be occurring while 10- and 11-year-old students play dodge ball. The instructor sees that one boy is not transferring his weight from the back to the front foot when throwing. This indicates that the child's level of overhand throwing is below average for his age. Skill activities that teach appropriate weight transfer must therefore be included in the youngster's program.

An *I CAN* evaluation sheet (Figure 8.8) shows how an entire class can be evaluated on the overhand throw. Note that specific levels of performance have been identified.

After testing students on other specific objectives to determine what skills they possess, the instructor can develop an individualized program for each child. Tables 8.6, 8.7, and 8.8 list specific items and activities that one might incorporate in formal or informal assessment.

If a particular skill is too complex to assess, the objective should be further broken down. A child's problem with developing and mastering a skill may be quite elementary, particularly when the child does not possess enough upper body strength to throw a ball an acceptable distance. The child's program should then contain specific activities to develop this basic strength component (e.g., prone to standing drills, modified push-ups, bear walk, crab walk, tennis ball squeezes, weight training).

Criterion-referenced assessment follows the concept of mastery learning in which several specifically defined objectives are attempted by the students. Assessment is conducted repeatedly to determine if objectives are being accomplished. Objectives should be revised continually to incorporate newly acquired motor skills.

The following example of how to establish and use criterion-referenced objectives involves a mildly ataxic cerebral palsied 11-year-old boy who is expected to play "kick baseball" in the regular 6th grade physical education class, but performs very poorly. The physical education instructor observes that the student is not succeeding due to a lack of eye-foot coordination and balance. The instructor therefore establishes cri-

I CAN

CLASS PERFORMANCE SCORE SHEET
PERFORMANCE OBJECTIVE: OVERHAND THROW

SCORING

Assessment:
X = Achieved
O = Not achieved

Reassessment:
⊗ = Achieved
∅ = Not achieved

FOCAL POINTS

a Overhand motion
  b Ball release
    a Eyes on target
      b Overhand motion
        a Arm exten./side orient.
          b Weight transfer
            c Hip and spine rotation
              d Follow through
                e Smooth integration
                  Angle of release 45°
                    Accuracy

STD.

10 ft distance, 2/3 times
20 ft target at 15 ft, 2/3 times
2/3 times
age/sex norm., 2/3 times
8 ft target at 50 ft, 2/3 times

PRIMARY RESPONSES
N Nonattending
NR No response
UR Unrelated response
O Other (specify in comments)

NAME	1 a	b	2 a	b	3 a	b	c	d	e	4	5 Primary responses*	COMMENTS
1. John G.	⊗	X	⊗	⊗	∅	⊗	⊗	∅	∅	∅	∅	Throws side arm
2. Katie	X	X	X	X	⊗	⊗	⊗	X	∅	∅	∅	
3. Susan	X	X	X	X	X	X	X	X	X	X	∅	Practice accuracy
4. Mark	X	X	X	X	∅	X	∅	⊗	∅	∅	∅	Faces target
5. John S.	X	X	X	X	X	X	X	⊗	∅	∅	∅	Follow through inconsistent
6. Scott	⊗	X	∅	⊗	∅	∅	∅	∅	∅	∅	∅	Throws underhand
7. Judy	X	X	∅	X	∅	∅	∅	∅	∅	∅	∅	Doesn't look at target
8. Cindy	X	X	X	X	⊗	X	⊗	X	∅	∅	∅	Faces target
9. Kirk	X	X	X	X	X	X	X	X	∅	∅	∅	Jerky
10. Joanie	X	X	X	X	X	⊗	⊗	X	∅	∅	∅	
11. Larry	X	X	X	X	⊗	X	X	X	∅	∅	∅	Arm Bent
12. Chuck	X	X	⊗	⊗	∅	⊗	∅	∅	∅	∅	∅	Throws underhand or side arm unless assisted
13. Linda	X	X	X	X	X	X	X	X	⊗	⊗	∅	Nearly mature
14. Sherry	X	X	X	X	⊗	X	⊗	X	⊗	∅	∅	Inconsistent beginning position
15. Greg	X	X	X	X	X	X	X	X	⊗	⊗	⊗	Nearly mature

FIGURE 8.8. The mature overhand throw is broken down into its observable components and an entire class is evaluated. (Reprinted with permission from J. A. Wessell, *Planning Individualized Education Programs in Special Education,* Northbrook, Ill.: Hubbard Scientific Co., 1977, p. 44.)

terion-referenced objectives for the student. These objectives will serve as an assessment instrument and as a subsequent skill-building program. The written program will be developed as follows:

- **First objective:** Student will balance on one foot (behavior) for 5 sec, three out of four consecutive attempts (criterion).
- **Second objective:** Student will kick (behavior) a 10-in. ball that is stationary in front of him (condition) 30 ft in the air, four out of five consecutive attempts (criterion).

TABLE 8.6
DEVELOPMENT PROFILE ITEMS[a]

Adaptive Behavior
- Discrimination of stimuli
- Leisure-recreation
- Manipulate environment
- Peers-playmates

Basic Knowledge
- Body awareness
- Spatial relationships

Fine Motor
- Building towers
- Copying activities
- Drawing
- Grasping
- Placing objects in container with one/both hands
- Stacking beads
- Tracing activities
- Turning pages of book
- Using small muscles of hands/fingers

Gross Motor
- Balancing
- Ball Handling
- Catching
- Climbing
- Climbing stairs
- Crawling
- Creeping
- Hand clapping
- Hitting objects
- Holding up head
- Hopping
- Jumping
- Kicking objects
- Maintaining good posture
- Physical fitness activities
- Reaching for object
- Riding tricycle
- Rocking activities
- Rolling activities
- Running
- Sitting with and without support
- Swinging
- Throwing objects
- Tossing objects
- Walking

SOURCE: Adapted from AAHPERD, *Testing for Impaired, Disabled, and Handicapped Individuals,* 1975, p. 75.
[a]Listed items and activities can be incorporated into formal or informal approaches for assessing each of these developmental characteristics to show growth and maturation of a child.

- **Third objective:** Student will kick (behavior) a 10-in. ball that is moving slowly toward him (condition) into an 8 × 24 ft soccer goal, four out of five consecutive attempts (criterion).

The instructor should note if additional skills of a more basic nature are needed to accomplish these objectives. Possibly the boy's leg strength is extremely poor, and appropriate hopping, jumping, and skipping activities should also be included in this program.

The *behavior, condition,* and *criterion* can always be modified. By using this type of assessment, the instructor can determine, on an individual basis, how students are doing, who needs more help in which areas, and who has acquired the necessary skills to advance to the next level of participation. When a child appears to need more time to learn with more opportunities for trial and error, the instructor may place the youngster in an adapted physical education class.

TABLE 8.7
PHYSICAL FITNESS TEST ITEMS[a]

Agility
    Leg thrusts
    Shuttle run (30 and 15 ft)
    Squat thrusts or burpee
    Line jumps
    Zigzag run

Balance
    Balance board activities
    Beam-rail-bench walks
    Object balance activities
    Hopping and skipping activities

Cardiorespiratory endurance
    Bench step cycling
    Hiking
    Jogging
    Rope jumping
    300 yard run
    600 yard run-walk
    6, 9, 12 min runs
    ½, 1, 1½ mi runs
    Swimming activities

Explosive power arms and shoulders
    Medicine ball throw
    Softball throw
    Volleyball throw

Flexibility
    Back extension activities
    Back lifts
    Bend, twist, and touch
    Floor touch
    Head, chest raise (prone position)
    Trunk flexion activities
    Windmill
    Goniometer

General coordination
    Ball bounce
    Roll progression
    Softball throw
    Standing long jump
    Running high jump

Leg power
    Mountain climber
    Squat jump
    Standing long jump
    Vertical jump
    Wall jump

Muscular endurance abdominal
    Curls
    Isokinetic activities
    Leg lifts
    Sit-ups
    V-sit

Physique
    Classification index
    Height
    Somatotyping
    Weight

Speed
    Dashes (25 to 100 yd)
    8 sec dash

Strength
    Dynometer
    Hand grip
    Isometric activities
    Isokinetic activities
    Tensiometer

SOURCE: Adapted from AAHPERD, *Testing for Impaired, Disabled, and Handicapped Individuals*, 1975, p. 25.

[a]Listed items and activities can be incorporated into formal or informal approaches for testing physical fitness components.

TABLE 8.8

MOTOR ABILITY, PERCEPTUAL-MOTOR DEVELOPMENT, AND PSYCHOMOTOR TEST ITEMS[a]

Balance dynamic
- Balance board activities
- Beam-rail-bench walks
- Bounce board activities
- Stepping stones
- Locomotor activities
- Stunts and self-testing activities
- Trampoline activities
- Hopping activities

Balance static
- Balance board activities
- Beam-rail-bench walks
- Stock stand series
- Stunts and self-testing activities

Balance object
- Carry object
- Finger and wand activities
- Stick activities

Fine motor coordination
- Building
- Grasping
- Gripping
- Lacing
- Manipulating
- Stacking
- Tapping

Gross motor eye-foot coordination
- Climbing stairs
- Kicking activities
- Motor planning and sequencing
- Rope jumping
- Line jumping

Gross motor eye-hand coordination
- Ball activities
- Catching activities
- Manipulative and manual activities
- Motor planning and sequencing
- Tapping activities
- Target activities
- Throwing activities

Gross motor coordination general
- Calisthenic activities
- Exercise
- Simultaneous activities
- Trampoline activities
- Tumbling and apparatus activities

Gross motor fundamental movements
- Balancing
- Batting
- Bouncing
- Catching
- Climbing

Subjective Assessment

Criterion-referenced assessment requires that the teacher make subjective judgments about an individual's performance. The quality of these judgments is directly related to the knowledge and expertise of the instructor. Herein lies the main drawback of the criterion-referenced approach. The gymnastic or springboard diving judge can make a reliable subjective evaluation. These people are highly trained and are able to reproduce reliable and consistent scores in their specific areas of expertise. While some experienced physical educators are able to determine student strengths and weakness with seeming accuracy, it is almost impossible to find a reliable consistency between the judgments of two or more instructors in all areas of physical education evaluation. It is therefore difficult to find agreement on the meaning of words such as "average" or "slow."

Crawling
Creeping
Dancing
Galloping
Hanging
Hitting
Hopping
Jumping
Kicking
Landing
Leaping
Lifting
Marching
Pulling
Pushing
Rolling
Running
Shifting
Sitting
Sliding
Skipping
Standing
Striking
Swinging
Throwing
Tossing
Walking

Spatial-body perception
  Bilateral activities
  Body abstraction
  Body awareness
  Body localization
  Directionality activities
  Identification of body parts
  Imitation of body movements
  Laterality activities
  Sensory-motor integration
  Shape-size-form differentiation and discrimination
Visual
  Acuity
  Constancy
  Equilibrium
  Figure-ground relationships
  Ocular control and pursuit
  Spatial relationships
  Tracking

SOURCE: Adapted from AAHPERD, *Testing for Impaired, Disabled, and Handicapped Individuals*, 1975, pp. 44–45.
[a]Listed items and activities can be incorporated into formal or informal approaches for assessing each of these motor, perceptual-motor, and psychomotor functions.

Although subjective assessment is used extensively by physical educators, its contribution to the IEP is, by itself, inadequate. P.L. 94-142 states specifically that all assessment data must include criteria that are both appropriate and objective, thus subjective observations should be used only to supplement other objective or criterion-referenced assessment.

Assessment Review

The assessment process must be completed before the multidisciplinary team can develop a student's IEP. Test results will reflect current performance and achievement levels of the individual. With completion of appropriate assessment, the first phase of the IEP is finished when the physical educator is able to supply the multidisciplinary team with the child's present level of physical fitness and motor ability.

Writing Basic Physical Fitness and Motor Proficiency Objectives Into the IEP

Fitness-oriented goals and objectives should appear on the student's IEP only if assessment ascertains that special fitness needs truly exist.

When assessment has identified low fitness levels among students who are guaranteed access to special services by P.L. 94-142, this becomes the basis for developing annual goals and short-term instructional objectives for each student. Annual goals should be stated in general terms that identify the area of physical education focus. Short-term instructional objectives should be stated in precise *behavioral* terms so both teacher and, when appropriate, student know unquestionably that the objective has been achieved. Short-term instructional objectives should be *developmentally sequenced* so achievement indicates step-by-step progress toward the annual goal.

Annual Goals

An **annual goal** relates to the student's current performance level and indicates what the student should be able to accomplish after 12 months in the program. We suggest that an annual goal be defined as a statement that includes a cluster of related behaviors in a given area (e.g., muscular strength, dynamic balance), which are appropriate to a child's needs and can be achieved by the end of the school year.

Teachers often ask the question, "How many goals should a child have?" There is no right answer; the number of goals a youngster should have depends on the child's specific needs. A child who is mildly mentally handicapped may have only one or two goals, both of which address the child's need to improve strength and endurance. A youngster who is severely physically and mentally handicapped has a greater number of needs and, therefore, a greater number of goals.

Specific examples of annual goals are to improve (1) upper body strength to the 35th percentile (2 pull-ups), (2) cardiorespiratory efficiency to the 15th percentile (1250 yd in 9 min run), and (3) static balance to the 20th percentile (8 sec right/left total). Werder and Kalakian (1985, p. 108) list three annual goals for object control skills: (1) Student will demonstrate a mature overhand throw with distance (30 ft) and accuracy (10 ft diameter target). (2) Student will grasp a 4-in. nerf ball nine of ten times. (3) Student will toe-kick a 10-in. playground ball for a distance of 20 ft, four of five times.

Short-Term Objectives

Short-term objectives are intended to be intermediate or en route objectives between the student's current performance level and that suggested by the annual goals. They are not as detailed as the instructional objectives used in daily planning, but they are specific to particular performance areas. They are to be used in measuring progress. Some examples of short-term instructional objectives are as follows: (1) Given a mat, the student will perform 20 curl-ups with knees bent and hands behind head, in 30 sec, (2) given a 3-ft square, the student will demonstrate nine of ten vertical jumps with feet together, full arm swing, and maintain balance when landing, and (3) given a basketball, the student will dribble to a line 30 ft away and return in 15 sec.

Werder and Kalakian (1985, p. 111) suggest the following guidelines when writing short-term objectives:

1. State the motor skill in behavioral terms, including positioning (e.g., 30- to 40-degree curl-ups with bent knees and hands clasped behind head).
2. Describe the "givens," the instructional cues, environmental boundaries, time limits, and equipment.
3. State criteria for attainment, the standard against which the student will be measured (e.g., nine of ten trials).

Summary

An individualized educational program (IEP) is a written statement incorporating the following: (1) the handicapped child's present levels of educational performance, (2) annual goals and short-term instructional objectives established for that child, (3) specific special education services available, (4) extent to which the child can participate in the regular education program, (5) projected dates for initiation of services and anticipated duration of services, (6) objective criteria and evaluation procedures used, and (7) schedules for determining annually whether instructional objectives are being achieved.

Individualized physical education programming might be described as the prescription of exercises and activities based on diagnostic pretest results. The IEP becomes a direct plan of action to meet both immediate and long-range motor needs of the handicapped child (Figure 8.9).

Appropriate assessment is critical to success of the IEP; assessment must be thoroughly planned to achieve maximum results. The adapted physical educator is instrumental in the selection, administration, and interpretation of motor and fitness tests for handicapped students. Test results should be forwarded to the multidisciplinary team for inclusion in the child's complete IEP.

References

AAHPERD. *Testing for Impaired, Disabled, and Handicapped Individuals.* Reston, Va.: AAHPERD, 1975.

PHYSICAL EDUCATION — IEP   (FRONT)

NAME __Warren__   AGE __14__   PE __X__   SWIM __X__
                       BIRTHDATE _____

LONG-TERM GOALS: • Mainstream for physical education and swimming.
                 • Participate in Adapted Physical Education classes for strength and range of motion
                   activities.

ANNUAL GOALS:

SCHOOL YR.	PROGRAM LEVEL	GOALS	COMMENTS
1986–87	Intermediate PE – 4	To improve upper body strength to the 35th percentile (2 push-ups) To increase elbow range of motion to the 85th percentile (160°)	May wish to use a wheelchair for some activities

(BACK)

OBJECTIVES: (INCLUDE PERFORMANCE CRITERIA)	STRATEGIES: (INCLUDE METHODS AND MATERIALS)	EVALUATION OF PERFORMANCE	COMPLETION DATE	
			ANT.	ACTUAL
Warren will . . . 1. perform on a 70% accuracy basis skills necessary for successful participation in flag football, basketball, modified volleyball, and softball.	1. Direct teaching and skill drills	1. Observations of performances. Skills tests.	6/87	
2. play each of the above sports in game situations on six different occasions.	2. Filmstrips, library books, officiating	2. Observations of performance. Written tests.	6/87	
Warren is an ATAXIC cerebral palsied male who walks with short crutches; he uses a wheelchair for some sports to free use of his hands. He has been mainstreamed once and after one unsuccessful semester returned to special school placement; intelligence is low normal. Motivation level is somewhat low. Sometimes Warren can be a real hard worker and other times he is really lazy-switch is not usually related to activity. He is an intermediate level swimmer.				

DATE ——————   PERSON(S) RESPONSIBLE ——————   POSITION ——————
LEA REPRESENTATIVE ——————   POSITION ——————
PARENT ——————

FIGURE 8.9. Example of an individualized educational program in physical education. (Adapted from AAHPERD, *Practical Pointers* 1(7):15, 1977.)

————. *Motor Fitness Testing Manual for the Moderately Mentally Retarded.* Reston, Va.: AAHPERD, 1975.

————. *AAHPERD Youth Fitness Test Manual.* Reston, Va.: AAHPERD, 1976.

————. *Special Fitness Test Manual for Mildly Mentally Retarded Persons.* Reston, Va.: AAHPERD, 1976.

————. *AAHPERD Health Related Physical Fitness Test Manual.* Reston, Va.: AAHPERD, 1980.

Broadhead, G. D., and Rarick, G. L. Family Characteristics and Gross Motor Traits in Handicapped Children. *Research Quarterly* 49(4):421–429, 1978.

Bruininks, R. H. *Bruininks-Oseretsky Test of Motor Proficiency: Examiner's Manual.* Circle Pines, Minn.: American Guidance Service, 1978.

Cratty, B. J. *Perceptual and Motor Development in Infants and Children,* 2nd ed. Englewood Cliffs, N.J.: Prentice-Hall, 1979.

Daniels, L., and Worthingham, C. *Muscle Testing,* 3rd ed. Philadelphia: W. B. Saunders, 1972.

Ekstrand, R. E., and Edmister, P. Mediation: A Process That Works. *Exceptional Children* 51(2):163–167, October 1984.

Gallahue, D. L. *Understanding Motor Development in Children.* New York: John Wiley & Sons, 1982.

Hayes, J., and Higgins, S. T. Issues Regarding the IEP: Teachers on the Front Line. *Exceptional Children* 44:267–273, 1978.

Johnson, B. L., and Nelson, J. K. *Practical Measures for Evaluation in Physical Education,* 4th ed. Minneapolis: Burgess Publishing, 1986.

Keogh, J., and Sugden, D. *Movement Skill Development.* New York: Macmillan, 1985.

Landis, J. Personal communication. Lincoln Developmental Center, Lincoln, Ill., 3 December 1985.

Lavay, B., and French, R. The Special Educator: Meeting Goals Through a Transdisciplinary Approach. *American Corrective Therapy Journal* 39(4):77–81, July/August 1985.

Polacek, J. J., Wang, P. Y., and Eichstaedt, C. B. *A Study of Physical and Health Related Fitness Levels of Mild, Moderate, and Down Syndrome Students in Illinois.* Normal, Ill.: Illinois State University Press, 1985.

Rarick, G. L., Dobbins, D. A., and Broadhead, G. D. *The Motor Domain and Its Correlates in Educationally Handicapped Children.* Englewood Cliffs, N.J.: Prentice-Hall, 1976.

Sage, G. H. *Motor Learning and Control—A Neurological Approach.* Dubuque, Iowa: Wm. C. Brown, 1984.

Sherrill, C. *Adapted Physical Education and Recreation: A Multidisciplinary Approach.* 2nd ed. Dubuque, Iowa: Wm. C. Brown, 1981.

Special Olympics. *P.L. 94-142: It's the Law—Physical Education and Recreation for the Handicapped.* Washington, D.C.: Special Olympics, 1980.

Stein, J. U. Individualized Educational Programs. *Practical Pointers* 1(6):8–9, 1977.

Thomas, E. D., and Marshall, M. J. Clinical Evaluation and Coordination of Services: An Ecological Model. *Exceptional Children* 44(1):16–22, 1977.

Werder, J. K., and Kalakian, L. H. *Assessment in Adapted Physical Education.* Minneapolis: Burgess Publishing, 1985.

Williamson, G. G. The Individualized Educational Program: An Interdisciplinary Endeavor. In *Unique Aspects of the Individualized Educational Program for the Physically Handicapped, Homebound, and Hospitalized,* edited by B. Sirvis, J. W. Baken, and G. G. Williamson. (Training manual for the CEC Institute on Individualized Educational Program Planning.) Reston, Va.: Council for Exceptional Children, 1978.

Winnick, J. P., and Short, F. X. *Physical Fitness Testing of the Disabled—Project Unique.* Champaign, Ill.: Human Kinetics Publishers, 1985.

CHAPTER 9

Mental Retardation

The adapted physical educator who teaches the mentally retarded must know about the nature and causes of mental retardation. Equally important, however, is the educator's awareness that the mentally retarded are indeed individuals who must not be stigmatized by descriptive data. Individual aptitudes, attitudes, and temperament are as typical of mentally retarded individuals as of individuals with normal intellect.

In learning about physical and motor performance characteristics of the mentally retarded, some generalizations can be made. It is important, however, to emphasize the retarded person's individuality. Some retarded persons cannot achieve physical and motor proficiencies commensurate with their chronological age; others achieve proficiencies that equal or surpass their nonhandicapped, chronological age peers.

Julian Stein relates an apropos story about the bumblebee, which, according to data gathered scientifically in wind tunnel experiments, cannot fly. The bumblebee's body is too heavy, its wings too short and without adequate surface area or correct configuration. The bumblebee is not, however, privy to this scientific information and does fly. The lesson is that many mentally retarded persons, like bumblebees, sometimes achieve significantly beyond what is expected.

Teachers and parents must ensure that accomplishments of the mentally retarded are not a product of limited expectation. Limited expectations or opportunity deprivation results in limited learning and performance, and becomes a self-fulfilling prophecy. Certainly expectations must be tempered with realism; however, low achievement expectations that result in unnecessarily low achievement are readily evident. Melton (1972), in addressing parents of the handicapped, made a point equally applicable to teachers when he warned that parents [teachers] of a handicapped child must be on guard against letting love and sympathy interfere with their judgment, causing them to be overindulgent or hesitant about encouraging the youngster to be as independent as possible and to do as much as possible.

A Definition

The definition of **mental retardation** put forth by the American Association on Mental Deficiency is widely accepted: "Mental retardation refers to significantly subaverage general intellectual functioning existing concurrently with deficits in adaptive behavior and manifested during the developmental period" (National Information Center for Handicapped Children and Youth 1983, p. 1). When, during this developmental period, the individual's intellectual and behavioral adaptations to society fall significantly below the norm, that person is designated *mentally retarded*.

Cegelka and Prehm (1982, p. 9) define mental retardation as "the condition which accounts for the lower end of the curve of intellectual abilities." They state that the study of mental retardation illustrates the extent to which the individual in a given group can differ in intellectual and behavioral characteristics from others in the group.

Deficits in Intellectual Adaptations

Intellectual adaptations significantly below the norm are defined as those that fall two standard deviations[1] below the mean, or average intelligence quotient (average IQ 100) (Cohen and Kaminer 1985).

Three commonly accepted measures of intelligence are the **Stanford-Binet** and **Cattell scales** (each with a standard deviation of 16) and the **Wechsler scale** (standard

---

1. Standard deviation (SD) is the measure that denotes the tendency for individual test scores to deviate from the mean, or average, score. The higher the standard deviation, the more spread or varied are the scores from the average. The lower the standard deviation, the more concentrated or clustered are the scores around the average.

deviation of 15). Intellectual deficits suggesting mental retardation, as measured by two standard deviations below the mean criterion for each of the above intelligence scales, would be as follows:

Stanford-Binet or Cattell   100 (Average IQ)
(1 SD = 16) $\underline{-32}$ (2 SDs below average IQ)
                             68

An IQ of 68 as measured by the Stanford-Binet or Cattell thus denotes two standard deviations below the average intelligence of 100. Intellectual function below this point as measured by the Stanford-Binet or Cattell is considered suggestive of mental retardation.

An IQ of 70 as measured by the Wechsler scale denotes two standard deviations below the average intelligence of 100.

Wechsler   100 (Average IQ)
(1 SD = 15) $\underline{-30}$ (2 SDs below average IQ)
                70

Intellectual function below this point as measured by the Wechsler would be considered suggestive of mental retardation.

In examining a normal distribution of intelligence across the general population, we find that two standard deviations below the mean fall at the 2.28th percentile. This means that about 98 percent of the general population (97.72 percent, to be exact) have IQs above the two standard deviations below the mean cutoff. Conversely, roughly 2 percent (2.28 percent, to be exact) have IQs (below) the two standard deviations below the mean cutoff. This is how the American Association on Mental Deficiency (AAMD) (1983) arrives at 2.3 (2.28 rounded off to 2.3) as the percentage of persons who, by reason of subnormal intellect, may be considered mentally retarded (Figure 9.1). This percentage of the U.S. population presently represents in excess of 6 million persons. Of this total, 780,831 were between the ages of 3 and 21 for the 1982–1983 school year (U.S. Department of Education 1984).

Degrees of mental retardation recognized by the AAMD are mild (designated Level I), moderate (designated Level II), severe (designated Level III), and profound (designated Level IV) (Table 9.1).

Mental Age as an Indicator of Intellectual Function

One practical appraisal of a person's functional intellectual status is to determine the individual's *mental age*. IQ scores are sometimes perceived as abstract statistics, but a measure of mental age can be a concrete indicator of intellectual maturity. A person with a mental age of 7, regardless of chronological age, can be expected to function as a normal 7-year-old. Morreau (1985) believes that mental age is the single best criterion for determining the child's academic status. Although mental age pro-

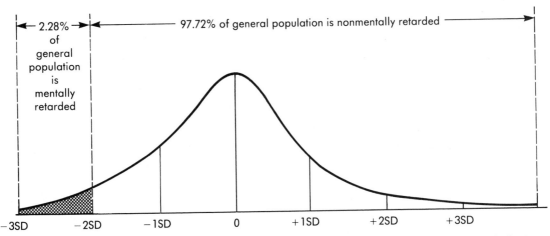

FIGURE 9.1. A normal curve showing percent mentally retarded and nonmentally retarded in general population.

vides primarily an estimate of academic status, it also supplies valuable information for the adapted physical educator who must determine the child's ability to deal with movement-centered or movement-related problems. Table 9.2 indicates the mental age expectancy level for each degree of mental retardation.

If not readily available, mental age can be estimated from the child's IQ and chronological age in months. Rothstein (1970, p. 216) provides the following example: A good rule of thumb to be used in estimating children's mental age is to multiply the

TABLE 9.1

AAMD DESIGNATED LEVELS OF MENTAL RETARDATION AND RESPECTIVE INTELLIGENCE QUOTIENT RANGES

Level	Degree of Retardation	IQ Ranges	
		Stanford-Binet or Cattell	Wechsler
I	Mild	67-52	69-55
II	Moderate	51-36	54-40
III	Severe	35-20	39-25
IV	Profound	19-below	24-below

TABLE 9.2
MENTAL AGE EXPECTANCY BY LEVEL OF RETARDATION

Level	Degree of Retardation	Mental Age Expectancy (years)	School Grade Equivalence
I	Mild (EMH)	8–12	3rd to 6th grade
II	Moderate (TMH)	3–7	Preschool to 2nd grade
III	Severe	1–3	
IV	Profound	0–1	

age in months by the last IQ record and divide by 100. Thus, a child tested at ten years (120 months) who had an IQ of 70 would have a mental age of 7 years (84 months).

Characteristics of Children by Level of Retardation

The intellectual deficit aspect of mental retardation is a handicap of degrees. The handicap may be so slight as to go unnoticed except when ability to deal with complex problems is required, or it may be so severe as to require complete custodial care. Most persons (approximately 89 percent) with intellectual deficits are termed mildly or educable mentally retarded.

The **educable** person's retardation (mild, EMH) is usually not apparent during preschool years. Once in school, however, the child's delayed development becomes apparent. As a teenager, the educable child's mental age is comparable to that of an intellectually average child in grade school. As adults, these persons blend readily into society and within limitations can achieve economic and social independence.

Persons with **moderate** or **trainable** (TMH) levels of mental retardation manifest developmental delays that become apparent during early childhood. For the trainable child, instructional emphasis is on systematic, repeated, rote experiences, which the child learns more by habit formation than by reasoning. While the goal of education promotes concept formation and abstract reasoning, training tends to foster appropriate conditioned responses. The trainable child or adult can achieve social and economic semi-independence, with support from others becoming necessary when stress levels are elevated.

The **severely mentally retarded** require constant supervision and support. They may achieve modest communication skills and may learn some self-care skills. Work can be undertaken by some, but only under close supervision. Severely retarded persons function effectively only when supervision is constant and the environment is highly structured.

The **profoundly retarded** are totally dependent on others for self-care. Communication abilities are grossly inadequate and there is little socialization or interaction. Lifelong, complete supervision is required.

Prevalence During School Years

The fact that mild and moderate retardation become apparent when the person is confronted by complex, abstract problems explains why these conditions are usually identified during the school years. Before and after the school years, identification drops markedly, suggesting that nonschool demands on learning and social adaptation are less acute. The preschool and postschool years permit handicapped children and adults to seek and find functional levels within their potential and incentive.

Deficits in Adaptive Behavior

The AAMD definition of mental retardation, as well as other definitions (Kolstoe 1972, Kidd 1979), includes maladaptive behavior among the identification criteria. Nihara et al. (1974) and Cegelka and Prehm (1982) believe that the major components of adaptive behavior and maladaptive behavior can be dichotomized and delineated. They cite **adaptive behavior** as exemplified by independent functioning, physical development, economic development, language development, number and time concepts, domestic activity, vocational activity, self-direction, responsibility, and socialization.

They cite **maladaptive behavior** as exemplified by violent and destructive behavior, antisocial behavior, rebellious behavior, untrustworthy behavior, withdrawal, stereotyped behavior and odd mannerisms, inappropriate interpersonal manners, unacceptable or eccentric habits, unacceptable vocal mannerisms, self-abusive behavior, hyperactive tendencies, sexually aberrant behavior, psychological disturbances, and use of medication.[2]

Assessment of social maturity and immaturity, or adaptive and maladaptive behavior, may be undertaken using social maturity and adaptive behavior developmental scales. Although adapted physical educators would not be involved directly in administering these scales, educators should understand the meaning and implications of maladaptive behaviors as they relate to mental retardation and how assessment can be undertaken. The more thoroughly the adapted physical educator understands the *total child*, the more effectively the educator will find the root causes of the child's behavior and thus avoid ineffective remediation attempts.

---

2. Reference is to illicit use (chemical dependency).

Causes of Retardation

While many causes of retardation exist, most mentally retarded persons (80–90 percent) present no demonstrable pathology. Among such persons, the exact cause or causes of mental retardation remain elusive. Among those who manifest a pathology, the following causative factors have been identified (Cohen and Kaminer 1985).

Infections (Prenatal or Postnatal)

Example (prenatal): Rubella.   Mothers who contract German measles (rubella) during the first three months (trimester) of pregnancy often give birth to children with a variety of congenital defects. Among these are deafness, cataracts, cardiac malfunctions, and mental retardation. Mental retardation is estimated to develop in 12 percent of children exposed prenatally to maternal rubella.

Example (postnatal): Meningitis.   Meningitis, an inflammation of membranous brain tissue, is believed to cause mental retardation among some affected children. In looking at samples of children who have survived meningitis, data suggest a distribution of intelligence that approaches near or low normal (Todd and Nevill 1967).

Intoxications

Kern - ik' Ter-us

Example: Kernicterus.   Kernicterus is a bilirubin (reddish yellow) staining of brain tissue. It often follows severe jaundice in the newborn owing to incompatible blood types of the mother and fetus (Rh factor). Although all affected children are not destined to be mentally retarded, they do, as a group, exhibit a subnormal level of intelligence.

Prenatal Trauma or Physical Defects

Example: Irradiation.   Exposure to high levels of radioactive substances during pregnancy creates greater risk of abnormal fetal development. Mental retardation is among the defects associated with maternal exposure to excessive doses of radiation.

Injury or Anoxia at Birth

Example: Difficult or complicated labor.   During difficult or prolonged passage through the birth canal, the fetus faces increased risk of cerebral damage. During delivery and prior to the child's breathing independently, umbilical cord compression or placental hemorrhage may occur. Either complication can deprive the fetus's brain of needed oxygen.

Postnatal Injury

Example: Blow to the skull.   Data supporting postnatal injury as a cause of mental retardation are sparse. Although postnatal trauma appears in the history of some mentally retarded persons, such trauma is more likely to occur among persons already mentally retarded (Nylander and Nylander 1964).

Metabolic Errors

Example: Phenylketonuria (PKU).   This disorder involves an inability of the child's body to metabolize protein. This metabolic defect allows substances that destroy brain tissue to accumulate in the body. Fortunately, PKU can be detected immediately after birth through a simple urine test. Retardation is then avoidable with control of the child's diet.

Chromosomal Disorders

Example: Down syndrome.   Down syndrome, until recently referred to as *mongolism*, is the most common clinically defined cause of mental retardation. Down syndrome may result from the child's having 47 instead of the usual 46 chromosomes. Chromosomes normally align in pairs. When the additional chromosome becomes attached to pair 21, Down syndrome, termed **Trisomy 21**, usually occurs (up to 95 percent of all cases).

Some Down syndrome children do have only 46 chromosomes. Among such children, a portion of chromosome 21 aligns with another chromosome, usually number 15 or 22. This chromosomal anomaly is termed **translocation**.

A third cause of Down syndrome, termed **mosaicism**, occurs when the individual has cells with different chromosome numbers. This difference occurs when, during cell division, one cell erroneously retains chromosome 21 intended for its sister cell. The sister cell dies, and the cell with the additional chromosome survives to generate additional abnormal cells (Priest 1985).

Approximately 13 percent of all pregnancies occur in women over 35 years of age. About half of all Down babies are born to women in this age group, one in every 300. Between the ages of 40 and 45, a woman's chance of bearing a child with Down syndrome is 1 in 100, and women 45 years and older have a 1 in 40 chance. It is interesting to note that reports from Texas, British Columbia, Japan, and Denmark show that only about 20 percent of infants with Down syndrome were born to older women. In general, women younger than 35 are responsible for more than 90 percent of all births, and they are having 65 to 80 percent of Down syndrome babies. Although the mother's age is an important factor, note that approximately 25 percent of all babies with Down syndrome can be attributed to a faulty sperm of the father (Holmes 1978). If the male's sperm or the female's eggs are exposed to physical or chemical forces, such as radiation or viruses, then it is theorized that as the individuals age, their physiological ability to produce normal healthy sperm or eggs decreases. The exact etiology of Down syndrome is, however, still uncertain.

The physical features of Down syndrome are clearly recognizable. In addition to the characteristic almond-shaped eye features, the most common diagnostic physical features are a fold in the skin in the corner of the eyes (epicanthal fold); a tongue too large for the small oral cavity; close-set, deep eyes that often are strabismic (cross-eyed); flaccidity (hypotonicity) of muscles (i.e., muscles appear to have little tone); thick, stubby hands; very small fingers; and short stature (bone growth stops at approximately 16 years of age). Average height for adult females is 4 ft 7 in., and for males, 5 ft. Many will experience foot problems, including weak or fallen arches.

Approximately 40 percent of Down syndrome infants have congenital heart defects. The majority of cardiac problems can be surgically corrected. Another congenital defect, **atlantoaxial dislocation condition (ADC)** has been identified as potentially dangerous for approximately 10 percent of all individuals with Down syndrome. This condition is defined as a malalignment or natural displacement of the C1 vertebrae in relation to the C2 vertebrae. An enlarged space between the vertebra allows excessive movement. If the individual should hyperextend or radically flex the neck, the spinal cord is exposed to possible damage. The national office of the Special Olympics now requires all Down syndrome individuals to be x-rayed before participating in competitive activities. Any individual who has ADC is not permitted to take part in gymnastics, diving, butterfly stroke in swimming, diving start in swimming, high jump, pentathlon, soccer, or any warm-up exercise placing pressure on the head or neck.

Share and French (1982) attribute the deficits in motor skill of Down syndrome children to hypotonia (i.e., lack of muscle tone). They theorize that this deficit is related to a smaller cerebellum or cerebellar impairment. Remember that the function of the cerebellum is directly related to synthesizing movement coordination in the body. In addition, thyroid and pituitary deficiencies, often found in these youngsters, result in body builds that are not conducive to strenuous or accurate movement.

The congenital and physical constraints of persons with Down syndrome have important implications for physical fitness and motor skill development. Owing to these constraints, the attainment of above average physical fitness and motor skills is difficult for individuals with Down syndrome.

Polacek, Wang, and Eichstaedt (1985) found that Down syndrome youngsters (ages 6–21 years) fall below the 10th percentile on all items in the *AAHPERD Health Related Physical Fitness Test* battery (1980). These items measure cardiorespiratory endurance, abdominal and hip flexion strength and endurance, excessive adipose tissue, and higher back and hamstring flexibility. The researchers confirmed that individuals with Down syndrome are far more flexible than other nonhandicapped and other mentally handicapped subjects. This facility is negative from the standpoint of coordinated movement and speed, both of which are related directly to degree of tonus of body ligaments and tendons. The hyperflexibility of Down syndrome youngsters is therefore not always a desirable trait. Evidence does exist, however, that this condition can be improved through progressive exercise programs.

Adapted physical educators must keep in mind the physical constraints of Down syndrome students when they make activity selections. For example, open-mouth breathing may cause problems during cardiorespiratory activities, and small hands and fingers can make catching and throwing difficult. When teaching throwing, the instructor should show the youngster how to hold the ball with three fingers across the seams, instead of teaching the regular two-finger grip. When foot problems are encountered, long periods of running may be difficult, and the adapted physical educator should choose alternative activities such as stationary bicycle riding or swimming. Pitt (1974, p. 19) believes that "Muscular development needs to be stimulated by exercises, by marching to music, and by the use of trampolines, on which many Down syndrome youngsters become very expert. Likewise, swimming is an enjoyable and helpful pastime that can also be taught to these children even at an early age." Caveny (1985) has found that use of the trampoline is extremely valuable. She believes that this activity contributes greatly to improved balance and motor planning.

When children reach their plateau in height, it is critical to maintain close supervision of diet, because individuals with Down syndrome have a tendency to gain weight. Glaze (1985) indicates that both males and females between ages 13 and 18 continue to gain weight despite the fact that they have reached maximum height in their early teens. Trainer (1978, p.104) states: "As some Down's youngsters grow older, they have a tendency to be fat. Today, through controlled diets and good physical education programs, the problem of obesity can be alleviated."

Share and French (1982) list developmental progressions of specific gross motor skills for Down syndrome children between the ages of birth and 6 years (Table 9.3).

Winnick (1979) has identified major physical and motor characteristics of Down syndrome children and adolescents and the resulting implications for movement experiences (Table 9.4).

Motor Characteristics

Although mentally retarded children generally achieve at lower levels of physical and motor performance, they tend to be more similar to their chronological age peers in physical and motor performance than in any other single respect. Mentally retarded children appear to have greatest achievement potential in this domain. Although physical and motor performance deficits do exist, such deficits are often more a matter of impoverished opportunity than impoverished potential. Many retarded persons, particularly the mildly retarded, often demonstrate levels of physical and motor proficiency that approximate those of their chronological age peers. Since physical education is, indeed, part of special education (a primary service under Public Law 94-142), improved physical and motor performances among the mentally retarded should become a trend.

Although data are available regarding intellectual and behavioral characteristics of the mentally retarded, less data are available about their physical and motor performance characteristics. Until recently, the education of mentally retarded children,

TABLE 9.3
DEVELOPMENTAL PROGRESSION OF SPECIFIC GROSS MOTOR SKILLS OF DOWN
SYNDROME CHILDREN

	Age of Onset (in months)			
Motor Skill	Normal	Down Syndrome	Difference in Months	Norm Rate (%)
1. Sitting				
Sits with head erect, but thrust forward and unsteady	3	3	0	100
Sits with head set forward	4	5	1	80
Maintains an erect sitting position	7	11	4	64
2. Standing				
While supported, bears small fraction of weight momentarily	3	3	0	100
Stands and maintains balance briefly, with hands held	8	13	5	61
Uses rail of crib to pull self to a standing position	10	18	8	56
3. Rolling				
On the verge of rolling over	4	5	2	1
Rolls from back to stomach	6	7	1	86
4. Rests weight on hands with chest off crib or surface	5	7	2	71
5. Partially turns on stomach	8	12	4	67
6. Creeps				
Creeps on hands and knees	10	15	5	67
Creeps up at least one or two steps	15	24	9	63
7. Walks				
Moves around freely while holding onto a rail or with both hands held	12	21	9	57
Walks with only one hand held	13	27	14	48
Walks a few steps without assistance, starting and stopping	15	30	15	60
Walks and seldom falls	18	30	12	60
Walks upstairs with one hand held	18	55	37	33
Walks downstairs with one hand held	21	36	15	58
Walks on tiptoes after demonstration	30	48	18	63
Alternated feet when going upstairs in adult fashion	36	54	18	67
Walks on a walking board	42	72+	30	58+
8. Seats self in small chair	18	30	12	60

continued

TABLE 9.3 *continued*
DEVELOPMENTAL PROGRESSION OF SPECIFIC GROSS MOTOR SKILLS OF DOWN SYNDROME CHILDREN

	Age of Onset (in months)			
Motor Skill	*Normal*	*Down Syndrome*	*Difference in Months*	*Norm Rate (%)*
9. Throwing				
Throws a ball	18	30	12	60
Throws overhand	48	72	24	67
10. Squats while playing	21	36	15	58
11. Kicks a large ball after demonstration	21	36	15	58
12. Runs well without falling (still not fast)	24	36	15	58
13. Jumping and hopping				
Jumps up with both feet off the floor after demonstration	30	48	18	63
Jumps from bottom stair, landing erect	36	54	18	67
Jumps while running	48	72+	24	67+
Hops on one foot	54	72+	18	75+
14. Rides a tricycle using pedals	36	60	24	60
15. Skipping				
Skips with one foot forward	48	72+	24	67+
Skips, alternating lead foot	60	72+	12	83+

SOURCE: Reprinted with permission from Share and French 1982.

under the guise of special education, was a classroom-centered phenomenon. Focus was largely on classroom-developed competencies for reading, writing, language, numbers, self-help, and socialization. The primary emphasis was on the child's mental retardation as a problem of intellect. The result of these attitudes has been the relative deemphasis of the mentally retarded child's movement-centered needs and potentials.

Before 1977, physical education of the mentally retarded seemed only a modest priority. This deemphasis occurred in part because many physical educators, although they taught children with special needs, perceived themselves primarily as teachers of children with physical and orthopedic handicaps. Most of these teachers did not consider themselves prepared to deal with the physical and motor performance needs of a mentally retarded child. As a result, the physical education needs of mentally retarded children often were not met.

Until recently, most information gathered in the physical education domain focused on the child's physical growth: collections of anthropometric data including length, height, weight, width, girth, and body fat. Little information was available regarding motor performance.

TABLE 9.4

CHARACTERISTICS OF THE CHILD WITH DOWN SYNDROME

Characteristics	Implications for Movement Experiences
Lag in physical growth. (Growth ceases at an earlier than normal age and generally results in shorter height and smaller overall stature.) Lag is evident in motor development.	The child may need to participate in activities geared for younger age groups.
The circulatory system is less well developed. Arteries are often narrow and thinner than normal, and less vascular proliferation is evidenced. Many children (especially boys) exhibit congenital heart disorders, heart murmurs and septum defects being the most common.	Although there is a need for the development of endurance, youngsters will have difficulty in endurance activities. It is necessary for all children to have a medical exam and for the instructor to develop a program with medical consultation.
Poor respiration and susceptibility to respiratory infections. (Underdeveloped jaw causes mouth to be too small for normal-sized tongue, inducing mouth breathing.)	Poor respiration may impede participation in endurance activities.
Perceptual handicaps.	Children may be clumsy and awkward. Activities to develop perceptual abilities should be emphasized.
Poor balance.	Since balance is important in most physical and motor activities, lack of balance will affect performance ability. Children need balance training.
Enjoyment of music and rhythmic activities.	The instructor should include rhythmic activities in the program to provide successful and enjoyable experiences and should use music as an aid in teaching.
Obesity.	General overall participation in activities that enhance weight reduction are recommended.
Flabbiness. (Hypotonicity, particularly associated with newborn infants.)	The instructor should provide opportunity for movement experiences at early ages and activities to increase strength at later ages.
Protruding abdomen, lack of muscle and ligament support around the joints, and pronated ankles.	Activities to enhance body alignment and to increase muscle and ligament support around the joints and abdominal exercises are recommended.
Ability to mimic.	Instructor should demonstrate activities and ask children to imitate them.

SOURCE: Reprinted with permission from Winnick, J. P. *Early Movement Experiences and Development: Habilitation and Remediation.* Philadelphia: W. B. Saunders, 1979, p. 229.

In reference to his review of research dealing with physical fitness and the mentally retarded, Newell (1985, p. 185) states: "The mentally retarded are generally less active than nonretarded individuals, and this alone contributes to many of the performance differences typically reported in studies with physical fitness orientation. . . ."

Thomas (1984) refers to the motor learning problems that affect mentally retarded (MR) individuals. She states:

> Training studies and other research have manipulated behavior to produce "normal" performance in MR individuals. That is, MR children can perform qualitatively like their chronological age counterparts when taught or forced to do so. Generalization and transfer are the greatest challenge for remediation. MR individuals can be both cued to attend and forced to rehearse, and exhibit normal retention. With more time (or trials), MR students can reach and maintain mastery. These individuals probably have less experience stored in LTS [long-term storage] than do normal individuals, and have increased difficulty in placing information there. They also have little knowledge about memory and ways to facilitate memory. All of these factors are alterable (p. 182).

In other words, with appropriate teacher cues, adequate trials, and enough practice time, mentally retarded students can and will develop long-term memory storage in relation to learning motor skills.

Newell (1985) identifies the problem of past research related to motor skill learning and the mentally retarded as follows: "Of more specific concern to the consideration of skill acquisition in the mentally retarded, is the realization that a very small range of motor skills have been utilized for analysis (often a key press or a simple unidimensional movement) and that problems of learning have been eliminated by the motor performance orientation" (p. 186).

Sugden (1978) and Reid (1980) found that the retarded child did not exhibit spontaneously an ability to remember movement cues. When subjects were prompted through instruction in the use of a strategy to recall movement, accuracy of recall was superior to the recall of retarded subjects who did not receive instruction. In reference to these studies, Horgan (1985) believes that the issue of spontaneity (i.e., acting without thinking) in adopting memory strategies for the recall of movement cues is fundamental to understanding memory structure of the mentally retarded. He substantiates his contention by his 1983 study in which he found no differences between his mentally retarded instruction subjects and two nonretarded instruction groups. His findings support the notion that the mentally retarded can make improvements in their movement accuracy equal to the improvements of their nonretarded counterparts. He qualifies his findings by stating that "the retarded *must* be made aware of effective means to assist them in coding, processing, and retaining movement information" (Horgan 1985, p. 201).

Francis and Rarick (1963) were among the first physical educators who sought systematically to determine physical and motor performance characteristics of mentally retarded children. Their data were drawn from (1) children classified as mentally retarded and assigned to special classes (IQ range 50–90), and (2) institutionalized children (IQ range 15–50). The researchers undertook to do the following: (1) determine age and sex trends in gross motor abilities, (2) compare motor achievement levels, (3) determine if interrelationships among gross motor functions of the retarded were different from those among functions of nonhandicapped children, (4) determine possible relationships between motor performance and mental retardation, and (5) devise tests of gross motor performance to be used for institutionalized children of very low intelligence.

Children included in the investigation were 284 public school educable children (CA 7½–14½) and 23 institutionalized children with retardation ranging from profound through trainable (CA approximately 10 years).

The investigators selected assessment items that (1) sampled different physical and motor abilities, (2) were easy to administer, (3) were easy to comprehend, (4) were reliable, and (5) were easy to standardize. Results for the educable mentally retarded children are shown in Tables 9.5–9.10.

Among institutionalized children (CA 7–12), average performances for the group were not reported, but their performances were compared with those of nonhandicapped nursery school children (CA 2½–5½). Figure 9.2 illustrates performance levels of institutionalized retarded children as compared with nonretarded nursery school children. For example, institutionalized children in this investigation exhibited target throwing skills roughly equivalent to those of nonretarded 3-year-olds.

Within the institutionalized group, children were identified as either Down syndrome or familial retarded with mean mental ages of 31 and 48 months, respectively. Each group's motor performance paralleled roughly that of nonhandicapped children of about the same mental age.

Among moderately and profoundly retarded institutionalized children (CA 7–12) performance was equivalent to that of nonretarded nursery school age children. Performance among the educable retarded was 2 to 4 years behind that of nonretarded chronological age peers. Among educables, the performance gaps widened with age.

TABLE 9.5
EMH GRIP STRENGTH (GRIP DYNAMOMETER)

| Chronological Age | Grip Strength—Right (kg) | | Grip Strength—Left (kg) | |
| | Mean | | Mean | |
	Boys	Girls	Boys	Girls
8	13.4	7.8	12.1	7.6
9	14.4	12.3	13.0	12.0
10	15.6	12.3	14.1	12.5
11	17.7	17.1	16.7	15.7
12	18.6	17.9	17.5	16.9
13	24.0	18.9	23.7	18.6
14	26.4	22.4	24.8	22.9

TABLE 9.6
EMH FLYING START 30 YARD AND REGULAR START 35 YARD DASHES

Chronological Age	35 Yard Dash (Gross Time in Seconds)		30 Yard Dash (Net Time in Seconds)	
	Mean		Mean	
	Boys	Girls	Boys	Girls
8	7.2	9.6	5.8	7.7
9	7.3	7.6	5.8	6.1
10	7.1	8.0	5.7	6.2
11	6.9	6.7	5.5	5.4
12	6.4	7.2	5.1	5.8
13	6.3	6.7	4.9	5.2
14	6.1	6.5	4.8	5.1

TABLE 9.7
EMH DYNAMIC STRENGTH

Chronological Age	Broad Jump (inches)		Vertical Jump (inches)	
	Mean		Mean	
	Boys	Girls	Boys	Girls
8	36.7	18.4	6.9	3.8
9	33.4	35.0	7.6	6.9
10	36.6	29.7	7.1	6.4
11	40.5	34.7	8.4	8.5
12	39.1	35.8	8.4	8.2
13	45.7	38.1	9.9	8.8
14	44.7	38.3	11.0	8.5

TABLE 9.8
EMH BALL-THROW FOR DISTANCE

Chronological Age[a]	Score (feet)	
	Mean	
	Boys	*Girls*
	Tennis Ball Throw	
8	41.0	19.0
9	53.2	31.3
	Softball Throw	
10	55.8	33.9
11	66.9	36.5
12	71.3	50.4
13	93.4	61.0
14	92.4	47.4

[a]Age 9 and under = tennis ball; 10 and over = regulation softball.

TABLE 9.9
EMH BALANCE BEAM

Chronological Age	Number of Steps Before Losing Balance	
	Mean	
	Boys	*Girls*
8	8.1	5.8
9	8.1	8.1
10	7.9	7.1
11	8.8	7.5
12	8.3	8.5
13	9.4	8.7
14	9.1	7.8

TABLE 9.10
EMH AGILITY

| Chronological Age | Agility Run (seconds)[a] | | Burpee Test | |
| | Mean | | Mean | |
	Boys	Girls	Boys	Girls
8	6.2	7.5	3.6	2.8
9	6.0	6.3	4.0	3.7
10	5.9	6.7	4.2	3.4
11	5.7	6.0	4.0	3.7
12	5.7	5.9	3.7	3.7
13	5.4	5.8	4.2	3.6
14	5.2	5.9	4.4	3.3

[a]From supine position, child rose as rapidly as possible, ran 10 ft to a table, picked up a small ball, turned around, and ran back to the starting line.

Chronological age and sex factors as they affect motor performance followed patterns similar to those observed in nonhandicapped children. Although the effects of age and sex in both the handicapped and nonhandicapped groups were noticeably similar, the performances of the retarded children were significantly below those of their nonretarded chronological age peers at every level.

Small, but significant, positive correlations were found between physical and motor performance and IQ. Similar correlations have been found among nonretarded children. The relationship between physical and motor performance and intelligence is not, however, fully understood. It is possible that a relatively higher intellect permits greater understanding of a task, which results in a better understood, better organized response. Perceptual-motor theorists (Barsch 1968a and b, Kephart 1960, Doman 1974) (see Chapter 7) suggest that cognitive genesis occurs in movement-centered proficiencies developed in nonhandicapped youngsters during early childhood.

Is There a Relationship Between Motor and Cognitive Development?

In recent years, investigators have endeavored to determine the precise nature of the motor development-cognitive development relationship. Thomas (1984) identifies one problem of the child with mental retardation in regard to motor learning. She states that "the same system controls all learning and memory, whether cognitive, motor, or affective. A problem in the memory system may affect motor skill acquisition

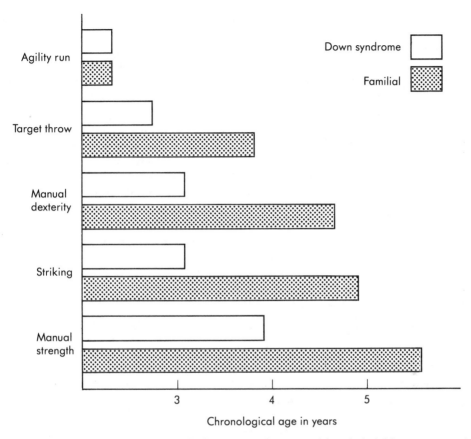

FIGURE 9.2. Motor achievement level of Down syndrome and familial children presented as age equivalent to performance of nursery school age children.

in infinite ways, including less understanding of task variables or verbal instructions, poor motor planning, slower processing, and inadequate socialization . . ." (p. 175).

Older studies also are still pertinent and shed light on how mentally retarded children learn motor skills. Corder (1966) investigated the effects of a systematic progressive physical education program on the intellectual development and social status of 24 educable retarded boys placed in one of three groups: (1) group receiving physical education, (2) "officials" group (served as teacher's helpers and interacted socially with the physical education group), and (3) control group (experienced neither physical education nor social interaction with the physical education group).

Inclusion of an officials group served to determine whether any observed performance improvement could be attributed to the physical education experience, or whether observed improvement might be due instead to the extra attention received. Improvement resulting from extra attention and not from any special program (i.e., physical education) would be an example of the *Hawthorne* or *extra attention effect.*

In the Corder investigation, significant improvement in IQ and self-concept was noted in the group receiving physical education. The control group did not gain in any of the measured attributes. The officials group and the physical education group both experienced significant IQ gains, indicating that the Hawthorne effect was operating and responsible for some of the gain. The fact that the IQ gain in the physical education group was somewhat higher than in the officials group suggests that other factors, perhaps the physical education experience, were responsible.

In a similar study, Soloman and Prangle (1967) undertook to determine the effects of physical education on intellectual function. The physical education group experienced significant gains in motor ability over a control group that had no physical education, but neither group gained in intellectual function. This lack of gain in intelligence conflicts with Corder's results. To explain these conflicting results in similar studies, Cratty (1974) suggests that the self-concept level of the children in each study should have been assessed. Perhaps a successful physical education experience produced an increased positive self-concept for the children in the Corder study, which resulted in turn in a posttest intellectual performance more consistent with potential. Perhaps children in the Soloman and Prangle study achieved a positive self-concept before the study began. In that case, the intellectual function test administered at the study's completion would not show IQ improvement. This analysis implies that children in the latter study, because of positive self-concepts, achieved more accurate scores on intelligence tests from the beginning.

State-of-the-art determination of the role that movement plays in achieving intelligence potential among the mentally retarded enables cautious assumption of an association between physical and motor proficiency and cognitive development. Gruber (1969, p. 598), in part, shares this persuasion:

> The role that physical education and recreation programs play in developing IQ in mentally retarded children is not entirely conclusive. However, those motor activities that require thought processes for execution do correlate to a higher degree with IQ than less complex activities. Hence, thought-provoking play activities may stimulate the development of independent reasoning by requiring the pupil to think through his movement patterns.

Cratty (1974, p. 24) cautions against making overzealous claims for the role that physical education plays in the retarded child's intellectual development. He suggests several possible positive outcomes of physical education for these children:

1. Movement capabilities often lead to vocational opportunities for the retarded.
2. Remediation of motor problems, coupled with learning of play skills, can lead to helpful social interactions among retarded children and between retarded and nonretarded children.
3. Physical activities help the retarded child achieve success in skills that have a performance level easily discernible both by the youth and by his observing teacher.

4. Academic tasks, when used to motivate physical activities, can be a powerful tool for improving academic abilities in retarded children.

5. Sustained and intensive programs of sensory-motor activity, coupled with other kinds of sensory stimulation, have been shown to improve basic adaptive behaviors of some profoundly and severely retarded youngsters.

6. When applied properly, various kinds of relaxation training involving reduction of excess muscular tensions may help reduce hyperactivity in some retarded youngsters.

7. Rhythmic motor activities may help some retarded youngsters to grasp concepts of self-control and pacing, and may enhance rhythmic components of language, writing, and reading.

8. Physical education programs, coupled with proper levels of exercise, can improve fitness of retarded youngsters and improve significantly performance of basic physical skills such as running, jumping, and swimming. Acquisition of these skills may in turn enhance significantly the child's self-concept.

Communicating and Relating in a Physical Education Setting

Mentally retarded children, like most of their nonhandicapped peers, are usually willing to obey the teacher if they understand what is being asked. The problem of understanding is, however, encountered often when the retarded child is confronted with communication abstractions. Language is a collection of abstract verbal symbols that have no "built in" meaning. The word "ball" is an abstraction without meaning until the symbol is connected with the concrete object. Mentally retarded children are not effective learners when abstracts are used. This explains the observed tendency in the retarded toward nonverbal expression.[3]

Werder and Kalakian (1985) warn that some mentally retarded youngsters may not understand the concepts of competition and trying their hardest. They simply do not comprehend statements such as "Run as *fast* as you can," or "Jump as *high* as you can," or "Do as *many* as you can." This is particularly true of students who function at or below the lower range of the moderately retarded. These individuals usually do not comprehend the significance of maximum performance. For such persons, strong, extrinsic motivators-reinforcers may be necessary to evoke the best response.

---

3. Note the difference between *verbal* and *vocal*. *Verbal* implies the ability to use language purposefully. Many mentally retarded children are good "word callers"—they use words, phrases, or sentences without understanding. "Word calling" or uttering sounds without meaning is *vocalizing*. The child's propensity for vocalizing gives a false impression of the child's ability to understand. To determine whether the child is verbalizing or vocalizing, observe whether appropriate, purposeful activity accompanies an utterance or ask the child to repeat or relate *in the child's own words* something just said.

Use of Short Sentences and Single-Syllable Words

When using language to communicate with retarded children, use single-syllable or few-syllable words and short sentences. Avoid slurring words (i.e., the subconscious running-together of words, which makes them difficult to understand), and avoid slang. Use consistency and repetition when communicating. Language should be consistent in that words should not be subconsciously interchanged. "Get the big ball" might be understood, but "get the large ball" might not be. Synonyms should be used in the physical education setting only when a conscious, controlled effort is being made to develop vocabulary. Language repetition is important as a way to give retarded children more than one opportunity to understand what has been said.

Using Physical Education to Help Overcome Nonverbal Behavior

Mentally retarded children who are nonverbal or who use language sparsely often will become more verbal as a result of a successful physical education experience. Because retarded children are similar to their nonretarded peers both physically and motorically, they often achieve movement-centered performance gains with relative ease. Success usually elevates self-concept, which may motivate the child to become a part of activity. Many activities in turn stimulate language use, and the child intensifies verbal communication. It is not uncommon for a nonverbal child to become more verbal during activity or when the conversation turns to activity. The child's willingness to verbalize about enjoyable physical education experiences should be used as a valuable adjunct to language development.

Problem of Newness

Mentally retarded children tend to be comfortable with consistency and repetition. Newness represents a departure from these factors and can be a stressful obstacle in the child's learning environment. To the mentally retarded, newness often means failure and uncertainty, so the child may consciously avoid any departure from what is comfortable and known. To guide the child into activities within, but presently beyond, his grasp, avoid unnecessary references to newness. This should eliminate or at least reduce psychological barriers associated with uncertainty that complicate the learning process. Newness must be introduced in small increments with progress measured (and praised) in inches rather than feet.

New or challenging experiences should be introduced early in a class period and early in the day, when children are mentally alert and physically fresh. This is especially important among retarded children whose attention span and physical stamina may be limited.

Whenever possible, new activities in physical education should be introduced when subsequent physical education periods follow relatively soon. Because retarded children often have short retention spans, new activities require immediate follow-up or they may be forgotten. Both quantity of intervening experiences and elapsed time between physical education classes can have a negative impact on the retention of new knowledges and skills.

Attention Span

The child's attention span should be considered when presenting activities. Generally, the attention span of retarded children is shorter than that of intellectually average children, but retarded children may remain interested in activities of their own choosing for a disproportionately long time. This raises the question of whether the children's attention span is truly short or whether teachers do not know how to or what maintains their interest. One plausible explanation for the child's short attention span, particularly when engaged in teacher-directed activities, might be the child's lack of communication skills. Children cannot be expected to remain interested in an activity that they simply do not understand. Children who do not understand a verbal instruction may need a *visual model*. If a visual model is too abstract for comprehension, use *tactile cues*, such as gently nudging the appropriate body part in the proper direction. Children who remain unable to execute a skill may need *actual physical assistance* (kinesthetic patterning) through the entire skill.

Before the children lose interest, change to a different activity or curtail the day's physical education instruction. A timely change or curtailment of activity serves a twofold purpose: (1) renders the activity worthwhile because it did not become boring, and (2) eliminates discipline problems stemming from loss of interest.

The Need for Structure

There is a need for structure in the mentally retarded child's learning environment to control variety and quantity of choices that the child must make. Children should be encouraged to make choices in accordance with their abilities and particularly when choice making is a desired result of the activity period. Choices that the children make should be a function of the learning environment structure and should be controlled by the teacher.

Examples of appropriate structuring include (1) having children hold hands to form a circle, (2) supplying a geometric figure on which the child can stand so she knows where to stand, (3) placing a colored ribbon around the hand (foot) when consistent use is desired, (4) having the whistle mean stop, turn around, sit down, and listen to the teacher, (5) not giving the child a piece of equipment (e.g., a ball) until the child is to use it, (6) selecting activities in which all children participate all of the time, while avoiding activities that eliminate children (those eliminated first often need physical education most), and (7) not asking a question unless you truly expect an answer. Avoid saying "do you want to play _____?" unless you are prepared to deal with a possible "no" answer. Say, "We are going to play _____." Even more confusing is the question "What shall we play?"

Need for structure will vary for different activities and for different children. Even a seemingly unstructured physical education environment should be consciously created (i.e., structured) by the teacher.

Praise and Recognition

Mentally retarded children, like all children, thrive on praise and recognition. Take advantage of every reasonable opportunity to praise a child's accomplishments, and especially praise efforts that precede accomplishments. Even a small effort or minor accomplishment may, in fact, be enormous for a particular child. For children who too often experience failure, praise is a most effective antidote to withdrawal, low motivation, and low self-esteem. Praise should be given publicly so the child derives satisfaction from knowing that others are aware of her achievement.

While praise is effective when given in public, reprimands are more effective if given privately. A reprimand among peers, which the child interprets as embarrassing, may cause needless lowering of self-esteem and unnecessary withdrawal. For some children, public reprimand may contribute to disruptive behavior because the child is seeking attention. In either case, address the child's behavior problem in privacy on a one-to-one basis. When speaking to the child, particularly in one-to-one communications, meet the child at his own level; kneel and talk eye-to-eye if necessary.

Culminating Activities

The final activity in the children's physical education day should be familiar and one in which all can participate successfully. A child who leaves the physical education environment feeling good about the experience will wish to return another day.

Often, a quiet activity is appropriate. High key activities near the end of a physical education period often evoke inappropriate levels of arousal, which the children bring into the academic classroom. The classroom teacher is then obliged to deal with the child's emotions before commencing instruction.

Use of Mental Age in Selecting Activities

Mentally retarded children often find activities more interesting and comprehensible when the activities are compatible with their mental age. When selecting activities for older retarded children or young adults, avoid activities that the older child perceives as "kid's stuff." The learner's negative perception of such activities does not motivate, improve self-esteem, or establish rapport with the teacher.

Often, the teacher need change only the name of a game or the character names to shed the game's "kid stuff" image. This is particularly true when the developmental level requires low-organized games suited to nonhandicapped elementary-age children.

Assessing Physical and Motor Performance

Pursuant to P.L. 94-142, adapted physical education must focus on development of (1) physical and motor proficiencies, (2) fundamental motor skills, and (3) skills in aquatics, dance, and individual and group games and sports (including intramural and lifetime sports).

Basic components of physical and motor proficiency were discussed in detail in Chapter 5. (See sections entitled "Organic Performance Components of Fitness" and "Motor Performance Components of Fitness," pages 61–65.)

Tables 9.11 and 9.12 show a few examples of physical and motor performance activities arranged by fitness component. Successful performance in one component does *not* ensure or even suggest successful performance in another. If a performance deficit occurs in any component, the physical educator must understand which specific activities will improve performance of that component. For example, strength activities will develop strength but not coordination or muscular endurance. Agility activities, which teach direction change capabilities, will not enhance flexibility.

Fundamental Motor Skills

Comprehensive assessment of the mentally retarded child requires evaluation of fundamental motor skills. Development of these basic motor skills (Table 9.13) increases the child's movement versatility in many activities. Conversely, children who lack fundamental motor skills cannot experience success in many physical education activities. Retarded children often experience more than their share of failure. When they show deficits in the most basic motor skills, skill development is required.

TABLE 9.11
PHYSICAL (ORGANIC) PROFICIENCY ACTIVITIES ARRANGED BY COMPONENT

Muscular Strength	Muscular Endurance	Cardiovascular Endurance	Flexibility
Isometrics Use of weights Pullups[a] Push-ups[a]	Backlifts[b] Leglifts[b] Pull-ups[b] Push-ups[b] Sit-ups[b]	Jogging Walking Swimming Cycling Jumping rope Stair climbing Extended wheelchair ambulation	Split Straddle split Toe touch Windmill Trunk twister

[a]These activities use muscular strength when fitness is low (i.e., child unable to repeat approximately ten).
[b]These activities use muscular endurance when fitness is high (i.e., child able to execute repetitions beyond ten).

TABLE 9.12
MOTOR PROFICIENCY ACTIVITIES ARRANGED BY COMPONENT

Balance	Coordination	Agility	Speed	Explosive Strength
Stork stand Balance beam Hop and land without losing balance V-sit (bent knees if necessary)	Ball throw Dribbling Manipulative activities Catching Jumping jack	Zigzag run Shuttle run Squat thrust Mirroring actions of teacher changing directions	Any activities requiring relatively short bursts of speed (e.g., running, wheelchair dashes)	Long jump Vertical jump High jump Throwing for velocity

Skill in Aquatics, Dance, and Individual and Group Games and Sports, Including Intramural and Lifetime Sports

The adapted physical educator will be asked to assess the retarded child's needs in aquatics, dance, and individual and group games and sports. Standard tools for assessing these skills, particularly for use with the retarded, are not readily available. Tests of

TABLE 9.13
BASIC MOTOR DEVELOPMENT SKILLS

Locomotor Skills	Receipt and Propulsion Skills	Axial Skills
Crawling	Throwing	Bending
Creeping	Catching	Twisting
Walking	Manipulating	Stretching
Running	Kicking	Pirouetting
Hopping	Striking	Swinging
Leaping	Dribbling (hand and feet)	Lifting
Jumping	Pushing	
Galloping	Pulling	
Sliding		
Skipping		

sport skill are, in some instances, the exception (Wessel 1976). Determining needs in the remaining sport areas depends on knowing the individual child and on the teacher's theoretical and practical competencies.

How Does One Select or Construct an Assessment Instrument?

In selecting an assessment instrument for use with mentally retarded children, the adapted physical educator must know which aspects of physical or motor performance are to be evaluated. Some standard tests are available. In other instances, tests must be constructed. When tests require construction because those available are unsuitable, determine first which components of physical or motor proficiency or which motor skills are to be evaluated. After making that determination, select performance items that evaluate performance in the specific area. For example, if coordination is to be assessed, observe the child skipping, dribbling, or following a pursuit rotor.[4] Here, *criterion references* might be used to evaluate the child's performance. A performance criterion would be stated in behavioral terms. The child would then be

---

4. The pursuit rotor resembles a phonograph with a small metallic disk positioned on and toward the outside of the turntable. The child, holding a metal-tipped stylus, attempts to maintain stylus contact with the disk as it revolves. Successful pursuit is calculated by continued contact between the moving disk and stylus as a measure of coordination.

assessed and periodically reassessed regarding achievement of the stated criterion. Examples of criterion referencing are as follows:

Performance Component— Coordination	**Actual Level of Performance**
Example One—The child will dribble an 8-in. playground ball, using the preferred hand, ten consecutive times without a break in rhythm.	_____
Example Two—The child will skip for 15 sec without a break in stride.	_____

The extent to which the child achieves the performance criterion determines the child's proficiency with respect to the skill in question. Criterion-referenced observations can be created for all aspects of performance in the physical or motor and motor skill performance domains.

In many instances, standardized or norm-referenced tests are also appropriate. Norms with which the child's performance can be compared generally accompany such tests. The following are a few available tests often used to assess physical or motor and motor skill proficiencies:

Health Related Physical Fitness Test Battery (AAHPERD)

This test battery (AAHPERD 1980) established norms for nonhandicapped children between the ages of 5 and 17. Test items include modified sit-ups, distance run (1 mi or 9 min run, 1½ mi or 12 min run), sit and reach, and the sum of adipose skin folds. Norms for the four test items are provided.

Polacek, Wang, and Eichstaedt (1985) found that this test battery is appropriate for administration to mildly or moderately retarded youngsters and youngsters with Down syndrome. These researchers also found that the three mentally handicapped subject groups, age 6 to 21 (N = 1298) averaged less sit-ups, ran less yardage, and possessed more adipose tissue than nonhandicapped peers of the same chronological age. In addition, comparisons revealed that the mildly mentally handicapped subjects (N = 276) ranked in the lower 25th percentile when compared with the nonhandicapped, and the moderately mentally handicapped (N = 718) and Down syndrome subjects (N = 304) usually fell below the 10th percentile.

Another interesting conclusion drawn from this study was that the moderately retarded and Down syndrome subjects are two distinct populations. Care should be taken when grouping them together for physical education purposes.

Special Fitness Test for Mildly Mentally Retarded Persons (AAHPERD)

This test (AAHPERD 1976) has norms established for educable mentally retarded persons age 8 to 18 years, and includes the following:

Item	Component Measured
Flexed arm hang	Arm, shoulder girdle muscular endurance (muscular strength in cases of low fitness)
Sit-ups (number executed in 1 min)	Abdominal, hip flexor muscular endurance (muscular strength in cases of low fitness)
Shuttle run	Agility
50 yard dash	Speed
300 yard run-walk	Cardiovascular endurance
Standing long jump	Explosive strength in lower extremities
Softball throw	Explosive strength in upper extremities

Motor Fitness Test for the Moderately Mentally Retarded (AAHPERD)

This test (AAHPERD 1975), with norms established for trainable mentally retarded subjects age 6 to 21 years, is similar in content to the instrument designed for use with the mildly retarded. On the test for the moderately retarded, however, the shuttle run has been eliminated. Additional items include recording height and weight, sitting bob and reach, hopping, skipping, and a tumbling progression.

In developing norms for this test, data were derived from a sample of approximately 1100 moderately retarded children. Whether these norms reflect accurately the performance capabilities of the general population of moderately retarded persons is uncertain. Recognizing this test limitation, one should use these norms with caution to assess the physical and motor performance of the moderately retarded.

Bruininks' Revision of the Oseretsky Scale of Motor Development

Oseretsky developed the original motor development scale. In 1948, Sloan (1955) revised the original test to improve its validity for practical settings. The most recent revision by Bruininks (1978) represents the most precise adaptation of the original scale. Bruininks alleges that specific motor behaviors fall into broad, general categories that comprise subtests of the composite test. Both subtest and composite test scores can be reported and used in the assessment process.

Bruininks also has developed a short form of the test that can be used as a quick, though less precise, measure of motor ability. Only items considered to be representative of each subtest are included in the short form. The short form may be used for initial screening or when administering the entire battery is not feasible.

The test measures motor ability in the 4½ to 14½ age range. Test results are interpreted in terms of motor age. A 9-year-old child performing at a 7½-year-old level would thus be exhibiting a 1½-year deficit in motor development as measured by the test.

Denver Developmental Screening Test

For many mentally retarded children, the physical and motor development tests and the motor skill performance tests previously mentioned are inappropriate. For these children, mental age, chronological age, or present level of physical and motor ability may be well below the ability levels measured by the instruments described. For these children, however, an assessment of physical and motor capabilities is essential, and such assessment can be done by using one of the available developmental scales.

Among the most used developmental scales is the *Denver Developmental Screening Test* (Frankenburg et al. 1975). This test measures developmental status among children 0 to 6 years. Gross motor, fine motor, language, and personal and social developmental status can be assessed. The results of any subtest enable the teacher to judge the extent to which observed behaviors are comparable to those of nonhandicapped children at any chronological age level from 0 to 6 years.

Portage Guide to Early Education

Like the *Denver Developmental Screening Test*, the *Portage Guide* (1975) measures developmental status for ages 0 to 6 years. Gross and fine motor abilities are arranged in sequence from elementary to complex on separate scales. Chronological age is provided adjacent to the behaviors to be observed, enabling the child's developmental status to be compared with that of nonretarded 0 to 6-year-old children.

The Portage materials also include a file of suggested developmental activities for children at any 0 to 6-year-old level. A child having difficulty with any developmental scale item can thus be directed to an activity designed specifically to facilitate improvement at that level. The activity file also provides recommendations for curricula to remediate identified problems. This "cookbook" curriculum approach should be used as a springboard for the teacher's imagination and innovativeness.

PROJECT A.C.T.I.V.E.

A.C.T.I.V.E. is the acronym for All Children Totally Involved Exercising. The program (Vodola 1977) allegedly affords physical education opportunities for all children regardless of handicap. Among the target recipients of Project A.C.T.I.V.E. are mentally retarded children.

Built into the Project A.C.T.I.V.E. curriculum are physical and motor performance assessments, activity prescriptions, and strong emphasis on parental involvement. Project materials that focus on low motor ability and vitality may be valuable in individualizing physical education instruction for mentally retarded children. Other materials focus on postural abnormalities, motor disabilities or limitations, nutritional deficiencies, communication disorders, and breathing problems and may also be applicable to some retarded persons.

I CAN

The *I CAN* program (Wessel 1976, 1979, 1980) is similar to Project A.C.T.I.V.E. in that it provides assessment tools, activity prescriptions, and teaching strategies. *I CAN* materials have been field-tested among trainable and severely retarded children (CA 5–14). Either physical education specialists or classroom teachers can use the materials. Like Project A.C.T.I.V.E., *I CAN* facilitates development of a child's individualized educational program (IEP) pursuant to P.L. 94-142. Specific *I CAN* programs focus on fundamental skills, body management, health and fitness, aquatics, and leisure and recreation, including team sports, dance and individual sports, backyard and neighborhood activities, and outdoor activities. The 1980 series includes preprimary motor and play skills.

Translating Assessment Into Individualized Education

Assessment based both on observations and on formal data-gathering procedures provides insight into a child's physical education status and potential. This information also provides insights on development of the child's physical education in the most appropriate (i.e., least restrictive) environment. Evaluation of assessment data should determine (1) whether special services are indicated for physical education, (2) whether related services such as physical therapy, occupational therapy, or special transportation arrangements might benefit the child, (3) annual goals, and (4) short-term instructional objectives.

Annual goals appearing on the child's IEP provide focus for the child's special physical education. Short-term instructional objectives serve as behaviorally stated steps toward achievement of the annual goals.

For example, if an educable mentally retarded child is functioning below the 40th percentile on all items of the AAHPERD *Special Fitness Test for the Mildly Mentally Retarded*, an annual goal similar to the following would be appropriate:

Annual Goal: The child will improve her physical and motor fitness level to at least the 50th percentile in all items appearing on the *Special Fitness Test for the Mildly Mentally Retarded*.

Appropriate short-term instructional objectives might be stated as follows:

1. During the first three weeks of physical education, the child will run-walk the perimeter of the school playground (follow the fence line), completing three laps during each physical education period (cardiovascular endurance).
2. During the third through fifth weeks of physical education, the child will ascend-descend a 13-riser flight of stairs, completing four consecutive laps during each physical education period (cardiovascular endurance).
3. The child will hop on the _____ (preferred or nonpreferred) foot five times without breaking rhythm during three consecutive physical education periods (rhythm, explosive strength).

In another example, assessment might suggest the child's need to engage independently in group activities. This observation could result from observations of the child's engaging successfully in parallel and partner play. For this child, an annual goal might be stated as follows:

Annual Goal: The child will participate independently in two group-oriented physical education activities.

Short-term instructional objectives leading to fulfillment of the annual goal might be stated as follows:

1. The child will be present during, but not participate in, group-oriented activities two weeks prior to actual participation.
2. The child will participate in one group-oriented activity assisted by an able student three times per week for three successive weeks.

These examples of annual goals and short-term instructional objectives are *examples only*. Individualized instruction, in the spirit of P.L. 94–142, implies that there can be as many annual goals and short-term instructional objectives as there are individual special needs.

Incentives to Encourage Effort and Achievement

Motivational charts should be created and placed where they are visible. Use stars to signify levels of achievement and effort.

Designate a "Student of the Week" and display the student's activity efforts, accomplishments, interest, or a combination of these on a bulletin board with the student's photograph. Certificates or ribbons also can serve as tangible recognition of the student's efforts.

Beyond the Physical Education Class, What Next?

While some mentally retarded children will not develop physical or motor proficiencies measurable beyond the early childhood level on the developmental scales, others will be able to participate in special and regular intramural and interschool athletic activities. P.L. 94-142 includes sports and intramurals as part of physical education, and Section 504 guarantees the child access to any school program provided that the child is capable of safe and successful participation. Mental retardation alone is no longer an acceptable criterion for excluding a child from intramural or athletic program participation.

Mentally retarded persons are becoming more visible in regular school sport programs. Retarded learners are often capable of physical and motor performance commensurate with their nonretarded, chronological age peers. If a retarded person is capable of participating safely and successfully as a member of the school's regular athletic team, no justifiable reason exists for denying that person such an opportunity.

The Special Olympics program, sponsored by the Joseph P. Kennedy Jr. Foundation, has enhanced opportunities for retarded persons to develop athletic skills and enjoy athletic experiences (Figure 9.3). The Special Olympics oath, "Let me win, but if I cannot win, let me be brave in the attempt," embodies the Special Olympics' emphasis on participation. The Kennedy Foundation reports that in any one year over 1 million mentally retarded persons, ages 8 and over, with IQs of 75 or less, participate in Special Olympics activities. The Special Olympics, Inc., offers 14 official events including soccer, softball, volleyball, athletics (track and field), gymnastics, basketball, aquatics (swimming and diving), bowling, alpine and Nordic skiing, figure and speed skating, floor and poly hockey, and wheelchair events. O'Brien (1985) states: "The international goal of the Special Olympics, Inc., is to reach at least 46 different countries and provide athletic opportunities to over 2 million mentally retarded individuals by 1986."

Special Olympics has also developed year-round fitness and sport skill development programs. These programs enhance both fitness for living and competence in Special Olympics sport events.

Mentally retarded children mainstreamed into regular school intramural or interscholastic athletic programs generally are not eligible for participation in Special Olympics. An objective of Special Olympics is to encourage and enable the participant's "graduation" into a regular school sport program.

Further information about Special Olympics programs is available from local Special Olympics chapters, the state director, or from the national office.

Summary

Mental retardation is a handicap of degrees. In its milder forms, it may escape notice during early years. In more severe forms, constant, lifelong custodial care may be indicated.

Causes of mental retardation are many; the most common *identifiable* cause is Down syndrome. The cause in the majority of cases (80 to 90 percent), however, cannot be pinpointed.

Although persons with mental retardation generally achieve lower levels of physical and motor proficiency than do their chronological age peers of normal intellect, they are more like their nonhandicapped peers in physical and motor proficiency than in any other respect. It is often difficult to ascertain the extent to which performance deficits are a function of impoverished intellect or lack of opportunity. Data indicate that physical and motor proficiencies often can approach the norms of the nonhandicapped when quality physical education is provided.

Retarded persons are capable of achieving both significant nonphysical and motor proficiency results. In the nonphysical realm, self-esteem may improve markedly as

A

B

FIGURE 9.3. (A) Special Olympics pageantry, and (B) competition.

proficiencies are developed that are important to the child and others. Physical education facilitates the socialization process by providing opportunities for give-and-take in group-centered settings. The inherently motivating nature of motor activities should stimulate achievement in conversation and in the three Rs.

A number of special teaching methodologies are appropriate for instruction of persons with mental retardation. Teachers are urged to use short sentences and to consider attention span when presenting activities. The mentally handicapped child has a special need for structure in the learning environment. Teachers must also keep in mind that any newness often stresses the child who may have come to associate anything new with failure.

Meeting the mandates of P.L. 94-142 makes assessment a necessity. In selecting an assessment instrument, the educator must first identify which aspects of physical or motor performance are to be evaluated. When appropriate standardized tests are unavailable, criterion references can be used to evaluate performance. Standard tests often used to evaluate the performance of the mentally handicapped are the *Special Fitness Test for the Mildly Mentally Retarded*, the *Motor Fitness Test for the Moderately Mentally Retarded*, the *Bruininks-Oseretsky Scale of Motor Development*, the *Denver Developmental Screening Test*, and the *Portage Guide*.

Achievement in physical education can be reinforced by incentives, which may include inexpensive tangibles such as badges, ribbons, certificates, or wall charts. The incentive program provided by the Joseph P. Kennedy Jr. Foundation also is recommended. Finally, the opportunity for sports participation is recommended through involvement in the Kennedy Foundation's Special Olympics program.

References

AAHPERD. *Motor Fitness Testing Manual for the Moderately Mentally Retarded.* Reston, Va.: AAHPERD, 1975.

————. *Special Fitness Test Manual for Mildly Mentally Retarded Persons*, rev. Reston, Va.: AAHPERD, 1976.

————. *AAHPERD Health Related Physical Fitness Test Manual.* Reston, Va.: AAHPERD, 1980.

American Association on Mental Deficiency. *Classification in Mental Retardation.* Washington, D.C.: The Association, 1983.

A New Kind of Joy. Washington, D.C.: Special Olympics, n.d.

Barsch, R. *Achieving Perceptual-Motor Efficiency.* Seattle: Special Child Publications, 1968a.

————. *Enriching Perception and Cognition.* Seattle: Special Child Publications, 1968b.

Bruininks, R. H. *Bruininks-Oseretsky Test of Motor Proficiency: Examiner's Manual.* Circle Pines, Minn: American Guidance Service, 1978.

Caveny, P. A. Personal Communication. Lincoln Developmental Center, Lincoln, Ill., 15 August 1985.

Cegelka, P. T., and Prehm, H. J. *Mental Retardation: From Categories to People.* Columbus, Ohio: Charles E. Merrill, 1982.

Cohen, H. J., and Kaminer, R. K. Mental Retardation. In *Current Diagnosis 7*, edited by R. B. Conn. Philadelphia: W. B. Saunders, 1985.

Corder, W. O. Effects of a Physical Education Program on the Intellectual, Physical, and Social Development of Educable Mentally Retarded Boys. *Exceptional Children* 32:357–364, 1966.

Cratty, B. J. *Motor Activity in the Education of Retardates,* 2nd ed. Philadelphia: Lea & Febiger, 1974.

Doman, G. *What to Do About Your Brain Injured Child.* New York: Doubleday, 1974.

Francis, R., and Rarick, G. L. *Motor Characteristics of the Mentally Retarded.* Washington, D.C.: U. S. Office of Education, Cooperative Research Branch, 1963.

Frankenburg, W. K., Goldstein, A., and Camp B. *Denver Developmental Screening Test: Reference Manual,* rev. Denver: LADOCA Project and Publishing Foundation, 1975.

Glaze, R. E. *Height and Weight of Down Syndrome Children as Compared to Normal Children Aged Ten to Eighteen.* Unpublished masters study, Illinois State University, Normal, Ill., 1985.

Gruber, J. J. Implications of the Physical Education Program for Children With Learning Disabilities. *Journal of Learning Disabilities* 2:593–599, 1969.

Holmes, L. How Fathers Can Cause the Down Syndrome. *Human Nature:* October 1978. In *Readings in Down's Syndrome,* edited by I. Newman and S. J. Feldman. Guilford, Conn.: Special Learning Corporation, 1980.

Horgan, J. S. Mnemonic Strategy Instruction in Coding, Processing and Recall of Movement Related Cues by the Mentally Retarded. *Perceptual and Motor Skills* 57:547–557, 1983.

————. Issues in Memory for Movement With Mentally Retarded Children. In *Motor Development: Current Selected Research,* Vol. I, edited by J. E. Clark and J. H. Humphrey. Princeton, N. J.: Princeton Book Co., 1985.

Kephart, N. C. *The Slow Learner in the Classroom.* Columbus, Ohio: Charles E. Merrill, 1960.

Kidd, S. W. An open letter to the Committee on Terminology and Classification of AAMD from the Committee on Definition and Terminology of CEC-MR. *Education and Training of the Mentally Retarded* 14:74–76, 1979.

Kolstoe, O. P. *Mental Retardation: an Educational Viewpoint.* New York: Holt, Rinehart & Winston, 1972.

Melton, D. *When Children Need Help.* New York: Thomas and Crowell, 1972.

Morreau, L. E. Public Education and the Mentally Retarded. Lecture given at the 1985 Region VI annual convention of the American Association on Mental Deficiency, Matteson, Ill., 14 August 1985.

National Information Center for Handicapped Children and Youth. *Mental Retardation.* Washington, D.C.: The Center, 1983.

Newell, K. M. Motor Skill Orientation and Mental Retardation: Overview of Traditional and Current Orientations. In *Motor Development: Current Selected Research,* Vol. I, edited by J. E. Clark and J. H. Humphrey. Princeton, N. J.: Princeton Book Co., 1985.

Nihara, K., Foster, R., Shellhaas, M., and Leland, H. *AAMD Adaptive Behavior Scale,* 1979 rev. Washington, D.C.: American Association on Mental Deficiency, 1974.

Nylander, B., and Nylander, I. (as cited by Heber). Acute Head Injuries in Children: Traumatology, Therapy, and Prognosis. *Acta Paediatrica* 152–157, suppl.:1–34, 1964.

O'Brien, K. Personal interview with the Illinois Special Olympics Program Director. Illinois State University, Normal, Ill., 5 August 1985.

Pitt, D. *Your Down's Syndrome Child . . . You Can Help Him Develop From Infancy to Adulthood.* Arlington, Texas: National Association for Retarded Citizens, 1974.

Polacek, J. J., Wang, P. Y., and Eichstaedt, C. B. *A Study of Physical and Health Related Fitness Levels of Mild, Moderate, and Down Syndrome Students in Illinois.* Normal, Ill.: Illinois State University Press, 1985.

Portage Guide to Early Education. Portage, Wis.: Cooperative Educational Service Agency No. 12, 1975.

Priest, J. H. Chromosomal Disorders. In *Current Diagnosis* 7, edited by R. B. Conn. Philadelphia: W. B. Saunders, 1985.

Reid, G. Overt and Covert Rehearsal in Short-Term Motor Memory of Mentally Retarded and Nonretarded Persons. *American Journal of Mental Deficiency* 85:69–77, 1980.

Rothstein, J. *Mental Retardation.* New York: Holt, Rinehart & Winston, 1970.

Sloan, W. The Lincoln-Oseretsky Motor Development Scale. *Genetic Psychology Monographs* 51:183–252, 1955.

Share, J., and French, R. *Motor Development of Down Syndrome Children: Birth to Six Years.* Sherman Oaks, Calif.: J. B. Share, 1982.

Soloman, A., and Prangle, R. Demonstrations of Physical Fitness Improvement in the EMR. *Exceptional Children* 34:1977–1981, 1967.

Sugden, D. A. Visual Motor Short-Term Memory in Educationally Subnormal Boys. *British Journal of Educational Psychology* 48:330–339, 1978

Thomas, K. T. Applying Knowledge of Motor Development to Mentally Retarded Children. In *Motor Development During Childhood and Adolescence,* edited by J. R. Thomas. Minneapolis: Burgess Publishing, 1984.

Todd, R., and Nevill, J. The Sequelae of Tuberculosis Meningitis. *Archives of Disease in Childhood* 39:213–226, 1967.

Trainer, M. C. Don't Take That *Baby* Home. *The Humanist,* July/August 1978. In *Readings in Down's Syndrome,* edited by I. Newman and S. J. Feldman. Guilford, Conn.: Special Learning Corporation, 1980.

U.S. Department of Education. *To Assure the Free Appropriate Public Education of All Handicapped Children.* Washington D.C.: The Department, 1984.

Vodola, T., Director. Project A.C.T.I.V.E. Grant sponsored by Elementary and Secondary Education Act, Title III-IV (c) and Division of Research, Planning, and Evaluation, New Jersey State Department of Education, 1977.

Werder, J. K., and Kalakian, L. H. *Assessment in Adapted Physical Education.* Minneapolis: Burgess Publishing, 1985.

Wessel, J. *I CAN.* Northbrook, Ill.: Hubbard Scientific Co., 1976.

———. *I CAN: Primary Skills.* Northbrook, Ill.: Hubbard Scientific Co., 1979.

———. *I CAN: Preprimary Motor and Play Skills.* East Lansing, Mich.: Instructional Media Center, Michigan State University, 1980.

Winnick, J., and Jansma, P. *Physical Education Inservice Resources Manual for All Handicapped Children Act* (P.L. 94–142). Brockport, N.Y.: by authors, 1978.

CHAPTER 10

Learning Disabilities

. . . and report cards I was always afraid to show
Mama'd come to school
and as I'd sit there softly cryin'
Teacher'd say he's just not tryin'
Got a good head if he'd apply it
but you know yourself
it's always somewhere else
I'd build me a castle
with dragons and kings
and I'd ride off with them
As I stood by my window
and looked out on those
Brooklyn roads

(Neil Diamond, "Brooklyn Roads")

In 1985 the Association for Children and Adults with Learning Disabilities adopted a definition of **specific learning disabilities** that stresses the potential of these disabilities to affect people throughout their lives:

> Specific Learning Disabilities is a chronic condition of presumed neurological origin which selectively interferes with the development, integration, and/or demonstration of verbal and/or non-verbal abilities. Specific Learning Disabilities exists as a distinct handicapping condition in the presence of average to superior intelligence, adequate sensory and motor systems, and adequate learning opportunities. The condition varies in its manifestations and in degree of severity. Throughout life the condition can affect self-esteem, education, vocation, socialization, and/or daily living activities.
>
> *(National Information Center for Handicapped Children and Youth 1985, p. 2)*

Possible Causes and Diagnosis

The U.S. Department of Education's Special Education Programs identified over 1.8 million learning disabled children in U.S. schools in 1983–1984. This is an increase of 127 percent over the 1976–1977 school year. According to the 1983–1984 statistic, 4.57 percent of children enrolled in the public schools were diagnosed as learning disabled and were receiving special education services.

The child with a learning disability possesses at least average intellectual abilities. In fact, some children with learning disabilities exhibit potential that exceeds the norm. Children are designated as having a possible learning disability when normal potential and opportunity exist, yet achievement is not in accordance with potential. Among learning disabled children, difficulties stem *not* from deprivation of information (i.e., negative environmental influences or sensory modality incapacity), but from *inability to utilize information adequately.* These children are identified as having emotional, motoric, sensorial, and intellectual integrity, but are unable to learn in the usual manner.

Learning disabilities have been attributed to various causes. As yet, the genesis of learning disabilities is not understood, and learning disabled children are homogeneous only to the extent that all are deficient in achievement despite seemingly normal potential and opportunity to learn. Cause-related theories range from genetic heredity to chemical imbalance. In some, the disability is believed to reside in the peripheral nervous system's inability to convert sensations accurately into electrical impulses. In such cases, the brain may be receiving portrayals of reality that are, in fact, distorted. In a few persons, learning disabilities may be associated with difficulties experienced during pregnancy or delivery. Inadequate prenatal care, prenatal maternal malnutrition, difficult delivery, prematurity, temporary anoxia at time of delivery, and Rh incompatibility are among complications seen in a disproportionate number of persons with learning disabilities. Although cause-and-effect relationships between these factors and the occurrence of learning disabilities cannot be drawn readily in many instances, such relationships are still suspected.

Learning disorders are generally categorized as **verbal** and **nonverbal.** Verbal non-achievement is characterized by disorders in spoken language, reading, written language, and arithmetic. Characteristic nonverbal disorders involve motor dysfunctions, problems of perception, problems of attention (distractibility and disinhibition), hyperactivity, perseveration, and social imperceptions. Disorders in more than one performance area occur frequently. This phenomenon suggests a possible interrelationship among the various dysfunctions.

For designation purposes, children with learning disabilities exhibit intelligence quotient (IQ) of 90 or above. In diagnosing learning disabilities, an IQ test and achievement tests are administered. Once IQ has been determined to be average or above, achievement tests are administered. Discrepancies between achievement potential, indicated by comparison of IQ scores with actual achievement as measured by achievement test scores, become the primary basis for the learning disabilities diagnosis.

Diagnosis of learning disability is a relatively new phenomenon. Until recently, learning disabled children often were misclassified as mentally retarded, emotionally disturbed, slow, or lazy. Incorrect diagnoses then led to improper educational placement and continued nonachievement.

While our understanding of learning disabilities is still incomplete, we now are aware that learning disabilities do exist independent of other conditions that affect learning and have similar symptoms. "Disability," as used in the term "learning disability" does *not* mean incapacity. Children with learning disabilities *can learn* in accordance with their potential provided that their unique learning needs are understood and accommodated.

A variety of characteristics have been associated with youngsters who have learning disabilities. A national task force tallied the numerous labels and terms related to this area and found 99 characteristics reported in the literature. The ten most frequently reported symptoms were: (1) hyperactivity, (2) perceptual-motor impairments, (3) emotional lability (frequent shifts in emotional mood), (4) general coordination deficits, (5) disorders of attention (short attention span, distractibility, perseveration), (6) impulsivity, (7) disorders of memory and thinking, (8) specific academic problems in reading, arithmetic, writing, spelling, (9) disorders of speech and hearing, and (10) equivocal neurological signs and electroencephalographic (EEG) irregularities (Hallahan and Kauffman 1982).

Learning disabilities have implications for physical education. Many problems involved in learning disabilities are exposed in movement-centered expression. Children with learning disabilities often exhibit problems in balance and coordination. These children have problems organizing time and space, which precipitates awkward and dysrhythmic movements. Writing and drawing problems involve an inability to execute fine motor coordinations.

Development of cognitive and verbal behaviors in learning disabled children affects their performance in physical education. Texts by Keogh and Sugden (1985), Thomas (1984), Sage (1984), and Gallahue (1982), although not intended specifically for the learning disabled, focus on learning through movement. Traditionally, development of such behaviors has been the responsibility of the classroom teacher. Efforts by the physical educator to reinforce cognitive and verbal learning are most successful when coordinated with the efforts of the classroom teacher.

Learning disabled children often manifest behavioral disturbances that have implications for physical education. Some children exhibit emotional disturbances, short attention spans, distractibility, and hyperactivity. Recognizing and understanding the cause of these behavioral traits enables the teacher to plan success-oriented physical education experiences.

This chapter focuses on (1) delineating specific learning and behavioral disorders among learning disabled children, (2) identifying teaching methods to accommodate these special learning needs, and (3) citing specific teaching strategies and remedial activities for physical education.

Nonverbal Disorders

Disorders of Motor Function

Deficits in motor ability are particularly distressing to learning disabled children. They experience feelings of ineptness in the presence of friends, peers, and important others, because awkwardness sets them apart. Much of the frustration of learning disabled children with motor dysfunction stems from their not being able to translate knowledge into required movement. Examples include inability to coordinate body motions on a swing, climb a jungle gym, tie one's shoes, or ride a bicycle or tricycle. Children with learning disability often experience difficulty in weaving individual body parts into coordinated body motion.

Such dysfunctions may stem from more than one cause. Although dysfunctions may be due to motor mechanisms, the child also may be trying to learn from a visual model, and may not be able to function when relying on visual cues. In another example, the child who does not function well when relying on auditory information will not experience success in an environment in which sound provides the primary sensory input.

Achievement tests administered to diagnose learning disabilities should yield information that will determine functioning and dysfunctioning modalities. This information influences the communication approaches chosen for use with each child.

Motor dysfunction may be associated with deficits in coordination, balance, agility, body image, tactile and kinesthetic awareness, spatial awareness, laterality, directionality, motor planning, and dysrhythmia. With the exception of motor planning and dysrhythmia, many activities to rehabilitate basic motor and perceptual-motor deficits are found in Chapters 5 and 7. To alter motor planning in which the child cannot execute a series of movements required for task completion, begin with discrete activities followed by serial activities. A **discrete movement** is the execution of a single motor act (e.g., bounce the ball and catch it). Following discrete skills, the child should execute movements in **simple series** in which the same skill is repeated. Dribbling a ball or continuous hopping are examples. Next, the child should execute tasks in **complex series.** This requires execution of many different discrete acts in sequential order (Figure 10.1).

Motor planning is similar to the classroom-related competence termed "sequential thinking." The final, desired result of motor planning and sequential thinking is the ability to **execute behaviors in proper sequential order.** For instance, some learning disabled children are unable to follow the steps necessary to complete the tasks required for long division. Given that there is some association between sequential thinking and motor planning, movement experiences requiring motor planning should be included in the special programming of certain learning disabled children.

The learning disabled child with **dysrhythmia** has difficulty organizing time. Tasks that require rhythm capabilities begin with noncomplex discrete acts (finger tapping, foot tapping, hand clapping). Initially, only a single cycle of a skill may be possible. Gradually, more cycles of a skill can be executed in correct rhythm.

The child with dysrhythmia needs concrete cues to achieve and maintain rhythmic performance. Among learning disabled dysrhythmic children, certain sensory modalities, although intact, may not function properly to provide meaningful information. If this occurs, the teacher must know which sensory modalities are functioning. This information can then be used to provide cues for the child in accordance with learning strengths. Cues may be tactile, kinesthetic, auditory, or visual (Figure 10.2). Once rhythmic behavior is established, these functioning cues should then be paired with cues that stimulate a dysfunctioning sensory modality. In this way, children can use their properly functioning sensory modalities to reinforce information being processed by the problematic modality. As proficiency improves, gradually "fade" cues to the stronger modality, and gently shift emphasis to and dependence on the modality being corrected.

Once rhythmic capabilities show improvement through reliance on heavily accented cues, gradually reduce the intensity of the cues. The objective should be a gradual fading that will not precipitate reversal to dysrhythmic behavior. For auditory cue fading, gradually reduce the volume of sounds that are heavily rhythmic. For visual cue fading, gradually alter an arm gesture to a hand or finger gesture. The goal of rhythm learning, which is accomplished to varying degrees by children with dysrhythmia, is achieving intrinsic or self-control of rhythm maintenance.

Early studies by Kephart, Getman, and Delacato produced theories that stated, in general, that motor activities, properly applied, could help young children overcome delays or disabilities in academic endeavors. Researchers have not, however, been able to prove a correlation between improvement of motor abilities and increased intellectual capacity. Cratty (1979) supports the case that good motor programs can have positive effects on academic performance. He states: "Although motor activity itself may not enhance learning in a direct way through movement, there are components of the motor task (i.e., doing *something* for increased periods of time) that may indeed positively transfer to academic learning. An increased number of studies suggest that (1) attention span influences learning, and (2) attention span may be improved by various techniques available to the classroom teacher" (p. 42). Gallahue (1982) agrees with Cratty and states: ". . . the value of perceptual-motor experiences to a general state of

FIGURE 10.1. Execution of discrete acts in sequential order. (A) "Go to the barrel." (B) "Place the beanbag in the barrel." (C) "Return to your chair." (D) "Sit down."

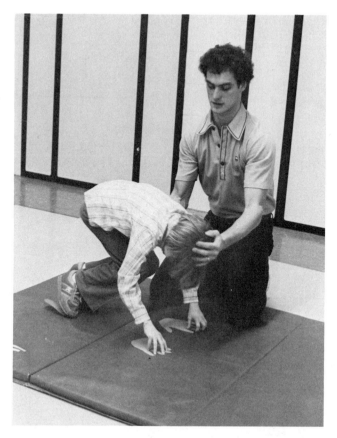

FIGURE 10.2. Pairing visual with tactile-kinesthetic cues.

readiness should not be dismissed. Enhancement of body, spatial, directional, and temporal awareness as a means of guiding the child toward improved movement control and efficiency in fundamental movement is worthwhile in itself. Practice in perceptual-motor activities will enhance perceptual-motor abilities. Whether these abilities have a *direct* effect on academic performance is questionable. One can be assured, however, that they do play an important role in developing and refining the child's movement abilities" (p. 317).

Further assistance in teaching learning disabled children with motor dysfunction can be found in Chapter 6, Fundamental Motor Skills.

Problems of Attention

Distractibility

Many learning disabled children are unable to concentrate on appropriate tasks. For children termed **distractible,** the typical learning environment is often overstimulating. Lights, bright colors, extraneous noises, and nonessential equipment and supplies all draw the distractible child's attention away from tasks. When teaching these children, remove nonessential stimuli from the learning environment. Equipment not in use should be put away; equipment to be used should be available only when needed. Whenever possible, activity should take place in a room or gym with softly colored walls without pictures. When outdoors, distractions are more difficult to control.

When using record equipment, ensure that records do not have distracting scratches. If the spoken word is important, there should be no background music. If rhythm is important, the recording should not include talking or singing.

For distractible children, limit the space in which activity occurs. When working one-on-one with the distractible child, have the child stand close to, and facing, a screen or wall to create a nondistracting visual field. To avoid having the teacher's visual presence be an unnecessary distraction, stand behind the child.

Concurrent with reducing distractions in the learning environment, the stimulus value of objects used for teaching should be enhanced. For example, a ball used for teaching should be a color that contrasts with the room.

Exuberant praise for tasks well done is contraindicated because it, too, is distracting. A low-keyed "well done" or "that's good" is not only sufficient, but more appropriate.

For distractible children, situations that include unpredictable movements by players or balls simultaneously in motion are contraindicated. By controlling the quantity and variety of environmental stimuli, the child may learn gradually to deal with more than one stimulus at a time.

Disinhibition

The child with **disinhibition** also exhibits attention problems. The inattention is, however, more covert than that of the distractible child. Random shifts in attention and daydreaming are characteristic behaviors. At times, the child with disinhibition will verbalize a thought that has just come to mind. Because such utterances are usually out of context with the activity, others often dismiss the child as being odd or strange.

Carlton and Rainey (1984) suggest that disinhibition problems may be reduced by establishing routines for the child at school and at home. Routines reduce anxieties over uncertainties in the environment. Attention shifts and drifts into daydreaming reflect the child's need to escape anxiety, which can be decreased through routine, thereby perhaps reducing disinhibition. The routine in physical education may require starting and ending each class in the same way. Special clothing, worn only for physical education, can help establish a frame of reference during physical education periods. Yahraes (1982, p. 22) agrees with Carlton and Rainey when he states:

> Remember that many learning disabled children need calm, "structured" surroundings. Schedule an activity—eating, playing, doing school work, reading with an adult—at the same time every day. In school, such a child is likely to do better in very small groups. Try to seat him or her in a spot that will minimize distraction from activities of other students. For children with little or no sense of space or direction, some teachers have found it useful to mark off the desk space on the floor with adhesive tape. The markings help the child to understand where he or she belongs and to gradually comprehend the meaning of left, right, back, and front.

Because it is appropriate to stand near the disinhibited child, the teacher can note shifts in attention as they occur. At that time, the child's attention should be gently, but firmly, reverted to appropriate tasks.

Another means to reduce disinhibition is behavior modification techniques. Ways to reinforce desired behavior, in this case attentive behavior, are presented in Chapter 12, Modifying Behavior in Physical Education Settings.

Hyperactivity

Symptoms of **hyperactivity** (also referred to as **attention deficit disorder** by Prazar and Friedman [1985]) may surface when the child begins regular school classes. Parents may not have noticed attention problems in the preschool years because the child was not required previously to concentrate in a room with other children.

The hyperactive child seems always to be in motion. These children find sitting or standing still for any length of time difficult or impossible. Hyperactive children will tap their feet, tap their pencils, and manipulate or exploit any object within reach. Such children routinely interfere with other children.

Hyperactivity in any child varies from day to day. Mood changes may reflect environmental influences, failure to take prescribed medications, or efforts to change medication or dosage to achieve more effective behavior control.

In most cases, hyperactivity disappears when the child reaches adolescence. Although hyperactivity will eventually pass, its effects on learning during critical early years may persist. For this reason, managing hyperactivity has both short- and long-term significance.

Efforts to manage hyperactivity are similar to those used to manage distractibility. The space in which activity occurs should be no larger than necessary to accommodate essential movement. Distractions, indeed, any source of unwanted activity, should be eliminated. Particularly with hyperactive children, equipment should be provided only when it is to be used. Verbal instructions should be brief to limit inordinate demands for sitting or standing still. For the hyperactive child, an error is committed if activity is used to help "blow off steam." These children often are not in control of their behavior. High-key activity intended to "blow off steam" will backfire, and the child may become even more hyperactive and distractible. In effect, misdirected efforts to "blow off steam" usually "fan the flames."

The physical education environment for hyperactive children must be structured to control the child's opportunity to make choices. For example, rather than ask children to get balls, the balls should be handed out. As the child becomes able to self-manage behavior in the physical education environment, the structure can be relaxed gradually.

On days when hyperactivity is a particular problem, activities should remain low key. At these times, activities that excite the child or call for creativity are contraindicated. Sometimes, pairing the hyperactive child with a youngster who is not hyperactive controls unwanted activity.

Occasionally, the child's ability to self-manage hyperactive behavior should be determined. This could be done by offering the child a cookie (or some other intense reinforcer) for which the child must abandon the unwanted behavior. If the child preempts the undesired behavior to accept the cookie, the youngster has demonstrated self-control. As the child learns to control his behavior to achieve positive consequences (e.g., a cookie), the teacher can rely more on behavior modification to achieve desired changes.

Perseveration

Perseveration is *uncontrolled* persistence in an activity. The child who perseverates is unable to stop an activity once it has begun.

Perseveration is different in character from long attention span, which implies the ability to persist in *purposeful* behavior. With perseveration, the child is out of control and continues the activity without purpose. Perseverators may incessantly rock, tap fingers, tap hands, tap feet, blink, cry, or laugh. The possible perseverations are limitless. The unifying characteristic is that, in all cases, the child is out of control and the behavior continues without purpose.

In a physical education setting, the perseverator may run but cannot stop. For example, the child may run, but may not be able to combine the run with a leap or jump. The youngster may begin dribbling a ball, but may not be able to stop. If asked to execute one forward roll, the child will persist in executing five or six.

In physical education, the perseverator should be given activities in which the motor responses are varied and change often. Changes may occur in required motor response and in the pace. The child should be eased gradually into activity in which *limited* persistence is required.

The perseverator will often need a cue to interrupt the unwanted behavior. Verbal cues ("Stop!"), visual cues (hand gestures), or tactile-kinesthetic cues (a tap on the shoulder) are examples.

When perseveration occurs predictably during a given activity, the child should be diverted from those circumstances. If ball bouncing evokes perseveration, the child should avoid ball bouncing. To avoid perseveration-evoking activity, the teacher should control task requirements and be prepared to intervene momentarily.

Social Imperception

Learning disabled children with **social imperception** are unable to comprehend the meaning of their actions or those of others. They are unable to interpret social expressions, gestures, and body language. These children often exhibit quantities and types of affection that are inappropriate. Social imperception may surface, for example, when the child "crashes" an orderly line, and is then angered by the angry response. The child's "in line" behavior is controlled in the teacher's presence, but when the teacher is absent, the child will misbehave. These children have difficulty making and keeping friends. They do not understand the implications of their actions, and classmates tire of the child's continued inconsideration.

Structure and close supervision are necessary for children with social imperception. These children should be taught in small groups so social dynamics can be monitored. The social implications of their activity and behavior must be explained. Repeated efforts must be made to show these chidren how social amenities, practiced in physical education, have relevance in other relationships as well.

The responses to social imperception should be empathetic but not permissive. The teacher must be understanding, but firm, in dealing with the child's socialization.

Verbal Disorders

Disorders of Auditory Language

Auditory language deficits manifest themselves in problems of receptive and expressive language and in auditory memory problems. The child with a **receptive language disorder** (i.e., *receptive aphasia*) has difficulty understanding the spoken word. For these children, words should be used sparingly at first. Instruction should be conveyed in phrases or simple sentences. As one means of expanding the child's receptive language capabilities, the teacher may gradually shift toward reliance on verbal cues. In many instances, the child will benefit from visual instructions that accompany verbal instructions. Visual supplements to verbal instructions could be pictures, demonstrations, or gestures. Tactile and kinesthetic cues also are indicated.

Use caution in substituting words that have similar meanings. For instance, the receptive aphasic child may respond when the teacher says "*throw* the ball," but may not respond to "*pitch* the ball." Likewise, the child may understand "big" but not "large," or "small" but not "little." The physical educator can expand the child's receptive language by consciously pairing a word that the child comprehends with another of similar meaning: "This is a big ball. It is also a *large* ball. Big and large are the same."

Articulate words clearly for children with receptive language disorders. Slurred words, idioms, and slang are a problem for them. To interpret verbal communication, the receptive aphasic child should be near the speaker so sounds can be plainly heard. In this position, the youngster can capitalize on visual cues including lip movements, facial expressions, gestures, and body language. Acoustics in the teaching environment should be good, and the environment should be free of extraneous sounds.

Children with **expressive aphasia** (expressive language problems) understand language, but are unable to verbalize that understanding. These children tend to be nonverbal. When they do verbalize, they exhibit limited vocabulary, incomplete phraseology, and poor syntax.

Because movement experiences seem to give satisfaction and a sense of well-being to children with expressive aphasia, such exercises become a prime source of conversation and vocabulary development. Many learning disabled children exhibit greater tendency to talk when engaged in activity or when the conversation turns to activity.

Children with **auditory memory problems** are unable to follow more than one direction at a time. They are also unable to carry out an instruction when time lapses between the instruction and the desired action.

For children with auditory memory problems, verbal instructions should precede *immediately* the desired response. When the child experiences difficulty in carrying out more than one direction at a time, the teacher must exercise caution in giving sequential verbal directions. Once the child performs a single verbal instruction on a consistent basis, two directions at one time may be given (e.g., go to Heather, and join hands). Gradually, the number of instructions may be increased.

The child with auditory memory problems is better able to perform multistaged auditory directions when mentally and physically fresh (i.e., early in the day, early in the period). As the school day or period wears on, the child may demonstrate less mature patterns of auditory memory behavior.

Disorders of Written Language

Difficulties in written expression may reflect lack of comprehension and also problems of fine motor coordination. Writing deficiencies also are known to result from a dissociation condition.

The child exhibiting **dissociation** is unable to visualize how parts merge to form a whole. Dissociation in movement is characterized by disintegrated responses or responses that overlook certain body segments. Dissociation in writing is manifested by letters or words written in disjointed fashion. The word "dog," for example, might be written as shown in Figure 10.3.

Remediating writing problems founded in lack of fine motor coordination and dissociation should concern the physical educator. To help remedy these problems, manipulative activities that use fine hand and finger muscles and activities that develop tactile and kinesthetic awareness of the hands and fingers are indicated. Ball handling and sand play are two examples of such activities. To select activities to promote fine motor coordination in a particular child, an occupational therapist should be consulted. To help remedy dissociation problems, activities that require total body action should be used. When children experience total body action (e.g., as in running, swimming, jumping jacks), they may begin to understand the association of body parts by sensing their body parts working simultaneously. Other relevant activities include having stu-

FIGURE 10.3. Dissociation in writing.

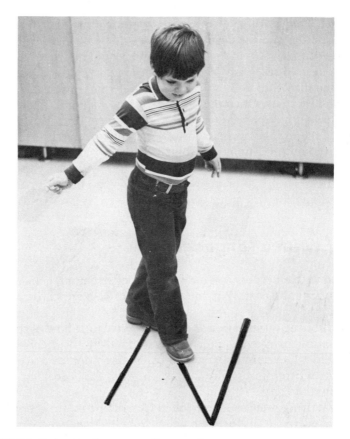

FIGURE 10.4. Heel-to-toe walking on letters—a concrete experience.

dents walk on lines that form geometric shapes, letters, or words (Figure 10.4). To make shapes, use tape that contrasts in color with the gym floor. Finally, children can be encouraged to develop writing skills by writing their own safety rules and by writing about their physical education experiences.

Disorders of Arithmetic

To assist the learning disabled child who has **arithmetic disorders,** give the child measured score-keeping responsibilities. This activity is motivating and will increase the child's interest in dealing with numbers and number concepts. The child also learns number concepts when instructed to hop five times or throw a ball at a target five times. A number card that requires an appropriate number of responses (e.g., clap your hands as many times as the number indicates) teaches number concepts.

Ask the child to use a tape measure and to outline the dimensions of a court. On the floor, place adjoining squares with numbers inside and ask the child to hop into two, three, or four squares, then total the points.

Number concepts also are learned through playing games (e.g., first, second, and third base; half court; quarters of play; nine innings; three strikes). The physical educator should be able to include many activities in which arithmetic and number concepts are learned through movement.

Disorders of Reading

Many learning disabled children experience difficulty in understanding the printed word. The child may understand the spoken word, but be unable to recognize printed words. Inability to comprehend the written word is termed **dyslexia** (a Greek word meaning "word blindness").

The physical educator can reinforce reading skills for dyslexic children by integrating written words and sentences with verbal directions. Signs that say "stop," "go," "fast," and "slow," when used simultaneously with the spoken word, provide help. Drawings accompanied by an appropriate printed word or phrase (e.g., four push-ups, run in place, touch toes) are appropriate for some activities. Students can read aloud their own simple written safety rules.

Children should be encouraged to read about sports, particularly the involvement of young people in sports, to stimulate interest in reading. A child who does not like to read, for whatever reason, will tend to want to read about the subject she likes. Stories about games and sports often motivate reading interest.

Summary

Children with learning disabilities possess normal or above-normal intelligence. For these children, difficulties in learning arise from an inability to assimilate available information. Although the learning and behavioral manifestations of learning disabilities are identifiable, the root causes are not understood.

The term *learning disabilities* covers a variety of *verbal* and *nonverbal* disorders. Verbal behaviors include disorders of written and spoken language, reading, and arithmetic. Nonverbal disorders include problems of perception, inattention, hyperactivity, perseveration, and social imperception. Each disorder has implications for learning in physical education.

Remember that motor disabilities have a strong influence on how children feel about themselves and how other children accept or reject them. Should a youngster possess low levels of motor ability, and should individualized physical education programming be called for, placement in the adapted physical education class is indicated. Meyen (1982, p. 340) warns: "To place a learning disabled child in a regular class where the disability will be further debilitating is foolish. For example, the child with difficulty in spatial orientation, directionality, and gross and fine motor coordination easily can become the subject of ridicule and failure if integrated into regular physical education class. The child's needs for physical education are vastly different from those of peers who may be ready for highly coordinated physical activities and competitive sports."

When learning disabilities are manifested in verbal disorders, activities can be prescribed in which verbal learning and verbal concepts are inculcated. This capitalizes on the motivating nature of movement experiences to overcome learning frustrations in problematic verbal areas. In dealing with children who have nonverbal disorders, Chapters 6 and 23 are particularly helpful. Effective methods of managing the difficult behaviors of some children with learning disabilities are discussed in Chapter 12.

References

Cratty, B. J. *Perceptual and Motor Development in Infants and Children*, 2nd ed. Englewood Cliffs, N.J.: Prentice-Hall, 1979.

Carlton, G., and Rainey, D. Teaching Learning Disabled Children to Help Themselves. *The Directive Teacher* 6(1): Winter/Spring 1984, 8–9.

Gallahue, D. L. *Understanding Motor Development in Children*. New York: John Wiley & Sons, 1982.

Hallahan, D. P., and Kauffman, J. M. *Exceptional Children*, 2nd ed. Englewood Cliffs, N.J.: Prentice-Hall, 1982.

Keogh, J., and Sugden, D. *Movement Skill Development*. New York: Macmillan, 1985.

Meyen, E. L. *Exceptional Children and Youth, An Introduction*, 2nd ed. Denver: Love Publishing, 1982.

National Information Center for Handicapped Children and Youth. *News Digest*, June 1985, p. 2.

Prazar, G., and Friedman, S. B. Behavioral Problems in Children and Adolescents. In *Current Diagnosis* 7, edited by R. B. Conn. Philadelphia: W. G. Saunders, 1985, 1066–1070.

Sage, G. H. *Motor Learning and Control*. Dubuque, Iowa: Wm. C. Brown Publishers, 1984.

Thomas, J. R. *Motor Development During Childhood and Adolescence*. Minneapolis: Burgess Publishing, 1984.

Yahraes, H. *Learning Disabilities: Problems and Progress*. Pamphlet #578. New York: Public Affairs Committee, 1982.

CHAPTER 11

Emotional Disturbance and Behavior Disorders

> *I can still feel the panic when I hear the phone ring . . . I automatically think someone is calling to tell me my son has just hurt a kid, or broken a window . . . even though things are better now. The teacher he has now has made a tremendous difference . . . I can get through a day without constant fear.*
>
> *(Common Sense From Closer Look 1979, p. 1)*

To imply that a child has an emotional disturbance is like saying that the child has a fever. Behavioral handicaps sufficient to be considered emotional disturbance have, like fevers, many causes and degrees of severity. Depending on the criteria used to define **emotional disturbance,** 2 to 22 percent of school-age youth manifest one or more of the conditions. Specific figures gathered from Public Law 94-142 data for the school year 1982–1983 show that 8.2 percent of legally handicapped children, between the ages of 3 and 21, are labeled as being emotionally disturbed (U.S. Department of Education 1984).

P.L. 94-142 defines serious emotional disturbance as follows:

A condition exhibiting one or more of the following characteristics over a long period of time and to a marked degree, which adversely affects educational performance: (1) an inability to learn which cannot be explained by intellectual, sensory, or health factors, (2) an inability to build or maintain satisfactory interpersonal relationships with peers and teachers, (3) inappropriate types of behavior or feelings under normal circumstances, (4) a general pervasive mood of unhappiness or depression, and (5) a tendency to develop physical symptoms or fears associated with personal or school problems.

(Federal Register 42, 23 August 1977, pp. 42478–42479).

An inability to learn is perhaps the single most commonly observed characteristic of all disturbed children. When all other factors that could impede learning have been eliminated, emotional disturbance becomes suspect. An inability to build or maintain interpersonal relationships includes more than an inability to get along with others. Such persons appear shy and do not convey warmth or sympathy toward others. They do not work well or play well either alone or with others. Children exhibiting unsatisfactory relationships usually are quite visible to their peers. When inappropriate types of behavior or feelings appear in these youngsters, they are often deemed "odd" by others. Such children may be overly aggressive and hyperactive, or overly passive and hypoactive. Mood variations may range from detachment to tantrums. General moods of unhappiness or depression are extremely common and are operative most of the time. These children experience virtually no joy in life. Finally, the tendency to develop illnesses, pains, or fears associated with personal or school problems is common. The anxieties stemming from perceived stress, whether real or not real, are sufficient to evoke psychosomatic illness ranging from nausea to headaches to ulcers.

Terms used to describe severe behavior problems include *emotionally disturbed, emotionally handicapped, psychological disorders,* and *behavior disorders* (National Information Center for Handicapped Children and Youth 1983b). Hallahan and Kauffman (1982, p. 146) explain their use of the term of **emotional disturbance** as follows: "We use the terms emotional disturbance and emotionally disturbed . . . to refer to the group of children who exhibit maladaptive social-emotional behavior . . . . We have chosen the term emotionally disturbed because we believe it is more familiar to students . . . and because it is the term used in P.L. 94-142 and government regulations."

Although there is inconsistency in both terminology and main points of emphasis, most definitions seem to agree that being emotionally disturbed involves the following: (1) behavior that goes to an extreme—behavior that is not just slightly different from the usual, (2) a problem that is ongoing—one that does not disappear, and (3) behavior that is unacceptable because of social or cultural expectations (Hallahan and Kauffman 1982).

A distinct difference must be made between *having* an emotional disturbance and *being* emotionally disturbed. Having an emotional disturbance in response to frustration, disappointment, or sadness is expected and normal. Striking out in a softball game is frustrating. Receiving a B instead of an A is disappointing. Experiencing the death of a friend evokes sadness. Responses to these situations are more or less disturbing, but these disturbances are transient and are consistent with normal expectations.

In contrast, being emotionally disturbed is characterized by behavior that is disordered to a *marked* degree and occurs over an extended period of time. Emotional disturbance generally does not go away of its own accord, and often becomes more pronounced in the absence of intervention.

While it is important to differentiate between being emotionally disturbed and having an emotional disturbance, this task is often difficult, particularly during the early stages, because early symptoms are usually present in everyone's behavior. According to Bower (1969, p. 178) "what one is attempting to define is the beginning of a process and not the ending—the sniffles and sneezes—as it were, rather than the full fever." Although true emotional disturbance often is difficult to diagnose in its initial stages, particularly in less than severe cases, timeliness of diagnosis is essential for effective intervention.

Degrees of Emotional Disturbance

Degrees of emotional disturbance include behavior disorders, neuroses, and psychoses. While less severe forms of emotional disturbance may not require remediation or are remediable through educational procedures, more serious forms require direct medical or psychiatric intervention. In the latter instances, educational procedures may supplement medical or psychiatric methods, with education often having to occur in relatively specialized settings.

Behavior Disorders

Children with behavior disorders exhibit a variety of symptomatic behaviors. While these behaviors are varied, they remain fixed over time and tend toward extremes. Terms that identify behavior disorders often overlap in definition, and in many instances, behavior disorders are interrelated. Common symptoms include delinquency, hypoactivity, withdrawal, pervasive anxiety, social maladjustment, aggression, tantrums, truancy, running away, extreme mood shifts, hypersensitivity, and hyperactivity. Prazar and Friedman (1985) are using a new term to describe hyperactivity; they call it an **attention deficit disorder.**

For students who cannot get along in school, generalizing why this behavior occurs is extremely difficult. The oversimplification is for the school to blame the parents, and for the parents to blame the school. Children with behavior disorders come from all economic levels of society, the very rich to the very poor. Every school has a small percentage of students who do not conform to the norms. These students seem to be searching for something that the school, the parents, other students, or the community are not able to provide.

Successful experiences are difficult for these children to accomplish. Too often, emotionally disturbed adolescents seem to search for activities that are considered antisocial or against the law. They tend to enjoy shocking everyone with whom they come in contact. They curse, fight, drink, use drugs, talk of their sexual exploits, and are usually negative toward anything considered by society as positive.

The adapted physical educator is faced with a difficult task. Remember, however, that all students will respond to positive and successful experiences. If the student is unable to meet the social obligations of the traditional physical education class, that is, cooperating with instructors and students, being on time, complying with established regulations, following game rules, and contributing to a "team effort," then the student must be placed in an individualized adapted physical education class. Figure 11.1 shows the range of physical education class placement alternatives for students with behavior disorders.

Implications for Physical Education

To remediate behavior disorders, the root cause must be understood. Hyperactivity, for example, may require drug therapy to improve behavior. L. B. Silver (1984, p. 75) believes that proper medication can calm many children who are hyperactive or easily distracted. He states: "Literally hundreds of studies have been done . . . , and the findings are consistent. There is improved attention span and decreased muscle-activity level. I feel safe in saying that psychostimulants (medications) are appropriate treatment when used correctly and followed up regularly." He also stresses that medication improves concentration and some motor skills.

Hypoactivity, withdrawal, or hypersensitivity may be a manifestation of a negative and fragile self-concept. Truancy may result from a fear of school failure, and delinquent behavior may result from a need for peer recognition. The child may perceive running away as less threatening than the home or school environment. All of these conditions, alone or in combination, are sufficient to precipitate social maladjustment.

The physical educator can mediate hyperactivity or aggressive behavior by structuring the child's learning environment. Often, this behavior is the result of having to make choices. Requiring children to sit while the teacher is speaking reduces disruptive or inattentive behavior. Requiring children to sit apart so they cannot reach each other further reduces disruption. For example, Earl is continually bothering his classmates to the detriment of both himself and his peers. The teacher should plan to reinforce Earl's behavior when he remains quiet or participates positively in assigned tasks. Such planned reinforcement by the teacher for being quiet and for other appropriate task-related behaviors could render unnecessary other less desirable procedures involving punishment. Imposing a penalty on Earl for bothering others at designated times only demonstrates to the youngster what he should *not* do, not what he *should* do.

The teacher must consciously plan activities that counteract the behavior disorder. For example, hyperactive children could engage in "catsup races" in which the person

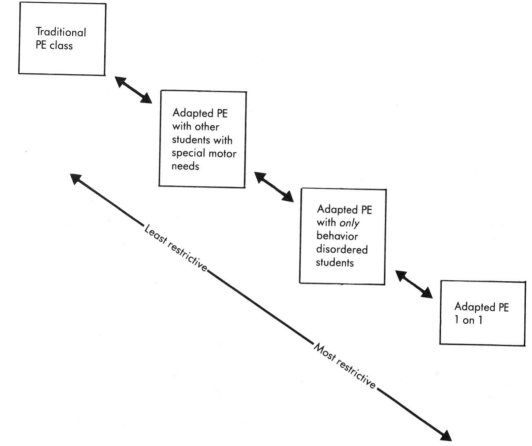

FIGURE 11.1. Appropriate PE placement of children with behavior disorders.

moving slowest is considered successful. Avoid placing overly aggressive children in activities that are highly competitive and overexciting. For the behaviorally disturbed child, activities should demonstrate cooperation (e.g., building a pyramid) rather than competition (e.g., dodgeball). Conscious relaxation techniques can also be used effectively. The child's attention should be focused on a situation, and the youngster encouraged to get his emotions calmed down. Specific methods of relaxation are described in Chapters 19 and 21.

Manifestations of inadequacy, such as hypoactivity, hypersensitivity, and withdrawal, can be mediated through the acquisition of motor skills that are important for positive recognition. The child may become more active once her skill levels are perceived as social assets. As motor skills improve, hypersensitivity and withdrawal may diminish in response to a gradually improving self-concept and increased positive recognition.

Pervasive anxiety related to physical education may result from the child's over-sensitivity to being hurt, either physically or emotionally, by negative activity experiences. The youngster probably needs to engage in activities that develop fundamental motor skills (see Chapter 6). Skill development allows less fearful participation to take place gradually. As confidence grows, the child's participation will contribute to the diminishment of anxieties.

Social maladjustment is often the result of a child's lacking the skills that facilitate the socialization process. During the school years, significant socialization occurs through play, which is a movement-centered phenomenon. The child with good motor skills is capable of participating successfully as a group member or on a team active in games or contests. Social adjustment is a by-product of efficient movement, which draws young people together in problem-solving situations. The socially maladjusted child often is poorly skilled and remains on the fringes of activities that could contribute positively to alleviation of his problems.

High school age students with behavior disorders often seem to revert, in at least one socioemotional characteristic, to a level found in very young children. In other words, they tend to be egocentric. The adapted physical education instructor should understand this deep-seated problem and attempt to meet it in a direct approach. Individuals are unlikely to want to share with others, or to contribute to a team effort, or to follow rules established for the good of everyone. Repeated conversations with behavior-disordered teenagers reveal a striking conclusion on the part of these youngsters: "If it doesn't help me, why should I do it?" These persons want and need to be self-satisfied. They want to be better looking, stronger, and smarter than everyone else, and their craving will not be diminished until the teacher recognizes this driving compulsion. For this reason, individualized activities in which students can work alone (i.e., weight training) tend to be more beneficial because the youngster does not have to share or cooperate for the good of others. The intrinsic value of weight training as a way to "feel good" is documented repeatedly by individuals engrossed in this sport. This activity should provide a deep feeling of self-attainment, thus helping to fulfill the driving need to feel good about oneself. In addition, both the long-range goals and the short-term objectives of a weight training program are ideal when attempting to meet the individualized needs of these students. These activities facilitate self-confidence, and thus help the youngster move closer to that day when he is able to take part in more socially oriented physical education activities. The instructor should be aware that this socialization process may take weeks, months, or even years, depending on the severity of the emotional disturbance.

The adapted physical education instructor should develop an individualized program with each student assisting in program planning and development. As socially maladjusted children acquire better motor skills, focus still should remain on the individual's skill development. Once skill development permits truly successful activity participation, then the introduction of activities requiring cooperation among children is important. Activities of a "New Games" nature are excellent because they require cooperation to achieve a common goal. These activities also do not designate winners or losers. The socially maladjusted child does not need to be designated a loser.

Behavior disorder symptoms and their causes suggest poor self-concept as a recurring factor. Teachers and clinicians often say, "Show me a child with a behavior disorder and I'll show you a child harboring a poor self-concept." Recognition that this association exists is the reason for including self-concept enhancement activities in remedial programs for children with behavior disorders. Physical education can make a unique contribution to the child's therapy. By acquiring efficient motor skills, the child becomes proficient in one aspect of human behavior that is almost universally admired. Good motor skills contribute to positive recognition from peers, parents, teachers, and important others. The child's growing awareness that his "likability quotient" is rising generates a cause-effect elevation in self-concept and interpersonal relationships.

Any behavior disorder, regardless of cause or symptom, is relatively more remediable during its early stages. In effect, "the time to bend the twig is when it is young." For children with behavior disorders, physical education presents "twig bending" opportunities. Acquired motor skills offer concrete indicators to the child that she does have self-worth. Because humans are movement-centered, each time a child moves with skill and is recognized positively, that child's worth is apparent.

Teachers must communicate their expectations to students clearly and firmly. Nothing is gained by beating around the bush or keeping the student guessing as to what the teacher has in mind regarding behavior, goals, and expectations. The student should know what is expected at all times (Caveny 1986).

Time Out

Time out refers to the procedure of temporarily removing the child from an enjoyable situation following an inappropriate behavior. In the physical education setting, the child who persists in disruptive behavior is told to sit outside the playing area, and is told why he must sit out on the side. For example, "No, Johnny, sit on the side for 3 minutes because you hit Bobby." When the time limit is up, it is critical that the instructor ask the youngster if he is ready to return to the game, and if he knows *why* he was told to sit out. The student must respond to the teacher's questions before returning to the activity.

The length of time used for a time out is contingent on the degree of misbehavior and on the mental and chronological age of the student. Fox (1982, pp. 74–75) describes the use of time out as follows: "The duration of the time-out is prespecified and relatively brief. The general rule of thumb is the younger the student, the shorter the duration of time. Also students who have lived in residential facilities typically require longer durations of time-out than those who live at home." In most cases, the typical time is less than 5 minutes.

Briskin and Gardner (1968, pp. 84–85) used the time out (TO) procedure with a 9-year-old child as described in the following account:

> This child was described as hyperactive, disruptive, and difficult to control in the school setting. Specific inappropriate behaviors included screaming and throwing things in fits of anger, crying or whining when not getting her way, not waiting her turn to engage in art projects and physical activities, hitting, biting, grabbing, rough pushing,

not responding to verbal instructions, and leaving the room, group, or activity without reason or permission. After an observational period revealed the average frequency of these behaviors in structured and unstructured activity periods throughout the school day, a TO procedure was initiated. Whenever any of these behaviors occurred during the three structured periods, Lisa was immediately removed from the classroom and seated outside for a two-minute period. The only verbal interaction during the TO consisted of a short statement informing Lisa why she was taken from the classroom: "You pushed Jill, you must sit in the chair." "You are whining; sit in the chair." Following the two-minute period, she was returned to the classroom.

As a means of strengthening desired behaviors to replace inappropriate ones, an additional procedure was used of providing prompt teacher praise and other forms of social interactions following occurrences of appropriate behaviors. Although initially Lisa voiced her objections when placed in TO, she soon accepted the action as an unpleasant consequence which she produced by her own disruptive behaviors. Within a few days inappropriate behavior was reduced from an average of 31 percent to 2 percent of the time spent at school. There was a concurrent increase in appropriate behavior which was maintained over a follow-up period. It is interesting to note that improvement in Lisa's behavior had pronounced positive effect on the teacher, aides, other children, and on Lisa's mother. All interacted more readily with Lisa and provided her with the social attention which apparently was quite valuable to her.

Another example of the successful use of time-out procedures is noted by Watson (1972). This example involved the modification of temper tantrums in a profoundly retarded psychotic child. From the beginning of a temper tantrum, the youngster was ignored completely by everyone in the environment for 5 minutes. As a result, the weekly tantrum frequency dropped, within about three weeks, from approximately 50 tantrums per week to a level of infrequent ocurrence.

Fox (1982, p. 74) cautions, however, about improper use of time outs. He states: "Some students will actually misbehave in order to receive time out, since they prefer the time out over the required educational activity. . . . However, if the density of reinforcement during the activity is high, the student will be less motivated to misbehave in order to escape or avoid it." In other words, the adapted physical educator must keep the activity interesting, stimulating, and rewarding for students; they should miss the activity when they spend time outside the setting.

Neuroses

Neuroses come in many forms and tend to be relatively common, particularly among adults. Among the most common neuroses are **phobias,** which are defined as fears that have no basis in reality.

Many superstitions provide examples of phobia-related behavior. Examples of such phobias are fear of the following: black cats, walking under ladders, broken mirrors, and Friday the 13th. Such phobias, however, represent only minor aberrations in behavior and generally do not become the focus of therapy or remediation.

Other phobias such as fear of confinement in small enclosures (e.g., elevators) or fear of heights can become serious and pervasive enough to limit the pursuit of a normal life-style. Among the more serious phobias occurring in certain school-age children is fear of school, or **school phobia.**

School phobia is a phenomenon that evokes feelings in the child ranging from fear to terror. Phobia related to school attendance is probably symptomatic of deep-seated problems in the child's family relationships. The child's fear of school is believed to be primarily the product of anxiety over separation from parents (i.e., separation anxiety). The fact that school is the object of the phobia appears incidental to the fact that school is the site where the child spends the majority of time away from parents. According to Levison (1969, p. 76), "The school itself, in some cases, may have only accidentally become the object of the phobia. The child may have experienced an attack of fear in school and, in remembering this attack . . . , will avoid the site where the attack occurred."

The separation anxiety involved in school phobia stems from the fear, which is very real to the child, that the parent may go away or be seriously harmed while the child is at school. Separation anxiety tends to be less of a problem in families that have strong and secure interpersonal relationships. Systematic planning will aid in the remediation of school phobias and is important to a positive prognosis. When intervention occurs at the onset of symptoms, the opportunity for complete remission appears most favorable. Treatment delayed by even a semester has been demonstrated to require prolonged therapeutic attention. The most serious problems are noted among children whose symptoms have been ignored during the early years. The prognosis is then poor, particularly among adolescents whose long-term symptoms have been ignored.

The specific term *school phobia* does not include aversions to school attendance founded more directly in school-related problems (e.g., nonachievement, shyness, truancy, awkwardness). Such maladjustments to school are addressed in the previous section on behavior disorders.

Neurosis also may manifest itself in **obsessions.** Obsessions are characterized by preoccupations in thought; they typically involve traits that would be perceived as desirable if they were not carried to extremes. Often observed obsessions are eating, not eating, neatness, cleanliness, and achievement. Obsessions lead to behaviors that are termed **compulsive.** Compulsive behavior is the overt manifestation of obsession. Persons who exhibit such behavior are therefore termed **obsessive-compulsive.**

Obsessive-compulsive behavior often manifests itself in quirks of movement behavior. Twitches of the head and neck, blinking, and facial grimacing are examples of such behavior. One problem in treating obsessive-compulsive behavior is that the observed behavior may be merely the outward sign of some deep-seated psychological trauma. In such cases, effective remediation requires identification and amelioration of the underlying problem.

Another form of compulsion occurring primarily among adolescent females is termed **anorexia nervosa.** The main symptom is total appetite loss, which stems from an extreme fear of ingesting food. Left untreated, the anorexic youngster may starve to death. The causes of anorexia nervosa are not thoroughly understood. Some believe that the condition results from a compulsive desire to avoid obesity. Among some adolescent females, extreme anxiety exists over physiological, including sexual, maturation. This anxiety manifests itself in loss of appetite, which, in turn, preempts physiological maturation. Therapy generally is medically oriented, long, and complex. A complete description of this condition is presented in Chapter 13, which deals with eating disorders.

Implications for Physical Education

The implication of physical education for children with neurotic behavior differs in accordance with the specific neurosis. Neuroses such as fear of heights, fear of enclosures, and obsessive-compulsive behaviors have direct implications for physical education. Neuroses such as school phobia and anorexia nervosa have indirect implications.

In the latter situations, the physical educator should focus on empathetic psychological support for the child who will undergo psychological or psychiatric treatment or both. While physical education may not directly affect the remediation of such neuroses, it can, through proper emphasis, ensure that students are not subjected to activities that evoke unnecessary added stress. Demands made on these youngsters must reflect concern for the individual's bouts with the perplexities of the neurosis. Physical education challenges should reflect cooperative efforts among understanding peers. Whenever possible, it is desirable to pair or group the child with neurosis with peers who show maturity in accommodating individual differences.

When evaluating such a child with neurosis, criterion-referenced rather than norm-referenced assessments should be used. The criterion-referenced instrument does not compare the child's performance with others. Instead, the child's performance becomes the norm, thereby avoiding anxiety over comparisons with others.

For persons with fear of heights, fear of enclosures, or obsessive-compulsive behaviors, the physical educator may have more direct impact on remediation. The child who fears heights may be coaxed gradually by empathetic support and positive reinforcement to experience activities above the gym or playground surface. For example, practice for walking a balance beam may begin by walking on a line. Next, the child may walk on a 2 × 4 in. board that remains directly in contact with the surface. Gradually, the board may be elevated above the surface. Throughout the progression, provide direct manual support, but only as needed. Gradually decrease manual support while continuing encouragement of the child's self-reliance.

Fear of enclosures can be mediated by activities that occur in open areas with few children. As progress permits, activities should be moved to relatively enclosed indoor settings. In each setting, increased numbers of children may be introduced into the learning environment, thereby gradually acclimatizing the child to enclosure and enclosures shared by others. For the child who fears enclosures, be sure to avoid darkness, eye shades, or physical confinement during the early stages of intervention.

Obsessive-compulsive behaviors may be mediated somewhat by engaging the child in activities that preempt the child's acting out of the obsession. Involvement in activity sufficiently demanding to preoccupy the child should reduce unwanted compulsive behaviors. Activities that are incompatible with the undesired behavior are also appropriate. For example, if the child's obsessive-compulsive behavior manifests itself in blinking or head and neck twitching, employ archery or a similar activity that requires head and eye steadiness. This may be particularly effective if positive reinforcement is forthcoming for behavior that results in performance accuracy.

Psychoses

Psychosis constitutes the most serious form of emotional disturbance. Its effect on personality is so pervasive that intense psychiatric attention and possible confinement are usually indicated. Although persons with neurosis may exhibit personality problems, they are generally able to function independently. Persons with psychosis, however, are so severely or profoundly hindered by personality disturbance that, without intervention, leading a normal life may never be possible. Early recognition and treatment are of paramount importance. Even with the most competent psychological and psychiatric intervention, however, the person with psychosis may never fully recover, and may require long-term supervision.

Four forms of schizophrenia comprise the most common kinds of psychosis (Randels and Marco 1985). They represent the types of psychosis for which the *adapted* behavior will function appropriately in an adapted physical education setting.

The **catatonic schizophrenic** individual assumes a posture and does not move for extended periods. The person in a catatonic state will not relate to, or otherwise acknowledge, the presence of others. She draws inward, excluding all else. Except for wide-open eyes, this person appears to be in deep sleep. Sherrill (1981) reports that persons who recover from catatonia recall that the catatonic state is characterized by some awareness of external activity. Their recollection, however, indicates that they were incapable of responding in a meaningful manner.

The **paranoid schizophrenic** harbors deep-seated fright, including fear of others. In some cases, the paranoid schizophrenic's extreme fears are exhibited in hostility toward others. This behavior is a manifestation of the individual's belief that others present a real and constant threat. At some stage in the progression of paranoid schizophrenia, the patient reveals inflated feelings of self-importance. In a hospital, the patient might believe, for example, that he is the doctor or hospital administrator. The paranoid schizophrenic not uncommonly assumes the personage of a famous person. Virtually all of this person's overt responses are tempered by the distorted belief that no one can be trusted.

Hebephrenic schizophrenia is characterized by the person's exhibiting behaviors that are not age appropriate. The hebephrenic schizophrenic regresses in behavior to a stage when life is perceived as having been less threatening. Inability to cope with adult stress and responsibility is believed to be the cause of hebephrenic schizophrenia. Childlike behaviors and mannerisms include gibberish, baby talk, inappropriate giggling, thumb sucking, escape into fantasies, and use of nonsensical word phrases.

Persons with **undifferentiated schizophrenia** do not manifest behaviors that permit clear-cut designation as to type. These persons exhibit behaviors characteristic of two or all three schizophrenias.

For further information concerning schizophrenia, consult the American Schizophrenia Foundation, Box 160, Ann Arbor, MI 48107.

Implications for Physical Education

When working with the schizophrenic child, do not become overwhelmed or angered by incongruous and disintegrated behaviors. On the contrary, the teacher's temperament must be marked by steadiness and empathy. Because teachers see children on a regular basis, they are in an advantageous position to influence the child's recovery process. A display of steady temperament from the teacher in a world otherwise characterized by chaos and disarray may be one of the few constants on which the recovering child can depend.

Empathy must not be misconstrued as synonymous with sympathy or permissiveness. The ability to empathize enables the teacher to perceive the child's dilemma through the eyes and mind of the child. Empathy facilitates understanding of the child's problem; sympathy evokes pity, which inhibits understanding of the child's circumstances.

Harsh discipline may drive the schizophrenic child into withdrawal and is contraindicated, but this caution should not be misconstrued as advocating permissiveness. The schizophrenic child needs limits, and must experience firm intervention when limits are exceeded. Permissiveness fails to fulfill this need, and in fact may precipitate reversions to maladaptive behavior. Firmness means not tolerating inappropriate behavior while avoiding punitive measures that might precipitate withdrawal.

When the child's behavior is inapproporiate, the child's attention should be drawn to an activity different from that which precipitated the maladaptive behavior. Timely and abrupt "changes of scenery" assist the child in regaining behavior control.

When possible, the teacher should avoid activities suspected of evoking schizophrenic responses. For example, if swimming evokes symptoms of catatonia or paranoia, avoid aquatic activities for that child. Instead, draw the child gradually toward aquatic experiences through successive approximations. Have the child squeeze wet sponges, then experience face washing with a wet towel. Subsequently, the child can engage in limited water play (e.g., with toy boats in a sink) or sit with feet immersed in water. Have the child sit at the side of the pool, then dangle legs in the water, and finally, enter the water with a teacher or aide in whom the child has confidence. At each stage in the approximation process, be firm (but not punitive), gently prodding, and provide intense reinforcement for behaviors that show progress toward the norm. Refer to Chapter 12, Modifying Behavior in Physical Education Settings, for additional insights regarding behavior shaping.

Avoid permissive responses to the child's fantasies, hallucinations, and other maladaptive behavior. Permitting unchecked reversions to such behavior disserves psychi-

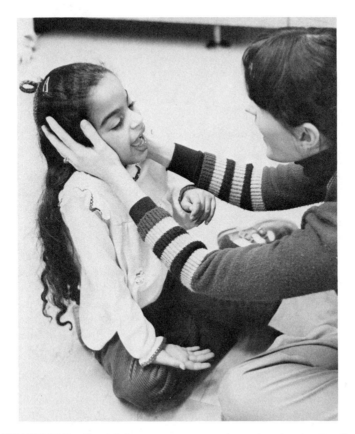

FIGURE 11.2. Establish eye contact to gain and maintain attention.

atric efforts and the child's recovery. Be ready to call the child back to reality. The verbal command "Listen to me," or "Look at me," may be sufficient. The child's head may need to be held to force eye contact (Figure 11.2). Should the child's eyes continue to wander, gently realign the child's head so that eye contact is reestablished, then, in close proximity to the child's eyes and speaking directly to the child, say "Listen to me."

Engaging the child alone in a reasonably challenging motor activity often will facilitate an attention shift to reality. For example, the child may be placed on the second or third rung of a climbing apparatus, then commanded, "Climb down." Because such a task requires concentration to negotiate the descent, the child may experience an attention shift back to reality.

The schizophrenic child, during initial contact with physical education, requires a carefully structured environment that offers security so the youngster can know what to expect from the surroundings. Knowing what to expect enables her to experience some reality, which ceases to be threatening. Positive experiences based in reality, although minimal at first, enable the schizophrenic child to realize that she can cope with reality.

Autism

The term **autism** is derived from the Greek word "autos," meaning "self." The autistic child functions as a separate entity to the virtual exclusion of all surroundings.

Autism is not a common disorder among children. When it does occur, it is serious and has potential long-term consequences. The condition occurs in approximately 5 to 15 children per 10,000 births, and is four times more common in boys than in girls. Autism usually is diagnosed during the first 3 years of age when the child's lack of communication with his surroundings becomes apparent (National Information Center for Handicapped Children and Youth 1983a). Some evidence indicates that there are several causes of autism, each with distinct neurological effects. Among these causes are untreated phenylketonuria (PKU), rubella, celiac (abdominal) disease, and chemical exposures in pregnancy. No known factors in the psychological environment of the child have been shown to cause autism. Over half of all children with autism eventually become institutionalized.

Some youngsters may exhibit autistic tendencies but are not classified as true juvenile autistics. Caveny (1986) believes that the true autistic child is uniquely different because of a neurological or psychological inability to control actions and responses. The other child, who at times exhibits autistic tendencies, seems nevertheless to be able to manipulate the environment and is able to psychologically come and go to meet immediate desires. The teacher often cannot distinguish between children with true juvenile autism and those who simply have autistic tendencies. Seeking a clear diagnosis from a school psychologist is recommended.

Autistic children are known to enjoy whirling, and observers have noted that they tend not to develop the associated dizziness, vertigo, loss of balance, nausea, or vomiting. They also have been observed to have abnormalities of posture and balance. Such findings suggest that these children have some form of vestibular dysfunction and some dysfunction in the central nervous system connections. In addition, Maurer and Damasio (1979) suggest that damage to the basal ganglia may have a direct bearing on autism.

The following characteristics exemplify the behaviors that autistic children manifest: (1) impaired or complete lack of social and emotional relationships, (2) repetitive nongoal-directed body motions or behaviors (e.g., constant rocking, hand waving in front of face, striking face with fist), (3) resistance to change and extreme distress when minor changes in environment or routine are undertaken, (4) peculiar perceptual and motor experiences such as "looking through" people, not seeing certain objects, not hearing some sounds and overreacting to others, walking on tiptoes, hyperactivity or passivity, apparent insensitivity to pain, (5) severe speech impairment and language difficulties, and (6) retardation in some areas, often accompanied by superior skill in other areas.

Additional information on autism is available from The National Society for Autistic Children, 169 Tampa Avenue, Albany, NY 12208.

Implications for Physical Education

Because autistic children cannot relate to external phenomena, they must be taught in small groups. During early stages or when symptoms are severe or both, individual instruction will be required.

Virtually all autistic children experience significant difficulty in understanding spoken language. In providing verbal directions to autistic children, always speak to the child in simple terms.

The autistic child functions best in individual activities. Dual or group activities, including team participation, often exceed the child's ability to understand the dynamics of participation. When the autistic child does participate as a group member, activities should not require extensive interpersonal cooperation. For example, participation in basketball might be inappropriate, but participation with a group in swimming, jumping on the trampoline, or tumbling might be suitable. These youngsters are receptive to being led through an activity such as jogging. The instructor or another student can hold the child's hand or arm and start jogging. The teacher should record the beginning and ending time and the distance covered. Positive verbal reinforcement should be given continually during the run. The child usually will terminate the experience when fatigued (Scholl 1986). By accurately recording progress and by making sure that the child jogs at least every other day, the instructor can assume that cardiovascular efficiency will improve.

Montileone (1983) was successful in gaining the autistic child's attention when he would "mirror the youngster's movements." The child tended to become very interested in what was happening and seemed to want to continue this experience.

When the autistic child does exhibit superior abilities in a specific area of motor performance, the teacher should capitalize on such abilities. Allowing the child an opportunity to excel will provide a sense of accomplishment and recognition by others.

Activities for autistic children must be monitored closely owing to an apparent inability of these youngsters to relate to pain. Care must be taken to ensure that the autistic child does not aggravate an injury, new or old, simply because the child does not relate to pain.

Summary

Estimates of the number of emotionally disturbed school-age youth in the United States differ because the definition of *emotional disturbance* varies among estimators.

The consensus is, however, that the majority of emotionally disturbed children are boys.

Emotional disturbance is a general term covering a broad spectrum of abnormal personality characteristics, which differ greatly in cause and degree. Having an emotional disturbance must be differentiated from being emotionally disturbed. In the former circumstance, behavior is neither aberrant nor chronic. In the latter, however, behavior is manifested to a marked degree and over a protracted period of time.

Emotionally disturbed children with behavior disorders exhibit behaviors that become fixed and tend toward extremes. Twelve types of behavior disorder have been delineated. Certain of these behaviors may be remediable as a result of medical supervision (e.g., hyperactivity) while for others remediation may be primarily in the educational model. In the former instance, the teacher's role in remediation may be simply supportive, while in the latter, it may be primary.

In some behavior disorders, there is indication that the individual possesses an egocentric personality and a poor self-concept. These are often the underlying causes of deviant behavior. Adolescents with this type of behavior disorder should be directed toward individualized physical education activities (e.g., weight training) that improve self-concept.

Good behavior management for emotionally disturbed children has much in common with good behavior management for all children. The best preventive action any physical education teacher can take is to make sure that the gym or playing field is a happy place where students take pride in their work and learn to treat others with respect. An exciting teacher, who uses a stimulating program, seldom has problems with students.

Neuroses discussed were phobias, obsessions, and anorexia nervosa. In cases of neuroses, the implications for physical education vary in accordance with both type and severity of condition. In all instances, however, the teacher should endeavor to be empathetic. Allowing the child's neurotic behavior disorder to trigger feelings of anger in the teacher, although understandable, is counterproductive.

Children with neuroses should be engaged in cooperative rather than competitive activities, and can be paired productively with nonhandicapped peers who have demonstrated a propensity for maturity. In many instances, behavior modification techniques can help alter the neurotic behavior. The introduction to behavior modification presented in Chapter 12 affords an opportunity to become familiar with the basic tenets, principles, and practices. Review of these tenets is particularly recommended for those working with emotionally disturbed children.

Psychoses are the most severe forms of emotional disturbance. The four types of schizophrenia (i.e., catatonic, paranoid, hebephrenic, and undifferentiated) are the most common psychoses. Without considerable special help, both medical and educational, the psychotic person may never achieve functional independence. Even with intervention, recovery is not guaranteed. Psychotic persons must not be expected to function in a mainstream physical education setting. Individualized attention in a special setting generally provides the most effective basis for safe, successful participation and gradual progress toward reality.

Autism, though not common, is significantly severe to warrant consideration. The autistic child appears to be self-stimulated to the exclusion of all else in the environment. Children with autism often require individual attention. Because the child does not relate to others, activities requiring cooperation often are not appropriate or possible. Some autistic children do not relate even to pain, so care must be taken in an activity setting that an injury does not go unrecognized.

The prognosis for children with autism is not encouraging. Presently, approximately one half of all autistic children require institutionalization. Despite the statistics, however, the autistic child should have full opportunity for successful physical education participation and recognition. Such opportunity may facilitate limited movement toward more normal relationships, although at present evidence does not exist to support this theory.

References

Bower, E. M. The Emotionally Handicapped Child and the School. In *Educating the Emotionally Disturbed Child: A Book of Readings*, edited by H. W. Harshman. New York: Thomas Y. Crowell, 1969.

Briskin, A. S., and Gardner, W. I. Social Reinforcement in Reducing Inappropriate Behavior. *Young Children* 24:84–85, 1968.

Caveny, P. A. Personal interview. Lincoln Developmental Center, Lincoln, Ill., 17 March 1986.

Common Sense From Closer Look. Forgotten Children . . . A Costly Crisis. Washington, D.C.: The Parents' Campaign for Handicapped Children and Youth, Fall 1979.

Federal Register. Final Regulations of Education of Handicapped Children, Implementation of Part B of the Education of the Handicapped Act. Department of Health, Education, and Welfare. Office of Education, 42(163), Part II, 23 August 1977, Section 121a.5, Definitions, pp. 42478–42479.

Fox, R. M. *Decreasing Behaviors of Severely Retarded and Autistic Persons*. Champaign, Ill.: Research Press, 1982.

Hallahan, D. P., and Kauffman, J. M. *Exceptional Children*, 2nd ed. Englewood Cliffs, N.J.: Prentice-Hall, 1982.

Levison, B. Understanding the Child With School Phobia. In *Educating the Emotionally Disturbed Child: A Book of Readings*, edited by H. W. Harshman. New York: Thomas Y. Crowell, 1969.

Maurer, R. G., and Damasio, A. R. Vestibular Dysfunction in Autistic Children. *Developmental Medicine and Child Neurology* 21(5):656–658, 1979.

Montileone, T. *Movement Exploration Activities*. Lecture given at Annual Convention of the American Corrective Therapy Association, Houston, 12 July 1983.

National Information Center for Handicapped Children and Youth. *Autism*. Washington, D.C.: The Center, 1983a.

———. *Emotional Disturbances*. Washington, D.C.: The Center, 1983b.

Prazar, G., and Friedman, S. B. Behavioral Problems in Children and Adolescents. In *Current Diagnosis 7*, edited by R. B. Conn. Philadelphia: W. B. Saunders, 1985.

Randels, P. M., and Marco, L. A. Schizophrenia. In *Current Diagnosis 7*, edited by R. B. Conn. Philadelphia: W. B. Saunders, 1985.

Scholl, R. Personal correspondence. Lincoln Developmental Center, Lincoln, Ill., 14 February 1986.

Sherrill, C. *Adapted Physical Education and Recreation: A Multidisciplinary Approach*, 2nd ed. Dubuque, Iowa: Wm. C. Brown, 1981.

Silver, L. B. *The Misunderstood Child: A Guide for Parents of Learning Disabled Children*. Bethesda, Md.: National Institute of Mental Health, 1984.

U.S. Department of Education. *To Assure the Free Appropriate Public Education of All Handicapped Children*. Washington, D.C.: The Department, 1984.

Watson, L. S. *How to Use Behavior Modification With Mentally Retarded and Autistic Children*. Columbus, Ohio: Behavior Modification Technology, 1972.

CHAPTER 12

Modifying Behavior in Physical Education Settings

Almost everything we do in life is controlled by consequences. Because behavior is also influenced by consequences, a given behavior can be modified by changing the consequences that are associated with it.

For example, a child involved in modified floor hockey might consciously remain on the fringes of the activity in which relatively little participation is ensured. This child is behaving according to expected consequences surrounding that action. Perhaps the child is avoiding energetic activity from fear of ridicule or of being hurt. Aversion to either outcome is sufficient to keep the child from the center of involvement. On the fringes, risk of ridicule or injury (however real or imagined) is greatly diminished. By avoiding the activity, the child experiences temporary relief from anxieties and fear of embarrassment or injury. Specific components of this situation in which the possible consequences of a behavior control that behavior are diagrammed in Figure 12.1.

In another situation, a child might be involved in the midst of activity. If the child perceives involvement as having positive consequences, the participatory behavior will continue.

SETTING: Modified Floor Hockey

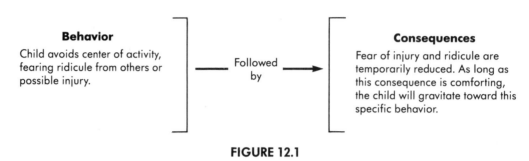

FIGURE 12.1

For example, when a child catches a ball and receives a smiling "good catch" response, positive consequences have resulted from the behavior. The child will probably continue to play catch. Specific components of this situation in which the consequences of the given behavior controlled that behavior are diagrammed in Figure 12.2.

In another situation, a child is removed from activity because her behavior has been inappropriate. For example, the child may have deliberately struck or pushed another child. Antisocial behavior has resulted in a consequence of removal from activity. If removal is aversive, the child may modify her behavior to avoid removal from activity for similar reasons in the future. Specific components of this situation in which the consequences of the given behavior may control that behavior in future are outlined in Figure 12.3.

These situations provide three examples of how consequences of behavior may influence further exhibition of that behavior. In the first instance, fear of ridicule and injury resulted in what behavioral psychologists call **aversive stimuli.** By avoiding the midst of the activity, a behavior termed an **avoidance response,** the child escapes the aversive stimulus. When the child's response to an ongoing stimulus is escape or avoidance, the behavior has been **negatively reinforced.**

In the second situation, the child's behavior was characterized by **approach** rather than avoidance. In this example, the child engaged in activity because a continued positive response was generated. Whenever the child engages in behavior because the behavior generates positive consequences, the behavior is said to be **positively reinforced.**

In the third situation, the child's inappropriate pushing resulted in removal from the activity. The consequence of this behavior, removal from activity, was calculated to be aversive to the child. In future instances, the child is expected to avoid behavior or behaviors that result in removal. When a consequence that is aversive to the child *follows* an undesirable behavior, that consequence is called **punishment.**

Both positive and negative reinforcement can *increase* and *maintain* the frequency of a given behavior. In positive reinforcement, a behavior increases in frequency as the direct result of a desirable consequence (e.g., food, recognition, money, praise, tokens, ribbons, patches or emblems, or privileges). In negative reinforcement, a behavior *increases*

SETTING: Child and a Friend Playing Catch

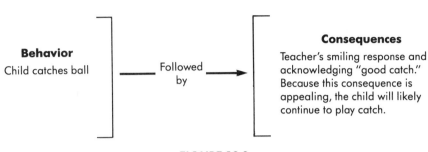

FIGURE 12.2

in frequency to avoid an undesirable situation (e.g., putting on a coat when cold, wearing sunglasses on a bright day, remaining on the fringe of an activity to avoid ridicule and embarrassment, feigning illness on the day of a swimming lesson owing to fear of water). In punishment, a behavior *decreases* in frequency to avoid aversive consequences (e.g., staying after school for disruptive behavior). Lavay (1985) believes that the physical education environment is an ideal setting in which to foster positive experiences and a genuine appreciation of physical education activities.

It is important to recognize that negative reinforcement and punishment, though often confused and used synonymously, are not the same. The examples demonstrate the basic differences. Negative reinforcement, like positive reinforcement, functions to *increase* a behavior, while punishment functions to *decrease* the frequency of a given behavior.

All Reinforcers Are Not Created Equal

We know that the consequences of behavior are capable of modifying behavior, but some consequences, whether positive or negative, are more *intense* than others. For instance, what is intensely satisfying, dissatisfying, or punishing for one person may not necessarily be the same for another.

If the consequence of a behavior has little relationship to the individual's likes or dislikes, wants or needs, it will have little impact on that individual's behavior. This is an important point to keep in mind when trying to modify behavior in an educational setting. For example, consider a situation in which the teacher tries to improve some component of a child's motor skill. Were the child marginally motivated or incapable of dealing with relatively abstract reinforcement (e.g., knowing how well she is progressing, or verbal praise), abstract reinforcement would not be particularly effective. To get this child's attention, a considerably more intense reinforcer or consequence should be used. Possible reinforcers might be edibles (food or drink) or tangibles (awards such as stars, ribbons, emblems, wall charts).

SETTING: Group Activity (Modified Soccer)

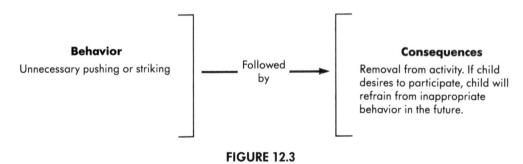

FIGURE 12.3

Lavay (1982) lists several methods for the application of reinforcers.

1. **Tangible reinforcers** are concrete rewards and usually given immediately following performance of the desired behavior. Administration of tangible reinforcers can present teaching problems and is most effective for young children or the low-functioning mentally retarded.
2. **Token economy system** is when the student is given a chip or point, which may later be exchanged for items that are of value to the student.
3. **Tally sheets** are a method for keeping track of points earned. If students are capable, they should keep track of their own points.
4. **Reinforcement menus** are a list of high-preference activities made available to students to choose from when they meet a specific criteria of performance or perform the desired behavior.
5. **No cost reinforcers** describes the physical education setting with its variety of equipment. The student can select from an assortment of readily available high-preference reinforcers. The instructor can give structured free time, allowing students to engage in various activities of their own choosing.

Long-term reliance on intense reinforcers, however, should be avoided. As student skill, interest, and attention improve, intense reinforcers should be replaced with less intense but equally effective reinforcers such as verbal encouragement and praise. In effect, move from reliance on *extrinsic* motivation to reliance on relatively *intrinsic* motivation. This is important, because long-term changes in behavior are more likely to occur when motivation to continue the behavior is self-imposed.

Punishment often is used to reduce the frequency of a child's disruptive behavior because it is effective. Punishment is, however, temporary; the undesired behavior remains subdued only as long as the threat of punishment exists. In other words, "while the cat's away, the mice will play."

Because punishment resolves problems only temporarily, more permanent means of reducing the frequency of an undesired behavior must be found. For instance, a child might be punished (e.g., made to sit on the sidelines) for exhibiting overly aggressive behavior, or as an alternative, might be positively reinforced (rewarded) for engaging in activity *incompatible* with the undesired response. One behavior is incompatible with another whenever both behaviors cannot be done at the same time. When a disruptive child is positively reinforced for attentiveness, attentive behavior will increase. Attentiveness is incompatible with disruption, and thus disruption should be reduced. This positive approach is desirable because (1) behavior improves as a result of positive rather than negative consequences, and (2) positive consequences or positive reinforcement generally provide the most effective means to influence long-term changes in behavior.

Sometimes, consequences that the teacher believes are aversive to the child are, in reality, not aversive at all.

People generally prefer to exhibit behavior that generates positive consequences. Some children, however, may not find positive consequences or reinforcement forthcoming. When a child does not gain attention or recognition in acceptable ways, he may seek attention in a less acceptable manner. When this occurs, the teacher may quite naturally respond with aversive consequences (punishment). Punishment in any form, even though aversive, represents attention, and attention, even though aversive in this instance, is more desirable to some children than no attention at all. In this situation, the teacher, in an effort to reduce unwanted behavior through punishment, has drawn attention to that behavior and created a situation that is positively reinforcing. Under these circumstances, even the smallest increments of good behavior should be positively reinforced. Positive reinforcement, coupled with ignoring (not reinforcing) undesirable acts, may improve the child's behavior.

Positive Reinforcement and Long-Term Positive Change

Positive reinforcement is the most efficient means of producing permanent behavioral change. Behavior that is punished remains subdued only as long as the threat of punishment is a consequence of behavior. Remove the threat of punishment, and the punished behavior will return. In many respects, punishment is treating a symptom of the problem rather than the problem cause. Likewise, negative reinforcement is not an efficient means of modifying behavior, because it requires a constant, ongoing negative consequence to produce a desired behavior. Take away the negative consequence, and the desired behavior also will disappear.

With positive reinforcement, the child will strive to achieve a desirable consequence of behavior. Often, the child needs no prodding to seek positive reinforcement or reward. She will initiate good behavior, because positive consequences mean satisfaction. Only in positive reinforcement does the child have a positive reason to continue the desired behavior.

Morreau (1985) believes that the instructor is the key to positive reinforcement, particularly for children who are having trouble identifying with appropriate behaviors. The students must have their reinforcers personalized. If they receive a star for a certain accomplishment, that star is even more valuable if the recognition is strongly reinforced by verbal praise from the instructor. M & Ms, Fruit Loops, and star charts may be replaced easily by a strong hug and a squeeze, and an enthusiastic comment such as, "I liked the way you dressed for PE today."

Conditioning Responses in Children

Conditioning responses were first explored systematically by the Russian scientist Pavlov. Because Pavlov's conclusions resulted from working with animals, some aversion exists to applying Pavlovian principles to educational settings. Actually, Pavlov's principles do apply to human behavior, and understanding these principles can assist the adapted physical educator in establishing a learning environment conducive to producing desirable behavior changes.

Pavlov demonstrated that responses could be **conditioned** by pairing events. In effect, experiencing one event signals the impending occurrence of another. Let us examine this phenomenon in an educational setting. The child who wears a particular piece of clothing only during physical education associates (pairs) that clothing with activity and physical education. This serves two purposes: (1) It signals when behavior and activity levels appropriate to physical education are expected, and (2) its absence signals that physical education activity is not appropriate (e.g., once the child has returned to the classroom). This approach of pairing events is particularly appropriate with mentally retarded youngsters or children with behavior disorders who experience difficulty in dealing with different arousal levels in various settings.

Physical education classes should begin and end in a consistent manner. The child then recognizes when the physical education period has come and gone by the activities that consistently begin and end each class. This helps the child achieve a level of arousal appropriate to the physical education or classroom setting. The final activity in any physical education class should be one in which everybody can find success. This leaves the child with a positive attitude about physical education and a desire to return again soon.

The adapted physical education instructor will often be assigned to teach the student who is unsuccessful in the traditional program. The student may be labeled uncooperative, disruptive, aggressive, withdrawn, and so forth. The regular physical education teacher was probably faced with the traditional problems. As he might explain, "I don't have time to discipline this student," or "This student won't listen to me." The following statement is often heard: "The student doesn't like PE, why should I have to force him to like it? If he doesn't conform—then I'll flunk him."

Students are frequently blamed for their inability to conform or follow the traditional program. Too many students are expected to enjoy and to never question the procedures of the teacher. The "hard-nosed drill sergeant" instructor will inevitably punish with some negative act those who are unable or not willing to conform. Extra push-ups, running laps around the gym or field, or detentions after school are common practices in many programs. In reference to negative student attitudes, one hypothesis is that the program or the teacher's approach may be the true cause of most youngsters' negative responses.

To identify why students are disruptive, one must be precise when labeling inappropriate behavior. Terms such as aggressive, uncooperative, hyperactive, or withdrawn need to be more specific. As Taylor and Marholin (1980, p. 273) state, "Behaviors presented in terms of traits, personality characteristics, and labels are too general and open to idiosyncratic interpretation to be of much value." Taylor (1984, p. 25) suggests that *aggression* might be better described as "strikes out at others with fists or other objects" or "verbally abuses others by using curse words or a loud tone of voice." Similarly, *hyperactivity* might be more specifically stated as "gets out of line at inappropriate times" or "does not sit still when rules are being given."

Operant conditioning is a method used to increase the probability that a behavior will be strengthened, maintained, or weakened. First, the adapted physical educator must identify specifically the behavior in question. After identification, the desired behavior must then be properly reinforced. Lavay (1982) lists five concerns:

1. Precise identification of the desired behavior must be measurable and observable.
2. Students must understand the reinforcement as well as why they are being reinforced.
3. Timing of the reinforcement is extremely important. At first, the student may need to be reinforced immediately so as not to become confused.
4. Individualize the reinforcement. What may be reinforcing to one student may not reinforce another.
5. Application of reinforcement must be consistent and direct. The particular behavior to be changed must be reinforced consistently.

The most important reinforcer is the positive and enthusiastic teacher. All children respond to a smiling face, a positive comment, and when appropriate, a hug, a squeeze, or a "high five." Instructors should, however, be extremely careful when making comments to students that they do not make the common mistake of continually telling every student "good job." Rewards should come when the student accomplishes the task *as desired*. If the youngster does not meet the task appropriately, the teacher is responsible for explaining or showing how to improve the skill. Instructors often will say "good job," when in reality the child has given a good effort but has not performed correctly. It is instead the teacher's responsibility to tell *how* to improve the task. For example, if the student is attempting a flank vault on the vaulting side horse and does not get her legs perfectly straight, the teacher must tell the student how to improve the vault. If the student does not understand by verbal comments, then show by demonstration. If there is still a communication problem, the instructor must provide physical guidance, that is, hands-on instruction. At this point, if and when the student accomplishes the skill in the correct manner, the instructor should, with genuine enthusiasm, reward the student with verbal and physical rewards. "Great vaulting! Did you feel it? Try it again." The hug or the "give me five" is also a major part of a job well done. Direct eye contact is extremely important and must be maintained throughout discussion with the youngster.

As Lavay (1985, p. 31) states: "In physical education, alternative teaching strategies are needed with students who are undisciplined and seem disinterested. . . . controlling student discipline and promoting interest in physical education, exists to those physical educators able to systematically incorporate behavior management programs in their teaching. In short, behavior management is simply good teaching!"

Seaman and DePauw (1982) provide an excellent description of behavior modification and its process (Figure 12.4). In this chapter, we offer only a brief, practical introduction to some major tenets of behavior modification. The fact that all behavior is controlled by consequences and that consequences can be controlled suggests that all teachers should understand behavior modification. By so doing, the teacher can avoid becoming the unwitting facilitator of undesirable behavior, and can become a more effective architect of the educational setting. Specifically, we encourage enrollment in at least one class that focuses on the modification of behavior in practical settings.

Summary

The consequences of any given behavior control that behavior. To the degree that the consequences of a child's behavior can be modified, the teacher can channel or mold that behavior.

Three major consequences of behavior include *positive reinforcement, negative reinforcement,* and *punishment.* Whenever possible, the teacher should rely on positive reinforcement, because it is most likely to influence long-term behavioral change.

The consequences of behavior, whether positive, negative, or punishment, vary in intensity. In any case, the reinforcement must be of sufficient intensity (e.g., consequence) to gain the child's attention. In certain instances, intense reinforcement may be necessary to gain the child's attention initially.

The principles underlying behavior modification are universally applicable. The teacher should rely heavily on behavior modification techniques. Reliance on these techniques is particularly important when behavior problems are significant (e.g., low motivation, bizarre behavior, emotional disturbance), but the principles of behavior modification are *always* in effect, whether or not they are consciously manipulated by the teacher.

Finally, the abridged approach to behavior modification presented in this chapter must not foster the assumption that behavior modification is simple. This text does not permit more extensive coverage. All teachers, particularly those who teach in settings in which student behavior is seriously problematic, should pursue further, in-depth study of the principles and practices of behavior modification.

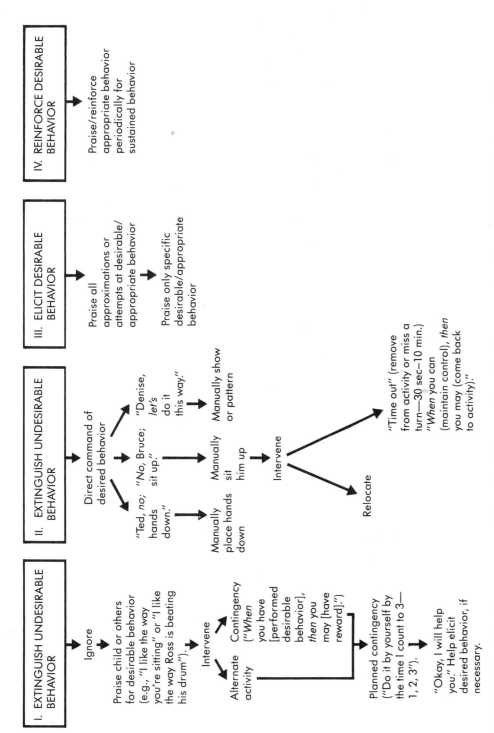

FIGURE 12.4. Behavior management flow chart diagrams key objectives: to extinguish undesirable behavior, to elicit desirable behavior, and to reinforce desirable behavior. (Used with permission from J. A. Seaman and K. P. DePauw, *The New Adapted Physical Education.* Palo Alto, Calif.: Mayfield Publishing, 1982, p. 332.)

References

Lavay, B. The Application of Operant Conditioning Techniques in the Physical Education Setting. Lecture presented at the New Mexico Association for Health, Physical Education, Recreation and Dance annual convention, Las Cruces, N. Mex., 22 October 1982.

———. Help! Class Out of Control. *Kansas Association for Health, Physical Education, Recreation, and Dance Journal* 53(2):29–31, 1985.

Morreau, L. E. Personal communication. Normal, Ill. July 1985.

Seaman, J. A., and DePauw, K. P. *The New Adapted Physical Education: A Developmental Approach.* Palo Alto, Calif.: Mayfield, 1982.

Taylor, R. L. *Assessment of Exceptional Students: Educational and Psychological Procedures.* Englewood Cliffs, N.J.: Prentice-Hall, 1984.

Taylor, R. L., and Marholin, D. A Functional Approach to the Assessment of Learning Disabilities. *Education and Treatment of Children* 3:271–278, 1980.

CHAPTER 13

Obesity, Overweight, and Other Eating Disorders

Jill was a 318-lb mass of flesh and flab. She was 14 years old, 5 ft 4 in. tall. She had always been heavy, almost from birth. She often took three helpings at mealtimes. Small children taunted her on the street. She was too large for necklaces, bracelets, and blue jeans. She wore the largest sizes available at the store for women, and when visitors came to her home, she fled to her room upstairs to keep out of sight.

Obesity has been a problem of human beings from the beginning of time. Evidence of obesity has been found in Stone Age diggings, in the ancient pyramids of Egypt, and in Greek sculpture. Overweight and obesity continue to be serious problems facing youth and adults in our society today. Approximately 20 percent of middle-aged males and 40 percent of middle-aged females are bordering on extreme overweight and obesity. Allsen, Harrison, and Vance (1980, pp. 1–2) state:

> Obesity is a major health hazard. If all deaths from cancer could be eliminated, two years would be added to a person's life span. If all the deaths related to obesity could be prevented, it is estimated that the life span would increase seven years! Some authorities indicate that life expectancy decreases approximately one percent for each pound of fat carried by an individual between the ages of forty-five and fifty.

No dimension of our physical condition is of greater interest to most people than an individual's weight. Overweight and obesity are the subjects of innumerable books, magazine articles, pamphlets, and newspapers. "Fat" is the target of many commercial enterprises that sell everything from special diets to reducing medicines or other "gimmicks" to produce small waistlines and little bottoms.

The problem of excess fat is not new. In fact, comparing present-day attitudes with attitudes of the early 1960s is interesting. Kraus and Raab (1961, p. 131) state: ". . . fat is unpleasing to our present aesthetic concepts. While a certain amount of it seems permissible and is accepted in the male, a 'slim, trim' waistline is a MUST for the woman who wishes to be attractive. Amazingly the desire for a slim figure is completely divorced from the desire for a functional body. . . . Yes, the problem of reducing is undertaken mainly for aesthetic reasons. The prevailing aim is to please contemporaries, to compete with the slimmer, and therefore, more attractive Joneses. While the important health problem is overlooked."

Who Is Fat?

To paraphrase nutritionist Jean Mayer: If individuals truly want to determine if they are fat, they should stand in front of a long mirror; take off all of their clothes and look at their body. If they *look* fat—they *are* fat! While this approach is not very scientific, it is realistic. Physical educators must keep in mind that the main reason why people want to lose weight is not for health purposes but because of vanity—a desire to look better in the eyes of other people.

Childhood obesity must be considered a major priority of adapted physical educators. According to current statistics, approximately one in every five youngsters is obese, and the alarming fact is that this figure is on the rise. The implications are many—including physical, psychological, and sociological. Early research by nutritionist Jean Mayer still holds true. He showed that obese high school students had less chance of gaining acceptance to college (when their obesity was known and a personal interview was required) than did students of average weight who were equally qualified. Other Mayer research demonstrates that even kindergarten children find fat children less desirable as playmates. Little wonder that obese children tend to exhibit personality disturbances!

Mayer and his associates also studied adolescent girls at a summer camp near Boston. In an effort to find out why obese girls were less active than their nonobese peers, three psychological tests were administered involving word association, sentence completion, and describing a picture story. The obese girls responded to the word association test with a larger number of food-related words such as "diet," "calories," "reducing," "fat," or "overweight." When completing the sentences, they used a much larger number of passive words. For example, in completing the sentence "When I am feeling bad, I . . ." the obese girls might add "sleep" or "cry." The nonobese girls, in contrast, finished with active concepts such as "work harder" or "visit with friends." Finally, in describing what they saw in a set of pictures, the obese girls described the boys and girls as passive. Things happened *to them* rather than their doing things. They also saw themselves as rejected (Mayer 1968).

As Thompson (Sinclair 1978, p. 44) states: "Among animals we shall see . . . how small birds and beasts are quick and agile, how slower and sedater movements come with larger size, and how exaggerated bulk brings with it a certain clumsiness, a certain inefficiency, an element of risk and hazard, a preponderance of disadvantage." Generally speaking, obese youngsters are far less active than boys and girls of normal weight. Numerous studies confirm that obese children take part in significantly lower levels of physical activity than their peers, whether they are in school, out of school, in summer camp, or at home (Bar-Or 1983).

Definition of Overweight and Obesity

A healthy individual possesses some adipose tissue (fat cells). A desirable percentage of body fat for the average person is estimated to be between 15 to 20 percent for adult females and 10 to 15 percent for adult males. Some highly conditioned male athletes have as little as 4 percent body fat.

By general consensus, a person is considered **overweight** in our society if her percentage of body fat is 10 to 20 percent above ideal weight. **Obesity** begins when the person is 20 percent over her ideal body weight. Sherrill (1986) has coined the phrase *super obese* for those individuals who reach a level of 50 percent above ideal weight.

These percentages have been applied traditionally to adults. Pollock, Wilmore, and Fox (1984, pp. 30–31) caution about applying these same percentages to children: "For individuals undergoing changes in bone material, i.e., increasing bone material in the youngster as he or she matures . . . the equations used to estimate relative fat from body density will be inaccurate, providing an overestimation of the actual fat concentration."

A major problem that must be addressed is how we determine ideal weight. One answer is that there are many ideal weights, which are determined by variables such as body type, age, and sex. As Roche (1985, p. 4) states, "*Standard* or *ideal* imply values for all time, with biologic interpretation of what ought to be. However, these reference data change from one survey to the next. External criteria of functional normality are desirable but difficult to include in surveys of large numbers of individuals. The large numbers are necessary to calculate stable estimates. . . . Only the questionnaire approach is practical, and its validity is questionable." Researchers are therefore not in agreement about the concept of "ideal weight."

Etiology of Fat

Genetic Factors and Obesity

A controversy exists as to whether certain individuals inherit an obesity trait from either or both parents. In other words, can the person control his potential to be obese? Because of an inherited predisposition to obesity, does the same caloric intake result in a greater accumulation of fat in some individuals (Hollenberg, Roncari, and Dijan, 1983)? This genetic trait may also predetermine how many new adipose cells are added during the developmental years (0–20), and how easily the fat is stored.

Foch and McClearn (1980) conducted a review of research dealing with genetic impact on obesity. They conclude from results of animal studies that there is a genetic code that controls obesity and is passed on to offspring. In a recent study by Aubert and associates (1985), the researchers found a new strain of mouse, which did possess all of the innate characteristics that induce obesity.

Research comparisons and conclusions regarding humans are not as conclusive. Most of the research tends to indicate that humans have a basic limit to the number of fat cells that any newborn child can possess and that the genetic code varies little among humans. Note that the initial birthweight of any baby has no bearing on how much the child will weigh as an adult. A large newborn baby (10 lb 6 oz) or a small baby (6 lb 4 oz) therefore have the same chance of being obese or of normal proportions.

Early studies by Gurney (1965) indicate that a strong correlation exists between the child's obesity and the parents' weight. He found that when both parents are obese, approximately 80 percent of their children are obese also. When one parent is obese, 40 percent of their offspring are obese. When, however, neither parent is obese, only 8 to 9 percent of their children are obese. The question is: What caused the obesity? Genetic factors or environmental conditions?

Excessive Caloric Intake

Katch and McArdle (1983, p. 133) summarize the cause of overweight as follows: "We can state with certainty that excess fat is the end result of an imbalance between the number of calories consumed and the number of calories expended to sustain daily activities." Astrand and Rodahl (1986, p. 571) concur: "If energy in-take [food] exceeds energy output [activity], the excess energy will be stored as adipose tissue."

Unneeded adipose tissue can develop in two basic ways. The first and rarer cause is related to glandular malfunction, including abnormality of the thyroid, hypothalamus, or pituitary glands. Glandular abnormalities are estimated to account for 3 to 10 percent of all obesity. The second, and by far more common cause of obesity is *excessive caloric intake*! People simply eat more than they can use, so the extra food is stored in the form of fat. As Katch and McArdle (1983, p. 161) state, "It is simply not possible to consume more calories than are expended without increasing body weight."

Adipose tissue is composed of fat cells. These cells are separated from each other by a matrix of collagenous fibers and yellow elastic fibers. Fatty lipids fill the existing cells, which become storehouses for future use. Individuals can increase fat storage from birth through adulthood.

Adipose tissue serves an important function. Bray (1983, p. 19) states: "Since adipose tissue is the major expandable depot for energy storage, excess calories, whether derived from carbohydrates, fat or protein, are converted into fatty acids and then stored as triglycerides in fat cells." Smith (1983, p. 245) describes the role of the fat cell when he comments: "The fat cell is uniquely adapted for its function to store energy as triglyceride in the cell and to release the stored lipids as fatty acids when needed by the body. The cell is capable of changing its diameter at least 10-fold to accommodate the stored triglyceride." When hundreds of thousands of fat cells become grossly enlarged, the result is obesity! Pollock, Wilmore, and Fox (1984) estimate that the mature obese adult has 90 to 150 billion fat cells, whereas the nonobese individual has only 20 to 30 billion, one third to one fifth as many.

Researchers agree that the obese person not only possesses more fat cells but possesses fat cells that are larger in size. This combination (i.e., more cells and larger cells) is the major cause of excessive overweight.

Studies by Spencer, Vinter, and Hull (1985); Faust and Miller (1983); Bray (1983); Oscai and associates (1974); and Salans, Cushman, and Weismann (1973) illustrate dramatically that the number of adipose cells does increase during the developmental years (i.e., the time when the musculoskeletal system is still growing). More specifically, fat cells can increase in number during the preschool years through the early teens. Salans et al. (1973) demonstrate that during the periods from age 0 to 5 years and from age 9 to 13 years, the number of fat cells increased significantly in their obese subjects.

Although this text deals primarily with school-age children, mention is made here of another theory that concerns the addition of new fat cells in adults. This occurs in adult onset obesity. Faust and Miller (1983, p. 46) explain: "However, when adult onset obesity is severe, there may be a substantial increase in the number of fat cells. . . . Since fat cell numbers begin to increase at about the time that fat cell size peaks, it has been suggested that at some level enlargement of the cells begins to produce locally acting signals which stimulate production of new fat cells. . . . It is thus reasonable to speculate that production of new fat cells will occur in man when fat cells get very large, and that the critical degree of enlargement will vary among individuals as well as across fat depots." This interesting theory may lead to new concepts of how additional fat cells are formed.

A distinct relationship exists between the body's muscle mass and adipose tissue. The amount and size of muscle tissue decreases in most older people, usually owing to lack of appropriate exercise. As the individual uses up less energy, the muscle mass decreases, and a larger percentage of body weight becomes fat. Ancel Keys, a researcher in weight control, showed that decreases in calories in different adult age groups at rest were related to decreased muscle mass rather than to age (Allsen, Harrison, and Vance 1980). A similar reaction can be observed in children and adolescents whose body mass is imbalanced toward fat. Dupont and Freedman (1983, p. 270) state: "The overweight individual has an increased proportion of 'inert body mass,' that is, tissue that does not participate in muscular exercise. Mostly fat, this 'dead weight' can approach 40–50% of body mass."

Cahill and Renold (1983, p. 4) summarize the processes that produce obesity: ". . . the calculation of the number of . . . fat cells in an organism, such as an experimental animal or man, has led to the concept that obesity in the formative years in man is associated with both *hypertrophy* (enlarged cells) and *hyperplasia* (increased number of cells), whereas obesity after completion of the growth phase is mainly hypertrophic (enlarged cells)."

Faust and Miller (1983) cite the example of a 120-lb female with approximately 20 percent body fat and average size fat cells. Through increased caloric intake, the girl increased the size of her fat cells until she was approximately three times her normal size. This represents about a 50 lb increase in weight. To return to normal body weight, the girl needs only to reattain her beginning fat cell size. The process of cell size reduction is accomplished by using the stored lipids (fat) for energy, that is, one reduces caloric intake so the body *must* use its stored fat. As a result, the girl returns to her beginning weight.

The only way to achieve and maintain a reduced fat cell size is by some form of continuous activity or dieting or both. Faust and Miller (1983, p. 41) believe that "Protocols of sustained alteration of activity or diet composition . . . can be at least moderately effective at keeping fat cells smaller than they otherwise would be" (Figure 13.1).

Katch and McArdle (1983) conducted a study with a group of nonobese subjects who had no previous personal or family history of obesity. The researchers report that each subject's body weight increased an average of 36 lb after the subjects were asked to intentionally overeat. At the conclusion of the 4-month eating program, the number and size of each subject's fat cells were compared with pretest figures. The average size of the fat cells increased significantly, with no corresponding change in fat cell number. At this time, the subjects reduced to their normal weight by restricting food intake. The researchers found that the subjects' body fat was reduced, and in addition that the fat cells returned to their original size (Figure 13.2).

What the research is telling us is this: if we could effectively control *excessive* caloric intake of youngsters (age preschool through junior high adolescents), we would be able to control the development of new and undesirable adipose tissue. Without the

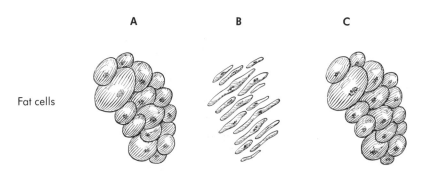

FIGURE 13.1. (A) Feeding results in slow production of fat cells filled with lipid. (B) After a period of food deprivation (starvation), fat cells have virtually no lipid, but all cells are present. No new cells are seen. (C) During refeeding, the fat cells refill with lipid, but no new cells are formed. (Adapted from Faust and Miller 1983, p. 43.)

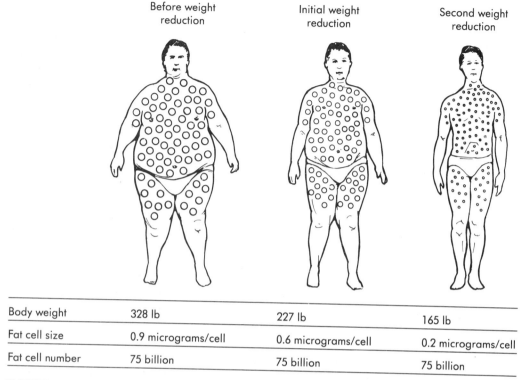

	Before weight reduction	Initial weight reduction	Second weight reduction
Body weight	328 lb	227 lb	165 lb
Fat cell size	0.9 micrograms/cell	0.6 micrograms/cell	0.2 micrograms/cell
Fat cell number	75 billion	75 billion	75 billion

FIGURE 13.2. Changes in adipose cellularity in obese subjects with weight reduction. (Data from J. Hirsch. Adipose Cellularity in Relation to Human Obesity, G. H. Stollerman, ed., *Advances in Internal Medicine*, vol. 17. Copyright © 1971 by Year Book Medical Publishers, Inc. Used with permission.)

addition of new fat cells, most individuals are able to control effectively the ravages of obesity. In other words, enormous extra numbers of fat cells are usually present when overweight and obesity begin.

A major problem develops when society attempts to control the feeding patterns of infants and very young children. Social customs, economic conditions, and misinformation often dictate what and how much parents feed their children. A common and erroneous practice endorses "giving the babies all they will eat, because chubby babies are happy babies." Little do the well-meaning parents know that they may be relegating their children to a life of frustration, which goes with being obese.

Once an individual's total number of fat cells has been established (approximately in the early teens), and if that number is excessive, then the individual will always fight a weight battle. Statements like the following are typical of such people: "Why is it that everything I eat turns to fat? My friend eats all she wants, but she never seems to gain a pound." Obesity researchers, using a specific technique to *count* the number of fat cells present, have supplied the answers to these questions. Put simply, more fat cells equal more fat.

This raises another question: if young children lose their "baby fat," and look normal during their developmental years, what are the chances that they will become overweight or obese as adults? Research indicates that the blueprint has been established and that under certain conditions these youngsters may face a continual problem of excessive weight.

The prepubescent years are critical and should be closely watched by parents, physicians, and physical educators. The educator's role is key and cannot be put aside because of embarrassment about bringing the child's obese condition to the attention of those involved. The adapted physical educator must assume a major responsibility and be a leader in developing a multidisciplinary approach to deal with the problem.

Steiner (1970) highlights this point when he notes that the problem of obesity is not given the attention it deserves. He tells of a 10-year longitudinal study involving 200 obese 9-year-old boys and girls. Seventy-four percent of the boys and 70 percent of the girls were determined to be still obese when the subjects turned 18 years old. One cannot help but ask questions like the following: Why weren't the parents seeking help for their child? Why wasn't the pediatrician prescribing diets and long-lasting behavior modification programs immediately? Why didn't teachers observe the emotional and social implications and try to intervene? Why didn't physical educators become involved when they observed motor and fitness difficulties? Responsibility and accountability must be shared by many, for programs are now available that deal with multiple aspects of the problem. Blackburn and St. Lezin (1984) describe the following weight control program: "A comprehensive, multidisciplinary approach to weight loss and weight maintenance emphasizes three points, in the following order: (1) behavior change, including cue control and food avoidance, (2) establishing increased activity patterns, and (3) establish techniques to produce weight loss" (p. 440).

Measuring Body Fat

A number of methods are considered acceptable and are commonly used today to measure body fat. These include anthropometric measures, underwater weighing, volume displacement, radiographic analysis, potassium-40 analysis, isotopic dilution, ultrasound techniques, computerized tomography, and nuclear magnetic resonance. Only one of these methods is easily adapted to the school setting, that is, anthropometric measurement (skinfold fat and body part circumference). In most situations, public school physical educators have the expertise to use skinfold thickness technique to determine existing percentages of body fat (Polacek, Wang, and Eichstaedt 1985; Hastad, Marett, and Plowman 1983; and AAHPERD 1980). The skinfold caliper is accepted as a comparatively accurate instrument in the hands of a trained and experienced physical education teacher.

Body Typing (Somatotyping)

Body typing, or somatotyping, deals with body type and the physical classification of the human body. Three general terms are used to describe individual body types: endomorphic, mesomorphic, and ectomorphic.

All children start life with a bone structure and basic muscle pattern that is pre-determined genetically. **Endomorphs** are short, stocky, heavy boned, soft muscled, medium shouldered, and wide hipped with ham-shaped limbs. **Mesomorphs** are medium tall, well set, medium boned, solid muscled, broad shouldered, narrow hipped, and have quite long limbs. **Ectomorphs** are tall, slender, light boned, thin muscled, narrow shouldered, narrow hipped, and long limbed. These classifications distinguish the three general body shapes, but many individuals are a combination of several types. Mathews and Fox (1976) believe that the pure somatotype does not exist, but that each person embodies components of all three types.

Nothing can be done to change an individual's body type, but much can be done to develop the best possible physique for the framework, including control of excessive fat.

Although height-weight-age charts are questioned by some, these charts can serve as a general guideline when programming is being developed for overweight and obese students. Appendix A provides desirable height and weight comparisons for boys and girls between the ages of 5 and 18 years.

Skinfold Thickness

National norm-referenced tables that show percentile ratings of triceps skinfold thickness have been established for children between 5 and 18 years of age (AAHPERD 1980). Tables 13.1 and 13.2 list the critical percentiles to be used with skinfold measurements. The AAHPERD *Health Related Physical Fitness Test Manual* (1980, p. 17) describes how the norms should be interpreted and used: "The criterion for a desired degree of fatness for children is above the 50th percentile. When children are below the 50th percentile but above the 25th percentile, it is recommended that their weight be maintained at the same level for the current year. For those below the 25th percentile, strong encouragement needs to be given to reduce body fatness until their skinfold fat data reaches a desired level."

Pollock, Wilmore, and Fox (1984, p. 215) state: "In some cases, and in particular with school children, the sum of skinfold measures should be used. In addition, various individual skinfold fat and circumference measures when taken serially over weeks or months can demonstrate a shift in body composition. For example, the gluteal and waist circumference measures are excellent in showing reductions in body fat with aerobic training, and biceps circumference increases with strength training."

Katch (1985, p. 73) warns that inaccuracies are highly possible when using skinfold measures alone. Researchers have established that some skinfold measurements are extremely inaccurate or impossible to use with obese individuals (Roche, Abdel-Malek,

TABLE 13.1

PERCENTILE NORMS FOR TRICEPS SKINFOLD FOR BOYS AND GIRLS AGE 6–18

| | Triceps Skinfold (mm) | | | | | | | | | | | | |
| | | | | | | Age | | | | | | | |
Percentile	6	7	8	9	10	11	12	13	14	15	16	17	18
						Boys[a]							
75	6	6	6	7	7	7	7	7	6	6	6	6	6
50	8	8	8	8	9	10	9	9	8	8	8	8	8
25	9	10	11	12	12	14	13	13	12	11	11	11	11
						Girls[a]							
75	7	8	8	9	9	9	9	9	11	12	12	12	12
50	9	10	10	11	12	12	12	12	14	15	16	16	16
25	11	12	14	14	15	15	16	17	18	20	21	20	20

[a]Based on data from Johnston, F. E., Hamill, D. V., and Lemeshow, S. (1) *Skinfold Thickness of Children 6–11 Years* (Series II, No. 120, 1972), and (2) *Skinfold Thickness of Youth 12–17 Years* (Series II, No. 132, 1974). U.S. National Center for Health Statistics, U.S. Department of HEW, Washington, D.C.

and Mukherjee 1985). The calipers do not fit around the "pinched" area. A logical blending of skinfold measurements and body part circumference measurements is more desirous and provides important information during initial assessment of individuals for excessive adipose tissue.

Body Part Circumference

The traditional method of measuring body part circumferences has led to conflicting conclusions, and is particularly questionable when attempting to identify valid norms. Extensive research by McArdle, Katch, and Katch (1981) involving individuals between the ages of 17 and 50 years addressed this point. Their study, however, is not directly relevant to school-age students. Frisancho (1981) developed an extensive set of norms using triceps skinfold, upper arm circumference, arm muscle circumference, arm muscle area, and arm fat area. He drew his data from the U.S. Health and Nutrition Examination Survey of 1971–1974. The age range of the 19,097 subjects was between 1 and 74 years. He concluded that arm circumference is not a good predictor of body fat, even when used in combination with triceps skinfold measurements. He presents

TABLE 13.2

PERCENTILE NORMS FOR SUM OF TRICEPS PLUS SUBSCAPULAR SKINFOLD FOR BOYS AND GIRLS AGE 6–18

Percentile	Triceps Plus Subscapular Skinfold (mm) Age												
	6	7	8	9	10	11	12	13	14	15	16	17	18
Boys[a]													
75	11	11	11	11	12	12	11	12	11	12	12	12	12
50	12	12	13	14	14	16	15	15	14	14	14	15	15
25	14	15	17	18	19	22	21	22	20	20	20	21	21
Girls[a]													
75	12	12	13	14	14	15	15	16	18	20	20	20	20
50	14	15	16	17	18	19	19	20	24	25	25	27	27
25	17	19	21	24	25	25	27	30	32	34	34	36	36

[a]Based on data from Johnston, F. E., Hamill, D. V., and Lemeshow, S. (1) *Skinfold Thickness of Children 6–11 Years* (Series II, No. 120, 1972), and (2) *Skinfold Thickness of Youth 12–17 Years* (Series II, No. 132, 1974). U.S. National Center for Health Statistics, U.S. Department of HEW, Washington, D.C.

specific norms,[1] including some for youngsters between the ages of 1 and 19 years, but cautions that these norms are to be used for white subjects only, as too few black subjects were sampled to develop accurate norms.

A third dimension of adipose tissue measurement, namely, the observation of where the main pockets of fat are located, has come recently into prominence. This observation is referred to as *distribution of fat*. In other words, through observation alone, a physical education teacher can see where unsightly fat is a problem. These areas (i.e., hips, waist, upper arms) are targeted as priority areas and become annual goals of a weight reduction program. For example, an annual goal might be: "To reduce circumference of hips from 44 in. to 41 in."

Although "spot reducing" is considered impossible, reducing the general size of a given area is quite possible. Fat cell size will not be reduced, but flabby muscle fiber can be firmed with a resulting decrease in circumference. An illustration may help to

---

1. These tables can be found in A. R. Frisancho's article entitled: New Norms of Upper Limb Fat and Muscle Areas for Assessment of Nutritional Status. *The American Journal of Clinical Nutrition* 34(11):2540–2545, November 1981.

clarify this controversy. When an individual participates in extensive abdominal strengthening exercises, the waist almost always becomes smaller in circumference because muscle fiber is firmed. Fat cell size around the waist is not, however, reduced.

MacIntyre (n.d.) conducted a research project at Pasadena City College entitled "A New Shape-Maker Program for Women." She found that when her experimental group ($N = 15$) used weight training exercises, they experienced significant size reductions over the control group subjects who did the same exercises without weight training. None of the subjects restricted their caloric intake during the 6-week period. She formed the following conclusions: (1) The hips seemed most sensitive to change. Average circumference reduction was 1⅜ in. with 95 percent of the subjects decreasing circumference. Some subjects lost up to 3 in. (2) The average decrease in upper arm circumference was ½ in., and 85 percent of the subjects decreased arm circumference. Some students lost as much as 1½ in. (3) Thighs also were sensitive to training, and average circumference reduction was almost 1⅞ in. Ninety percent of the subjects had measurement decreases. Some subjects showed reductions of more than 2 in. The regimen lasted for 6 weeks, 3 days per week, 40 min per day. The specific exercises used by MacIntyre are discussed later in this chapter under the heading "Weight Training Programs."

A more general approach is therefore suggested in reference to measuring and using body part circumferences as indications of overweight. This approach involves actual measurement of the body part circumference with a cloth tape measure (or, to be more accurate, with a steel tape). The measurement should occur at those sites shown in Figure 13.3, and be recorded to the nearest quarter inch. This process allows one to record existing size and plan for future size reduction. Accuracy and consistency of measurement are possible when the physical education teacher uses this technique regularly. In addition, the student can observe actual improvement. Charting or plotting of each student's progress is highly recommended.

To determine desirable body weight, Katch and McArdle (1983, p. 130) list the following formula, example, and description:

$$\text{Desirable body weight} = \frac{\text{Lean body weight}}{1.00 - \% \text{ fat desired}}$$

Suppose that a 200-lb teenage boy who has 25 percent body fat wishes to lower his body fat to 18 percent. The computations would be:

Fat weight = 200 lb × .25 = 50 lb
Lean body weight = 200 lb − 50 lb = 150 lb
$$\text{Desirable body weight} = \frac{150\,\text{lb}}{1.00 - .18}$$
$$= \frac{150\,\text{lb}}{.82}$$
$$= 182.9\,\text{lb}$$

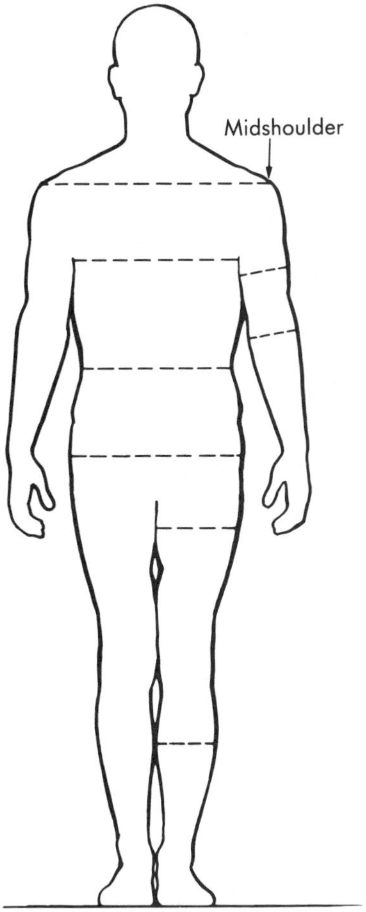

Midshoulder

Name _____		Date _____			
Year 19____ – 19____		Year in School _____			
	Sept.	Nov.	Jan.	April	June
Weight					
Shoulder					
Chest (normal)					
Chest (expanded)					
Left biceps					
Right biceps					
Left forearm					
Right forearm					
Left thigh					
Right thigh					
Left calf					
Right calf					
Waist					
Hips					

Measure each area at the same spot every time you measure. Don't let the tape sag.

FIGURE 13.3. Sample body circumference chart. Measuring each area at the same spot every time you measure is important for accurate record-keeping. Be careful not to let the tape sag.

Desirable fat loss = Present body weight − Desirable body weight

= 200 lb − 182.9 lb
= 17.1 lb

If this boy loses 17.1 lb of body fat, his new body weight of 182.9 lb will have a fat content equal to 18 percent of body weight. The physical educator should recommend an approximate range for desirable body weight. This boy's range would be 180 to 185 lb.

A Change in Life-Style: The Weight Reduction Program

Weight reduction programs are generally ineffective because individuals are usually unable to change their life-style. As Blackburn and St. Lezin (1984, p. 439) comment, "Treatment of either obesity or overweight by conventional diet programs or by emphasizing weekly weight change without comprehensive therapy has yielded extremely poor results. Successful treatment must emphasize a multidisciplinary approach to obesity therapy, involving diet, exercise, and behavior modification."

A major concern of all physical educators who work with overweight and obese students is that the weight lost will be put back on when the exercise and diet programs are reduced or stopped. Franklin (1984, p. 111) illustrates the negative and positive variables that contribute to sustained participant interest and enthusiasm when attempting to lose weight (Figure 13.4).

Parents should become actively involved in all programs that deal with the obese youngster because total family cooperation is needed for success to occur and continue. Some parents may be apprehensive and may balk at the thought of segregating their child from peers and from the traditional curriculum. The educator must convince the parents of program quality and must be prepared to explain the exciting and stimulating activities that comprise the new program (e.g., "The Trim Team"). Program participation should not become a stigma, but should be in demand when parents and students realize that activities are individualized. The educator also should ask parents to contact the child's pediatrician for diet recommendations, perhaps even a prescribed diet. Be sure to mention that the child's progress will be monitored closely and that ongoing results will be sent home regularly.

Physicians in general tend to be unaware of the contribution that physical education programming can make to the management of childhood obesity. Sintek and Bishop (1985) surveyed 96 pediatricians and 97 family physicians and found that few believed that physical educators were playing a major role in reduction of student obesity. The physicians did believe that physical education programming had the potential to make an important contribution. The researchers suggest that a gap exists between physical educators and the medical profession. They recommend accordingly that physical education departments disseminate information to physicians telling how physical education programming can be used in obesity management. Physical educators might make oral presentations at local or regional medical society meetings. The presentation should include a video-cassette showing school settings and how school personnel (i.e., physical educator, school nurse, health teacher, and school psychologist) can help manage childhood obesity through cooperation with the student's physician and family.

Behavior modification is a necessary component of all successful weight loss programs. Students must be made aware that permanent changes in their appearance will result if they are able to control caloric intake and continue an ongoing regimen of moderate exercise.

The goal of a sensible eating plan is to help students restructure and change eating habits by extinguishing problem eating patterns and replacing those undesirable behav-

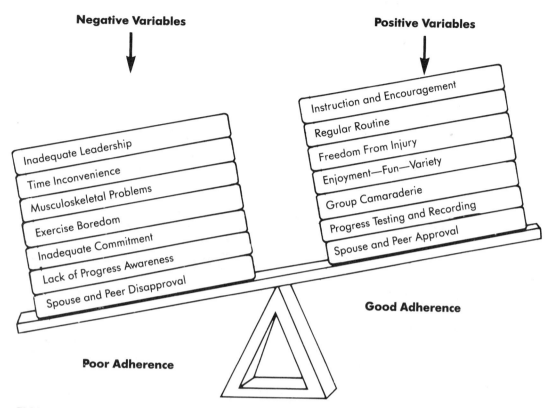

FIGURE 13.4. Variables affecting compliance with physical conditioning programs. Negative variables often outweigh positive variables, resulting in poor program adherence. (Reprinted by permission of the publisher from Figure 1, page 111 in BEHAVIORAL MANAGEMENT OF OBESITY by Jean Storlie and Henry A. Jordan (eds.). Copyright 1984, Spectrum Publications, Inc., Jamaica, New York.)

iors with normal eating patterns. The process is further complicated when parents dictate when and what the student eats. Recruiting the parents' cooperation at all times is therefore necessary. The physician's diet and suggestions, if these are forthcoming, are also integral parts of the program.

Goal setting and contracting are useful and successful techniques. For example, an ideal body weight is a desired outcome and is therefore a program goal. To achieve this goal, the instructor should help the student clarify and state which life-style features and behaviors must be changed if the program is to be successful. The student must indicate exactly *what* is to be accomplished and *how* these goals are to be achieved. Exercise descriptions must be specific, that is, exercise duration and frequency must be provided for each activity. This leaves no room for misunderstanding or misinterpretation of what is expected of the student. Both long-range goals and short-term behavioral objectives should be listed. The short-term behavioral objectives, or mini-goals, give the student a sense of accomplishment, thereby reinforcing the long-range goals. Storlie and Jordan (1984, p. 28) provide an excellent example of a weight loss contract (Figure 13.5).

Diet and Weight Control

Caloric intake must be reduced if individuals are to lose weight. Guyton (1979) describes what happens to an individual who undergoes the extreme process of starvation. He states: "During starvation, essentially all the stored carbohydrates in the

NUTREXERCISE Weight Loss Contract

I, _____, hereby contract to lose _____ pounds per week to lose a total of _____ pounds while involved in the NUTREXERCISE Program. This will place me at my short-term goal of _____ pounds by _____ (date). To achieve this weight loss I will engage in the following exercise program:

Activity	Duration	Frequency
_____ for	_____ minutes	_____ times/week
_____ for	_____ minutes	_____ times/week
_____ for	_____ minutes	_____ times/week

This will burn approximately _____ calories per day on an average. In addition to the exercise program, above, I will decrease my calorie intake by _____ calories per day to lose the _____ pounds per week.

To decrease my calorie intake, I will use the following dieting techniques:
_____ Avoid empty calorie food, specifically _____
_____ Portion control, specifically _____
_____ Selecting low calorie foods, specifically _____
_____ Decrease luxurious calories, specifically _____
_____ Other, specifically _____

Through these life-style changes, I will:
_____ Maintain my short-term goal
_____ Continue to lose _____ pounds per week to achieve my long-term goal of _____ pounds by _____ (date).
With the best of my intentions, I sign below to confirm my commitment to and understanding of this weight loss program.

_____   _____
Date   Signature of participant

_____   _____
Date   Signature of instructor

FIGURE 13.5. Sample weight loss contract. (Reprinted by permission of the publisher from Figure 2, page 28 in BEHAVIORAL MANAGEMENT OF OBESITY by Jean Storlie and Henry A. Jordan (eds.). Copyright 1984, Spectrum Publications, Inc., Jamaica, New York.)

body, which amounts to about 300 grams of glycogen in the liver and muscles, becomes used up within the first 12 to 14 hours. Thereafter, the person exists on his stored fats and proteins. For the first 2 to 4 weeks, almost all of the energy used by the body is derived from the stored fats, but eventually even these are almost depleted, so that finally the proteins must also be used. Most tissues can give up as much as one-half of their proteins before cellular death begins. Therefore, for at least another few days to a week, the body can derive its energy from proteins. But finally, death ensues because proteins are the necessary chemical elements for the performance of cellular functions. This usually occurs 4 to 7 weeks after starvation begins" (p. 423).

We do not imply that individuals should go on starvation diets. On the contrary, most experts agree that a dieting individual should lose no more than 2 lb per week. In addition, **all diets must be written by a physician.** If anyone else writes or gives a specific diet to an individual, that person can be held liable for any negative results stemming from weight loss. Only the physician has access to all of the patient information needed to write a program for healthy weight reduction. The physician will take into account basic metabolic rate, vitamin and mineral levels, and potential complications unique to each person. Blackburn and St. Lezin (1984) suggest that routine evaluation by a physician should include not only physical examination and routine biochemical and metabolic tests, but also psychological testing, exercise fitness assessment, and nutritional history.

When a diet is prescribed by a physician, it should (in comparison with prediet intake) contain at least 500 fewer calories per day for a 1 lb loss per week, and 1000 fewer calories per day for a 2 lb loss per week. It is critical that the new diet be comprised of a *balanced* cutback of the basic nutrients, that is, carbohydrates must constitute 50 to 55 percent of the diet, while fats make up 30 percent, and proteins 15 to 20 percent. Any major deviation from the above percentages should be closely monitored by the physician.

Some "fad diets" on the market today encourage severe reductions and departures from the critical nutrient balance. These wonder diets do not meet required carbohydrate, fat, or protein percentages. For example, Dr. Stillman's "Quick Weight Loss Diet" prohibits carbohydrates, allows proteins, and requires the individual to drink eight glasses of water per day. Stillman then developed a second diet with the following suggested percentages: 5 percent carbohydrates, 5 to 15 percent fat, and up to 90 percent protein. His diet allowed for selected vegetables, breads, and dairy products, plus 10 glasses of water per day. Stillman claims that the diet causes the body to burn more calories because of an increase in metabolism, which accelerates breakdown of stored fat. Critics of the Stillman diet cite several potential problems, including fatigue, a breakdown of existing body protein and bone cells, and a high rise in blood cholesterol. Of major concern is the diet's nutritional imbalance. It is basically a protein and water diet, and in addition, it is high in saturated fat and cholesterol.

The "Last-Chance Diet" is another example of nutritional imbalance that is potentially dangerous. The individual is instructed to eat no food with the exception of a liquid protein supplement, which is to be taken four or five times per day. This type of diet was designed originally for people who were grossly obese and under strict physician supervision. At present, however, anyone can purchase liquid protein in drug or food stores, or in health food shops. It is readily available to anyone. Even though liquid protein supplements control the loss of lean body mass, other irregularities occur if one ingests these supplements as the main food source. Mineral and vitamin stores are reduced, and dehydration develops. Low blood sugar, anemia, and menstrual abnormalities are recorded. Several persons have died of heart attacks, which were attributed to low potassium levels.

The "Scarsdale" diet promises a 20-lb weight loss in 2 weeks, and stresses high protein and low carbohydrate intake. No sugar, alcohol, or oils are allowed, but carrots and celery are unlimited. If the specific meal plan is followed faithfully, the dieter usually consumes approximately 1000 calories per day. People on this diet tend to complain of fatigue. As with all diets, any imbalance of essential nutrients over an extended period of time is potentially harmful.

The "Beverly Hills" diet is based on the concept that you can lose weight and stay slim all your life, while eating all of your favorite foods, by following the "conscious combining" technique. For the first 11 days, the dieter eats nothing but fruit, and lots of it, letting one type digest before eating another. The more fruit the dieter eats, the more weight she supposedly loses. The second week, vegetables and bread are added; the third week, lobster. In the fourth week, the dieter begins a morning regimen of bran. The conscious combining process means that common food types are eaten together. For example, proteins are eaten with other proteins, but not with carbohydrates or fats. This diet is extremely dangerous, and doctors have warned that lack of natural salt combined with ingestion of large amounts of fruit may cause severe water loss through diarrhea, which can lead to serious illness and even death.

It is generally true that fad diets enable people to lose significant weight over a short period of time, but the negative side effects of such diets do not justify their use. Katch and McArdle (1983, p. 165) state: "There is simply no compelling evidence to support the contention that the popular 'fad' diets have any advantage over a calorically-restricted, well-balanced diet."

Of the publicized diets, the "Weight Watchers'" diet appears to take the most reliable approach to weight loss. It involves a balanced and planned diet with three variations: Full choice (1200 calories per day), Limited choice (1100 calories), or No choice (1050 calories). The "No choice" plan spells out 7 days of menus, which are to be followed for as long as 2 weeks, then the dieter switches to one of the other plans. The diet stresses a 1 to 2 lb loss per week until the desired weight is reached, then an appropriate maintenance plan is developed. A major component of the diet is the ongoing behavior modification support group technique, plus involvement in a regular exercise program.

Students should be strongly discouraged from following cure-all diet programs described in magazines. Instead, dieters should use only the restricted meal plans given to them by a physician. In addition, they should be encouraged to eat well-planned meals, but in smaller quantities. The physical educator should have students record their daily food intake for 1 week to determine approximately how many calories are consumed. The students also should include specific information regarding (1) time of day when food is eaten, (2) how much food is eaten, (3) place where food is eaten, (4) people food is eaten with, and (5) immediate feelings or mood at time of eating (Fig-

ANALYSIS OF DAILY FOOD INTAKE DAY		Mon	Tues	Wed	Thurs	Fri	Sat	Sun

Time of Day	Food	How Much?	Where Were You?	With Whom?	How Do You Feel?

FIGURE 13.6. Sample page from a weekly food diary.

ure 13.6). This approach gives the instructor an opportunity to help the student understand not only how much he eats but also the reasons why he eats. For example, the chart may show that whenever the youngster becomes bored, food is eaten. By identifying this problem, the teacher and student can take positive steps to help the youngster do something else when boredom sets in. For example, take a walk, ride a bike, jump rope, phone a friend, or read a magazine.

Jones, Shainberg, and Byer (1974, pp. 109–110) list the following rules for successful and healthful dieting:

1. Know what your desirable weight should be.
2. Count calories.
   a. 1 pound of weight = 3500 calories
   b. A reduction of 3500 calories per week = 1 pound lost per week
   c. A reduction of a mere 500 calories per day = 1 pound per week
   d. A planned diet (prescribed by a physician):
      (1) Should contain calories necessary to maintain desirable body weight
      (2) Must include all basic foods—proteins, fats, carbohydrates, vitamins, and minerals (or equivalent supplements) and water

(3) Do not cut out foods you like; just cut down on amounts you eat
(4) Remember that fats contain more calories per pound than any other foods
  (a) Some foods are very high in fat content—bacon, ham, chocolate, nuts, oils, and the like.
  (b) Fried foods retain the fats they are fried in
(5) If the reduced weight is to be maintained over a long period of time, a diet should include a change in eating habits.

Exercise and Weight Control

A question often arises as to what types of exercise promote weight loss. Some argue that an individual must perform exercise equivalent to an extremely heavy amount of work just to lose 1 lb. For example, Katch and McArdle (1983, p. 175) state: "Usually cited is the fact that one must chop wood for 14 hours, golf for 20 hours, perform mild calisthenic exercises for 22 hours, or play Ping-Pong for 28 hours or volleyball for 32 hours just to reduce body fat by one pound." They continue:

> Understandably, such a commitment is overwhelming and very discouraging to the overweight person who plans to lose up to 20 or 30 pounds or more. From a different perspective, however, if you played golf only two hours (about 350 kcal per day) two days per week (700 kcal), it would take about 5 weeks or ten golfing days to lose 1 pound of fat (3500). Assuming you could play golf year round, playing golf two days a week would result in a 10-pound loss of fat during the year. While most of us would probably not play golf this frequently (nor are we likely to play golf for 20 consecutive hours) the point is that the calorie expending effects of exercise are cumulative; a calorie deficit of 3500 kcal is equivalent to a 1-pound loss, whether the deficit occurs rapidly or systematically over a long time.

Dietz and Gortmaker (1985) found a direct correlation between inactivity (television watching) and obesity. They conclude that obese and superobese children between the ages of 12 and 17 years watch significantly more television than their nonobese peers. In reference to this study, the editors of *Nutrition Reviews* (1986) suggest that additional studies are needed to address the issue of whether it is television and the consequent inactivity of television watching that cause obesity, or whether overweight children simply choose to watch more television. Possibly these youngsters are so uncomfortable when they attempt to take part in organized physical activities that they therefore avoid recreational endeavors. They also may not possess the motor skills necessary to be successful in games and sports. As a result, they spend an excessive amount of time in front of the television set.

The early research of Oscai and associates (1974) resulted in important and dramatic findings regarding development of new fat cells and size of existing fat cells when an extreme exercise program was imposed on experimental animals. Although comparisons between animals and humans are clearly imperfect, the research implications are nevertheless meaningful. The researchers used carefully controlled groups of rats and subjected the experimental groups to extensive bouts of swimming. Results showed that the exercised groups had a final lower body weight and reduced total body fat content than did the sedentary control groups. In addition, the swimmers had significantly less fat cells in later life than did the inactive groups. The researchers concluded that progressive and extensive exercise during the developmental growth period curtails successfully development of fat cells. If, therefore, appropriate and ongoing exercise were provided to young human children early in life, such an exercise program might reduce the number of potentially developing fat cells.

Increased activity and low caloric intake can, either separately or together, induce fat loss (Figure 13.7). Early research by Parizkova (1968) demonstrated a significant difference in percentage of body fat of active and inactive adolescents. The most active males were shown to have an average body fat content of 9.9 percent, as compared with an average content of 15.9 percent in the least active males. Novak's study (1966) found a significant difference in body fat when he compared male adolescent athletes with nonathlete controls, and Lundgren (1968) determined that female athletes also had lower levels of body fat than nonathletes (although not necessarily lower body weight).

Bar-Or (1983) compares the merits and disadvantages of diet and exercise as ways to treat childhood obesity. His results are summarized in Table 13.3.

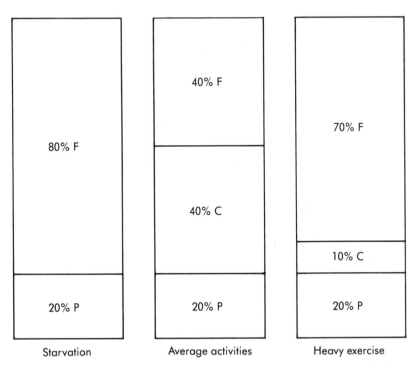

FIGURE 13.7. Percent of calories derived from each of the three major food groups—carbohydrate (C), protein (P), and fat (F)—depends on the individual's activity level. During heavy exercise, 70 percent of the calories utilized come from fat.

TABLE 13.3
MERITS AND DISADVANTAGES OF DIET AND EXERCISE AS WAYS TO LOSE WEIGHT

Effect	Diet	Exercise
Weight loss	Yes	Yes
Fat loss	Yes	Yes
Fat-free mass	Loss	Gain
Growth retardation	Possible on extreme diets	No
Increased fitness	None or some	Yes
Reduction of adipose size	Yes	More than in diet(?)
Feeling of hunger	Yes	No
Rate of weight loss	Fast or slow	Slow
Carry-over effect	No	No

SOURCE: Modified with permission from Bar-Or, O. *Pediatric Sports Medicine for the Practitioner.* New York: Springer-Verlag, 1983, p. 211.

Blackburn and St. Lezin (1984) believe that exercise, along with diet and behavior modification, is an important component of a weight reduction program. They state: "During this period [of the weight loss program], progressively more demanding aerobic exercises are introduced" (p. 440) (Figure 13.8).

Katch and McArdle (1983, p. 171) comment on the role of exercise in a weight reduction program: "Clearly, physical activity can be used by itself or in combination with mild dietary restriction to bring about an effective loss of body fat. Perhaps equally important, the feelings of intense hunger and other psychologic stresses may be minimal compared with a similar program of weight loss that relies exclusively on caloric restriction."

Appetite and Weight Loss

Skinner (in Rogers 1985, p. 159) addresses the relationship of exercise to increased hunger drive when he states: "It turns out that if you exercise very hard before you eat, you will actually eat less because of an increase in body temperature and change in hormonal levels. The centers for the thermoregulatory system, appetite and sleep, lie right next to each other in the brain stem. When you affect one you affect the other. This explains why you get sleepy after you eat a big meal and why, if you increase your body temperature by exercising, you reduce your appetite." In further reference to exercise and appetite, Williams (1983, p. 197) poses and attempts to answer the question: "Does exercise affect the appetite? Research has shown that sedentary persons who begin an exercise program do not increase food consumption above normal. The same has been shown for obese individuals, the appetite actually decreasing in some cases."

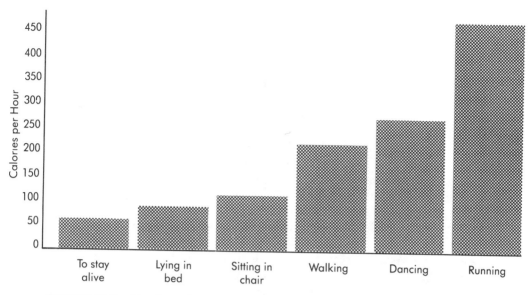

FIGURE 13.8.   Number of calories needed per hour to perform various activities.

Bar-Or (1983, pp. 212–213) agrees: "Studies with rats, a dog, and monkeys have indicated that when a highly sedentary animal increases its level of physical activity, appetite may *decrease* rather than increase. In adult humans, cross-sectional and longitudinal data confirm this pattern." The same phenomenon has also been described in children. Overweight 8- to 10-year-old boys attended a 4-month program of one or two extra physical education periods per week. By the end of the program, their daily caloric intake had decreased by an average of 12 percent, and those who had two extra physical education periods had a greater decrease in caloric intake than did those with only one extra period.

The effectiveness of a prescribed exercise program is largely dependent on regularity and duration. Research indicates that individuals do not achieve optimal training levels until regular physical conditioning has persisted for at least 20 weeks (Franklin 1984). This is not to say that improvement is not occurring before the 20-week mark, but truly significant levels of conditioning usually take this amount of time to develop. In addition, regularity of ongoing exercise tends to become a part of the individual's daily life-style. The person will, in most cases, come to look forward to the opportunity to exercise.

Developing the Exercise Program

There is little doubt as to the benefit of a prescribed exercise program for all individuals, especially for youngsters who are considered overweight or obese.

Several guidelines have been established to assist the physical educator in development of excellent programs. Franklin (1984, pp. 115–128) lists ten key points for successful programming:

1. Minimize injury with a moderate exercise prescription.
2. Emphasize exercising in a group.
3. Emphasize variety and fun in the program.
4. Include modified recreational games in the conditioning program format.
5. Play music during workouts.
6. Incorporate effective behavioral and programmatic techniques.
7. Establish a regular workout schedule.
8. Use fitness testing periodically to assess training results.
9. Provide progress charts to record exercise achievements.
10. Recognize individual accomplishments through a reward system.

Obese youngsters seldom perform physical activities on an equal level with their peers. Bar-Or (1983, pp. 199–200) offers the following explanation of the obese child's inadequate performance: "One reason for his deficient performance is a greater metabolic cost of exercise. In physiologic terms, obese children require a higher O_2 uptake to perform a given task. Their *maximal* O_2 uptake, in contrast, is often lower than that of leaner children. . . . A high submaximal O_2 uptake might reflect either reduced mechanical efficiency at the muscle subcellular level or mechanical 'wastefulness' due to the carrying of excessive weight and to their clumsy execution of movement. Based on current knowledge, the latter seems to be true." When, therefore, obese children lose weight, several important changes should be noted: (1) improved oxygen uptake, (2) improved mechanical efficiency, and (3) reduction of clumsiness.

Research associated with cardiorespiratory efficiency and obesity is highlighted by a study completed by DeMeersman et al. (1985). Their conclusions show that obese girls between the ages of 7 and 12 were significantly less efficient than nonobese subjects in the area of maximum VO_2. Specifically, obese subjects began to show evidence of fatigue 3 min before the control group.

Haymes, McCormick, and Buskirk (1975) conducted a study to determine if differences exist between lean (15.5 percent fat) and obese (31.2 percent fat) 9- to 12-year-old boys. Both groups walked on a treadmill in a dry-heat atmosphere. Rectal temperature and heart rate rose faster and reached higher levels among the obese subjects. Bar-Or (1983) finds that obese children sweat more profusely and thus tend to lose body fluids more readily. He stresses that "One should therefore be alert to the possibility of fluid deficiency in any obese child with recent exposure to heat" (p. 290).

In addition, the obese child has an increased proportion of inert body mass, that is, tissue that does not participate in muscular exercise. In most obese individuals, the O_2 used in 1 min and oxygen consumption in general are often double that of normal weight subjects at any given level of work. DuPont and Freedman (1983) believe that the work required to breathe is increased in obese subjects because of altered chest wall configuration owing to excess fat in the thorax and abdomen. This results in an increase in chest wall resistance to breathing.

An exercise program should consist of three parts: (1) cardiorespiratory, (2) weight training, and (3) motor skill development. The cardiorespiratory program should emphasize activities that contribute to ongoing exercise with an aerobic component. These activities facilitate reduction of body weight through the process of making the fat cells smaller. The weight-training activities help develop a firmer muscle base, and in the early phases of the program assist in reducing the size of specific body parts, although little if any reduction in fat cell size will be noted. Finally, the motor skill development phase of the program should be introduced. This phase is necessary because the obese individual may not have had the opportunity to develop normal eye-hand coordination or movement skills.

Developing a Cardiorespiratory (Aerobic) Program

LaPort et al. (1985, p. 148) provide an important perspective on cardiorespiratory programming. They state: "Aerobic training programs typically are not reaching the highest risk groups for disease . . . the obese. . . . Aerobic training programs in the high-risk groups . . . are unlikely to be successful on a large scale. It is more reasonable to increase the activity levels of these groups with a walking program. Moreover, the epidemiological evidence suggests risk of disease is likely to decrease by merely increasing activity irrespective of its aerobic nature."

The basic concepts and progressions of a traditional aerobic program should be included in the program planning of obese students. A major difference between the obese and normal weight individual is that the overweight youngster will not enjoy the idea of extended effort because of the discomfort encountered when activity is continued beyond a 1-min duration. Even climbing a long flight of stairs is an unpleasant task for the obese child. The program progression *must* begin at a low level of performance and must *not* demand an established criterion level (e.g., walk-jog 1 mi in 15 min). Instead, have the student walk-jog around the basketball court until discomfort is felt. Have him record the number of laps completed and the time it took him (e.g., 8 laps in 3 min:15 sec). Graphs or bar charts that document performance help to motivate youngsters. The next session (no more than 2 days later) should use the previous record as a goal to surpass, that is, longer sustained effort and more laps should be achieved in the second session. Again, record laps and time at the end of the activity. Immediate positive reinforcement by the teacher is a *must*, including both verbal and physical praise. As a result of their past physical education experiences, these youngsters are accustomed to negative reinforcement whether covert, as in the case of continual lack of personal success, or overt, as when peers make fun of them and their performance.

Research indicates that if the cardiorespiratory system is to be strengthened, individuals must take part in *at least* 12 min of continuous exercise per day. Anything less than 12 min is considered nonbeneficial cardiorespiratory activity. The problem encountered by obese individuals is that long-range goals appear to be all hard work and no fun. For example, the physical educator may say on the first day of class: "I want everyone to run for 12 minutes and I will record your time." This is an extremely difficult challenge (both physically and psychologically) because obese students will have had problems in the past when endurance activities were presented to them. The instructor must not "turn off" students before they have a chance to find out that the new program is truly individualized and that the program will start at their existing ability level and progress at a slow and reasonable rate. For an obese youngster, the beginning level of cardiorespiratory activity performance may be only 2 min 25 sec, and the 12-min goal may be as far away as 3, 4, or 5 months. Indeed, most obese individuals can be expected to perform at very low levels of efficiency, so the program should begin with a combination of walking and mild jogging. The jogging-running guidelines developed by the President's Council on Physical Fitness and Sports (n.d.) list several paces, ranging from slow walk (3 mph) to fast running (10 mph). (This walk-jog-run pace chart can be found in Appendix B.)

Jumping rope has been identified as an excellent aerobic conditioner; in addition, agility and strength should also improve. A jumping surface that is firm but somewhat cushioned, such as a low-pile carpet or a composition (rubberized) running track, is best. If possible, avoid using hard surfaces for exercise because of the possibility of foot and ankle strain. One suggested rope jumping program (King Features 1986) includes a 5-min warm-up walk, then a slow stretching of ankles, calves, shins, and upper legs prior to beginning rope jumping. The alternate day, 15-week training schedule for this program is shown in Table 13.4.

Aerobic dance is also an excellent activity for stimulation of the cardiorespiratory system. The dances are designed to keep individuals moving throughout the routines (Doherty 1985), which typically contain stretching and bodytoning movements that provide a total body workout.

TABLE 13.4
ROPE JUMPING TRAINING SCHEDULE

Week	Jump	Rest	Repeat	Total Jump Time
1	15 sec	45 sec	8 times	2 min
3	15 sec	15 sec	12 times	3 min
5	30 sec	15 sec	8 times	4 min
7	1 min	30 sec	7 times	7 min
9	2 min	1 min	5 times	10 min
11	3 min	1 min	5 times	15 min
13	6 min	1 min	3 times	18 min
15	8 min	2 min	3 times	24 min

SOURCE: Used with permission from King Features. Jumping Rope Can Slim and Trim. *The Pantagraph*, 13 February 1986, p. C1.

Hooper and Noland (1984, cited in Doherty 1985) investigated the effects of an 8-week aerobic dance program on 22 subjects who exercised for 45 min per day, 3 days per week for 8 weeks. Body weight decreased significantly as a result of the program, and the researchers concluded that participation in the program improved cardiorespiratory fitness.

Weber (1974) conducted a study to determine the energy cost of three intensities of aerobic dancing. The intensity of each routine ranged from low to medium to high. Results indicated that aerobic dance routines of different intensities produce various kilocalorie per minute scores. Moderately intense aerobic levels are comparable to ice skating at 9 mph, or bicycling at 10 mph. High-intensity aerobic dance programs equal 30 min of vigorous basketball or running at 5½ mph. Weber found that aerobic dancing, if performed regularly at desired intensity levels, can benefit individuals engaged in the program.

Rockefeller (1980) studied the effects of a 3 times-per-week, 10-week-long aerobic dance program on the physical characteristics of 21 college-age women. Measurements of the subjects' energy expenditures while dancing indicated that aerobic dance was sufficiently intensive to improve cardiorespiratory endurance and to aid in weight control.

Any kind of gross motor activity causes the body to use calories. Adapted physical educators must recognize that activities have to be enjoyable and involve a variety of experiences if students are expected to be enthusiastic about the program. Obese students should be encouraged to take part in exercise activities outside of school as well, but convincing them to walk, jog, or run on their own time may be difficult. Table 13.5 shows some of the exercise alternatives available for cardiorespiratory conditioning.

A nationally validated program has been developed to emphasize weight reduction among school-age students. In 1984, the Joint Dissemination Review Panel approved the program entitled "Physical Management." The program was then entered in the National Diffusion Network as an exemplary model of a physical education program for overweight youth. Physical Management is offered only to overweight students, either as an alternative to the required physical education program or as an elective for upperclass students. The class meets for 1 hour each school day and addresses four different areas that may affect weight control: nutrition education, physical conditioning, behavior change, and positive image building. Each area is considered effective in its own right, and students are required to participate in all four program areas. The *AAHPERD Health Related Physical Fitness Test* battery is used to determine initial levels of fitness and is repeated each quarter (Solberg 1985). For more information about the program, contact Physical Management Program, P.O. Box 891, Billings, MT 59103.

Developing a Weight Training Program

Development of muscle strength through a progressive resistive exercise (PRE) program is highly recommended for obese teenagers. One question is frequently asked: Will the use of weights increase the size of specific body parts instead of decreasing measurements? In answer, one must remember that the majority of obese individuals

TABLE 13.5
ACTIVITIES AND CALORIES USED

Activity		Approximate Calories Burned		
		Per Hour	In 15 Min	In 5 Min
Walking				
	2 mph	200	50	17
	5 mph	650	162	54
Swimming				
	Slow	400	100	33
	Fast	800	200	67
Biking				
	Slow	300	75	25
	Fast	600	150	50
Tennis				
	Singles	450	112	37
	Doubles	350	87	29
Badminton		350	87	29
Racketball		550	137	46
Jogging		600	150	50
Fast dancing		600	150	50
Bowling		250	62	21
Golf		250	62	21

usually have a flabby muscle base on which large amounts of fat are deposited. The physiological process of strength development must begin with a firming of the muscles before any increases in muscle size occur. In fact, Pollock, Wilmore, and Fox (1984) found that after a 10-week strength training program, females doubled their strength but exhibited little or no change in muscle girth. MacIntyre's research (n.d.) confirms this finding: a 6-week weight training program for females resulted in significant circumference loss in the upper arms, hips, thighs, and abdominal region of the experimental group. Both groups exercised for 40 min per day, 3 days per week. MacIntyre describes one subject as follows: "Bea S., age 18. Her initial weight was 142, final weight 140. During the program she lost 4 and ¼ inches. She reduced her hips by 2 inches, thighs by 1 and ⅛ inches, and abdomen by 1 and ⅜ inches. Her comments: 'I was worried that I would get fatter using weights—but I actually slimmed down in the areas I needed most. Frankly, I didn't expect to lose anything, so I was impressed. I have the body type that is very muscular and the fat is very firm and hard to remove—but it happened!' "

MacIntyre's program consists of a progressive overload series of lifting 3-lb weights. The following schedule was used: weeks 1 and 2 = one set of 10 repetitions, weeks 3 and 4 = two sets of 10 repetitions, and weeks 5 and 6 = three sets of 10 repetitions. The exercises used are as follows:

1. **Area: Abdomen**—Sit on chair with buttocks on edge of chair. Cross legs at ankles. Top leg should have weight. Bring knees to chest and extend legs almost fully. Repeat. Make certain to keep feet level with chest. (Individuals with lower back problems should not do this exercise.)
2. **Area: Waist and Thighs**—Recline on back with a 3-lb weight on each leg. Bend knees until heels hit buttocks. Extend legs straight upward. Legs are lowered to right side then brought back to center. Repeat on left side.
3. **Area: Back of Upper Arm**—Standing, bend at waist so torso is perpendicular to floor (or as nearly so as is comfortable). Hold arms at sides and raise one arm backwards as far as possible while holding weight. Change arms.
4. **Area: Inner and Outer Thigh**—Rest on side, legs straight, with pillow under hips. *Raise* both legs while keeping body in a straight line. Lower legs and repeat.
5. **Area: Thigh (front)**—Standing, raise left knee to waist height. Extend foot. Return foot to floor and repeat action with opposite leg.
6. **Area: Hips**—Lie on back, arms at sides. Lift left leg (with weight) straight up and lower it over to right side without letting it touch the floor. Return to starting position. Repeat with right leg.

Developing a Motor Skill Program

Malina (1984) believes that girls who excel in motor performance during adolescence generally have more slender physiques than those who perform poorly, that is, a correlation appears to exist between being overweight and having a low motor skill level.

The physical educator should determine existing levels of motor skill performance by administering a general motor ability test battery. Care must be taken to use appropriate test items that will provide valid and reliable information. Most test batteries are developed for children 14 years of age and younger (i.e., Bruininks-Oseretsky, Denver Developmental Screening Test, Purdue Perceptual Motor Survey, and Ohio State University Sigma Scale). For those youngsters who fit the age norms, the educator should look for performance that falls *below* the 25th percentile. While these norms may not be appropriate for all students, the test items can be used to measure objectively (how many, how fast, how far) the existing levels of eye-hand coordination and of static and dynamic balance. Once a deficiency is noted, specific corrective activities should be included in the student's individualized educational program (IEP). Instruction in new motor skills can be added as an exciting dimension of cardiorespiratory and strength-building activities.

Obesity and Students With Disabilities

Although some disabled individuals are highly conditioned and participate with and compete against nonhandicapped individuals, the great majority of persons with handicaps tend to function at lower activity and physical fitness levels. Blair (1985, p. 154) provides a theoretical continuum of physical activity based on estimated cardiovascular fitness (Figure 13.9).

Of major concern are those individuals who are confined to wheelchairs or bedridden. How can a nutritional balance be maintained when exercise and nutrition become greatly imbalanced? The result is often extra weight. One solution is to continue to provide exercise, even if it is of a nonambulatory type. In addition, caloric intake should be supervised carefully. An average 6.9 percent decrease in basal metabolic rate is common during periods of immobilization (Mitchell 1985). This causes major problems when physicians attempt to determine optimal nutritional intake for individuals who become immobile. In attempting to adjust protein and energy balances, physicians usually rely on ideal body standards, which are based on healthy active individuals. These norms are not appropriate for the immobile bedridden patient or the nonactive wheelchair-bound child. Doctors may reduce caloric intake by standard dietary formulations that contain adequate amounts of nutrients, but if adequate protein, vitamins, and minerals are provided in these formulas, an excess of calories is almost always given. The result is an increase in body fat! In reference to this problem,

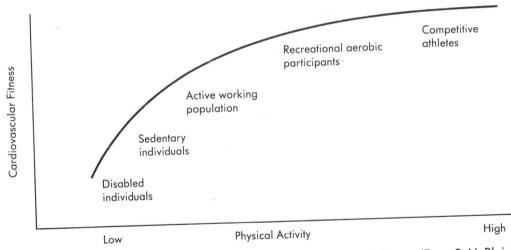

FIGURE 13.9.   Theoretical association between activity and physical fitness. (From S. N. Blair. Physical Activity Leads to Fitness and Pays Off. *The Physician and Sportsmedicine* 13(3):154, 1985. Reprinted by permission of THE PHYSICIAN AND SPORTSMEDICINE, a McGraw-Hill publication.)

Mitchell (1985, p. 91) states: "This [added obesity] is particularly undesirable . . . since it is more difficult to care for heavy patients. These patients are likely to develop serious infections and decubitus ulcers [bed sores]."

While dietary balances are the direct responsibility of the physician, the adapted physical educator must be constantly aware that exercise and activity are extremely important in control of and reduction of body fat. The physical educator should send a copy of all exercise programs to the child's physician for informational purposes. Based on the activity program, including progressions and periodic accomplishments, the physician can make appropriate dietary prescriptions and alterations. In most cases, the physician will not be able to provide as effective a progressive strength and cardiorespiratory conditioning program as the adapted physical educator.

Some handicapping conditions tend to increase the chance of obesity, particularly if the disability restricts movement potential. A classic example is the boy who has Duchenne muscular dystrophy. The condition progressively destroys muscle tissue, which is replaced by fat and connective tissue. Movement becomes more and more difficult as the condition progresses, thus creating a distinct calorie-energy imbalance. The result is the characteristic obesity found in the totally wheelchair-bound boy. Shepherd (1984) believes that these individuals are affected directly by a combination of inactivity, overeating, and inappropriate diet, the principal causes of obesity. She advises that low carbohydrate, high-protein eating habits be developed early in life before onset of severe obesity.

For those individuals who manually roll their own wheelchairs, as is the case with many students who have spinal cord injury, the physical educator should help students develop methods to increase their cardiorespiratory efficiency. The traditional walking, jogging, and running are not viable options. The routine of using an arm crank device has been established as a technique to develop cardiorespiratory efficiency. Burke et al. (1985) found that competitive wheelchair basketball (30 min full-court practice session) was an appropriate way to develop an acceptable level of cardiorespiratory endurance. These researchers concluded that although upper arm endurance workouts were not as productive as a running regime (60 to 75 percent as effective), such workouts are nevertheless of sufficient intensity to develop positive levels of fitness. They suggest that the differences in workout effectiveness may be due to smaller available muscle mass, fewer motor units recruited, increased peripheral resistance of arm exercise, and restricted blood flow during arm exercise. Despite these observations, note that an overload of the cardiorespiratory system is definitely possible for individuals in wheelchairs, and should be included in their workouts.

Down syndrome youngsters are prone to obesity because their developmental growth period ends at about 16 years of age. The boys' height averages 5 ft, and the girls' height 4 ft 7 in. As adolescents, these youngsters do not need as many calories because the growth spurt has ceased. Their metabolism will begin its natural slowdown, and the normal amount of calories will result in added fat. If exercise is not increased, then the possibility that adipose tissues will be added is further enhanced.

Most teenagers (both handicapped and nonhandicapped) are continuously hungry, although they do not always eat nutritionally beneficial foods to satisfy hunger. In fact, they tend to enjoy and crave candy, soft drinks, chips, and other nonessential foods.

Caveny (1986) observed that when institutionalized Down syndrome adolescents were given a specific low fat diet (1200 calories), they were able to lose weight and eventually to maintain weight loss on an 1800 calorie diet. A main concern at the institution was that residents, during their free time, were eating sweets (e.g., candy and soft drinks), and were experiencing the same food cravings that most teenagers experience. The new maintenance diet seemed, however, to keep their weight at a reasonable level.

The Down child also has a tendency to stand, walk, and run in an inefficient way. Youngsters often shuffle their feet instead of walking with a normal gait pattern. This condition involves an external rotation at the knee in which the tibial tubercle is turned to the outside. The individual thus walks with a typical "Charlie Chaplin" gait. This abnormal walking characteristic is observed often in nonhandicapped obese people, and it is suggested that obesity is the cause of the "toe-ing" out gait. For the Down child, this gait is not a congenital defect, but is learned through several years of incorrect walking. In addition, these youngsters also tend to have fallen arches by the time they enter their teenage years. This condition also is generally brought about by excessive stress on the longitudinal arch of the foot. The extra weight carried by the obese person is undoubtedly a causative factor.

These developmental problems cause Down children to avoid movement experiences because of the discomfort they experience when walking, jogging, or running. The etiology of the problems is associated directly with hypotonicity. This genetic "looseness" of joint ligaments does not have to persist. The newborn Down child exhibits the "floppy baby syndrome," but significant improvement occurs during the first year of life. If manipulation and strengthening programs are provided at an early age, many of the problems associated with hypotonicity would probably not exist (e.g., shuffling gait and fallen arches). When the gait pattern is more efficient, the youngster should be able to participate more successfully in movement and cardiorespiratory endurance activities. Activity success should lead in turn to more effective weight control.

Down youngsters are hypothesized to have such a pronounced problem with obesity because their level of ongoing aerobic exercise is significantly lower than that of other children. Most nonhandicapped teenagers are given extensive physical fitness opportunities in their public school physical education program. In addition, many children and adolescents are involved in community programs that promote dancing, swimming, team sports, gymnastics, or tennis. When youngsters are physically active, they burn up excess calories that could develop into unwanted fat. The problem for Down children is that they usually are *not* offered opportunities similar to those offered to nonhandicapped children. One solution is to ensure that trained adapted physical educators are available to provide Down youngsters with appropriate physical fitness programming.

Children with myelomeningocele spina bifida also have trouble with extra weight when they become wheelchair-bound. This is a typical problem of children who are active at one time in their early years, but whose condition or disease significantly reduces activity level in later years. These youngsters tend to continue eating the same amounts of food that they ingested when they were more active. Overweight and obesity thus begin to creep into their lives.

Other Eating Disorders

Anorexia Nervosa

The condition of **anorexia nervosa** is defined by the American Psychiatric Association (1980) as having the following characteristics: (1) intense fear of becoming obese, which does not diminish as weight loss progresses, (2) disturbance of body image, for example, claiming to "feel fat" even when emaciated, (3) weight loss of at least 25 percent of original body weight or, if under 18 years of age, weight loss from original body weight plus projected weight gain expected from growth charts may be considered to constitute the 25 percent, (4) refusal to maintain weight over a minimum normal weight for age and height, and (5) no known physical illness that would account for weight loss. Mitchell (1985) believes that anorexia nervosa is a result either of depression, a psychological alteration, or a dysfunction of the hypothalamic appetite-satiety center. Although many measurable endocrine abnormalities are well documented as being present in youngsters with anorexia nervosa, these abnormalities may be the result rather than the cause of the condition. In fact, the condition occurs mainly in white teenage girls of upper socioeconomic class.

The basic aim of treatment is to regain weight. The long-range goal is to increase and maintain weight over a period of months, to work to achieve a degree of self-acceptance, and to diminish preoccupation with food (Giles 1985). To do this, the anorexic person must attempt to maintain an adequate diet and to avoid binging, vomiting, laxative abuse, or too much physical activity. Close articulation with the student's parents, physician, and school counselor will be necessary.

Bulimia

Bulimia (bulimarexia) is often directly associated with anorexia nervosa. It is a process used to rid the body of food before the food is digested, that is, to vomit or to use laxatives. Those who have bulimia are mostly women (95 percent). Indeed, an estimated 15 to 20 percent of college-age women may practice forced vomiting or use of laxatives to stop food digestion and promote weight loss. Most bulimics start in their teens when societal pressures seem the most intense. The long-range dangers of bulimia are lack of proper nutrients, including inadequate amounts of carbohydrate, protein, fat, minerals, and vitamins. The major concerns in advanced stages of the condition are possible starvation or life-threatening electrolyte imbalance.

Anorexia nervosa and bulimia are similar in that the individual who has either condition is obsessed with thinness. There are, however, important differences between the two. Unlike the anorexic, who eats almost nothing, the bulimic compulsively overeats and resorts to purging to keep from gaining weight. The individual manages, however, to maintain a near-normal weight and to appear outwardly quite healthy. In contrast, the anorexic continues a near-starvation diet to promote weight loss even after becoming grotesquely thin.

Exercise and activity prescriptions should be carefully controlled because overload strength and cardiorespiratory conditioning programs may be too intense for the student. The individual's energy level is usually limited, and she may possess all of the characteristics of an anemic person. A yoga exercise program is ideal, and can provide much needed body conditioning, flexibility, and positive relaxation (see the yoga exercise program in Chapter 19). Giles (1985, p. 515) suggests: "The anorexic patient is often anxious and frightened before meals and may suffer severe physical discomfort and feelings of guilt after eating. Scheduled yoga sessions . . . will help reduce these responses and alleviate some of the problems of after-meal supervision." Scheduling adapted physical education classes for these students immediately after lunch may be appropriate.

Summary

Overweight and obesity are major problems that affect directly the physical, social, and emotional well-being of over 25 percent of our school population. The causes of excessive adipose tissue in children and adolescents are strongly associated with too much food taken in and too little exercise to burn off extra calories. In only a small percentage of cases (less than 10 percent) can obesity be attributed to other causes.

The number and size of adipose cells can be controlled, especially during the developmental years. A strong correlation exists between lack of physical activity and obesity. Physical educators must take a major role in programming for obese students. Indeed, if the physical educator does not take an active part in helping students control obesity, then who will? The educator has the opportunity to assess existing levels of adipose tissue; to write appropriate progressive physical fitness programs and strength-promoting activities; to place students in positive class settings; to teach, encourage, and motivate students during weight loss programs; and to evaluate progress. Finally, the educator should keep open lines of communication with parents, physicians, school nurses, and school counselors.

Richard Sartore (1982, p. 30) wrote the following poem, "Skipping Gym":

> The teacher asked—
> Why skip gym?
> Responded the student,
> With a nervous grin
>
> My shorts are dirty.
> My shirt's all worn,
> My feet hurt,
> and my sneeks are torn.

The other day
I planned to come,
But then it happened—
Both hands went numb.

When playing games,
I feel low.
Always picked last
What a blow!

Kids laugh,
Especially when I run.
Being called FAT BOY,
Is surely no fun.

Tell me teacher,
Now that you know,
If you were me,
Would you go?

References

AAHPERD. *AAHPERD Health Related Physical Fitness Test Manual.* Reston, Va.: AAHPERD, 1980.

Allsen, P. E., Harrison, J. M., and Vance, B. *Fitness for Life,* 2nd ed. Dubuque, Iowa: Wm. C. Brown, 1980.

American Psychiatric Association. *Diagnostic and Statistical Manual of Mental Disorders (DSM III).* Washington, D.C.: The Association, 1980.

Astrand, P., and Rodahl, K. *Textbook of Work Physiology,* 3rd ed. New York: McGraw-Hill, 1986.

Aubert, R., Herzog, J., Camus, C., Guenet, J., and Lemonnier, D. Description of a New Model of Genetic Obesity: The db Pas Mouse. *Journal of Nutrition* 115(3):327–333, 1985.

Bar-Or, O. *Pediatric Sports Medicine for the Practitioner.* New York: Springer-Verlag, 1983.

Blackburn, G. L., and St. Lezin, E. Obesity. In *Conn's Current Therapy,* edited by R. E. Rakel. Philadelphia: W. B. Saunders, 1984.

Blair, S. N. Physical Activity Leads to Fitness and Pays Off. *The Physician and Sportsmedicine* 13(3):153–157, 1985.

Bray, G. A. Obesity: What Comes First? In *The Adipocyte and Obesity: Cellular and Molecular Mechanisms,* edited by A. Angel, C. H. Hollenberg, and D. A. K. Roncari. New York: Raven Press, 1983.

Burke, E. J., Auchinachie, J. A., Hayden, R., and Loftin, J. M. Energy Cost of Wheelchair Basketball. *The Physician and Sportsmedicine* 13(3):99–105, 1985.

Cahill, F. F., Jr., and Renold, A. E. Adipose Tissue: A Brief History. In *The Adipocyte and Obesity: Cellular and Molecular Mechanisms,* edited by A. Angel, C. H. Hollenberg, and D. A. K. Roncari. New York: Raven Press, 1983.

Caveny, P. A. Personal communication, 8 March 1986.

DeMeersman, R. E., Stone, S., Schaefer, D. C., and Miller, W. W. Maximal Work Capacity in Prepubescent Obese and Nonobese Females. *Clinical Pediatrics* 24(4):199–200, 1985.

Dietz, W. H., and Gortmaker, S. L. Do We Fatten Our Children at the Television Set? Obesity and Television Viewing in Children and Adolescents. *Pediatrics* 75:807–812, 1985.

Doherty, L. L. *Selected Physiological Effects of Aerobic Dance Among Moderately and Severely Mentally Retarded Adults.* Master's Thesis, Illinois State University, Normal, 1985.

Dupont, D. C., and Freedman, A. P. Pulmonary Disorders and Exercise. In *Exercise Medicine,* edited by A. A. Bove and D. T. Lowenthal. New York: Academic Press, 1983.

Faust, I. M., and Miller, W. H., Jr. Hyperplastic Growth of Adipose Tissue in Obesity. In *The Adipocyte and Obesity: Cellular and Molecular Mechanisms,* edited by A. Angel, C. H. Hollenberg, and D. A. K. Roncari. New York: Raven Press, 1983.

Foch, T. T., and McClearn, G. E. Genetics, Body Weight, and Obesity. In *Obesity,* edited by A. J. Stunkard. Philadelphia: W. B. Saunders, 1980.

Franklin, B. A. Exercise Program Compliance. In *Behavioral Management of Obesity,* edited by J. Storlie and H. A. Jordan. New York: Spectrum Publications, 1984.

Frisancho, A. R. New Norms of Upper Limb Fat and Muscle Areas for Assessment of Nutritional Status. *The American Journal of Clinical Nutrition* 34(11):2540–2545, 1981.

Giles, G. M. Anorexia Nervosa and Bulimia: An Activity-Oriented Approach. *The American Journal of Occupational Therapy* 39(8):510–517, 1985.

Gurney, R. C. Skinfold Thickness and Body Fat in Children. *Human Biology* 37:206–215, 1965.

Guyton, A. C. *Physiology of the Human Body,* 5th ed. Philadelphia: W. B. Saunders, 1979.

Hastad, D. N., Marett, J. R., and Plowman, S. A. *Evaluation of the Health Related Physical Fitness Status of Youth in the State of Illinois.* DeKalb, Ill.: Northern Illinois University Human Performance Laboratory, 1983.

Haymes, E. M., McCormick, E. R., and Buskirk, E. R. Heat Tolerance of Exercising Lean and Obese Prepubertal Boys. *Journal of Applied Physiology* 39:457–461, 1975.

Hollenberg, C. H., Roncari, D. A. K., and Dijan, P. Obesity and the Fat Cell: Future Prospects. In *The Adipocyte and Obesity: Cellular and Molecular Mechanisms,* edited by A. Angel, C. H. Hollenberg, and D. A. K. Roncari. New York: Raven Press, 1983.

Jones, K. L., Shainberg, L. W., and Byer, C. O. *Instructor's Manual to Accompany Health Science,* 3rd ed. New York: Harper & Row, 1974.

Katch, F. I., and McArdle, W. D. *Nutrition, Weight Control, and Exercise,* 2nd ed. Philadelphia: Lea & Febiger, 1983.

Katch, V. L. Body Composition and Sports Medicine: Clinical Considerations. In *Body-Composition Assessments in Youth and Adults,* Report of the Sixth Ross Conference on Medical Research. Columbus, Ohio: Ross Laboratories, 1985.

King Features. Jumping Rope Can Slim and Trim. *The Pantagraph,* 13 February 1986, pp. C1–C2.

Kraus, H., and Raab, W. *Hypokinetic Disease.* Springfield, Ill.: Charles C Thomas, 1961.

LaPort, R. E., Dearwater, S., Cauley, J. A., Slemenda, C., and Cook, T. Physical Activity or Cardiovascular Fitness: Which Is More Important for Health? *The Physician and Sportsmedicine* 13(3):145–150, 1985.

Lundgren, H. Changes in Skinfold and Girth Measurements of Women Varsity Basketball and Field Hockey Players. *Research Quarterly* 39:1020, 1968.

MacIntyre, C. A New Shape-Maker Program for Women. Pasadena City College, Pasadena, Calif., no date.

Malina, R. M. Physical Growth and Maturation. In *Motor Development During Childhood and Adolescence,* edited by J. R. Thomas. Minneapolis: Burgess Publishing, 1984.

Mathews, D. K., and Fox, E. L. *The Physiological Basis of Physical Education and Athletics,* 2nd ed. Philadelphia: W. B. Saunders, 1976.

Mayer, J. *Overweight: Causes, Cost and Control.* Englewood Cliffs, N.J.: Prentice-Hall, 1968.

McArdle, W. D., Katch, F. I., and Katch, V. L. *Exercise Physiology.* Philadelphia: Lea & Febiger, 1981.

Mitchell, C. A. General Discussions of Assessments in the Disabled. In *Body-Composition Assessments in Youth and Adults,* Report of the Sixth Ross Conference on Medical Research. Columbus, Ohio: Ross Laboratories, 1985.

Novak, L. P. Physical Activity and Body Composition of Adolescent Boys. *Journal of the American Medical Association* 197:1969, 1966.

Obesity and Television Viewing in Children and Adolescents. *Nutrition Reviews* 44(1):9, 1986.

Oscai, L., Babirak, A., Dubach, B., and Spirakis, C. Exercise or Food Restriction: Effect on Adipose Tissue Cellularity. *American Journal of Physiology* 227:901–904, 1974.

Parizkova, J. Longitudinal Study of the Development of Body Composition and Body Build in Boys of Various Physical Activity. *Human Biology* 40:212, 1968.

Polacek, J. J., Wang, P. Y., and Eichstaedt, C. B. *A Study of Physical and Health Related Fitness Levels of Mild, Moderate, and Down Syndrome Students in Illinois.* Normal, Ill.: Illinois State University Press, 1985.

Pollock, M. L., Wilmore, J. H., and Fox, S. M., III. *Exercise in Health and Disease.* Philadelphia: W. B. Saunders, 1984.

President's Council on Physical Fitness and Sports. *Jogging/Running Guidelines.* GPO number 907-798, p. 6, n.d.

Roche, A. F. Discussion of S. L. Newman, Clinical Assessment of Adipose Tissue in Youth. In *Body-Composition Assessments in Youth and Adults,* Report of the Sixth Ross Conference on Medical Research. Columbus, Ohio: Ross Laboratories, 1985.

Roche, A. F., Abdel-Malek, A. K., and Mukherjee, D. New Approaches to Clinical Assessment of Adipose Tissue. In *Body-Composition Assessments in Youth and Adults,* Report of the Sixth Ross Conference on Medical Research. Columbus, Ohio: Ross Laboratories, 1985.

Rockefeller, K. Aerobic Dance. In *Exercise, Science, and Fitness,* edited by E. J. Burke. Ithaca, N.Y.: Mouvement Publications, 1980.

Rogers, C. C. Of Magic, Miracles, and Exercise Myths. *The Physician and Sportsmedicine* 13(5):156–166, 1985.

Salans, L. B., Cushman, S. W., and Weismann, R. E. Adipose Cell Size and Number in Nonobese and Obese Patients. *Journal of Clinical Investigation* 52:929–941, April 1973.

Sartore, R. L. Skipping Gym. *JOPERD* 53(9):30, 1982.

Shepherd, R. B. *Physiotherapy in Pediatrics,* 2nd ed. London: William Heinemann Medical Books Limited, 1984.

Sherrill, C. *Adapted Physical Education and Recreation,* 3rd ed. Dubuque, Iowa: Wm. C. Brown, 1986.

Sinclair, D. *Human Growth After Birth,* 3rd ed. New York: Oxford University Press, 1978.

Sintek, S., and Bishop, P. Physician's Perceptions of Using Physical Education for Managing Childhood Obesity. *The Physician and Sportsmedicine* 13(5):119–124, 1985.

Smith, U. Regional Differences and Effect of Cell Size on Lipolysis in Human Adipocytes. In *The Adipocyte and Obesity: Cellular and Molecular Mechanisms,* edited by A. Angel, C. H. Hollenberg, and D. A. K. Roncari. New York: Raven Press, 1983.

Solberg, E. Physical Management Helps Flabby Kids Shape Up, Slim Down. *The Executive Director* 12(2):24–25 (1985).

Spencer, S. A., Vinter, J., and Hull, D. The Effect in Newborn Rabbits of Overfeeding on Fat Disposition, Gross Energetic Efficiency, and Metabolic Rate. *Pediatric Research* 19(1):127–135, 1985.

Steiner, M. M. *Clinical Approach to Endocrine Problems in Childhood.* St. Louis: C. V. Mosby, 1970.

Storlie, J., and Jordan, H. A., eds. *Behavioral Management of Obesity.* New York: Spectrum Publications, 1984.

Weber, H. Aerobic Dance: A Step to Fitness. *The Physician and Sportsmedicine* 7(8):98–103, 1974.

Williams, M. H. *Nutrition for Fitness and Sport.* Dubuque, Iowa: Wm. C. Brown, 1983.

CHAPTER 14

Postural Deviations

This chapter provides information regarding body alignment and function problems. Procedures are included that are best suited for prevention of disability, improvement of impaired function, and maintenance of the optimum activity level.

Postural deviations are often disabling conditions that restrict the individual from participating in the regular physical education program. Many posture-related abnormalities can be improved with corrective activities. The student who has postural defects that result in poor coordination needs to correct the problem or to compensate for it. Acquisition of skills essential to coordinated movement is integral to the student's adapted physical education curriculum.

Good body alignment is necessary if an individual is to function efficiently. Indeed, before 1970 most adapted physical education programs in universities and public schools dealt primarily with body mechanics and corrective procedures. Today, postural evaluation and corrective programs are still the responsibility of the physical education program.

The correction of postural deviations is approached from physiological, mechanical, psychological, and aesthetic aspects. The prevention of chronic disabilities that develop from strain and stress is important. Indeed, the value of prevention cannot be overemphasized. Poor body alignment, whether occupational or a result of faulty posture habits, eventually limits normal function. Repeated conscious correction of faulty alignment leads to improved posture habits. A student with mild spinal curvature may feel comfortable although the curvature is visible in a mirror. When the position is corrected, the posture may seem strange, but the mirror reflection is now straight. The person must constantly correct or overcorrect until proprioceptive recognition produces proper position and the former unbalanced (but correct) alignment becomes comfortable.

The physical educator must identify postural deviations early and determine whether the deviation is structural or functional. Vertebral abnormalities, such as scoliosis and lordosis, are observed easily (e.g., a "swayed" back or one low shoulder). Knee problems (bowlegs or knock-knees) are also readily apparent when students are in shorts. Improper foot placement, such as feet turned out (duck walk) or turned in (pigeon-toed), is a key factor when determining reasons for poor running or jumping performance.

Since physical educators see children frequently and share directly in the postural examination, they are able to detect deviations from normal and are obligated to identify individuals who need special corrective activities.

Most postural deviations result from incorrect sitting, standing, walking, and running habits. The adapted physical educator has responsibility for identification and referral (to parents or physicians or both) of all significant abnormalities. As mentioned before, early identification is extremely important.

Most atypical body postures can be corrected through positive verbal reinforcement. Teachers must remind students to "point your toes straight ahead when you walk, walk tall, pull your stomach in, lift your left shoulder," and so forth. This continual reference to correct postural position can be important for the student. The instructor's comments should be encouraging and positive, never disparaging.

The adapted physical educator can be the motivating force when developing postural rehabilitation programs. Such programs, however, should be developed and conducted *after* the student has received a physician's written approval to participate in a rehabilitation program. *Written approval* (commonly referred to as a **prescription**) should describe the student's condition, provide remedial suggestions, and in some cases, list specific progressive exercises and activities.

Physicians need the expertise of adapted physical education teachers to implement these written prescriptions and to detect structural and functional deviations in the early stages. Every deviation from normal, however slight, should be corrected as soon as possible.

Physician Cooperation

Cooperation of the medical profession in any rehabilitation or corrective physical education program is mandatory! Too often, physicians excuse individuals from phys-

·ical education participation or do not involve the physical educator in rehabilitation programs. This approach is inopportune and probably results from physicians being unaware of new directions in adapted physical education. It is vital that physicians be informed that adapted physical education is truly an individualized program to meet each child's needs. AAHPERD's newspaper *Update* (January 1978, p. 6) states:

> Experience indicates that when physicians are aware of and understand what is intended in individualized physical education programs they are most often supportive and become the greatest supporters and proponents of the program. Physical educators have the responsibility to make contacts with . . . local medical associations so that they are aware of these new directions and emphases in physical education in general and adapted physical education in particular. This also dictates that physical educators assume the responsibility of developing and implementing appropriate and continuing public information and public relations programs and activities designed to acquaint various publics and populations about these programs.

Program Organization and Administration

The corrective program is an integral part of the adapted physical education class. Remedial programs for various disabilities can be conducted during the same class period.

There are two classifications of students with postural deviations: (1) Those who would benefit from exercises to improve a specific disability, and (2) those who cannot participate in the regular class even with activity modification.

For students to derive maximum benefits from an individualized corrective program, exercises should be administered a minimum of 3 days per week or, ideally, 5 times per week. Again, instruction in specific exercises should be given by the adapted physical educator only with the written consent of the family physician.

Screening Program

All students should be **screened** to determine which ones have postural deviations. This should identify major problems. The adapted physical educator must not attempt to recognize all deviations or specific degrees of misalignment, but only marked deviations (Logan 1972). Additional assessment of those identified in the initial screening should be done later.

The postural screening chart in Figure 14.1 should be used to assess a group of five to eight children. This body alignment chart will (1) identify major postural deviations (information is forwarded to parents suggesting physician involvement), (2) provide a record of beginning deviation level and a basis for future evaluation, (3) serve as a foundation for writing an individualized corrective program, and (4) provide a posture concept for the student.

STUDENT'S NAME _____   AGE   SEX   GRADE   DATE

Stand approximately 15 ft away from the student. To check body line, hold a pencil vertically at arm's length and use it as a guide to determine if the body line goes through the ear, shoulder, hip, knee, and ankle. If most of the weight falls in front of the pencil, then the body line is forward.

CHECK THE PROPER COLUMN BELOW:

	CORRECT	INCORRECT
SIDE VIEW		
1. Body line	Correctly balanced _____	Forward _____ Backward _____
2. Knees	Correctly balanced _____	Hyperextended _____ Too flexed _____
3. Abdomen	Contracted _____	Protruding _____
4. Lumbar curve	Correctly balanced _____	Hollow _____ Too flat _____
5. Chest	Correctly balanced _____	High _____ Depressed _____
6. Upper back	Correctly balanced _____	Protruding _____
7. Shoulders	Correctly balanced _____	Round and forward _____ Back _____
8. Head	Correctly balanced _____	Forward _____ Back _____
BACK VIEW		
9. Feet	Parallel _____	Toes out _____ Toes in _____
10. Knees	Parallel _____	Knees out _____ Knees in _____
11. Hips	Parallel _____	Right high _____ Left high _____
12. Scapula	Parallel _____	Right protruding _____
		Left protruding _____
13. Shoulders	Parallel _____	Right high _____ Left high _____
BACK VIEW (BENDING FORWARD)		
14. Upper back	Parallel _____	Right protruding _____
		Left protruding _____

FIGURE 14.1. Postural screening chart. (Adapted from Barratt et al. 1968, p. 33.)

The student's attire should not conceal the body. Gym suits, undershirt-type jersies, and shorts are acceptable. Loose fitting clothes do not allow the instructor to see enough of the individual's body. Boys and young children should remove shirts.

To assess, have students line up with their left side facing the teacher. Students should stand comfortably with arms at sides (check items 1 through 8 of Figure 14.1). Have students turn around and face away from teacher. The youngsters should stand comfortably with arms at sides (check items 9 through 13). Have students bend forward with arms hanging down, relaxed, without touching toes (check item 14). Have each student march in a straight line across the area. (The teacher should pick a line on the floor for the student to follow.) Call the child to a halt and have each student walk 20 to 30 ft while observing her gait. Look for deviations that were not evident during the standing evaluation.

Functional and Structural Deviations

Functional deviation describes a condition that is correctable through exercise. The deviation is caused by improper posture, fatigue, or occupation. Without correction, the condition may become painfully disabling and cause inefficient physical performance. If the condition is allowed to progress, it may eventually be corrected only through surgery.

Structural deviation is due to bony abnormalities and deformities. Correction of these deviations requires plaster casting, orthoses (braces), or surgery. These skeletal problems often result from birth defects, disease, or injury.

There are tests to determine whether a postural deviation is functional or structural. The instructor must not diagnose a condition (diagnosis is the legal responsibility of a physician), but she can make general observations and give recommendations to parents, the school nurse, or directly to the child's physician. Identification of postural problems is important and is a primary responsibility of the adapted physical educator.

Anatomy and Conditions of the Foot

Anatomy

The 26 bones in the foot (Figure 14.2) are held together by ligaments, and balance and position are maintained by muscular tension (Figure 14.3). Two major arches, the longitudinal and the transverse, reduce the jar of walking and running, and add resilience and flexibility to the foot. Low arches are normal, and unless they cause pain or discomfort in walking or running, nothing need be done. For example, a "flatfooted" college female, who performed without pain or disability, became a national pentathlon

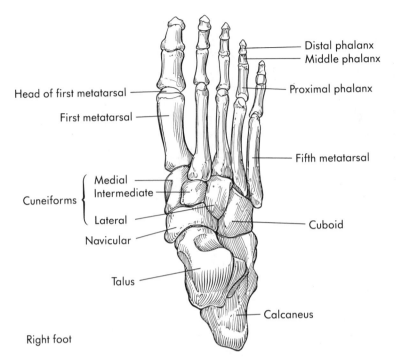

FIGURE 14.2. Bones of the foot.

track champion. Successful competition is often possible, although postural alignment is defective.

The foot is capable of many movements. *Inversion* is shown by lifting the inside of the foot and walking on the outside edge. *Eversion* is the opposite—walking on the inside edge of the foot. *Abduction* is outward rotation of the tibia, described as the duck walk. *Adduction* is the inward rotation of the foot, described as pigeon-toed walking. *Dorsiflexion* describes walking on the heels with the toes raised. *Plantar flexion* is walking on the toes. *Pronation* is a combination of eversion, abduction, and dorsiflexion. Although pronation is associated with flatfeet, these three movements are not always found together.

Flatfeet

The acquired **flatfoot** is not easily identified unless the student is standing. When bearing weight, the foot assumes a flattened appearance. **Pes planus** and **pes valgus** describe the condition of flatfeet. *Pes* is the anatomical term for "foot."

Blackman (1984) describes the flatfeet observed in babies: The feet tend to look flat because of a thick layer of fat tissue on the sole of the foot. With time, this fat

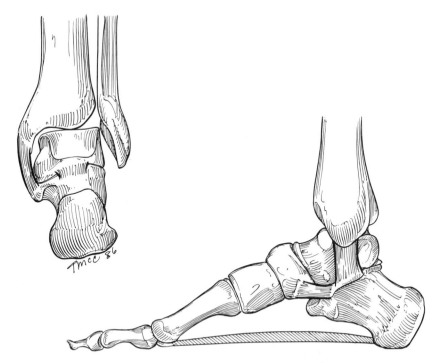

FIGURE 14.3. Normal alignment of the foot.

disappears and the arch usually becomes evident. He adds: "In the otherwise normal child, treatment for flat feet is necessary only rarely—corrective surgery almost never. Children beyond the age of three who experience discomfort may use arch supports to distribute weight evenly" (p. 180).

Students with pronated feet usually develop an awkward gait, toeing out and lacking spring in their walk. They complain frequently of aching legs. This pain often leads to nonparticipation in walking, running, or jumping games and activities. Further pronation results in atrophy from inactivity. This abnormal foot position is the result of structural inadequacy, fatigue, poor muscle tone, inactivity, overweight, improper footwear, or poor walking technique.

The pronated foot and flatfoot usually involve the longitudinal arch, which loses stability from ligamentous laxity, and abnormal bone formation, which results in poor foot functioning. The talus (ankle bone) is not supported and drops down medially toward the inside arch. The navicular (foot bone) also drops down medially, as does the first cuneiform bone. The foot's declining progression (Figure 14.4) is as follows: (1) The medial (inside) of the ankle becomes lax. (2) The talus (ankle bone) moves toward the floor and to the inside of the foot. (3) The calcaneus (heel bone) flattens, and the ligaments of the inside arch stretch. (4) The plantae fascia (ligamentous tissue on the bottom of the foot) is stretched. (5) The heel bone everts (turns outward), and (6) the forefoot spreads and flattens (Figure 14.4).

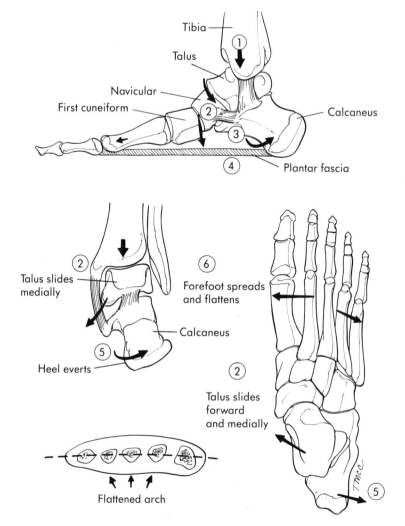

FIGURE 14.4. Mechanism of the pronated foot. (Modified from Cailliet 1968, p. 84.)

Foot Exercises and Activities

Treatment begins with removal of the cause, so longitudinal arch support is encouraged. Arch supports, prescribed by the physician, must be worn in both gym and street shoes. The use of orthotic arches does not improve the condition but does promote proper foot positioning. Subotnick (1983) believes that appropriate exercises are needed in addition to foot supports to increase flexibility and to build strength. Many obese children develop flatfeet. In such cases, loss of weight is beneficial and should be strongly suggested to the parents. Exercise is important for the obese, and the adapted physical educator must encourage the student to engage in activity. Proper walking is the best exercise, and the student must not be allowed to avoid walking (Cailliet 1972).

Rathbone and Hunt (1966) have identified four specific objectives for rehabilitation of the foot: (1) to improve circulation, (2) to relieve the pressure on nerves of the foot, thus reducing back pain, (3) to strengthen the muscles that hold the arch in position, and (4) to ensure efficient foot positioning while walking and standing, which, through practice, becomes habitual.

If students incur ankle injuries that require rest, alternative activities such as cycling or swimming are strongly suggested. Pollock, Wilmore, and Fox (1984) believe that general fitness can be maintained in this fashion while the jogging injury has a chance to heal.

Wilson (1976) suggests progressive exercises for rehabilitation of ankle injuries. The program develops strength, flexibility, and range of motion for "weak" ankles. The following activities are from the program and are for strengthening and improving flat or pronated feet or both. All exercises should be done with bare feet.

1. First stage (check for range of motion):
   a. Dorsiflexion: point toes upward as far as possible.
   b. Plantar flexion: point toes downward as far as possible.
   c. Inversion: turn sole of foot inward.
   d. Eversion: turn sole of foot outward.
2. If the above exercises can be done in full range of motion, without pain, do the following exercises:
   a. Rotate foot in small circles: ball of foot down first, then in, up, and out.
   b. Alphabet: sit on table with knee straight and ankle only extended over the table edge. Using foot, print the entire alphabet in capital letters.
3. If the above exercises can be done in full range of motion, without pain, do the following exercises:
   a. Towel exercise: sit on a chair with foot on towel, use toes to pull towel under foot. After completing this exercise successfully, place a 1 lb weight on the towel to offer resistance (use toes to pick up towel, *not* slide it along floor).
   b. Marble pick-up: use toes to pick up marbles, small pieces of sponge rubber, or small stones.
   c. Toe raises: stand with feet 1 ft apart, toeing in. Raise up on toes as high as possible without pain. Repeat this exercise with toes pointed straight ahead and pointed out.
4. If the above exercises can be done in full range of motion, without pain, do the following exercises:
   a. Repeat range of motion exercises (see no. 1 above) with the teacher providing resistance to the exercises with the hand.
   b. Hopping exercise: hop as high as possible while standing and moving.

Repetitions should follow the general progressive resistive exercise pattern of ten repetitions, three sets of each.

Anatomy and Conditions of the Knee

Anatomy

The knee is an articulation of the femur, the patella, and the tibia. Weight-bearing and locomotion place considerable stress and strain on the knee joint. Strong knee joint extensor muscles (quadriceps) and flexor muscles (hamstrings), combined with tough ligaments, provide a strong functioning joint. The knee joint has been criticized structurally because it is vulnerable to front-back or inside-outside displacement (Hollinshead 1962). Football, soccer, and field hockey generate many knee injuries. Today, modern athletes can become conditioned to sustain greater joint stress by participating in weight training and flexibility programs, particularly for the knee. Pollock, Wilmore, and Fox (1984) have found that knee injuries can be caused or aggravated by an endurance conditioning program. They stress the use of proper footwear and running on soft, even surfaces, such as grass, to reduce or eliminate the problem. Exercises for development and rehabilitation of knee-related muscles must include the three main muscle groups—quadriceps, hamstrings, and calf.

Knees and Good Posture

In good posture, the knees are relaxed and bent slightly to provide "spring." They should not be thrust back or locked, as in poor posture. This hyperextension, or "back knees," is called **genu recurvatum** (Figure 14.5B) (see also Figure 14.8A). The condition results from weak muscles of the gastrocnemius (calf) and excessive strength of the quadriceps. Treatment consists of exercises designed to regain muscle balance by improving weaker muscles and stretching the overpowering muscles.

When the knees are locked, the buttocks are forced outward, and the entire body tenses. An individual who stands habitually with locked knees must be reminded to "loosen the knees." Continued positive verbal reinforcement by the adapted physical educator should provide essential correction of the standing position. In severe cases, bracing may be necessary.

Bowleg and Knock-Knee

Bowleg (genu varum) and **knock-knee** (genu valgum) (Figure 14.5C and D) are the result of weak knee ligaments or imbalance in the growth centers during the preteen growth spurt. These conditions can be partially corrected by progressive resistive exercises and by corrective footwear recommended by the student's physician (Goldenson 1978). In small children, these conditions generally do not require treatment, although lifts or wedges are sometimes placed in shoes. Mild bowing of the legs is typical in infants and in very young children, and usually corrects itself between the ages of 18 months and 2 years (Blackman 1984).

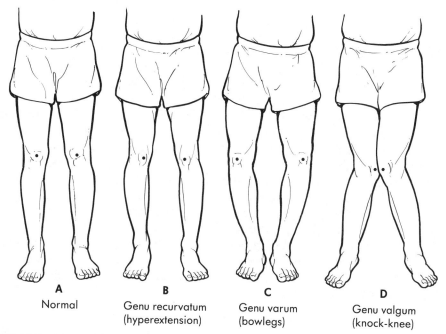

A
Normal

B
Genu recurvatum
(hyperextension)

C
Genu varum
(bowlegs)

D
Genu valgum
(knock-knee)

FIGURE 14.5. Normal knee alignment and common abnormalities. (Modified from Logan 1972, p. 93.)

Bowleg is observed when the feet are placed together and the knees are separated. The normal knee position is vertical. Knee alignment is correct if an imaginary line can be drawn that intersects the ankle midpoint, the knee midline, and the anterior superior iliac spine of the pelvis.

Poor muscle development that results in bowleg can be improved by proper leg alignment. Ballet dancers often place extreme stress on the knee joint. The ballet first position technique may reinforce negative knee alignment. The fifth position, flexing and hyperextending the knees, allows for external rotation. These positions leave the dancer with extensively stretched knee ligaments. To balance this, the instructor must be sure that the dancer assumes the fifth position without preliminary flexing of the knees (Sweigard 1974). The damage created by overstretching knee ligaments is similar to the harm caused by repeated deep knee bends or duck walking.

Knock-knee is common in children between the ages of 2 and 6 who have severely pronated feet. This is not a major problem unless it persists beyond age 8. When the protruding bones inside the ankle are less than 3 in. apart, minimal treatment only is recommended (Cailliet 1973).

Treatment, prescribed by a physician, usually consists of an inner wedge support in the shoes. Stretching exercises should be employed by the adapted physical educator. The legs should be manipulated to align correctly and the position held for the normal isometric count of 6 sec. The exercise should be repeated ten times for a total of three sets.

Osgood-Schlatter's Disease

Osgood-Schlatter's disease is a partial separation of the tibial tuberosity from the tibia and is caused by intense strain and pull from the patellar ligament (the patellar ligament is a continuation of the extremely strong quadriceps tendon) (Figure 14.6). This can be the result of disease, a sudden blow, or prolonged strain. Individuals between the ages of 9 and 14 will complain of sharp pain whenever running, jumping, or kicking. If the condition is considered severe and if continued activity could cause further damage, the physician will restrict movement completely. A leg cast ensures that knee movement is eliminated while the damaged area heals. Surgery is seldom indicated. When tearing has occurred, the surgical procedure involves tendon splitting, multiple drilling of the tibia, bone grafting, or a combination of these (Cailliet 1973).

Corrective treatment requires avoidance of excessive, explosive, or rapid movements of the knee joint. Therapeutic activities include isometric muscle-setting exercises for the quadriceps, straight leg raises from both supine and prone positions, and toe raises. These exercises follow rehabilitation treatment for post-surgical knee to ensure that the knee's muscle strength does not weaken owing to inactivity during the nonflexion and extension phase.

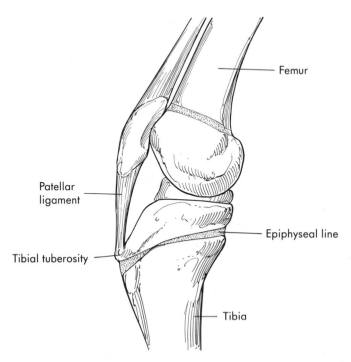

FIGURE 14.6. Osgood-Schlatter's disease may produce late deformity of the anterior portion of the epiphysis.

Corrective programs must always have the physician's endorsement. Rehabilitation of Osgood-Schlatter's disease must therefore follow the physician's prescribed recommendation. C. Weiss, M.D. (1984, p. D-9), endorses physical activity when he states: "There is no evidence at all, if they are willing to put up with some discomfort, that continuing physical activities will cause any long-term damage. . . . Depending on the motivation of the child, often we restrict activities for a few weeks, put them on anti-inflammatory medications, basically aspirin, and very occasionally use splints. If we restrict running, jumping, and cycling, we encourage swimming and weight-lifting for the upper body."

The adapted physical education teacher is responsible for suggesting to the doctor exercises for the student and requesting specific activity guidelines. Many physicians are eager to cooperate with the physical educator in giving the student specific exercises (e.g., quadriceps muscle setting, toe raises, and so forth) with exact limitations (weight, reps, and sets).

Besides providing exercises for rehabilitation, the adapted physical educator must develop additional exercises. A comprehensive upper body training program should be incorporated in the disabled student's program. Alternative or modified programs should be provided for individuals who are excused from regular physical education classes.

Knee Strengthening Exercises

The following exercises should be used when the knees are weak or need rehabilitation owing to injury or surgery. Individuals with low levels of explosive leg power, poor kicking ability, and below-normal running speed can benefit from knee strengthening exercises. These students do not need a physician's written prescription to participate in an exercise program. For rehabilitation and corrective programs, however, the adapted physical educator must have the physician's written approval.

Knee joint stability requires firm muscles, and maintenance of knee muscle strength requires use and stimulation. Injury and pain reduce the individual's use of the knee, resulting in weakness owing to atrophy. The instructor should develop exercises to stimulate the knee muscles without causing damage or injury. If pain develops during exercise, the student should be told to discontinue exercise immediately. The muscle is indicating, through pain, that it has reached its limit of participation.

If the student is recuperating from knee surgery or has Osgood-Schlatter's disease, begin with isometric muscle-setting exercises. These are appropriate when joint motion is not desirable, or when the leg is in a pressure dressing or cast.

Quadriceps Setting

The student should assume a supine or sitting position. The leg is straightened, then tensed and held in an isometric contraction for a 6-sec count. The knee should be kept as straight as possible. Begin action by having the student pull the kneecap upward as he pushes down simultaneously on the back of the knee. The student should perform up to ten repetitions. Record the number completed. A minimum 2-min rest period is recommended before starting the second set of ten repetitions. A third set of ten should follow after a similar rest. This regimen should be done one to three times per day. A student with Osgood-Schlatter's disease should use *only* these exercises and should not progress further without a physician's recommendation.

When three sets of 10 repetitions can be completed successfully without discomfort, the student should increase to 12 and then 15 repetitions. As strength improves, the next phase can be taught.

Straight Leg Raises

When leg strength is desired, straight leg raises, even for those in a cast, are appropriate. Ladley (1971) has stated that strengthening of the knee can be done more effectively if a 3-in. pad or block is placed under the knee. The leg is then straightened and held for a 6-sec isometric count. Cailliet (1973) has suggested that simultaneous dorsiflexion of the foot during these exercises improves quadriceps efficiency. Again, three sets of 10, 12, and 15 repetitions should be the student's goal.

Flexion and Extension Exercises

To develop the knee's full range of motion, the student should assume a standing position supported by a chair, table, or wall. The leg is bent slowly upward and then lowered slowly. When this motion can be executed without pain, flexion and extension can be performed while sitting on a table edge or lying face down on the floor or a table. Apply *no additional weight or resistance* to the leg. Toe raises should be included in the exercise regimen because they develop calf (gastrocnemius) strength, which provides necessary support for the knee. When in standing position, the heels should be raised.

Progressive Resistive Exercises

In progressive resistive exercise, extra resistance is added gradually. This is done by the teacher who applies pressure against the desired movement. When three sets of 10, 12, and 15 movements can be completed, the student should switch to a weight machine or weighted boot. The student can begin with 5 lb and increase the weight in 5 lb increments as the leg strengthens. A final weight of 30 to 35 lb is usually adequate for male high school students. (The adjusted maximum weight will be less for females.) In rehabilitation, use the nonaffected leg as a guide. For example, if the "good" leg can lift 30 lb, the other knee should reach that same level.

Endurance Exercises

The final phase of knee strengthening should include stair walking, jumping jacks, hopping on both legs, hopping on affected knee, jogging, bicycle riding, and shallow knee bends (never go lower than the position assumed when sitting in a chair).

Normal knee strength is usually attained within 3 to 6 weeks.

Anatomy and Abnormalities of the Vertebral Column

Anatomy

The vertebral column, or spine (Figure 14.7), is composed of 33 bones, which protect the delicate spinal cord. The vertebral column supports the body in an upright position. It defies gravity, conserves energy, absorbs shock, and permits locomotion and purposeful movement. Antigravity support and flexibility are demanded constantly of the vertebral column (Cailliet 1974).

From a posterior (back) view, the normal vertebral column appears to be a straight line. From a lateral (side) view, three natural curves appear—one at the neck, one at the upper back, and one at the lower back. Strong trunk muscles assist the vertebra in maintaining the normal upright postural position.

Postural Abnormalities of the Vertebral Column

When one or more of the spine's natural curves is increased or decreased, changes often occur, which, if left unattended for several years, become permanent structural defects. When an individual continues to use improper posture, the deviation will eventually affect the individual's mechanical efficiency. An extreme example of such alteration is the ancient Chinese custom of tightly wrapping the feet of baby girls to restrict growth. The result of this procedure was extreme bone compression and permanently damaged feet.

Spinal deformities (Figures 14.8A–C) include increased convex curvature (kyphosis), forward curvature (lordosis), and lateral curvature (scoliosis).

Most lower vertebral deviations result from abnormal tilting of the pelvis. When growing stops, usually in the late teens, the sacroiliac becomes firm and rigid, restrict-

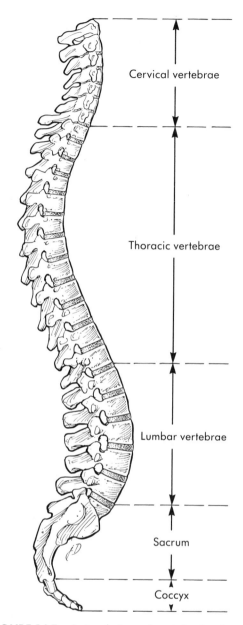

FIGURE 14.7. Lateral view of vertebral column.

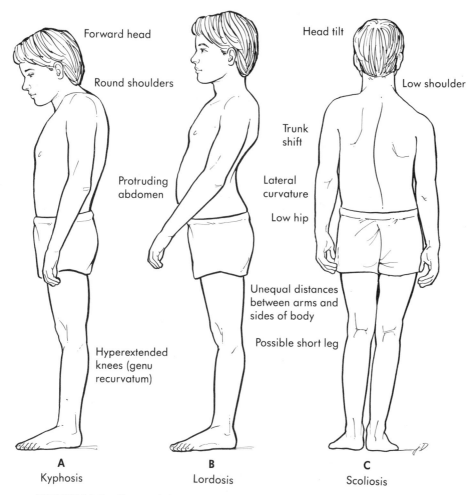

FIGURE 14.8.   Postural deviations. (A) Kyphosis. (B) Lordosis. (C) Scoliosis.

ing movement. As a result, when the pelvis tilts forward, backward, or sideward, the lower back vertebrae also curve in the same direction. Increased forward curvature of the lower back is called **lordosis.** Abnormal tilting of the pelvis to the side, causing lateral curvature, is called **scoliosis.**

Lordosis

Lower back pain syndrome is a common disability. Physicians have three classifications for lower back pain as follows:

1. Traumatic back pain is caused by an injury that irritates the sensitive tissues of the muscles and ligaments.

2. **Referred back pain** signals that something is wrong in another part of the anatomy. The pancreas, stomach, liver, prostate, and heart all use back pain as their distress signal.
3. **Structural deformity** of the back bones, innate or acquired, also can result in lower back pain. A tumor of the spine, an arthritic condition, or many different diseases may be the underlying cause of the deformity.

Unlike muscles, ligaments cannot repair themselves. When overstretched for a long period of time, they will resemble an overstretched rubber band. This can happen as a result of strain from poor posture or from a sprain, which is the tearing of ligaments. Usually the ligaments in the lumbosacral region (at the spine's base) become so badly stretched that the surrounding muscles fail to protect the joint from sudden movement (e.g., straightening up too quickly or lifting a heavy object quickly). Strained or torn ligaments relax their support of the vertebrae, causing pain in the lower back (Tolarski 1982).

When the back is strained or sprained, a localized swelling occurs. As ligaments and muscles swell, excess fluids irritate the nerves, which causes a dull ache and sometimes muscle spasms.

Lordosis usually occurs as a result of strains or sprains, but chronic lower back pain often results from a ruptured disk. Injury or violent stress from falling or jumping can cause the intervertebral disk to tear away (i.e., a slipped disk). A disk fragment may then protrude against the spinal nerve root and cause pressure, which radiates pain downward, toward the leg.

All corrective and rehabilitation programs for lower back pain must be prescribed by a physician, because the pain must be medically diagnosed prior to treatment. Almost all persons with generalized lower back pain exhibit no apparent reason for the discomfort, but persons with disk problems are usually able to identify when and how the injury occurred.

Kraus and Raab (1961) estimate that approximately 80 percent of the U.S. population experiences lower back pain caused by "hypokinetic disease" (i.e., pain caused by diminished exercise). The large muscles that hold the body in different positions while we execute various movements are not exercised by sedentary individuals. As a result, abdominal muscles sag from neglect, back muscles (used to keep the body erect) are used mainly while stationary, and upper back leg muscles are not stretched, often resulting in shortened hamstrings.

Cailliet (1981) believes that low back pain is related directly to *both* static and dynamic ("kinetic") abnormalities. He believes that static abnormalities are the result of faulty posture, and that correction of these faults through continued use of proper posture techniques should result in a pain-free condition. Adequate flexibility, good muscle tone, and proper concept of good kinesthetics are essential for maintenance of proper posture. In reference to problems encountered when individuals are moving, Cailliet (1981, p. 142) states: "Insofar as movement requires muscular effort, sometimes strength, and sometimes endurance, and at times both, good muscle conditioning is paramount. . . . Proper performance constantly practiced will result in everyday function free of pain, owing to the proper use of a properly conditioned machine."

Stress and strain on the lower back are considered responsible for prolonged pain. Most lordosis is attributed to an abnormal forward tilting of the pelvis (Figure 14.9), which exerts pressure on nerves in the lumbar region of the back. With increased lumbar curvature, the center of gravity of the body is moved forward from its normal position, and as a result, the back muscles are subjected to intense strain. The hip extensors and the hamstrings also become shortened and inflexible.

The anterior longitudinal ligament (Figure 14.10) that connects the vertebrae is sensitive to strain, and when constantly stretched, will cause pain in the lower back.

The rectus abdominis muscle controls the tilt of the pelvis and the curvature of the lumbar region. By holding the pelvis up, the lower back is flattened and the lumbar curve reduced. The abdominal muscles should be tensed, pulling the pelvis upward. Raising the chest and drawing in the stomach should be done repeatedly. The adapted physical educator can remind the student of this exercise.

The iliopsoas muscles are found on the upper, inner surface of the pelvis and lumbar vertebrae. These muscles produce strong running, provide leg lifting for the long jump, and are responsible for kicking actions. When the iliopsoas muscles are overstrengthened, as in the performance of supine straight leg lifts, the lower back is pulled forward and the lumbar curve assumes a lordosis position. The strength of this muscle group is evident in young children under age 5 who have a protruding, down-

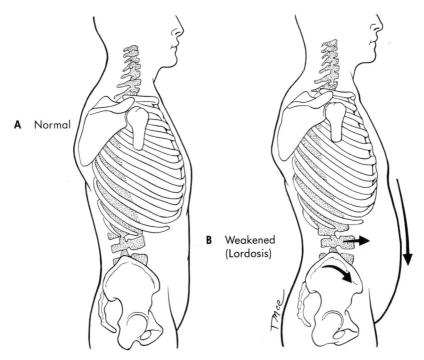

A Normal

B Weakened (Lordosis)

FIGURE 14.9. Lordosis is apparent when comparing normal abdominal muscle strength (A) with a weakened muscle wall (B), which produces forward tilting of the pelvis.

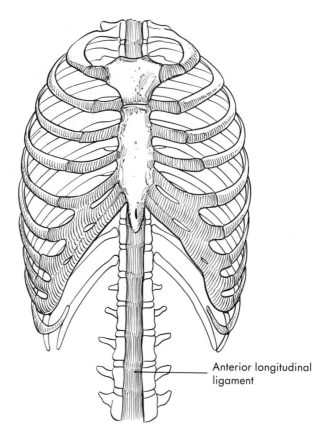

Anterior longitudinal
ligament

FIGURE 14.10. Position of anterior longitudinal ligament.

ward sagging abdominal wall. This "pot belly" is typical of all preschool children. The iliopsoas muscle is being stretched from the original prenatal tightness that held the baby in the fetal position. Normal and natural play activities will firm the abdominal muscles and allow the pelvis to assume its correct position. A school-age child thus requires a comprehensive physical education program.

The hamstring muscles originate on the pelvis. The natural pull of the hamstrings is almost directly downward and has little effect on the backward tilt of the pelvis. An inability to touch the floor reveals inflexibility of the hamstrings, and muscle tightness indicates limited elasticity of intramuscular connective tissue. It is important that this muscle group be stretched.

Exercises for Lordosis

The Paul Williams (1953) exercises (Figure 14.11) to reduce lower back pain are commonly prescribed by physicians. All exercises are aimed at reducing excessive lumbar curve, increasing abdominal muscle strength, stretching hip flexors, stretching

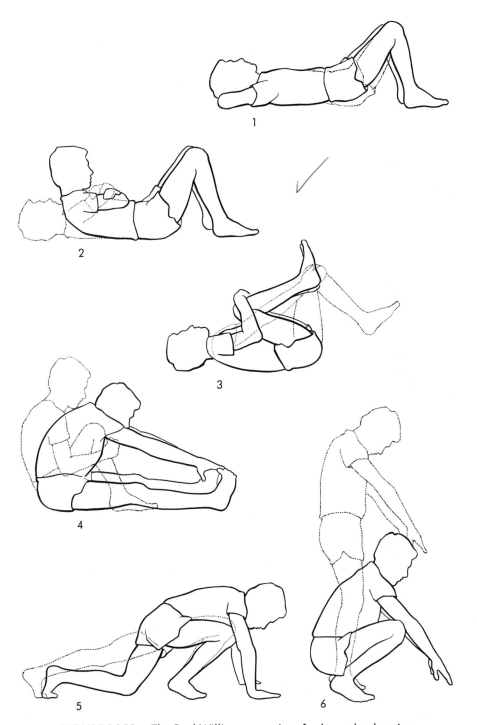

FIGURE 14.11. The Paul Williams exercises for lower back pain.

hamstrings, and correcting posture by learning to hold the pelvis in an upward and backward pain-free position. The exercises should be performed on a padded mat. Each exercise should be repeated 10 times on the first day, and increased by 1 for each successive day until a maximum of 30 per day is reached. Strength and flexibility should improve within 20 days and pain should be reduced. Kraus and Raab (1961) stress that the program must be continued even after pain stops. Too often individuals return to an inactive life-style and experience subsequent return of pain.

Exercise 1—Pelvic Tilt (back lying). Bend knees and put soles of feet flat on floor. Pull up and in on the abdominal muscles and pinch buttocks together. This lifts the tailbone off the floor while pressing the small of the back down against the floor. Hold position for a 6-sec isometric count. The exercise strengthens abdominals and buttocks, and reduces low back curve. Repeat exercise 10 times and increase by 1 each day to reach 30. (All remaining exercises should follow this pattern of 1 per day increase to a maximum of 30 per day.)

Exercise 2—Abdominal Strengthening (back lying). Bend knees with soles of feet flat on floor. Fold arms across chest; raise shoulders off floor. Hold position for a 6-sec isometric count. Repeat 10 times on first day. This exercise develops abdominal muscle strength.

Exercise 3—Stretching Lower Back (back lying). Lie with knees bent and one hand hooked around each knee. Keep knees apart to avoid hitting chest. Pull knees slowly and evenly toward armpits. Keep head and lower back flat. This stretching exercise need not be held for the 6-sec count. Do not release grip on knees during exercise. Do not pull knees over shoulders. This exercise is intended to lift buttocks off the floor.

Exercise 4—Hamstring Stretching (sitting up). Straighten one leg; bend other leg and place foot flat on floor. Drop flexed knee outward and bend forward to reach toes of extended leg. The stretch is felt in the extended leg. Repeat 10 times on first day. This stretching exercise need not be held for the 6-sec count. Repeat for other leg.

Exercise 5—Iliopsoas Stretching (modified single-leg treadmill position). Kneel on one knee; bend other leg at hip and knee with foot flat on floor under shoulder. Begin a forward and backward rocking motion with head bent downward to ensure that no arching of the back occurs. Complete 10 repetitions with one leg; repeat exercise with other leg.

Exercise 6—Flat-Footed Squat (standing position). With feet 12 in. apart and turned slightly out, squat while keeping heels flat on floor. Keep head curved downward during the exercise. Arms should be downward, elbows dropped between knees, fingers touching floor as squat is executed. Repeat minimum of 10 times.

These exercises, modified from Williams (1953), develop minimal strength levels and increase flexibility of those muscles that cause lower back pain. The following postural suggestions for individuals with lower back pain syndrome (Williams 1953) may reduce the chances of lordosis returning: (1) When walking or standing, keep toes straight ahead with most of weight on heels. (2) Try to form a crease across the upper abdomen by holding chest up and forward, and at the same time elevating the front of the pelvis. Walk as if you are going up an incline. (3) Avoid wearing high heeled shoes as much as possible. (4) Sit with buttocks "tucked under" so hollow in lower back is gone. (5) When possible, sit so knees are elevated higher than hips. This is especially important when driving (driver's seat forward) or when riding as a passenger in an automobile. (6) Sleep on back with knees propped up, or on side with one or both knees drawn up. (7) Do not lift loads in front of you above the waistline. (8) Never bend backwards. (9) Do not bend forward with knees straight, always squat. (10) Avoid standing as much as possible, and (11) learn to live 24 hr a day with the hollow in the lower part of your back reduced to a minimum.

Scoliosis

Scoliosis is a lateral (side-to-side) curvature of the spine accompanied by twisting vertebrae. Some curves are caused by birth defects and disease, but most are idiopathic (i.e., of unknown origin) (Figure 14.12).

One out of every 10 persons has some degree of scoliosis. Two to 3 in every 100 will have a progressive condition. One out of every 1000 cases will require surgery (National Scoliosis Foundation 1985).

Scoliosis is classified according to the child's age at onset because of both diagnostic and prognostic factors (Cailliet 1975). If the curvature develops during the first 3 years of life, it is termed *infantile*. If developed between the 3rd and 12th year in girls and between the 3rd and 14th year in boys, it is termed *juvenile*. If developed after age 12 in girls and after age 14 in boys but before maturity, it is called *adolescent scoliosis*. Of all idiopathic scoliosis cases, 90 percent occur in girls. No pain or other symptoms are present, only a slight lateral curvature of the back. This may go unnoticed for some time; even the parents may be unaware of the abnormality. The individual with scoliosis usually does not experience pain in the early years. Curves that are moderate to severe will become more pronounced in adulthood, and may increase during pregnancy. Left untreated, scoliosis can cause obvious physical deformity, pain, arthritic symptoms, heart and lung complications, and can limit activity (National Scoliosis Foundation n.d.).

The physical educator should observe these deviations when students are relaxed and postures are easily identified. The instructor may wish to know if the curve is *functional*, that is, caused by abnormal postural positions, or overstrengthening of back muscles, or if it is *structural*, a deformity of the vertebrae. Structural deviations are usually found in children with birth defects or bone disease (Figure 14.13). Over several years, functional scoliosis can result in permanent spinal changes and then becomes a structural deviation (Blackman 1984).

Highly noticeable curvatures should be diagnosed by an orthopedic surgeon who may recommend surgical correction, fusion, or casting. Common treatments include orthotic devices (Boston and Milwaukee braces, Risser localizer cast, Harrington rods), spinal fusion (joining of the vertebrae), and grafts and revisions. There is a strong

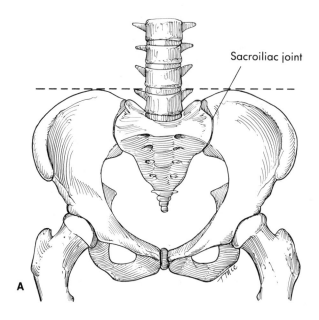

Sacroiliac joint

A

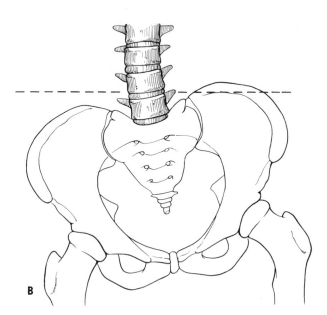

B

FIGURE 14.12.   (A) Normal pelvic structure. (B) Lateral tilting of the pelvis resulting in scoliosis.

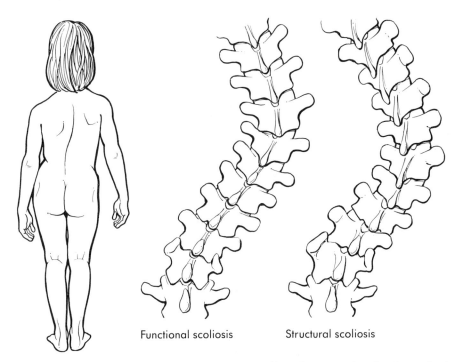

Functional scoliosis   Structural scoliosis

FIGURE 14.13. Comparison of infantile and congenital scoliosis: With infantile scoliosis, the bony parts of the spine are normally developed. With congenital scoliosis, they are malformed.

correlation between scoliosis and the lateral tilting of the pelvis seen in children with one leg shorter than the other. When the pelvis tilts, the sacrum also tilts and the spinal column curves (Figure 14.13). The resulting scoliosis condition is a regular "C" or a reverse "C." When the original curve is not altered, a secondary curve develops that will progress to an "S" or reverse "S" curvature. The curve may involve any segment of the spine and may be of any length. Table 14.1 lists specific terms relating to scoliosis and other postural deviations.

Screening for Scoliosis

Because idiopathic scoliosis does not develop until the rapid growth period of adolescence, a postural examination is not necessary before children reach the age of 10. Screening is recommended when children are between ages 10 and 13, the typical junior high school age.

This screening is the responsibility of the adapted physical education instructor. The school nurse should be recruited to assist in the evaluation.

Setting up the Scoliosis Evaluation

1. Appoint a committee to plan the screening program. Include the school administrator, school nurse, physical education teacher, physician or orthopedist, PTA or parent representative, and corrective, physical, or occupational therapist.

TABLE 14.1

COMMON TERMS RELATING TO SCOLIOSIS AND OTHER POSTURAL DEVIATIONS

Term	Description
Scoliosis	Side-to-side (lateral) curvature of spine
Functional	Flexible; tends to correct when person bends forward
Structural	Rigid; does not tend to correct when person bends forward
Infantile	Develops before 3 years of age
Juvenile	Develops between 3 years of age and puberty
Adolescent	Develops between puberty and maturity
Adult	Develops after maturity
Idiopathic	Due to unknown cause; heredity is probable factor
Congenital	Present at birth
Neuromuscular	Due to neurological or muscular diseases

SOURCE: Adapted from Bigge, J. L., and O'Donnell, P. A. *Teaching Individuals With Physical and Multiple Disabilities.* Columbus, Ohio: Charles E. Merrill, 1976.

2. Choose grade levels to be screened. Grades five, six, seven, eight, and nine are suggested, or children between the ages of 10 and 13.
3. Plan a training session, taught by an orthopedic physician or therapist, for individuals who will screen, record scores, and assist children in dressing.
4. Provide a screening device (Figure 14.14).
5. Provide screening forms (Figure 14.1).
6. Schedule testing time and place. Secure a private area where 50 to 70 children can be evaluated in 1 hr, or about 1 student every 30 sec.
7. Inform all students to be screened about the reasons for the program.
8. Plan a rescreening session for children who show curvature of the spine or a rib hump or both (approximately 10 percent will show deviation).
9. Plan a referral system. Send letters to parents with suggestions for further referral to physicians.
10. Collect statistics: number screened, grade level, number of boys and girls referred and the results, and exercise program prescribed for each child.

Advanced Screening Test to Determine Degree of Scoliosis

For observation, the student's back must be exposed. Gym suits or trunks should be lowered to below the hip line (a two-piece bathing suit is appropriate for girls). Small dots (use washable marking pen) should be placed on each of the spinous processes of the upper lumbar, thoracic, and cervical vertebrae. While standing behind the grid, the student should assume two positions. First (refer to the postural screening chart in Figure 14.1), from a rear view, look for one overdeveloped hip, one low shoulder, a

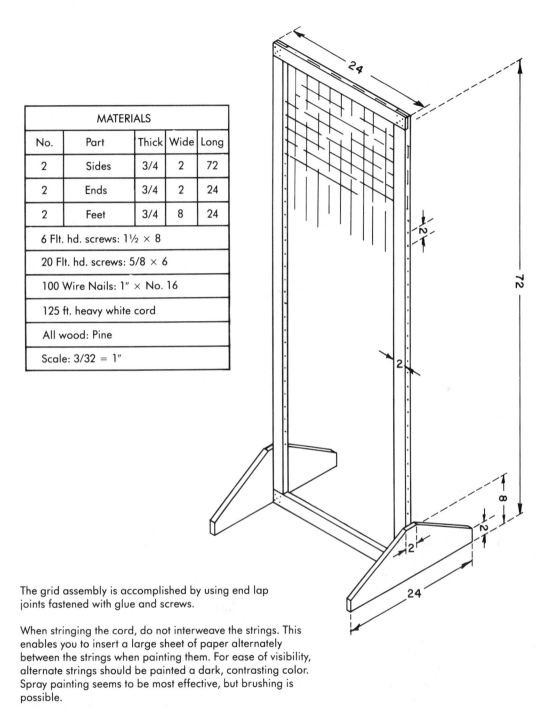

MATERIALS				
No.	Part	Thick	Wide	Long
2	Sides	3/4	2	72
2	Ends	3/4	2	24
2	Feet	3/4	8	24
6 Flt. hd. screws: 1½ × 8				
20 Flt. hd. screws: 5/8 × 6				
100 Wire Nails: 1" × No. 16				
125 ft. heavy white cord				
All wood: Pine				
Scale: 3/32 = 1"				

The grid assembly is accomplished by using end lap joints fastened with glue and screws.

When stringing the cord, do not interweave the strings. This enables you to insert a large sheet of paper alternately between the strings when painting them. For ease of visibility, alternate strings should be painted a dark, contrasting color. Spray painting seems to be most effective, but brushing is possible.

FIGURE 14.14.   A screening grid used for identification of postural deviations. (Grid plans and drawing courtesy of J. Wozniak, LaCrosse, Wis.)

prominent scapula, or an open area or angle between arm and body. Take a Polaroid photograph to document whether a curvature exists. This technique serves as an objective assessment (pretest) of the student, and provides information for further evaluation (posttest). Second, have the child bend forward at the waist and drop head and arms in a relaxed manner (i.e., the Adam's position). This position determines whether the curvature is functional or structural. Examine closely for a rib hump or prominence in the thoracic or lumbar region. If the curvature disappears when in the forward bending position, the curve is functional. Functional scoliosis can be remedied by repeated stretching, bending, pushing, and reaching exercises. The muscles that cause the deformity are overstretched or overdeveloped, and rehabilitation activities restore muscle balance.

Scoliosis Exercise Program

All exercise programs to rehabilitate a regular "C" curve must be approved by a physician. To correct lateral curvature, the students should understand that they are attempting to push and stretch the spine back to its normal position. The following exercises are from Daniels and Davies (1965, pp. 137–139) for remediating regular "C" curve scoliosis (these exercises also can be used to correct a reverse "C" curve if the exercises are reversed):

1. **Starting Position:** Prone lying, right arm upward, left arm at side. **Exercise:** Move right arm in an arc overhead toward the left, press down with left hand, and slide left hip up. The effect is a reversal of the curve, with both stretching and strengthening taking place where needed.
2. **Starting Position:** Prone lying, right arm extended forward, left arm at side. Partner holds feet firmly to floor. **Exercise:** Trunk is extended, right arm pushed forward, and left arm pushed backward. Hold 3 counts, relax, and repeat.
3. **Starting Position:** Right side lying, left hand on side of thigh, right arm supporting head, feet held firm by partner. **Exercise:** Raise trunk laterally, sliding left hand down side of left thigh. This is a strenuous exercise and requires some conditioning before its use.
4. **Starting Position:** Kneeling on right knee, extend left leg sideward. Right arm is overhead, left hand pressed against ribs, fingers to rear. **Exercise:** Lateral trunk flexion to left, right arm is moved in arc overhead and toward the left, while left hand presses against ribs. Use forceful, stretching, lateral trunk movement.
5. **Starting Position:** Standing, feet a few inches apart. **Exercise:** Raise left heel and left hip. Extend right arm in arc overhead to left. Press left hand against ribs on left side.
6. **Starting Position:** Stride stance, arms horizontal at sides. **Exercise:** Lateral trunk flexion to left, left hand sliding down side of left leg, right arm extended in an arch overhead.
7. **Starting Position:** Straight hanging position on horizontal bar or stall bars, forward grasp. **Exercise:** Straight hanging, followed by lateral trunk flexion to left. Movement accentuated by raising left hip and moving feet to left.

Summary

Many factors influence posture and postural abnormality. Some deviations are structural (inherited), but the greater number are functional (acquired). The physical educator has an excellent opportunity to observe and evaluate students and to determine if an abnormality exists. Early identification of postural deviations is of extreme importance and can lead opportunely to needed remediation if proper programs are administered. Physicians must give a written prescription for all corrective exercises, and physical educators must provide ongoing progress reports to the medical profession and to parents.

References

AAHPERD. Questions and Answers about P.L. 94-142. *Update*, p. 6, January 1978.

Barratt, M., et al. *Foundations for Movement*, 2nd ed. Dubuque, Iowa: Wm. C. Brown, 1968.

Blackman, J. A. (ed). *Medical Aspects of Developmental Disabilities in Children Birth to Three*, rev. 1st ed. Rockville, Md.: Aspen Systems Corporation, 1984.

Cailliet, R. *Foot and Ankle Pain*. Philadelphia: F. A. Davis, 1968.

———. *Knee Pain and Disability*. Philadelphia: F. A. Davis, 1973.

———. *Low Back Pain Syndrome*. Philadelphia: F. A. Davis, 1974.

———. *Scoliosis: Diagnosis and Management*. Philadelphia: F. A. Davis, 1975.

———. *Low Back Pain Syndrome*, 3rd ed. Philadelphia: F. A. Davis, 1981.

Daniels, A. S., and Davies, E. A. *Adapted Physical Education*, 2nd ed. New York: Harper & Row, 1965.

Goldenson, R. M., ed. *Disability and Rehabilitation Handbook*. New York: McGraw-Hill, 1978.

Hollinshead, W. H. *Textbook of Anatomy*. New York: Harper & Row, 1962.

Kraus, H., and Raab, W. *Hypokinetic Disease*. Springfield, Ill.: Charles C Thomas, 1961.

Ladley, G. An Investigation Into the Effectiveness of Various Forms of Quadriceps Exercises. *Physiotherapy* 57:356, 1971.

Logan, G. A. *Adapted Physical Education*. Dubuque, Iowa: Wm. C. Brown, 1972.

National Scoliosis Foundation. One in Every 10 Persons Has Scoliosis. Belmont, Mass.: The Foundation, n.d.

———. *The Spinal Connection* 2(1):2, Spring 1985.

Pollock, M. L., Wilmore, J. H., and Fox, S. M., III. *Exercise in Health and Disease*. Philadelphia: W. B. Saunders, 1984.

Rathbone, J. L., and Hunt, V. V. *Corrective Physical Education*, 7th ed. Philadelphia: W. B. Saunders, 1966.

Subotnick, S. I. Foot Orthoses: An Update. *The Physician and Sportsmedicine* 11:103–109, August 1983.

Sweigard, L. E. *Human Movement Potential—Its Idiokinetic Facilitation*. New York: Dodd, Mead, 1974.

Tolarski, C. School Teaches Patients How to Overcome Back Pain. *Medical Center News—The University of Chicago* 6(4):2, Fall 1982.

Weiss, C. Young Athletes Are Prone to Lower-Leg Pain. *Chicago Tribune,* p. D-9, 5 May 1984.

Williams, P. C. Conservative Management of Lesions of Lumbosacral Spine. In *Instructional Course Lectures,* edited by J. W. Edwards. Ann Arbor, Mich.: American Academy of Orthopedic Surgeons, 1953.

Wilson, H. The Rehabilitation of Ankle Injuries. *The First Aider* 45(5):4, 1976.

CHAPTER 15

Chronic Musculoskeletal Disorders

Chronic musculoskeletal disorders that may be congenital, acquired, progressive, or permanently disabling or a combination of these do not soon pass. Their long-term nature, coupled with often occurring secondary complications, generates many significant and far-reaching consequences for the child.

When a condition is **chronic,** the normal course of that condition occurs over a period of years. Recovery and rehabilitation, even if complete, are accomplished over a protracted period of time. The term *chronic* is applicable to *congenital* as well as *acquired* conditions.

Congenital refers to any condition that occurs during fetal development. The child with a congenital disorder is born with a birth defect or a genetic defect that later manifests itself in disability. **Acquired** refers to conditions not founded in genetic anomaly. Onset of these conditions occurs sometime after birth.

Progressive describes those conditions, congenital or acquired, that continue to worsen. Some disorders, despite all known intervention efforts, are relentlessly progressive.

Permanent refers to any residual loss of function that remains even after a chronic disorder has run its course. Permanent disability usually implies the need for some form or forms of lifelong adjustment.

Depending on the nature and extent of the child's musculoskeletal disorder, the adapted physical educator will observe significant interruption in many facets of the child's developmental progress. The educator needs to keep in mind, however, the fact that the affected child, despite musculoskeletal disorder, is climbing the same developmental ladder as her nonhandicapped peers. In the affected child's case, the handicapping condition simply makes the climb more difficult, and often limits the child's progress. The adapted physical educator should not envision the child as handicapped, but rather as a child whose musculoskeletal disorder happens to limit normal development. The focus should not be on the handicap but on curricular modifications that circumvent limitations. As always, emphasize ability, *not* disability. Even when musculoskeletal disability may be permanent or progressive, appropriate medical attention, therapy, and adapted physical education can facilitate significantly the child's physical, motor, and psychosocial development.

The musculoskeletal disorders discussed in this chapter were selected because they recur in the adapted physical education setting. The conditions are those that the child's physician and others would expect an adapted physical educator to understand. When obscure or rare musculoskeletal disorders are encountered, the educator should consult with the appropriate therapists or the attending physician.

Limb Deficiency

Limb deficiency has far-reaching consequences physically, motorically, and psychosocially. Depending on the site or sites of limb deficiency, physical and motor impairment may range from relatively mild to relatively severe. In addition, psychosocial implications influence the child's feelings toward self and his feelings toward others, and others are influenced in their feelings toward the child. Developing a positive psychosocial attitude in the child and in how others react to the child will create a positive environment in which the child can grow and develop. Because children (and adults) tend to be very conscious of even slight differences that set them apart from others, the obvious limb deficiency presents a significant psychosocial dilemma.

Classmates of a child with a prosthesis may reject that child unless the teacher provides a positive setting and acceptance. Kieran et al. (1981, p. 56) make the following suggestions: "Children are often more straight forward in their questions and explanations than adults are. If a child is somewhat accepting of the handicap, he or she may act as a 'teacher,' explaining what happened and how the prosthetic device (if any) works. Touching the disfigured area often helps to satisfy young children's curiosity. Once the curiosity has been satisfied, the children will probably play together like all other children."

Limb absence may be either *acquired* or *congenital*. Acquired amputation refers to limb loss by accident (traumatic amputation) or surgery (surgical amputation). Surgical amputation most often occurs owing to a malignant bone tumor. The child with an acquired amputation was born with an intact body, but has experienced a problem subsequent to birth necessitating amputation.

Congenital amputation refers to missing limbs or portions of limbs at birth. Characteristics of the various congenital limb amputations are **amelia** (absence of limb or limbs), **hemimelia** (congenital absence of all or part of distal half of limb), and **phocomelia** (congenital absence of proximal portion of limb, the hands or feet being attached to the trunk by a small bone).

Congenital amputation may be transverse, taking the limb in full cross-section, or paraxial (Greek for "along the axis"), taking only a side or center portion of the limb (Figure 15.1).

Males incur more amputations from all causes at the rate of 2:1 from disease, 10:1 from trauma, and 1.2:1 from congenital causes and tumor (Dunham 1981). The three major causes of amputation that most directly affect school-age individuals are cancer, trauma, and congenital deformity. Trauma involves crushing injuries or lacerations

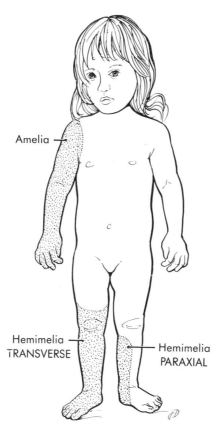

FIGURE 15.1. Types of amputations.

that are so extensive that reconstruction is not possible. The destroyed tissue and attendant loss of blood may threaten the person's life. Amputation resulting from **congenital deformity** is performed when the limb is not capable of functioning and there is extensive loss of nerve supply or muscle power. Individuals with congenital underdevelopment or malformation of the limbs have been helped by amputation of the nonfunctional limb and fitting of a prosthesis.

Activity Considerations

When amputation is elective and planned in advance, physical conditioning activities should be provided in preparation for surgery and convalescence. Following convalescence and return to the physical education setting, the child will need psychosocial support as well as physical and motor rehabilitation. The educator should discuss the child's amputation with classmates to satisfy their curiosity and alleviate apprehension about the amputee. This effort will help to resolve social problems for the amputee and his peers.

Recommended activities for the amputee involve moving the joints above the amputation site as pain permits. Stretching activities prescribed by the physician following surgery and return to school usually are done by, or in cooperation with, a physical therapist. Moving the affected limb through reasonable ranges of motion and strengthening appropriate muscles will prevent debilitating contractures that can occur following amputation.

The following list of progressions is designed for a below-the-knee amputee. A mat program is a combination of exercises that involve different functional skills such as rolling, crawling, and kneeling. Such skills are commonly taught in a sequence that follows their normal development in childhood. Each section of this mat program for a unilateral amputee stresses skill development. The exercises build on one another to increase strength and coordination. The activities are (1) rolling, (2) assuming a long sitting position, (3) seated push-ups, (4) moving forward, backward, side to side in a long sitting position, (5) assuming a kneeling posture on all fours, (6) crawling and resisted crawling, (7) assuming a high kneeling position, and (8) balance activities in a high kneeling position (O'Sullivan, Cullen, and Schmitz 1981).

Maintaining proper range of motion in the limb is vital to achieving correct body mechanics, and the strengthening of appropriate muscle groups allows for eventual motor control and management of the artificial limb or **prosthesis** (Figures 15.2–15.4). The sound limb and all unaffected body parts should be exercised as well to maintain a desirable physical condition. Lower extremity amputees need activities to strengthen upper extremities for crutch or cane walking.

Congenital amputee children may have had few opportunities for preprosthetic care or motor skills enlightenment. It is important to note that comprehensive early attention facilitates a positive prognosis. As the congenital amputee child continues to grow and develop, regular evaluation serves as the basis for prosthesis fitting, refitting, and activity prescription. The adapted physical educator, by virtue of professional

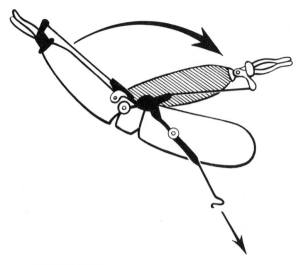

FIGURE 15.2.   Above-the-elbow prosthesis.

Prosthesis
Prosthetist

preparation and practical or clinical experience, can provide valuable input by evaluating the child's progress as related to potential and prognosis.

When attempting to understand prosthetic devices, the adapted physical educator should determine if modifications are possible that will allow the youngster to take active part in a specific skill or game. In many cases, the person who makes the prosthesis, called the prosthetist (pros' thet ist), will offer suggestions for adapting the artificial equipment. For example, the split hook is an extremely functional hand substitute that can be modified to add a device on which a baseball glove is securely attached, and easily opened and closed by the player.

A new type of artificial equipment that is becoming popular are the myoelectric prostheses. This equipment involves movement of the artificial limb through an electric signal initiated by the person. At present, such prostheses are generally reserved for light work, with the conventional prosthesis used as a back-up for heavy-duty tasks. Shaperman (1985) has found, however, that myoelectric hands have greater grip strength than those operated by body power. In reference to the traditional prosthetic devices operated by body power, Adams et al. (1982, p. 51) state: "The stump is used as a source of energy for control of the prosthesis. . . . Force and motion can be obtained by means of a cable that is connected between the prosthetic device and a harness across the chest or shoulder."

Myoelectric
move limb via electric signal

Problems of Balance

Balance appears to pose one of the most pervasive problems confronting amputees, particularly acquired amputees who are in the early stages of rehabilitation. Initially, the child is not accustomed to the limb's absence and its effect on the body's center of

FIGURE 15.3. Below-the-elbow prosthesis.

gravity. Learning to manage the prosthesis can be disconcerting also because of its awkwardness in not moving counteractively to the other member. Normal arm counteraction for balance in walking or running is complicated by limb absence and prosthetic replacement.

For lower extremity amputees, balance is a problem particularly when amputation is above the knee (AK). Below-the-knee (BK) amputees often walk quite normally with little or no indication that the limb is missing. Generally, the level of lower extremity amputation and whether the amputation is AK or BK will determine the child's balance capabilities and skill development. These factors should serve as a guide in selecting appropriate activities.

Swimming

Swimming is an enjoyable and valuable activity for amputee children. It serves to condition and to ensure that affected body segments can move through the desired range of motion. Depending on need, swim fins may be strapped to the limb or to a special prosthesis to enhance performance and enjoyment.

Problem of Increased Perspiration

Amputees encounter increased perspiration during activity because the amputee's cooling surface is reduced owing to missing a limb or limbs (Blakeslee 1963). Encourage

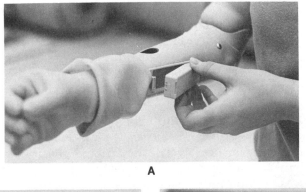

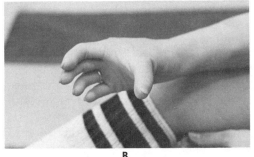
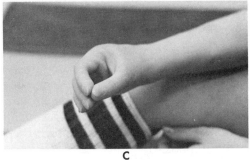

FIGURE 15.4. (A) Battery activates servo. (B) Tensing the stump causes prosthetic hand to open. (C) Relaxing the stump causes hand to close.

the amputee to wear lightweight clothing to reduce fatigue and to absorb perspiration. On days that are warm or humid or both, this problem needs to be monitored closely.

Low Energy Output and Obesity

Because of low motivation and low self-concept, many amputee children adopt a sedentary behavior pattern. While amputation may limit movement and decrease efficiency to some degree, low energy output nevertheless tends to be a characteristic behavior even among unilateral below-elbow amputees. This suggests that in some cases the sedentary behavior pattern may be a function of attitude rather than disability.

Some amputees, particularly BK amputees, become obese with age as a result of inactivity. This tendency should be countered with an activity program that is both satisfying and within the child's potential.

Lasko and Knopf (1984) stress the importance of developing the amputee's level of cardiorespiratory efficiency. They state: "The aerobic capacity of the amputee should be maintained as much as possible. Swimming is an excellent choice for even the bilateral amputee. Swim fins may be attached to the stumps by special prostheses. Arm crank ergometry may be another choice for those with limited weight bearing capabilities" (p. 198).

Increasing the energy output of amputees is important, because good muscular condition is required to manage the prosthesis. Limited muscular strength and endurance render the prosthesis unmanageable and encourage sedentary behavior.

Among low-energy amputees whose sedentary behavior appears more a function of attitude than disability, a negative self-concept is probably the culprit (Blakeslee 1963). Amputee children who have been treated as invalids will reflect the limited expectations of those adults around them. Telling children through words and deeds that they are invalids becomes a self-fulfilling prophecy.

Many low-energy amputees can achieve physical and motor proficiencies well beyond their present performance levels. The adapted physical educator should be patient but persistent, empathetic but gently prodding to help the amputee child find enjoyment, success, and improved self-image through movement.

Playground Activities and Sports

Surprisingly, amputee children often enjoy participating in climbing and hanging activities. For upper extremity amputees, this presents a unique challenge because the pull against the prosthesis, which occurs in hanging activities, is identical to the force exerted to remove the appliance. Resourceful amputee children do discover ways of stabilizing the prosthesis so it will not come loose. Below-the-elbow amputees become proficient climbers by using a forceful tensing of the stump in the prosthesis socket to hold it in place (Blakeslee 1963).

Amputee children can participate in many sports, depending on each specific case. Skiing is one activity that appears to be gaining favor among unilateral lower extremity amputees. Unilateral upper extremity amputees can participate in baseball or softball when they learn to catch and throw with the same hand (Blakeslee 1963, pp. 299–300). This is done by catching the ball, tossing it into the air, quickly tucking the glove under the affected arm, catching the ball with the unaffected hand, and throwing it. Upper extremity amputees with controls that open and close the hook learn to time opening the hook by tossing beanbags for distance or accuracy or both (Bleck and Nagel 1982, p. 20). Lower extremity amputees can enjoy archery and weight training.

While engaging in sports, some amputees will discard their prosthesis because it gets in the way. If removal of the prosthesis has the physician's approval, there should be no other cause for concern. Under such circumstances, the child is often the best judge of how she performs most efficiently.

When introducing the amputee to a variety of activities, do not overprogram the child so that he never becomes proficient at any one activity. Enjoyment of an activity is determined by the child's skill in that activity. Realistic activity selection for the amputee should reflect some variety but also some focus so the child can develop skill (Figure 15.5).

Spinal Cord Injury

Spinal cord injury is not a musculoskeletal condition; it is a neuromuscular condition. This disability is not caused by a dysfunction of either muscle or bone, but by

FIGURE 15.5. Girl with below-the-elbow amputation uses nonimpaired arm to serve while boy with muscular dystrophy "sets up" ball.

trauma to the spinal cord nerves that innervate skeletal muscles. The condition is being seen increasingly in schools and is characterized by chronic, permanent orthopedic disability.

In the United States, the leading cause of death between ages 1 and 25 is accidents. Many persons who undergo accidents sustain permanent injuries, particularly to the spinal cord. When permanent spinal cord injury occurs, disability results below the injury site in the form of muscle paralysis (Figure 15.6). This happens because the nerves responsible for innervating those muscles do not function owing to spinal cord trauma.

Generally, the higher the site where trauma on the spinal cord occurred, the more pervasive the loss of muscle function. Permanent injury to the neck area (cervical vertebrae) will involve all four limbs (quadriplegia). Permanent injury to the spinal cord below the neck will involve the lower extremities (paraplegia). When the lesion is complete, loss of function below the injury site will be total. In some instances, the lesion may be partial only, resulting in *some* residual muscle function below the injury site. For example, some quadriplegics (i.e., persons with cervical lesion) are able to walk.

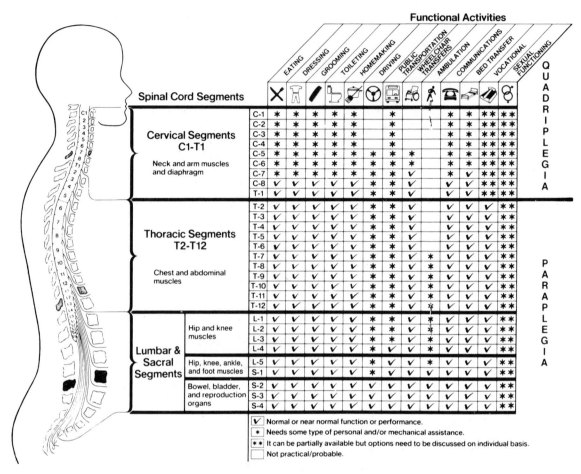

FIGURE 15.6. Functional activity for spinal cord injuries. (Used with permission of the Harmarville Rehabilitation Center, Pittsburgh, PA 15238.)

Prior to spinal cord injury, opportunities for educational, psychosocial, and physical and motor development were probably normal. This should be considered a plus in helping the person who faces post-accident rehabilitation and adjustment, for the skills of noninvolved extremities will remain intact (Tindall 1985). When involvement is partial, rehabilitation may restore function according to potential with modifications occurring in sport skills, equipment, and rules to restore and continue participation.

Although spinal cord injury is significant, persons with this injury generally do not encounter multiple handicaps or the degree of complications experienced by those with other orthopedic impairments (i.e., muscular dystrophy is progressive; cerebral palsy may affect intelligence, vision, and speech; arthritis is painful; hydrocephaly may accompany spina bifida). Fewer complicating conditions mean that spinal cord injury often is more manageable and responsive to rehabilitation than other orthopedic conditions.

Historically, persons with spinal cord injury have been relatively active in developing and maintaining physical and motor proficiencies and sport skills. Such activity levels began shortly after World War II when soldiers returned paralyzed from war injuries. These active life-styles over the years have provided positive role models for others who have sustained spinal cord injury.

Beyond physical education, opportunities to participate in sports are expanding. National wheelchair athletic associations are active in many sports. Several states have formed adapted athletic associations so orthopedically impaired athletes can engage in interscholastic athletic competition (see Chapter 24, Opportunity in Sport).

Activity Considerations

Activities that use primarily noninvolved or partially involved extremities are appropriate. Although the available options are more varied for persons with spinal cord injury located lower on the spinal cord, many options do exist for persons with higher site lesions. Persons with higher site lesions are now engaging in activities and sports previously considered inappropriate or not possible. White water kayaking, racquetball, tennis, and skiing are among these expanding opportunities. Further information regarding sport opportunities and activities can be found in the publication *Sports n' Spokes*. Another organization that supports activity opportunities is Courage Center, 3915 Golden Valley Road, Golden Valley, MN 55422.

Finally, yet another excellent source of programming for individuals with disabilities is found in the journal *Palaestra: The Forum of Sport and Physical Education for the Disabled*. This periodical is edited by Dr. David Beaver and can be obtained by writing to P.O. Box 508, Macomb, IL 61455.

The person with spinal cord injury often can participate in the physical education mainstream, sometimes with and sometimes without modification. Bowling, table tennis, archery, weight lifting, and swimming may be performed with little modification. Many racket and ball games require only modest modifications for participation. For example, in softball, the spinal injured participant may play a position that requires minimal amounts of rapid mobility (e.g., pitcher). On offense play, the person may bat as others do, and "run" a distance that challenges the batter and the fielders. In court and racket games, the ball might be permitted to bounce more than once and still be considered playable. Such rule modifications should be applied only as needed to equalize the challenge for all players.

Should the disability limit the student's grasping functions, several modifications are appropriate. A rack ("the third hand") can be mounted on a wheelchair so a bowling ball is "held" until needed. Pushing devices can be purchased or made to give added control and strength to enable the nonimpaired hand and arm to impart more velocity. Tape or Velcro on paddles, mallets, or rackets provides grip assistance.

In track and field activities, only jumping events will be inappropriate. Participation in putting and throwing events is both possible and desirable, though the weight and dimensions of the projectile may require modification. When appropriate, a softball or baseball might replace the shot put. Participation in running events often requires little or no modification, except for the wheelchair. In some instances, an efficient wheeler may move even faster than a conventional runner. Distances should be modified to equalize opportunities and challenges. When wheelchair and other participants engage in highly mobile activities, the chair must not impose unnecessary risk or produce interference for other athletes.

Sometimes positive results can be achieved when nondisabled students use wheelchairs or crutches to participate in races with the spinal injured student. The activity should, however, remain appropriate for all participants so the educational integrity is not compromised.

The spinal cord injured participant needs to learn to move in and out of the wheelchair independently. Based on the student's capabilities, the physical educator should teach him efficient ways to exit and enter the chair and how to right himself after a fall during active play. To develop exit and entry skills, the student must develop arm and shoulder muscle strength. Isometric grip activities, flexed arm hang, pull-ups, and dips are appropriate exercises.

The National Wheelchair Athletic Association, to equalize competition for persons with spinal neuromuscular conditions, has developed a participant classification system. The system is revised periodically to make it more sensitive to different degrees of residual muscle function. The system classifies participants by lesion site. (This classification is discussed in Appendix C and Chapter 24.)

Muscular Dystrophy

Muscular dystrophy is a degeneration of muscle tissue. As muscle cells degenerate, fat and fibrous tissue emerge. Although the condition appears to be inherited, the cause is not known. In some cases, muscular dystrophy (MD) develops with no previous family history. Such cases are considered to be the result of genetic mutation. Approximately 200,000 persons in the United States have muscular dystrophy (Hopkins 1985).

Muscular dystrophy is a general term that refers to numerous diseases that cause muscle cell deterioration, and in most cases (depending on the specific disease), result in premature death. Death occurs not because of muscle cell deterioration, but from complications usually involving heart failure or respiratory failure or both.

Four forms of muscular dystrophy affect school-age children: Duchenne, Becker, limb-girdle, and facioscapulohumeral. The last three will be described only briefly because prevalence does not justify in-depth consideration, but Duchenne and Becker will be discussed thoroughly.

Duchenne Muscular Dystrophy

Duchenne MD, also called *childhood MD* or *pseudohypertrophic MD*, is an extremely progressive condition and is perhaps the most catastrophic of all childhood afflictions.

In 1982, according to Siegel, the Muscular Dystrophy Association estimated that there were approximately 10,000 children with Duchenne MD living in the United States. The condition occurs only in males. Detailed examination of medical records has not confirmed any report of Duchenne MD in girls (Siegel 1982). A strong connection exists between the etiology of Duchenne and the inherited recessive X-linked type, which is passed from the mother to her male offspring. The female, who is the carrier, has a 50 percent chance of having a son with Duchenne MD. She also possesses the potential to pass the "carrier" condition on to 50 percent of her female children (Hopkins 1985).

When physicians attempt to diagnose a child with muscular dystrophy, they use a combination of tests including manual muscle testing, biopsy, electromyogram (EMG), and blood cell analysis. If the blood test reveals an excessively high level of *cretine phosphokinese (CPK)*, the cell walls of the muscle tissue are assumed to be breaking down. This leads to the conclusion that the child has Duchenne MD (De Lisa and Tipton 1979).

Gardner-Medwin (1979, p. 659) provides insight into this condition. He explains: "Life with the boy with Duchenne MD, for both the affected child and his parents, is punctuated by a series of crises. After the diagnosis itself, the next major crisis to be faced is the moment when he loses the ability to walk, usually between the age of 8 and 11 years. It is found that parents seem to fear this moment more than any other except death itself. Perhaps it is partly because the wheelchair has become the universal symbol of disability, but certainly the loss of their own boy's ability to walk confirms in a graphic and inescapable way the prognosis they had been given and had been hoping against hope might be wrong."

Although symptoms usually are present during the first year of life, they may go unnoticed. Clinical signs develop between the ages of 2 and 6. The boy may have trouble climbing stairs and difficulty rising from a sitting or lying down position. The clumsiness becomes more prevalent, and there is a tendency to fall more often. The distinctive characteristic of this type of MD is the seeming enlargement (pseudohypertrophy) of calf muscles (Figure 15.7). This is caused by the destruction of muscle cells, which are replaced by adipose (fat) and connective tissue. Muscle normally makes up approximately 40 percent of our total body weight. Approximately 33 percent of muscle mass has to be lost for function of the large postural muscles to be impaired. For those with Duchenne MD, the progression of muscle cell loss, resulting in weakness, is rapid with no remission. The proximal muscles, particularly in the pelvic region, begin to lose strength first. These are followed closely by involvement of muscles in the chest, abdomen, and shoulders.

The complications of Duchenne-type MD reflect the severity and extent of muscle weakness. The cause of death in most cases involves the cardiorespiratory system. The child may be unable to cough strongly and may have difficulty clearing secretions. These problems become particularly severe when the boy is immobile in a wheelchair and scoliosis develops. The inability to control the muscles used in breathing results in major complications, including congestive heart failure and stasis pneumonia, which are the most common causes of death (Hopkins 1985).

At this time, no cure exists for Duchenne MD, and no treatment has yet been found to correct the underlying pathology or to stop the progression of the disease (Siegel 1982). One of the complications occurring as a direct result of muscle weakness

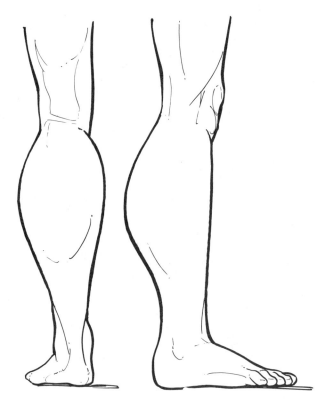

FIGURE 15.7. Calf manifesting pseudohypertrophy in Duchenne muscular dystrophy.

is muscle contracture. This is particularly problematic after the youngster is confined to a wheelchair. Owing to a lack of leg use, the foot begins to turn inward and point down (complex equinocavovarus). The ankle joint becomes frozen in place, and the foot becomes totally useless. After this occurs, putting shoes on the boy is almost impossible. Some controversy exists regarding the use of orthotic devices (braces) by children who are beginning to have difficulty walking. Although each case should be considered individually, some experts reason that if the child will eventually become wheelchair bound, why extend the inevitable. Gardner-Medwin (1979, p. 661) believes "that the provision of a well-chosen wheelchair, electrically powered if necessary, gives the boy much more practical independent mobility than does 'bracing for ambulation,' that the surgery and the exercises which must be continued use up precious time and energy that might have been devoted by the family to other activities, and that to concentrate attention on walking instead of on activities at which the boy could continue to succeed is psychologically wrong . . . . The boys themselves seem to take to wheelchairs with relief, and indeed with enthusiasm . . . ." The Muscular Dystrophy Association stresses that if a youngster is put into a manually operated wheelchair, it is critical that the boy propel himself! This helps maintain existing muscle strength and thus slows muscle atrophy and attendant complications.

During the early stages, affected children may be treated more harshly by peers than are other chronically disabled children because the boy exhibits no visible manifestations of the disease. Peers mistake early stages of the illness for ineptness and weakness. The educator must recognize this and enlighten peers to encourage empathy for the child's dilemma.

The earliest signs of Duchenne MD include clumsiness of gait and tendency to fall. The child may seem to be running "funny." Tiptoeing usually appears early and is caused by already weakened dorsiflexors. Other early signs of muscle weakness include swaying of the back and protruding abdomen. Gower's sign (named for W. R. Gower who gave the first comprehensive account in English of the disease in 1879), also a sign of muscular weakness, appears when the child "walks up" the thighs using the hands for support in rising from a sitting position (Figure 15.8).

As the disease progresses, many children become obese, presumably because of overeating and low energy output. Advancing obesity, coupled with decreasing muscle strength, motivates the child negatively, and activity is further diminished. Parent cooperation to reduce food intake is imperative, while activity levels require maintenance to retard fat accumulation.

Becker Muscular Dystrophy

Becker MD is similar to Duchenne MD in that all victims are male and the condition is X-linked recessive in its genetic trait (e.g., mother passes it on to her son). It is less severe than Duchenne, and progresses more slowly, although following a similar course. Muscle weakness, however, is less pronounced and much more benign in its outcome. This type is differentiated from Duchenne by later onset (10 to 15 years of age), prolonged ambulatory capability, less severe muscle contracture of the foot and ankle, and nonprogressive scoliosis.

Limb-Girdle Muscular Dystrophy

Limb-girdle MD can occur in either sex. It is a slowly progressive muscular dystrophy, usually beginning in childhood, marked by weakness and wasting in the shoulder or pelvic girdle. One girdle usually becomes symptomatic, with the other subsequently becoming involved. Disability typically becomes severe within 20 years. Skeletal deformities and muscle contractures occur late in the course of the disease. The person becomes disabled by middle life, and usually dies earlier than normal.

Facioscapulohumeral Muscular Dystrophy

Facioscapulohumeral MD can occur in either sex. Symptoms may appear either in childhood or adult life. Progress of the disease is insidious, interspersed with prolonged periods of apparent arrest. Muscles of the face and upper extremities are pri-

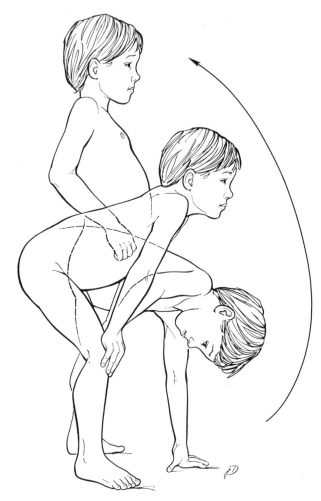

FIGURE 15.8. Gower's sign.

marily involved. The person becomes aware of the progressive nature of the disease when unable to fully close the eyes, whistle, or drink through a straw. Weakened facial muscles cause a pouting appearance, and speech may become slurred. Persons with this muscular dystrophy have a normal life-span.

Activity Considerations

Persons with *limb-girdle* or *facioscapulohumeral MD* usually survive into adulthood. Quiet forms of recreation, including billiards, table tennis, fishing, and darts, provide activity for those with limited ambulation capability or those who are in a wheelchair.

During school years, activities that develop manipulative skills can prepare the person for clerical or bench-type work. During the advanced stages of limb-girdle or facioscapulohumeral MD, work may require close supervision or a sheltered workshop environment.

Kaneda (1980) believes that owing to the benign course and later onset of *Becker MD* (as compared with Duchenne) a greater potential exists for rehabilitation and resultant productivity. He states: "contractures and scoliosis are more amenable to conservative treatment. . . . programs should include muscle strengthening and range of motion exercises with special attention to the ankle joint, to retain maximum function for as long as possible" (p. 1485).

For individuals with *Duchenne MD*, the critical point to remember is that the dystrophy (i.e., destruction of muscle cells by the disease) cannot be controlled, slowed down, or cured. The adapted physical educator must provide activities that will not allow *atrophy* to take place, for when dystrophy and atrophy are combined, the individual deteriorates at a much faster rate. Strength and range of motion therefore must be maintained, and muscle contractures must if possible be reduced.

That range of motion exercise is necessary to prevent disabling muscle contractures is an accepted fact. The value of strengthening exercises, however, has been questioned. Some physicians express concern that short-term strength gains made by exercising dystrophic muscle may be followed by greater weakness in the long run. In other words, the natural muscle cell destruction that takes place during heavy exercise could have a negative effect on Duchenne boys because they cannot replace destroyed muscle cells as do nonhandicapped children. This theory is strongly contested by de Lateur and Giaconi (1979) who found that Duchenne subjects showed no evidence of overwork weakness. Their research used a 30-month follow-up study and concluded that in addition to range of motion exercises, a program for patients with Duchenne MD may safely contain submaximal strengthening exercises that stay within the comfortable tolerance of the patient.

An analysis of the existing gait pattern is appropriate and should be done for all ambulatory students. Observe the stance and gait semiannually until the boy approaches the point of being unable to walk. The essential limiting factor is muscle weakness, but muscle contracture, itself largely secondary to weakness and abnormal posture, may also play a part. Extensive weakness develops first in the quadriceps muscles and in the extensors of the hips. A little unguarded flexion of the knees or hips while the boy is standing or walking results in "jackknifing" and a sudden fall. Consequently, these joints must remain fully extended whenever they are bearing weight, and at all times the body's center of gravity must be carried directly above them both. This explains the typical posture, the wide-based gait on the toes with the shoulders and head thrust back, inducing the characteristic lumbar lordosis. The boy often will stand squarely on one leg, the other "half-astride," balancing on the plantar-flexed forefoot. This posture usually results in mild but critical contractures of the hip flexors on the side of the "balancing" leg, especially of the iliotibial band (tensor facia lata). Less often, these contractures develop on both sides, which results in the restriction of full hip extension (as well as adduction) and is the final limiting factor in preventing the boy from walking. At the same time, equinus contractures of the foot develop as a result of the constant equinus posture (standing on the toes), which is necessary for balance. Failure to understand the secondary nature of these contractures has led in some cases to inappropriate surgery in the form of cutting and lengthening of the Achilles tendon (tenotomy), after which the boy is usually unable to walk at all. Although most boys with Duchenne MD develop severe hip and ankle contractures, their ability to walk may be prolonged by continued elongation (stretching) exercises of the hips. A few boys, however, will lose their walking ability without any contractures, simply because of extreme muscle weakness. Treatment, therefore, should begin at approximately 5 or 6 years of age. Have the student lie prone on a mat and actively stretch the hip flexor. Ankle contractures are more difficult to prevent. The instructor should stretch the plantar flexors, internal rotators, and adductors. In addition, strengthening exercises should be continued for dorsiflexion, external rotation, and abduction.

The time when the boy is finally *unable to walk* usually occurs between a few months and two years after the child becomes unable to climb stairs. His walking will become increasingly slower and more precarious; he often prefers to walk touching walls and holding on to furniture. He appears to be increasingly anxious about falling. At this point serious consideration should be given to use of a wheelchair.

Breathing exercises are extremely important and should be included, particularly for those confined to a wheelchair. Breathing is always improved when appropriate posture is maintained. The youngster may have difficulty sitting in the chair because of increased scoliosis or lordosis (a direct cause of weakened abdominal muscles). Diaphragmatic breathing exercises should be taught, as explained in Chapter 21 on allergies, asthma, and other respiratory conditions.

Siegel (1982) stresses the importance of assessing the existing physical fitness condition of the boys. He believes that measuring the strength and functional ability of the child with MD at regular intervals is important. In this way, subtle changes can be noted regarding progressive weakness, and the child's physical education program can be modified appropriately.

Table games and activities that encourage reaching and manipulating small objects should be selected. For young children, an elevated sandbox under which the wheelchair fits will encourage the child's upper extremity use and assist in maintaining manipulative skills. For older students, billiards, modified table tennis, fishing, and darts should be encouraged.

Obesity is a natural result of the combination of reduced exercise and the inability to maintain a desirable balance between exercise and caloric intake. Obesity is also often a result of psychic overeating (a response to anxiety) and parental pampering. The youngster with minimal energy demands should have his caloric intake reduced.

Finally, because of the progressively debilitating nature of the disease, emphasis should be placed on enjoying the present. Adapted physical education is a rich source of enjoyment and draws attention away from a treatment-oriented existence.

Spina Bifida

Spina bifida is a congenital anomaly wherein the bony casement of the spinal cord fails to close (Figure 15.9). The condition occurs in 2 to 4 per 1000 births (Howell 1978). Spina bifida has replaced poliomyelitis as the major cause of paraplegia in young children (Dumars 1985). The National Information Center for Handicapped Children and

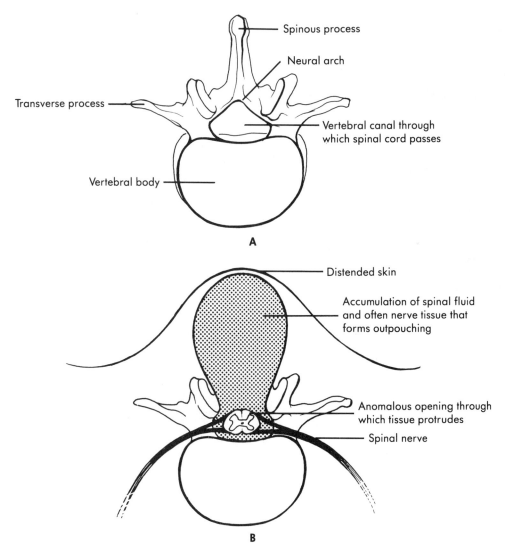

FIGURE 15.9. (A) Normal vertebrae. (B) Anomalous vertebrae.

Youth (1983) estimates that approximately 40 percent of all people in the United States have spina bifida occulta, but few even know it.

Three categories of spina bifida occur with specific designations dependent on the tissue that protrudes through the abnormal vertebral opening.

Spina bifida occulta is the least serious and is different from the other bifidas in that the meninges do not protrude through the defective bony encasement. Many persons with occulta are asymptomatic, and their condition goes unnoticed until accidental discovery by X-ray. Sometimes the site of the occulta may be marked by a tuft of hair or dimple. Loss of muscle function below the occulta site is uncommon. When disability occurs, it is not severe.

The next two types are referred to collectively as **spina bifida manifesta.** Of those who have manifesta, 4 percent have spina bifida meningocele and 96 percent have spina bifida myelomeningocele.

Spina bifida meningocele is a hernial protrusion of the meninges through a defect in the vertebral column. The meningocele (sac) contains no spinal nerve tissue, and paralysis does not occur. Surgical repair generally involves removal of the hernial protrusion.

Spina bifida myelomeningocele is a hernial protrusion of both spinal cord and meninges through a defect in the vertebral column (Figure 15.10).

During the latter part of the first month of pregnancy, the spinal cord (myelo-) and vertebrae around it do not develop properly in children born with spina bifida manifesta. In the normally developing fetus, the spinal cord forms a straight column, first covered by membranes (meningo-) and then by a bony spine. In the child with myelomeningocele, the membranes push out at some point along the back. As the spinal

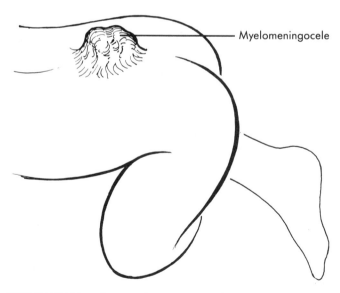

Myelomeningocele

FIGURE 15.10. Outpouching at anomalous vertebrae site.

cord develops further, it does not follow a straight line but pushes out instead into the membranous sac (-cele), where it does not form in the normal way. Some or all of the nerves coming out of the vertebrae below the sac are not attached properly to the spinal cord and are thus unable to supply the brain with proper messages (Wolraich 1984).

In myelomeningocele, the spinal cord is subjected to permanently damaging trauma, resulting in partial or total absence of muscle function below the vertebral defect. The higher the site on the vertebral column, the more extensive the loss of function. Where partial muscle function remains, muscle pull imbalance occurs. Such imbalance in the lower extremities may result in hip dislocation and club or rocker bottom feet. Where only partial function remains in muscles controlling the spinal column, abnormal spine curvatures, including scoliosis (S curve), lordosis (swayback), or kyphosis (humpback), can occur.

Some disagreement appears in the literature over incidence patterns. Bleck and Nagel (1982) suggest that racial or genetic patterns do not exist. Dumars (1985) disagrees and believes that inheritance is responsible for the transmission of a large variety of structural malformations, including spina bifida. In addition, Travis (1976) cites race and social class as significant contributors to incidence. For reasons not explained, spina bifida is three times as common among low socioeconomic whites than among high socioeconomic whites in the United States. Occurrence among blacks is one half that of the combined white incidence. Mysteriously, Jews and Chinese show high incidence, while Irish and Sikhs show low incidence.

Complications That Accompany Spina Bifida

Hydrocephalus (*hydro,* water; *cephalus,* brain) occurs in 80 percent of all myelomeningocele cases (Howell 1978). Normally the cerebrospinal fluid travels inside and around the brain and spinal cord and is eventually absorbed into the bloodstream. In spina bifida, some interference usually occurs in the circulation and absorption of this fluid. Hydrocephalus is characterized by abnormal accumulation of cerebrospinal fluid within the skull. As a result, pressure on the brain reaches intolerable levels. Enlargement of the head occurs, accompanied by brain atrophy, mental deterioration, and spastic paralysis in the lower limbs.

Retarded hydrocephalic children are usually vocal, but distinction must be made between vocalizing (mimicking sounds) and verbalizing (understanding). Only the latter is meaningful communication.

Surgically implanted shunts or drainage systems in the cranial cavity can release spinal fluid pressure. Although an implant does not reverse damage, it can reduce significantly further brain damage.

Another major problem involves uneven muscle pull, which results in paralysis and deformity of the lower extremities (Figure 15.11). Fractures are common because affected bones become weak and brittle and paralysis inhibits the child's ability to react protectively and prevent injurious falls. Because of paralysis, hypoactivity occurs precipitating obesity.

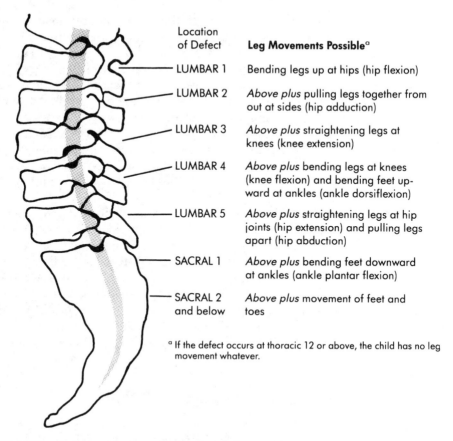

Location of Defect	Leg Movements Possible[a]
LUMBAR 1	Bending legs up at hips (hip flexion)
LUMBAR 2	*Above plus* pulling legs together from out at sides (hip adduction)
LUMBAR 3	*Above plus* straightening legs at knees (knee extension)
LUMBAR 4	*Above plus* bending legs at knees (knee flexion) and bending feet upward at ankles (ankle dorsiflexion)
LUMBAR 5	*Above plus* straightening legs at hip joints (hip extension) and pulling legs apart (hip abduction)
SACRAL 1	*Above plus* bending feet downward at ankles (ankle plantar flexion)
SACRAL 2 and below	*Above plus* movement of feet and toes

[a] If the defect occurs at thoracic 12 or above, the child has no leg movement whatever.

FIGURE 15.11. Relationship between level of defect and leg movement in children with spina bifida. Incomplete lesions account for variations among children with myelomeningocele. (Reprinted with permission of Aspen Systems Corporation, copyright 1984, from M. L. Wolraich. Myelomeningocele. In J. A. Blackman, *Medical Aspects of Development Disabilities in Children Birth to Three,* p. 163.)

Bowel and bladder dysfunction that accompanies paralysis is no problem during infancy, but becomes a problem during school years. The nerves involved in bladder control come from the second, third, and fourth sacral segments of the spinal cord. Most youngsters with myelomeningocele will usually not feel the urge to urinate and will not have control of the urinary sphincter muscle. This is potentially dangerous because the urine cannot be passed. If not cared for properly, this condition can cause permanent damage to the kidneys. The child may have to use a catheter, which allows the urine to be passed into a urine collection bag. The nerves involved in bowel control also come from the lower section of the spinal cord, and the youngsters frequently are not able to control their bowel movements. This results in constipation and bowel movement accidents (incontinence). The obvious social problems encountered by incontinence are compounded by urinary tract infections. Many children do, however, eventually gain some control over bowel and bladder functions. Best (1978, p. 55) comments: " . . . the teacher of the child with spina bifida will need to be conscious of the physical needs of the child as they relate to bladder and bowel control. If the child is wearing an external urine collection bag, or if the child attends school wearing diapers, the teacher needs to be alert to the requirements of personal hygiene for the child, not only for cleanliness and infection control, but because of the social implications for the child if he/she is shunned by classmates as a result of odor or altered personal appearance."

The ultimate life expectancy of children with spina bifida is not certain. Recent successful medical treatment is making adult survival increasingly common. In a recent follow-up of children with myelomeningocele, 80 percent were walking and 20 percent were confined to wheelchairs. Hydrocephalus was arrested in 38 percent of the cases. An IQ of 80 or above was found in 89 percent of the cases. Seventy-nine percent had graduated from high school, and 27 percent pursued postsecondary education (Bleck and Nagel 1982).

Activity Considerations

When spina bifida results in nerve damage and limited, unbalanced muscle function, braces equalling the child's body weight may have to be worn. The awkwardness of braces tends to discourage the child's involvement in movement-centered efforts. The child's motivation to participate in physical activities may match her perceived limited capacity. Perceived limitations may not be accurate, however, but may be simply reflections of the limited expectations that others hold. Past excuses from physical exertion, including physical education, only reinforce inactivity and withdrawal.

In reality, many persons with spina bifida can enjoy pursuits that need not be sedentary. Appropriate activities for wheelchair-bound children include darts, fishing, catch, modified bowling, and archery. Progressive resistance upper extremity exercises are also indicated for the wheelchair-bound child. When crutch assisted or other limited ambulation is possible, the child may participate in modified ambulatory activities. Activities for the wheelchair-bound child are also appropriate for the crutch- or brace-assisted child who may also participate in modified ball games, low-organized games, and relays. Activity modification varies from child to child. An activity can be modified to suit the child's physical limitations, and also, when present, the child's mental retardation.

In almost all spina bifida cases, swimming is an excellent activity for strengthening weak muscles and maintaining desirable range of motion. Swimming is particularly valuable because it is enjoyable and permits the exercise of extremities that cannot function under the stress of gravity or weight bearing.

Problems with muscle weakness of the lower extremities must be anticipated from the beginning to avoid development of joint deformities caused by muscle contractures.

This can be helped by proper positioning and by range-of-motion exercises. Regular treatments, at least three times per week, will assist in allowing the child to grow stronger and will increase the chances of some form of ambulation. Some youngsters will be able to walk without assistance, while others will require braces and assistive devices such as canes or crutches. Walking and weight-bearing exercises are important to prevent osteoporosis, which could lead to easy bone fracturing.

Upper extremity activities and exercise that conditions arms and shoulder girdle are excellent for children with spina bifida who walk with crutches or who transfer themselves to and from the wheelchair. The adapted physical educator should know the child's capabilities and should understand biomechanical principles so she can educate the child in appropriate techniques for maneuvering in and out of a wheelchair.

Spina bifida children with unbalanced muscle function will develop debilitating muscle contractures that result in skeletal deformities. Bracing, which minimizes the progress of contractures, and stretching exercises may be prescribed by the child's physician.

Because the spina bifida child experiences no feeling in affected extremities, the educator must watch for skin irritations and sores resulting from braces or shoes. Skin breakdowns should be reported to the school nurse or the child's physician.

Wheelchair ambulation may be necessary in some cases, but many opt for the wheelchair unnecessarily. These children perceive themselves as less deviant sitting in the wheelchair than dragging paralyzed extremities along behind crutches. Others recognize that wheelchair ambulation is more efficient. Regardless of the child's ability to walk, standing is physiologically more desirable than sitting. Standing, even for those who cannot walk, is psychologically beneficial, improves urinary system function, reduces susceptibility to fractures, and improves circulation.

Juvenile Rheumatoid Arthritis

Juvenile rheumatoid arthritis (JRA) strikes very young children and affects girls more often than boys. The disease usually strikes during the midelementary years, but confirmed diagnoses have been made in 6-week-old infants. Approximately 250,000 children in the United States are affected by JRA, making it a major crippler of young children (Spencer 1985). Unlike arthritic adults, 20 percent of whom experience remission, 60 to 70 percent of children with JRA experience almost complete recovery within 10 years (Bleck and Nagel 1982). Approximately one third recover completely, one third experience mild to moderate residual crippling, and one third experience severe crippling. Duration of disease activity is not predictable; some cases last only months, while others persist for years.

In 1977, the American Rheumatism Association established specific criteria for the diagnosis of juvenile rheumatoid arthritis. The condition involves the onset of symptoms at or before age 16 and persistent disease activity for at least 6 weeks. Disease activity is characterized by observable swelling or effusion (fluid in the joint capsule) of one or more joints and is accompanied by at least two of the following signs: limitation of motion, heat, pain, or tenderness. Inflammation is what causes swelling, heat, and pain, and is directly responsible for the damage caused to joints. This joint destruction can lead to deformity and crippling. The inflammation caused by arthritis is usually chronic and persistent.

Frequent remission indicates that the disease of rheumatoid arthritis comes and goes. Nearly all victims go through periods when the condition seems to disappear. While X-rays and blood tests might still reveal signs of it, the person feels perfectly well. No consistent pattern emerges as to when these relief periods occur, but the individual should be strongly encouraged to take part in any and all physical activities during the pain-free time.

Splinting is used occasionally to give tender joints added rest and to prevent or control contractures. Quite often, removable casts are used at night and for periods during the day. Several different materials are now available to make lightweight molded splints. For example, a splint for the wrist would permit active use of the fingers and hand while protecting the painful or deformed wrist joint.

Juvenile rheumatoid arthritis occurs in three forms: systemic, polyarticular, and pauciarticular (Pachman 1984).

Systemic Arthritis

Systemic arthritis, often called **Still's disease,** occurs in approximately 20 percent of all affected children. Symptoms are systemic and include pink rash, swollen lymph nodes, anemia, lethargy, and high, spiking fever that occurs daily. Arthritis is often only a minor manifestation of the illness, and may not appear until months after other symptoms have passed, making the disease difficult to diagnose. Attacks may persist for months, disappear, and reappear months or years later. While complete recovery is not assured, prognosis tends to be good.

Polyarticular Arthritis

Polyarticular arthritis (arthritis in five or more joints) affects 40 percent of children with JRA. The distinction between this and systemic disease is not clear-cut, except that in polyarticular arthritis severe pain occurs in five or more joints. Severity of joint pain is the child's major problem and the problem that parents, physician, and adapted physical educator must confront. Most often, affected joints include the knees (Figure 15.12), ankles, wrists, neck, fingers (Figure 15.13), elbows, and shoulders. When the jaw (mandible) is involved, bone growth can be retarded, resulting in a receding chin.

Children with polyarticular arthritis live in pain and tend to avoid movement, which provokes pain. While the disease is active, these children will sit motionless with affected joints flexed (Figure 15.14). Continued flexion in affected joints, if not

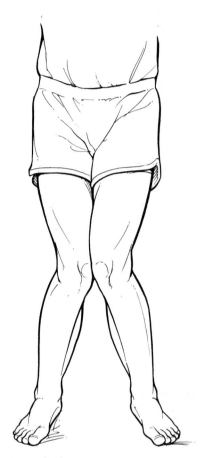

FIGURE 15.12. Arthritis in lower extremities can result in knock-knee.

therapeutically altered, results in chronically disabling deformities and muscle contractures (Figure 15.15). The extended duration of this disease also results in affected children being small for their age and sexually immature.

Pauciarticular Arthritis

Pauciarticular arthritis (four or fewer involved joints) affects approximately 40 percent of all arthritic children. Unlike children with systemic arthritis, these children do not have systemic symptoms. Manifestations of the disease usually are limited to pain and inflammation only at affected joints. These children appear quite well. Damage to affected joints tends not to be permanent even when the disease duration is lengthy.

The most serious concern is not arthritic joint pain and inflammation, but inflammation of the iris and the muscles controlling the eye, which, if untreated, leads to

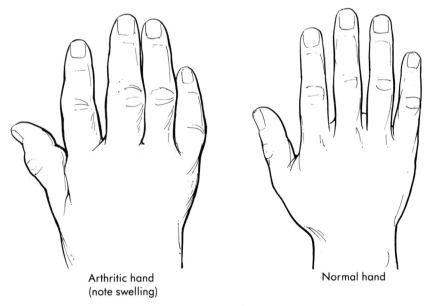

Arthritic hand
(note swelling)

Normal hand

FIGURE 15.13.   Arthritic hand compared with normal hand.

FIGURE 15.14.   Child with polyarticular arthritis often prefers to sit motionless in flexion.

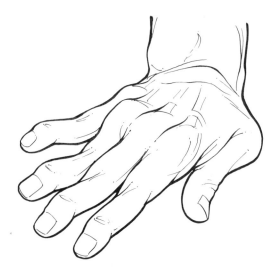

FIGURE 15.15. "Swan neck" deformity caused by arthritis.

blindness. Initial symptoms are often mild and may go unnoticed or seem of little concern. Children with red eyes who rub their eyes often or complain about bright lights should be referred immediately to an ophthalmologist. Early intervention minimizes or eliminates loss of residual vision. Delayed intervention risks permanent visual impairment or blindness.

Activity Considerations

The child with JRA usually takes medication for joint pain and inflammation. Aspirin is used often because of its effectiveness, but side effects may occur from its overuse. These include stomachaches, behavioral changes, ringing in the ears, increased bruising following mild trauma, and a feeling of "stuffed up" ears. Because aspirin has been implicated in Reye's syndrome (pronounced "rise"—an acute and often fatal childhood disease involving inflammation of the brain and enlargement of the liver), the physical education teacher should be alert for persistent vomiting and unusual irritability in the student (Pachman 1984).

Sometimes hearing loss results temporarily from aspirin consumption and contributes to maladaptive behavior merely because the child cannot hear effectively. If hearing loss is suspected, the child should be tested to ensure that it is not due to another cause. Because acoustics often are poor in physical education environments, the educator should make sure that the child can hear. When aspirin is no longer needed, the child's temporary hearing loss will disappear.

When aspirin fails to reduce discomfort, various gold compounds or cortisone may be prescribed. The adapted physical educator can be of assistance by ensuring that the child has, indeed, taken the prescribed dosages of medicine. Some children avoid medication, even at the expense of pain, because of self-consciousness over being "different."

Like aspirin, physical movement in appropriate quantities is important. Although affected joints also require adequate rest, exercise designed to prevent or correct deformities and contractures also is imperative. When exercise is indicated but pain is significant, hot paraffin applications or hot baths should precede movement.

Immediately before the exercise program, a thorough warm-up should be done. The application of heat to involved joints helps reduce the early onset of pain. Muscle strengthening and flexibility exercises also help to control pain and reduce the chances of joint deformity. Isometric exercises are particularly beneficial because they induce muscle contraction with no joint movement. These isometric contractions should be held for a 6-sec count at maximal effort. Range of motion exercises should include active, assistive, and passive activities, depending on the condition of the student. Anderson (1982) stresses that isometric exercises should be done twice daily.

Limb movement activities that maintain or rehabilitate motion often can be done by the child. Many children, however, because they cannot see the long-range value of such activities, are disinclined to inflict discomfort on themselves. When prescribed activity is the child's responsibility, the adapted physical educator must monitor the student regularly to ensure program execution.

During the active stages of JRA, the physician often recommends exercise of affected joints once or twice a day. Range of motion is determined by the degree of pain that the child can tolerate. Activities often are performed in warm water, which reduces pain and increases range of motion. Inflicting pain is unavoidable when trying to minimize the effects of JRA. The adapted physical educator and other helping persons must be patient when working with the child, otherwise treatment can turn into battle!

During acute stages of JRA, jarring and jumping activities, including batting, catching, trampolining, jumping rope, hop scotch, roller skating, skate boarding, and wrestling, should be avoided. Swimming, tricycling, and bicycling activities are indicated because affected joints can experience ranges of motion without being traumatized. These activities are valuable because they are inherently more motivating than activities that are purely therapeutic.

Children with JRA often exhibit daily mood changes that may include frustration, depression, and anger. Following a comfortable night, the child may be active and happy; following a painful night, the child may exhibit fatigue and irritability. The teacher should understand such moodiness and endeavor to respond with empathy (The Arthritis Foundation 1977).

While some JRA children withdraw and cease activity, others require monitoring to ensure adequate rest. The psychosocial need to participate with peers makes some children with JRA poor judges of activity level.

Active children who acquire JRA late in childhood are psychologically vulnerable to their new confinement. During childhood, activity often implies friendships, and these children may lose friends when they are no longer active. Slipping into anonymity is a serious psychological blow at an age when being accepted by others is pervasively important.

Because some children need to excel or compete to build self-esteem, activities should be selected to satisfy that need. The child should participate in activities requiring skill without joint trauma. Vigorous competitive activities should be avoided because of real or imagined peer, parent, or teacher pressure to pursue activity beyond the threshold of pain.

Congenital Hip Dislocation

Congenital hip dislocation is a malformation of the hip joint, which results in femoral head displacement from the hip socket (acetabulum) (Figure 15.16). Displacement occurs in three stages:

1. **Unstable stage.** An abnormally shallow acetabulum makes the hip susceptible to dislocation. The affected limb appears shorter than the nonaffected limb. Gluteal and thigh folds may increase in number and prominence on the affected side.
2. **Subluxation stage.** The femur, although still in contact with the acetabulum, rides upward and outward from its acetabular seat.
3. **Dislocation stage.** The femur becomes completely displaced outside the acetabulum.

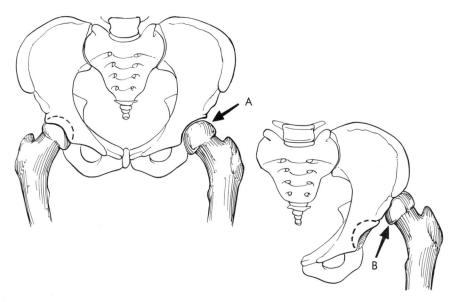

FIGURE 15.16. (A) Hip susceptible to dislocation (note shallow socket). (B) Hip in dislocation stage.

Incidence is high among those of Latin descent but is rare among blacks. Incidence is ten times more common among children who had breech delivery. Incidence is relatively low in cultures that carry infants with legs straddled on the parent's hip, and relatively high in cultures that swaddle the infant's legs together in adduction and extension (Blackman 1984). The condition usually occurs unilaterally and is more common among girls than boys.

Early identification and management of congenital hip dislocation are important. If allowed to progress unchecked, severe arthritis can result, requiring complicated medical corrective procedures.

The child with congenital hip dislocation walks with a limp (unilateral) or a duck-like waddle (bilateral). In either case, pain may not be evident. Unfortunately, the young child's condition may go unnoticed until limping or waddling becomes apparent when walking commences.

The Trendelenburg test is a diagnostic aid to identify congenital hip dislocation. The child stands on one foot and flexes the nonweight-bearing extremity at both hip and knee. When the Trendelenburg test is positive, the nonweight-bearing hip tends to sag because weakened thigh abductors on the affected side are unable to support the pelvis in a normal parallel-to-the-ground attitude (Lasko and Knopf 1984) (Figure 15.17).

Activity Considerations

Efforts to reduce congenital hip dislocation include casting, traction, and splinting.

Delayed treatment retards normal hip development, and prolonged dislocation precipitates abnormal development of affected bone and soft tissue. The child whose condition is not treated early will probably need surgical reduction, requiring removal and reconstruction of malformed bone tissue.

During the course of treatment, the school-age child will have protracted periods of lower extremity immobility. At this time, upper extremity exercises should be used to improve energy levels for maintenance of overall physical condition.

If the child must remain immobile for an extended period, nonlocomotor activities should be brought to the child. When treatment limits interaction with peers, play and learning experiences should be arranged to improve social and emotional growth.

Once mobility is again permitted, swimming is an appropriate activity because it facilitates range of motion development and provides resistance for hip joint muscles when weight bearing is not appropriate. When activity is indicated, the child's physician will prescribe strength and flexibility exercises.

If the child has been immobilized during early childhood when locomotor skills develop and normal posture occurs, opportunities to learn basic locomotor skills and postures should be provided.

The child who has been immobilized for a long period will need to learn social skills if activity and play experiences are to be positive. The adapted physical educator must be empathetic and accentuate the positive, yet limit reinforcement when behavior is inappropriate. The child's classmates also must be helped to understand the

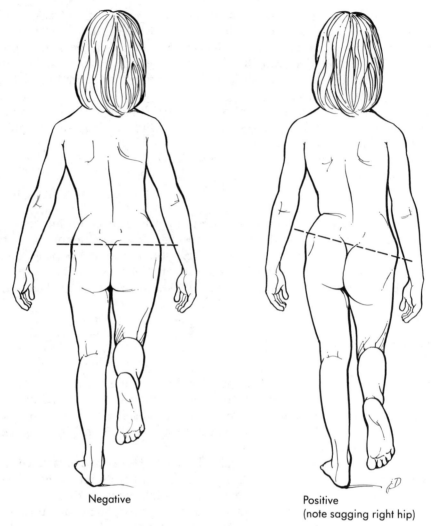

Negative

Positive
(note sagging right hip)

FIGURE 15.17. Trendelenburg test.

child's condition. In this way, the physical educator can assist the child in creating positive peer relationships.

Osteochondritis Dissecans

Osteochondritis dissecans occurs most often during the teen years when bone and articular cartilage split from the parent bone into the affected joint. Sometimes split-

BONE AND ARTICULAR CARTILAGE SPLIT FROM PARENT BONE

ting progresses to such an extent that complete separation from the bone occurs. **Osteochondritis** means "inflammation of bone and cartilage," and **dissecans** means "cutting out from" (Bleck and Nagel 1982, p. 200).

The condition appears to result from an interruption in blood supply beneath the affected articular surface, usually considered joint trauma. Boys contract the condition more frequently than girls, which lends some credence to the trauma theory. Historically boys have engaged in more vigorous physical activities that increase the likelihood of trauma to vulnerable anatomical structures. Perhaps this theory will be tested as girls become increasingly involved in similar trauma-producing activities.

Approximately 90 percent of osteochondritis dissecans occurs in the knee joint. Other joints sometimes affected include the elbow, hip, ankle, and shoulder. On occasion, the condition occurs bilaterally.

Mild disability in the affected joint is an initial symptom. The loosened osteochondral piece may protrude into the joint cavity, causing the youngster to recount several troublesome problems. Pain, particularly with palpation, and mild swelling are noted initially. As the condition worsens, the joint will lock, and pain becomes more definite. Should the condition continue to progress, loss of joint function becomes significant, resulting in muscle atrophy crossing the joint.

If complete osteochondral separation occurs, surgery is required to remove or replace detached tissue. Reattachment of the separated osteochondral body to the parent bone is the preferred procedure when the body is large and has separated from a weight-bearing surface.

Activity Considerations

Two major factors influence the nature and course of therapy and activity prescriptions: (1) Age of the child when the condition is first diagnosed, and (2) whether the bone and articular cartilage have merely loosened or have actually broken away from the parent bone and entered the joint cavity (Bleck and Nagel 1982).

If the child is young and the osteochondral body has not dislodged totally, treatment may involve only simple immobilization. Spontaneous healing often occurs within 3 to 6 months. In older children, longer time spans, extending 3 to 4 years, may be required for spontaneous recovery. Generally, the younger the child at the condition's onset, the less eventful the recovery and the more favorable the prognosis.

Activity for such children is limited only at the affected site. The paired extremity should be exercised to maintain function and prevent atrophy. The other healthy extremities also need exercise to maintain desirable energy output, function, and fitness. Virtually any physical education activity that does not traumatize the affected joint is indicated.

As recovery permits, passive, then nonweight-bearing exercise, followed by weight-bearing progressive resistance exercise is prescribed by the physician. During nonweight-bearing stages of recovery, swimming is a most effective treatment for recovery of joint function and maintenance of body fitness.

When an osteochondral body has broken away from the bone, or when conservative management has proved ineffective, surgery is indicated. In such cases, although recuperation and rehabilitation time may be extended, the principles underlying the selection of rehabilitative and adapted activities remain essentially unchanged.

Full weight-bearing activity may resume once recovery is complete and the joint reassumes normal function. In some cases, however, the affected articular surface may become permanently irregular. When this occurs, the adapted physical educator should interest the child in activities that will spare the anomalous joint unnecessary trauma. Subjection to trauma increases susceptibility to degenerative arthritis.

Perthes' Disease

Perthes' disease, sometimes referred to as **Legg-Perthes,** or **Legg-Clavé Perthes,** is that member of the osteochondritis dissecans family that occurs specifically in the femur head. Perthes' disease deserves particular attention because of its crippling potential when permitted to progress untreated.

As with other forms of osteochondritis dissecans, Perthes' disease results in a loss of blood supply to bone underlying the affected articular surface. Interruption of blood supply to the femoral head causes death (necrosis) of affected tissue and degeneration of the femoral surface. Subjection of the femoral head to stress during the disease increases the probability of significant damage and permanent degenerative arthritis disability. When Perthes' disease bone degeneration results in a flat and irregular femoral head, the condition is termed **coxa plana** (Figure 15.18).

Perthes' disease occurs unilaterally in 85 percent of all cases, and is most common in boys age 4 to 10 years. The disease occurs four times more often in boys than in girls. If intervention is early, prognosis is favorable (Bleck and Nagel 1982).

Initially, the child with Perthes' disease will complain of knee, thigh, or hip pain. A physician often becomes involved when parents note a limp in the child's walk.

Three methods of treating Perthes' disease are as follows:

1. **Recumbancy Treatment.** Bed rest is prescribed. Initially, casts, bracing, or traction may be used to reduce irritation and discomfort. If the child has not been casted, swimming and other nonweight-bearing activities are encouraged. The primary disadvantage of these methods is the child's isolation from peers and others during critical developmental years. The primary advantage is that treatment minimizes trauma to the diseased femoral head.
2. **Ambulatory Treatment.** This method permits the child to attend school and to remain among peers during the years of recovery and rehabilitation. In ambulatory treatment, the leg is placed in a sling or braced so it does not bear weight. In either case, the child walks with crutches (Figure 15.19).
3. **Operative Treatment.** In this method, bone grafting or drilling into the affected

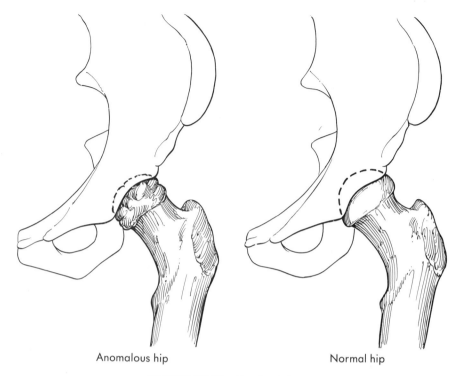

Anomalous hip   Normal hip

FIGURE 15.18. Perthes' disease.

growth center is done to speed healing. The joint cavity (acetabulum) may be repositioned to allow for bone regeneration and molding into a more favorable socket.

Activity Considerations

In general, the activity indications and contraindications appropriate for osteo-chondritis dissecans are also appropriate for Perthes' disease. The educator's primary concern is developing physical fitness and motor skills in unaffected body segments. In so doing, the affected hip joint must not be traumatized. If ambulatory treatment has been prescribed, activities that strengthen arm and shoulder muscles for crutch walking should be encouraged.

Because the 2 to 3 year period during which the disease runs its course may seem like an eternity to a child, the 4- to 10-year-old requires considerable psychosocial support during the years of recovery and rehabilitation. Particularly important is the child's development of skills using unaffected body parts. Such efforts will maintain a desirable level of overall fitness, and allow the child to remain active in the mainstream of peer relationships.

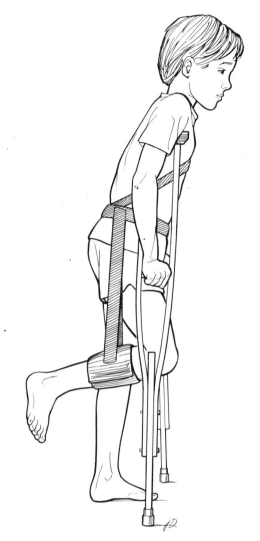

FIGURE 15.19.   Hip joint immobilization in treatment of Perthes' disease.

Coxa Valga and Coxa Vara

An angle is formed where the neck of the femur joins the femur's long shaft or axis. **Coxa valga** and **coxa vara** refer to abnormal variations in that angle. The term *coxa*, meaning hip region, identifies the site of angular deviation. The terms *valga* and *vara* identify whether the angle is inordinately open or closed, respectively. The angle of the normal adult femur, between the femoral neck and shaft, is between 120 and 140 degrees (Powell 1976). In coxa valga, the angle is inordinately open, causing the distal (knee) portion to be displaced abnormally away from the body's midline. In coxa vara, the angle is inordinately closed, causing the distal portion to be displaced abnormally toward the body's midline.

Of the two angular abnormalities, coxa valga occurs less often. Etiological factors to which coxa valga may be attributed include, but are not limited to, congenital hip dislocation and muscle pull imbalance (Powell 1976). Etiological factors underlying the valgus condition determine appropriate prescriptions for medical requirements, physical therapy, and adapted physical education activity.

Significant reduction in the femoral neck-shaft angle (coxa vara) depresses the femoral neck, which results in abnormally fitting joint surfaces. Continued reduction in the angle precipitates upward displacement of the greater trochanter and inward rotation of the femur at the hip joint.

Bilateral coxa vara produces a waddling, ducklike gait. Unilateral coxa vara appears as a lowering of the pelvis on the affected side. Narrowing of the femoral neck-shaft angle may give the affected limb a significantly shortened appearance. Coxa vara may be congenital or acquired. Congenital coxa vara is due to constitutional or developmental disorder such as achondroplasia (dwarfism). Acquired coxa vara may be due to fracture, osteotomy (removal of diseased bone tissue) as treatment for osteoarthritis, rickets, or other bone dystrophies. Congenital coxa vara may be treated surgically (osteotomy). Because coxa vara describes a symptom rather than a cause, medical treatment, physical therapy, and adapted physical education must also proceed according to cause.

Slipped capital epiphysis is the most commonly observed cause of coxa vara among school-age children. Because of the chronological age range during which slipped capital epiphysis occurs, it is often called adolescent coxa vara. Apparently, during adolescence, a weakening of the epiphyseal or growth center junction occurs. This weakened junction increases susceptibility to slippage, hence the coxa vara condition.

Adolescent coxa vara appears most often in children 12 to 15 years of age. Those most susceptible tend to be sexually immature, obese, or rather tall and thin. Approximately 20 percent of those suffering adolescent coxa vara experience bilateral involvement (Bleck and Nagel 1975). The condition appears earlier in girls, probably because they experience the adolescent growth spurt sooner than boys. Boys, however, contract the condition more often than girls, probably because boys traditionally engage in activities more stressful to the epiphyseal growth center (Bleck and Nagel 1975). With the recent increase in girls' participation in vigorous activities and sports, the adapted physical educator may witness a proportionate rise in adolescent coxa vara among girls.

Adolescent coxa vara is a three-stage process:

1. *Preslippage stage* shows symptoms that include a slight limp on the affected side accompanied by some limitation of internal rotation.
2. Through trauma or minor injury, the femoral portion of the epiphysis may *slip upward, accompanied by outward rotation.*

3. *Upward slippage* becomes more extensive. Limitations in abduction and internal rotation become pronounced. As slippage continues to worsen, the femur neck begins to assume a "horse-neck" appearance (Figure 15.20).

Activity Considerations

Adolescent coxa vara, if diagnosed during the preslippage stage, may be managed by the immediate removal of weight-bearing stress and by crutch walking. Where slippage has occurred, repositioning and pinning may be required. In advanced, untreated cases, surgical correction may be required. In any event, activity involving the affected structure must be eliminated for a protracted period.

When significant involvement of the lower extremities occurs, energy output is greatly reduced, which increases the chance of obesity and a decline in physical fitness. Problematic weight gain may require a reduction in caloric intake. Activity prescriptions will vary depending on the extent of slippage and the child's progress through the rehabilitation process.

Initially, when the affected femur cannot bear weight and is casted or braced, muscle tensing exercises in the affected limb may be prescribed. These exercises should prevent or reduce atrophy in the extremity. During the time when the affected part

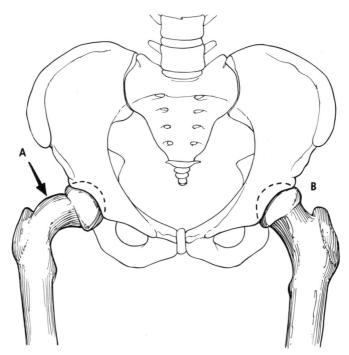

FIGURE 15.20. (A) "Horse-neck" appearing femoral neck. (B) Normal femoral neck.

limits activity, other body segments should be exercised. Because mobility is limited, activities probably will consist of exercises rather than active games.

The child's physician determines when the affected femur can be exercised. Generally, nonweight-bearing activities are prescribed to rehabilitate range of motion. The child will regain weight-bearing capability eventually and is then allowed progressive weight-bearing exercises and activities to facilitate the return to normal function. During this period, swimming activities can provide calorie expenditure for weight management, exercise for physical fitness, and morale-boosting enjoyment.

Talipes (Clubfoot)

Talipes (clubfoot) is a deformity of the foot characterized by foot malalignment in relation to the leg. The condition may be acquired or congenital, with congenital being the more prevalent. Talipes can occur in conjunction with spina bifida, hydrocephalus, or congenital hip dislocation. Depending on the configuration, the deformity occurs in 1 to 4.4 per 1000 births. The condition is twice as common in boys as in girls. According to these statistics, talipes is among the most frequently occurring chronic musculoskeletal disfigurements.

Talipes has four cardinal positions: **talipes varus** (foot angled inward or inversion), **talipes valgus** (foot angled outward or eversion), **talipes equinus** (foot angled directly downward or plantar flexion), and **talipes calcaneus** (foot angled directly upward or dorsiflexion) (Figure 15.21).

Combinations of these deformities are often present, with **talipes equinovarus** (foot turned inward-downward) the most prevalent form-combination.

The clubfoot may be a rigid or flexible deformity, depending on when the clubbing started to occur during pregnancy. The earlier the occurrence began, the more rigid the deformity. Early occurrences tend to result in bone deformities (i.e., in rigidity), while later occurrences tend to involve soft tissue and minimum bone abnormality (i.e., flexibility). Regardless of time of occurrence during pregnancy, if left untreated, the condition worsens and becomes more rigid.

As with many congenital deformities, early intervention encourages a positive prognosis. Too often, however, prompt treatment that provides greater potential for correction is not followed up with therapy and exercise. Visits to the doctor may become less frequent, and only when serious deformity has reappeared is the child reassessed. The adapted physical educator therefore must become alert to cessation or reversal of rehabilitation progress. Interruption in progress requires alerting the child's physician immediately.

Activity Considerations

Conservative clubfoot deformity correction includes casting or bracing to achieve a more normal anatomical position (Figure 15.22). If the foot does not respond, surgical

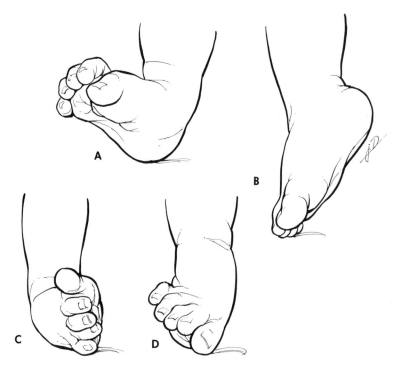

FIGURE 15.21.   Four cardinal talipes positions. (A) Foot angled inward or varus (inversion). (B) Foot angled outward or valgus (eversion). (C) Foot angled downward or equinus (plantar flexion). (D) Foot angled upward or calcaneus (dorsiflexion).

correction may be needed. More rigid deformities (owing to early onset during pregnancy or late postnatal intervention) generally respond only partially to manual pressure. In such cases, surgery is the preferred procedure.

Congenital clubfoot, corrected initially by manual pressure or surgical correction followed by manual pressure, requires constant supervision during the growth years. Progressive exercises to improve muscular condition in the affected foot and in ankle muscles are a valuable adjunct to corrective treatment, but exercise alone does not constitute adequate remedial attention.

No single activity prescription suits all children with clubfoot. Activities must be determined for each child. Severe involvement limits vigorous, weight-bearing activity, which may not even be possible for some children. Following casting and bracing, hightop corrective footwear may render vigorous, weight-bearing activities awkward. Some children with clubfoot do participate in vigorous, weight-bearing activities, including organized youth sport programs. In any case, the adapted physical educator should encourage vigorous activity involvement when appropriate.

Modification or limitation of lower extremity activity need not limit activity to the upper extremities. When lower extremity activities are limited, however, an activ-

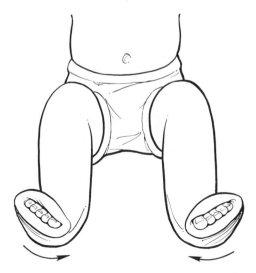

FIGURE 15.22. Talipes casted into progressively more normal anatomical positions.

ity regimen for the upper extremities can help maintain a desirable level of fitness and energy.

For a child or adolescent, an abnormality in locomotor patterns results in an emotional handicap as significant as the physical handicap. The child's clubfoot does not alter his psychosocial and emotional needs. In addition to physical rehabilitation, helping the child establish a positive level of self-esteem is a significant responsibility of the adapted physical educator.

Dwarfism

Many etiological factors cause growth inhibition. The most common form is inherited **achondroplasia** (dwarfism), which is characterized by shortened limbs and a height seldom exceeding 1.4 m. The bridge of the nose is flattened or depressed, and the forehead may appear to bulge. Hands and feet tend to be foreshortened, but fingers are normal length.

Achondroplastic dwarfism is not associated with deficiencies in intelligence. Apart from the mechanical problems that dwarfed stature creates, regular physical and motor activities and typical life pursuits characterize the person's achievement motivations.

Activity Considerations

Foreshortened limbs tend to reduce the individual's motor skill performance to less than normal levels (Figure 15.23). Typical performance limitations occur in body

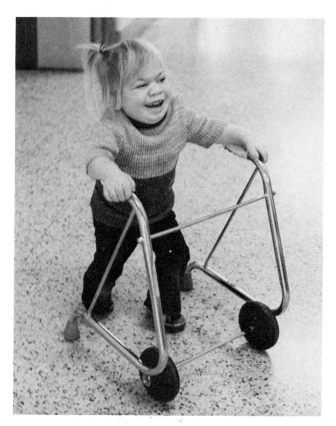

FIGURE 15.23.   Child with dwarfism and an orthopedic disability ambulates with the aid of a walker.

projection skills because shortened lower extremities reduce force application against a surface (i.e., explosive strength). Likewise, disproportionately short upper extremities reduce potential for distance throwing. Activities that use implements (e.g., golf, tennis, softball, or badminton) create performance problems because the implements are of disproportionately large size. To some degree, this limitation can be overcome by "choking up" on the shaft, or cutting down the shaft size.

Using sport implements that require simultaneous arm action (e.g., golf club, softball bat) creates a complication. Disproportionately short arms and a characteristically broad trunk and shoulders necessarily place the implement inordinately close to the body. This trunk and arm compaction inhibits significantly freedom of movement during the swing, thus limiting potential for normal striking achievement.

None of these limitations should be construed as contraindications, but achievement expectations of both child and teacher should be realistically modified. When expectations are modified in accordance with potential, the child can participate safely and successfully in the regular physical education program.

Summary

Chronic musculoskeletal disorders are those that persist over protracted periods. They may be congenital or acquired, nonprogressive or progressive, temporary or permanent. Musculoskeletal disorders encompass any ailment of long duration that affects the muscular or skeletal system, or both.

There are many musculoskeletal disorders. In this chapter, we focus on those that tend to occur among school-age persons and those that occur with relative frequency.

Limb deficiencies, either congenital or acquired, require special consideration when planning activity programs. Equipment may need to be adapted, and in some cases game rules should be modified. Prosthetic devices (artificial limbs) are often worn during the physical education class, so the instructor must be aware of possible limitations caused by their use.

Those with spinal cord injury are often confined to a wheelchair, and activities must be planned with this in mind. Development of upper body strength should be emphasized, along with improvement of cardiorespiratory efficiency. Extensive sport competition is now available for these individuals.

Duchenne muscular dystrophy (pseudohypertrophic MD) is a progressive, terminal disease. The condition must not be further complicated by excessive inactivity, which results in yet more physical atrophy. Strength maintenance and range of motion development should be major program components.

Spina bifida is a congenital condition that affects the spinal cord directly. The most common and most limiting type is myelomeningocele, which usually necessitates constant use of a wheelchair. In addition, paralysis of the lower limbs is present, and bladder and bowel control are often difficult to achieve. Activities involving upper arm manipulation and strength are suggested.

Juvenile rheumatoid arthritis usually develops before the child is 6 years old, and is characterized by at least two of the following symptoms in one or more joints: swelling, pain, heat, and limitation of motion. Activities should be provided to maintain and possibly increase range of motion. When pain is present, the instructor can limit activities to mild bending, stretching, and reaching. Swimming in a pool with water temperature above 85°F is desirable.

Congenital hip dislocation involves displacement of the femur head out of the hip socket. Activities should be planned that allow the student to exercise in a sitting position. Upper body strength development is suggested.

Osteochondritis dissecans involves the knee joint in 90 percent of the cases. Pain and mild swelling usually occur, and if the condition worsens, small osteochondral pieces may break off and lodge in the joint. Immobilization or restricted use of the joint may then be prescribed by the physician. Activities that involve running or jumping are contraindicated. The adapted physical educator should provide activities that enhance upper body strength. Cardiorespiratory exercises are also recommended.

Perthes' disease is a member of the osteochondritis dissecans family. The condition occurs specifically at the head of the femur and warrants particular attention, for if left untreated, the individual may be permanently crippled. Activities described for osteochondritis are appropriate.

Coxa valga and coxa vara are abnormal variations in the angle of femur attachment to the hip. These conditions result in improper anatomical positioning of the femur, so running, jumping, and leaping are more difficult. Physicians commonly prescribe removal of all weight-bearing stress. Activities during the nonweight-bearing period should focus on the upper body. When the physician directs, mild, progressive weight training activities can be developed.

Talipes (clubfoot) is often encountered in conjunction with spina bifida or congenital hip dislocation. Mild cases involve casting, whereas severe cases require surgery. Following a period of immobilization, activities should involve a progressive exercise program. Walking, jogging, and running are difficult, and the instructor will note marked differences between students. The physician's written prescriptions should guide the rehabilitation activities.

Dwarfism is a congenital defect caused by inhibition of the growth process. Shorter than average limbs and height are the major characteristics. General activities may have to be adapted, including equipment modifications.

In all cases involving student rehabilitation, the adapted physical educator must receive written instructions from a physician. In addition, the physician should be kept informed of the student's progress during the rehabilitation phase.

References

Adams, R. C., Daniel, A. N., McCubbin, J. A., and Rullman, L. *Games, Sports, and Exercises for the Physically Handicapped,* 3rd ed. Philadelphia: Lea & Febiger, 1982.

Anderson, R. Exercise in Management of Arthritis and Rheumatic Diseases. *Cardio-Gram* 9(2):3, February-March 1982.

The Arthritis Foundation. *Arthritis in Children.* Atlanta, Ga.: The Foundation, 1977.

Best, G. A. *Individuals With Physical Disabilities.* St. Louis: C. V. Mosby, 1978.

Blackman, J. A. (ed.). *Medical Aspects of Developmental Disabilities in Children Birth to Three,* rev. 1st ed. Rockville, Md.: Aspen Systems Corporation, 1984.

Blakeslee, B. *The Limb Deficient Child.* Berkeley: University of California Press, 1963.

Bleck, E. E., and Nagel, D. A. *Physically Handicapped Children: An Atlas for Teachers,* 3rd ed. New York: Grune & Stratton, 1982.

de Lateur, B. J., and Giaconi, R. M. Effect on Maximal Strength of Submaximal Exercise in Duchenne Muscular Dystrophy. *American Journal of Physical Medicine* 58(1):26–36, 1979.

De Lisa, J. A., and Tipton, N. M. Exercise Effect on Creative Phosphokinase Elevation in Motor Neuron Disease. *Archives of Physical Medicine Rehabilitation* 60(9):397–400, 1979.

Dumars, K. W. Approach to Genetic Disease. In *Current Diagnosis 7,* edited by R. B. Conn. Philadelphia: W. B. Saunders, 1985.

Dunham, C. S. Amputations. In *Disability and Rehabilitation Handbook,* edited by R. M. Goldenson. New York: McGraw-Hill, 1981.

Gardner-Medwin, D. Controversies About Duchenne Muscular Dystrophy. Bracing for Ambulation. *Developmental Medicine and Child Neurology* 21(5):659–662, 1979.

Hopkins, L. C. Muscular Dystrophies. In *Current Diagnosis 7*, edited by R. B. Conn. Philadelphia: W. B. Saunders, 1985.

Howell, L. Spina Bifida. In *Disability and Rehabilitation Handbook*, edited by R. M. Goldenson. New York: McGraw-Hill, 1978.

Kaneda, R. R. Becker's Muscular Dystrophy: Orthopedic Implications. *Journal of the American Orthopedic Association* 79:332–335, 1980.

Kieran, S. S., Conner, F. P., Von Hippel, C. S., and Jones, S. H. *Mainstreaming Preschoolers: Children With Orthopedic Handicaps.* Belmont, Mass.: CRC Education and Human Development, 1981.

Lasko, P. M., and Knopf, K. G. *Adapted and Corrective Exercise for the Disabled Adult.* Dubuque, Iowa: Eddie Bowers Publishing, 1984.

Muscular Dystrophy Association. *Muscular Dystrophy.* New York: The Association, 1980.

National Information Center for Handicapped Children and Youth. *Spina Bifida.* Washington, D.C.: U.S. Department of Education, 1983.

O'Sullivan, S. B., Cullen, K. E., and Schmitz, T. J. *Physical Rehabilitation: Evaluation and Treatment Procedures.* Philadelphia: F. A. Davis, 1981.

Pachman, L. M. Juvenile (Rheumatoid) Arthritis. In *Conn's Current Therapy 1984*, edited by R. E. Rakel. Philadelphia: W. B. Saunders, 1984.

Powell, M. *Orthopedic Nursing*, 7th ed. Edinburgh, Scotland: Churchill-Livingstone, 1976.

Shaperman, C. Myoelectric Stimulation of Prosthetic Limbs. In *Current Diagnosis 7*, edited by R. B. Conn. Philadelphia: W. B. Saunders, 1985.

Siegel, I. M. *101 Questions and Answers About Muscular Dystrophy.* New York: Muscular Dystrophy Association, 1982.

Spencer, C. H. Juvenile Rheumatoid Arthritis. In *Current Diagnosis 7*, edited by R. B. Conn. Philadelphia: W. B. Saunders, 1985.

Tindall, S. C. Trauma of the Central Nervous System. In *Current Diagnosis 7*, edited by R. B. Conn. Philadelphia: W. B. Saunders, 1985.

Travis, B. *Chronic Illness in Children.* Stanford, Calif.: Stanford University Press, 1976.

Wolraich, M. L. Myelomeningocçle. In *Medical Aspects of Developmental Disabilities in Children Birth to Three*, rev. 1st ed., edited by J. A. Blackman. Rockville, Md.: Aspen Systems Corporation, 1984.

CHAPTER 16

Seizures and Convulsive Disorders

Questions often asked are: Is it appropriate for a child who has seizures to participate in physical education activities? Will developmental exercises and physical fitness activities precipitate a seizure? What happens if the child's head is bumped during a game? What should I do when a convulsion occurs? Will competitive games cause undue stress? Is it better to assign the individual to a study hall or a class involving sedentary activities such as checkers, chess, or shuffleboard?

These questions plague physical educators, parents, physicians, and individuals who have seizures. Today, researchers and the medical profession have an extensive understanding of the intricacies of seizure disorders. As a result, a more positive approach is taken to activity for seizure-prone youngsters.

Unnecessary overprotection has perpetuated the belief that physical exertion is inappropriate for individuals with convulsive disorders. Forche (1973) states that the most crippling effects of these disorders are not the convulsions, the momentary lapse of consciousness, or the apparent daydreaming, but the witnessing of expressions of confusion and horror on the faces of teachers and classmates. If the child is assigned to a study hall while classmates attend physical education class, the child will not make the team. She may even find it difficult to make friends. Although the child takes medication regularly and rarely or never has a seizure, she may still be held back by fearful parents and teachers from the necessary experiences of playing games, being on teams, and roughhousing with peers.

Seizures are estimated to occur in 1 to 2 percent of the U.S. population (Berg 1984). Medical authorities state that approximately 1 in 50 school-age children has seizures. Seizures occur in children of all races and age groups and afflict both sexes. **Seizure disorder** (commonly, and inappropriately, called **epilepsy**) is not a disease and is not contagious. Of all new cases, 77 percent occur before the age of 20 years (Bruni and Wilder 1985).

In the nervous system, all movement and activity is initiated by electrical discharges in the brain. In most people, the excitability of the nerve cell is controlled by an intricate system of checks and balances so the discharge level seldom gets out of control. There is, however, a level at which these controls cease to operate, and an uncontrolled discharge then produces a seizure. In some individuals, this level is lower than in others, and may vary depending on such factors as time of day, onset of illness, fatigue, or emotional stress.

None of us is able to control our environment. We all respond differently to emotional situations. For example, the opossum may seem to "play possum" to confuse its attacker. In reality, the opossum is overcome with fear and simply faints, thereby giving the impression of being dead. When humans experience emotional situations that they cannot endure, they, like the turtle, pull into their shells and hide. Their emotional threshold has been overcome, the brain "turns off" the world, and the child faints. One hypothesis is that the seizure-prone individual possesses a lower emotional threshold and thus experiences seizures when under stress.

Abnormal Brain-Wave Patterns

Abnormalities of brain function during seizures cause abnormal brain-wave patterns. Three anomalous patterns caused by different types of seizures are shown in the electroencephalographic (EEG) recordings in Figure 16.1. The second recording shows a spike and dome picture that occurs during **petit mal** (pet-tee mahl) seizures. A person in this condition becomes suddenly unconscious for 3 to 10 seconds. These episodes may occur every few minutes or every few hours, or the person may function for months without a seizure. Petit mal seizures result from abnormality of the reticular activating system of the brain. Transmission of normal alpha waves to the cerebral cortex is stopped temporarily. Instead, the spike and dome pattern is transmitted, and the person "falls asleep" for a few seconds until the alpha wave pattern is reintroduced.

The third recording in Figure 16.1 shows the brain-wave pattern in grand mal (grahn mahl) seizures. In this condition, the cerebral cortex becomes extremely excited

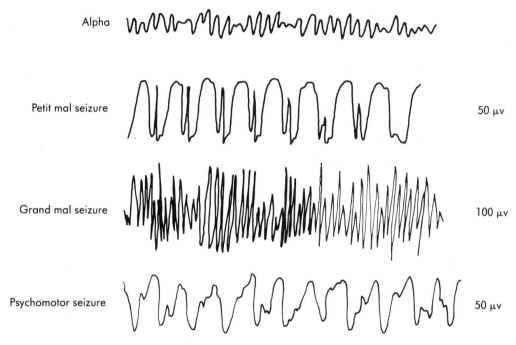

Alpha

Petit mal seizure — 50 μv

Grand mal seizure — 100 μv

Psychomotor seizure — 50 μv

FIGURE 16.1. Normal (alpha) and abnormal brain-wave patterns as seen on an electroencephalogram. (Modified from Guyton 1979, p. 343.)

and sends many strong signals throughout the brain at the same time. When these signals reach the motor cortex, they cause rhythmic movements, called **clonic convulsions,** throughout the body. **Grand mal** seizure results from abnormal reverberating cycles that develop in the reticular activating system. One portion of the brain stimulates another portion, which stimulates a third portion, which restimulates the first portion. The cycle continues for 2 to 3 minutes until the neurons of the system fatigue and the reverberation ceases. At the beginning of a grand mal attack, individuals may experience violent, abnormal, hallucinatory thoughts. Once most of the brain is involved, the person no longer has any conscious thoughts, because signals are being transmitted in all directions rather than through discrete thought circuits. Even though the brain is violently active, the person becomes unconscious of her surroundings. Following the attack, the brain and the muscles are so fatigued that individuals often sleep for at least a few minutes and sometimes as long as 24 hours (Guyton 1971).

The most common characteristic of this disorder is the **seizure.** The seizure is, however, merely a symptom of the condition. In the past, some of the words used to describe a seizure were "epileptic convulsion," "spell," "fit," and "attack." "Seizure" is defined medically as an episode of impaired consciousness, which may or may not be associated with convulsive movements. Some loss of consciousness almost always occurs during a seizure. The individual's brain turns off the outside world because of an inability to control the overabundance of electrical (nerve) activity. These individuals possess a low convulsive threshold. It is important to understand that such conditions are common and can be treated. For the majority of children who have seizure disorder, limiting activities is not necessary.

Etiology

Children and adolescents who experience seizures are in one of two general categories: (1) those who have experienced brain damage (lesion), or (2) those who have inherited a low threshold for seizures. Some of the possible causes of seizures are identified in Table 16.1.

Lesions can occur as a result of any damage to the brain. A direct blow to the head during an accident, disease, an extremely high fever, or lack of oxygen (anoxia) are all possible causes of brain damage. The resultant seizures are termed *symptomatic, acquired,* or *focal,* because the seizure cause is easily identified.

TABLE 16.1
CAUSES OF SEIZURES OCCURRING AT DIFFERENT AGES

Neonatal (first month)
  Birth injury—anoxia or hemorrhage
  Congenital abnormalities
  Metabolic disorders—hypoglycemia, hypocalcemia
  Meningitis and other infection

Infancy (1 to 6 months)
  As above
  Infantile spasms

Early Childhood (6 months to 3 years)
  Febrile (high fever) seizures
  Birth injuries
  Infection
  Trauma
  Poisons and metabolic defects
  Cerebral degenerations

Childhood and Adolescence
  Idiopathic
  Birth injury
  Trauma
  Infection
  Cerebral degenerations

SOURCE: Modified from Laidlaw and Richens 1976, p. 33.

Seizures are common when an injury penetrates the skull, especially when the motor area of the brain is affected, and when a depressed fracture and intracranial bleeding occur. Seizures may occur soon after the injury (usually within 2 weeks) but may be delayed up to 1 year.

Most seizures are *idiopathic*, that is, they have no apparent cause. These seizures may be inherited, for studies show that parents of children with seizure disorder often have unusual EEG readings (Simmons 1974). As Dr. L. D. Bushes (Epilepsy Foundation of America 1976) states: "There is, in general, a significant heredity factor in epilepsy. . . . What is inherited is not some form of epilepsy, but a greater or lesser degree of resistance . . . that produces epilepsy" (p. 8).

Seizures are commonly classified within specific age groups. Table 16.2 identifies these classifications by age group.

Diagnosis

Neurologists determine whether or not an individual has the potential for seizures. Careful neurological examination may reveal specific lesions or tumor. These tests involve safe and painless X-rays, EEG, and the newer computer tomography (CT). Bruni and Wilder (1985) report that physicians, using CT scanning, are now able to identify tumors, cerebral atrophy, hydrocephalus, infarctions (dead cells), subdural hematomas (bruises), cystic lesions, and arteriovenous malformations, all of which may be the cause of seizures. CT scanning is most helpful in diagnosing children who have partial (focal) seizures.

TABLE 16.2

Etiology and Age: Convulsive Disorders

	Newborn	Infancy	Childhood	Adolescence
Severe perinatal injury	———	———		
Metabolic defects	———	———		
Congenital malformation		———	———	
Infection		———	———	
Genetic		———	———	———
Perinatal injury	———	———		
Genetic disease	———	———	———	
Myoclonic syndromes	———	———	———	
Postnatal trauma			———	———
Brain tumor				
Vascular disease				

Once the condition is diagnosed, the physician makes a thorough evaluation to determine what is causing the seizures. Even if the main cause can be identified and treated, however, most individuals who suffer from seizure disorder require ongoing treatment with antiepileptic drugs (Delgado-Escueta 1984).

If a diagnosis is confirmed, the EEG may reveal that the excessive discharges always begin in the same brain area. For example, irregular EEG waves may occur only in a small area of the temporal lobe. If this area can be identified specifically, that small portion of the brain may be removed. Cole (1971, p. 94) cautions about the dangers of this surgical procedure: "Surgery is performed in only a small percentage of cases— only if the seizures are incapacitating and do not respond to available drugs, and if the difficulty is in a section of the brain which can be safely cut."

Types of Seizures

The system known as the International Classification of Seizures identifies two major categories of convulsive disorder: (1) partial seizures (e.g., psychomotor), and (2) generalized seizures (e.g., petit mal and grand mal) (Berg 1984).

Partial seizures are limited to one part of the brain; generalized seizures imply that all brain cells are involved. Among children and adolescents, generalized seizures are more common. One type of generalized seizure (grand mal) consists of a convulsion combined with a complete loss of consciousness. Another type, petit mal, resembles a brief period of fixed staring (National Information Center for Handicapped Children and Youth 1983).

Seizures are classified by observable characteristics. Four varieties are commonly found in school-age individuals.

Petit Mal Seizures

Petit mal seizures are considered *absence* seizures, and are identified by a temporary loss of consciousness without convulsions. These seizures last for a few seconds only. Minor rhythmic movements of the eyes or eyelids are the only observable symptoms. Consciousness is regained, but total amnesia exists for the brief period of attack. The person may look around for a moment and then resume previous activity. If engaged in listening before the attack, the person experiencing the seizure will have missed only a sentence or two. The petit mal seizure usually occurs only in childhood, and is the most common type of seizure in school-age children.

The following account is taken from a case study of a young woman who experienced petit mal seizures (Alvarez 1972, p. 138):

> Sure, I have always had brief spells of being "out" for a half a minute. There are seconds when I am gone, and then I return. I have brief vacant intervals. . . . Often I must have been unconscious for a few seconds . . . I have vacant spells in my thoughts that scare

>

the life out of me. I am slow in my work because of the momentary spells when I know nothing. Often after such a spell I wonder what happened to me. Sometimes my vision shuts off for a few seconds. And, brief spells of unconsciousness interfere with my reading, because I miss a number of words. Once, when I was reading, I woke to find my book on the floor of the room . . . and I knew I must have had some sort of spell in which I was "out." Too often also, I must keep going unconscious because I drop things and break them.

Such seizures fortunately disappear in adult life. The use of medication is extremely successful for youngsters who experience petit mal seizures; control of seizures is effective in up to 80 percent of all cases (Laidlaw and Richens 1976).

Grand Mal Seizures

Grand mal seizures are probably responsible for most of the misunderstanding and fear that surround convulsive disorders. The seizure that accompanies all grand mal attacks is alarming to observe. Remember, however, that the individual feels no pain because of unconsciousness.

Grand mal seizures, although fairly common among children, are experienced more by adolescents and adults. Approximately 10 percent of all seizures are grand mal.

Some people who have grand mal seizures experience a vague, poorly described warning that a seizure is about to occur. This warning is called an **aura.** Not all grand mal seizures are preceded by an aura; for some individuals, seizure occurs without warning. The adapted physical education teacher should ask each child if seizure onset is predictable. The child should be instructed to inform the teacher immediately when he experiences an aura. Such warnings give the instructor time to prepare for the attack by removing the child to a less hazardous place and having the child lie down.

Injuries from seizures can occur from a fall to the floor or from striking the head or other body parts on a hard surface (e.g., floors, walls, gymnastic equipment, tables). Any advance seizure warning could prevent a falling injury. Emergency procedures to follow during a grand mal seizure are discussed on page 397.

Three types of brain wave patterns appear during a grand mal seizure. Initially, the brain experiences fast activity and starts "buzzing." This begins the **tonic phase,** during which the child may cry out or make a gasping, gurgling sound. These sounds arise because the respiratory muscles are contracting. If standing, the individual will fall with boardlike rigidity in the direction in which he is leaning. After falling, the child will lie rigid, and because tonic contraction inhibits breathing, he may become blue. The child may also bite the inside of the mouth or tongue, or may urinate or defecate if the bladder or bowel is full.

The tonic phase progresses quickly into a rapid jerking of the muscles. These generalized spasms are the convulsive or **clonic phase.** During the spasms, the person may gasp for air between convulsive movements. Swallowing does not occur, so the child may froth at the mouth because of saliva buildup.

These movements gradually slow and disappear, and the individual seems to relax. The brain waves are at highest intensity and most erratic during the tonic-clonic phases of the seizure. When these phases pass, the person then experiences the **postseizure stupor phase.** If a brain wave recording were made during this phase, it would show very, very slow movement, for the brain is exhausted, as are all of the body muscles. The seizure stops because the body is physically and mentally unable to continue and is literally "fatigued out"—all available energy has been used.

A grand mal seizure can last for a few seconds or many minutes. The longer the individual continues in the convulsive state, the more fatigued she will be during the postseizure phase. Following the convulsion, the person may complain of a headache or a tired feeling. If the seizure has been extremely violent or prolonged, the child may ask to sleep. This is common, and the individual should be allowed to sleep. The sleeping phase allows the child's body to recover from an exhausting experience.

For most individuals, on any given day a seizure is a single happening, but some persons do experience one grand mal seizure after another. This critical situation is called **status epilepticus.** Immediate emergency medical care should be obtained. Although deaths do occur when individuals experience status epilepticus, the condition is usually encountered only in severely involved seizure-prone individuals whose seizure disorder is poorly controlled by medication. Status epilepticus is comparatively rare.

Psychomotor Seizures

Few children have psychomotor seizures (Wright 1975) (see Figure 16.1 for EEG brain wave patterns). Persons experiencing a **psychomotor seizure** usually behave in a confused and irrational manner: they may wander around, make aimless gestures, or repeat whatever action was being performed when the attack began. The following case history (Livingston 1963, p. 36) identifies a typical psychomotor experience of a 16-year-old female. Her father gave the following description of her "spells."

> My daughter and I were sitting in the restaurant eating lunch. . . . Suddenly she stopped talking and complained of feeling funny in the stomach . . . she had a blank and dazed expression in her eyes which lasted for a moment . . . she began repeating the questions: "Where am I?" "What day is this?" "What time is it?" She continued to repeat these questions . . . for about fifteen minutes. Then she . . . took a fork and began hitting it against the table . . . for about ten minutes. Following this she sat down again and then she seemed to relax. . . . For a moment she appeared somewhat confused, but then recovered completely. I spoke to her frequently during the course of the spell, but she did not seem to hear me and she did not answer the questions. When she recovered completely, I asked her what happened and she had no recollection of the disturbance.

During a psychomotor seizure, the individual may become involved in abnormal behavior, mutter meaningless phrases, or appear wide-eyed and terrified. During this state, the person may respond to a question, but usually does not understand the question and the reply is often inappropriate. Individuals may repeat prelearned material, count, or state their name over and over again.

Behavior abnormalities are three times as common in individuals with psychomotor seizure disorder as in persons with other forms of seizure disorder (Rutter, Graham, and Yule 1976). In an estimated one fourth of all psychomotor episodes, the person actually moves around. The potential for danger is evident if the person walks or runs into a dangerous environment (e.g., toward a flight of stairs, glass windows, or doors). The teacher should restrain the child so injury does not occur. The idea that the person, while experiencing this type of seizure, might injure others intentionally is totally *incorrect*. In reality, the person is unaware of what is happening. Another child, positioned in the path of the seizure-disordered person, could conceivably be bumped or possibly knocked down by accident. Restraint is therefore necessary for the safety both of the child and others.

Akinetic Seizures

Drop or **akinetic seizure** describes a condition common in children in which the youngster falls unconscious to the floor. A second type of drop attack occurs when a sudden weakness of the legs forces the child to fall to the knees, but consciousness is not lost. Drop seizures are usually recurring, but they are brief and not of a convulsive nature. During the attack, the student generally falls forward and injury to forehead or chin can result. To prevent injury, these children should, when ambulating, wear protective head devices with padded straps for the chin.

Although there are other, less common forms of convulsive disorder, grand mal, petit mal, psychomotor, and drop seizures are the most common types found among school-age children.

Medication

Most children with seizure disorder must take medication to control the occurrence of seizures. These medications are **anticonvulsants,** which limit the spread of abnormal electrical discharges in the brain. Anticonvulsants are neither sedatives nor tranquilizers. Table 16.3 lists the common anticonvulsants, their uses, and side effects.

The long-range goal of medication is to eliminate seizures completely without negative side effects. In general, the amount of medication prescribed is based on a rough estimate of the condition's severity and the possibility of complete seizure control. In the drug management of seizures, children generally have a better prognosis than adults. For example, 60 to 75 percent of youngsters with petit mal seizures become seizure-free when put on drug treatment.

In cases for which a specific cause of the convulsive disorder has been identified, appropriate treatment is usually determined easily. In over half of all children with recurring convulsions, however, no cause can be determined. Treatment generally con-

TABLE 16.3

COMMON ANTICONVULSANTS, THEIR USE, AND SIDE EFFECTS

Type of Drug		Type of Seizure	Common Side Effects
Brand Name	*Generic Name*		
Dilantin	Phenytoin (fee-nit-o-in)	Grand mal	Unsteady gait, blurred vision, double vision, gum hypertrophy, increased hair growth in females
Luminal	Phenobarbital (fee-no-bar-ba-tol)	Grand mal	Hyperactivity or irritability in young children, sluggishness in school-age children
Primidone (pry-mo-dōne)	Mysoline (my-so-leen)	Grand mal	Stomach upsets, dizziness, drowsiness, irritability (temper outbursts)
Tegretol[a]	Carbamazepine (car-ba-maza-peen)	Grand mal	Dizziness, blurred vision, drowsiness
Depakene	Valproic acid	Grand mal and petit mal	Nausea, vomiting, and weight gain
Clonopin	Clonazepam (clo-noz-a-pam)	Petit mal	Drowsiness, ataxia, behavior changes
Tridione (try-dee-own)	Trimethadione (try-metha-down)	Petit mal	Nausea, drowsiness
Zarontin	Ethosuximide (eth-o-sucks-a-mide)	Petit mal	Nausea, fatigue, dizziness, and drowsiness

[a]Safety and effectiveness of Tegretol (carbamazepine) for use in children under age 6 years has not been established (Berg 1984).

sists of daily doses of anticonvulsive drugs (Berg 1984). When the specific convulsive disorder has been identified and the most appropriate drug prescribed, the drug dosage is then increased gradually until control of the seizures is attained. Once the seizures are controlled, that drug dosage is continued. If the seizures recur, the drug dosage is increased further until side effects become evident. If seizures still continue, a second appropriate drug usually is administered, again in gradually increasing dosages until control is gained. Changes of drug dosage are not advised until a given dosage has been tried for at least 7 days.

Seizures usually occur when individuals are not taking medication. The importance of regular, consistent intake of the prescribed drug cannot be overemphasized. The person with seizure disorder should have a schedule for taking medication, which should be administered in a few daily doses to make the schedule easy to follow (Massey, Folger, and Riley 1980).

The physical educator should know when the student is adding, deleting, or changing medication. Parents should be asked to inform the instructor when changes are being made to ensure that physical activities are within the child's safety limits. For example, gymnastic units involving high balance beam activities may not be appropriate without additional spotting.

If a child is having regular seizures (i.e., daily), the physician may be experimenting with the medication. Safety becomes a critical issue and the physical education instructor must be constantly aware of dangers that could arise. This does not mean that the child should be excused from physical education, but rather, that the program must be adapted to compensate for any possible risks.

The adapted physical educator should become familiar with the most common types of medication used to treat seizure disorders.

The drug of first choice by many physicians for treatment of grand mal seizures is valproic acid (Depakene) (Delgado-Escueta 1984).

Phenytoin (Dilantin) is often prescribed for grand mal seizures because it does not sedate or cause sleepiness. Livingston (1963) states that balance and equilibrium may be impaired as a result of overdosage, but the impairment usually disappears within 1 to 2 weeks after dosage reduction. Dilantin may cause blurred vision or double vision, which can be a problem in activities that involve catching balls. A chronic side effect, when Dilantin has been administered for a long time, is gum hypertrophy, which causes the gums to bleed during tooth brushing. In females, Dilantin may produce excessive hair growth on the extremities and face.

Phenobarbital (Luminal) is prescribed for grand mal seizures, but is not as much used as Dilantin because it causes hyperactivity or irritability in young children and sluggishness in older children. Either side effect is undesirable in school because attention and performance may be impaired. When a child experiences negative side effects from phenobarbital, another drug is prescribed.

Petit mal seizures are usually controlled with the following medications: Ethosuximide (Zarontin) will control simple staring spells or absence seizures. Trimethadione (Tridione) is as effective as Zarontin and has fewer negative side effects.

"Drop" or akinetic seizures are resistant to anticonvulsant drugs, so steroid therapy is often recommended.

The type and amount of medication required are determined by trial and error. The physician may spend a year or more adjusting medications to achieve the proper dosage.

Children may need to bring medications (pills, tablets, liquid) to school. These medications should be kept in a cool place and not be exposed to excessive temperatures. For example, capsules may melt when left in direct sunlight or near excessive heat, and potency may be reduced. All anticonvulsive medications should be kept in one specific school area, such as in a refrigerator in the nurse's office.

The physical education teacher is not expected to administer or alter a student's medication program, but she should be familiar with the common side effects of the prescribed drug. Because of the teacher's close contact with the student, she can usually identify whether the individual's performance or behavior has become markedly better or worse. The educator should consult with the nurse and with the parents before and during administration of a medication program.

Controversial Issues Regarding Seizure Disorders

All physical educators ask: "What situations or activities precipitate a seizure?" Many of the old, ultraconservative restrictions imposed on children with seizure disorder were based on fears that rarely materialized. The possibility of **head injury** has been the main reason given for excluding students who experienced seizures from physical education activity. The concern was that a blow to the head, either from falling or from being hit, would cause a seizure. The original injurious damage to the brain is nonprogressive, however, and further brain damage is highly unlikely. The chances that a given seizure-prone individual will have a seizure as a result of head injury are the same as for a person who has never had a seizure.

Livingston and Berman (1974, p. 172) state: "Over the past 36 years, we have followed at least 15,000 young children with epilepsy, many of whom have been under our care during their entire scholastic careers. Hundreds of these patients have played tackle football and many have participated in boxing, lacrosse, wrestling and other physical activities which render the participant prone to head injuries. We are not cognizant of a single instance of recurrence or aggravation of epileptic seizures related to head injury in any of these athletes."

Black's (1974) study involving 301 head-injured students between the ages of 5 and 14 found no difference regarding the risk of seizure when he compared seizure-prone children with children who had never experienced a seizure. Both groups were found to possess an 11 to 12 percent chance of having a convulsive reaction to a head injury caused by contact with a hard surface or a blunt object.

Craig (1974) also supports the contention that head injury caused by participation in sports (including football) will not cause seizures. He emphasizes the importance of proper head protection for all individuals, and indicates that head injuries should not be a factor when considering physical education and athletic programming for individuals who have had seizures.

Hyperventilation is known to produce seizures in some individuals. Forced deep breathing can be used by physicians to induce a petit mal seizure. This is common practice and is used routinely for EEG examination. The question therefore arises whether deep breathing, as experienced in extended periods of running, swimming, fatiguing exercise, and circuit training, brings on petit mal seizures? Henderson (1978, p. 44) responds: "It is known simple hyperventilation may precipitate a petit mal episode. However, the hyperpnea (abnormal increase in the depth and rate of respiration) of exercise is a precise adjustment to the metabolic needs of the individual related to oxygen requirements and metabolic acidosis. . . . Evidence is lacking that hyperpnea of exercise precipitates an epileptic attack." Livingston and Berman (1974) conclude that hyperventilation caused in confined settings (such as a physician's office) is distinctly different from the increased breathing rate induced by physical exercise. They believe that physical activities do not cause an individual to hyperventilate so as to bring on a seizure. In a 3-year-long research project involving seizure-prone individuals and vigorous physical activities, Rose (1973) observed that rapid breathing, when occurring naturally as a result of vigorous exercise, did not increase seizure incidence, and that changes in blood chemistry during exercise appear to have a protective effect that actually reduces the chance of having a seizure. The conclusion is that labored breathing caused by exercise will not bring on seizures.

Emotional or stressful situations are thought to precipitate seizures, but identifying exactly what triggers an attack is difficult, if not almost impossible. There is no doubt, however, that seizure frequency is linked to the individual's psychological well-being and that seizure cause is related directly to the emotional intensity of a specific situation. Some children can definitely relate seizures to moods, but it is difficult to decide whether a highly stressful state caused the seizure, or whether the seizure was caused simply by worrying that an attack might occur.

Among children with seizure disorders, the emotional stress encountered is essentially the same as that observed in individuals who suffer from other chronic disorders such as asthma and heart disease. These psychological barriers consist primarily of anxiety or depressive states or both, feelings of insecurity and inferiority, and antisocial tendencies. If the students can be relieved of strong pent-up emotions, and can be offered positive reinforcement through successful participation in physical education activities, then many stressful situations will be ameliorated. Some children are intensely fearful that they will experience a seizure in the presence of their peers. This burden may become so intense that the constant worry charges the brain's electrical impulses to a state of potential explosion. Medication can help control the child's anxiety, but being active, stimulated, and happy will also help to ward off seizures.

Fatigue is another potential cause of seizures. The physiological effects of fatigue can be analyzed in terms of what happens just prior to the seizure episode. The body is demanding rest and relief from exhausting daily activities. Fatigue is defined as a state of increased discomfort and decreased efficiency, which results from prolonged or excessive exertion. In short, fatigue is the loss of power or capacity to respond to stimulation (Dorland's Illustrated Medical Dictionary 1981). Few physical education programs reach this combined intensity. If such conditions do occur and if the physical demand is excessive, the child with a seizure disorder should be told to reduce the demand or pace.

Loss of sleep may be a potential cause of seizures. The instructor should look for signs that indicate fatigue. Is the student distinctly more lethargic than the other children? Does he seem overtired and listless? If the student is interested, active, and attentive, all disorder tends to be suppressed. Scott (1969) maintains that idleness and frequent rests pose greater seizure problems than do exertion and concentration.

Many students have seizures only when they sleep. Those who experience attacks while sleeping have fewer problems, physically and socially, and require few restrictions of their daily activities.

About fatigue, Livingston (1963, pp. 58–59) states: "I have found it very difficult to evaluate the significance of fatigue as a precipitating factor of seizures in epilepsy. However, I believe that the general attitude of treating an individual with epilepsy as if he had tuberculosis or rheumatic fever and consequently encouraging or forcing him to take frequent rest periods *should be discouraged*. I believe that, if possible, the patient should be instructed and encouraged to conduct himself in the same manner as his normal associates" [italics added].

Menstruation has caused seizures in some women. This occurrence is highly individual and is not considered common or even occasional for the majority of females who have had seizures. If menstruation does seem to cause seizures in a given individual, then modified programming during that time is necessary. The young woman's medical history will indicate the relationship between menstruation and seizure onset.

An example of a rare seizure is **photosensitive epilepsy,** which is provoked by repetitive flashing lights or a flickering television set. Few individuals will have a seizure under these conditions. If, however, a photosensitive individual is present in the class (which would be rare), the child's medical history should list the potential cause, and steps can be taken for program modification.

First Aid for Grand Mal Seizures

Teachers are usually enlightened and helpful, and if fully informed about the possibility of a convulsive episode, they review what to do (or what not to do). Cardinal rules are:

1. Remain calm. Students assume the same emotional reaction as their teacher. Remember that the seizure is painless for the child.
2. Clear the area so the child is not injured by hard or sharp objects.
3. Do not force anything between the child's teeth.
4. Do not restrain the child. The seizure cannot be stopped once it has begun. Oxygen should not be administered; it may actually prolong the seizure.
5. Cradle the head in your hands to prevent violent banging against the floor. If saliva accumulates, turn the head to the side so it can drain out.
6. Do not call a doctor unless the seizure lasts for more than 5 minutes or is followed immediately by another major seizure without the child regaining consciousness.
7. Stay with the child until all movement has ceased, consciousness has been regained, and confusion has subsided. A small child can be carried to a rest area; an older youngster may be allowed to lie where he is until able to talk. If tired, the individual should be permitted to rest until normal activities can be resumed.
8. Observe carefully the details of the attack, which should be reported to the school nurse and to the child's parents.
9. Turn the incident into a learning experience for the entire class. Explain what a seizure is, that it is not contagious, and that it is nothing to cause fear.

General Guidelines for Teachers

Teachers, like parents, must not be overprotective toward seizure-prone individuals. There are few school situations in which the child cannot participate. Safety and common sense should dictate which activities are potentially dangerous.

When a child with seizure disorder is placed in the class, the instructor should plan a short private interview with the student to develop a complete picture of the child. Both the physical education teacher and the school nurse should interview the child. This personal contact demonstrates to the youngster that the teacher is concerned and interested. Too often, educators are embarrassed to discuss handicaps with the individuals involved, perhaps fearing that such discussion might be construed as an intrusion. The following questions can be used as guidelines for the educator's interview with the child:

1. When was the last time that you had a seizure?
2. How often do you have seizures?
3. What causes your seizures?
4. Do you know when you are going to have a seizure?
5. What happens to you when you have a seizure?
6. Do you lose consciousness?
7. How long does your seizure usually last?
8. How do you feel when you wake up after a seizure?
9. Do you take medicine? If so, what kind, and do you bring it to school?
10. Where do you keep your medicine when it's at school?
11. Do the other students know that you have seizures?

Answers to these questions should give the physical educator a thorough understanding of the student's seizure pattern. In most instances, the seizure pattern will be consistent, which should alleviate normal apprehension and prepare the instructor to handle calmly a seizure if it occurs.

Social Acceptance

The public's attitude toward seizures is a major cause of concern for persons with seizure disorders. Unfortunately, most attitudes include pity and negative feelings as well as a strong belief that seizure-prone individuals should be protected from injuring themselves or others. The uninformed public often entertains inaccurate images of mental deficiencies, physical deformities, and other bizarre abnormalities as typical characteristics of those who have seizures. The informed educator must reinforce the fact that having seizures is *not* contagious and is *not* a progressive condition.

Misconceptions are bred through lack of knowledge about the condition. Physicians who deal with seizure-prone children believe that the major problem is *not* keeping the disorder under control medically. Seizure control can usually be accomplished. The real difficulty lies in dealing with the psychological problems surrounding the disorder. For example, parents may be instructed by the doctor to give the child's teacher full details about the seizures, their nature, and frequency. Many parents, however, believe that if the child's classmates know about the condition, they will be suspicious or fearful or will reject the child completely. The physician can help avoid these problems by explaining the condition to the parents (and the child), thereby reducing the emotional impact of the terms "seizure," "epilepsy," and "convulsion." The adapted physical educator should reassure the parents that their youngster will be helped to achieve normal status in the school environment.

The stigma of seizure disorders may follow the adolescent into adult life if the school does not dispel old fears and myths. Open discussion of seizures with all children helps to establish a positive, straightforward understanding of the condition, thus erasing the mystery and much of the fear. The role of the school, therefore, is to educate, *not* to hide the facts. Ignoring the situation is not acceptable; openly discussing the problem can lead to understanding. Achievement and success in the physical education class can be a strong motivating influence for children who have seizures, especially when the class attitude is one of acceptance and understanding.

Physical Education Activity Recommendations

All children are subject to risks, and in the physical education environment these become more common. Potential dangers must be accepted. Only through the efforts of conscientious teachers who preplan carefully can serious injuries be avoided. As previously discussed, the seizure-prone child must be allowed to participate in physical education; his exclusion from physical education classes or from athletic competition could mean a future as an inactive invalid. As Livingston and Berman (1974, p. 171) state, "Enlightened physicians and educators today believe that once a patient's seizures are under reasonable control, he should lead a normal life and participate in sports and other physical activities." Laidlaw and Richens (1976) also endorse activities such as football (soccer) and physical education class, which are supervised by a trained instructor.

The key to determining which activities are best for a given child depends entirely on the individual's degree of seizure control. If daily attacks are occurring, the instructor should not use games involving heights, rope climbing, high balance beams, or stair climbing.

Swimming and water skills must be closely supervised. The child should wear a bright colored bathing cap for immediate identification from other swimmers. A buddy system should be used, and the "buddy" should understand what her responsibilities are if a seizure occurs. Laidlaw and Richens (1976) state that seizures seldom occur while the person is swimming, even in special schools for children who have seizures.

If, however, a seizure should occur while the child is in the pool, he should be floated face up, with jaw supported. The convulsing child need not be pulled onto the pool deck. Israel (1968) states that breathing temporarily stops during the initial phases of seizure, so a convulsing swimmer will not inhale water. As he emerges from the seizure, however, the exhausted muscles relax and the danger of drowning is imminent.

Safety should be of major concern when selecting activities for these students. Most seizure-prone youngsters in the public schools have their condition under control by regular administration of prescribed medication. They should have few or no restrictions and normal programming is indicated.

When the child is not under control or when the physician is determining correct medication, the adapted physical educator should consider the following: (1) What specific activities are presently scheduled for the student? Will the student be asked to climb ropes or walk on a high balance beam? Will the activity involve lifting weights above the head? Does participation include carrying or lifting other students, as in relays? If so, appropriate spotting techniques, including use of spotting belts, should be used so the individual can participate. (2) Where will the activities take place? Is the playing surface hard, such as a gym or playroom floor, an asphalt court, or a pool deck? What injuries could occur if the student falls? Should the child wear protective headgear? If the area is undesirable and possibly dangerous, the child should be placed in an adapted environment that includes mats or composition flooring. Wrestling rooms and tumbling areas are examples of ideal playing surfaces. These restricted areas are not suitable teaching stations for many physical education activities, however, and the child's program could become restrictive and shortsighted were his physical education limited to this environment for an extended period of time. The instructor's responsibility is to provide a diversified curriculum for a well-rounded motor program.

Most children whose seizures are not under control will probably possess lower motor skill proficiency because they have been excluded from programs and have not developed normal skill levels. Assessment of general motor ability may indicate that they should have a well-rounded developmental concentration involving basic strength, balance, locomotor skills, agility, and eye-hand coordination.

Since a blow to the head will probably not cause a seizure, exclusion from contact sports is uncalled for! General safety precautions used by all students in the physical education and interscholastic programs will suffice for students whose condition is under control.

Livingston and Berman (1974) list the following suggestions for determining which involved students should engage in contact sports: (1) **Frequency of seizures**—Patients who experience frequent seizures (daily to weekly) should not participate. (2) **Time of seizure occurrence**—Patients whose seizures occur only in sleep should be evaluated in the same manner as individuals who are not subject to seizures.

If the patient is interested, active, and attentive, all disorder tends to be suppressed. In other words, for the seizure-prone person, activity is good therapy. When bored, the child's disorder tends to increase. Fewer seizures are experienced when youngsters are participating in physical activities, including football and baseball. Indeed, abnormalities in the EEGs of seizure-prone patients frequently *increase* during the resting state.

The cardiorespiratory efficiency of children who have seizures should be improved,

TABLE 16.4

FIFTIETH PERCENTILE SCORES FOR 600 YARD RUN FOR BOYS AND GIRLS ON AGE/TEST SCORES IN MINUTES AND SECONDS[a]

	Age									
	9	*10*	*11*	*12*	*13*	*14*	*15*	*16*	*17*	*18*
Boys	2:33	2:33	2:27	2:19	2:10	2:03	1:56	1:52	1:52	1:52
Girls	2:56	2:56	2:53	2:47	2:41	2:40	2:37	2:43	2:41	2:41

SOURCE: Scores taken from AAHPERD 1976, pp. 43, 51.

[a]The 50th percentile scores can be used to determine appropriate levels of cardiorespiratory efficiency for seizure-prone students. When reaching this suggested level, the student can be programmed for longer distances.

for one major concern is that overfatigue may cause seizures. Rose (1977) notes that seizures may be related to degree of cardiovascular fitness. A gradual and progressive program to increase fitness and to minimize undue fatigue therefore seems indicated.

The seizure-prone individual may possess a low level of physical fitness, probably because she has been excused too often from physical activity. Assessment of existing physical fitness levels should determine the individual's placement in regular or adapted physical education activities. The *AAHPERD Youth Fitness Test* (1976) is an ideal assessment tool for this purpose. To eliminate extreme fatigue, two endurance test items should not be given on the same day. For example, the sit-up test and the endurance run should be administered on alternate days. The endurance run should be limited to the 600 yard run. When the student becomes more efficient through the fitness program (i.e., fitness increased to at least the 50th percentile), the program can include longer distances or timed runs or both. Table 16.4 includes the 50th percentile norms for the 600 yard run for boys and girls.

Summary

Seizures are chronic disorders of the brain characterized by recurrent attacks involving loss of consciousness or convulsions or both. There are two categories of seizure: (1) symptomatic or acquired, due to specific disease or damage to the brain, and (2) idiopathic, which includes those individuals who have inherited a low threshold for seizures.

Most seizure-prone individuals can be aided by medication. Physical activity need not be restricted for the school-age child unless seizures are not under control. For those who have frequent attacks, the adapted physical education teacher should modify the activity or the activity area. Seizure-prone individuals should not be excused from physical education activities because of their disorder. Safety is a main precaution in program planning.

The student with seizure disorder may enter the physical education program with below normal levels of physical fitness and motor skills owing to previous excuses from physical education programs. Assessment is necessary to determine appropriate placement.

Continual communication among the physical educator, the school nurse, the parents, and the physician is necessary. When properly understood and medically supervised, the seizure-prone individual can lead a normal life; his condition need not interfere with daily school activities. Too often, people do not understand what happens during a seizure, and stigma and prejudice are directed at the child. This social problem must be dealt with and an understanding attitude developed in classmates. A positive success-oriented physical education experience can contribute greatly toward the child's acceptance in the school and community.

References

AAHPERD. *AAHPERD Youth Fitness Test Manual.* Reston, Va.: AAHPERD, 1976.

Alvarez, W. C. *Nerves in Collision.* New York: Pyramid House, 1972.

Berg, B. O. Epilepsy in Infancy and Childhood. In *Conn's Current Therapy* 1984, edited by R. E. Rakel. Philadelphia: W. B. Saunders, 1984.

Black, P. In Samuel Livingston and Wulfred Berman, Participation of the Epileptic Child in Contact Sports. *Sports Medicine* 2(5):172, 1974.

Bruni, J., and Wilder, B. J. Epilepsy and Other Convulsive Disorders. In *Current Diagnosis* 7, edited by R. B. Conn. Philadelphia: W. B. Saunders, 1985.

Cole, W. New Understanding, New Hope, for Children With Epilepsy. *Parent's Magazine and Better Family Living* 46(4):52–53, 94–96, 1971.

Craig, T. AMA Reviews Its Stand on All Sports. *National Spokesman* 7(4):5, 8, 1974.

Delgado-Escueta, A. V. Epilepsy in Adolescents and Adults. In *Conn's Current Therapy* 1984, edited by R. E. Rakel. Philadelphia: W. B. Saunders, 1984.

Dorland's Illustrated Medical Dictionary, 26th ed. Philadelphia: W. B. Saunders, 1981.

Epilepsy Foundation of America. *Answers to the Most Frequent Questions People Ask About Epilepsy.* Washington, D.C.: The Foundation, 1976.

Forche, C. The Child With Epilepsy. *Journal of Health, Physical Education, and Recreation* 43(4):83–86, 1973.

Guyton, A. C. *Basic Human Physiology: Normal Function and Mechanisms of Disease.* Philadelphia: W. B. Saunders, 1971.

———. *Physiology of the Human Body,* 5th ed. Philadelphia: W. B. Saunders, 1979.

Henderson, J. P. *Sports and Epilepsy,* edited by R. M. Palulonis. Monroe, Wis.: American Medical Association, 1978.

Israel, K. First Aid for Swimmers Simple. *Michigan Education Association News* 10(1):22, 1968.

Laidlaw, J., and Richens, A. *A Textbook of Epilepsy.* Edinburgh, Scotland: Churchill-Livingstone, 1976.

Livingston, S. *Living With Epileptic Seizures.* Springfield, Ill.: Charles C Thomas, 1963.

Livingston, S., and Berman, W. Participation of the Epileptic Child in Contact Sports. *Sports Medicine* 2(5):170–173, 1974.

Massey, E. W., Folger, W. N., and Riley, T. L. Managing the Epileptic Patient. *Postgraduate Medicine* 67(2):134–143, 1980.

National Information Center for Handicapped Children and Youth. *Epilepsy.* Washington, D.C.: The Center, 1983.

Rose, K. Physical Stress and Epilepsy: An Investigation. *National Spokesman* 6(6):6,1973.

———. The Effect of Exercise on EEG and Blood Chemistry of Epileptics. In *The Best of Challenge,* vol. 3. Reston, Va.: AAHPERD, 1977.

Rutter, M., Graham, P., and Yule, W. A Neuropsychiatric Study in Childhood. In *A Textbook of Epilepsy,* edited by J. Laidlaw and A. Richens. Edinburgh, Scotland: Churchill-Livingstone, 1976.

Scott, D. *About Epilepsy.* New York: International Universities Press, 1969.

Simmons, H. E. *The Psychoendocrine Aspects of Epilepsy.* Sacramento, Calif.: General Welfare Publications, 1974.

Wright, G. N. Rehabilitation and the Problem of Epilepsy. In *Epilepsy Rehabilitation.* Boston: Little, Brown, 1975.

CHAPTER 17

Cerebral Palsy

Physical education activities for cerebral palsied individuals are often therapy based. Their capacity for developmental exercise and learning physical and motor skills has been underestimated. The entire physical education experience should be planned to serve the developmental, rehabilitation, and recreational needs of these youngsters.

Cerebral palsy is also known as Little's Disease, after the London orthopedist William Little (1810–1894). Winthrop M. Phelps, M.D., originally coined the term *cerebral palsy* in the early 1900s. He identified *cerebral* as a causative lesion located in the brain, and indicated *palsy* to be the consequence—loss or impairment of motor functioning.

Approximately 750,000 people in the United States (16 out of every 5000) have some degree of cerebral palsy. One third of these are under 21 years of age. Cerebral palsy is the most frequently occurring physical disability among school-age children (Sherrill and Mushett 1984). The National Information Center for Handicapped Children and Youth (1982) estimates that 10,000 babies are born each year with this disorder, and another 2000 acquire it in their preschool years.

A Definition

Cerebral palsy has been defined by the United Cerebral Palsy Research and Education Foundation Program (1975, p. 1) as follows: "Cerebral palsy is a clinical picture, usually manifesting itself in childhood, with dysfunction of the brain in which one of the major components is motor disturbance." In addition, cerebral palsy is described as "a group of conditions usually originating in childhood, characterized by paralysis, weakness, lack of coordination, and any other aberration of motor function caused by pathology of motor control centers of the brain. In addition to such motor dysfunction, cerebral palsy may include learning difficulties, psychological problems, sensory defects, convulsions and behavioral disorders of organic origin."

Mental Retardation

Because the etiology of cerebral palsy is destruction of brain cells, there is a high incidence of mental retardation. An estimated 60 to 70 percent of persons diagnosed as having cerebral palsy also possess some degree of mental retardation (Healy 1984). This, too, will have a negative effect on the child's learning ability.

Motor Deficits

According to Bobath (1966), cerebral palsy is manifested by abnormal tonus (muscle stiffness), abnormal patterns of posture, and abnormal patterns of movement.

Severely involved infants are usually diagnosed at birth; more mildly involved children are identified during the early months of life as developmental lags become apparent. Degree of involvement may vary from mild (no functional incapacity or obvious disability) to severe (little or no functional ability). Brain damage will not worsen, but nothing can be done to restore those brain cells already destroyed. The child will have permanent lesions and will be relegated to a life involving distinct movement problems. Although the disorder is not progressive, physical growth, compounded by paralysis and atrophy, may contribute to development of further deformities.

Bobath and Bobath (1967), experts on the treatment of cerebral palsy, reinforce the importance of suppressing abnormal posture and movement behaviors and enhancing normal patterns. The corrective program requires early intervention, and any delay can cause irreversible structural damage to muscles and joints.

Laskas et al. (1985) reinforce the Bobath neurodevelopmental treatment approach when they identify two fundamental premises: (1) motor development follows a sequential order in both nonhandicapped and handicapped children, and (2) through controlled sensorimotor experiences, normal patterns of motor behavior can be elicited in the child with a damaged central nervous system (CNS).

Cerebral palsied individuals must expend extreme energy to make muscles obey their commands. As a result, they often become lethargic and unmotivated when attempting new movement experiences. They require exciting and stimulating motor activities that provide independence through physical education. Early and appropriate psychomotor programs are important, because proper corrective physical education activities can direct the child with cerebral palsy toward a more normal life-style.

Seizures

The brain injury that caused cerebral palsy also causes seizures in 35 to 45 percent of all affected youngsters. Some studies (Healy 1984) report that 60 percent of all children with cerebral palsy have seizures. Scarring on the cerebral cortex, damage to basal ganglia inside the brain, or injury to the cerebellum are major causes of seizure activity. All types of seizures have been identified—grand mal, petit mal, psychomotor, and akinetic.

Etiology

Cerebral palsy is directly related to **brain cell destruction.** The brain controls motor skills by initiating, coordinating, and integrating movement activities of increasing complexity. To do this, the brain must achieve an exacting and delicate balance between many interacting and opposing forces. In cerebral palsy, the damaged brain cannot achieve this balance correctly. Owing to imperfect coordination, the child has an improper balance between voluntary and involuntary controls, stimulating and suppressing influences, and flexion and extension movements.

The cause of cerebral palsy is linked to the time when the brain destruction occurred. These time periods are divided into two major categories with subdivisions: (1) congenital (prenatal and natal, including 2 weeks of neonatal), and (2) acquired (postnatal).

Certain groups of infants, including those with extensive intracranial bleeding, prolonged birth anoxia, very low birth weight, and abnormal neurological symptoms (low APGAR scores) are possible candidates for cerebral palsy (Campbell and Wilhelm 1985).

Prenatal

A major cause of brain damage during the prenatal period is insufficient oxygen reaching the fetus. This occurrence is known as **anoxia** or **hypoxia.** Restriction of oxygen to the mother, as in carbon monoxide poisoning, dense smoke inhalation, or drowning, will affect the fetus directly. The oxygen supply to the fetus also is reduced in cases of maternal anemia, umbilical cord twisting or knotting, or premature separation of the placenta from the uterine wall.

Certain viruses have been identified as the cause of cerebral palsy because they invade the placenta and infect the fetus. An example is the **rubella virus.** The rubella epidemic of 1964–1965 caused death or serious neurological consequences to approximately 50,000 unborn children. Rubella, known as German or three-day measles, has mild symptoms beginning with low-grade fever, a rash on the face that spreads over the body, and swelling of the lymph glands. It usually lasts 1 to 3 days with no apparent aftereffects. If, however, a pregnant woman develops rubella within the first 3 months of pregnancy, when the fetal brain is developing, the fetus is threatened. Possible results are miscarriage, premature birth, stillbirth, or birth of a child with a disorder such as cerebral palsy.

Rubeola (regular measles) should not be confused with rubella. Vaccination against rubeola does not provide protection against rubella, and all children should be inoculated against both types of measles. Vaccination reduces the probability of the child's catching the disease at school and exposing the mother.

Cytomegaloviruses and **toxoplasmosis** are two major infections that also cause fetal damage when they strike pregnant women. In the United States alone, cytomegalovirus infections damage approximately 3000 fetuses annually. Toxoplasmosis during pregnancy is devastating to the fetus and may affect almost 6000 children in utero (i.e., when the baby is still inside the mother) every year (Sternfeld 1978).

Another prenatal cause of cerebral palsy is **Rh hemolytic disease** or **erythroblastosis fetalis.** This condition, commonly called the **Rh factor** and usually identified as blood incompatibility between parents, afflicts approximately 2000 babies born in the United States each year. Half of these infants survive but have permanent brain damage. This accounts for about one tenth of all cerebral palsy cases.

The major concern of the United Cerebral Palsy Association is preventing **premature births,** which are associated with brain damage, particularly when the birth weight is 1500 g (3 lb 5 oz) or less.

Sternfeld and Berenberg (1981) believe that the widespread use of newborn intensive care units has saved the life of many prematurely born babies and has helped preserve intact the central nervous system of babies who weigh above 1500 g at birth. New studies conducted during pregnancy and the newborn period are progressing rapidly. For example, ultrasound studies performed during pregnancy now monitor the fetal position. Physicians can tell if the fetus is at risk if, for example, the placenta is in a dangerous position. Caesarian section can then be performed properly without damage to the baby, which might otherwise have occurred. In certain instances, brain surgery can now be done in utero. For example, if the baby is developing hydrocephalus, excess fluid can be drained off, before the infant is born.

Natal (Perinatal)

This period begins when the mother identifies labor pains, continues through delivery, and terminates when the baby is 2 weeks old. Complications that arise during this time are usually the result of anoxia, prolonged labor, improper use of forceps, small birth canal, breech delivery, or other abnormal birth position. Poor surgical and delivery techniques that contributed to this type of problem in the past have been all but eliminated today.

The United Cerebral Palsy Association warns physicians (particularly obstetricians) that infants born under the following conditions should be closely monitored: (1) abnormal pregnancy (bleeding, infection, toxemia), (2) prematurity (less than 2000 g birth weight or less than 36-week gestation period), (3) difficult labor and abnormal infant pulse and respiration, (4) abnormal respiration and cyanosis occurring after the first 24 hours, (5) seizures, including flexion spasms, developing in the neonatal period, (6) poor feeding and sucking, or more than 15 percent weight loss in the first 10 days of life, (7) excessive sleeping during the neonatal period, and (8) neonatal jaundice for any reason (United Cerebral Palsy Association, n.d., pp. 1–2).

Postnatal

The following causative factors may develop after birth: severe blows to the skull, meningitis, encephalitis, ingestion of arsenic or lead, carbon monoxide poisoning, or any other anoxia. All destroy brain cells and can lead to cerebral palsy.

Kempe (1977) identifies the most common cause of postnatal brain injury as **child abuse.** Sternfeld (1977) states that more than 1500 cases of cerebral palsy are caused by child abuse each year.

Severity Classification

The Information and Research Utilization Center, an AAHPERD division concerned with physical education and recreation for the handicapped (1976, p. 5), classifies severity of neuromotor involvement of the cerebral palsied in its publication *Physical Education and Recreation for Cerebral Palsied Individuals:*

> *Mild* cases of cerebral palsy include individuals who need no particular care and may attend school. They walk adequately and use their arms although not as skillfully as noninvolved individuals. They may have difficulty speaking but can be understood. *Moderately* involved persons have problems with speech and locomotion. Although they usually are able to attend school, many need help in living skills. They are often confined to wheelchairs that they can maneuver by themselves. *Severely* involved persons are often confined in bed or limited to a wheelchair that is propelled by others. Most severe cases cannot hold or release objects at will.

Topographic Classification

Clinical classifications of cerebral palsy are made by reference to involved body parts. Love and Walthall (1977, p. 72) list the following definitions: "*Monoplegia* involves one limb (rare). *Paraplegia* involves legs only and is usually spastic. *Hemiplegia* includes the lateral half of the body involving the hand and the leg on the same side; usually spastic. *Triplegia* involves three extremities, usually the legs and an arm. *Quadriplegia* involves all four extremities. Individuals may be spastic, rigid, or athetoid. *Diplegia* involves both legs with possible hand involvement. *Double hemiplegia* indicates a quadriplegia in which arms are more involved than the legs."

Rusk (1971, p. 478) explains the confusing topographic classification: "With respect to terminology applicable to topographic distribution of neuromotor deficit, we find it less confusing to use the term quadriparesis [paresis means slight or incomplete paralysis], with greater involvement of the right or the left side rather than to use the term double hemiplegia. Likewise, quadriplegia with greater involvement of the lower extremities avoids the uncertain meaning of diplegia."

Physiological Classification

The type of cerebral palsy is determined by observing clinically the child's reflex patterns. Although different forms are associated with damage to a particular area of the brain, this is less important than the clinical observations of physicians, physical educators, and therapists.

Spastic

This is the most common type of cerebral palsy, including 50 to 60 percent of all cases (Healy 1984). Muscle movements are explosive, jerky, and poorly coordinated. A spastic muscle (hypertonic) is stiff and movements are awkward. **Spasticity** tends to affect flexor, adductor, and internal rotator muscles of the body. The classic picture of an individual with spastic cerebral palsy includes plantar flexion of the feet, which makes the child walk on the toes, flexion of the knees, and flexion of the hips. Flexor muscles in the upper limbs are also spastic and cause finger, wrist, and elbow flexion. The shoulder is usually adducted and internally rotated (Figure 17.1).

Spasticity is characterized by presence of the **stretch reflex,** the principal diagnostic sign. The stretch reflex is an increased tendency of the muscle to contract when stretched rapidly; the reflex does not occur when the muscle is stretched slowly. Harris (1978a) states that affected muscles display elevated tone because their stretch receptors have increased sensitivity. When force is applied to stretch the spastic muscle, there is increased resistance to movement, but at a certain point, a rapid decrease in resistance occurs. This is similar to the action of a pocket knife upon opening: there is tension on the blade, but at a certain point, it springs open. Children with spastic cerebral palsy can hold a limb in either extreme extension or extreme flexion, but they cannot regulate muscle contraction sufficiently to control movements between these extremes.

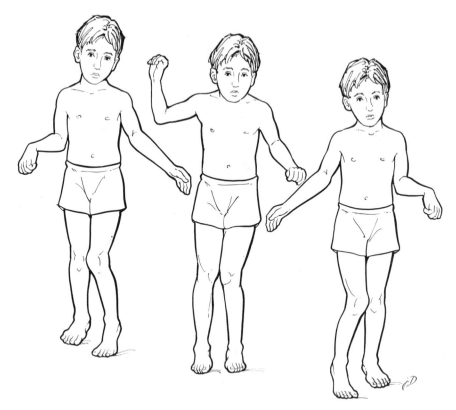

FIGURE 17.1. Typical gait of child with cerebral palsy, spastic diplegia, or paraplegia. Thighs are together (adducted), turned in (internally rotated), and flexed, plus flexion of the knees and tiptoeing (equinus of the feet).

Another clinical sign is an exaggeration of the deep tendon reflexes (patellar tendon knee jerk) or ankle clonus, which is characterized by a jerking reaction caused by sudden and forceful flexion, or a bending of the foot back toward the leg.

The least restricting form of cerebral palsy is **mild spasticity.** Affected children have no apparent movement difficulties until they begin to ambulate or to try to use extremities in refined tasks. They are usually able to walk, and should be thoroughly tested to determine general motor ability and physical fitness. Many can participate in regular physical education activities.

Children with **moderate spasticity** have differing degrees of muscle tone, ranging from normal to hypertonic. Bigge and O'Donnell (1976) point out that spastic children move with less difficulty if activities are done slowly and easily. Furthermore, youngsters have more purposeful movements if they are not overstimulated, overworked, or emotionally stressed. When these children are excited or are trying hard to execute a given task (e.g., hitting a badminton birdie), the high-tone muscles become even more tense. The attempt to move quickly induces an **extensor spasm,** which they cannot control. The muscles that extend or straighten the arms, legs, and body suddenly become extremely tight, throwing the head back, straightening the arms and legs, and stiffening the body. An extensor spasm can literally push the child off a chair (Kieran et al. 1981).

The spastic child's range of motion is also impaired. The more involved youngsters perform motor skills in a primitive fashion, with little selectivity or refinement. Deformities, such as contractures, can occur. A **contracture** develops when an individual does not, or cannot, voluntarily use certain muscles and joints. The muscles shorten and pull continually until the joint becomes totally closed, frozen in an immovable position.

The physiological nature of contracture is explained by the fact that muscle tissue will adapt in length to habitually shortened positions over time. Because muscles have the ability to shorten by active contraction, they eventually will adapt to the shortest length if proper stretching exercises do not maintain an adequate range of motion (Cherry 1980).

Prolonged, gentle manual stretching (elongation) or positional stretching will reduce contractures effectively. Complete range of motion exercises should be performed at the beginning and end of each physical education period (Figure 17.2). If, after several months of exercise, no measurable change in the joint angle appears, parents should consult an orthopedic surgeon.

Children with **severe spasticity** have little or no fluctuation in muscle tone. Purposeful movement, except when aided, is extremely limited. Movements are small, labored, and limited to midrange. Owing to lack of movement and minimal change of position, these youngsters are prime candidates for contracture deformities. Initiation of voluntary movements is minimal and abnormal reflexes occur frequently. Equilibrium and protective reactions are often absent (Bigge and O'Donnell 1976).

If the condition has been present for many years, the spastic child is likely to perceive the condition quite differently from the way nonhandicapped children see themselves. Spastic children have no other frame of reference. Consequently, they experience the midrange as a fleeting transitional state; they cannot be expected to exert precise control over movement. The adapted physical educator must provide opportunities for stretching, strengthening, and controlled movement activities for these children.

Spastic hemiplegia is the most common type of cerebral palsy. The main abnormality is in adduction of the hip joint causing flexion on the affected side. The calf muscles are tight and the dorsiflexors are weak, which gives the common appearance of the toe-walker with heel raised. For better control (i.e, dorsiflexion and eversion of the foot), a short leg brace is worn. The upper extremity is also involved; the elbow is flexed, the forearm is internally rotated, and the wrist and fingers are flexed.

The Information and Research Utilization Center (1975, p. 152) lists specific questions to ask when evaluating the motor performance of the spastic hemiplegic child: "Is the affected hand used for holding, helping, transferring, playing, assisting the dominant hand, or is it completely ignored?"

FIGURE 17.2.   Gentle range of motion exercises should be done at the beginning and end of each physical education period. (Photograph courtesy of Photo Associates Limited)

Teaching Suggestions for a Child With Spastic Cerebral Palsy

1. To relax clenched fists, bend the student's hand down at the wrist (Figure 17.3).
2. To counteract simultaneous flexion of both legs (when child is creeping), hold back the foot of one leg each time the opposite leg is moved forward.
3. To prevent contractures, avoid activities that stress flexion; encourage the child to change positions frequently.
4. To improve arm extension of the hemiplegic child, hold the affected hand when playing or walking. The thumb will thus be held properly with the arm extended and swung in rhythm.

Athetoid

This type of cerebral palsy includes approximately 25 to 30 percent of all cases. The child with **athetosis** (or **dyskinesia**) exhibits slow, uncontrollable, irregular twisting movements of the extremities (Figure 17.4). For instance, the hand or arm may twist repeatedly to one side or the other, then backward, then forward. These children are constantly moving, without selectivity of movement, and they lack control in the midranges. Contractures are not common because muscle tone is in a state of fluctua-

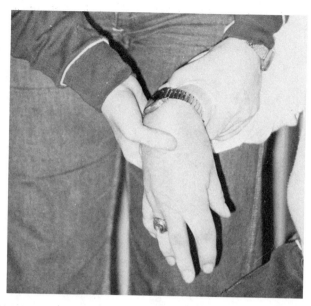

FIGURE 17.3. Clinched fists are often relaxed by bending the hand down at the wrist. (Photograph courtesy of Photo Associates Limited)

tion. Their gait is often lurching or stumbling. Protective and equilibrium reactions are present, but exaggerated, unpredictable, and jerky.

Speech may be difficult, and facial expressions may be constant grimacing. Communication boards (a board with words and letters that is attached to the wheelchair to which the child can point) are commonly used.

Another form of athetosis is **choreoathetosis.** When severe, any activity creates uncontrollable spasms that prevent useful limb function. Children with choreoathetosis experience involuntary, sinuous movements, more proximally than distally. These children often seem to make flying motions with the arms and legs when they attempt to move quickly.

Positioning Suggestions for the Child With Athetosis

1. To reduce unsteady and uncoordinated movements, support the child's body to allow concentration on one or two body parts (hand, head, or arm).
2. To reduce unsteady and uncoordinated arm and hand movements, place a hand on the student's shoulder to support or stabilize.
3. To increase movement independence, help the child devise ways to inhibit unnecessary movements (e.g., hold one flailing arm with the other while walking to avoid being thrown off balance by uncoordinated arm movements).

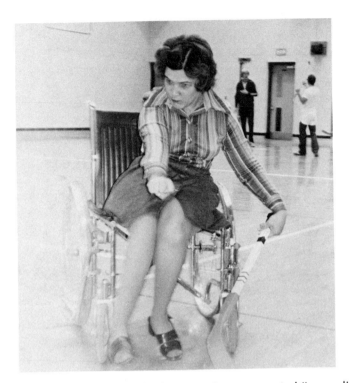

FIGURE 17.4. The athetoid individual will often experience unwanted "worm-like" movements when attempting to move.

Ataxic

The individual with **ataxia** exhibits an inability to maintain normal balance compounded by lack of coordination. Depending on degree of involvement, many functions that require postural stability are affected. Activities that require fine hand movements are performed poorly. Walking is characterized by frequent lurches and lunges. These problems are all directly related to damage of the cerebellum.

The cerebellum collects information from moving body parts and determines how momentum affects the movements. Even before each part reaches its destination, the cerebellum sends feedback signals to begin appropriate reversal contractions of opposing muscles to slow and stop movement. This causes the hand, for example, to be brought to rest with ease and accuracy. All movements are essentially pendular; when an arm is moved, momentum begins and must be overcome before arm movement can be stopped. Because of momentum, all pendular movements tend to overshoot. The cerebellum normally prevents this, but in persons with a damaged cerebellum, conscious control does not initiate the proper motor signals to appropriate muscles. The arm thus overshoots and oscillates back and forth several times before it reaches its mark. Guyton (1979, p. 322) explains this phenomenon: "If a person who has lost his cerebellum tries to run, his feet will overshoot the necessary points on the ground for maintenance of equilibrium and he will fall. Even when walking, his gait will be very severely affected, for placement of the feet can never be precise; he falls first to one side, and then overcorrects to the other side, and must correct again and again, giving him a broken gait."

Ataxia also affects eye-hand coordination, which may be so severely impaired that the child finds it extremely difficult to bounce a ball, strike a badminton birdie, or catch a football. Precise movements are almost impossible owing to excessive overshooting of the arm movement.

Initial Physical Education Program Considerations

The aim of physical education for children with cerebral palsy is to improve posture and locomotor function. After a thorough evaluation, level of posture and locomotion development and deficiencies or delays that interfere with further development should be identified.

The Information and Research Utilization Center (1976, p. 146) identifies the following treatment aims for those with cerebral palsy: "(1) improve function by conservative [nonsurgical rehabilitation] as well as active surgical means, (2) prevent deformity, (3) if deformity develops, correct or relieve it, and (4) to achieve the maximum degree of habilitation or rehabilitation possible." Habilitation involves the treatment of neuromuscular symptoms, stretching contractures, establishing voluntary control, assessing developmental level and personality factors, and treating other accompanying conditions such as visual, speech, and hearing handicaps and seizures.

Too often physical educators have not been involved in planning the motor development program of the cerebral palsied individual. Harris (1978b) determined through research that improvement in static control of posture and in dynamic control of movement can be obtained by relaxing tight muscles and strengthening weak muscles, thus correcting muscle imbalance. The adapted physical educator plays a key role in implementing this type of corrective program.

Perceptual-motor training should also be included. Such training is appropriate for both ambulatory and wheelchair students. Cratty (1980) identifies six major components involved in the learning of perceptual motor skills: (1) impulse control, (2) body image, (3) perceptual-motor competencies, (4) seriation, (5) pattern recognition, and (6) decision making and problem solving. The physical educator plays a major role in the first three. **Impulse control** encompasses relaxation training, controlling movements, and prolonging tasks. **Body image training** includes learning body parts, body planes, and position in space. **Perceptual-motor competencies** include learning balance, agility, locomotor skills, eye-hand coordination skills, and ball throwing, striking, and catching. These perceptual motor skills often develop very slowly in children with cerebral palsy.

To teach the desired skills, the instructor must start at the child's level of motor development rather than at chronological age development level. The instructor must use teaching skills that enhance the child's learning. For example, physical educators should present tasks in sequential steps that are achievable, using repetition and concrete examples with oral instructions.

Although the ultimate goal is maximum function and independence, short-term goals must coincide with present developmental levels. The cerebral palsied child will show only small gains, so the instructor must not set goals too high. Unachievable goals produce only frustration and nonparticipation. Each session must contain activities that allow the child to experience some success.

Development and maturation of the child with cerebral palsy must not be judged in reference to the developmental level of same-age peer without a handicap. The whole child must be considered, and physical components as well as emotional, social, and intellectual aspects of the curriculum must be evaluated. A multidisciplinary approach is important for cerebral palsied children because they usually possess additional handicapping conditions. Adapted physical educators often contend with children who are nonverbal, inactive, and uncooperative. The teaching techniques used for dealing with nonhandicapped children or mildly retarded children do not always apply. Frequently, the child with cerebral palsy is functioning at a motor developmental level far below the level of walking or running.

Assisting the youngster with cerebral palsy requires a true multidisciplinary approach. The therapist can provide expertise in assessment and rehabilitation of school-age children functioning at the level of able-bodied youngsters who are less than 18 months old. The adapted physical educator must work closely with the therapist during initial assessment and when planning each child's motor program. The related services provided by the therapist are an important part of most cerebral palsy programs and greatly enhance the physical educator's effectiveness.

An individualized program can be developed after a complete assessment of malfunction, which includes manual muscle tests, evaluation of range of motion, status of bones and joints, and evaluation of coordination. The initial assessment and follow-up require careful study by professionally trained individuals.

Owing to the nature of the handicap, the child's ability to learn through spontaneous interaction with her physical environment is limited. Objects, symbols, and sensory stimulation must therefore be provided for movement. Specifically, the child must learn basic motor skills, beginning with rolling, crawling, creeping, kneeling, sitting, standing, and walking. The adapted physical educator must teach the child how to move with braces, crutches, or a walker; how to sit while playing on the floor; how to increase limb and body mobility; how to compensate for involuntary muscle action; how to adjust for unresponsive muscles; and how to strengthen other muscles. Developing comprehensive opportunities for the child with cerebral palsy is challenging work for the physical educator.

Assessment

The initial assessment goal is to determine the level and degree of function already acquired by the nervous system so progress can begin from that point. Because different skills emerge as the child grows, various testing tools are needed for each age group.

Motor skill assessment of the child with cerebral palsy is often the same as assessment used for nonhandicapped children to age 6 years. The physical educator should be involved in assessment of skills that require muscle tone, strength, and coordination to perform voluntary movement (i.e., rolling over, sitting, walking, running, hopping, and jumping). Defects, as evidenced by failure to perform these tasks at an appropriate age, are specific indicators of the individual's performance level. Performance of these tasks should be acquired progressively during the formative years; inability to perform a task adequately may be normal at age 6 but inappropriate at age 9. Developmental norms for a given task must be understood to assess their significance. An interesting example is cited by Johnston and Magrab (1976, p. 139):

> A newborn baby responds to stimulus, such as a rattle, by a total body response, that is, flailing of arms and legs and general total body excitement. As the nervous system matures during the next four months, that response is limited and directed to the arms, which reach out in an attempt to grasp the object. This process of inhibition progresses over the years so that by the age of six years the child can do fine finger manipulations with only a minimum amount of overflow movement perceived in the resting hand. This overflow movement is usually entirely lost by age 9 or 10 years. Therefore, at the age of six, there will normally be overflow activity that cannot be inhibited voluntarily, whereas, at the age of nine years, the presence of uninhibited overflow activity is considered abnormal and a sign of possible brain immaturity or dysfunction.

Specific assessment is necessary to determine the degree of maturation and organization of the brain in terms of measurable motor skill performance. A few functional irregularities are not necessarily evidence of significant brain damage. For example, a clumsy child will exhibit distinct motor difficulties, but in most of these children, no brain damage is present.

The purpose of appropriate assessment tools is to determine gross psychomotor abnormalities, which serve (1) to identify existing levels of motor performance, (2) to determine appropriate placement in a least restrictive environment, and (3) to obtain pertinent information for multidisciplinary staffing.

Primary Reflexes

Basic infantile reflexes are found in newborn children and are necessary for early survival. These reflexes are the source of such necessary functions as breathing, sneezing, coughing, and digesting. Other reflexes play an extremely important role in the development and acquisition of postural skills and voluntary movements. Pediatricians and therapists routinely assess these reflexes to determine the present level of neurological function and the existing level of motor development. Winnick and Short (1985, p. 50) describe the importance of this information: "If reflexes, when elicited, are uneven in strength, too weak or too strong, or inappropriate at a particular age, neurological dysfunction may be suspected. Various reflexive behaviors are quite predictable and are expected to appear at particular ages and to be inhibited, disappear, or be replaced by higher order reflexes at later ages. Failure of certain reflexes to disappear, be inhibited, or be replaced may inhibit the development of voluntary movement." For example, if children still possess a positive tonic neck reflex at the age when they should be creeping on all fours, the abnormal tonic neck reflex will cause unwanted flexion of the arms or legs and will inhibit creeping.

Zemke (1985) explains that caution must be used when attempting to determine which children still exhibit a primary reflex. She has found that 3- to 5-year-old *nonhandicapped* children still possess mild levels of asymmetrical tonic neck reflex. This would indicate that the assessment of basic primary reflexes should be done only by highly trained professionals.

Hoskins and Squires (1973, pp. 119–20) describe 16 developmental reflexes.

1. **Flexor withdrawal**—supine; quick tactile stimulus to the plantar surface of the foot elicits abrupt, uncontrolled flexion of the total lower limb.
2. **Extensor thrust**—supine; child with one leg flexed, opposite leg extended; light pressure applied to ball of flexed foot elicits total, uncontrolled extension of the flexed leg.
3. **Crossed extension**—supine; child with one leg flexed, opposite leg extended; when extended leg is passively flexed, opposite leg extends with adduction, internal rotation of the hip.
4. **Asymmetrical tonic neck reflex**—supine; child actively or passively turns head approximately 90 degrees to one side to elicit extension of limbs on nose side and flexion of limbs on skull side.
5. **Symmetrical tonic neck reflex**—prone; flexion of head (chin to chest) causes flexion of upper extremities, extension of lower extremities. Extension of head causes extension of upper extremities, flexion of lower extremities.
6. **Tonic labyrinthine**—supine; child suspended. The position of face upwards elicits limb extension, or extensor tone in limbs. **Tonic labyrinthine**—prone; child suspended. The position of face downward elicits limb flexion, or predominant flexor tone.
7. **Moro reflex**—supine; several stimuli elicit same response; abrupt loud noise near child's head, sudden movement of supporting surface, or dropping child backwards from semisitting position results in sudden opening (extension and abduction) of upper extremities, with opening of hands, followed by flexion to the midline.
8. **Neck righting**—supine; when head is passively turned and held, thorax should follow. If not, reflex is not present.

9. **Labyrinthine on head**—supine; in suspension, when head is slightly lowered, head and trunk should rise to vertical position.
10. **Plantar grasp**—supine; pressure on sole of foot at base of toes causes flexion of toes.
11. **Positive supporting reaction**—upright; when child is bounced on feet, extension of both lower limbs with plantar flexion of feet occurs.
12. **Placing reaction**—upright; when dorsum of foot brushes table, foot is lifted and placed on table top.
13. **Primitive stepping**—upright; with some weight-bearing on soles of feet, when child leans forward, one foot will step forward, followed by other foot.
14. **Body righting on body**—supine; when child is passively rotated at shoulder or hip, normal, if segmental, rotation of shoulders, trunk, pelvis follows.
15. **Landau**—prone; when child is suspended by chest, head actively or passively dorsiflexes. Extension of trunk and lower extremities is elicited, or ventro-flexion of head elicits flexion of spine and lower extremities.
16. **Upper extremity protective extensor thrust**—upright. When body and head move suddenly toward floor, immediate extension of upper extremities with abduction and extension of fingers to protect head should occur.

The functions to be tested can be separated into three distinct categories: general, prewalking, and walking.

General Assessment

Traditional range-of-motion, muscle tone, and muscle strength tests should be included in each student's full evaluation. Body alignment also should be considered, because physical educators are often the first to notice problems such as scoliosis, lordosis, or kyphosis, hip dislocation or subluxation (partial dislocation), and leg length differences. Abnormal body alignment should be determined so physical educators can recommend specialized positioning in the wheelchair, assistive standing devices, or adaptations for lying down in proper posture.

Assessment of each child should include the following:

1. Leg length evaluation from the anterior border of the superior iliac crest to the inferior border of the internal malleolus, and from the top of the greater trochanter to the lower border of the lateral malleolus. X-rays (by the physician) that show leg length may be of help.
2. Contractive evaluation, especially of the ankles, knees, and hips.
3. Examination for scoliosis or lordosis.
4. Observation for obvious hearing or vision deficits.
5. Presence of abnormal amount of motor function or activity (hyperactivity and hyperkinesia).
6. Sensory impairment including impaired responses to pain, temperature, and

vibration. The inability to recognize objects by touching or feeling them (aster-ognosis) may be present.

Assessments are the responsibility of the adapted physical educator. Should any of the previous evaluations be difficult or not within the teacher's capability, then direct assistance should be sought from a therapist. Washburn (1976) stresses that the assessment of students classified as moderate to severe should involve special therapists.

Prewalking Assessment

This assessment should be repeated with the student in several positions (supine, prone, sitting on floor, kneeling, and standing). Head control also should be evaluated in all positions, and hip mobility should be evaluated in the sitting position. The student's ability to change position should be noted, and attention given to the child's technique for each transition and the degree of difficulty experienced.

The **supine** or **back-lying position** should begin with a warm-up consisting of slow, random movements of the arms and legs. This position minimizes the effect of gravity against which the cerebral palsied person constantly struggles to maintain postural stability and dynamic balance. Assessment in this position is critical because the fundamental movement problems that interfere with more complex skills can be identified. Particular attention should be paid to the resting position of body parts (when there is no deliberate attempt to move the part), including hips, knees, ankles, elbows, wrists, thumbs, and fingers. The degree of muscle tone needed to maintain these resting positions is determined by moving or attempting to move each joint toward and away from the neutral position. The degree of movement achieved in each direction, the rate at which these movements are made, and the direction against which the greatest resistance is encountered should be noted. The body sides should be compared for imbalance in neuromuscular abnormalities. Note whether the joint positions and distribution of muscle tone are maintained or modified when positions are changed.

Finally, check the child's ability to produce voluntary joint movement. This should be done at points throughout the obtainable range of motion, particularly the extremes. If the child can produce voluntary joint movement, apply slight resistance to determine the strength behind the movement.

Have the student roll over into the *prone* or *front-lying position*. Note arm strength and skills used to roll over. If the child reaches the prone position, note whether there is sufficient neck strength to lift the head off the mat and sufficient control to keep it centered. If unable to lift the head, note whether assistance is required to turn the head to one side so the child can breathe freely.

Have the child assume the *hands and knees position* by using the arms to push up until the shoulders and head are supported by resting on the elbows. If the student is unable to attain this position, place his arms in the proper position and have the child stay in this position. If the student can prop his body weight on the elbows, then have him execute a push-up by extending the elbows. If able to do this, have the student maintain support on the hands and bring the knees up and forward into a kneeling or hands and knees position. If unable to accomplish this, move the student's legs into place. Support the shoulders if necessary, and have the child maintain this position. While the student is in the kneeling position, test for head control by asking him to move his head up and down and from side to side voluntarily.

Have the child reach the *sitting position on the floor* by lowering him into the prone position, then ask the child to roll over into the supine position. (The child's capability determines the amount of assistance required.) From there, place the child in the sitting position by pulling him up by his arms. The child may not tolerate sitting with knees extended because of limited hip flexion. To place the child in a sitting position requires the following technique: While the child is in supine position, bend legs and knees into full flexion position with knees held against chest. When this position has been maintained for 1 min, rock the child forward slowly into an upright position (lift from back of child under shoulders while keeping his knees pressed against the chest). When upright position is reached, the student will be seated with knees flexed, ankles in neutral position, and soles flat on the floor. If the child can tolerate this position, note degree of spine curvature, shoulder protraction, and hip flexion. Assess head control in this position by requesting the child to move his head voluntarily in all directions. Release the child cautiously to determine if he is able to maintain position independently.

If the student is able to tolerate this initial sitting position without marked kyphosis and shoulder protraction, attempt gradually to extend the knees. Determine how far the knees can be extended without losing the sitting position. If the child cannot tolerate the normal sitting position, attempt to teach side-sitting (i.e., resting on one hip and leg with the corresponding arm supporting the upper body). Alternate sides frequently to avoid developing one-sided bias to posture.

The **standing position** is accomplished by lowering the child into supine from sitting and asking the child to roll into prone, and then to rise to the hands and knees position again. If successful, the child should attempt rising to the standing position. The child can grasp a chair to pull up against or to assist with balance. If able to stand by using a chair for assistance, attempt to teach the child to reach the standing position from the hands and knees, without a chair, by raising first one knee and then pushing on the raised knee with one hand and on the floor with the other. If the child is unable to stand alone, then lift and support at shoulders or waist or both to assist with weight-bearing and balance. The flexion-extension positions of the ankle, knee, and hip joints, and any tendency toward increased adductor tone and inward rotation of the femur, should be noted.

Observe whether or not spontaneous arm movements occur to maintain balance. To assess head control while standing, ask the student to move the head voluntarily in all directions (Harris 1978a).

Figure 17.5 is a motor control assessment chart that uses the basic positions of supine, prone, sitting, kneeling, squatting, and standing.

A complete motor assessment tool, which evaluates motor patterns, was developed by Banham (1978, pp. 112–116) for children with cerebral palsy. Figure 17.6 shows a modified version. Items 1 through 34 can be used for prewalking assessment.

FIGURE 17.5. Cerebral palsy basic motor control assessment chart. (Adapted from materials and tests of Karel and Berta Bobath.)

NAME _____

BIRTH DATE _____ DIAGNOSIS _____

KEY: 0—Cannot be placed in test posture.
1—Can be placed in test posture but cannot hold.
2—Can hold test posture momentarily after being placed.
3—Can assume an approx. test posture unaided, in any manner.
4—Can assume and sustain test posture in a near normal manner. (Note any abnormal detail)
5—Normal

EXAMINER:

Test Postures & Movements	NAME: Date	Remarks	NAME: Date	Remarks	NAME: Date	Remarks
SUPINE						
1. Hips and knees fully flexed, arms crossed, palms on shoulders						
2. Hips and knees fully flexed						
a. Extend right leg	R.		R.		R.	
b. Extend left leg	L.		L.		L.	
3. Head raised 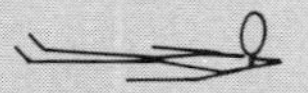						
PRONE						
4. Arms extended beside head Raise head in midposition						

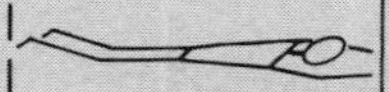

continued

		R.					
		L.					

5. Arms extended beside body, palms down

6. a. Flex right knee, hips extended
   b. Flex left knee, hips extended

7. Trunk supported on forearms, upper trunk extended, face vertical

8. Trunk supported on hands with elbows and hips extended

SITTING ERECT
9. Soles of feet together, hips flexed and externally rotated to at least 45°

10. Knees extended and legs abducted, hips 90-100°

FIGURE 17.5 continued

Test Postures & Movements		Date	Remarks	Date	Remarks	Date	Remarks
11. Legs hanging over edge of table a. Extend right knee b. Extend left knee		R. L.		R. L.		R. L.	
KNEELING 12. Back and neck straight (not hyperextended) a. Weight on knees b. Weight on hands		A. B.		A. B.		A. B.	
13. Side sitting, upper trunk erect, arms relaxed a. On right hip b. On left hip		R. L.		R. L.		R. L.	
14. Kneeling upright, hips extended, head in midposition, arms at sides							
15. a. Half kneeling, weight on right knee b. Half kneeling, weight on left knee		R. L.		R. L.		R. L.	
SQUATTING 16. Heels down, toes not clawed, knees pointing in same direction as toes, hips fully flexed, head in line with trunk							

STANDING & COMPONENTS

17. Standing correct alignment

18. Pelvis and trunk aligned over forward leg. Both knees extended
    a. Right leg forward
    b. Left leg forward

	R.	L.	R.	L.	R.	L.

19. Bear weight on one leg in midstance
    a. Shift weight over right leg
    b. Shift weight over left leg

	R.	L.	R.	L.	R.	L.

20. Heel strike, rear leg extended and externally rotated, heel down. Both knees straight
    a. Right heel strike
    b. Left heel strike

	R.	L.	R.	L.	R.	L.

State of California
Department of Public Health
Bureau of Crippled Children Services
Revised June 9, 1964

CHILD'S NAME _____ DATE _____

BIRTH DATE _____ AGE _____ IQ _____ FMR SCORE _____

DIAGNOSIS _____ HAD SURGERY: YES _____ NO _____

INVOLVEMENT: GENERALIZED _____ SPECIFIC _____

SEVERE _____ MODERATE _____ MILD _____

RIGHT SIDE _____ LEFT SIDE _____ RECORDER _____

Instructions: Check statements in the appropriate column: True, Completely or Usually; True, Partially or Rarely; Not True or Never, according to observations of the infant made during the preceding week. Allow 2 points for each check mark in the left-hand column (Completely True), 1 point for each check mark in the middle column (Partially True), and no points for check marks in the right-hand column (Not True). Add all the points to give a total score and write the total FMR score in the places indicated on the form.

TRUE USUALLY OR COMPLETELY	TRUE RARELY OR PARTIALLY	NOT TRUE OR NEVER	HEAD The child has:
_____	_____	_____	1. Held head steadily when sitting, not letting it flop over uncontrolledly.
_____	_____	_____	2. Lifted head spontaneously, or on request, from lowered position.
_____	_____	_____	3. Raised chin from mat when lying on belly.
_____	_____	_____	4. Raised head from mat when lying on back.
_____	_____	_____	5. Raised head and chest from mat when lying on belly.
_____	_____	_____	6. Turned head to left or right, in search of sound, person or object.
			TRUNK The child has:
_____	_____	_____	7. Sat trunk erect, with or without support.
_____	_____	_____	8. Sat trunk erect, without support, 1 or more minutes.
_____	_____	_____	9. Raised self from lying to sitting position.
_____	_____	_____	10. Rolled unaided from lying on back to side position, spontaneously or when encouraged.
_____	_____	_____	11. Rolled completely over from lying on back to prone position, spontaneously or when encouraged.
_____	_____	_____	12. Pivoted around completely, spontaneously or to attain an object when lying on belly.

FIGURE 17.6. Functional motor scale for cerebral palsied children. (Adapted from K. M. Banham, Duke University.)

TRUE USUALLY OR COMPLETELY	TRUE RARELY OR PARTIALLY	NOT TRUE OR NEVER	
_____	_____	_____	13. Propelled self forward when lying prone, using arm and body movements.
_____	_____	_____	14. Raised chest from mat supporting body on extended arms, when lying on belly.
_____	_____	_____	**ARMS** The child has:
_____	_____	_____	15. Controlled arm movements, directing them toward desired object when reaching.
_____	_____	_____	16. Crawled on hands and knees, trunk away from floor, spontaneously or to reach an object or person.
_____	_____	_____	17. Brought two hands together, spontaneously, manipulating and feeling them.
_____	_____	_____	18. Clapped hands together on request, or in imitation of person clapping
_____	_____	_____	19. Thrown object away with some thrust, not merely releasing hold and letting it drop.
			HANDS The child has:
_____	_____	_____	20. Grasped small objects on contact with hand.
_____	_____	_____	21. Released objects from grasp voluntarily or on request.
_____	_____	_____	22. Held thumb out of palm of either hand.
_____	_____	_____	23. Reached, grasped, and held small object for several seconds.
_____	_____	_____	24. Transferred objects from one hand to the other.
_____	_____	_____	25. Pointed with index finger, or poked it in holes.
_____	_____	_____	26. Picked up tiny objects between first finger and thumb.
			LEGS AND FEET The child has:
_____	_____	_____	27. Flexed legs at knee, while taking hold of toes.
_____	_____	_____	28. Pulled self to standing position, holding furniture or person's hand.

continued

FIGURE 17.6 *continued*

TRUE USUALLY OR COMPLETELY	TRUE RARELY OR PARTIALLY	NOT TRUE OR NEVER	
_____	_____	_____	29. Made alternate stepping movements when held with feet touching floor in attempt to move upward.
_____	_____	_____	30. Raised self from sitting to standing, independently, without support of furniture.
_____	_____	_____	31. Sat on floor, knees flexed, legs crossed in tailor fashion.
_____	_____	_____	32. Squatted low, with both knees flexed.
_____	_____	_____	33. Stood erect, hand held.
_____	_____	_____	34. Stood erect, unsupported for half a minute or more.

LOCOMOTION, USING ARMS AND LEGS
The child has:

_____	_____	_____	35. Taken steps sideways, with or without support of hand or furniture.
_____	_____	_____	36. Walked forward, with or without hand support.
_____	_____	_____	37. Walked with both heels touching ground.
_____	_____	_____	38. Walked, legs together, not wide apart to keep balance.
_____	_____	_____	39. Walked across room independently without support of furniture or person's hand.
_____	_____	_____	40. Walked quickly, both heels touching ground, not crossing feet over or scissoring.
_____	_____	_____	41. Walked backwards, independently.
_____	_____	_____	42. Walked up steps with support of wall, rail, or person's hand.
_____	_____	_____	43. Walked up steps independently, or holding rail, wall, or hand.
_____	_____	_____	44. Walked down steps independently without support of wall, rail, or person's hand.

TRUE USUALLY OR COMPLETELY	TRUE RARELY OR PARTIALLY	NOT TRUE OR NEVER	
————	————	————	45. Run with hand held.
————	————	————	46. Run about independently without hand support, indoors and outdoors.
————	————	————	47. Moved about independently on wheeled chair or toy, or by propelling self by hands and arms on floor.
————	————	————	48. Raised or pulled self from sitting to standing, unaided.
————	————	————	49. Climbed and seated self on adult chair, unaided.
————	————	————	50. Pedalled tricycle or other pedalled toy without assistance.
————	————	————	TOTAL NUMBER CHECKED
————	————	————	SCORE TOTAL FMR SCORE ————————

Walking and Locomotor Assessment

Walking and locomotor assessment should be conducted when the child can stand with reasonable ease. If children are unable to balance but have sufficient lower extremity extensor tone to support body weight, then assist them to walk. During independent or assisted ambulation, observe head control, arm position and movements, trunk stability, pelvic movements, knee and ankle joint positions during swing and stance phases, toe-in or toe-out, tendency to adduct or scissor, and overall quality of gait.

The modified version of Banham's functional motor scale (1978) lists 15 items (see Fig. 17.6, items 35–50) that are appropriate for identifying developmental walking levels.

Hoskins and Squires (1973, p. 120) have developed an assessment tool, the *Test for Gross Motor and Reflex Development,* that is validated for use with cerebral palsied children. The test items shown in Table 17.1 are directly related to the developmental progression for walking.

Activities and Rehabilitation

Developmental and corrective exercises are necessary and should be integral components of all physical education programs for children with cerebral palsy. A study by

TABLE 17.1

A DEVELOPMENTAL PROGRESSION FOR WALKING

No.	Item
1	Pulls to feet at rail: child can pull to standing position at rail or furniture
2	At rail, lifts foot: child stands holding rail; can lift and replace one foot at a time
3	Cruises: standing at rail or furniture, child moves along sideways holding on
4	Walks, hands held: hold child's hands, and he walks forward
5	Lowers to floor from standing: without "falling," child moves with control to sitting
6	Walks, one hand held: walks with one hand held
7	Walks few steps alone: walks alone without support for two or three steps, then falls or holds on
8	Stands momentarily alone: stands without support briefly, then falls or holds on
9	Walks, starts, stops: initiates walking, steps, and can stop with control
10	Stands independently: stands alone steadily and indefinitely
11	Runs stiffly: runs, but not smoothly and lacks complete control
12	Squats in play: maintaining full flexion of hips and knees, bearing weight on feet, child is able to balance in play
13	Upstairs, one hand held: child can climb stairs if one hand is held
14	Small chair, seats self: child climbs onto a small chair from standing, and sits
15	Downstairs, one hand held: walks downstairs if one hand is held
16	Upstairs, holds rail: child can walk upstairs holding rail with one or two hands
17	Walks and runs: walks and runs well independently, with heel-toe gait
18	Up, down stairs, marks time: brings second foot to lead foot on each step
19	Kicks large ball: kicks a large ball, maintaining balance
20	Jumps with both feet: jumps, keeping two feet together
21	Walks backwards: walks backwards with control at least four steps
22	Walks on tiptoes: walks on tiptoes keeping heels off floor for ten consecutive steps
23	Rides tricycle: rides a tricycle independently
24	One foot, momentarily: can stand on one foot without support for at least ten seconds
25	Jumps high: can jump up off floor with two feet together, at least twelve inches
26	Upstairs, alternate feet: can walk upstairs alternating feet independently
27	Jumps distance: jumps ahead with two feet at least seventeen inches
28	Stands on one foot steadily
29	Downstairs, alternate feet: walks downstairs alternating feet independently
30	Hops on one foot: is able to hop at least five hops

SOURCE: Modified from PHYSICAL THERAPY (Vol. 53:120, 1973) with the permission of the American Physical Therapy Association.

Bullock and Watter (1980) of 78 children over a 6-month period, revealed a decrease of 86 percent in abnormalities of school-age children and a decrease of 75 percent in abnormalities of preschool-age children when appropriate developmental and corrective exercises were used. In the control group of cerebral palsied children who did not do the exercises, a 7 percent increase in the number of abnormalities was seen in the school-age children and a 14 percent increase was seen in the preschool-age children. Any delay in programming could leave the cerebral palsied child with more severe motor problems than were present when the child entered school.

An important concept to keep in mind when setting goals for the child with spastic cerebral palsy is that proper muscle balance at affected joints must, if possible, be restored. To accomplish this goal, Harris (1978a) advocates relaxing "tight" muscles (i.e., those with hypertonicity) to cause contraction of the weak antagonists. With every movement, therefore, one muscle, or set of muscles, releases tension while the other increases it. If proper muscle balance is present when movement is initiated, changes in tension of both agonistic and antagonistic muscles should improve during motion. The balance of reciprocal muscle action can thus be maintained throughout the motion, resulting in better control. Harris has found that when the cerebral palsied child understands completely how the muscle should work, the child will be able to "feel" variations of tone throughout the midrange. This should teach the child to make distinct movements with controlled acceleration and deceleration.

Relaxation of tight muscles is extremely important. All passive and assistive exercises must use slow and continuous action. Fast movements are contraindicated and usually cause uncontrolled movement.

All affected joints should be moved passively into, or past, the neutral position in the opposite direction from deviation. Place the student in a position so that each joint can be observed, and any pain or discomfort that occurs can be observed or related during the procedure.

During activity, the student should be told what will happen and what is actually happening when joint positions change. Horgan (1980, p. 28) observes that verbal stimulation and positive involvement in the learning and performance of motor skills is important for cerebral palsied children. He states: "Motivational reinforcement treatment does in fact aid in the acquisition of motor skills by the spastic child, as shown by the results in this study, that may have important clinical implications. The continued use of motivational or reinforcing stimuli may be profitably adapted to school work, therapy, recreation and activities of daily living. Any method which has the potential for improving the motor function and efficiency of the cerebral palsied child is worthy of consideration."

Applying force smoothly and slowly is absolutely necessary. Prolonged, slow stretching will fatigue the stretch receptors and eventually relax the spastic muscles. The degree of resistance, the time required to bring the joint into the neutral position, and whether any opposing muscle spasms occur are important progress indicators of exercise effectiveness. Harris (1978a) found that when the "slow stretch" process was repeated, the joint was usually more readily brought into the neutral position than on the first day of the program. As the activity program continued over a few months, the abnormal resistance of the originally spastic muscles to stretch was overcome entirely and the joint position was neutralized.

Relaxation and Stretching Exercises

The child should be in a supine position for the following exercises. Since this position is stable, the student can relax, and the teacher can move each joint individually. *Athetoid* children show less tendency to involuntary movement while resting in this position, and tight muscles of the *spastic* students relax considerably after a few moments of random, passive manipulation of the head and extremities while in the supine position.

Exercises for the foot and ankle.   Exercises begin with the ankle brought passively into the neutral position by prolonged, slowly increasing force to the ball of the foot. The calf muscles (gastrocnemius-soleus) will relax during this procedure. Finally, ask the student to bend the ankle backward *voluntarily*.

Knee exercises.   Exercises require that the leg be extended passively to the maximum and then slowly extended voluntarily until the hamstrings relax. Gravity can be used by lifting the leg and resting the heel on a low support (rolled-up blanket or mat). The leg's weight will stretch the hamstrings and gradually extend the knee joint, then ask the student to extend the knee voluntarily. Elevate the thigh and hold, then ask the child to extend the knee and align the lower leg with the thigh. As the child's strength increases, the thigh is held at progressively steeper angles.

In most cases, voluntary movements of the ankle and knee joints are possible, even during the first exercise. If voluntary movement occurs, introduce the student immediately to resistance exercises involving movements such as : (1) dorsiflexing the ankle while resisting upward movement of the foot, and (2) extending the knees in a bilateral extensor thrust with the feet pushing upward against the teacher's midriff.

Exercises for the elbow.   Elbow exercises include passively extending the biceps using the prolonged slow-stretch process, and then holding in extended position until relaxation can be felt. The student should flex the elbow first, allowing the forearm to dangle across the chest. The teacher then holds the upper arm and asks the student to extend the elbow and raise the forearm upward. The upper arm should be held in many positions; the force of gravity provides resistance while the procedure is repeated. Finally, to provide resistance, grasp the student's wrist and resist the elbow extension motion.

Exercises for the wrist.   Exercises involve slow stretching of the flexors, and while holding the child's forearm, having the child extend the wrist and align the back of the hand with the forearm.

Exercises for the hand and fingers.   These exercises require that the child's fingers and hand be closed. In the young child whose upper extremities are involved, normal grasp is not well developed. Palmar grasp (grasping with the hand) is often crude. When the thumb has been held flexed and adducted inside the palm with the fingers flexed over it, the web of the thumb becomes shortened. These fisted fingers can be extended by passively hyperextending the wrist, firmly stroking the back of the hand in a distal-to-proximal direction, and shaking the forearm so the hand is forcibly altered toward wrist extension. Once the fingers are extended, the student should passively "brush" the hands past each other to engage the opposing sets of fingers and pull one open with the other. To aid voluntary finger extension, have the child squeeze the fingers into a fist with maximum voluntary effort while the teacher squeezes down on the child's fisted hand. The "feeling" of extreme opposition to extension provides the child with an awareness against which opening the fingers can be better sensed, or a rebound phenomenon may be involved (Harris 1978b).

Once the fingers are fully extended, passive manipulation of the child's forearms, as in "drumming" on the chest or abdomen with open hands, keeps them effectively extended. Finally, ask the student to alternately flex and extend the fingers.

When there is voluntary movement in the student's hand, provide games that involve pushing, reaching, grasping, and releasing, followed by activities that require placement and grasp, progressing from crude palmar grasp to pincher grasp. It is best to start with wooden blocks and toys large enough to be picked up easily, but small enough to fit in the student's hand. Progression to smaller objects will occur rather rapidly. Pegboards and cupcake pans are excellent tools for hand and finger development (Figure 17.7). When the child shows flexion and extension control, use a stopwatch to determine how long it takes the student to complete a task. Objective evaluation for both speed and endurance is then possible.

Muscle Strengthening Exercises

For proper muscle balance, spastic muscles must be relaxed and their antagonists strengthened. Traditional methods used to stimulate weak muscle action include repetitive tapping, stroking, or brushing the weak muscle. A quick stretch in the direction

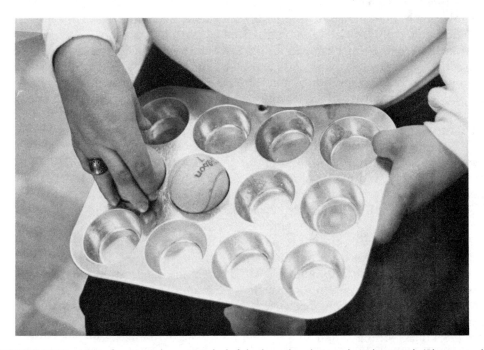

FIGURE 17.7.   Use of a cupcake pan is helpful when developing hand control. (Photograph courtesy of Photo Associates Limited)

opposite that of the desired movement, prior to the movement, is particularly effective. Extremely useful is the student's voluntary effort. Passive manipulation of the arm or leg in the desired direction may assist the child to understand what is being asked. For true control, the child must understand what movement is being attempted. Clear instructions will establish learned responses. For example, "Press your knees together so you can feel this pillow being squeezed."

An extensive study by Harris (1978a, 1978b) indicates that development of strength in spastic cerebral palsied children should be included in all exercise programs. He states: "The subjects responded very enthusiastically to incorporation of newly learned muscle activation and relaxation patterns into activities which they could continue practicing independently in order to sustain proper muscle balance and to strengthen both of the opposing muscles or muscle groups. Exercises such as push-ups, sit-ups, and knee-bends, traditionally used for physical fitness training, were effective in strengthening weak muscles and improving coordination once muscle balance had been approximated through rudimentary single-joint exercises practiced in supine position" (1978a, p. 24).

Development of strength requires exercises and activities involving progressive resistance, which should be matched to the age and status of the child. Motivational and recreational stimuli, from work and conditioning to diversified games and sports, are essential to a stimulating program. Progressions and goals should be written and improvements recorded on colorful graphs and charts. Measurable accomplishments (i.e., how much, how many, how far) are reinforcing, and accurate evaluations fulfill the requirements of a complete individualized educational program.

Muscle strengthening exercises for the head and neck. These exercises should be done in the prone position. The child should be encouraged to roll from the supine to the prone position. Students may "pin" an arm under them when rolling over, but if the shoulder is lifted by the teacher, the child can usually lift the arm high enough to clear it. Prone-lying is one position tolerable to the cerebral palsied child if the head can be lifted far enough to avoid covering the nose and mouth. The head may be turned or lifted to one side. If the child is weak, lift the shoulders and place the child in an "elbow-propped" position. The child may require support to perform head and neck exercises. Ask the child to move the head up and down. If neck muscles are too weak to accomplish this, cup the forehead to support the head and ask the child to continue holding it up. The ability to hold the head against gravity, or even to slow the rate at which the head falls, indicates strength development.

Muscle strengthening exercises for the shoulders and upper arms. These should be done with the child in the prone position and supported on the forearms and elbows (i.e., elbow-propped position). When the child can hold this position for a few seconds (increase to 10 sec), place additional weight on the upper back by pressing down on the shoulders. This exercise strengthens the triceps muscles. For additional strength in the triceps and the challenge of a new position, the child should assume the hands and knees creeping position. When able to hold up to 10 sec, increase the child's strength by pressing down on the shoulders.

Muscle strengthening exercises for the abdominals and back. These exercises include isometric contraction of the abdomen, such as "sucking in your stomach" and holding for a 6-sec count. Have the student then assume the supine position and hold the instructor's hands; pull the child to sitting position. By pulling with her own arms, the child uses abdominal muscles. The child should be lowered in the same way, which also uses her abdominal muscles for control. Finally, have the child raise her head and shoulders off the mat and hold this position for a 6-sec maximum count. Repeat.

Straight leg lifts are contraindicated even though they develop strength in the abdominal and hip flexor muscles. The iliopsoas muscle group (major hip flexors) is unusually tight in children with spastic cerebral palsy so additional strengthening is undesirable. Prone leg lifts and prone chest raises are beneficial because they emphasize the action of hyperextension.

Muscle strengthening of the knee joint. Exercises to strengthen the knee joint are necessary for the child to learn to walk. Teaching children to walk by having them walk increases spasticity if they lack sufficient balance and strength to support themselves. Specific quadriceps strengthening exercises in the supine position prepare the child for standing and walking.

Strength in the quadriceps (knee extensors) is gained by extensor thrust exercises against resistance in the supine position. Half knee bends and hopping in place, while supported, should be performed constantly to prepare for independent standing and walking. To develop strength, place the child supine on a scooter board and have him push with the feet. A "stand-box" develops antigravity muscles and balance, but does not develop strength when progressive resistance is necessary.

A Case Study

The following is a clinical description of an 18-year-old male with severe quadriplegic spasticity. When first encountered, he was in a wheelchair with his legs uncontrollably crossed and hands secured between his knees to avoid flailing. Although now confined to his wheelchair, he had walked before he was 9 years old. At approximately age 9, he stopped walking and has been confined to a wheelchair since. His movements pass rapidly from one motion to another, with no control in the midrange. When asked to elevate his extended leg while in the supine position, it shot immediately overhead. He could not estimate his arm or leg movements with any accuracy, and he had problems judging passive movements as well.

This student had little opportunity for participation in physical education classes. A developmental program was initiated as follows: (1) muscle balance was reestablished to strengthen the muscles opposing dominant tendency toward abduction and extension for both upper and lower extremities, and (2) resistance exercises were provided to facilitate the adductors and flexors in both upper and lower extremities. The student was placed in a supine position, and elbow flexion movements were resisted by the instructor. After repetitions of elbow flexion against heavy resistance, the student was asked to move the elbow slowly through the entire range of motion. By facilitating the elbow flexors, it was possible to teach controlled elbow extension movements. Controlled hip flexion was also accomplished by moving the hip extensors through resistance exercises in the prone position. (If the hypertonic muscles have something to pull against, voluntary control is improved.) The student was then returned to his wheelchair, and given resistance exercises to strengthen adduction of the arms. After the repetitions, the student was asked to adduct voluntarily his extended arms and to press the palms of his hand together at the midline. This was difficult, but once accomplished, produced a generalized relaxing effect that enabled the student to sit quietly without tenseness in a normal sitting position.

Balance Improvement

Bobath (1959, p. 13) believes that upright positioning is a learned response that progresses through specific levels of development. He states: "As the child passes from a stage of primitive reflex activity and learns to right himself and get his balance, he gradually begins to use the automatic patterns for voluntary activity." This concept is extremely important, because many cerebral palsied children have neuromuscular conditions that limit head, neck, and body control. These individuals have primitive patterns of abnormal flexion and extension that inhibit normal body posture and foster physical deformities that interfere with further functioning. According to Connor and Baken (1976), these abnormal patterns interfere with attention to stimuli, perception of stimuli, and voluntary control of responses to stimuli.

Research in motor control indicates that effective positioning of the body and maintenance of stability are prerequisites to skilled performance. For example, it is difficult, if not impossible, for most performers to execute even the simplest gross or fine motor act effectively (e.g., kicking, throwing, writing, jumping) unless appropriate postural adjustments occur to support such movements (Williams, McClenaghan, and Ward 1985). These reactions occur automatically in most able-bodied skilled individuals. For such persons, little, if any, conscious attention is given to positioning or balance—allowing the performer to concentrate instead on information related to movement execution. Williams, McClenaghan, and Ward (1985, p.171) state: "In certain pathological conditions [e.g. cerebral palsy], stabilizing postural reactions do not occur spontaneously and precision movement of the extremities is, at best, effortful and slow." Williams, Fisher, and Tritschler (1983) believe that for children with motor development delays, postural reactions are often slow and inappropriate, and the execution of skillful movement is difficult and ineffective.

Some children with athetosis have difficulty sitting because of involuntary writhing movements and equilibrium reactions that are only partially developed. Stable sitting posture is poor because of the increase in extensor tone (tonic labyrinthine reflex) throughout the body when the head is extended. When the child sits with the head erect, there is a tendency to topple backwards. The most stable sitting position is the reverse tailor position.

Adequate head and trunk control are extremely important when positioning the child. Emphasis should be on symmetry and righting, equilibrium, and protective reactions. The appropriate chair and accessories should place the child in the most normal sitting position possible. This will maintain a posture that inhibits primitive reflexes and allows better control of the head and upper extremities.

When seating a child, the buttocks should be close to the back of the chair to obtain an angle of 90 degrees, thus providing adequate hip flexion. The chair depth should not permit the back of the knees to touch the front of the seat when the child's hips are properly placed. The most ideal position is found by inserting the index and middle fingers between the back of the child's knees and the seat edge; the fit should be comfortable, not too loose or too snug.

The feet should be placed firmly on the floor or on the foot rests of the wheelchair, creating an angle of 90 degrees. Angles greater than 90 degrees (including the knees and hips) generally produce extensor hypertonus due to lack of support at the hips. Tactile and kinesthetic input occur when the feet are in constant contact with a supporting surface. Writing or support boards attached to the chair allow for hand use. The child's forearms should form an approximate 90-degree angle with the upper arm. The desk surface should be ½ to 1 in. (1.25 to 2.5 cm) higher than the child's elbows to provide adequate stability and movement (Carrington 1979).

All good positioning involves sitting, prone, supine, and standing positions that discourage the child's natural but abnormal reflexes. Most spastic children are dominated by flexion movements, so the spastic child should always be placed in positions that discourage flexion activities (i.e., the supine position is suggested, but if the prone position is used, the person should be placed on an incline board so body weight will restrict any flexion activities). Movement skills involving extension, external rotation, and abduction should be integral components of programs for the student with spastic cerebral palsy. For the child with athetosis, whose major actions are usually unwanted trunk extension, positioning should be with flexion, such as placing the student on her side.

Vestibular stimulation is important to improving motor performance of children with cerebral palsy (Ayres [1975], Clark, Kreutzberg, and Chee [1977], and Ivy and Roblyer [1980]). The vestibular mechanism is made up of two kinds of receptors, the **semicircular canals,** which respond to angular acceleration, and **otolith organs,** which respond to linear acceleration. The vestibular mechanism understands where the head is in space, that is, it signals whether the head is upright, upside down, or in some other position. In addition, it is sensitive to sudden changes in direction of body movement. Sage (1984) believes that the vestibular mechanism is also important in the visual component of balance, because it assists in visual fixation during head and body movements.

The biophysics of the vestibular mechanism (semicircular canals) is sensitive only to angular acceleration, that is, a change in angular velocity. These sensitive areas receive stimulation only at the beginning and ending of rotation. The more rapid the change in angular velocity, the greater the angular acceleration stimulus to the semicircular canals (Guyton 1979).

The otolithic organs are fluid-filled sacs called the **utricle** and the **saccule.** Each sac has a patch of hairlike nerve endings. The sacs are located between the semicircular canals, and feed information into the vestibular nerve, which leads into the auditory nerve. The utricle is approximately horizontal in the upright head and the saccule is approximately vertical. Sage (1984, p. 172) explains how the otolithic organs function: "Since the hair cells of the utricle are set on a horizontal plane (whereas those of the saccule lie on a vertical plane), the utricle is maximally stimulated when the head is bent either forward or backward. . . . The saccule appears to be maximally stimulated when the head is bent to the side and when the body is raised or lowered in space."

Chee and his associates (1978) found that semicircular canal stimulation improves gross motor skills in preambulatory cerebral palsied children, and that stimulation also reduces unwanted reflexes. Striking improvements were seen in equilibrium, gross motor coordination, alertness, and curiosity. In research involving 23 subjects between the ages of 2 and 6 years, including athetoid and spastic children, 16 sessions were given in 4 weeks, using vertical and horizontal circular stimulation. The subjects were rotated at least 60 sec before being stopped to receive the full benefit of the stimulus. These researchers concluded that the treatment enables the vestibuloocular reflex to mature to a level similar to that of normal, ambulatory children of the same age. Not all children, however, are able to tolerate rotary vestibular stimulation. Children with serious cardiovascular disorders and those susceptible to recurrent seizures should not be given this stimulation unless specifically designated by the child's physician.

Walking Progressions

Teaching and assisting with walking are an important part of the physical education program of the child with cerebral palsy. The need for cane, crutches, walker, braces, or other special devices is the physician's decision.

Preliminary strengthening exercises should be included in the program. Preparatory to crutch walking, progressive resistive exercises for the latissimus dorsi, triceps, and biceps are indicated as well as for the quadriceps, hip extensors, and abductors. Crawling and creeping, rolling, sitting, and balance precede ambulation. If the student does not have enough strength in the leg and hip muscles, the spastic child will have negative muscle reactions when the body attempts antigravity actions. Do not encourage the child to try independent walking before initial lower extremity strength is developed.

For students learning correct patterns of gait, parallel bars can be used for balance. Balance is a prerequisite for successful ambulation. The cerebral palsied child is often affected by unwanted movements caused by unsteadiness (the muscles react in anticipation of falling). Harris (1978b, p. 26) describes a technique to aid in standing balance:

> A procedure in which the subjects were continuously thrown off balance, but prevented from falling by a number of surrounding individuals who acted as "catcher" (i.e., who caught them before they tilted very far and returned them to the upright position) had a remarkably relaxing influence on the children. During this procedure, they began to develop compensatory movements of arms and trunk necessary for independent bal-

ance. It would appear that the children tense their muscles so much in fear of falling, while attempting to stand entirely on their own, that normal compensatory movements are impossible and they are certain to fall. (In a sense, they cannot stand because they are afraid to fall.) If they are secure in the knowledge that they will not be allowed to fall past a certain point, however, they can develop independent balancing skills.

Once the student has developed sitting control, standing balance, alternating leg movements, forward progression in the parallel bars, and free standing, she is ready for gait training, either unassisted or with crutches, and with or without orthotic devices (braces).

When children use long leg braces, they can begin ambulation by standing in the parallel bars. The hip locks can be opened to allow flexion and extension of the hip joints. Stand behind the child and grasp the wrists. At the count of *one*, move the child's left arm forward to grasp the bar; at the count of *two*, push the right leg forward with the (instructor's) right knee; at the count of *three*, move the right arm forward; and at the count of *four*, move the left leg.

When able to walk in the parallel bars unassisted, the child should be fitted with crutches and placed against a wall to learn standing balance with crutches. With the crutches held properly under the arms and the hip locks open, the child should be instructed to shift the weight and raise the crutches. This procedure should be followed to move away from the wall. Next, have the child walk unassisted with a four-point crutch gait. When this is accomplished, open one knee lock; later, open the other knee lock so the child can develop a normal reciprocal walking pattern.

For the child who does not need braces, toe dragging is a problem. If no abnormality prevents the child from lifting the toes, place bricks or a ladder on the floor to force the child to lift the foot up and over for forward progression. For toeing in, toeing out, and differences in length of step, ask the child to walk in footprints on the floor (painted rubber or plastic). This game can involve several students and works well with young children.

Orthotic Devices or Braces

Orthotic devices (braces) prevent contractures, restrict unwanted movement, and give support. A passive corrective brace is often used to prevent spastic muscles from reproducing deformity, particularly at night. Night braces prevent deformity from recurring after stretching or surgery. The most common braces are ankle splints for control of plantar flexion deformity (talipes equinus), knee splints to control knee flexion deformity, and adduction splints to control hip adduction contractures. Night braces are not often prescribed for the upper extremities, but a "cock-up" wrist splint is prescribed occasionally to control wrist flexion and improve hand function.

Supporting braces for lower limbs are used to control deformity and to provide walking stability. The basic principles of brace use are simple: If the ankle and foot alone require support, a below-knee brace is used. If the knee also requires support, a long leg brace is used. If hip control is inadequate, a pelvic band is added to the full-length leg brace.

Bracing for children with athetosis is controversial. The primary problem is generalized involuntary movement in the trunk and extremities. Secondary problems are weakness and varying degrees of loss of motor control. Fixed contractures are not usually found. For young children with moderate to severe athetosis, bilateral double-bar long leg braces with spinal bracing may be used initially. With increased control and maturity, trunk bracing is often removed. Surgical correction of deformities is frequently considered to minimize bracing.

Rusk (1971) strongly recommends orthotic devices for children delayed in sitting, standing, and walking. He believes that these youngsters derive great physical and psychological benefit from standing in an erect position by means of braces. Weight-bearing develops better bone formation and stimulates growth, and the vertical position also provides better circulation and prevents postural atrophy. Braces guide the movement of extremities into normal patterns and align skeletal components, minimizing deformities.

Surgical Techniques

If deformity occurs and rehabilitation does not provide positive results, surgery can improve function. Surgical release of contractures, transplant of muscles and tendons, or release of tight joint capsules offers many advantages to children who have severe cerebral palsy. Nerve blocks and nerve crushing also prove beneficial.

Specifically, surgery is done in the following ways: (1) soft tissue surgery to release contractures by dividing tendons, muscles, or joint capsules, (2) neurectomy, the division of selected peripheral nerves to denervate (to deprive the muscle of its nerve supply) spastic muscles, and (3) bone surgery to correct deformity by adding or removing bony parts.

Mital (1979) describes the effects of elbow surgery on 26 children with spastic cerebral palsy. Patients exhibited 30 to 45 degrees or more of flexion contracture. After surgery, the average gain in extension was 40 degrees. All but two patients had considerable functional improvement in reach, two-handed activities, and independent use of limbs.

During the last decade, Dr. Irving Cooper's surgical procedure of implanting electrodes on the brain has captured the imagination. The electrodes are stimulated by an implanted radio frequency receiver activated by a transmitter carried outside the body. (The erroneous phrase "brain pacemaker" is used frequently by the media and hence by the public. This treatment is called **chronic cerebellar stimulation**.) Since its introduction in 1972, more than 700 persons have undergone this implant procedure. Research shows positive improvement in motor control and muscle tone and a reduction of joint stiffness for the majority of patients (Sternfeld 1978).

Programming for Cardiorespiratory Improvement

Students with cerebral palsy are sometimes reluctant to walk because of the strain placed on the cardiorespiratory system. As ambulation becomes more strenuous, walking tends to decrease and time spent in the wheelchair increases, which means that the more severely involved become wheelchair-bound. Such inactivity can cause reduced aerobic capacity and inferior lung function. A vicious cycle is created in which ambulation level and other physical functions decrease continuously.

Rothman (1978) found that when spastic cerebral palsied youngsters did breathing exercises, they increased their breathing capacity significantly beyond the capacity of a control group that did not do exercises. After exercising for 5 to 7 min each day for 8 weeks, the experimental group's vital capacity was increased by 0.46 liters. The average increase was 31 percent over pretest values. Rothman used the Bobath treatment, which inhibits abnormal breathing patterns and teaches the child proper breathing technique. The following eight exercises were used in the study:

1. **Diaphragmatic breathing.**[1] This is considered the most important exercise.
2. **Expiratory exercise using abdominal muscles.** While seated, the child blows a Ping-Pong ball across the table for different distances. This exercise enhances cough production and forces expiration.
3. **Inspiration and expansion of the chest.** In the supine position, the child inhales while elevating arms above the head, and exhales while lowering arms.
4. **Stimulation of inspiration.** A belt is placed around the lower ribs and crossed in front of the seated child. The child exhales as the belt is tightened and inhales as the belt is loosened.
5. **Strengthening anterior abdominal musculature, especially rectus abdominus.** The child is supine and exhales while bringing knees to chest; inhales as knees are lowered.
6. **Strengthening anterior abdominal musculature, especially rectus abdominus.** A sit-up exercise with knees flexed and feet flat on floor.
7. **Strengthening lateral abdominal muscles and internal and external obliques.** Same as exercise 6, but the child moves an elbow toward opposite knee.
8. Same as exercise 1, but a 5-lb weight is now applied to abdominal area to provide resistance to diaphragm movement.

The exercise schedule is in Table 17.2. The first exercise was performed each day of the schedule. All other exercises were performed for 2 weeks. The exercise schedule allows for the increase in exercise difficulty. These exercises were performed 5 to 7 min per day.

Wall pulleys can be used to develop cardiorespiratory efficiency in the cerebral palsied child. The use of pulleys is particularly effective for those who are nonambu-

---

1. Refer to Chapter 19 for an explanation of how to do correct diaphragmatic breathing.

TABLE 17.2

BREATHING EXERCISE SCHEDULE FOR THE CEREBRAL PALSIED CHILD

Week	Exercise	Week	Exercise
1	1, 2, 3	5	1, 6, 7
2	1, 2, 3	6	1, 6, 7
3	1, 4, 5	7	1, 8
4	1, 4, 5	8	1, 8

latory or have great difficulty walking. Physical educators often ask about methods to stimulate cardiorespiratory efficiency if the child cannot run or walk. Even a bicycle ergometer or a stationary bike may not be within the capabilities of a handicapped child. Amundsen and associates (1980) state that wall pulleys and arm exercises are a highly productive way to increase heart rate and systolic blood pressure. The exercise routine is as follows:

- **Wall-pulley pulling** is done while facing the pulleys. Start with the right elbow in full extension and fists pointing at the pulleys. Based on four counts to a cycle, on count one, the right arm is pulled to approximately full elbow flexion (hand to chest); on count two, the right arm is returned to the starting position; counts three and four are identical to one and two, but with the left arm.
- **Wall-pulley pushing** is performed with the student facing away from the pulleys and using the same count. This second exercise is desirable for spastic cerebral palsied children because they need to develop strength in the extensor arm muscles. Repetitions should be counted and recorded. This serves as a measure of existing strength and helps in setting goals for future workouts.

Games and Activities to Improve Eye-Hand Coordination and Object Release

Dropping or Releasing Skills

Milk Bottle Drop

Place the milk bottle at the side of wheelchair. Drop clothespins into the bottle— 5 chances, 5 points for each successful try. Materials: 1 milk bottle, 5 clothespins.

Waterfall

Drop coins into a glass placed in a bucket filled with water—3 chances, 5 points for each coin that falls in the glass. Materials: 1 bucket, 1 large drinking glass, 25 coins (or metal slugs, disks, washers).

Pushing or Sliding Skills

Miniature Shuffleboard

Slide small disks onto chalk target—3 chances. Disks that stop within designated circles receive 5 points. Materials: 6 checkers or disks, target outline.

Bombs Away

Set large box or wastebasket on the floor at far edge of a table. Slide disks along the table so they fall off far edge. Count number of disks falling into the box—10 chances, 2 points for every victory. Materials: 20 checkers or disks, 1 large box (or wastebasket), 1 long table.

Ball Rolling Skills

Cupcake Bounce

Bounce Ping-Pong balls into cupcake tin or egg carton from a distance of 6 ft—3 chances, 5 points per successful bounce. Materials: Cupcake pan or egg carton, 6 Ping-Pong balls.

Volleyball Bounce

Bounce volleyball into wastebasket from a distance of 6 ft—3 chances, 5 points per successful bounce (any type of ball can be used). Materials: 1 wastebasket, 2 volleyballs.

Goal Bounce

Bounce large ball into basket or box positioned 8 ft away—3 chances, 5 points per ball in the basket. Materials: 1 wastebasket or box, 1 large ball.

Underhand Throwing Skills

Coffee Can Toss

Set up 5 coffee cans in irregular order. Throw beanbags or small balls into the cans—5 chances, 5 points for each bag in a can. Materials: 5 coffee cans, 10 beanbags.

Chair Toss

Toss rings at legs of upturned chair—5 tosses, 5 points per ringer. Materials: 1 chair, 10 rope, plastic, or wire rings.

Horse Shoe Pitch

Throw 3 rubber or cardboard horseshoes at stake 6 ft from toss line—5 points per ringer, and 1 point for closest. Materials: 6 cardboard or rubber horseshoes, 1 stake.

Tossing or Flipping Skills

Toss the Discus

Sail paper plate for distance. Measure distance thrown. Materials: Several paper plates.

Paper Plate Flip

Sail paper plates into bushel basket from 15 ft (move closer if necessary)—5 chances, 5 points for each basket. Materials: Several paper plates, 1 bushel basket.

Ring the Bottle

Toss rubber jar rings at bottles set in triangular shape—5 chances, 5 points per successful try. Materials: 6 large pop bottles, 12 jar rings.

Card Flip

Toss playing cards into wastebasket set at an angle facing the child. Count number of cards that fall into the basket. Materials: 1 deck of playing cards, 1 wastebasket.

Bottle Cap Pitch

Fill washtub with water, and float a small pie plate. From 5 ft away, pitch the bottle caps (one at a time) onto the plate—5 chances, 5 points per successful try. Materials: Bottle caps, washtub, small pie plate.

Lifetime Sport Skills and Athletic Competition

When planning game and sport activities, the following general considerations described by Huberman (1976) are helpful. Children who have spastic cerebral palsy relax with repetitive movements, but persons with athetoid cerebral palsy perform better if they relax *before* movement. The spastic children show more accuracy in fine movements, even though their performance is labored and less skillful in larger motor activities. Those with athetoid cerebral palsy display the reverse. For example, the spastic child will throw more accurately, but the athetoid child can throw farther and her walking or running is faster and freer than the labored gait of the spastic person. Children with ataxia pose a special problem and should, initially, move fewer parts of the body at one time (i.e., keep the rest of the body still when moving the limbs).

In 1978, the first national cerebral palsy competitive sports games were held in Detroit, Michigan. These games provided fun and competition for individuals who ordinarily do not have that opportunity. No entry was withheld because of lack of experience, fear of failure, or fear of embarrassment. Anyone 15 years of age or older and diagnosed as having cerebral palsy could compete.

The 1985 National Games of the Cerebral Palsy/*Les Autres* (a French term meaning "The Others") were held at Michigan State University. Approximately 850 athletes, including not only the cerebral palsied (who comprised 90 percent of the athletes) but also *Les Autres*, a group of handicapped individuals who are not able to participate in one of the other national organizations governing sports for physically challenged athletes. Eligible physical conditions included (but were not limited to) multiple sclerosis, muscular dystrophy, osteogenesis imperfecta, Friedreich's ataxia, arthrogryposis, dwarfism, and various forms of cerebral palsy.

The athletes competed in 16 sports, including archery, cycling, golf, horseback riding, table tennis, track and field, soccer, wheelchair soccer, bowling, boccia, basketball, power lifting, swimming, target shooting, cross-country, and slalom.

The classification system used to equalize competition was as follows:

Class I. Quadriplegic, wheelchair-bound. Moves chair with arms slowly.
Class II. Quadriplegic, wheelchair-bound. Moves chair with feet (1) forward, (2) backward.
Class III. Quadriplegic or triplegic, uses wheelchair but not wheelchair-bound. Moves chair with arms.
Class IV. Paraplegic, ambulates with assistive devices. Uses wheelchair for racing.
Class V. (a) Quadriplegic, ambulates with assistive devices. Racing events on feet. (b) Paraplegic, ambulates with assistive devices. Racing events on feet.
Class VI. Quadriplegic, ambulates with assistive devices. Racing events on feet.
Class VII. Hemiplegic, ambulates without assistive devices. Racing events on feet.
Class VIII. (Swimming only)—Hemiplegic with severe involvement in one arm.

The National Association of Sports for Cerebral Palsy (NASCP) currently has approximately 2000 members (Sherrill and Mushett 1984). Many cerebral palsied individuals are capable of serious athletic competition. Too often, they are expected to possess extremely low levels of motor performance, and normal physical education activities are considered, mistakenly, to be beyond their reach. While many cannot compete on an equal basis with nonhandicapped peers, they can perform identical activities, and with modifications can be integrated into the regular program.

Summary

Healy (1984, p. 34) summarizes the problems surrounding this disorder as follows: "Cerebral palsy is the result of a permanent brain injury and is therefore lifelong. While the brain damage itself is nonprogressive, the resultant muscle control problems are not. However, their progress can be halted—or at least postponed—with proper therapy, including frequent elongation (stretching) of stiff muscles and proper positioning. In some cases, surgery is necessary to release tight muscles and tendons, particularly of the ankles and hips, or to treat dislocations of the hips. Other orthopedic disorders, such as scoliosis and contractures of the joints, may become more problematic as the child gets older."

The characteristics of cerebral palsy can range from mild to severe, depending on the child's age and the location and extent of the brain damage. The condition involves general body weakness, paralysis, and an inability to control muscle reflexes. A youngster with mild involvement will appear awkward and clumsy, but is able to move easily and freely in a physical education class. Lack of coordination extends to poor eye-hand coordination. A severely involved youngster is unable to sit unaided, speaks unintelligibly, and requires almost total physical care. Most cerebral palsied children fall somewhere between these two extremes.

Cerebral palsy is a nonprogressive condition that cannot be cured. The condition is often further categorized as spastic, athetoid, or ataxic. The child who is spastic may be very rigid; the legs scissor and the increased activity of deep tendon reflexes often causes muscle contractures. The child with athetosis makes involuntary movements. This child may know where to place balls in a cupcake pan, but arm movements are so uncontrolled and explosive that he frequently misses the pan entirely. The child who has ataxia lacks balance and depth perception. She is unable to stand easily, and when she attempts to take a step forward, as when hitting a ball, she almost falls. Furthermore, her stroke timing is poor.

Children with cerebral palsy also have a high incidence of additional handicaps. Mental retardation is found in at least 60 percent of all cases. Sensory disabilities are common and include hearing, seeing, and perceptual motor impairment. Speech and communication disorders are encountered often.

The initial assessment of motor abilities and capabilities of these children is an integral part of their physical education programming. Basic motor skills and early childhood activities are commonly included in the program. Many youngsters, because they must expend great energy to make their muscles obey their commands, become lethargic and unmotivated when asked to explore the world of movement through physical education. The adapted physical educator must make sure that the child's program does *not* become a mere extension of the therapy program. The child's physical education should include games, skills, and activities that provide enjoyment, challenge, and stimulation. Finally, evaluation of the child's progress is essential for future planning.

References

Amundsen, L. R., Takahasi, M., Carter, C. L., and Nelson, D. H. Response During Wall-Pulley Versus Bicycle Ergometer Work. *Physical Therapy* 60(2):173–178, 1980.

Ayres, J. *Sensory Integration and Learning Disorders*. Los Angeles: Western Psychological Services, 1975.

Banham, K. M. Measuring Functional Motor Rehabilitation of Cerebral Palsied Infants and Young Children. *Rehabilitation Literature* 39(4):111–116, 1978.

Bigge, J. L., and O'Donnell, P. A. *Teaching Individuals With Physical and Multiple Disabilities*. Columbus, Ohio: Charles E. Merrill, 1976.

Bobath, K. The Neuropathology of Cerebral Palsy and Its Importance in Treatment and Diagnosis. *Cerebral Palsy Bulletin* 8:13–33, 1959.

———. *The Motor Deficit in Patients With Cerebral Palsy*. London: Clinics in Developmental Medicine, 1966.

Bobath, K., and Bobath, B. The Neuro-Developmental Treatment of Cerebral Palsy. *Physical Therapy* 47:1039–1041, 1967.

Bullock, M. L., and Watter, P. A Study of Effectiveness of Physiotherapy in the Management of Young Children with Minimal Cerebral Dysfunction. *Physical Therapy* 60(1):105, 1980.

Campbell, S. K., and Wilhelm, I. J. Development from Birth to 3 Years of Age of 15 Children at High Risk for Central Nervous System Dysfunction. *Physical Therapy* 65(4):463–469, April 1985.

Carrington, E. G. A Seat Position for a Cerebral-Palsied Child. *American Journal of Occupational Therapy* 32(3):179–181, 1979.

Chee, F. K. W., Kreutzberg, J. R., and Clark, D. L. Semicircular Canal Stimulation in Cerebral Palsied Children. *Physical Therapy* 58(9):1071–1075, 1978.

Cherry, D. B. Review of Physical Therapy Alternatives for Reducing Muscle Contracture. *Physical Therapy* 60(7): 877–881, July 1980.

Clark, D. L., Kreutzberg, J. R., and Chee, F. K. W. Vestibular Stimulation Influence on Motor Development in Infants. *Science* 196(4295):1228–1229, 1977.

Connor, F. P., and Baken, J. W. Designing Materials for Physically Handicapped Learners. In *Language Materials and Curriculum Management for the Handicapped Learner*, edited by F. B. Withrow and C. J. Nygren. Columbus, Ohio: Charles E. Merrill, 1976.

Cratty, B. J. *Adapted Physical Education for Handicapped Children and Youth*. Denver: Love Publishing, 1980.

Guyton, A. C. *Physiology of the Human Body*, 5th ed. Philadelphia: W. B. Saunders, 1979.

Harris, F. A. Muscle Stretch Receptor Hypersensitization in Spasticity. *American Journal of Physical Medicine* 57(1):16–28, 1978a.

———. Correction of Muscle Balance in Spasticity. *American Journal of Physical Medicine* 57(3):123–138, 1978b.

Healy, A. Cerebral Palsy. In *Medical Aspects of Developmental Disabilities in Children Birth to Three*, rev. 1st ed., edited by M. A. Blackman. Rockville, Md.: An Aspen Publication, 1984.

Horgan, J. S. Reaction Time and Movement Time of Children With Cerebral Palsy. *American Journal of Physical Medicine* 59(1):22–29, 1980.

Hoskins, T. A., and Squires, J. E. Developmental Assessment: A Test for Gross Motor and Reflex Development. *Physical Therapy* 53(2):117–125, 1973.

Huberman, G. Organized Sports Activities With Cerebral Palsied Adolescents. *Rehabilitation Literature* 37(4):103, 1976.

Information and Research Utilization Center (IRUC) in Physical Education and Recreation for the Handicapped. *Physical Education and Recreation for Impaired, Disabled, and Handicapped Individuals—Past, Present, and Future.* Reston, Va.: AAHPERD, 1975.

————. *Physical Education and Recreation for Cerebral Palsied Individuals.* Reston, Va.: AAHPERD, 1976.

Ivy, A., and Roblyer, D. D. Vestibular Stimulator for Handicapped Clients. *Physical Therapy* 60(3):309–310, 1980.

Johnston, R. B., and Magrab, P. R. *Developmental Disorders Assessment, Treatment, Education.* Baltimore, Md.: University Park Press, 1976.

Kempe, H. In *Report of the Medical Director,* L. Sternfeld to the Members of the Corporation. Washington, D.C.: Annual Conference, United Cerebral Palsy Association, 22 April 1977.

Kieran, S. S., Connor, F. P., von Hippel, C. S., and Jones, S. H. *Mainstreaming Preschoolers: Children With Orthopedic Handicaps.* Belmont, Mass.: CRC Education and Human Development, 1981.

Laskas, C. A., Mullen, S. L., Nelson, D. L., and Willson-Broyles, M. Enhancement of Two Motor Functions of the Lower Extremity in a Child With Spastic Quadriplegia. *Physical Therapy* 65(1):11–16, January 1985.

Love, H. D., and Walthall, J. E. *A Handbook of Medical, Educational, and Psychological Information for Teachers of Physically Handicapped Children.* Springfield, Ill.: Charles C Thomas, 1977.

Mital, M. A. Lengthening of the Elbow Flexors in Cerebral Palsy. *Journal of Bone and Joint Surgery* 61(4):515–522, 1979.

National Information Center for Handicapped Children and Youth. *Cerebral Palsy.* Washington, D.C.: The Center, 1982.

Rothman, J. G. Effects of Respiratory Exercises on the Vital Capacity and Forced Expiratory Volume in Children With Cerebral Palsy. *Physical Therapy* 58(4):421–425, 1978.

Rusk, H. A. *Rehabilitation Medicine,* 3rd ed. St. Louis: C. V. Mosby, 1971.

Sage, G. H. *Motor Learning and Control—A Neurological Approach.* Dubuque, Iowa: Wm. C. Brown, 1984.

Sherrill, C., and Mushett, C. A. Fourth National Cerebral Palsy Games: Sports by Ability . . . Not Disability. *Palaestra* 1(1):24–27, Fall 1984.

Sternfeld, L. *Report of the Medical Director,* L. Sternfeld, to the Members of the Corporation. Washington, D.C.: Annual Conference, United Cerebral Palsy Association, 22 April 1977.

————. *Report of the Medical Director.* New York: United Cerebral Palsy Research and Educational Foundation, 7 April 1978.

Sternfeld, L., and Berenberg, W. *Twenty-Five Years of Cerebral Palsy Research.* Report at the Board of Directors' Meeting of the United Cerebral Palsy Research and Educational Foundation, 2 June 1981.

United Cerebral Palsy Association. *Doctor, Only Through Early Diagnosis Can You Control Cerebral Palsy.* New York: The Association, n.d.

United Cerebral Palsy Research and Educational Foundation Program. New York: United Cerebral Palsy Association, 1975.

Washburn, K. B. *Physical Medicine and Rehabilitation—A Practitioner's Guide.* Flushing, N.Y.: Medical Examination Publishing, 1976.

Williams, H. G., Fisher, J. M., and Tritschler, K. A. A Descriptive Analysis of Static Postural Control in 4, 6, and 8 Year Old Normal and Motorically Awkward Children. *American Journal of Physical Medicine* 62:12–26, 1983.

Williams, H. G., McClenaghan, B., and Ward, D. S. Duration of Muscle Activity During Standing in Normally and Slowly Developing Children. *American Journal of Physical Medicine* 64(4):171–189, 1985.

Winnick, J. P., and Short, F. X. *Physical Fitness Testing of the Disabled—Project UNIQUE.* Champaign, Ill.: Human Kinetics Publishers, 1985.

Zemke, R. Application of an ATNR Rating Scale to Normal Preschool Children. *The American Journal of Occupational Therapy* 39(3):178–180, March 1985.

CHAPTER 18

The Hearing Impaired

An interview with Jimmy, age 12, diagnosis: mild hearing loss (43 dB).

Question: Have you ever had problems when playing sports?
Response: I went into a game once and the kid told me where to play. I did not hear him and the coach yelled at me.
Question: If you cannot hear the directions, do you tell the teacher you cannot hear?
Response: No. I do not want to be embarrassed.
Question: Has it happened a lot?
Response: Yes. The other day we were playing some games and all the kids had numbers. We had to go out and get the ball and see who could make the first shot. I did not understand. I did not hear the directions so I just had to watch and see how to play. I wasn't very happy.

Hearing impaired individuals must learn to cope—to develop their social, emotional, and physical personalities—without normal hearing. Success usually requires the ability to communicate effectively. There are few deaf students on college campuses or participating in classroom learning situations. Hearing loss makes the educational hurdle difficult. The physical educator has a challenging opportunity to help those with hearing impairment to develop a more normal way of life.

Many recreational activities readily available to the nonhandicapped are often missed by individuals with hearing impairment. For example, the hearing impaired cannot totally enjoy television, radio, records, movies, or concerts.

Through physical education, the potential arises for enjoyment through movement: from grace and beauty (dance) to intense physical exertion (athletic competition), from recreational individualism (jogging) to recreational adult competition (bowling or golf). Moving and doing replace sitting and listening. Physical education must provide the hearing impaired with opportunities to learn and enjoy movement skills to establish a solid foundation for future leisure time activities, sports, and individual pursuits.

Because the majority of hearing impaired children possess at least average motor ability, they are able to participate successfully in regular physical education classes. Deaf individuals have excelled in statewide and national gymnastics, dance, and wrestling competitions in which they competed with the nonhandicapped.

Motor deficiencies of the hearing impaired child generally stem from not having played with other children and not having participated in early childhood activities. Overprotective parents, while eager to seek educational (intellectual) endeavors for their children, sometimes overlook the importance of organized movement activities. Not being able to run, jump, or play as well as the children in the nonhandicapped peer group is further compounded if the child is not offered (or is denied because of handicap) a comprehensive developmental physical education program. Motor deficiencies become strikingly evident as the child grows. The hearing impaired child must have stimulating movement experiences as soon as the hearing deficiency is diagnosed. Delayed intervention too often ensures that the child's motor abilities will be below the national norms for nonhandicapped children.

How Many?

The number of hearing impaired children (ages 5–17) in the United States is estimated to be between 76,000 and 90,000 students. Figures 18.1 and 18.2 identify the distribution by sex and ethnic group within the United States (Gallaudet Research Institute 1985).

The National Information Center on Deafness (1984) states that one out of every eight hearing impaired students will be classified as **deaf** (90 dB loss).

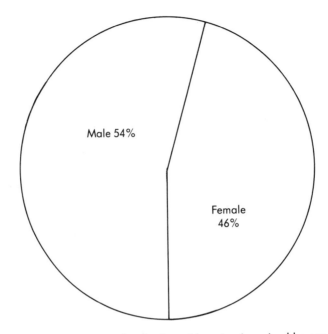

FIGURE 18.1. U.S. distribution of hearing impaired by sex.

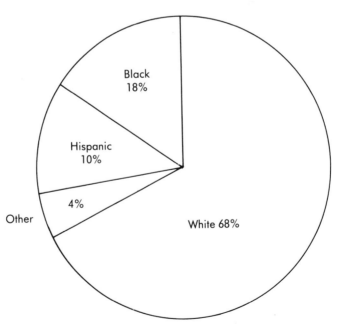

FIGURE 18.2. U.S. distribution of hearing impaired by ethnic group.

Hearing Impaired Defined

The term **hearing impairment** identifies individuals with measurable hearing loss resulting from defects in the hearing apparatus or process. Four descriptive variables are used to identify specific subgroups. They are: (1) degree of hearing impairment, (2) age of onset of hearing impairment, (3) type of hearing impairment, and (4) etiology of hearing impairment.

Distinction between levels of hearing loss is measured with an audiometer, an instrument that gauges the loudness of sound in units called decibels (dB).

Individuals who have a **moderate hearing loss** (less than 70 dB) are often considered "hard of hearing," whereas those who have a **profound loss** (greater than 90 dB) are considered deaf. The category **severe loss** (71 to 89 dB) is a transition category between hard of hearing and deaf. Table 18.1 lists classifications and educational implications of hearing loss.

TABLE 18.1

Classifications and Educational Implications of Hearing Loss

Classification	Decibels (ISO)[a]	Educational Implications
Normal	−10 to 26	
Slight	27 to 40	Student needs favorable seating and lighting; may have difficulty hearing faint or distant speech; will not usually experience difficulty in school situations.
Mild	41 to 55	Needs hearing aid in some cases; favorable seating and possible special class placement, especially for primary children; understands conversational speech at distance of 3–5 ft; may miss as much as 50% of class discussions.
Moderate	56 to 70	Needs hearing aid by evaluation and auditory training; lip reading instruction; conversation must be loud to be understood; will have increasing difficulty with school situations requiring participation in group discussions.
Severe	71 to 89	Needs full-time special program for deaf children with emphasis on all language skills, concept development, lip reading, and speech; individual hearing aid by evaluation; may hear loud voices about 1 ft from ear.
Profound	90+	Needs full-time special education program for deaf children, with emphasis on all language skills, concept development, lip reading, and speech; continuous appraisal of needs in regard to oral and manual communication; relies on vision rather than hearing as primary avenue for communication; speech and language are likely to deteriorate.

SOURCE: Modified from Bernero, R. J., and Bothwell, H. *Relationship of Hearing Impairment to Educational Needs.* Illinois Department of Public Health and the Office of the Superintendent of Public Instruction, 1966.

[a]ISO = International Standards Organization.

Quigley and Kretschmer (1982) advise caution when determining the differences between deaf and hard of hearing. They state:

> We stress again the need for clearly stated definitions or at least descriptions of deaf individuals. . . . It is inappropriate to generalize findings obtained with what we would term hard-of-hearing individuals (less than 90 dB) to deaf individuals (greater than 90 dB). It should be recognized that 90 dB is a somewhat arbitrary line. Other authors use varying points on the decibel scale to define "deaf." . . . The important point is that the sensorineural impairment is of sufficient severity that the individual, even with amplification, must rely on vision as the primary channel for receptive communication. We contend that any impairment of less than 90 dB is not sufficient severity to produce such an effect and, therefore, should not be classified as deaf (p. 104).

Figure 18.3 shows the distribution of hearing impaired students in the United States by degree of hearing loss (Gallaudet Research Institute 1985).

Special educators also distinguish between deafness and less severe levels of hearing loss by how the child learns language. Deaf children who have little or no hearing ability during the first 3 years of life will not have learned language in the normal way; these children are classified as educationally deaf (prelingually deaf). Children who become hearing impaired *after* 3 years of life will, in most cases, have learned language in the usual way. These youngsters are considered to be advanced in their ability to understand and articulate new language experiences. The Gallaudet Research Institute (1985) estimates that 94% of all hearing losses occur before age 3.

The physical educator should obtain school medical records (often available through the school nurse) to develop a complete picture of the hearing impaired child (e.g., cause of deafness, age at which deafness occurred, use of hearing aid, degree of hearing loss, balance difficulties, eye-hand coordination problems). When the degree of hearing loss is recorded in a student's medical file and only one score is noted, that score is for the better ear.

In a 1981 research project, Sarff, Ray, and Bagwell found that 32 percent of their fourth, fifth, and sixth grade subjects had minimal hearing loss (10 to 40 dB loss). Seventy-five percent of the sixth grade students who had a minimal hearing loss were *also* deficient in one or more of the basic academic skill areas of reading, language arts, or mathematics. This 3-year longitudinal study showed that students improved their achievement significantly after amplification of the teacher's voice. This research highlights the importance that hearing plays in learning. Even minimal hearing loss must be identified early if teachers are to meet the educational needs of the child.

Anatomy and Physiology of the Ear

Figure 18.4 shows a diagram of the ear. Hearing involves two basic components: (1) the reception and conduction of sound waves, and (2) the nerve function by which impulses are set up and transmitted to the brain.

Individuals hear in three ways. First, the auricle (fleshy, outside ear) directs sound

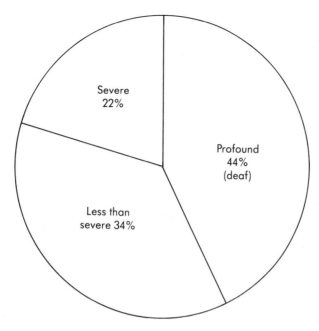

FIGURE 18.3.   U.S. distribution of hearing impaired students by degree of hearing loss.

waves through the ear canal. Sound waves vibrate the eardrum, which vibrates across three small bones of the middle ear. The stapes, the innermost of the three small bones, moves in and out of the oval window, stimulating the fluid in the cochlea. This, in turn, stimulates nerves that lead to the brain. A second method of hearing involves the sound waves passing through the eardrum (or a hole in the eardrum) to a secondary eardrum covering the oval window. This covering vibrates fluid in the cochlea, which in turn stimulates nerves leading to the brain. A third way to hear occurs when the bones of the skull that surround the ear carry sound waves directly to the inner ear, striking the cochlea. This method is often associated with use of a hearing aid, which is placed behind the outer ear and is grounded directly on the mastoid bone. The cochlea, where all sound waves must ultimately go, contains over 25,000 hairlike sensory receptors. These generate nerve impulses to the brain.

3 ways to hear

Etiology of Hearing Impairment

heredity – 50% of cases.

Among the causes of hearing impairment are <u>heredity</u>, accident, and illness. An unborn child can inherit hearing loss from the parents. In about 50 percent of all cases

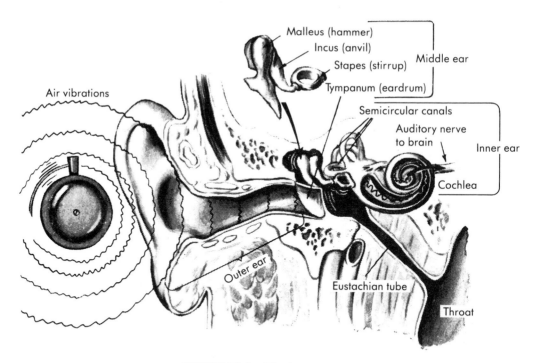

FIGURE 18.4.   The human ear.

of deafness, genetic factors are a probable cause (National Information Center on Deafness 1984). Accidents, illness, and ototoxic drugs are responsible for hearing loss in the remaining cases. Rubella or other viral infections contracted by the pregnant mother may cause destruction of parts of the hearing apparatus of the fetus. Complications during the birth process, such as anoxia, may also affect hearing. Illness or infection may cause permanent deafness in young children. For example, mumps is one of the leading causes of unilateral sensorineural deafness in children and young adults. Loss of vestibular reactions may accompany the hearing loss (Marcy 1980). Central hearing loss can occur from congenital brain abnormalities, tumors, or lesions of the central nervous system.

New medical and surgical techniques to correct conductive hearing loss have greatly improved the prognosis within the last few years, but medical correction of sensorineural hearing loss is still in the experimental stages. Current research involving the cochlear implant (which provides electrical stimulation to the inner ear) may provide a way to medically correct profound sensorineural hearing loss. Schein (1984, p. 234) states: "The number of cochlear implants performed is increasing dramatically. . . . Approximately 1,000 cases are known worldwide, with the United States having about half of the reported number."

Hearing Defects

If any part of the ear structure fails to function normally, partial or total deafness results. Deafness may be caused by either conduction or nerve failure. Conductive deafness is caused temporarily by a simple swelling due to infection in the external auditory canal. Nearly all forms of conductive deafness can be corrected by use of an electronic hearing aid. Deafness due to nerve deterioration is more serious. Sound is conducted to the inner ear, but an abnormality there, in the auditory nerve, or in the brain, prevents the proper electrical signal from being generated, transmitted, or received.

Sensorineural deafness results from damage to the microscopic sensory hair cells of the inner ear or to the nerves. This type of hearing loss often affects certain frequencies more than others. Even with amplification to increase sound level, the person still perceives distorted sound. This distortion, which accompanies some forms of sensorineural deafness, can be so severe that successful use of a hearing aid is impossible.

Central deafness is attributed to damage or impairment to the nerves of the central nervous system.

Mixed hearing losses are those in which impairment occurs both in the outer or middle and inner ear. Table 18.2 lists definitions, causes, and treatment of various types of hearing impairment.

Acoustical Trauma

In modern society, we are assaulted by extremely high levels of noise pollution. Intense exposure to high decibel noise over an extended period of time can cause serious hearing impairment. Loud rock music, home power tools, and industrial noise are all potential causes of acoustic trauma (Figure 18.5). While industrial noise used to cause most of acquired hearing loss (not attributed to aging), ear specialists say that recreational noise—from rock concerts to auto racing—has become the major threat to hearing today.

Acquired hearing loss is usually gradual, subtle, and cumulative. Extremely high levels of sound, as experienced when listening to amplified rock music (110 to 130 dB), is known to damage the delicate hearing mechanism of the ear. Depending on length and intensity of exposure, damage can be temporary or permanent. When damage is permanent, the sensory hair cells in the inner ear lose their ability to relay sound. Dr. Hawley Jackson (1985, p. 1), a Long Beach, California, otologist states: "Kids often say that they have ringing in their ears for days after going to a rock concert. Ringing is an indication of trauma or injury to your inner ear. Ringing is your body telling you that you have damaged your hearing." Ear specialists warn that one risks hearing loss if exposed to 95 to 100 dB for 2 hours or more.

TABLE 18.2

Definitions, Causes and Treatment of Hearing Impairments

	Type		
	Conductive	*Sensorineural*	*Central*
Definition	Those conditions arising from some mechanical blockage of sound transmission in the outer or middle ear (outside central nervous system).	Conditions arising from damage to neural pathways between inner ear and brain: 1. Congenital—nerve injured or destroyed before or during birth. 2. Acquired or adventitious—hearing loss occurring after birth.	Any interference with sound transmission from brain stem to and including auditory cortex.
Cause	Physical obstruction (e.g., impacted wax or middle ear infection) to conduction of sound waves to inner ear. Major cause of conductive hearing loss related to middle ear pathology is *otitis media*, inflammation or infection of the middle ear.	1. Genetic factors, Rh blood factor, premature birth, and diseases such as German measles, mumps, or influenza (when contracted by mother during early pregnancy). 2. Complications of childhood diseases such as spinal meningitis, encephalitis, scarlet fever, or influenza, or accident that damages nervous system so hearing ability is affected.	Diseases of the brain that affect auditory pathway (e.g., cerebral tumor or abscess, arteriosclerosis, cerebral hemorrhage, and multiple sclerosis).
Treatment and Prognosis	Hearing may be seriously impaired, but deafness is never total. Hearing aids improve hearing loss that results from conduction difficulties.	Usually more serious than conductive loss and less likely to be improved by medical treatment. Proper treatment usually involves educational as well as medical intervention.	Patient can "hear" but does not understand what he hears. Generally treated as a form of receptive language disorder (i.e., aphasia).

SOURCE: Adapted from AAHPERD 1976, p. 3.

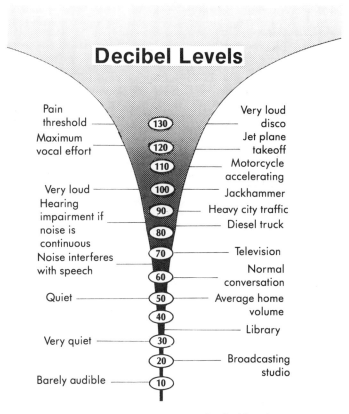

Decibel Levels

Pain threshold	(130)	Very loud disco
Maximum vocal effort	(120)	Jet plane takeoff
	(110)	Motorcycle accelerating
Very loud	(100)	Jackhammer
Hearing impairment if noise is continuous	(90)	Heavy city traffic
	(80)	Diesel truck
Noise interferes with speech	(70)	Television
	(60)	Normal conversation
Quiet	(50)	Average home volume
	(40)	
		Library
Very quiet	(30)	
	(20)	Broadcasting studio
Barely audible	(10)	

FIGURE 18.5. Comparative decibel levels.

The Federal Occupational Safety and Health Administration has set standards to determine when damage could occur. Sustained sound over 85 dB, the equivalent of heavy street traffic, is enough to impair hearing gradually. An average person can probably withstand a noise level of 85 dB for 7 to 8 hours per day without damage. A few more decibels, however, can make a significant difference. If the noise level increases to 90 dB, a 3 hour per day exposure can be damaging.

Physical Education: Adapted or Regular?

Most hearing impaired children can perform successfully in the regular, unrestricted physical education class. Physiologically, they usually possess adequate physical development. They should not be placed in an adapted physical education setting without reliable and valid assessment. Accurate testing of general motor ability should be completed before the individual is programmed for and placed.

Vance (1968) found that although girls with normal hearing scored higher than deaf girls on seven of nine selected motor tests, only two of the tests were significant at the 0.05 level. He questions whether inferior motor ability is inherent in those who are congenitally deaf. Inferior ability may result instead from limited variety of experiences, from differences in child-rearing practices, or from inadequate training of deaf children at an early age. In the past, hearing impaired children were not offered a comprehensive physical education or movement oriented program supervised by a qualified physical educator. Marked differences may have developed in the hearing impaired population simply from lack of participation and *not* because of poor innate motor ability.

Gallaudet College in Washington, D.C., is an institution of higher learning for the deaf. The college gave all incoming freshmen a national physical fitness test. After 1 year of physical education, the students were retested and surpassed the national averages for hearing students (Wisher 1969). Arnheim and Sinclair (1979, p. 5) believe that the hearing impaired child can overcome significant movement difficulties. They state, "the most important sense organs to the acquisition of skilled movement are organs of vision, touch, and kinesthesis. . . . Hearing, or audition, is important but not as important as the aforementioned three sense organs." A concentrated perceptual-motor program that stresses vision and kinesthesis will enable hearing impaired children to participate successfully in physical activities with their nonhandicapped peers (Figure 18.6).

FIGURE 18.6. Activities that stress development of vision and kinesthesis must be provided. (Photograph courtesy of Photo Associates Limited)

Balance and the Hearing Impaired

Balance not Always. Affected

Too often we assume that all hearing impaired persons possess significant balance deficiencies. Indeed, destruction or impairment of the inner ear can leave the child with a distinct balance problem, but not all hearing impairments stem from inner ear difficulties (Wisher 1974). Unless the semicircular canals, which contain the corti and the endolymph organs, are damaged, balance is not necessarily affected (Figure 18.7) (Pennella 1979).

Balance is affected by vision, muscle proprioceptors, and the vestibular mechanism of the inner ear. The importance of vision in maintaining balance is emphasized by Guyton (1971, p. 470): "After complete destruction of the vestibular apparatuses, and even loss of most proprioceptive information from the body, a person can still use his visual mechanisms effectively for maintaining equilibrium."

Lindsey and O'Neal (1976) compared the static balance of 8-year-old deaf and normal hearing children and found that vision played an important role in balance. Elimination of visual input on static balance tasks increased task difficulty for both deaf and normal hearing persons, but the deaf were more seriously impaired. Grimsley (1972) also identifies vision as a major contributor to balance performance. Using a dynabalometer, he compared the balance of normal hearing, congenitally deaf, and

FIGURE 18.7. Hearing impairment but no balance problems. (Photograph courtesy of Photo Associates Limited)

acquired deaf children, and concluded that exclusion of visual input impairs balance performance. Grimsley's study also determined that deaf children can learn a balance skill as well as their peers who have normal hearing.

Balance, or the ability to maintain equilibrium in the presence of disrupting conditions (Cratty 1979), is a basic yet complex skill composed of several performance units. Deficiency in balance ability has a negative influence on more complex skills such as running, hopping, and jumping, as well as the highly coordinated activities of throwing and catching (Figure 18.8).

Two distinct measures of balance characterize general motor ability: one is **static balance** (e.g., standing in place on one foot), and the other is **dynamic balance** (e.g., walking on a balance beam). When one compares trends observed in tests of static and dynamic balance, and when one consults correlative or factorial studies comparing these two measures, one finds that the two types of balance are indeed independent and distinctly different (Cratty 1979).

In a discussion of how damage to the vestibular mechanism affects dynamic balance in activities that involve running agility, Guyton (1979, p. 311) makes the following statement:

FIGURE 18.8.   Kinesthesis, including balance, is necessary to perform successfully the act of throwing. (Photograph courtesy of Gary Geiger and the Illinois Special Olympics)

... a person can still maintain his equilibrium provided he moves slowly. This is accomplished mainly by means of proprioceptor information from the limbs and surfaces of the body and visual information from the eyes. . . . If he begins to fall forward, the pressure on the anterior parts of his feet increases, stimulating the pressure receptors. This information transmitted to his brain helps to correct the imbalance. At the same time, his eyes also detect the lack of equilibrium, and this information too helps to correct the situation. Unfortunately, the visual and proprioceptor systems for maintaining equilibrium are not organized for rapid action, which explains why a person without his vestibular apparatuses must move slowly.

This problem becomes significant when a youngster attempts to change directions, as when playing a game of tag or touch football. Among children who have been diagnosed as having temporary or permanent vestibular damage, the physical education teacher should be aware that activities involving rapid change of direction may be difficult for that student. This problem should not be interpreted as one about which the teacher can do nothing. The instructor must now provide extensive skills work and drills to "overload" the child's proprioceptor and visual systems, thus attempting to compensate for vestibular weaknesses. Figure 18.9 shows the vestibular mechanism of the semicircular canals in the inner ear.

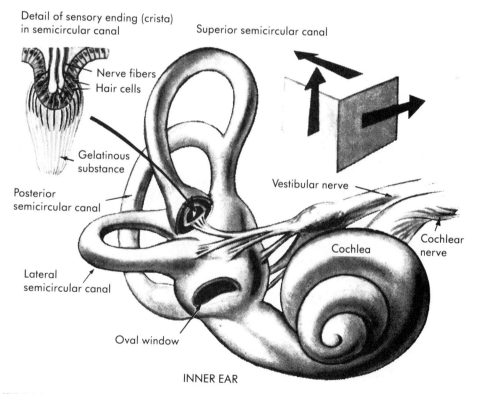

FIGURE 18.9. Semicircular canal (vestibular mechanism) in the inner ear. Cube indicates that regardless of direction of head movement, information will be transmitted to the brain.

An important conclusion resulted from research conducted by Clark, Kreutzberg, and Chee (1977) when they attempted to increase semicircular and vestibular input. Preambulatory nonhandicapped infants were exposed to sessions of mild semicircular canal stimulation on 2 days per week for 4 weeks. The vestibular stimulation effected a significant improvement in gross motor skills. The magnitude of the semicircular canal treatment provided in the study was similar to that produced by cessation of prolonged whirling enjoyed by older children on small manually propelled merry-go-rounds and in games such as ring-around-a-rosy. The researchers concluded, based on study results, that through a planned vestibular stimulation program, young and old children alike may receive positive benefits to aid in remediation of gross motor deficits, including static and dynamic balance.

All hearing impaired children who have obvious balance problems must be tested to determine their static and dynamic levels of balance ability.

Tests of Balance

Static Balance

Several tests for static balance are valid and reliable. Arnheim and Sinclair (1979) evaluated 1563 boys and girls between the ages of 4 and 12 by using a modified version of the "stork stand" and a homemade balance board. Test description and norms are shown in Figure 18.10 and Table 18.3, respectively.

Dynamic Balance

Past research is vague about which dynamic balance testing scales are best. The purpose of initial general motor screening is, however, to identify individuals with distinct motor disabilities. A general forward walking balance beam test will identify those individuals with dynamic balance problems. Figure 18.11 describes a dynamic balance test that is reliable and appropriate for initial screening. (See also Table 18.4.)

Activities for Improvement of Static and Dynamic Balance

To remedy major balance problems, additional practice sessions should be scheduled for the physical education class. Individual sessions of 5 to 20 min should be held before or after school, at recess, during the lunch hour, or during study hall. These sessions would consist of exercises planned by both teacher and student. Encourage

Flat foot,
hands on hips

PURPOSE: To test static balance with eyes open and with eyes closed.

MATERIALS: Blindfold, stopwatch, 2 by 4 in. balance board with actual width of 1.75 in.

PROCEDURE: Tester demonstrates on board, explaining that first the preferred foot and then the other foot will be tested. While child is balancing (with shoes on), hands must be kept on hips with nonsupporting foot hooked behind knee of support leg. Child is first given one trial for each foot on the board with eyes open, then the test is repeated with eyes closed or blindfolded.

TIME LIMIT: Ten sec per trial, for each of four trials.

SCORING: Record total number of seconds child maintains balanced position with eyes open both for right foot and left foot, then repeat with eyes closed. Record cumulative score for the right and left foot and their total by adding the scores obtained for both eyes open and eyes closed.

FIGURE 18.10. Stork stand test. (Adapted from Arnheim and Sinclair 1979, p. 123. Drawing from Moran and Kalakian 1977, p. 55.)

TABLE 18.3
Static Balance[a]

	Male Percentiles						Female Percentiles				
10	30	50	70	90	Age		10	30	50	70	90
9	14	17	19	20	4		8	12	16	19	21
9	17	19	22	23	5		10	15	17	20	24
12	19	21	24	27	6		10	17	21	23	25
11	20	22	26	29	7		12	18	21	24	26
11	20	23	27	30	8		12	20	24	27	28
11	18	21	26	31	9		13	18	22	26	33
10	19	24	25	31	10		10	18	23	26	31
12	20	22	27	29	11		12	18	21	25	29
11	17	21	26	29	12		12	16	21	24	28

SOURCE: Adapted from Arnheim and Sinclair, 1979.

[a]It should be noted that any child scoring in the 30th percentile or lower (as indicated in the shaded area above) is considered to possess a major balance disability. Adapted programming involving static balance activities is therefore necessary.

PURPOSE: To test dynamic balance while moving forward with eyes open.

MATERIALS: A regular balance beam, 4 in. wide and a minimum of 6 ft long. The beam should be placed in secure and stable position either directly on the floor or at a maximum height of no more than 10 in.

PROCEDURE: Child walks forward on balance beam heel-to-toe, with hands on hips. Child must make six consecutive steps correctly to achieve a maximum score. Have child stand at one end of beam. Say: "Place your feet on the beam like this (demonstrate). Place your hands on your hips. When you walk down the beam, hit the toe of your back foot with the heel of your front foot (demonstrate). Walk to the end of the beam. Remember, keep your feet on the beam and your hands on your hips as you walk. Ready, begin." Remind child as needed to walk heel-to-toe and to keep hands on hips.

SCORING: Trials: Administer second trial only if child does not achieve a maximum score on first trial. Stand at one side of beam and count child's steps, keeping track of both correct and incorrect steps. A step is incorrect if child (1) does not touch heel of front foot to toe of back foot, (2) moves back foot forward to touch heel of front foot. After six steps have been taken, tell child to stop. If child places one or both feet completely off beam before taking six steps, stop trial and record number of steps taken on beam. Record number of correct and incorrect steps. Use "1" for correct steps and "0" for incorrect steps. For example, 1-1-0-1-1-0 equals a score of 4.

FIGURE 18.11. Walking forward heel-to-toe on balance beam. (Adapted from Bruininks 1978, pp. 57–58.)

TABLE 18.4
Dynamic Balance (Walking Forward Heel to Toe on Four-Inch Balance Beam)[a]

Male	Age	Female
1[b]	4	1
1	5	1
2	6	2
2	7	3
2	8	3
2	9	3
3	10	3
4	11	4
4	12	4

[a]Any child scoring less than the minimal levels listed above is considered to possess a major dynamic balance disability. Adapted programming involving dynamic balance activities is therefore necessary.

[b]Number of correct steps taken.

the parents' cooperation to improve skills by practicing at home. Table 18.5 lists activities for home and classroom.

Static and dynamic balance can be practiced by using positions and movements such as kneeling, sitting, standing, walking, galloping, hopping, skipping, leaping, running, and jumping. Balance is an important aspect of kinesthesis, the sense of the body's position in space. Balance is therefore a critical skill to improve.

Static or Stationary Balance Skills

Students should learn to control their bodies in stationary positions. Many balance activities that are comparatively easy to perform with the eyes open become difficult to do with the eyes closed. The balance skill should be practiced with the eyes closed since this requires exclusive use of body proprioceptors and vestibular mechanisms. Static balance (Figure 18.12) can be taught individually or with full class participation.

Dynamic or Moving Balance Skills

The simple skills of hopping, leaping, jumping, and running require balance proficiency, particularly when chasing, stopping, starting, and dodging. The child with low proficiency in dynamic balance will have difficulty competing successfully unless activities to improve balance deficiencies are planned. The program should stress take-off from one or both feet and landing in a gentle, controlled manner. Learners should practice jumping for distance and height. Their bodies must be under control when airborne and when landing. Explosive power for the jump comes from the upper and lower leg muscles, with a strong thrust from the foot and ankle. Some students will be deficient in muscular leg power, so leg strengthening exercises should be included for these students.

During a controlled landing, executed with good balance, the weight is absorbed gradually by the ankle, knee, and hip joints, which bend as toes and feet touch the ground. The arms and shoulders also absorb weight and provide for smooth integration of the total skill. Figures 18.13 and 18.14 show a progression of dynamic balance skills.

Teaching Suggestions

1. Be sure students are aware that a hearing impaired child may need assistance.
2. Teacher and students should learn the child's name sign.
3. Be sure that directions and explanations are clearly understood by the student. Manual signs and demonstrations reinforce directions.

TABLE 18.5

Adapted Activities for Home and Classroom

Balance
1. Children assume hand and knee position on floor.
    a. Each child raises one hand in air; alternate hands.
    b. Each child raises one leg in air; alternate.
    c. Each child raises right arm and right leg; alternate sides.
2. Children balance on tiptoes for count of ten.
3. Children stand on one foot for count of five; alternate feet.
4. Rocking horse—children stand with hands on hips and feet astride; lean forward keeping knees stiff and lifting heels from floor; rock backward lifting toes from floor.
5. Children walk forward and backward on knees.
6. Children jump on right foot with eyes closed; alternate feet.
7. Children stand on both feet with eyes closed, jump and turn while in air (use ¼ and ½ turns only).
8. Use suggested balance beam activities described in Figure 18.11.

Basic Body Movements
1. Children practice walking; check that arms and legs alternate and swing freely; music may be added.
    a. Walk fast.
    b. Walk slow.
2. Children walk on tiptoes with arms over head.
3. Children walk backward bringing knees up high.
4. Children walk sideways using shuffle step (slide).
5. Children walk sideways using crossover step.
6. Children walk backward on tiptoes with arms over head.
7. Children walk in squatting position.
8. Children alternate between walking "small" and walking "tall."
9. Children place big toes together and walk.
10. Children place heels together and walk.
11. Children walk on heels, slow and fast.
12. Children, with feet together, jump forward one step, backward one step, forward three steps, sideways to left and right.

Eye-Foot Coordination
1. Place strips of masking tape on floor.
    a. Children walk forward heel to toe.
    b. Children walk forward on tiptoes.
    c. Children walk forward with giant steps.
    d. Children walk sideways each direction on tiptoes.
    e. Children walk backward.
    f. Children straddle tape while walking.
    g. Children use crossover step.
2. Lay pieces of rope in looping pattern and direct children to step in loops without touching rope.
3. Children sit on chairs facing partners, roll ball back and forth between each other by catching and pushing the ball with feet only.
4. Play hopscotch.

FIGURE 18.12. Examples of static balance. (Copyrighted by C. B. Eichstaedt, 1979.)

FIGURE 18.13. Locomotor activities to improve dynamic balance. (Copyrighted by C. B. Eichstaedt, 1979.)

FIGURE 18.14. (Copyrighted by C. B. Eichstaedt, 1979.)

ACTIVITIES INVOLVING DYNAMIC BALANCE

1 Jump then squat land		
2 Jump and keep your arms and legs spread apart when you jump	**3** Hop like a bunny	**4** Run and jump as far as you can
5 Jump as high up as you can	**6** Stand then jump as far as you can	**7** Jump straight up
8 Jump and put your hands on your knees	**9** Jump and put your arms and legs out	**10** Jump and only spread out your arms
11 Jump up and clap your hands under your legs	**12** Jump up and put your arms and legs in front of you	**13** Jump up and clap your hands above you

continued

FIGURE 18.14. *continued*

Jump up and touch your toes **14**	Jump up and turn half way **15** around before you land	Jump up and clap your hands **16** in front of you then behind you
Jump up and turn all the **17** way around before you land	Take a short run, then split **18** jump	Take a short run, then stag **19** leap
Take a short run, then **20** scissors high jump	Run, then take off with one **21** foot from a low box or step	Run, then take off with both **22** feet from a low box or step

4. Show the student how to perform the action. The teacher should guide the child's body through the desired movement if necessary.
5. For safety, be sure that hearing impaired students know exactly what they are to do. Do not assume that they understand the first time an activity is explained. Hearing impaired students may be embarrassed to admit that they do not understand and may nod their heads "yes" along with everybody else. Dangerous activities, such as those that require spotting, must be explained clearly and demonstrated visually before the activity begins.
6. Avoid lengthy explanations and constant changes in rules and regulations.
7. Hand signals are absolutely necessary. All students should use regular and official hand signals, even when playing without a referee.
8. Always know the location of the hearing impaired students in the teaching area.

Special Motor Activities for the Hearing Impaired

Many activities are needed to motivate and foster positive attitudes when the child is placed in the individualized adapted physical education class. Long-range goals will ultimately be attained through short-term objectives. Interesting and continuing activities are important.

Dance and Creative Movement

The hearing impaired, including the totally deaf, can learn new rhythms and complicated dances. A drum or other striking implement is extremely valuable for teaching rhythm to children with different degrees of hearing loss. They learn to feel the vibrations from the air compression, and the vibrations serve as a cue to movement. It is very difficult for the deaf to dance by feeling vibrations in the floor. Although the hearing impaired person may be skillful at receiving tactile cues, floor vibrations are not very useful because most dance forms involve airborne movement. The hearing impaired individual learns to dance by counting specific beats (e.g., three-fourths time). Music then is added for the hearing audience who may be watching the performance.

Swimming

Some children may have ventilation tubes or prescribed medicine in their ears. For these children, avoid underwater swimming skills and submersion activities. Other swimming activities are encouraged. For those with tubes or medication, cotton in the ears and a tight bathing cap will keep water out of the ears. Quick immersion usually does not get the cotton wet.

The swimming student will not be able to lip-read because of distance from the poolside speaker. A buddy system should be used, and lifeguards should know which students are hearing impaired.

Basketball

When playing basketball, hearing team members should hold up arms or give visual signals to indicate to hearing impaired students that play has stopped.

Touch or Regular Football

Hearing impaired students must learn to respond to movement of teammates or opponents. They should learn silent signal counting by working with the quarterback. Since deaf students cannot hear an official's whistle, they should be taught the same rules of not "piling on" that hearing players learn.

Gymnastics and Tumbling

The hearing impaired child needs to learn by observing skills and activities—one good demonstration may be worth ten thousand words. Manual assistance is extremely helpful also.

Trampoline

Trampoline participation is an excellent activity for those with balance and coordination disabilities. Primary skills involving trampoline stunts allow a hearing impaired student to improve the proprioceptors and usual balance components. Do not give verbal instructions while the child is moving or bouncing on a trampoline since lipreading is then almost impossible.

Hearing Aids

Hearing aids for sound amplification are effective correction for certain hearing disorders, such as a conductive loss in the external or middle ear. A **hearing aid** is a small, personalized unit that increases sound. Israel (1975, p. 22) describes several styles:

> The traditional body-type aid consists of a small pocketworn unit (containing the microphone, amplifier, volume control, and battery). The unit is connected to the ear by a cord, at the end of which is the loudspeaker (usually referred to as the "button" or "receiver"). The ear-level type hooks around the top and back of the ear and contains all the basic components . . . in a single shell. The eyeglass type is similar to the ear-level type, but is built into the temple portion of a pair of eyeglasses. The all-in-the-ear type is a subminiature aid which fits directly into the . . . hollow portion of the outer ear. All these aids require some form of ear mold and none . . . are invisible to the observer.

Hearing aids can be worn in one ear (monaural) or in both ears (binaural), and are designed to meet each person's need. The y-cord, which includes wires attached to an instrument worn on the body (Figure 18.15), is popular with many students.

In reference to new advances in hearing aids, Osnowitz (1985, p. 4a) states: "The industry has undergone radical change. . . . Hearing aid makers have refined the technology required to put the entire hearing aid inside a person's ear, and in some cases entirely inside the ear canal. . . . It puts the components closer to the eardrum."

Karchmer and Kirwin (1977) show that the extent of hearing loss also determines the specific type of aid that suits the child best. The relative proportions of binaural and y-cord use increase steadily with severity of hearing loss. Monaural aid use declines correspondingly, although monaural aids still account for the majority of use even among students with profound hearing loss.

Children who wear hearing aids obtain different levels of effectiveness, and some may even give a false impression that they are benefiting from its use when they in fact are not. If the aid is functioning properly, the child's auditory input will be improved.

The hearing aid should be used during physical education activities unless possible damage to the unit could occur or the unit inhibits activity. The child's hearing aid can be held securely by an elastic "tube top." This allows the child to run and jump without bouncing or jarring the hearing aid against his chest.

Activities such as basketball or touch football are rough enough to cause a sharp

FIGURE 18.15. Instructors now have the advantage of using wireless transmitters to amplify sound. (Photograph courtesy of Photo Associates Limited)

blow to the player's chest. The hearing aid therefore should be removed for safety during such activities. If wires are used for the hearing aid, the teacher may have difficulty spotting the child who is tumbling or vaulting. The hearing aid should be removed in these instances.

Total Communication and the Physical Education Teacher

Sign language is now accepted as part of the education of hearing impaired children. Significant educational advances result when deaf children are exposed to a combination of communication methods (oral, speechreading, lipreading), amplification of sound (hearing aids), fingerspelling, and signing, rather than an exclusive focus on any one of the highly controversial extremes of rigid oral or rigid manual communication (Schoenwald-Oberbeck 1984, Grove and Rodda 1984).

Since communication is vital, sign language and fingerspelling are necessary instruction tools for physical education instruction. Birch (1975) suggests that regular classroom teachers who deal with the hearing impaired child should be given training programs to learn signing and fingerspelling. Since signing is desirable, a workable

FIGURE 18.16.   A working composite of approximately 50 signs, which will greatly assist the instructor of hearing impaired students. (Adapted from Eichstaedt and Seiler 1978, pp. 20–21; modified by Howorka 1986.)

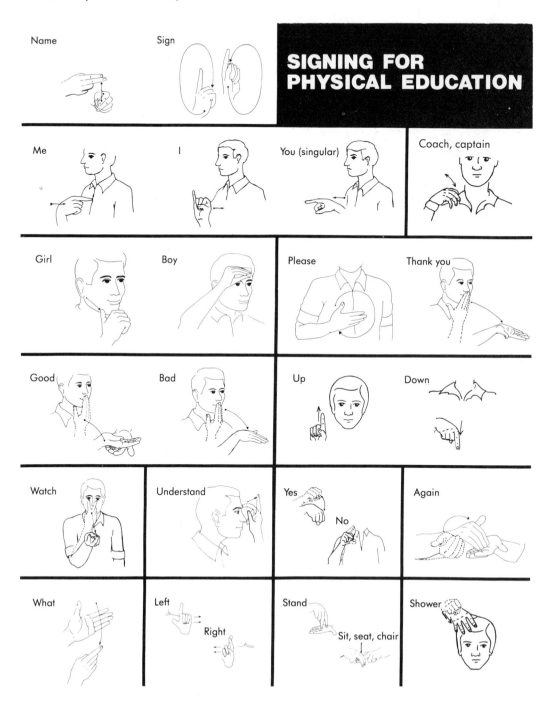

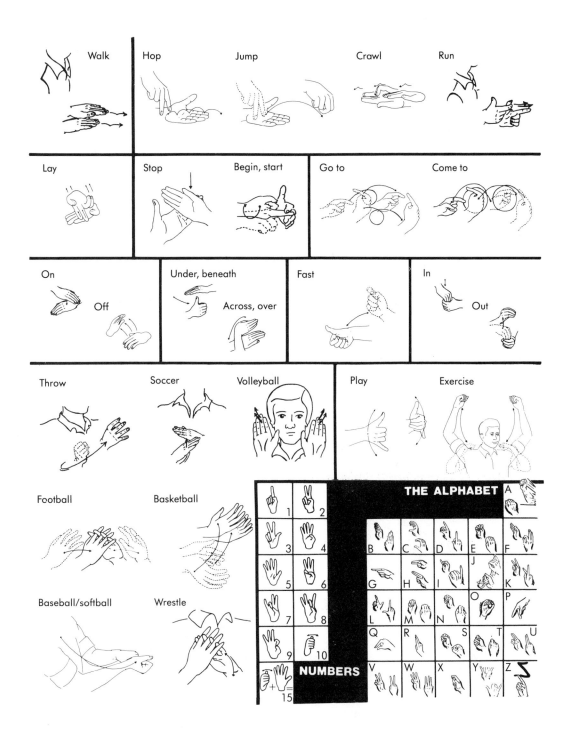

Walk

Hop

Jump

Crawl

Run

Lay

Stop

Begin, start

Go to

Come to

On

Off

Under, beneath

Across, over

Fast

In

Out

Throw

Soccer

Volleyball

Play

Exercise

Football

Basketball

Baseball/softball

Wrestle

THE ALPHABET

NUMBERS

composite of approximately 50 signs used commonly in physical education and athletics will assist the instructor of hearing impaired students (Figure 18.16).

Physical educators frequently use a single word or phrase to explain, encourage, correct, or control learning situations. Some familiar expressions are: "Jump over, run to your left, come to me." "Good girl! Try again." "Crawl under. No, watch me." "Stop! Begin again." "Sit down, stand up, run to boys." Such commonly used activity words are converted easily to signs, can be learned readily, and should become workable tools for every physical educator.

In many typical physical education situations, the hearing impaired student should be directly in front of the instructor so directions and commands will be understood. Both the hearing impaired and the normal hearing child can benefit from signing. Many hearing impaired children can read lips, but not if the instructor is too far away. When explaining new concepts, rules, stratagems, or skills, use simple terms. Avoid unusual cliches or idiomatic statements. If you must use idioms, explain what they mean.

Hearing impaired students will be unable to lip-read from the outfield, from across the swimming pool, or from the other end of the basketball floor. Use consistent signs and gestures as you would for nonhandicapped students.

Meeting the Hearing Impaired Individual for the First Time

Ask the person, "Can you read my lips?" If the individual says *yes*, continue conversation in a normal voice; do not shout. Speak distinctly but do not overenunciate your words. Face the person and do not turn your head while speaking. Do not cover your mouth or speak with something in your mouth. People with a mustache are more difficult to understand. If the individual does not understand, use a paper and pencil.

If you do not understand what a hearing impaired person is trying to say, ask her to repeat the statements. Pretending to understand when you do not only leads to confusion and frustration. If you cannot understand, ask the individual to write.

Fingerspelling

The basic English alphabet can be learned in a short time. It is easier to fingerspell than to read fingerspelling. The dominant hand, held at shoulder level with palm out, spells the letters. Spelling slowly increases accuracy and eliminates confusion. When receiving, if a letter is lost, continue interpretation, for the remaining letters may suggest the total word. Figure 18.16 shows the alphabet finger positions both as the receiver and the sender view them.

Signing

1 Deas not Word

Most signs are for concept only—the idea and not the word is stressed. The concept of *good* is signed in the following way. The left hand is held open, palm up before the chest. The right hand, also open, touches the lips. The right hand is brought down so the back rests on the left palm (see Figure 18.16).

Signing often requires shortening extraneous words or deletion of word endings. "Go out to left field" is simply "go" and then point to left field. Use common everyday gestures because most hearing impaired students are familiar with them. Pointing, motioning, demonstrating, and signaling are perfectly acceptable (Eichstaedt and Seiler 1978).

Formal signing and fingerspelling as explained in *A Basic Course in Manual Communication* (O'Rourke 1973) can serve as the foundation for communication with hearing impaired individuals. *The Joy of Signing* (Riekenhof 1985) is also an excellent illustrated source for learning sign language and the alphabet.

Summary

Hearing impairment in varying degrees constitutes one of the most common disabilities affecting school-age children. Eight out of every 1000 students under age 20 have significant hearing loss. Hearing disabilities range from slight to total loss of sound perception. Statistics indicate that only 1 out of every 8 hearing impaired children is deaf.

Most motor activities can be included in the hearing impaired child's physical education program. Students may possess low levels of static or dynamic balance or low levels of both, but the great majority possess normal motor and physical capabilities. All hearing impaired youngsters should be properly assessed and given the same test battery as normal hearing children.

Hearing impaired students have a communication handicap and suffer from inability to understand verbal instruction. All physical educators should be able to use minimal fingerspelling and signing to facilitate communication with hearing impaired students.

References

AAHPERD. *Physical Education, Recreation, and Sports for the Individual With Hearing Impairments.* Reston, Va.: AAHPERD, June 1976.

Arnheim, D., and Sinclair, W. A. *The Clumsy Child,* 2nd ed. St. Louis: C. V. Mosby, 1979.

Birch, J. W. *Hearing Impaired Children in the Mainstream.* Minneapolis: University of Minnesota Press, 1975.

Bruininks, R. H. *Bruininks-Oseretsky Test of Motor Proficiency: Examiner's Manual.* Circle Pines, Minn.: American Guidance Service, 1978.

Clark, D. L., Kreutzberg, J. R., and Chee, F. K. W. Vestibular Stimulation Influence on Motor Development in Infants. *Science* 196(4295):1228–1229, 1977.

Cratty, B. J. *Perceptual and Motor Development in Infants and Children,* 2nd ed. Englewood Cliffs, N.J.: Prentice-Hall, 1979.

Eichstaedt, C. B., and Seiler, P. Communicating With Hearing Impaired Individuals in a Physical Education Setting. *JOPER* 49(5):19–21, 1978.

Gallaudet Research Institute. *Today's Hearing Impaired Children and Youth: A Demographic and Academic Profile.* Washington, D.C.: Center for Assessment and Demographic Studies, The Institute, 1985.

Grimsley, R. *The Effects of Visual Cueness and Visual Deprivation Upon the Acquisition and Rate of Learning of a Balance Skill Among Deaf Individuals.* Ph.D. dissertation, University of Georgia, Athens, Ga., 1972.

Grove, C., and Rodda, M. Receptive Communication Skills of Hearing-Impaired Students: A Comparison of Four Methods of Communication. *American Annals of the Deaf* 129(4):378–385, 1984.

Guyton, A. C. *Basic Human Physiology: Normal Function and Mechanisms of Disease.* Philadelphia: W. B. Saunders, 1971.

———. *Physiology of the Human Body,* 5th ed. Philadelphia: W. B. Saunders, 1979.

Howorka, S. Personal Communication, Normal, Ill., 1986.

Israel, R. H. The Hearing Aid. *Volta Review* 77(1):22, 1975.

Jackson, H. In W. Murray, *Chicago Tribune,* Section 6, pp. 1, 4–5, 24 March 1985.

Karchmer, M. A., and Kirwin, L. A. *The Use of Hearing Aids by Hearing Impaired Students in the United States.* Washington, D.C.: Office of Demographic Studies, Gallaudet College, 1977.

Lindsey, D., and O'Neal, J. Static and Dynamic Balance Skills of Eight Year Old Deaf and Hearing Children. *American Annals of the Deaf* 121(1):49–55, 1976.

Marcy, M. Mumps. In *Current Diagnosis 6,* edited by H. F. Conn and R. B. Conn, Jr. Philadelphia: W. B. Saunders, 1980.

Moran, J. M., and Kalakian, L. H. *Movement Experiences for the Mentally Retarded or Emotionally Disturbed Child,* 2nd ed. Minneapolis: Burgess Publishing, 1977.

National Information Center on Deafness. *Deafness: A Fact Sheet.* Washington, D.C.: Gallaudet College, 1984.

O'Rourke, T. J. *A Basic Course in Manual Communication.* Silver Spring, Md.: National Association of the Deaf, 1973.

Osnowitz, P. Hearing Aids Open Deaf World. In J. Williams, *The Daily Pantagraph,* p. 4a, 10 December 1985.

Pennella, L. Motor Ability and the Deaf: Research Implications. *American Annals of the Deaf* 124(3):366–372, 1979.

Quigley, S. P., and Kretschmer, R. E. *The Education of Deaf Children.* Baltimore: University Park Press, 1982.

Riekenhof, L. L. *The Joy of Signing.* Springfield, Mo.: Gospel Printing House, 1985.

Sarff, L. S., Ray, H. F., and Bagwell, C. L. Why Not Amplification in Every Classroom? *Hearing Aid Journal,* October 1981, pp. 43–52.

Schein, J. D. Education of Deaf Children. *American Annals of the Deaf* 129(3):324–332, 1984.

Schoenwald-Oberbeck, B. A Communication Program for Enhancing Interaction in Families With a Hearing-Impaired Child. *American Annals of the Deaf* 129(4):362–369, 1984.

Vance, P. C. Motor Characteristics of Deaf Children. Unpublished doctoral dissertation, Colorado State University, 1968, *Dissertation Abstracts International*, p. 1145-A, 1968.

Wisher, P. R. Status of Physical Education for the Hearing Impaired. *Physical Education and Recreation for Handicapped Children: Proceedings of a Study Conference on Research and Demonstration Needs.* Washington, D.C.: National Recreation and Park Association and AAHPERD, 1969.

CHAPTER 19

Visually Handicapped: The Blind and Partially Sighted

Approximately 6.4 million persons in the United States have some visual handicap, that is, they have less than normal vision even with corrective lenses. Of these, 1.7 million are severely visually impaired—they are either legally blind or function as if they were legally blind. Approximately 400,000 of these severely visually impaired individuals have no usable vision at all.

In the 1983–1984 school year, the actual number of visually handicapped persons (age 0 to 21) served by Public Laws 94-142 and 89-313, was 31,576 (U.S. Department of Education 1985). This represents one of the smallest groups of handicapped children served. The only smaller group is in the deaf-blind classification.

The majority of visually handicapped children in the United States attend public school, and a need exists for all visually handicapped students to be integrated into sighted society. Dr. Charles Buell (1980), a pioneer in physical education and recreation for the visually handicapped, estimates that two thirds of the visually handicapped children in public schools are not given vigorous physical education opportunities, even though physical fitness training is probably needed more by the blind student than by the student with normal vision.

Definitions

The term **visually handicapped** covers three general categories: **blind, legally blind,** and **partially sighted.** The American Foundation for the Blind prefers that the word **blind** be used to describe a complete loss of sight, and that all other degrees of visual loss be described as **visual impairment**.

Legally blind describes visual acuity (clarity or clearness) that does not exceed 20/200 in the *better eye* with corrective lenses or a visual field of less than a 20-degree peripheral angle. Simply put, a person is legally blind if he can see at a distance of 20 ft what a person with normal vision can see at 200 ft. Table 19.1 lists specific degrees and definitions of visual acuity, ranging from normal vision to total blindness.

Persons identified as **partially sighted** (often referred to as **functionally blind**) must possess a visual acuity of better than 20/200 but not greater than 20/70 in the better eye after correction. Although these individuals may have a great deal of useful vision, they may be unable to read newspapers or to see a television image.

Students are handicapped to the degree that the visual impairment prevents them from living as they wish. A visually impaired person who wants to participate in games such as tennis or racquetball will find poor vision more of a handicap than the person

TABLE 19.1
Degree of Visual Acuity

Visual Acuity	Description
Normal vision: 20/12 to 20/25	Healthy young adults average better than 20 / 20 acuity.
Near-normal vision: 20/30 to 20/70	Causes no serious problems, usually explored for potential improvement or possible early disease.
Moderate low vision: 20/80 to 20/160	Strong reading glasses or magnifiers usually provide adequate reading speed.
Severe low vision ("legal blindness"): 20/200 to CF10'[a]	Gross orientation and mobility generally adequate, but difficulty with traffic signs, bus numbers, etc. High-power magnifiers for reading.
Profound low vision: CF8' to CF4'	Increasing problems with visual orientation and mobility. White cane useful. Highly motivated individuals can read visually with extreme magnification. Others rely on braille, talking books, or radio.
Near blindness: less than CF4'	Vision unreliable except under ideal circumstances. Must rely on nonvisual aids.
Total blindness (no light perception)	Must rely on other senses entirely.

SOURCE: Modified from *California Department of Education and Rehabilitation Manual,* 2nd ed., Sacramento, California: Department of Developmental Services, 1978, p. 29.
[a]CF = central field

who enjoys jogging or swimming. In other words, people are severely handicapped when they consider themselves to be severely handicapped.

Physiology of the Eye

The eyeball is the receiving unit of the visual system. The eye is protected by the lids and rests in a bony pyramid (orbit or socket) filled with fat. The fat absorbs shock and facilitates eye movement, which is accomplished by four rectus muscles. The muscles provide motion upward, downward, toward the nose, and away from the nose. Two oblique muscles provide angular as well as upward and downward movement.

The eyeball has three layers (see Figure 19.1 for a cross section of the eye). The strong outermost protective coat is composed of the cornea (clear window and major refractive surface) and opaque sclera (white in color). The middle coat (uvea) carries the blood supply in its three structures: (1) the iris, which gives color to eyes, (2) the ciliary body, which produces the fluid of the aqueous humor and allows adjustment for distant vision (i.e., accommodation), and (3) the choroid, the blood supply for the retina. The front segment of the inner coat contains pigment that prevents light scattering, and in its posterior portion, the retina, which is the receptor organ. From the

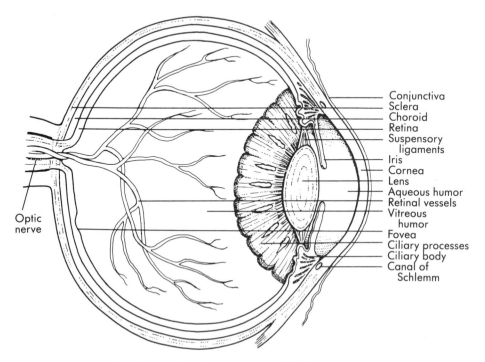

FIGURE 19.1.   Cross-section of the human eye.

retina, nerve fibers form the optic nerve and carry impulses to the brain, which integrates these impulses with input from other sense systems and projects composite images, called **vision** (Figure 19.2).

Optical functions are associated primarily with physiological control of the external and internal muscles of the eye, which aid in fixation, tracking, accommodation, focus, and movement. Impairment or disease in the tissues or structures restricts function and produces irregular development of muscular skills. Often, several functions may occur simultaneously; one function may be uniform whereas others occur intermittently from day to day. In visually impaired individuals, some visual functions may occur under certain conditions only and not in other situations. This variation in eye function can result from the nature of the impairment or disease or from the visibility characteristics of the environment or from a combination of the two.

When a student possesses irregular, malfunctioning, or incomplete vision, the instructor needs to match eye-hand activities with the student's visual ability level. Success in this endeavor may be difficult, if not impossible, if eyeballs are too small, or move too fast, or if the environment is dark. Student frustration can be avoided if the instructor modifies equipment, rules, or playing area accordingly.

Causes of Visual Defects

Table 19.2 describes common visual handicaps. Diseases of the retina cause the greatest loss of vision, and contribute to approximately 40 percent of all blindness. The

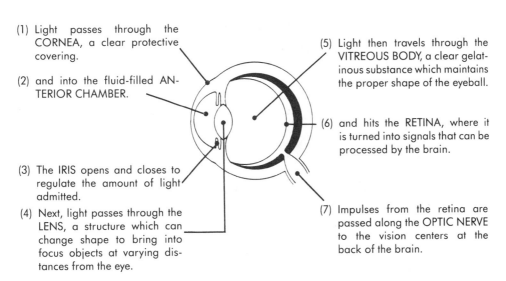

(1) Light passes through the CORNEA, a clear protective covering.

(2) and into the fluid-filled ANTERIOR CHAMBER.

(3) The IRIS opens and closes to regulate the amount of light admitted.

(4) Next, light passes through the LENS, a structure which can change shape to bring into focus objects at varying distances from the eye.

(5) Light then travels through the VITREOUS BODY, a clear gelatinous substance which maintains the proper shape of the eyeball.

(6) and hits the RETINA, where it is turned into signals that can be processed by the brain.

(7) Impulses from the retina are passed along the OPTIC NERVE to the vision centers at the back of the brain.

FIGURE 19.2. How light is transmitted to the brain. (Reprinted with permission of Aspen Systems Corporation, copyright 1984, from D. P. Schor. Visual Impairment. In J. A. Blackman, *Medical Aspects of Developmental Disabilities in Children Birth to Three*, p. 227.)

TABLE 19.2
Common Visual Abnormalities

Term	Description
Albinism	Hereditary condition characterized by a lack of pigment throughout the body, including the eyes. It is usually accompanied by a nystagmus condition (see below). Children with albinism are very sensitive to light and must sometimes wear tinted glasses.
Amblyopia	Commonly called "lazy eye," an eye deviation in which the wandering eye does not focus on the same object as the good eye.
Astigmatism	Blurred vision caused by defective curvature of refractive surfaces of the eye, as a result of which light rays are not sharply focused on retina.
Cataract	Condition in which the normally transparent lens of the eye becomes cloudy or opaque.
Glaucoma	Condition in which fluid pressure inside the eye is too high. Depending on the type of glaucoma, visual loss may be gradual, sudden, or present at birth. When visual loss is gradual, it begins with decreasing peripheral vision.
Hyperopia	Condition in which the eyeball is too short from front to back, causing farsightedness.
Myopia	Condition in which the eyeball is too long from front to back, causing nearsightedness.
Nystagmus	Involuntary, rapid movement of the eyeballs from side to side, up and down, in a rotary motion, or in a combination of these.
Retinitis pigmentosa	Hereditary degeneration of the retina beginning with night blindness and producing a gradual loss of peripheral vision. Although some persons with this disease lose all vision, many do retain some central vision.
Retrolental fibroplasia	Visual impairment caused by oxygen given to incubated premature babies.
Strabismus	Eyes not simultaneously directed to the same object as a result of muscle imbalance of the eyeball. Crossed or deviated eyes are examples.

SOURCE: Adapted from Corn and Martinez 1977, pp. 23–24.

retina and the optic nerve are outgrowths of the brain and do not regenerate when injured.

Detachment of the retina occurs when the retina detaches from the choroid and floats in vitreous space. Prolonged detachment results in permanent visual loss following reattachment. This condition can be caused by a tumor, fluid underneath the retina, or strands of vitreous humor attached to the retina, which contract and detach the retina, as in diabetes. The condition often results from unknown causes as well. In idiopathic detachment, holes occur in the retina edges because of vitreous pressure. Vitreous fluid flows through these holes, stripping the retina away from the choroid. If the detachment continues, all central vision will be lost.

Surgical repair of a detached retina requires closing holes by diathermy and sewing plastic over the holes, thereby allowing the choroid to once again contact the retina. Fluid is released by puncture, and in most cases, the retina returns to normal. Approximately 60 percent of people with a detached retina in one eye will develop the condition in the other eye. Untreated retinal detachments usually result in blindness, glaucoma, or phthisis bulbi (shrinking and wasting of the eyeball), with resultant enucleation (surgical removal).

Premature infants who are placed in incubators are also susceptible to detached retina. In this case, the blood vessels in the infant's retina become accustomed to the high levels of pure oxygen administered in incubators. When the baby is returned to natural room air, too little oxygen is available for transfer by existing blood vessels to the infant's system. New blood vessels then grow, not on the retina but toward the center of the eye, and scar tissue develops. Immediate surgery is necessary, but the condition often is not diagnosed soon enough for surgery to be effective. New surgical procedures are being used, but the prognosis is questionable. Machemer (1985, p. 188) states: "One cannot expect full vision even if the retina is completely reattached, since many alterations have occurred in the retina during the disease's progress."

A child with retinal detachment must not jar or bump the head or eyes. Running and jumping are therefore contraindicated, but other noncompetitive activities are encouraged. All activities should be checked with the physician prior to participation.

During the past several years, a major preventive campaign has been undertaken to vaccinate school-age children throughout the United States against *rubella*, or German measles. This precaution is not only to safeguard the children, but to protect their mothers as well. As a childhood disease, rubella is usually quite mild, but when the virus attacks women in the first 3 months of pregnancy, its effects on the unborn child can be devastating. In the rubella epidemic of 1964 and 1965, almost 40,000 unborn children were affected by rubella. One of the common prenatal results of the virus is the formation of congenital cataracts. Many of today's young adults with multiple handicaps were conceived during this epidemic. In addition to loss of vision, they also suffer from deafness, heart conditions, mental retardation, and neurological impairment. When planning a physical education program for blind individuals, the physical educator must make sure that the child's physician provides specific information regarding any additional handicapping condition that the child may possess (Osborne and Clark 1985).

Visual Aids: Glasses and Contact Lenses

Many visual aids are available for severely visually impaired youngsters. These include headborne aids (which look like ordinary glasses), contact lenses, magnifiers (hand-held and on stands), telescopic lenses, and optical enlargers. Contact lenses do not supply sufficient magnification for the most severely handicapped. Eyeglasses, therefore, should be worn during most physical education activities. For safety, all eyeglasses should have unbreakable plastic or case-hardened lenses. Pop-out lenses or protective coverings over the glasses can also be used.

Professionals Who Work With the Visually Handicapped

Ophthalmologist—A physician who specializes in diagnosis and treatment of defects and diseases of the eye. Physical education activity restrictions should come from this physician.

Optometrist—A licensed, nonmedical practitioner who measures refractive errors (irregularities in the size or shape of the eyeball, or surface of the cornea) and eye muscle disturbances. The optometrist's treatment is limited to prescribing and fitting glasses.

Optician—A maker of glasses who grinds lenses according to prescription, fits them into frames, and adjusts frames to the wearer.

Orientation and mobility specialist—One who teaches visually impaired students how to familiarize themselves with new surroundings and to travel independently; also works with young children to develop concepts of body image and spatial awareness. The services of this individual are especially helpful to the very young or a newly blinded person.

Common Concerns About Vision

1. Glasses do not always correct limited vision. While some visually limited children may be aided by corrective lenses, correction is not possible for many, and many who benefit from correction will still have limited vision.
2. Holding a book close to the eyes does not harm vision. This is often done by visually handicapped children to compensate for print size.
3. If a television is functioning properly, sitting close will not harm the eyes.
4. Sight cannot be conserved. Unless informed otherwise, encourage a child to use her eyes.
5. Dim light will not harm the eyes. Because of some eye conditions (e.g., cataracts or albinism), a child may require dim lighting to feel more comfortable.
6. Loss of vision in one eye does not reduce vision by 50 percent. While there is loss of vision on the affected side and a general loss of depth perception, a loss of half of the visual system has *not* occurred.

Physical Activity—How Much and for Whom?

Blind and partially sighted students can participate in many of the same physical activities that sighted individuals enjoy provided that the visually impaired children have learned basic motor skills, possess minimal levels of physical fitness, and have had some opportunities for interesting movement experiences.

Concern has been expressed that blind students are not given appropriate physical education opportunities. Seelye (1983) found that only 46 percent of the blind students in her study tested above minimal levels of physical fitness, whereas 95 percent of sighted children and 84 percent of partially sighted subjects passed the test. She states (1983, p. 117): "Apparently, existing school and home activities weren't meeting their [blind students] needs. The . . . students were not allowed to participate in physical education activities designed for sighted students—either because the teacher believed they were unable to participate or because they were actually unable to do so."

Teachers tend to set visually handicapped students apart as being different from sighted students. They believe (often based on misunderstanding or lack of knowledge) that the blind and partially sighted must be coddled, that their motor abilities are limited, and that their activities must be restricted. In reality, if students with visual problems are given the opportunities, they can live life as fully as others. The quality of their physical well-being depends largely on the availability of good physical education programming.

Some visually handicapped students may be reluctant to attempt new activities for fear of failure or bodily injury. The student needs support and encouragement from teachers, peers, and family to realize the joy of becoming involved with nonhandicapped people through physical education and recreational experiences. The physical educator should discuss with the student the possible fears and apprehensions surrounding new physical encounters. The student may be cautious and exhibit a reluctance to try new activities. The teacher's role is to instill confidence with verbal and tactual explanations. Given an understanding approach, the student often becomes enthusiastic.

Regular or Adapted Physical Education . . . Or Both?

Initially, the visually handicapped student must be assessed for general motor ability and physical fitness. Outstanding deficits, observed by objective, criterion-referenced, and subjective testing, should be noted and recorded. These results serve as the basis for appropriate placement in physical education classes. As with other handicapping conditions, placement is likely to be a combination of regular and adapted physical education classes.

The most severely visually impaired students will use tactual and auditory perception to explore, recognize, and learn. The physical education teacher should use these same sensory skills to provide an individualized program that enables the student to regain self-confidence and develop new motor proficiencies. The adapted physical education specialist should evaluate motor, tactual, and perceptual capabilities, and provide instruction in perceptual skills and physical functioning.

The visually impaired individual can succeed in the regular class with nonhandicapped children when jogging, distance running, sprinting, weight training, swimming, gymnastics, wrestling, and tumbling are offered. For participation in team-oriented visual-motor activities, such as softball or volleyball, extreme modification is required if the visually handicapped student is to participate. It is questionable also if such modification is beneficial to the nonhandicapped students. The severity of an individual's handicap will dictate the student's ability to participate in eye-hand coordination activities in the regular class. When the handicapped student is relegated to menial and watered-down activities, however, the child has been inappropriately placed.

Adapted physical education placement should allow for the special adaptation of certain games and sports to make them more suitable for the student. Beep balls, wiffle balls with bells inside, or beach balls with noisemakers are useful equipment when adapting activities for the visually handicapped.

When the student is placed in a regular physical education class, determine if the child can engage in effective physical competition and meaningful social interaction. Although the child may need to cope with visual and emotional stresses not usually encountered by nonhandicapped students, the chances are that he will soon become a fully participating class member if emphasis is put on individual improvement and not on specific levels of performance. For example, if the student improves cross-country performance by reducing his time by 5 percent (i.e., 1½ mi run pretest 12:10, posttest 11:34), a significant gain was made, and participation in the regular class therefore proved successful. The only modification involves the "buddy system," in which the blind student holds the arm of a sighted person during events such as the 1½ mi run.

Unique Characteristics of the Blind

Mannerisms or "blindisms" are often exhibited by blind individuals. These are repetitive or stereotyped movements not directed toward attainment of any identifiable goal. Cratty (1971) observed 200 blind children and reported a number of rocking movements. Interchild comparisons showed a range of postures, stances, and accompanying body movements.

Common mannerisms identified in the literature are (1) bending the head forward, (2) waving fingers in front of the face, (3) putting fist or fingers in the eyes, (4) rocking backward and forward, (5) whirling rapidly around and around, and (6) hitting or slapping oneself.

Eichel (1979) discovered that certain activities reduce the occurrence of mannerisms, and in some cases, the mannerisms ceased completely. In her study, the blind children showed few, if any, mannerisms while eating, playing on swings, deeply absorbed in activity, or listening to records. The frequency of mannerisms increased when the child became angry, frustrated, bored, anxious, or excited. Mannerisms also increased slightly when the children were left alone.

Past research generally supports the assumption that mannerisms result from a lack of appropriate stimulation. By providing interesting and challenging activities, the adapted physical educator can help the child to replace unacceptable mannerisms. As with other handicapping conditions, the educator should stress activities that develop the following psychomotor components: balance and coordination, posture and gait, ability to walk a straight line, dexterity or agility, stamina or endurance, and reaction time.

Internal (Kinesthesis) and External Orientation

[handwritten: Bad Posture Habits]

Severely visually handicapped children may need orientation training to help them recognize the environment and its temporal and spatial relationships. The blind often possess certain bad habits, including poor posture (head drop, head thrust, rounded shoulders, forward tilt of pelvis) and a shuffling gait resulting from tight hamstrings and pronated feet. These characteristics develop when children have no visual model after which to pattern themselves. After a few years of repeated poor posture, bad habits become permanent. The adapted physical educator must provide constant positive correction and remind the individual to stand erect and walk with the feet in proper placement.

[handwritten: Have no Visual Model]

Exercises are best performed in reference to a vertical surface such as a wall. Sensation of limb position in space is aided by exercising in front of a large fan. The correct "feel" of the upright position can be learned only though repeated stimulation of body proprioceptors. Tumbling, trampoline, or other activities that increase kinesthetic awareness can lay the groundwork for posture improvement. Sensory stimulating activities, such as using a full-sized mannequin to demonstrate body parts and position, help the student acquire an appropriate body image. A sequential program of balancing that progresses from crawling and creeping to standing balance may be needed to reinforce specific psychomotor patterns.

[handwritten: Use a Mannequin]

Mobility Training

Mobility training is based on an understanding of six basic concepts: right, left, up, down, forward, and backward. Table 19.3 identifies the developmental progressions for blind children between the ages of 2 and 6.

The adapted physical education instructor should stress two important hearing skills, sound discrimination and sound location, as well as improving degrees of concentration, memorization, retention, and environmental awareness. Severely visually impaired students should be given practice in walking unaided in a straight line while maintaining good posture (Klee and Klee 1985).

TABLE 19.3

Determinants for Mobility Training—Developmental Progressions of Blind Children Between the Ages of 2 and 6

Skill	Age Range (months)
Walks sideways	14
Points to four body parts	18
Walks straight line	18—30
Walks backward	20—30
Walks on tiptoe	20—30
Moves from one room to another without difficulty	24
Moves about yard without difficulty	24
Hops on two feet	25—30
Distance jumps 14 to 24 in.	28—30
Hops on one foot	30
Balances on either foot for 5 sec	31—36
Runs	36—48
Comprehends "on top of," "under," "inside"	42
Comprehends texture	48
Identifies most body parts	48—60
Learns left from right	60—72
Identifies variety of objects by tactual exploration	60—72

SOURCE: Adapted from Ferrell 1979, p. 148.

The Sixth Sense

Blind persons have a "sixth sense," or develop more acute hearing or more sensitive smell and touch than nonhandicapped people. At one time, the belief was common that blind people could tell colors by using their fingertips or could develop a special sensitivity wherein the skin produced its own little "eyes." None of this is true, but many blind persons do develop, through necessity and training, other senses to a greater degree than sighted individuals. The adapted physical education program should provide activities that bombard the individual's available senses. Many trial and error experiences usually will be necessary for permanent motor learning to occur. For example, children with normal motor ability learn the beginning trampoline skills of bouncing, stopping, and starting in a few minutes, but blind children need more trials to stimulate kinesthetic awareness.

Sighted people rely on sight to perform many activities that could be learned through other senses. For example, the coins in one's pocket can be identified through touch, but a sighted person will look to ascertain their value. Without dependence on sight, the person must organize and process the sense information through another

CONGENITALLY

ADVENTITIOUSLY

framework, which provides a reasonably reliable and realistic impression of the environment and becomes the basis for analysis and intellectual judgment. Here, the major difference between *congenitally* blind persons and *adventitiously* blind persons becomes apparent. Children who are born blind or who become blind before age 4 will not have enough visual memory to coordinate their sensory perceptions. Adventitiously blind children (blinded later in life through disease or accident) rely on the same sensory input as the former group but within the framework of visual memory. The once sighted child remembers the appearance of a ball, a basketball backboard, a swimming pool, and a climbing rope if these were experienced before blindness.

SOUND
REFLECTION

Hearing provides identification, direction, distance, size, and structure. Visually handicapped students learn to identify sounds and to discriminate and select those that are important and useful. They learn to localize sounds and to use sound reflection, sound shadows, and echo location. This phenomenon is called **object perception.** The ability to perceive extremely close objects by feeling a sensation change or pressure on the face can be developed by anyone who can hear, whether sighted or blind.

Touch, or tactual stimulation, involves anything touched by any part of the body or anything that touches the body. The student learns about the object's size, weight, volume, density, texture, and surface through tactual exploration. Important to touch are the sensations of hot or cold, changes in air current, and changes in temperature.

Kinesthetic awareness is useful for detecting lateral tilts in surfaces, gradients, distances, and in position, movement, and posture. Equilibrium is vital to balance and turning.

Complex sensory information is learned through interaction of the senses. The tactile discrimination of shape and form occurs through kinesthetic awareness when one feels the position of a batting tee. Kinesthesis makes many habitual activities automatic. A blind person relies on kinesthesis to put on a gym shoe and to get from the locker room to the gymnasium without counting steps.

The Congenitally Blind

The congenitally blind child may possess distinct motor ability deficiencies. According to research, these children usually need to improve large muscle control and balance.

Learning reflects experience, that is, interaction with the environment. The absence of motor development in the congenitally blind is difficult to explain but probably reflects a general lack of learning experience. Gagné (1970) stresses "learning by doing," that is, concepts are learned in actual situations. The most widely accepted motor development theories about blind children emphasize two main points. First, blind children are unaware of the movement potential of many parts of their body because they lack opportunities to experience movement. Parents as well as school personnel often limit the congenitally blind child's physical experiences. P.L. 94-142 should ensure that all blind students receive appropriate and necessary physical education experi-

Touch Feeling + Modeling

ences. Second, motor development specialists claim that overprotection may hamper the child's motor development by instilling fear of bodily harm or by preventing practice. Cleaves and Royal (1979) state that early visual experience of spatial relations establishes a method for processing information, which affects all subsequent cognitive and motor learning experiences. Since blind children cannot see objects or movement, it is extremely difficult for them to copy or imitate. For example, if the adapted physical education instructor wants the students to imitate "lame dogs," few congenitally blind children will understand what the teacher means. Only through touching, feeling, and modeling can the blind child understand this concept.

The blind child who does not explore the environment by reaching out or moving toward objects or by other nonvisual stimuli usually becomes accustomed to stationary activities or to being guided in movement through space. Blind children cannot see to imitate the motor performance of others, so they cannot benefit from demonstrations of skilled movement. Congenitally blind students generally have a poor body image. For blind children to move skillfully and efficiently, they need to understand their body and its parts in relation to the surrounding space.

The Adventitious, or Newly Blinded

Newly blinded persons must come to terms with their new circumstances and develop new skills. The person must strive for alertness beyond that of most sighted persons. The individual will no longer be able to walk, run, and jump as she used to. Simple acts become complex undertakings, to be thought through and planned in advance, therefore many movement opportunities must be provided!

The Visually Impaired or Partially Sighted Are Not Blind

Remember that visually impaired individuals can see. They may not see distant objects, and their vision may be blurred or they may have restricted visual fields, but most can localize contrasting light and dark. Physical education instructors must be as conscientious about teaching these students to use their residual vision as they are about teaching the other senses to students who are blind.

The student who can localize light can move about indoors and locate lights, windows, and doors. Some visually impaired students, although unable to read words or numbers on a Universal Weight Lifting Machine, can set the amount of weight by memorizing the number of 10-lb plates and inserting the holding pin appropriately.

Teaching Techniques

The child learns tasks involving manipulation of materials, equipment, or his own body more quickly if his hands are placed and guided through the movement required to complete the task, and if the teacher provides tactual as well as verbal feedback.

The teacher needs to speak clearly and loudly enough to be easily understood. A blatant violation of this is nodding the head in response to a blind child's question. The teacher must not use ambiguous statements such as "Throw the ball over there," and must not point or use nonverbal gestures. A quiet-spoken teacher may be giving inappropriate feedback to a student's performance. This teacher must learn to praise through voice or tactile contact, or the student may not receive the message.

B. F. Skinner once claimed that the most valid proof of effective teaching is knowing students have learned a skill so well that they can perform it without thinking. Walking is so automatic that most people never think about it until a critical situation arises. We become very conscious of walking, however, when we maneuver on an icy sidewalk—our steps become short and our pace slows, because we are acutely aware of not wanting to slip and fall. Too often physical education teachers do not provide enough practice sessions for total learning to occur. Extensive practice is essential for all slow motor learners.

Specific Suggestions for Teaching the Visually Handicapped

Introduce the student to classmates. Other students will have questions that the visually handicapped student may wish to answer. Shaking hands does not have to be awkward. Anticipate the situation and encourage contact between the blind student and others.

If the student prefers not to bring attention to her handicap, she may use special aids and assistance only when absolutely necessary. In general, the teacher should respect the child's wishes, but if the child obviously requires aids or assistance, discuss these needs with the special education teacher.

When the visually handicapped student brings adaptive aids into the physical education area, encourage the use of the aids and answer questions that others have about them.

When approaching an unfamiliar blind student, always state your name. Voices are not easy to identify, particularly in noisy areas. When a blind person is alone in the room, announce your entry, especially if you are wearing gym shoes or going barefoot.

Do not shout at a blind student. Blind individuals are not hard of hearing. When uncertain about whether assistance is needed by the student, ask. Offering help is always appropriate.

When speaking to the visually handicapped person, it is acceptable to use words such as *see*, *look*, or even *blind*. These words are part of everyone's vocabulary. The blind child will use them to express feelings regarding *seeing*, and in phrases such as "*See* you tomorrow."

The adapted physical education teacher must provide extra locker space to accommodate any special aids, such as the student's cane. A lock with a key is preferable to a combination lock. The key can be worn around the student's neck or carried by the instructor. The locker should be easily identifiable by position, as at the end of the row. Assist the blind student to the locker room, the showers, toilets, and activity areas. Most blind students will learn the routine and floor patterns quickly. Be constantly aware of unusual hazards such as stairways, objects protruding from walls, and slippery floors. Use verbal cues to guide the student around the activity area.

Encourage the student to assume leadership roles (i.e., team captain or activity leader) just as you would any nonhandicapped student. Because children are sensitive to peer criticism, be aware of this problem and encourage positive interactions between the students. The blind child may not be aware of events, such as facial expressions or arm movements. Verbal cues become extremely necessary when working with the visually handicapped.

Disciplinary rules apply equally to both visually handicapped and the nonhandicapped.

Manual Assistance, or the Sighted Guide

Assistance for the blind student is appropriate. The individual may choose (or need) to have a sighted guide. For safety, the blind person should grasp the guide's upper arm, above the elbow, with the thumb on the outside and the fingers on the inside of the guide's arm. A younger child can hold an adult's wrist. Both student and guide should hold upper arms close to the body. This automatically positions the student one-half step behind the guide, and is also an acceptable position for jogging or running.

When approaching doorways or objects, the guide should press his elbow close to his body or behind his body so the blind student understands to walk directly behind the guide. Verbal cues are important. Inform the student when approaching stairways or curbs and whether ascending or descending.

Body Image and Spatial Awareness

Failure to develop body image and a sense of position in space are common problems of the visually handicapped child. Limited vision does not enable one to see mirror reflections, which help in understanding body contours. Movement limitations and irregularities limit one's exploration of one's body potential and the conception of how one's body relates to the world.

Beginning instruction starts with stroking the child's different body parts. A terry cloth, silk scarf, velvet glove, or feather can be used. Each part should be stroked gently and named. For example, stroke the leg and say: "Suzie's leg." Repeat the action with the opposite leg. As this is done repeatedly, body awareness increases. The stroking routine also reduces the tactile defensiveness commonly found in blind children. Introduce the child's hands to various textures; use sand, whipped cream, flour, and corn meal.

The child's proprioceptors must be developed to maintain static and dynamic balance. The body must experience different and unusual balance situations. The instructor should increase the child's proprioceptive awareness by attaching small weights, such as beanbags or sandbags, to the body. The added weight requires more effort to move, thus intensifying awareness of those parts.

The child's relationship to space must be clarified. This sense develops early when auditory stimuli help determine direction and distance of objects. Talk to the child from different positions around the room. Use a beep ball to let the student experience differences in direction of movement. Let the student throw objects to assist in learning the concept of up and down. Have the child throw or drop an object; pick it up, hand it back to the child, and have the youngster do it again. In this way, the child experiences space, a concept that should be reinforced by the instructor through sound, touch, and movement.

The blind child cannot see or copy images and therefore must be taught to feel. Imagery plays an important role in stimulating and understanding movement. For the blind youngster, tactual stimuli suggest certain qualities of movement. Skills involved in locomotion (walking, hopping, galloping, sliding, and jumping) help children to sense movement. The qualities of lightness, heaviness, softness, and hardness assist in feeling movement. Tactual materials such as clay, wire, rubber bands, and balloons allow children to understand these concepts.

Clay can assume many shapes and is self contained. It has the quality of heaviness. It can be made into numerous shapes such as flat, long, round, and thin.

Wire is hard, but pliable and flexible; thin, but strong; long, but form producing. It can be shaped, but its major feature is hardness. When shaping wire, the student becomes aware of the interaction between muscle resistance and skeletal articulation. The student knows that force will change the wire's shape. The child can imagine this force as muscle strength and the wire's firmness as resistance of the skeletal frame. The concepts of bend-straighten, toward-away from, right-left, and parallel-perpendicular can be taught using wire.

Rubber bands establish an image of elasticity. They provide an opportunity to experience flexibility, "stretchiness," and contracting ability of the child's muscles. A rubber band has no specific dimensions; it can be stretched up, down, forward, backward, and sideward. As the student moves, this action is compared with elasticity and lightness.

Balloons produce images of both lightness and airiness. Body shape can imitate a balloon that is flat and shriveled before inflation. Movement is experienced as traveling lightly off the floor at different levels. A balloon can explode, suggesting jumps and leaps from a crouched position, followed by collapse.

These stimuli alone provide an infinite number of movement possibilities and should enable blind students to experience movement shapes and qualities. They also enable the teacher to introduce a movement vocabulary.

The following lesson outline should serve as a guide when using clay, wire, rubber bands, or balloons. Structure each lesson to encourage time for relaxation and breathing exercises; explore a new movement (e.g., time and energy factors, body involvement, relationship of body parts); create imitations (e.g., "Move as if you were carrying something heavy," "Crawl on the floor, like a worm"); and verbally analyze where the movement occurs in the body.

Encourage the students to move in response to suggested emotions (happy, sad, angry, funny); to act out words (descriptive words such as lazy, sleepy, sticky; or action words such as wiggle, crawl, bounce, shiver, squirm); and to experience movement sequences (dropping and falling, holding and stopping, tearing and breaking). For locomotion, the students should be encouraged to move from place to place, including different levels or heights (high, medium, or low to the ground, tall or short), to interpret different sizes or shapes during movement, and to move to a beat or a piece of music.

Gross Body Movement

Gross body movements usually precede fine motor coordination activities and should be encouraged at an early age. Place the child on a bare floor or mat and allow free movement, assisting when necessary. Rolling, scooting, crawling, and other gross movements involve the entire muscular system (Figure 19.3). Place the child on her back and guide her into rolling and gradually toward creeping independence.

Various activities and toys can also develop body control. Simple, guided gymnastics and postural exercises are effective. Swimming fosters movement exploration and body self-awareness while developing coordination. Heavy toys develop muscle strength and endurance. Large beach balls, rocking boats, swings, teeter-totters, hobby horses, animals filled with sand, medicine balls, and boxes filled with heavy material all stimulate mobility, balance, and strength.

If the student's walking techniques are poor, improvement is necessary to run effectively. Teach the child to maintain balance without spreading the feet. Encourage free arm movement by swinging the child's arms during a walk. Reinforce the heel-toe technique by having the child begin steps with the heel, roll to the balls of the feet, and end on the toes. Discourage the child from shuffling the feet. If necessary, move the child's feet up and down to demonstrate walking without shuffling. Walking on a mattress helps the student learn to lift the feet.

Developing Concepts

When attempting to develop concepts of size, such as big and little, use items familiar to the student. Do not talk about a "little" ball and then provide only a small

FIGURE 19.3. Gross body movements, such as rolling, should be encouraged.

ball. Children learn more quickly by experiencing concept comparisons. Provide the student with several examples of a concept and one example that does not fit the concept. The nonexamples allow the child to eliminate certain attributes and reinforce common characteristics.

Concepts should be taught that stimulate greater environmental awareness. For instance, the child should learn comparisons—big child-little ball, little child-big tree. Action concepts can be taught by having the student respond physically to action verbs. When a story mentions the act of spinning around and around, the student can sit on the floor and experience spinning.

Visually handicapped students with additional physical impairments may need assistance to explore their world. Their environment may be small because of insufficient mobility. If they have severe vision loss, their concepts of the world are even more limited.

Methods to Increase Visual Tracking

There are four basic ways to improve the visually impaired child's ability to catch, kick, and strike objects. These include (1) increased ball size, (2) structured programming and repetition, (3) increased lighting, and (4) appropriate figure-ground contrasts (Gardner 1985).

Increasing the size of the object being tracked assists visually impaired youngsters. An example would be using an inflated beach ball instead of a volleyball. Not only is the ball larger, but it also moves more slowly. This combination should enhance the student's chances of success.

Barraga (1977) explains the process of improving visual tracking through repetition. The concept includes systematic instruction and opportunities to "learn" how the ball looks as it travels through space. She believes that visual functioning is enhanced, including the improvement of speed and accuracy, through extensive trial and error. In other words, the child's performance improves through practice while motor learning is occurring.

The instructor should consider improving the lighting in the gymnasium. Increasing bulb wattage and replacing any dead bulbs in the ceiling lights are possible solutions to lighting problems. These adjustments may be all that is necessary for successful participation. Inadequate light may also be experienced when the children are outside on a dark and gloomy day, or toward evening when the sun has gone down. Adjusting the class time or, on a gloomy day, changing the setting to indoors can solve such problems.

The ball color and background against which it is thrown contribute to the success of a visually impaired child. For example, brown or tan colored balls are much more difficult to see than white or yellow balls. Kligerman (1981) conducted an experiment using figure-ground reversals with cerebral palsied, learning disabled, and visually impaired populations. The use of a light foreground on a dark background improved the visual and perceptual motor functioning of these students.

Gardner (1985) finds that the background color (i.e., yellow chalk on a green chalkboard) enhances the visually impaired child's ability to read the writing on a chalkboard. Another important finding of his study is that the amount of luminance contrast available is critical. How dark the foreground is in comparison with the background, or vice versa, is the major contrast factor controlling visibility for the visually impaired. Consideration therefore must be given to the actual color and hue of the gymnasium and playroom walls. They must be of sufficient contrast to provide an appropriate background when visually impaired students are attempting to track a moving object such as a ball or badminton birdie.

A Special Exercise Program

Many visually handicapped adults do not get enough physical activity and are therefore not physically fit. Since physical activity patterns are formed in early childhood, the visually handicapped child must be exposed to many athletic and developmental activities. Strength, muscle tone, and flexibility can be improved by performing specific exercises that are commonly identified with hatha-yoga (Krebs 1979). The visually handicapped student needs to develop good hand and finger coordination, head and neck control, and skill in using body parts that are developmentally delayed.

Mobility is thought to correlate directly with the blind student's ability to function academically. Many body image and spatial movement concepts that seeing children learn automatically (e.g., bending, stretching, and reaching exercises) reinforce academic skills such as reading readiness (e.g., left to right and top to bottom progression), printing and cursive handwriting (e.g., muscle strength from stretching wrists and fingers), mathematics (counting), and geometry (parallel, triangle, line, and straight).

The following exercises do not involve special equipment. They can be practiced in the gymnasium, outdoors, in the classroom, or at home. All movements should be gentle and never forced; the child should perform the exercises slowly. The breath is never held, and breathing is done through the nostrils rather than through the mouth. The amount of time that each exercise is held can be decreased or increased according to the student's progress.

General Exercises

Krebs (1979) suggests the following exercises:

Breathing (Figure 19.4A): (1) Sit with head, neck, and back in a straight line and pull the shoulders back. Cross the legs. Place the hands palms down on the knees. (2) Breathe in (through the nose) as the abdomen ("tummy") pushes out like a balloon. (3) Breathe out and pull in the abdomen. (4) Place hands flat on abdomen sideways, with fingers together and fingertips touching, to feel the movements.

Slow, controlled, rhythmic breathing should accompany all exercises. Check for proper posture before beginning the breathing exercise. Begin inhalation and exhalation, each to the count of three. Start with five complete rounds (inhalation and exhalation). Visually check the student's abdominal region and hand for proper movements (the fingers should come apart as the abdomen is expanded on inhalation). This exercise may also be practiced while lying on the back with the face upward. Breathing exercises are very relaxing and increase efficiency of the lungs.

Neck rolls (Figure 19.4B): (1) Sit with head, neck, and back in a straight line and pull the shoulders back. Cross the legs. Place the hands palms down on the knees. (2) Let the head drop forward with the chin pointing down, toward the chest. Keep the back straight. (3) Slowly roll the head to the right shoulder so the ear is pointing down toward the shoulder. (4) Roll the head backwards so the nose is pointing toward the ceiling. (5) Roll the head to the left shoulder so the ear is pointing down toward the shoulder. (6) Roll the head forward with the chin pointing down toward the chest and repeat steps 3 through 5.

Neck rolls should be done slowly with continuous movement. Begin with two complete rolls to the right, then reverse the instructions for the left side. Neck rolls stretch the muscles of the neck, improve posture, and relieve tension.

Tiptoe stretch (Figure 19.4C): (1) Stand up straight with arms straight down touching the body sides. Place feet together; pull abdomen in and shoulders back. Make sure that head, neck, and back are in a straight line. (2) Rise up on the toes. Keep both legs straight. (3) Stretch arms and hands up slowly over the head until fingers are pointing up, toward the ceiling. Place palms together and keep elbows straight. (4) Hold to the count of five. (5) Slowly lower arms straight down by sides and rest heels back on floor.

FIGURE 19.4. General exercises: (A) breathing, (B) neck rolls, (C) tiptoe stretch, (D) tree, (E) triangle, (F) hero, (G) standing forward bend, (H) frog, (I) cobra, (J) bow, (K) seated forward bend, and (L) relaxation.

If students have difficulty at first, have them practice against a wall. Balancing a book on the head will help students correct postural alignment problems. This exercise strengthens the toes and ankles, tones the leg muscles, and improves balance ability. Posture (standing and walking) can be improved by practicing the Tiptoe Stretch exercise.

Tree (Figure 19.4D): (1) Stand up straight with arms straight down touching body sides. Place feet together and pull abdomen in and shoulders back. Make sure that head, neck, and back are in a straight line. (2) Place sole (bottom) of right foot high up on inside of left thigh. Keep left leg straight. (3) Stretch arms and hands up over head with fingers pointing up, toward ceiling. Place palms together and keep elbows straight. (4) Hold to count of five. (5) Lower right foot to the floor. Arms are lowered gradually until they are straight down, touching sides. (6) Place sole of left foot high on inside of right thigh, keeping right leg straight. Repeat steps 3 through 5.

Triangle (Figure 19.4E): (1) Stand up straight with arms straight down touching sides. Place feet together and pull abdomen in and shoulders back. Make sure that head, neck, and back are in a straight line. (2) Jump, spreading legs apart to right and left sides. (3) Raise arms straight up 90 degrees, sideways, in line with shoulders and parallel to floor. Keep palms facing down toward floor and fingers stretched straight out to sides. (4) Turn right foot so it is pointing toward the right and bend down sideways, toward floor. Place right hand on ankle. Keep both legs straight. (5) Stretch left arm up with fingertips pointing toward ceiling and palm forward. Left arm should be in line with right shoulder. (6) Point nose toward hand in air. (7) Hold to count of five. (8) Slowly straighten by raising body up sideways, then jump so feet are together. (9) Repeat reversing instructions for left side.

Students should try to keep both legs (knees) straight and bend sideways while doing this exercise. The arms and fingers should be stretched straight up. The Triangle develops chest, leg, and hip muscles, stretches side and back muscles, and strengthens ankles.

Hero (Figure 19.4F): (1) Stand up straight with arms straight down touching sides. Place feet together and pull abdomen in and shoulders back. Make sure that head, neck, and back are in a straight line. (2) Jump, spreading legs apart to right and left sides. (3) Raise arms straight up sideways in line with shoulders (parallel to floor). Keep palms facing down toward floor and fingers stretched straight out to sides. (4) Turn right foot so it points toward right, and turn head so nose is pointing toward right hand. (5) Bend right knee slowly so thigh is parallel to floor. Keep left leg straight. (6) Hold to count of five. (7) Slowly straighten knee and jump so feet are again together with legs straight and arms straight down at sides. (8) Repeat, reversing instructions for left side.

In this exercise, the fingers and arms should be stretched out sideways, while the pelvic area faces forward. The Hero exercise strengthens leg and back muscles and tones abdominal muscles.

Standing forward bend (Figure 19.4G): (1) Stand up straight with arms straight down touching sides. Place feet together and pull abdomen in and shoulders back. Make sure that head, neck, and back are in a straight line. (2) Bend slowly forward from waist. Bring head down toward knees, and let arms and hands reach down toward floor. Keep legs straight. (3) Hold to count of five. (4) Raise the body slowly, keeping head down until body is erect. (5) Place hands pointing straight down by sides.

The Standing Forward Bend should be done very slowly. Students should only bend as far forward as they comfortably can while keeping the knees straight. This exercise improves posture and relaxes tight neck and back muscles.

Frog (Figure 19.4H):   (1) Sit on floor with legs together and straight out in front, and hands, palms down, resting on floor beside hips. (2) Bring soles of feet together. (3) Place hands around the feet and pull feet toward the body. (4) Hold to count of five or ten. (5) Straighten legs and rest hands on floor beside hips.

Check for correct posture before starting the Frog. Students should try to bring knees as close to floor as possible without pushing the knees down. This exercise increases the leg flexibility for activities such as running and jumping.

Cobra (Figure 19.4I):   (1) Lie face down, flat on floor. Keep body in a straight line with arms straight down by sides. Put feet together with toes pointing back, away from body. (2) Place hands with palms down on floor, under shoulders. Elbows are bent by sides, and forehead is on the floor. (3) Slowly lift forehead, nose, and chin off floor. (4) Bring head up and back so nose is pointing toward ceiling. (5) Keep elbows bent and hold to count of five. (6) Lower head slowly to floor. (7) Place arms straight down by sides.

The pubic bones remain in contact with the floor during this exercise. The Cobra expands the chest, strengthens the wrists, and tones the spinal region.

Bow (Figure 19.4J):   (1) Lie face down, flat on floor. Keep body in a straight line and arms straight down by sides. (2) Hold ankles with hands. (3) Raise chest, knees, and thighs off floor. Keep nose pointing forward. (4) Hold to count of three. (5) Gently remove hands from ankles and return to starting position.

The arms should be straight in this exercise. The Bow eases tension in back and shoulders, and stretches chest and abdominal muscles.

Seated forward bend (Figure 19.4K):   (1) Sit on floor with legs together and straight out in front and hands, palms down, resting on floor beside hips. Pull shoulders back and keep head, neck, and back in straight line. (2) Raise hands up, straight over head, with fingers pointing toward ceiling. (3) Bend forward slowly from waist. Keep legs straight and together. (4) Hold legs (or ankles) with hands. (5) Hold to count of five. (6) Slowly raise body and hands to position 2. (7) Lower hands, palms down, so they rest on floor beside hips.

At first the back may be rounded when students do this exercise. Practice, relaxing, and normal breathing will gradually enable the children to flatten the back. The knees should not bend. The Seated Forward Bend strengthens abdominal muscles, stretches hamstrings, increases spinal flexibility, and massages abdominal organs.

Relaxation (Figure 19.4L):   (1) Lie flat on back with feet slightly apart, toes pointing away from each other and arms straight down by sides with palms up. (2) Close the eyes and open mouth slightly. Continue to breathe through nose. (3) Wiggle feet. Relax feet. (4) Raise legs, keeping them straight, a little above floor. Lower legs slowly to floor. Relax legs. (5) Raise arms straight up, a little above floor. Lower arms slowly to floor. Relax arms. (6) Stretch fingers. Relax fingers. (7) Roll head gently from side to side (ear on floor). (8) Make a silly face and stick out your tongue. Relax face. (9) Relax entire body. Lie quietly for a few minutes. (10) Roll onto left side. Pull knees up to chest. Sit up slowly.

Students who have difficulty relaxing should concentrate on the breathing (inhalation and exhalation). Relaxation eases body tension and is restful yet energizing.

Physical Fitness for the Blind

For the totally blind student, quick vigorous movement in an unfamiliar or physically complex area increases the risk of collision or falling and suffering injury. The amount of healthful, invigorating physical activity (i.e., brisk walking, jogging, running, climbing, or hiking) performed by blind students often declines sharply or becomes nonexistent if the children are not stimulated by daily activities. Lack of appropriate physical education opportunities causes loss of stamina, strength, and agility. Without these, students may settle for a daily routine that consists of sitting, standing, lying down, and walking slowly over short distances. This low level of participation is totally insufficient to stimulate vital organs. In the absence of an effective cardiorespiratory program, the incidence of future adult heart disease and degenerative muscle disease rises significantly. The low physical fitness level of many blind persons means fewer calories burned, yet food may become a primary source of personal gratification to the sedentary individual. Obesity, which has complex side effects, often results (Weitzman 1985). Regardless of weight, once one's body composition starts to shift away from lean muscle toward fat, one's strength-to-weight ratio falls sharply, and relatively easy physical activity may seem strenuous and fatiguing.

Weitzman (1985, pp. 97–98) suggests the following brisk walking program for blind individuals:

> Because walking is low intensity exercise (which is what makes it safe), much more of it must be done to stimulate the body to develop greater efficiency and stamina. The ratio of walking three miles at an 18 minute per mile pace gives virtually the same aerobic benefit as running a mile in eight minutes and consumes twice as many calories. Compared to sitting, standing, or shuffling along, walking at a brisk pace forces the cardiovascular-pulmonary system to process two to three times as much oxygen and aerate the body. Over a period of four months, walking three to five miles daily will stimulate the adaptive changes at the tissue level. . . . The ability to work longer and harder without fatigue increases.

The Braille Institute of America in Los Angeles developed a walking program for its students. Instructors found that all students, after program participation, were able to walk farther and faster without serious fatigue. The students also demonstrated gains in agility through their improved performance on the Braille Institute Youth Center obstacle course. Students were occasionally overheard boasting about their new physical accomplishments. A few students enjoyed, perhaps for the first time in their life, the feeling of physical and ethical superiority over the majority of indolent, sighted persons (Weitzman 1985).

Special Equipment

Many pieces of physical education and athletic equipment can be altered to allow visually handicapped students to participate in regular or adapted activities.

Balls should be yellow or bright orange so they can be located easily by the visually impaired. Large softballs, preferably 16 in. in diameter, should be used. These balls travel shorter distances at reduced speeds, and can be seen more easily. Medicine balls and cage balls can also be included in the class equipment.

Audible balls emit a beeping sound for easy location. They should be rugged enough for kicking, throwing, dropping, or hitting. The sound, which is activated by removing a small plug, is generated by a battery-powered solid-state circuit with the components properly located within to maintain balance. Different-sized audible balls are available, including basketballs, soccer balls, softballs, and playground balls. The **National Beep Baseball Association** was developed to encourage the blind and nonhandicapped to compete in softball. Special equipment includes a beep softball (16-in.), cone-shaped rubber bases with internal buzzers, batting tee, and blindfolds for partially sighted and normal players.

A beep baseball contest lasts for six innings unless more are needed to break a tie. A team has three outs per inning. The first and third bases are 4-ft-high rubber or pliable plastic cones, and are placed 90 ft down their respective lines and 5 ft off the foul line. This is to prevent a runner from colliding with a defensive fielder (Figure 19.5). There is no second base as in regulation baseball or softball. The bases contain sounding units that give off a buzzing sound when activated. The batter does not know which base will be turned on. When the ball is hit, the umpire activates one of the bases. The runner must identify the correct sound-cone and run to it before the ball is fielded by a defensive player. If the runner is safe, a run is scored. In other words, there is no running from one base to another. Players do one of three things when batting. (1) They hit the ball and earn a safe call scoring a run. (2) They hit the ball and make an out if they are retired by the defense. (3) They strike out. The batter is allowed five, rather than the traditional three, strikes, and the fifth strike must be a clean miss.

To better understand how the game is played, keep in mind that each team has its own sighted pitcher and catcher. The catcher sets the target where the batter normally swings. The pitcher attempts to place the ball on the hitter's bat; the ball is pitched from a distance of 20 ft. According to the rules, a pitcher is obligated to verbalize two words clearly. He must say "ready" just before the ball is about to be released. This alerts all players that the ball may soon be hit. As the ball is being released, the pitcher says, "pitch." The batter allows a split second of time to pass before swinging. If contact is made, one of the two bases is activated, and the game then becomes a race between the runner and the defense. Note that a hit ball must travel at least 40 ft to be considered fair. A hit ball that does not reach the 40-ft line is counted as a foul. A hit ball that rebounds off the pitcher is ruled no pitch (1983 World Series of Beep Baseball).

Most Beep Baseball equipment is available through Telephone Pioneers of America. Local telephone offices usually can provide information regarding specific contacts.

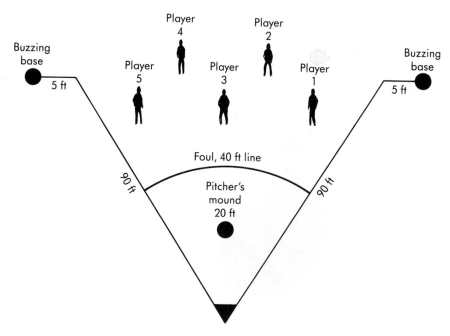

FIGURE 19.5.   Beep baseball field dimensions and player placement.

Other special sport equipment enables visually impaired persons to participate in a variety of sports. A description of some of this equipment follows:

An *audible goal-locator* is a motor driven noisemaker that emits clicking sounds. It plugs into a regular electrical outlet and can be attached to a basketball backboard or soccer goal, or can be used to provide orientation in a swimming pool or gymnasium.

Guide wires enable the blind to run at top speed without fear of tripping over objects or curbs (Figure 19.6). The person grasps a short rope tied to a metal ring, which slides along a wire stretched 100 yd without intervening supports. The athlete can run back and forth to develop endurance.

Bowling rails are usually aluminum poles 9 ft long, 36 in. high, with 7/8-in. diameter rail. The rail includes formed metal bases into which four bowling balls are placed for ballast. This equipment is portable; the parts slide together easily.

Athletic Competition

The U.S. Association for Blind Athletes holds national championships. In 1979, more than 800 blind and visually impaired athletes participated in the annual com-

FIGURE 19.6. Guide wires enable visually impaired individuals to participate in running activities. Both speed and endurance can be developed. (Photograph courtesy of Gary Geiger and the Illinois Special Olympics)

petition. The sports included track and field, swimming, wrestling, goal ball, and gymnastics. Demonstrations were held in competitive power lifting, sailing, Nordic and Alpine skiing, and crew racing. The goal of this association is to develop independence in blind and visually impaired persons through athletic programs that do not have unnecessary restrictions. The organization sponsors blind athletes in national and international competition, and organizes informational programs to raise public awareness.

To be eligible to compete nationally, a person must have ¹/₂₀th or less normal vision. Buell (1979) notes that the times and distances achieved by blind athletes compare favorably with those of sighted peers. In fact, 90 percent of a blind athlete's competitive experiences involve opponents with normal vision.

The 1980 U.S. Blind Olympic Team was selected from participants who competed at the Fourth National Championships for the Blind, cosponsored by the U.S. Association for Blind Athletes.

Summary

The adapted physical educator must be able to evaluate the visually handicapped student's motor, tactual, and perceptual capabilities. If students are to have a positive attitude toward physical activity, then perceptual-motor skills, coordination, balance, activities for orientation training, mobility skills, and physical fitness must be taught. Lifetime sports and recreational games should be an integral part of the curriculum.

Equipment and program adaptations are often necessary if the visually handicapped are to be placed in regular programs to the greatest extent possible. Physical educators have in fact found that accidents and injuries occur less among blind students than among the rest of the student body.

Because tactile, kinesthetic, and auditory perception are the primary ways in which the visually handicapped explore, recognize, and learn, the adapted physical educator's main focus should be on improving physical performance through the training of these senses. When this occurs, students regain self-confidence and feelings of independence and discover that they can enjoy the psychomotor world.

References

Barraga, N. C. *Increased Visual Behavior in Low Vision Children.* New York: American Foundation for the Blind, 1977.

Buell, C. E. Blind Athletes Prepare for the Olympics. *IRUC Briefings,* 1979, p. 5.

————. Physical Education and Recreation for the Visually Handicapped. Lecture given at Illinois State University, Normal, Ill., 26 March 1980.

Cleaves, W. T., and Royal, R. W. Spatial Memory for Configurations by Congenitally Blind, Late Blind, and Sighted Adults. *Journal of Visual Impairment and Blindness* 73(1):13–19, 1979.

Corn, A. L., and Martinez, I. *When You Have a Visually Handicapped Child in Your Classroom: Suggestions for Teachers.* New York: American Foundation for the Blind, 1977.

Cratty, B. J. *Movement and Spatial Awareness in Blind Children and Youth.* Springfield, Ill.: Charles C Thomas, 1971.

Eichel, V. J. A Taxonomy for Mannerisms of Blind Children. *Journal of Visual Impairment and Blindness* 73(5):167–178, 1979.

Ferrell, K. A. Orientation and Mobility for Preschool Children: What We Have and What We Need. *Journal of Visual Impairment and Blindness* 73(4):148, 1979.

Gagné, R. M. *The Conditions of Learning.* New York: Holt, Rinehart & Winston, 1970.

Gardner, L. R. Low Vision Enhancement: The Use of Figure-Ground Reversals With Visually Impaired Children. *Journal of Visual Impairment and Blindness* 79(2):64–69, February 1985.

Klee, K., and Klee, R. Group Training in Basic Orientation, Mobility and Hearing Skills. *Journal of Visual Impairment and Blindness* 79(3):100–103, March 1985.

Kligerman, J. *The Effects of Color Reversal on Stimulus and Response Materials on the Performance of Learning Disabled and Normal Learning Children on the Bender Gestalt Test.* Unpublished Doctoral Dissertation, Columbia University, New York, N.Y., 1981.

Krebs, C. S. Hatha Yoga for Visually Impaired Students. *Journal of Visual Impairment and Blindness* 73(6):209–216, 1979.

Machemer, R. RPB Seminar Highlights Latest Research Findings. *Journal of Visual Impairment and Blindness* 79(4):188, April 1985.

1983 World Series of Beep Baseball. *Beep Baseball in a Nutshell: Batting and Fielding.* St. Louis Park, Minn.: The World Series Program, 25–27 August 1983.

Osborne, N. G., and Clark, J. F. J. Rubella. In *Current Diagnosis 7*, edited by R. B. Conn. Philadelphia: W. B. Saunders, 1985.

Seelye, W. Physical Fitness of Blind and Visually Impaired Detroit Public School Children. *Journal of Visual Impairment and Blindness* 77(3):117–118, March 1983.

U.S. Department of Education. *To Assure the Free Appropriate Public Education of All Handicapped Children.* U.S. Office of Special Education and Rehabilitative Services, Division of Educational Services, Special Education Programs, Washington, D.C., 1985.

Weitzman, D. M. An Aerobic Walking Program to Promote Physical Fitness in Older Blind Adults. *Journal of Visual Impairment and Blindness* 79(3):97–99, March 1985.

CHAPTER 20

Cardiovascular Conditions, Heart Disease, and Abnormalities of the Blood

The adapted physical educator commonly encounters students with restrictions owing to cardiovascular problems. Despite these problems, most affected students lead normal lives and engage in a variety of physical activities. New medical and surgical techniques have greatly improved the prognosis of these students. Restricting activity intensity may be necessary for some, but for others, little or no restriction is necessary.

Cardiovascular abnormalities that occur during fetal development are considered **congenital.** Other conditions that occur later and affect a previously normal heart are **acquired,** or **degenerative.** This chapter discusses the cardiovascular problems that are commonly found in school-age children.

Heart function may be impaired as a result of heredity, injury, or disease (Figure 20.1). The heart or its main blood vessels may be malformed (congenital heart defects), the heart muscle may be diseased (myocarditis), the protective sac that surrounds the heart may become infected (pericarditis), or the valves inside the heart may be damaged (rheumatic fever).

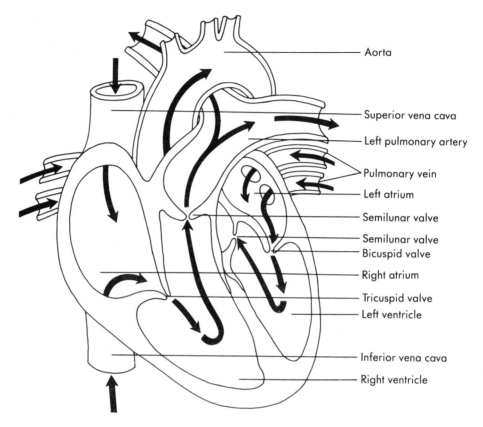

FIGURE 20.1. The human heart and circulation pathways.

Congenital Heart Disease

Congenital heart disease is more common in children than acquired heart disease. Some form of congenital heart defect occurs in approximately 8 of every 1000 live births (Vargo 1985). Table 20.1 lists frequency and type of congenital childhood cardiac anomalies.

The fetal heart begins to take recognizable shape during the first trimester of fetal life. This is when abnormalities also develop. The major cardiovascular structure is formed by the 7th week, so severe abnormalities of the heart and major blood vessels usually occur before the 8th week. Rubella, if contracted by the mother during the first 2 months of pregnancy, can cause fetal heart defect. (See Figure 20.2 for a diagram of the fetal heart.)

Although specific causes of congenital malformations are largely undocumented, maternal illnesses such as rubella, mumps, or influenza during the first 3 months of pregnancy are known to cause defects. X-rays and some drugs have similar detrimental

TABLE 20.1

CONGENITAL CARDIAC ANOMALIES SEEN AT JOHNS HOPKINS HOSPITAL CARDIAC CLINIC, 1963–1972[a]

Anomaly	Percentage (%) of All Congenital Heart Disease
Ventricular septal defect	26
Pulmonic stenosis	14
Tetralogy of Fallot	11
Atrial septal defect	9
Patent ductus arteriosus	8
Aortic stenosis	6
Coarctation of the aorta	5
Endocardial cushion defect	5
Transposition of the great vessels	3
Total	87

SOURCE: From Freedom, R. M., Pieroni, D. R., and Ho, C. S. Congenital Heart Disease. In *Current Diagnosis 4,* edited by H. F. Conn and R. B. Conn, Jr. Philadelphia: W. B. Saunders, 1974, p. 323.

[a]Total number of patients studied (0 to 16 years) was 2956.

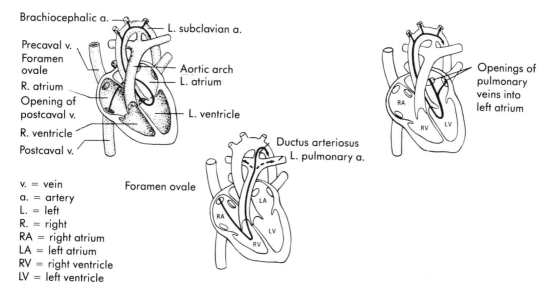

Brachiocephalic a.
L. subclavian a.
Precaval v.
Foramen ovale
Aortic arch
L. atrium
R. atrium
Opening of postcaval v.
L. ventricle
R. ventricle
Postcaval v.
Ductus arteriosus
L. pulmonary a.
Foramen ovale
Openings of pulmonary veins into left atrium

v. = vein
a. = artery
L. = left
R. = right
RA = right atrium
LA = left atrium
RV = right ventricle
LV = left ventricle

FIGURE 20.2. Chambers, openings, and circulation in the fetal heart.

effects. Heart defects, however, are common to all races in all parts of the world. Most inborn heart defects are probably not inherited, but a mother with a congenital heart defect has a 2 percent chance of passing the malformation on to her child.

At least 90 percent of children with congenital heart defects can be categorized in one of four groups. In order of frequency, the groups consist of (1) septal defects, (2) constriction of the aorta, (3) patent ductus arteriosus, and (4) the tetralogy of Fallot (fal-low). All are correctable by surgery.

The problem underlying septal defects occurs during formation of the septum, the dividing wall of either the atria or ventricles. An abnormal septal opening (**patent foramen ovale**) between the two upper chambers (atria) of the heart is the most common and least important of congenital defects. This condition is an abnormal opening that remains after birth. In fetal development, the normal foramen ovale allows blood to move from the right to left atrium, bypassing the nonfunctioning lungs. After birth, this opening slowly closes, so by the end of the 1st year, the opening is sealed. When the opening does not close within the normal time, this slight defect makes it impossible for the child to develop normal cardiorespiratory efficiency. A physician can determine accurately if the defect is present.

Any larger hole in the atrial wall is considered serious and must be corrected surgically for the child to live a normal, active life. Open heart surgery corrects this type of problem.

The most severe congenital heart defect is **tetralogy of Fallot,** which produces cyanosis (blueness of the skin caused by lack of oxygen in the blood). The condition is caused by a narrowing (stenosis) of the pulmonary valve leading from the right ventricle to the pulmonary artery. Stenosis of the pulmonary valve restricts the flow of unoxygenated blood to the lungs. As a result, almost 75 percent of the blood returning to the heart may pass directly from the right ventricle into the aorta without becoming oxygenated. Three other changes occur as a result of this condition. First, the septum is shifted to the right, further narrowing the pulmonary opening. Second, an opening develops in the ventricle wall, which allows blood to pass. Third, the right ventricle wall is enlarged owing to the increased pumping action required to force blood through the narrowed pulmonary valve. These four complications gave the condition its name—tetralogy (*tetra,* four).

Surgery is necessary to correct the tetralogy of Fallot defect. Boyd (1971) notes that the child's improvement following surgery is dramatic. Cyanosis and shortness of breath are often eased immediately.

Epstein and associates (1973) state that in ten subjects who had complete surgical correction of tetralogy of Fallot, resting cardiorespiratory signs were normal except for small residual ventricular outflow. During upright exercise of sufficient intensity to lower pulmonary arterial oxygen, eight patients showed increased cardiac output, less than that attained by normal subjects. Residual cardiac dysfunction thus tends to remain despite corrective surgery. In 1976, James and his colleagues studied 43 asymptomatic patients, 1 to 14 years of age, following surgical correction of tetralogy of Fallot. Maximum heart rate and physical working capacity were lower in these patients when they were compared with age-matched controls. Impaired cardiac performance was evident in the individuals who had had surgery. Interestingly, the patients who had surgery while they were young developed more efficient working capacities than the youngsters who had surgery during adolescence.

Patent ductus arteriosus is a congenital heart defect that affects approximately 1 in every 5500 babies. The fetal blood vessel that joins the pulmonary artery and the aorta normally closes immediately in newborn infants, specifically, when the baby takes his first breath. In some babies, the vessel may take almost 1 month to close completely. If it fails to close, the condition is known as patent ductus arteriosus. During the first few months, the child does not require increased oxygen, but when active walking, running, and jumping begin, the youngster cannot sustain effort because of low cardiac and respiratory reserve. The heart muscle therefore enlarges and the left ventricle hypertrophies because of the abnormally excessive work load to pump a greater than normal blood output. Without corrective surgery, people with this condition die between the ages of 20 and 40 owing to pulmonary congestion and increased work load imposed on the heart. The surgical treatment involves tying off (ligating) the ductus arteriosus so the blood flows through normal pathways.

The abnormal myocardial growth associated with heart defects is distinctly different from the desired hypertrophy of the heart muscle that results from progressive exercise. A healthy heart does and should increase in size when positive aerobic programs are employed.

Many children experience a **heart murmur.** Two out of every 3 healthy babies have an innocent heart murmur that results from slow development of the circulatory system. This is of no consequence, and most children outgrow these functional murmurs in adolescence (American Heart Association 1974).

The physician detects a heart murmur with a stethoscope. Murmurs are generally low in intensity and quite difficult to identify. They indicate an imperfection in the heart valves and may sound like indistinct gurglings or hissings as valves close improperly. The blood is being squeezed backward (regurgitated), and not enough blood is being moved forward into the system.

The physician determines which heart murmurs are "normal" and which are associated with heart disease. A serious murmur often is associated with cardiac malformations such as ventricular septal defect, atrial septal defect, and patent ductus arteriosus. Murmurs commonly result when valves are damaged and do not close completely. Rheumatic heart disease is a known cause of acquired heart murmurs.

Murmurs are also heard in normal hearts. During intense exercise, the blood may flow through valves and chambers of the heart so rapidly that a turbulence is produced. This turbulance can be heard when the blood in the chamber collides with the incoming stream; it is a phenomenon of no consequence.

Children with murmurs generally have lower fitness levels, particularly in activities involving endurance.

When a student has been identified as having a congenital heart defect, the adapted physical educator should refer to the child's medical history to determine if and when surgery was performed on the youngster. If the child underwent surgery several years ago, then the individual may now be able to take part in normal physical activities. The teacher should request a physician's recommendation for activity level of any child who is presently under physician care for cardiac problems.

Physical Activity for Children With Congenital Heart Defects

Some children with mild heart conditions can participate in organized sports (Gersony 1975). Students with decreased exercise tolerance tend to limit their activities. Labored breathing (dyspnea), headache, and fatigue in cyanotic youngsters are indications that the activity is too strenuous. Activity intensity should be lowered and smaller gradients established for children exhibiting these symptoms.

For the adolescent with congenital heart disease, Mahoney (1984, p. 172) states: "The physician should discourage a sedentary lifestyle and encourage physical activity in programs such as physical education but stress with school personnel that the child should be allowed to rest when fatigued." He recommends strongly that physicians give an **exercise stress test** to students with recorded heart defects to measure exercise tolerance. The test results should provide valuable information regarding activity level. If the student has a dilated heart or significant left or right heart obstructive lesion, the individual should not participate in competitive sports. Participation in such organized sports as baseball, golf, and bowling is acceptable.

The physical educator should look for general warning signs when teaching students with cardiac abnormalities. Common complaints are fatigue, shortness of breath, chest pain, cyanosis (blueness of lips and fingernail beds), and fainting. Poor growth and small chest development also indicate that the child is having problems stimulating the cardiovascular system sufficiently.

Acquired Heart Defects

Rheumatic heart disease sometimes results from acute rheumatic fever, which involves inflammation of the joints. The joint inflammation is secondary, however, to the more serious complication involving the heart itself (myocardium). Carditis (inflammation of the heart) is the most serious possible consequence of rheumatic fever. Carditis may result in congestive heart failure or even death during the acute phase of the disease. Later manifestations are valve deformity, specially of the mitral and aortic valves (Lynfield 1985).

The incidence of acute rheumatic fever has decreased greatly in the United States. The disease is, however, still the commonest cause of acquired heart disease in children and young adults (Peter 1984).

Rheumatic heart fever is caused by a streptococcal infection, usually accompanied by a sore throat. The disease generally strikes children between the ages of 5 and 15, causing high fever, weakness, considerable chest pain, and tender, swollen joints. When the heart muscle or valves are damaged, the damage usually occurs during the acute stage of the disease. During this stage, bed rest and antibiotic treatment are commonly prescribed. Most children who contract rheumatic fever escape permanent cardiac damage. If the disease is not treated quickly, however, permanent damage is more likely to occur.

For those individuals who contract rheumatic fever, medication usually has to be continued throughout adolescence and sometimes into young adulthood. The medication of choice to prevent recurrences is usually penicillin or erythromycin.

When damage occurs as a result of rheumatic fever, the mitral valve, located between the left atrium and left ventricle, is usually the affected valve. The valve edges become scarred, so the valve cannot close tightly. As a result, blood regurgitates into the atrium instead of flowing normally. When this occurs, the work load of the heart is greatly increased, and if damage is severe, congestive heart failure may occur. If the valve edges fuse, as often happens, less blood flows between the chambers and mitral stenosis (i.e., narrowing) occurs. In some cases, the opening may become no larger than a buttonhole, whereas the normal mitral valve opening accommodates two fingers.

For those individuals who sustain heart damage from rheumatic fever, medication usually has to be continued throughout the person's lifetime. An exception is sometimes made for those youngsters who reach their 18th birthday without recurrence of rheumatic fever for the last 5 years. If these individuals are not exposed frequently to persons with streptococcal infection, then medication can be discontinued (Peter 1984).

New surgical procedures give children with damaged hearts the opportunity to lead a normal life. The heart can now be reconstructed, abnormal openings closed, and valves repaired. Because of these procedures, rehabilitation and physical education for the child with a damaged heart is now possible.

Boyd (1971) states that bed rest is important because any strain on the heart will sustain inflammation with a subsequent increase in damage to the valves and heart muscle. He stresses, however, that there are limits to the value of rest. While the heart muscle recovers from infection, graduated exercise can be resumed so the patient can prepare to lead a normal life again. Complications have a direct bearing on when activity should begin. Again, the physician should prescribe appropriate beginning levels and intensity of activity.

School-age children often experience mild cardiac problems following a bout with rheumatic fever, but they tend not to develop permanent damage. The physician will prescribe restricted activities in the physical education class. Lynfield (1985) suggests that three common conditions result from rheumatic fever: polyarthritis, mild carditis, and cardiac enlargement. All are considered temporary, and with proper rehabilitation, the heart should return to normal function.

Polyarthritis involves most body joints with attendant swelling and pain. General rehabilitation directs that the student return to school if no symptoms recur and if cardiac findings remain normal. Competitive sports and strenuous physical activity should be deferred for a month. Mild bending, stretching, reaching, and flexibility exercises are indicated, which means placement in the individualized adapted physical education class.

Mild carditis, without heart enlargement, is managed in the same way as polyarthritis with extended medical treatment. The child may return to school after 2 weeks of normal temperature and pulse rate. Competitive sports should be avoided for 2 months. Adapted physical education programming is recommended.

Cardiac enlargement involves a further delay in returning to school. The physician often requires an individual with carditis and heart enlargement to wait 1 month following the conclusion of drug treatment before returning to school. Initially, activity should be mild. In fact, the student may be in school half days only and physical education may be excluded for the first week. If half days are tolerated, the child may return to the full school program, but she may be told to avoid strenuous activity for 2 to 3 months after heart size is normal.

Damage to heart valves owing to rheumatic fever or congenital abnormalities may lead to **bacterial endocarditis,** which is a severe infection of the heart lining. Problems occur when the infection attacks valves already damaged by rheumatic fever or attacks at the site of congenital malformation. Antibiotics have helped reduce the mortality rate and have limited disease severity. Houd (1978) warns, however, that the incidence of this disease has increased recently, particularly among drug addicts.

Exercise training is recommended for patients with valvular heart disease. The results of training are, however, controversial. Auchincloss and Gilbert (1973) studied the effects of a 2-week physical fitness training program on 7 patients who had multiple rheumatic valve abnormalities. The patients were given a progressive work load on a treadmill with exercise periods of 30 to 60 min once or twice daily. All 7 subjects increased their exercise tolerance, but the increase was significant in only two individuals. Increased exercise tolerance was not the result of increased heart efficiency, because lower maximal oxygen uptake was not achieved, nor was increased tolerance the result of increased physical fitness, because a lower heart rate with similar oxygen consumption was not attained. The researchers concluded that improved exercise tolerance was probably secondary to familiarity with the testing procedure. The study was limited to a 2-week training period. With prolonged training (more than 2 weeks), better conditioning might be attained by students with valvular heart disease.

Functional Classification of Patients With Heart Disease

Table 20.2 lists functional classifications of heart disease developed by the American Heart Association. Physicians use these classifications when writing exercise prescriptions, but note that patient classification according to functional capacity gives only part of the information needed to plan individualized activities. An activity recommendation or prescription should be based on information from many sources. The functional classification is simply an estimate of what the patient's heart will allow. Classification should not be influenced by the presence of structural lesions or by an opinion as to treatment or prognosis.

TABLE 20.2

FUNCTIONAL CAPACITIES OF PATIENTS WITH HEART DISEASE

Class	Description
I	Patients with cardiac disease who do not have resulting limitation of physical activity. Ordinary physical activity does not cause undue fatigue, palpitation, dyspnea, or anginal pain.
II	Patients with cardiac disease resulting in slight limitation of physical activity who are comfortable at rest. Ordinary physical activity results in fatigue, palpitation, dyspnea, or anginal pain.
III	Patients with cardiac disease resulting in marked limitation of physical activity who are comfortable at rest. Less than ordinary activity causes fatigue, palpitation, dyspnea, or anginal pain.
IV	Patients with cardiac disease resulting in inability to pursue any physical activity without discomfort. Symptoms of cardiac insufficiency or of anginal syndrome may be present even at rest. If any physical activity is undertaken, discomfort is increased.

SOURCE: Adapted from Love and Walthall 1977, p. 96.

Therapeutic Classification of Patients With Heart Disease

Table 20.3 lists therapeutic classifications of cardiac patients. These classifications are a guide to permissible activity for each functional class. The therapeutic recommendations should be translated into daily physical activity, such as running a number of yards, climbing a number of stairs, lifting a number of pounds, or standing for a limited time. Play programs for each child should be individualized by specifying type and duration of outdoor and indoor activity.

Differences between functional and therapeutic classifications should be determined. The student's functional capacity does not always determine the amount of physical activity that should be permitted. At the onset of rheumatic carditis, for example, the child may not experience discomfort while playing baseball, but rest is imperative and only sitting activities are allowed. This child would be designated as Class I (functional) and Class E (therapeutic). A discrepancy often exists between the amount of activity that a student can undertake and the activity that should be attempted so the disease is not aggravated. Physical activity is recommended not only on the basis of amount of effort possible without discomfort, but also taking into account the nature and severity of the cardiac disease.

EXERCISE WITHOUT DISCOMFORT.

TABLE 20.3
THERAPEUTIC CLASSIFICATION OF PATIENTS WITH HEART DISEASE

Class	Description
A	Patients whose physical activity need not be restricted.
B	Patients whose ordinary physical activity need not be restricted, but who should be advised against severe or competitive physical efforts.
C	Patients whose ordinary physical activity should be moderately restricted, and whose more strenuous efforts should be discontinued.
D	Patients whose ordinary physical activity should be markedly restricted.
E	Patients should be at complete rest, confined to bed or chair.

Summary of Activity Planning for Students With Cardiovascular Conditions

1. **Type of exercise**
   a. Should affect overall physical fitness.
   b. Must be aerobic—affect cardiorespiratory system.
   c. Should be gradually progressive.

2. **Sample programs**
   a. Cooper's aerobics are applicable if discussed with the physician.
   b. Begin mild strength building exercises, which may include lightweight lifting; progress to rhythmic endurance exercises such as walking, jogging, running, or swimming.
   c. Minimum of three sessions per week: progressive calisthenics, walk-jog activity, noncompetitive group activity.

3. **Keys to remember**
   a. Each patient is different—there are no norms.
   b. Consult a physician before finalizing exercise program.
   c. No exercise alone.
   d. Stop at any sign of fatigue.
   e. Progress slowly and safely.

4. **Conditions that contraindicate exercise**
   a. Poor exercise environment (e.g., extreme heat, extreme humidity).
   b. For any heart disease patient, stop exercise at first sign of symptoms such as shortness of breath or emotional stress.

Role of Exercise in Rehabilitation of Cardiovascular Defects

Exercise should not begin until a written prescription is received from a physician. Communication with the physician is necessary before planning physical fitness activities for the disabled student. Abnormalities should be noted, such as condition of heart, septal defects, or cardiac surgery results. All reasons for restricting the person's physical activities should be understood as well as the intensity at which programming should begin.

Exercise Procedures

Physical fitness programs should begin at a low level of physical activity and continue in a progressive fashion on a daily basis. The individualized program should continue through the logical sequence of passive, assistive, active, and progressive exercises in the supine, sitting, and standing positions. Table 20.4 reviews specific exercise techniques.

Students should be taught to measure their heart rate. This procedure acts as a built-in safety device should the student push herself beyond a safe limit. In addition, attaining an understanding of how the heart responds to and recovers from exercise is a positive learning experience.

Beginning Program of Progressive Calisthenics

Begin a cardiorespiratory program with mild bending, stretching, and reaching activities. Weiss and Karpovich (1947, p. 447) list 42 calisthenics that are graded and

TABLE 20.4
TYPES OF THERAPEUTIC EXERCISE

Exercise Type	Description
Passive Exercise	Body part or limb is moved through a range of motion by another person.
Assistive Exercise	Body part or limb is moved through the beginning range of motion by the individual, then the teacher or therapist completes the final phase of exercise.
Active Exercise	Body part or limb is moved by the patient without assistance.
Resistive Exercise	Body part or limb is moved through the range of motion while additional weight or resistance is applied.

designated by energy expenditures. These exercises (Figure 20.3) develop cardiovascular endurance and prevent physical deconditioning. The exercises should be done by number and at the designated count per minute to promote the indicated energy cost. Use a metronome to time the exercise, and select only prescribed exercises for a student's program. Exercises that require less energy expenditure should be used for warm-up. Those that require greater energy expenditure should not be used until prescribed by the physician.

Precautions

Once the student achieves a minimal level of cardiorespiratory efficiency (as determined by the child's physician), an assessment test should be administered to determine exact degree of fitness.

Be sure the student takes a rest period before participation in the exercise program. Activity must be stopped at onset of fatigue, chest pain, or dyspnea.

Crowe, Auxter, and Pyfer (1981) recommend the following procedures when developing programs for students with cardiac disorder:

1. Reduce exercise cadence.
2. When using progressive exercises, start in a lying down position, then progress to a sitting position and finally a standing position.
3. Keep number of repetitions low.
4. Check for cardiac stress; check heart rate and watch for shortness of breath.
5. Be sure amount of exercise is congruent with student's reaction.
6. Use aerobic exercise within the child's established physical bounds to provide maximum improvement.

A Test and Exercise Program for Students With Cardiovascular Abnormalities

Objectives

The test should be usable in the following ways:

1. As conditioning agent and evaluation method
2. As a means to compare pulse rate when student is semiactive with resting pulse
3. To increase cardiovascular efficiency
4. As a home exercise program
5. As an exercise substitute for strenuous activity in physical education class
6. To monitor student's convalescence by measuring overall cardiac efficiency
7. To provide greater student self-confidence

The Test

Have the child perform the following:

1. **Chest pass.** Using both hands, pass and catch a large, lightweight ball 15 times to partner. Stand 10 ft from partner.
2. **Knee bends.** From standing position with arms extended straight out, bend knees to half squat position, hold 5 sec, and return to upright position. Repeat ten times.
3. **Inhale-exhale exercise.** Deep breathing exercise:
   a. Stand on toes and inhale through nose to count of five.
   b. Exhale through pursed lips to count of ten; return to normal standing position, feet spread apart. Repeat ten times.
4. **Bounce pass.** With both hands, bounce large, lightweight ball to a partner 15 times.
5. **Squat thrusts.** From standing position:
   a. Take deep knee bend; place hands on floor in front of feet in squat-rest position.
   b. Jump and extend legs backward so body is in front-leaning rest position, with body weight resting on hands and toes.
   c. Return to squat position.
   d. Stand erect; repeat five times.
6. **Running in place.** Spot running: raise and lower feet enough to clear floor. Count right foot contacts only to count of 50.

Equipment

1. Ruler
2. Lightweight ball (rubber playground ball or basketball)
3. Stopwatch
4. Graph paper

Exercise Procedure

Pulse rate is calculated from 1 min stopwatch reading.

1. Have student rest in chair for 5 min.
2. Take student's resting pulse rate.
3. Have student perform six listed semiactive exercises without rest period.
4. When exercises are completed, have student return to sitting position and take student's pulse immediately.
5. Allow a 1-min rest.

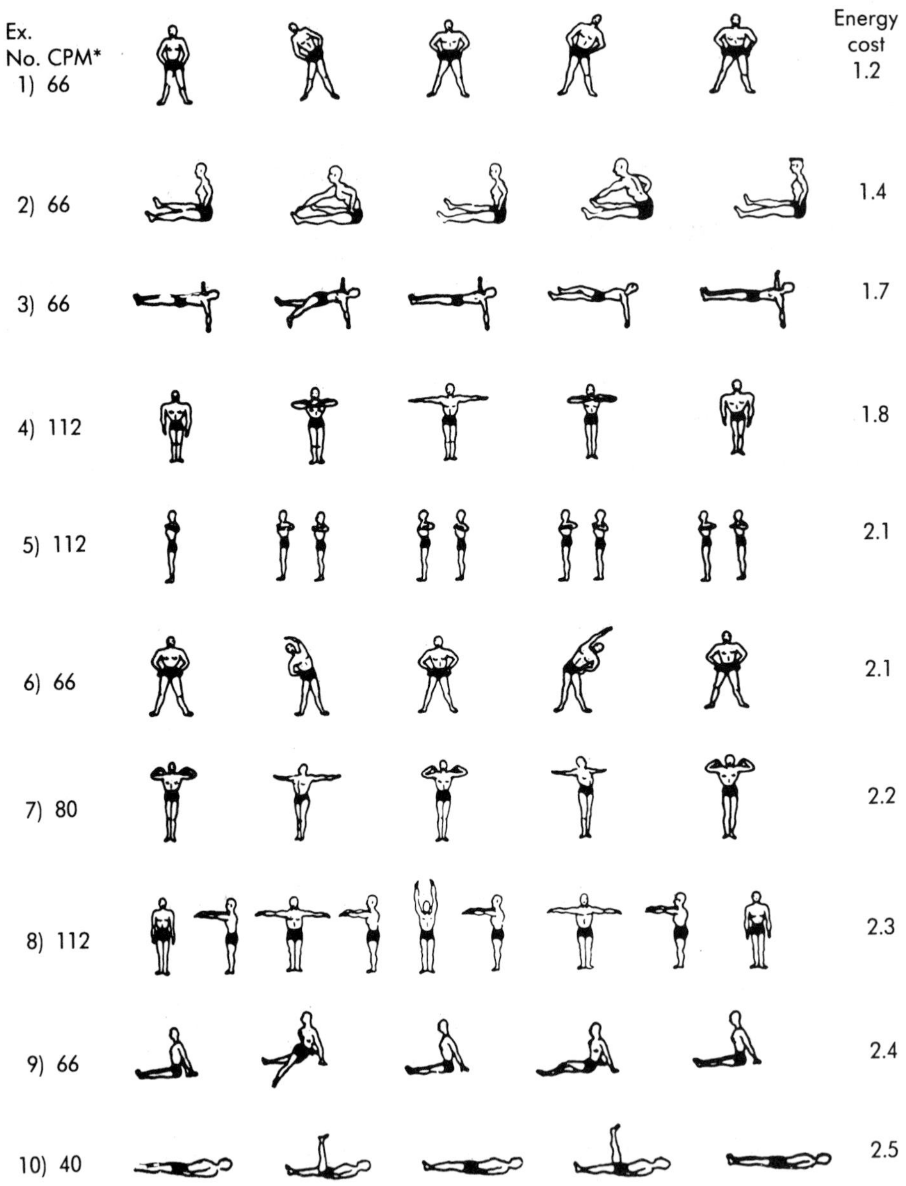

Ex. No. CPM*						Energy cost
1) 66						1.2
2) 66						1.4
3) 66						1.7
4) 112						1.8
5) 112						2.1
6) 66						2.1
7) 80						2.2
8) 112						2.3
9) 66						2.4
10) 40						2.5

*CPM = counts per minute.
Note: The first figure in each exercise shows the starting position for that exercise. All exercises are performed in four counts, except exercise 8, which is performed in eight counts. For example, in exercise 1, the count is: 1, trunk bent right; 2, return; 3, trunk bent left; 4, return.
Exercise 5. Two figures represent each count: 1, elbows back and return; 2, elbows back and return; 3, elbows back and return; 4, elbows back and return.
Exercise 8. The alternate figures in this exercise show the side view.

FIGURE 20.3. Progressive exercise program for rehabilitation of the cardiac patient. (Reprinted with permission from Weiss and Karpovich 1947, p. 447.)

Ex. No.	CPM*						Energy cost
11)	112						2.6
12)	66						2.8
13)	112						2.9
14)	66						2.9
15)	66						3.0
16)	80						3.1
17)	40						3.2
18)	80						3.3
19)	66						3.3
20)	66						3.4
21)	66						3.6

*CPM = counts per minute.

Exercise 13. Second to fifth figures show first two counts of this exercise: 1, trunk bent right, return half way; 2, trunk bent right, return half way; 3, trunk bent right; 4, return.

Exercise 18. Second and third figures show the side view.

Exercise 19. The right knee is raised in the second figure, and the left knee is raised in the fourth figure.

Ex. No. CPM*						Energy cost
22) 66						3.8
23) 66						3.9
24) 40						4.0
25) 80						4.1
26) 66						4.1
27) 80						4.3
28) 66						4.4
29) 80						4.4
30) 80						4.6
31) 80						4.6
32) 80						4.7
33) 66						4.7

*CPM = counts per minute.
Exercise 30. The second figure shows the side view.

Ex. No.	CPM*						Energy cost
34)	80						5.0
35)	66						5.1
36)	66						5.1
37)	66						5.7
38)	80						6.4
39)	66						6.5
40)	66						6.8
41)	80						7.8
42)	66						9.3

*CPM = counts per minute.

Exercise 38. Fingers touch toes of the opposite foot. The second and fourth figures show the side view.
Exercise 41. Two figures represent each count: 1, right knee raised and returned, arms circled outward; 2, left knee raised and returned, arms circled outward; 3, repeat count 1; 4, repeat count 2.

6. Wait 2 min after exercise and take student's pulse again.
7. Allow a 1-min rest.
8. Wait 4 min following exercise and take student's pulse.
9. Allow a 1-min rest.
10. Wait 6 min following exercise and take student's pulse.
11. Plot pulse rate on a graph.

Abnormalities of the Blood

Diseases of the blood usually affect the blood cells—red, or erythrocytes (*erythros*, red), and white, or leukocytes (*leukos*, white). A third element, blood platelets, or thrombocytes (*thrombos*, clot), are responsible for blood clotting. Some problems occur when there are too few or too many of a given cell type. In other instances, the blood cell count is normal, but the cells display abnormalities and do not function properly.

Anemias

Anemia refers to a deficiency of red blood cells. Some anemias are caused by physical problems; others are hereditary and result in fragile red blood cells. Anemia means, literally, "lack of blood," which is not completely accurate. The term describes a condition in which the oxygen-carrying capacity of the blood is reduced. For example, following a hemorrhage, inadequate production or abnormal disintegration of hemoglobin or red blood cells occurs, resulting in a decrease in hemoglobin. Hemoglobin, the oxygen-carrying protein in red blood cells, is responsible for carrying oxygen to body cells (Walter 1982).

Anemia greatly increases the heart's work load. The increased cardiac output compensates for the symptoms of anemia. In the anemic individual, each cell carries smaller quantities of oxygen. The body compensates for this by increasing blood flow so that almost normal quantities of oxygen are delivered to the tissues.

Anemic children can sustain adequate health as long as their activity rate is low, even though their red blood cell concentration may be reduced by one fourth. When these youngsters exercise, however, the heart is incapable of pumping sufficient quantities of blood. During exercise, therefore, extreme tissue anoxia develops because of the body's great demand for oxygen.

Anemia in children is commonly caused by poor diet, resulting in iron deficiency. The physical educator usually will witness excessive fatigue and inability to sustain effort. Less frequent symptoms are headache, cold hands, sore mouth and tongue, difficulty swallowing, indigestion, easy bruising, and brittle or sore nails (Robinson 1985). Boyd (1971, p. 464) states: "Every patient with severe anemia is pale and suffers from shortness of breath and palpitation. The shortness of breath (dyspnea) is due to the fact that there are not enough red blood cells to carry oxygen from the lungs to the tissues. Just as dyspnea may result from disease of the heart or lungs, equally so, it may result from disease of the red blood cells."

Approximately 30 percent of 9- to 11-year-old girls experience significant anemia. The physical educator can expect some anemia to be present during, and immediately following, the menstrual cycle. This should not excuse young women from physical education, but could mean that their performance may be less efficient, particularly during endurance activities. If chronic loss of blood occurs, as in heavy, prolonged menstruation, iron absorption may be inadequate. Red blood cells form but contain inadequate hemoglobin, which means that less oxygen is carried to the body's tissues.

Hereditary anemia is a serious blood disease. Two types are prevalent, sickle-cell anemia and Cooley's anemia.

Sickle-Cell Anemia

Sickle-cell anemia, a condition in which the red blood cells appear twisted and sickle-shaped, occurs almost exclusively among blacks (8 to 10 percent of the black population in the United States is affected). A milder condition, **sickle-cell trait,** occurs when the defective sickle-cell gene is inherited from one parent only, and seldom causes serious or life threatening complications (Pearson 1975). Inheritance of the defective gene from both parents causes extensive cell sickling with death occurring in 50 percent of the affected population before age 20. This condition is known as true sickle-cell anemia.

No effective treatment has been found for individuals with sickle-cell anemia. The severe reduction of hemoglobin causes weakness and an inability to sustain effort, as in chronic anemia. Overexertion or oxygen shortage causes the red blood cells to become sickle-shaped. The cells bunch up in tiny capillaries, impede blood flow, clot, and in the most serious cases, cause death. Because the red blood cells are unusually shaped, delicate, and fragile, they tend to break down and are easily destroyed, thus causing serious anemia.

The general health of an individual with sickle-cell anemia can vary greatly. At times, she may appear to be healthy; at other times symptoms of severe anemia are present. When the disease is most active, the child will seem to be undergoing an acute crisis and the anemia is intensified. At such times, the child experiences sharp abdominal pain similar to acute appendicitis (Boyd 1971). No medical treatment is available for these painful episodes. The individual's body cannot concentrate urine, so the person requires greater than normal amounts of fluid because dehydration occurs. The child should be allowed to drink a lot of water, particularly when involved in continuous activity. The teacher should remind the student to drink water both during and after the physical education class.

From age 10 to 20 years, the child may experience chronic ulcerations (open sores) on the legs. These usually respond well to antibiotics. The physical educator should stress and encourage thorough showering after activities. If the student has medication and sterile dressings on the ulcerations, fresh medication and coverings should be applied following a shower.

The activity program for these children should be planned with the same constraints as the program for children who have anemic tendencies. If the child with sickle-cell anemia has difficulty keeping up with the peer group, individualized developmental programming with slower progressions is recommended.

Cooley's Anemia

Cooley's (Mediterranean) anemia is a hereditary condition in which red blood cells are small, have fragile membranes, and are ruptured easily. This condition is commonly called thalassemia. A mild form develops when the defective gene is inherited from one parent only, and is of no major consequence to the physical education teacher. When two defective genes are inherited, however, the condition becomes serious and is termed "thalassemia major." When this condition occurs, severe anemia, skeletal abnormalities, and Down syndrome facial features are present.

The gene responsible for defective hemoglobin formation occurs among eastern Mediterranean people and is known as Mediterranean anemia. This condition is found in people of Greek, Italian, and Armenian heritage.

The physical education programming designed for these children should consist of slow progressive developmental activities. Routines that induce fatigue or require intense cardiorespiratory exertion are not appropriate. Lifetime skills and games are recommended.

Mononucleosis

Infectious mononucleosis is a viral infection caused in 90 percent of cases by the Epstein-Barr virus. Between 10 and 20 percent of those who have been previously infected by the virus have the virus present in their saliva for some months following infection. Among young adults, the disease is commonly spread through salivary transfer during kissing. The asymptomatic virus carrier, who has the virus in the saliva, passes the virus to the susceptible person (Schooley and Dolin 1985).

The infection is characterized by sore throat, fever, and swelling of the lymph glands. Symptoms include general overall weakness, feverishness, chills, sore throat, and headache. The condition is fairly common among teenage students and occurs typically during the late teenage years. Seventy to 80 percent of all documented cases occur in persons between the ages of 15 and 30. It is not uncommon, however, for youngsters between ages 11 and 14 to contract the disease, although the infection is usually not as severe as in older individuals (Adams et al. 1982).

The disease is rarely fatal, but results in general weakness that may persist for a few weeks to several months. Mononucleosis has an acute phase, lasting from 10 to 14 days, followed by a 2- to 4-week convalescent period.

The acute phase requires bed rest until the temperature is normal for one entire day. Rose (1975, p. 40) states: "To prolong bed rest beyond this time only results in deconditioning with its effects of fatigue . . . and a sense of invalidism. In the student, this can be catastrophic. Encouraging the patient to be up and about his daily activities, insisting only on at least 8 hours of rest each night, and avoidance of unreasonable physical and psychological strain, will hasten recovery without increasing complication morbidity. There is no rationale for the prolonged bed rest previously recommended."

Normal physical activities are permissible, with the possible exception of those that are fatiguing. Contact sports should not be allowed for approximately 1 month to prevent a severe blow to the spleen (located immediately below the heart and above the abdomen). In uncomplicated cases, normal stamina returns within 3 to 6 weeks once the fever ends (Hoagland 1974).

Hepatitis (inflammation of the liver) is a common side effect of infectious mononucleosis but recovery is usually complete. With proper medical treatment, the student should return to full activity within 10 to 14 days (Rose 1975).

Hemophilia

Hemophilia pertains to a hereditary condition, contracted by males only, in which the blood clots very slowly or not at all. A cut or bruise can cause excessive blood loss, but the hemophiliac will not bleed to death from a cut finger. A bump or blow, however, can produce painful internal bleeding into vital organs, muscles, and joints.

The term **hemophilia** is used to identify several different blood coagulation deficiencies that cause indistinguishable bleeding tendencies. Each classification lacks a specific plasma protein. This lack of specific proteins, or factors, has been identified and the most common are as follows: lack of factor VIII:C (classic A hemophilia) which includes about 80 percent of all cases, and lack of factor IX (Christmas disease, or B hemophilia) which includes approximately 15 percent of all cases (Hussey and Olive 1985). Both A and B types are inherited by the son from the mother. Hemophilia is therefore described as a sex-linked recessive trait. The female carries the abnormal trait and has a 50 percent chance of passing the abnormality to a male child. The female carrier also has a 50 percent chance of transmitting the abnormality to a female child, who will not contract the condition but will herself become a carrier. An affected male transmits the condition to all of his female offspring, who become carriers. A male hemophiliac will not, however, transmit the abnormality to his sons. Males must inherit the condition from the mother, or in rare cases, develop hemophilia as a new disease.

Approximately 1 in every 4000 U.S. males will be born with this disease. Of all genetic diseases, hemophilia has the greatest mutation rate, approximately one third of all cases occur in families with no prior history of affliction (National Hemophilia Foundation n.d.). Ninety percent of all hemophiliacs are under age 25.

Another blood coagulating abnormality, von Willebrand's disease, affects both males and females. The condition is even more common than hemophilia A if patients with milder forms of the disease are included. Factor VIII:VWF is lacking (Goodnight 1984).

Those students who have hemophilia should be classified as having a physical handicap. They therefore become eligible for adapted physical education programming.

The Bleeder

Any cut, abrasion, or bruise, excessive or stressful movement, or continual use of a joint can cause bleeding in the child who has hemophilia. The most disabling complications result from bleeding into a joint (hemarthrosis) or muscles (hematoma) (Hussey and Olive 1985). Approximately 80 percent of all individuals who have hemophilia have had joint hemorrhages. Once bleeding occurs in a joint, it tends to recur. Knees, ankles, and elbows are the most commonly involved joints, although bleeding can also occur in wrists, shoulders, and hips.

Medical Treatment of Bleeding Episodes

Treatment involves the replacement of the missing clotting factors by intravenous injection of factor VIII (type A) and factor IX (type B). These factors are contained in plasma, or dehydrated concentrate. In general, moderate and severe hemophilia are treated with concentrate. These injections may be given in a hospital setting or by a parent or the patient himself. Individuals generally are taught to administer the "factors" to themselves at home at the earliest sign of bleeding (Goodnight 1984).

When the concentrate is administered early following onset of bleeding, the incapacitation period is shortened considerably. The physician may place the affected part in a plaster cast or bulky wrap to restrict movement for a time. Isometric contraction ("muscle setting") without joint movement is appropriate. The physician may recommend crutches if the child's hip, knee, or ankle is involved. Physician contact is strongly suggested prior to the rehabilitation period.

When the youngster begins a strength development program or a cardiorespiratory routine, plasma concentrate should be injected before exercise, which requires that the parent or physician be consulted. New developmental activities could cause joint bleeding, and injections are helpful when bleeding is anticipated. As new muscle strength is developed, it will provide support for joints, and bleeding episodes will become less frequent and less severe. The need for concentrate will be reduced gradually and finally discontinued.

Prolonged running and excessive stopping and starting, as in soccer or field hockey, may be too demanding. Slow progressive walking and jogging are recommended. Progressive aerobic programs, as suggested by Cooper, are highly desirable for the individual with hemophilia.

General First Aid for Students With Hemophilia

Students who have hemophilia usually know when internal bleeding is occurring, even before swelling or other external signs are evident. The child's statement indicating that bleeding is happening is probably reliable and should be taken seriously.

Since most bleeding involves joints or soft tissue, cold compresses or ice packs should be applied and the body part elevated. This facilitates vasoconstriction and should be continued for 8 to 12 hours following injury. *Aspirin and aspirin-containing compounds should not be given to children with hemophilia* because these medications increase frequency and severity of bleeding in people with coagulation disorders.

Following an acute bleeding episode, the hemorrhage site may be quite painful and temporarily incapacitated. Quick or strenuous movements should *not* be done. *Mild* stretching and *mild* range of motion activities are acceptable.

Specific Complications of Hemophilia

Hemarthrosis occurs when bleeding into a joint is characterized by a swollen, painful, and slightly warm joint. When lower extremities are involved, weight bearing should not be allowed for 3 to 5 days. Gradual resumption of weight bearing may begin over the next 5 days (Davis 1975). Swimming and upper body activities that allow the student to sit or lie down are acceptable.

Joint damage occurs from repeated bleeding into the same joint with resultant damage to cartilage and bony structure. Arthritic problems may develop, including limited range of motion, joint stiffness when one position is maintained for a prolonged time, and varying degrees of pain and discomfort. Rehabilitative surgery (e.g., joint replacement, joint bracing, or wedging out of nonosseous contractures) is performed on hemophiliac individuals with severe joint destruction and deformity.

Boone (1974) states that in addition to joint damage, the muscles weaken because of recurrent periods of pain and immobilization. As muscles weaken, joint support diminishes, which makes the joint more susceptible to additional trauma from normal activities with resultant bleeding and greater chronic disability. A vicious cycle is thus established.

Hematoma (muscle and soft tissue bleeding) causes problems because of localized symptoms for which a single dose of concentrate is generally adequate. Bumping the affected area should be avoided. If this happens, ice, compression, and elevation should be administered quickly. Swimming is a fine activity to perform during rehabilitation. If adequate modifications can be made to reduce the chance of reinjury, students should not be excused from physical education.

One complication that sometimes occurs involves the child's biting his tongue. A hematoma generally develops. The student should be forewarned to tell the teacher and the school nurse if this happens.

Hematuria, blood in the urine, occurs often in hemophiliac individuals. It is not life threatening and generally responds to factor replacement injections. Restrictions in the physical education program are not indicated.

Physical Education Activities for the Child With Hemophilia

Because educators and parents tend to be overcautious with the hemophiliac child, many children with this disorder are excluded from regular physical education programs and playground activities. The concern of parents and educators is valid but is not necessarily best for the child. The adapted physical educator is responsible for understanding the adults' concerns and for providing information about activities that will be used in the child's program. The teenage youngster can help by actively avoiding situations that are likely to result in bleeding episodes. In most cases, the hemophiliac individual should be restricted from contact sports. This frequently creates problems in managing the young child who may resent the fact that he is forced to behave differently from his peers.

The educator should encourage and provide activities that are less likely to cause bodily injury (e.g., tennis, golf, badminton, swimming, archery, and jogging). Boone (1974) points out that a number of hemophiliac children play Little League baseball, and participate in intramural basketball, soccer, and other sports.

Davis (1975, p. 251) suggests that avoidance of normal activities because of the possibility of *some risk* is inadvisable. He states: "There is no altogether satisfactory solution to the problem of allowing the patient to experience a 'normal' childhood and at the same time to avoid potentially injurious activity. Encouragement of the hemophiliac to obtain as high a level of formal education as his abilities permit is beneficial."

Because of the multiple problems associated with hemophilia, ideal medical treatment occurs when a team of medical and nonmedical professionals is developed (Carrai and Handford 1983). The adapted physical educator should be a contributing team member who participates in development and implementation of the individualized activity and rehabilitation program.

Each hemophiliac male differs in physical ability, severity of joint involvement, and frequency and kind of bleeding episodes. All variables must be considered when the student's individualized physical education program is being planned. For example, a boy who experiences repeated bleeding in the elbow joints should not be placed in an upper body weight training program because this activity would keep his affected joints chronically irritated. He can participate in isometric exercises that develop similar strength, however, but do not cause unnecessary flexion or extension of the elbow joints. The prescribed program should be flexible enough to accommodate the bleeding variability. The boy should not play tennis or run while recovering from a bleeding episode of the knee. Modified activities such as swimming or weight training while sitting are advisable in that instance. When knee bleeding has stopped and swelling is reduced, he can resume usual activities.

Summary

With proper medical treatment and appropriate physical activity, most young people with heart damage or abnormality can live long and useful lives. Restriction of physical activity may be necessary for some but not for others. Many students with heart disease are fully capable of participating unrestricted in the activities of daily life, and some may engage in strenuous activity. In other cases, heart disease may require curtailment of intense physical demands (Figure 20.4). The physician is the key to program constraints.

The more common heart and blood conditions among school-age youth include congenital heart defects, rheumatic heart disease, the anemias, mononucleosis, and hemophilia. All have a direct bearing on school attendance and participation in adapted or regular physical education classes. Each individual must be evaluated carefully to determine the extent and significance of the child's fear and anxiety and the relationship of those feelings to symptom aggravation.

Rehabilitation and physical education programming for all children with cardiovascular abnormalities are fundamentally similar. Although individual conditions may

FIGURE 20.4. Modified activities should be stimulating and interesting, without undue stress.

differ, the heart expresses distress or impairment in a limited number of ways. Many students with mild heart disease do not require program restrictions. Those who do require activity restrictions should experience activity in quantities that stimulate but do not distress the cardiovascular system. The educator should work with the physician to plan a program of permitted and restricted activities, which can be varied depending on the functional and therapeutic classification of each individual. Once a heart problem is identified, the adapted physical educator should provide interesting activities to meet the child's psychomotor needs.

Exercise training for cardiac and pulmonary rehabilitation has been conducted successfully through a number of aerobic exercise programs with duration varying from 3 months to 2 years. Most specialists in exercise rehabilitation agree that an exercise prescription of 50 percent of the maximum VO_2 may be necessary to provide beneficial physiological changes (Woods 1982–1983). Some individuals may be unable to reach this level of cardiac output because they experience warning signs such as dyspnea, feelings of anxiety, or extreme discomfort before the level is attained. In these cases, training sessions must be adjusted to lower activity levels with anticipation of gradual activity increase in the future.

For children with heart disease, planned programs must begin early in life with special attention devoted to growth and development. Because developmentally disabled children experience fewer opportunities for unrestricted and uninterrupted exercise and activity, they are potential candidates for heart disease. The adapted physical education teacher should be concerned with prevention of cardiorespiratory disabilities in handicapped children.

The early years are the time when lifelong behavior patterns are established. During this period, birth through adolescence, the caliber of the individual's total life is determined (Amsterdam, Wilmore, and DeMaria 1977).

References

Adams, R. C., Daniel, A. N., McCubbin, J. A., and Rullman, L. *Games, Sports, and Exercises for the Physically Handicapped*, 3rd ed. Philadelphia: Lea & Febiger, 1982.

American Heart Association. *You and Your Heart*. New York: The Association, 1974.

Amsterdam, E. A., Wilmore, J. H., and DeMaria, A. N. *Exercise in Cardiovascular Health and Disease*. New York: Yorke Medical Books, 1977.

Auchincloss, J. H., Jr., and Gilbert, R. Short-Term Physical Training in Patients With Rheumatic Heart Disease. *Chest* 64:163–169, 1973.

Boone, D. C. Physical Activity for a Child With Hemophilia. *Physical Therapy* 54:7–12, 1974.

Boyd, W. *An Introduction to the Study of Disease*, 6th ed. Philadelphia: Lea & Febiger, 1971.

Carrai, E. B., and Handford, H. A. Problems of Hemophilia and the Role of the Rehabilitation Counselor. *Rehabilitation Counseling Bulletin* 26:155–162, 1983.

Crowe, W. C., Auxter, D., and Pyfer, J. *Principles and Methods of Adapted Physical Education and Recreation*, 4th ed. St. Louis: C. V. Mosby, 1981.

Davis, W. E. Hemophilia and Allied Conditions. In *Current Therapy 1975*, edited by H. F. Conn. Philadelphia: W. B. Saunders, 1975.

Epstein, S. E., Beiser, G. D., and Goldstein, R. E. Hemodynamic Abnormalities in Response to Mild and Intense Upright Exercise Following Operative Correction of an Atrial Septal Defect or Tetralogy of Fallot. *Circulation* 47:1065–1075, 1973.

Gersony, W. M. Congenital Malformations of the Heart. In *Current Therapy 1975*, edited by H. F. Conn. Philadelphia: W. B. Saunders, 1975.

Goodnight, S. H., Jr. Hemophilia and Related Conditions. In *Conn's Current Therapy 1984*, edited by R. E. Rakel. Philadelphia: W. B. Saunders, 1984.

Hoagland, R. J. Infectious Mononucleosis. In *Current Diagnosis 4*, edited by H. F. Conn and R. B. Conn, Jr. Philadelphia: W. B. Saunders, 1974.

Houd, H. Cardiac Disorders. In *Disability and Rehabilitation Handbook*, edited by R. M. Goldenson. New York: McGraw-Hill, 1978.

Hussey, C. V., and Olive, J. A. Hemophilia and Other Inherited Coagulation Disorders. In *Current Diagnosis 7*, edited by R. B. Conn. Philadelphia: W. B. Saunders, 1985.

James, F. W., Daplan, S., and Schwartz, D. C. Response to Exercise in Patients After Total Surgical Correction of Tetralogy of Fallot. *Circulation* 54:671–679, 1976.

Love, H. D., and Walthall, J. E. *A Handbook of Medical, Educational, and Psychological Information for Teachers of Physically Handicapped Children.* Springfield, Ill.: Charles C Thomas, 1977.

Lynfield, J. Rheumatic Fever. In *Current Diagnosis 7*, edited by R. B. Conn. Philadelphia: W. B. Saunders, 1985.

Mahoney, L. T. Congenital Heart Disease. In *Conn's Current Therapy 1984*, edited by R. E. Rakel. Philadelphia: W. B. Saunders, 1984.

National Hemophilia Foundation. *What You Should Know About Hemophilia.* New York: The Foundation, n.d.

Pearson, H. A. Sickle Cell Anemia. In *Current Therapy 1975*, edited by H. F. Conn. Philadelphia: W. B. Saunders, 1975.

Peter, G. Rheumatic fever. In *Conn's Current Therapy 1984*, edited by R. E. Rakel. Philadelphia: W. B. Saunders, 1984.

Robinson, S. H. Anemia. In *Current Diagnosis 7*, edited by R. B. Conn. Philadelphia: W. B. Saunders, 1985.

Rose, K. D. Infectious Mononucleosis. In *Current Therapy 1975*, edited by H. F. Conn. Philadelphia: W. B. Saunders, 1975.

Schooley, R. T., and Dolin, R. Epstein-Barr Virus (Infectious Mononucleosis). In *Principles and Practice of Infectious Diseases*, 2nd ed., edited by G. L. Mandell, R. G. Douglas, Jr., and J. E. Bennett. New York: John Wiley & Sons, 1985.

Vargo, T. A. Congenital Heart Disease. In *Current Diagnosis 7*, edited by R. B. Conn. Philadelphia: W. B. Saunders, 1985.

Walter, J. B. *An Introduction to the Study of Disease*, 2nd ed. Philadelphia: W. B. Saunders, 1982.

Weiss, R. A., and Karpovich, P. N. Energy Cost of Exercise for Convalescents. *Archives of Physical Medicine* 28:447, 1947.

Woods, D. Y. Exercise Rehabilitation in COPD. *Cardio-Gram* 10(1):6, 1982–1983.

CHAPTER 21

Allergies, Asthma, and Other Respiratory Diseases

Although I've had asthma since I was three I never thought of it as a handicap. I always loved sports. I wasn't going to be kept from taking part even when I couldn't breathe. Over the years I have participated in athletics and found them easier. I know that my lungs have gotten stronger and my stamina has increased greatly. I participated in track for three years at my high school. My first year I was only able to do half of the workout. I remember that I often had to go back to the locker room to take a pill. I was always optimistic so I would keep my medicines in the locker room, hoping to have no need of them on the field.

My second year I made it through almost every workout. But every day when I came home from track I would be wheezing. My mom thought I was crazy for pushing myself so hard, but I had to prove that I could do the same as the other kids. I would get frustrated when I would have to sit out for a rest. Sometimes the other kids would even think I was using my asthma as an excuse to get out of a workout! I really wished I could have traded places with them, so they could feel what it is like not to be able to breathe. Well, last year I was finally able to make it through a whole workout without getting an asthma attack. It was an important event for me. Finally, everything—all the other practices—was worth it.

(Taken from a letter from Erika Benowitz, 1985 Asthma Athlete of the Year, *The Allergy and Asthma Advance* 3(4):12, March/April 1985.)

Physical education programs have traditionally excluded allergic or asthmatic persons for fear that an exercise-related attack would have irreparable or fatal consequences. This attitude has denied asthmatic students the opportunity to develop physical and motor skills. Now, with the cooperation of the physician, parent, and adapted physical educator, the asthmatic child need not be relegated to a nonactive life.

The adapted physical educator must be familiar with the anatomy and physiology of the respiratory system, the causes and characteristics of allergies and asthma, the relevant medical terminology, and those drugs and medicines used to control asthma and allergies. Finally, and most important, the educator must know how to develop and teach a progressive program of rehabilitation.

Allergic and asthmatic disorders rank first among children's diseases. Of the millions who suffer from respiratory conditions, most cases occur in infancy or childhood. Many asthmatic youngsters are further hampered by poor appetite, loss of sleep, and inability to compete with others, all of which result in frustration and personality changes.

The Asthma and Allergy Foundation of America (April 1984, p. 12) provides these statistics: "Approximately 35 million people in this country—about one out of seven—suffer from asthma or allergies. Some of these people are so incapacitated as to be unable to perform any work, while many others lose part of their employment time. In children, one out of every four days' absence from school is due to asthma."

Allergies and asthma are directly related to a malfunctioning of the human immune system. According to the National Institute of Allergy and Infectious Diseases (NIAID), recent research in immunology is vitally important to an understanding of the immune system, which appears to be the key to treating a number of diseases. A normal immune system protects the individual from a vast array of infectious microbes. When the immune system is altered, the individual may suffer from a variety of common disorders, including allergies and asthma. The immune system is the body's main defense against disease, and many respiratory conditions appear to be linked directly to a faulty response of the immune system. Specifically, the antibody associated with certain types of allergies and asthma is the serum **immunoglobulin E (IgE).** This antibody often is found in elevated concentrations in the blood during a negative response or attack.

The Breathing Process

Pulmonary ventilation (respiration) is the exchange of oxygen and carbon dioxide between the atmosphere and cells of the body. Through respiration, we take in oxygen for the body's cells and release carbon dioxide, the cell's waste product, to the atmosphere. The respiratory system (Figure 21.1) includes those muscles and organs that accomplish the process of respiration (Figure 21.2). Any impairment or reduced effectiveness of this system has a direct bearing on programs developed by the adapted physical educator.

The process of lung expansion and contraction involves (1) downward and upward movement of the diaphragm to lengthen or shorten the chest cavity, and (2) elevation and depression of the ribs to increase and decrease the anteroposterior diameter of the chest cavity (Figure 21.3). Raising the front portion of the rib cage increases the anteroposterior dimensions of the chest cavity. Normal, quiet breathing is accomplished almost entirely by diaphragm movement (Guyton 1979). Diaphragm contraction pulls the chest cavity downward and increases its length. Upward movement is caused by simple relaxation of the diaphragm or by contraction of the abdominal muscles. The diaphragm is responsible for about 65 percent of pulmonary ventilation, with the respiratory muscles responsible for the remainder.

In children with chronic bronchial asthma and chronic bronchitis, progressive damage occurs to the pulmonary structure. Because of this damage, the lungs lose their recoil property, become distended, and weaken and depress the diaphragm. The weakened diaphragm is unable to rise against the distended lung, and is no longer responsible for breathing. The body compensates for diaphragmatic weakness by using accessory chest muscles when extra effort is needed. This results in increasingly shallow and labored breathing. If this faulty breathing pattern persists, the diaphragm will eventually perform only about 30 percent of the work load, while the chest and accessory muscles do the remaining 70 percent.

Edwards (1979, p. 81) states: "In respiratory failure resulting from airway obstruction, the lung volume increases, and the diaphragm becomes low and flattened. Muscle fibers must shorten considerably to generate force in the presence of this alteration in geometry." Druz and associates (1979) find that patients with obstructive lung disease may possess a functionless diaphragm. They rely instead on rib cage and accessory muscles for virtually all ventilation requirements.

Anatomy of the Respiratory System

Air initially enters the body through the nose or mouth or both. The nose acts as a filter, and warms and moistens the air for the deeper respiratory organs. Although the mouth allows more air to enter the body than does the nose, physicians encourage nose breathing because of the filtering and moistening processes. Individuals with chronic nasal congestion (from allergies) often become mouth breathers, thereby increasing their chance of acquiring upper respiratory infections.

The nose and mouth empty into the throat (**pharynx**). The voice organs (**larynx**) are located between the pharynx and the windpipe (**trachea**). Food or water may occasionally enter the larynx, causing the muscles to contract and expel the particles or liquid. The epiglottis protects the larynx during swallowing.

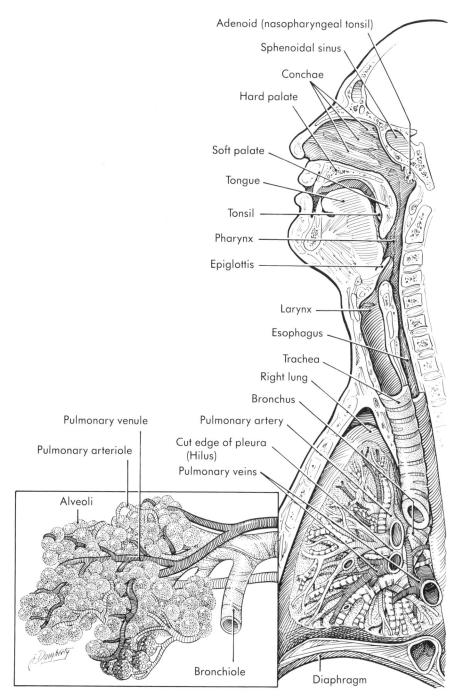

Adenoid (nasopharyngeal tonsil)

Sphenoidal sinus

Conchae

Hard palate

Soft palate

Tongue

Tonsil

Pharynx

Epiglottis

Larynx

Esophagus

Trachea

Right lung

Bronchus

Pulmonary artery

Cut edge of pleura (Hilus)

Pulmonary veins

Pulmonary venule

Pulmonary arteriole

Alveoli

Bronchiole

Diaphragm

FIGURE 21.1. Respiratory system.

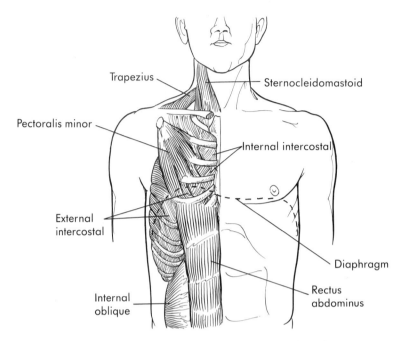

FIGURE 21.2.   Muscles that assist in breathing.

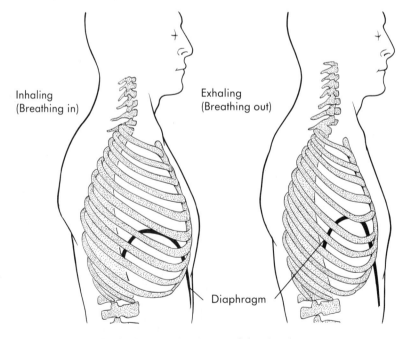

FIGURE 21.3.   Movement of the diaphragm.

The trachea is protected by cartilage, which keeps it open at all times so air can pass continually through the trachea to the lungs.

The trachea divides into two smaller tubes, the primary right and left **bronchi** (Figure 21.4), which are lined with ciliated mucous membranes. Each primary bronchus enters the lung and divides into secondary bronchi, which continue to branch and form increasingly smaller structures called **bronchioles.** The smooth muscles of the bronchioles are controlled by the autonomic nervous system, which causes them to dilate (expand). The smooth muscles are also innervated by the parasympathetic nervous system, which stimulates the muscles to contract. Uncontrollable contraction of these muscles during an asthmatic attack is called **bronchospasm** (Figure 21.5). This condition leads to significant reduction of oxygen to and from the lungs.

The bronchioles split into microscopic branches called **alveolar ducts,** which terminate in **alveolar sacs.** Each alveolus has direct contact with the body's circulatory system. It is at this point that the exchange of gases occurs, with oxygen diffusing into the bloodstream and carbon dioxide diffusing into the alveoli to be transported out of the body. The total surface area available for exchange of gases between lungs and blood is increased tremendously by the alveoli.

Ciliated mucous membranes line the nose, mouth, and respiratory system, including the smaller bronchioles. When these membranes become irritated, additional amounts of mucus are produced.

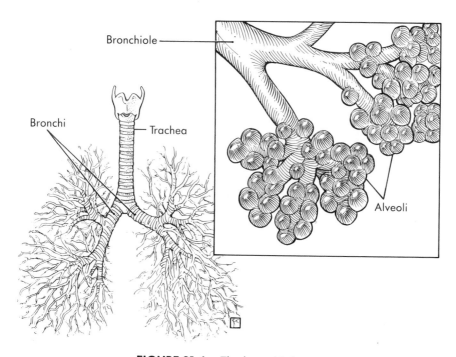

FIGURE 21.4. The bronchial tree.

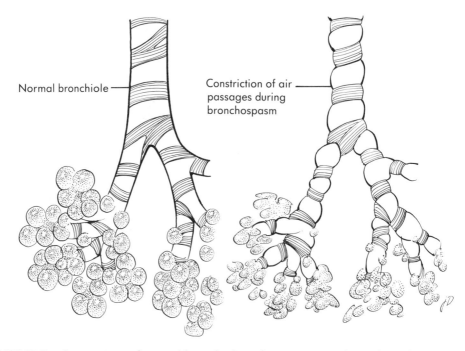

Normal bronchiole

Constriction of air passages during bronchospasm

FIGURE 21.5.   Comparison of normal bronchiole with appearance during bronchospasm.

Diseases and Infections of the Respiratory System

The common cold, influenza (flu), and bronchitis usually do not result in long-term impairment of the upper respiratory tract. These infections do interfere with normal passage of air in the respiratory system and force mouth breathing. Infection occurs in the mucous membranes, and as a result, excessive mucous is produced, which interferes with respiration. These conditions result in lowered resistance and development of secondary bacterial infections. Table 21.1 identifies the terminology used to describe common respiratory abnormalities.

The Common Cold (Rhinitis)

A cold is the most common infectious disease. It is a contagious filterable virus that causes mild to severe epidemics. The infected person develops no immunity and can suffer several colds within the period of a few months. Many different viruses, including the influenza virus, contribute to school outbreaks of respiratory tract infection.

To lessen the chance of contracting a cold, direct contact with individuals who have cold symptoms should be avoided. Children with a virus should be kept at home.

TABLE 21.1

ABNORMAL RESPIRATORY TERMINOLOGY

Term	Definition
Anoxia (ah-nok'se-ah)	Absence or lack of oxygen; reduction of oxygen in body tissues below normal physiologic levels.
Eupnea (youp'ne-ah)	Normal, resting breathing.
Dyspnea (disp'ne-ah)	Difficult or labored breathing. A person suffering from an asthmatic attack exhibits dyspnea.
Tachypnea (ta-kip-ne'ah)	Shallow, rapid breathing.
Hyperpnea (hy-perp-ne'ah)	Excessively deep breathing. This condition often follows vigorous exercise.
Apnea (ap-ne'ah)	Stopping of breathing.
Cough	Reflex response to foreign material in the pharynx, larynx, or trachea. This response consists of a pressure buildup in the lungs and the sudden opening of the glottis. Air rushes out with great force, clearing the bronchi and trachea.
Sneeze	Reflex response to foreign material in the nasal cavity. Initially, more and more air is inspired and then expelled with great force through nasal and mouth cavities. Expulsion of air acts to expel foreign material from the body.

SOURCE: Modified from Landford, T. R. *Integrated Science for Health Students.* Reston, Va.: Reston Publishing, 1976, p. 574.

The infection produced by the cold virus is usually acute, but may pass within a few days. Often, however, secondary infections occur immediately, which may develop into a chronic condition. Early medical attention will reduce the chance of spreading.

The common cold usually attacks the nose and throat and spreads to the chest. Mucous membranes that line the nose and throat become swollen, red, and dry, giving a "stuffed-up" feeling. Irritated tissues soon produce a watery fluid, which drains from the nose. If a secondary infection complicates the condition, the inflammation creates thick mucus, and the individual should take antibiotic medication prescribed by a physician.

The adapted physical educator should be aware that a person's physical state is impaired by a cold, particularly in the advanced stages. The student will not be able to perform effectively due to restricted breathing. The program, therefore, should be modified to include less strenuous exercises that stimulate (but do not fatigue) the respiratory system. Light calisthenics, including bending, stretching, and reaching activities, are encouraged. All activities can be performed except those that produce fatigue. Close contact between individuals should be avoided, and extreme chilling is also contraindicated. The infected child need not be excused from outdoor activities or swimming, but extreme temperature differences could have a negative effect.

The following parental questions concerning appropriate handling of individuals with colds are typical: Is there scientific evidence that chilling or getting wet causes one to "catch cold," or are colds actually caught from a virus passed from person to person? Should a child be excused from gym or recess and from showering? The physician's reply (Thosteson 1979, p. 9) indicates the medical attitude toward the cold condition:

> Neither temperature nor wetness of an individual causes virus colds. Too much coddling—no recess, no gym, no showers—following a cold is nonsense. It is probable, but not provable, that severe chilling can impair resistance to viruses. But so do loss of sleep and poor nutrition. 'Severe chilling' is not the same as outdoor activity. Nor will a gym class cause anybody to catch a cold. Showering after gym is no more conducive to catching a cold than taking a bath at home. A youngster with a cold should be kept at home for his own good and so not to pass cold germs along to others. But when the child is well, alert, and active with no fever, there's no reason to refrain from recess, gym, showers, or all the normal school activities.

Allergies

Allergy (hypersensitivity) is an inherited abnormality in the body's immune system. When some individuals come in contact with certain elements in the environment, an unusual or negative reaction occurs. These elements could include materials inhaled (pollen, dust, smoke), eaten (chocolate, eggs, milk), physically contacted (poison ivy, animal dander), or injected (bee sting, penicillin). Each individual's allergic reaction will vary greatly, depending on which specific body tissue is involved. Reaction in tissue of the nose and eyes is commonly called hay fever. If the musculature of the bronchial tubes is affected, the resulting condition is asthma. If the intestine walls or bowels react, the result is abdominal cramps or diarrhea or both. If the skin reacts, the result is hives or rash. The material that causes the negative reaction is called an **allergen** or **antigen.** In any given individual, the same allergen may affect different tissues similarly, therefore, ragweed pollen may cause both hay fever and asthma in one individual.

An allergic reaction creates swelling in the affected cells. Irritated cells release chemicals called **histamines,** which are normally found within all cells. Histamines are responsible for many serious reactions (Walter 1982). The effects of histamines on blood vessels and on bronchioles are particularly dangerous when breathing is impaired. Histamine causes **dilation** (enlargement) of the arterioles of the capillaries of the nose and eyes. This dilation allows a greater blood supply to flow into the capillaries and raises the capillary pressure so blood flows profusely into the tissues. Vasodilation and fluid accumulation in tissues of the nose and eyes are responsible for the discomfort that the hay fever victim experiences. Sneezing and excessive fluid accumulation are common symptoms.

When experiencing allergic symptoms, the individual will suffer ill health and perform poorly. Loss of appetite, loss of interest, and general fatigue occur. The child may seem disinterested in physical activity and may be as uncomfortable as the person suffering from a severe cold.

Dr. Gene S. Rachelefsky, Director of the Pediatric Allergy Clinic at UCLA (Respiratory Allergy in Athletes 1978, p. 58), explains that the allergic child's physical health is generally below normal. He has found that loss of sleep is common among youngsters with an active allergy condition. He states: "When allergic individuals lie down to sleep they toss and turn because they can't breathe well. Their nose is stuffy; they might cough from postnasal drip or low-grade wheezing. In short, they don't get enough rest."

Allergists have found that when allergic symptoms are treated with appropriate medication, the child's sense of well-being also improves. Strength and energy return when the allergy is under control.

Antihistamine drugs are commonly used to counteract the allergic person's release of histamines. These drugs prevent some of the negative effects of allergy, but in many individuals the antihistamine drugs themselves produce undesirable side effects. A student's reaction time may be significantly impaired, and drowsiness also may occur.

Hay Fever (Allergic Rhinitis)

Hay fever is an allergic condition of the upper respiratory tract caused by airborne pollens or spores. It is characterized by sneezing, nasal drainage, nasal congestion, and itching of eyes, nose, palate, and throat.

The individual usually develops sensitivity during the school-age years (rarely before the age of 3), although onset can occur at any time. The allergic condition may increase in severity for several years and then stabilize (Haynes and Caplin 1974). The body tends to develop immunity to the allergen.

Most allergic children have a family history of allergic or asthmatic conditions. Generally, the earlier the age of onset, the stronger the family history.

Characteristics of the Allergic Child

Typical characteristics of an allergic child include an upward lifting or rubbing of the nose with the palm of the hand, or wrinkling of the nose or mouth from side-to-side. The child often will sneeze in *paroxysms* (sudden attacks) of five or more sneezes. Hay fever activity is strictly seasonal, occurring in spring, summer, or autumn, depending on the person's hypersensitivity to different trees, grasses, or plant pollens. Seasonal hay fever is caused by windblown particles. When the pollen count is extremely high, physical education activities should be planned for indoors.

Pollen seasons vary geographically, but throughout the United States, the first to appear are tree pollens (March to June in the East and Midwest); next are grasses (mid-May to July in much of the country, but almost all year in the Southeast). These pollens cause "rose fever" in spring and early summer. In August through October, ragweed pollen is the most common cause of hay fever. The allergic reaction to ragweed can produce severe hay fever.

Allergists should be consulted to determine what allergens are causing hay fever. A child's history and a physical examination assist in the diagnosis of an allergic condition and the suspect allergens. Skin tests done by a physician can determine the specific allergens involved. These tests are reliable for inhaled allergens, but less so for food allergies.

Once a physician determines the allergen, the individual can be desensitized by repeated small injections of the allergen before the critical season arrives. About 80 percent of those who undergo desensitization experience an 80 percent reduction of symptoms (Hirsch 1984). The Asthma and Allergy Foundation of America pamphlet *Allergy in Children* (October 1979) emphasizes that the most successful principle in allergy treatment is removal of the cause. The allergic individual, if at all possible, should be kept away from the source of the allergen. Excluding the child from all outdoor activities because of pollen allergies should, however, be done only as a last resort.

The instructor must keep track of daily pollen counts. These are usually reported during peak seasons on radio, TV, and in most newspapers. High pollen levels mean that individuals with hay fever or asthma will not perform well in activities involving excessive cardiorespiratory output (e.g., cross-country, soccer, field hockey). Although the allergic child may be unable to participate fully when the pollen count is high, she should not be excluded or sidelined. Being a scorekeeper or captain does not meet the individual's physical needs either. Appropriate placement or indoor activity is preferable to an outdoor program of nonactivity. A well-planned regular physical education program should allow for modifications, or the child should be placed temporarily in an individualized adapted physical education setting. Exclusion from physical activity or assignment to meaningless watered-down programs is not acceptable.

Allergic Reaction to Bee and Insect Stings

Allergic reactions can result from insect stings, specifically, the stings of bees, hornets, wasps, yellow jackets, and fire ants. The **antigen** (allergic substance) of the insect venom is responsible for more deaths in this country than snake bites.

In most of the United States, 85 percent of insect reactions are caused by hornet, wasp, yellow jacket, or fire ant stings. In California, however, 85 percent of reactions are caused by honey bee stings. The fire ant, commonly found in the South, is becoming a new threat, and is estimated to cause approximately 13.8 percent of life-threatening anaphylactic reactions.

Insect sting fatalities are caused by local respiratory obstruction: swelling (edema) of the larynx and exaggerated reaction (anaphylaxis) (Asthma and Allergy Foundation, Sept./Oct., 1983). An unusual or exaggerated allergic reaction usually occurs within 5 to 30 min following the sting (or injection, as with penicillin reaction) but can occur up to an hour later. The individual may develop a flush, itching of palms, soles, or groin, generalized or localized swelling, hives or other eruptions, shortness of breath, asthma, blurring of vision, or faintness.

When involved in outdoor activities, students should not use scented perfume or lotions, or wear dark or floral printed clothing. They should never go barefoot lest they step on a stinging insect. If stung by a bee (the only insect that leaves a stinger), the student should have the school nurse remove the venom sac with a pin or pointed knife—being careful to avoid squeezing the sac and thus injecting more venom into the skin. Students who react negatively to stings should be given medication to ward off severe reactions. Most school nurses are capable of administering available medication (usually epinephrine). The child should then be taken to an emergency medical facility.

Chronic Obstructive Pulmonary Disease

Chronic obstructive pulmonary disease (COPD), or **chronic obstructive lung disease (COLD)** (Walter 1982), refers to several related conditions that can result in an inability to expel air completely and rapidly from the lungs. Common types of COPD include **chronic bronchial asthma, chronic bronchitis**, and **emphysema.** Two million people in the United States are known to have COPD. The symptoms are chronic cough; wheezing, particularly on exertion or during periods of respiratory infection; and breathlessness, either constant or during short but active periods. A standard classification scheme for measuring degree of severity of COPD is found in Tables 21.2, 21.3, and 21.4.

The majority of patients suffering from COPD have chronic bronchitis and emphysema, which are closely associated with cigarette smoking or the constant breathing of cigarette smoke. In the latter category are children of families with heavy smokers; the air found in the home is highly contaminated. Moderate, regular exercise should be encouraged for individuals diagnosed as having chronic bronchitis or emphysema.

Individuals in the advanced stages of COPD frequently have been allowed a life of self-imposed nonactivity. This occurs when parents, relatives, or medical practitioners are ill-advised. The major goal of treatment is the resumption of physical activity within each individual's capability, such as daily walking on level surfaces, or indoor exercising using a stationary bicycle, rowing machine, or treadmill (Ostrow 1978).

Rehabilitation of the COPD Individual

In rehabilitation of the COPD individual, Degré and associates (1979) showed that a 33 percent increase in maximal work capacity is possible. The increase probably results from more effective use of oxygen rather than an increase in cardiac output or stroke volume. To increase work capacity, physical education programming must be designed to improve cardiorespiratory and musculoskeletal function, thus reducing the

TABLE 21.2

STANDARD CLASSIFICATION OF GRADING BREATHLESSNESS

Grade	Description
1	Can keep pace walking with person of same age and body build without breathlessness on level ground, but not on hills or stairs.
2	Can walk a mile at own pace with dyspnea, but cannot keep pace with a normal person on level ground.
3	Becomes breathless after walking about 100 yd (92 m), or for a few minutes on level ground.
4	Becomes breathless while dressing or talking.

SOURCE: From Disability and Rehabilitation Handbook by R. M. Goldenson (ed.), p. 535. Copyright © 1978, McGraw-Hill. Used with the permission of McGraw-Hill Book Company.

TABLE 21.3

CLASSIFICATION OF ASTHMA

Term	Description
Slight asthma	Attacks of short duration once or twice a month
Moderate asthma	One or two attacks per week last minutes to hours
Marked asthma	Frequent attacks, almost daily, lasting hours to days
Intractable asthma	Nonremitting, resulting in minimal physical activity and incomplete response to intensive drug treatment

TABLE 21.4

CLINICAL ASSESSMENT OF ASTHMA

Grade	Description
A	Children who had five or less episodes of wheezing by age 14. Most had no attacks after 7 or 8 years of age.
B	Children with continuing history or episodic asthma over 3 to 5 year period. Most had ceased to wheeze by 10 years of age.
C	Children with long-standing history of episodic asthma, and who had wheeze in 12 months before study. Most of these have had several episodes each year since infancy.
D	Children with long-standing history with evidence of chronic unremitting asthma in 12 months before examination. They had periods of persistent asthma in preceding year, or their longest symptom-free period during that time was less than 1 month.

increased breathing demands of physical exertion. The adapted physical education program should be progressive and include exercises to improve breathing pattern. In the absence of physical exercise, a reduction in lean body mass occurs in healthy individuals. Inactivity therefore multiplies disease complications. Specific breathing exercises can be found on pages 560–562.

The physical and social aspects of rehabilitation for COPD individuals must be improved. Psychologically, the person gains independence and confidence when freed from the role of invalid. No longer must these students be excused from physical education programs and sent to study halls as they once were.

Rehabilitation programs require the total cooperation of the child's family. A non-supportive home environment destroys the work of the adapted physical educator. The positive influence of teachers and parents during physically uncertain and trying times provides a solid base for the child's pursuit of an active life-style (Fregosi 1979).

Despite inability to reverse the underlying disease process, the future prognosis of children who are in well-designed physical education programs is good. With increased exercise tolerance and improved self-care, the youngster's anxiety and depression often are reduced. Progressive resistance exercises should be written for all respiratory conditions. Remember that any exercise program for COPD individuals requires the physician's approval. A. J. Ryan (Respiratory Allergy in Athletes 1978, p. 65) states, "I think that atopic (allergic) disorders are rarely a prohibition to competitive or recreational sports. In fact, individuals with respiratory allergies should be encouraged to exercise within their limitations."

Rehabilitation guidelines for individuals with COPD should include a comprehensive approach to exercise training (Woods 1982–1983). Although the resultant increase in exercise tolerance is often small, the activity is usually a positive motivational device. Exercise training for rehabilitation should be developed through progressive aerobic programs. Remember, however, that the student who suffers from *severe* COPD may not tolerate a 50 percent max VO_2 exercise prescription well. Training sessions, therefore, must be adjusted to accommodate dyspnea (labored breathing), and feelings of anxiety when breathing becomes difficult.

Belman and Wasserman (1982) note little change in pulmonary function, exercise heart rate, or cellular characteristics after training, in spite of increased endurance capacity. These researchers suggest that the following can be expected to occur if a progressive and ongoing program is developed and properly implemented:

1. Improved aerobic capacity
2. Increased motivation
3. Desensitization to sensation of dyspnea
4. Improved muscle function
5. Improved technique of performance

These changes in exercise performance usually give the student a great psychological boost. A progressive, ongoing program helps break the vicious cycle of atrophy that comes from deconditioning.

Asthma

For the affected child, asthma means labored breathing accompanied by wheezing, a sense of chest constriction, and frequent coughing, gasping, and apprehension. To the adapted physical educator, the child with asthma poses a fascinating and rewarding challenge. The child's most important physiological needs can be accommodated in the physical education class without expensive or complicated equipment.

Taplin and Creer (1978, p. 17) provide a simple definition of **asthma:** "Any episode involving worsening of breathing that interrupts ongoing activities or requires some procedure (such as resting and using a nebulizer) to resume normal and comfortable breathing."

Asthma is not contagious. Those affected experience breathing difficulty because air flow through the bronchial tubes is obstructed owing to swelling of mucous membrane linings, contraction of muscles surrounding the bronchial tubes, or plugging of tubes by thick mucus (Asthma and Allergy Foundation of America, *Handbook for the Asthmatic*, 1979). The resulting reduction of the airway occurs mainly during expiration, when airway diameter is smallest. The main problem in any pulmonary disorder is discharge of air to allow fresh air in. As breathing becomes difficult (see Figure 21.5), swelling of the passageway and increased secretion of mucus further restrict air exchange. The typical asthmatic attack can be compared to an individual trying to breathe adequately through a straw.

The etiology is related directly to an increased amount of histamines in the bloodstream, which cause the inner walls of the bronchial tubes to swell and the smooth muscles surrounding the bronchial tubes to contract. This combination of negative reactions is called **bronchospasm.**

The disease is potentially reversible at any stage, and in the absence of secondary complications, does not lead to further lung disease (Cavanaugh 1974). Asthma is extremely common and affects approximately 3 percent of children and adults in the United States. Feldman and McFadden (1977) identify asthma as the most common chronic disease of childhood.

Asthma Characteristics

The cough that accompanies asthma is often the first complaint of the young asthmatic child. An increased cough reflex occurs particularly during physical activity and may result in coughing attacks. Coughing is caused by the presence of excessive amounts of mucus, which obstruct the bronchial airways. If a child begins coughing, the instructor should encourage continued coughing to improve drainage of the obstructing fluid.

Jim Hart, professional football quarterback, has been affected continually by asthma. An asthmatic attack for him is a serious wheezing and breathlessness that occurs in cooler and colder weather and at peak periods of exercise. His problems are more likely to occur during practice than during a game, and are most likely to occur during warm-up exercises at the beginning of practice. He sometimes must limit the number of wind sprints he runs during practice sessions (Asthma and Allergy Foundation, Sept./Oct., 1983).

Types of Asthma

The three asthma classifications are based on distinct features and are as follows:

1. **Extrinsic** asthma usually develops in childhood, although it can occur in adulthood. It is commonly associated with allergies to external materials such as pollens, house dust, mold spores (found in damp areas), and animal danders. Persons with this form of asthma usually have positive skin tests. More males are involved than females; in childhood cases the ratio is 2:1 (Bierman, Pierson, and Shapiro 1975).
2. **Intrinsic** asthma, less prevalent than the extrinsic type, is nevertheless commonly encountered by the physical educator. This type includes exercise-induced asthma and psychosomatic asthma.
3. **Mixed** asthma has features of both intrinsic and extrinsic asthma. It often begins in late childhood, appears to be more severe during adolescence, and seems to affect more girls than boys.

Marley (1977) argues that specialists do not agree with the terms *extrinsic, intrinsic,* and *mixed,* and suggests that these designations may not be appropriate. He classifies childhood asthma by taking into account such factors as school absenteeism, school performance, use of medication, and occurrence of exercise-induced bronchospasm. His classification scheme is as follows: Class I—occasional asthma, Class II—chronic asthma resulting in dependence on bronchodilators, and Class III—intractable asthma resulting in curtailment of studies.

Exercise-Induced Asthma (EIA)

Exercise-induced asthma (EIA) is also referred to as **exercise-induced bronchospasm.** With this type of asthma, excessive and prolonged exercise precipitates muscular constriction of the bronchial tubes. This narrowing of the airways suggests that EIA is caused by formation and release of a histamine that tightens bronchial muscles (Sly 1976). McFadden (1981) suggests the *heat-flux hypothesis* as the cause of EIA. He explains that air temperature and humidity are important factors. When an individual breathes in, inhaled air is warmed and humidified as it travels through breathing passages on its way to the lungs. Outside air can be very cold or very dry or both and yet still be warm and moist by the time it reaches the lungs. The lining of the breathing passages heats and humidifies the air. As one would expect, the colder the inhaled air is, the harder the lining of the breathing passages must work to do the job. McFadden theorizes that EIA is caused by this heating and humidifying action of the lining. In asthmatics, the rush of air through the air passages during exercise drains the lining of its heat and moisture content. The greater the rush of incoming air, the greater the heat and moisture loss. These losses lead in turn to bronchioconstriction, or bronchospasm.

When EIA is mild, it is apparent only when measured with mechanical pulmonary devices. When more intense, it may cause wheezing and labored breathing (dyspnea). This constriction occurs differently in different asthmatic children and depends also on duration and intensity of exercise.

When the asthmatic who suffers from EIA begins to exercise, the airway passages increase in size (bronchodilation) during the first few minutes of mild exercise. The child may actually breathe easier at this time than during a resting period. As exercise continues, the student appears to experience no breathing problem for the next few minutes. In studies by Silverman and Anderson (1972) and Sly (1970), an exercise-induced asthmatic attack usually occurred after 6 to 8 min of treadmill running.

When assessing EIA response, researchers find that the most reliable and convenient exercise is treadmill walking or running at 3 to 3.5 mph for 6 to 8 min at a 15 to 20 percent grade. Sly (1972) used 14 asthmatic children (walking on a treadmill, 3 mph, at a 10 percent grade) to determine effects of exercise. He found that walking for 1 to 2 min increased forced expiratory volume in 1 sec ($FEV_{1.0}$), but continuation of exercise for 6 min (total now 8 min) showed a significant decrease of $FEV_{1.0}$. This reduction in breathing effectiveness continued for another 10 min. At 18 min subjects recovered and increases in FEV were noted. All subjects returned to normal resting rates in approximately 50 min (Figure 21.6). None were given medication before, during, or after exercise.

Hendrickson and Nielsen (1983) studied the effects of an exercise program on asthmatic children. The researchers used 42 subjects (25 boys and 17 girls with a mean age of 10.5 years) to examine the cardiopulmonary response to exercise before and after endurance training. The experimental group (N = 28) participated in 90 min of supervised physical training (ball games, running, gymnastics, circuit training and team games) twice a week for 6 weeks. All subjects used inhaled medication before exercise to prevent EIA. In the endurance trained group, EIA percentage reduction in peak expiratory flow (PEF) fell significantly from a mean of 44 percent at baseline to 30 percent after training. Resting forced expiratory volume (FEV_1) did not change significantly. After training, significant decreases were observed in both heart rate at rest (from 94 beats per min to 88 beats per min) and postexercise heart rate (from 178 beats per min to 167 beats per min). No change in EIA or physical fitness was observed in controls during the same period. The study findings thus suggest that endurance training in asthmatic children can reduce EIA and increase aerobic capacity.

The Asthma and Allergy Foundation of America (July 1984) estimates that 60 to 90 percent of all asthmatics are susceptible to EIA. EIA also affects about 40 percent of all children who have hay fever or other allergies that involve the nasal passages.

For EIA to develop, exercise must be fairly strenuous and sustained. The accepted amount in a research setting is running hard enough to raise the heart rate of nonath-

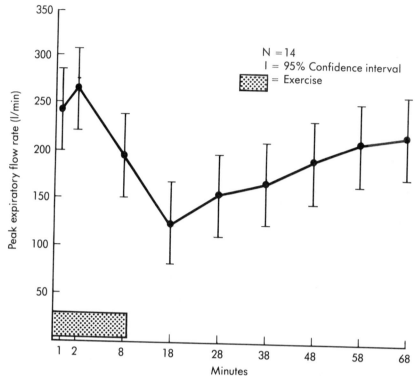

FIGURE 21.6. Mean peak expiratory flow before, during, and after treadmill exercise (walking 3 mph, 10 degree grade) in 14 asthmatic children. (From R. M. Sly. Exercise and the Asthmatic Child. *Pediatrics Digest* 14:42, 1972. By permission of Medical Digest, Inc.)

letes to 170 beats per min in children, or 150 beats per min in adults. These numbers are about 50 beats per min below the appropriate maximum for each age group.

For students who experience EIA, an adapted physical education program should be initiated as soon as the diagnosis is clear. The student must be encouraged to build up a gradual tolerance of exercise. Softball and touch football are less apt to provoke EIA than basketball, field hockey, or soccer. Despite the apparent restrictions, those who desire to be endurance runners or basketball players usually find that they can be successful with proper precautions and monitored programming. In a California study (Asthma and Allergy Foundation, July 1984), a group of 15 youngsters with severe asthma ran for 4 days per week for 6 weeks, gradually increasing the running distance to 2 miles. Although about half developed EIA repeatedly, an aerosol bronchodilator reversed their symptoms readily. As the weeks passed, the involved runners were able to run greater distances in a given period of time.

An exercise test that is used by physicians (Marshall and Bierman 1985) can employ a treadmill, bicycle ergometer, or free running to access an individual's exercise tolerance. For EIA, pulmonary function tests are generally administered before exercise and at 1, 5, 10, 15, and 20 min into exercise. Test results are usually expressed as a percentage of change from baseline. In general, a decrease of 15 percent in either FEV_1 or PEF rate is considered abnormal. A change of 30 to 40 percent is considered moderately severe, and more than 45 percent a severe response.

Outgrowing Asthma

Siegel, Katz, and Rachelefsky (1976) note that some children seem to "outgrow" asthma at age 5 or 6 because of a dramatic increase in the size of the airway passages at this age. Dr. J. Fink (1984) believes that approximately 30 percent of childhood asthmatics will outgrow their asthmatic condition. In general, asthma is more severe in the younger child and tends to become less severe with growth and development of the child's lungs. By age 6, adult configuration of the lungs is reached and disease severity tends to wane, as measured by number of hospital admissions (Marshall and Bierman 1985). In those youngsters who still have asthmatic symptoms in adolescence, asthma may become more severe and require more intense medication and therapy.

Asthma Medication and Drugs

Since the basic cause of hyperreactivity is unknown, current asthma therapy is not curative, but aims, rather, at control of the asthmatic condition. Present methods of treatment are either through use of oral or inhaled medication. The wide range of drugs now available makes control of symptoms, normal lung function, and a completely normal life-style reasonable therapy goals for most children (Leffert 1984).

Two general types of medications are prescribed: (1) those that prevent an attack from occurring, and (2) those that relax the constricted bronchial muscles once an attack has begun (Katz-Smith 1986).

Oral theophylline is the most useful drug for preventing occurrence of an asthmatic attack. It builds up the child's system to control frequency and severity of attack. Because children tend to be rapid metabolizers of theophylline, slow-release preparations are used. When the drug is taken on a regular basis and in appropriate dosages, it becomes the accepted choice of physicians to prevent or control EIA (Respiratory Allergy in Athletes 1978). Possible adverse effects include stomach upset, heartburn, nausea, anorexia, and central nervous system (CNS) stimulation. CNS stimulation can be a problem in some youngsters, who may develop highly undesirable behaviors. For these children, physicians suggest that the medication dosage be increased more gradually over a more prolonged period of time.

Beta-adrenergic (beta-2) drugs relieve the difficult breathing associated with acute attacks of bronchial asthma. They affect nerve terminals of the sympathetic nervous system, which activate muscles of the bronchial tubes. In this way, the drug produces dilation of the airways (i.e., increases size of airways and thus improves ability to breathe). Beta-adrenergic is available in oral preparations but is more effective when taken by inhalation. *Albuterol* is the most beta-2 specific and longest lasting drug now available, but it is not recommended for children. *Metaproterenol* is almost as effective and is the drug of choice (instead of albuterol) for children.

These beta medications are useful both as a preventive, before exercise, and after an attack has begun. The drug acts to reverse an acute bronchospasm rapidly and effectively. The best example of the use of the beta medications is before exertion to prevent EIA. Because of the 3 to 6 hour duration of action, the drug can be used as protective medication three or four times a day.

Cromolyn is used to block the release of histamine that occurs normally in allergic reactions. This drug acts to prevent the sequence of tissue changes that produce constriction of bronchial tubes and development of asthma. The medication will *not* relieve an asthma attack that has begun. The major advantage of the drug is an absence of adverse side effects, so it may be the drug of choice for students who experience negative CNS overstimulation from other asthma medications.

In the past, corticosteroids were used, but because of excessive side effects, these are now prescribed only if the child is not responding to bronchodilators or in the event of a severe attack (Katz-Smith 1986).

Athletic Competition and Illegal Drugs

Forty-one American Olympic medalists at the 1984 summer games in Los Angeles demonstrated that asthma need not be a barrier to outstanding athletic achievement. Sixty-seven of the 597 members of the U.S. team (11 percent) were helped by a medical screening and counseling program organized by the U.S. Olympic Committee and sponsored by the American Academy of Allergy and Immunology's Rehabilitation and Sports Medicine Committee. The U.S. athletes included medal-winning cyclists Alexei Grawal, Bill Nitts, and Steve Hegg; heptathlon silver medalist Jackie Joyner; sprinter Jeannette Bolden; swimmer Nancy Hogshead; Greco-Roman wrestler Dave Schultz; volleyball team member Paul Weishoff; and basketball player Sam Perkins. The screening committee, led by Dr. William Pierson, surveyed 438 of the 597 members of the Olympic team, looking for allergic and EIA symptoms. Of the total surveyed, 67 team members had a history of asthma or EIA, or had taken asthma medications.

The use of specific medications is monitored closely in athletes who participate in international competition. In the past, sport officials have disqualified some athletes from competition because of drugs used to control asthma. These officials are concerned that certain drugs give the athlete added physiological benefits that produce better performance. Under Olympic rules, ephedrine, a heart stimulant similar to adrenalin, is banned. Many over-the-counter drugs contain ephedrine or pseudoephedrine. The use of these medications by nonhandicapped athletes may enable them to increase their cardiorespiratory efficiency and thus have an unfair advantage. Because improper and illegal use of drugs gives some athletes an unfair advantage, officials administer blood and urine tests to all athletes. For those athletes with respiratory conditions, certain medications are identified as legal and acceptable to control asthma. None of these medications contains an illegal stimulant to the cardiorespiratory system.

Over-the-counter antihistamines are not banned but often have negative side effects such as drowsiness, drying up of secretions, and slowing of reaction time. Competitive athletes should always consult a physician regarding the medications that they plan to take.

Excessive Use of Aerosols

A major concern exists that excessive use of aerosols is dangerous. Many physicians now strongly suggest that children and adolescents use oral medication (pills or liquids) instead of inhalants. In the past, some youngsters used aerosols indiscriminately at the slightest feeling of respiratory discomfort. Feldman and McFadden (1977, p. 1244) voice this concern: "The major drawback to aerosol therapy with the hand-held freon-powered nebulizer is the potential for abuse. The excessive use of aerosols was incriminated in the increase of asthma mortality in England and Wales in the early 60's."

Appropriate use of inhalers means that the individual does *not* use the medication more than once every 3 hours. Patients tend to step up their dosage when symptoms worsen. This procedure is definitely contraindicated. A physician should be consulted if the condition worsens despite proper use of medication.

Inhaled medications do (in most cases) relax bronchial muscles and are considered an immediately effective treatment for asthmatic attack. The teacher should know what medication the physician has prescribed, and what the student should do if an attack occurs. When an aerosol is used, the teacher should have the atomizer available in the activity area in case substantial breathing difficulties develop.

When oral medication is prescribed, the teacher should know the student's schedule for taking the drug. The teacher can then determine if sufficient time has elapsed for the medication to "block" EIA. A 1-hour time lapse is recommended after taking the medication and before exercising.

Most physicians agree that some medication is necessary to treat asthma, but in each case treatment must be considered individually. As Feldman and McFadden (1977, p. 1239) explain, " . . . its [the condition's] course is extremely variable from patient to patient and is marked by unpredictable exacerbations (increase in severity). . . . A treatment regimen for a given patient is determined empirically and is based upon the severity of the patient's disease and his response to various modalities. The treatment schedule becomes more complicated with increasing severity of disease, but the clinical response is usually satisfying for both the physician and the patient, and chronic disability can be avoided in all but the most severe cases."

Role of Exercise in Rehabilitation

The asthmatic's situation is often paradoxical. The child usually needs a well-rounded physical education program including strength development, cardiorespiratory activities, and lifetime recreational skills, but he may have been excluded from those activities for fear that even mild exercise would precipitate an attack. This overly conservative approach relegates the asthmatic child to an inactive world. Although medication is important to most rehabilitation programs, it cannot duplicate the effects of a well-planned exercise regimen (Cox 1976).

Caution must be used when developing a specific program for the asthmatic individual. Once the program is written, a copy must be sent to the child's physician for possible alteration and final approval (signature).

Findheisen (1975) suggests that vigorous physical activities, such as long distance running, competitive swimming, bicycling, and cross-country skiing, can improve cardiorespiratory function in adolescent asthmatics. Younger asthmatics also improve significantly when activities involve running and catching, particularly when offered three times per week for a minimum of 5 months. Approximately 8 weeks after initiation of an exercise program, Findheisen found that the number of attacks decreased or students stopped having acute asthmatic attacks altogether. The study participants also improved their dynamic pulmonary function, normalized respiratory rate, and increased their tidal volume during exercise. Finally, the students decreased their dependency on bronchodilators.

Puthoff (1972) identifies three major physical education goals for asthmatics: (1) improvement of cardiorespiratory efficiency, (2) development of upper body strength, including the breathing muscles, and (3) opportunity to learn lifetime recreational skills. Earlier researchers also suggest that breathing exercises and relaxation methods be taught.

McElhenny and Peterson's original study (1963) establishes two specific guidelines that are still useful: (1) increase gradually time and effort required to develop strength, endurance, and skill, and (2) provide individual instruction and encouragement to practice basic body skills. These researchers found a 30 percent reduction in number of asthmatic attacks and an equivalent lessening of dependence on drugs and medications when the physical fitness program occurred twice a week for 4 months.

To provide positive and measurable change in the asthmatic child's condition, the activity program must be of sufficient frequency, intensity, and duration. Taplin and Creer (1978) suggest that the asthmatic individual must be taught to recognize early the signs of an asthma attack and to initiate proper treatment while the episode is still relatively mild. The child often knows when an attack is beginning. The most common symptoms include shortness of breath, coughing, chest tightness, and in some cases, wheezing. Note, however, that the symptoms are specific to each individual. When aware of an attack, the person should slow her pace drastically or stop. Jones (1984) suggests that when students experience an attack, they should relieve themselves immediately by administering aerosol medication and then sitting on the floor, leaning back slightly on straight arms, with legs pointed straight ahead. If the student is participating in a well-controlled progressive exercise program, the adapted physical educator can terminate the exercise for that day and use the student's final recorded performance as the next day's goal. For example, when a student experiences discomfort during a cardiorespiratory workout that includes walking and jogging around the gym floor, the instructor should stop the student, record distance covered (e.g., three and one-quarter laps) and activity time (2 min, 35 sec). These standards then become the goal to surpass during the next workout.

Potential for EIA is a concern. Haas, Castillo, and Lustig (1976) indicate that gradually increased submaximal exercise will not elicit EIA. To prevent occurrence of EIA, they believe that students should *not* be encouraged to proceed beyond their limits. An overenthusiastic physical education teacher may tend to push a little too hard.

The student should increase activity level gradually until mild exercise can be sustained for 15 min periods four times per week. For the more severe asthmatic, this achievement level may take several months to reach. Pace and progression should be geared to each student's existing ability.

Breathing Exercises

Fregosi (1979) suggests that, besides being progressive, programs should include activities to improve breathing pattern. Many asthmatic children breathe in a rapid, inefficient manner. They use only the upper chest muscles, which are mechanically inefficient for breathing. They tend also to contract their abdomen while inhaling, which restricts the amount of air drawn into the lungs. When inhaling, students should be taught to use the lower and upper chest and the diaphragm and abdomen increasingly.

Appropriate training programs can increase the breathing (ventilatory) muscles in strength and endurance (Leith et al. 1979). Breathing exercises also teach proper use of respiratory muscles. Although diaphragmatic and lower rib breathing is important for children and adults, thoracic breathing, which is undesirable for adults, is important in children to promote physical development. The respiratory chest muscles, which tend to atrophy in the asthmatic individual, should be exercised adequately. Chest expansion can be taught with synchronized breathing and combined with light calisthenics (Haas, Castillo, and Lustig 1976).

Sherrill (1986, p. 423) recommends that the following interaction take place when teaching breathing exercises: (1) Provide each child with an exercise mat, waste paper container, and box of tissues. (2) Encourage the child to blow the nose and cough up phlegm. (3) Explain to the child that the exercises may initially detract from one's sense of well-being. (4) Warn the child to expect coughing and wheezing during the first few seconds of abdominal breathing.

Stress that the diaphragm must contract (downward) to its maximum. Breathing should be relaxed, not forced. A relatively short inspiration should follow, with contraction of abdominal muscles during expiration while exhaling through pursed lips. Expiration should take twice as long as inspiration (i.e., inhale for 3 sec and exhale for 6 sec—a ratio of 1:2). Pursed lips and slow respiration promote efficient exchange of oxygen and carbon dioxide in the lungs. Labored breathing (dyspnea), which always accompanies an asthmatic attack, is somewhat relieved by pursed-lip breathing. Slow respiration, pursed-lip breathing, and diaphragmatic breathing exercises all force the individual to breathe slowly. These measures help prevent the panic that often occurs when bronchospasm develops (Wanner and Sackner 1975).

Children who learn to relax and use pursed-lip breathing are often able to control an asthmatic attack effectively. Wood, Krauls, and Lecks (1970) believe that control is possible because the child is distracted from attack anxiety.

Authorities on bronchial asthma in children (Siegel, Katz, and Rachelefsky 1976, p. 937) recommend the following breathing exercises:

> The patient lies supine with his knees drawn up and one hand resting over the thorax. This allows greater diaphragmatic excursion. . . . During the procedure, expiration occurs first with the chest and as much as possible with the upper part of the abdomen. A similar exercise, done in the sitting position with the hands placed over or resting on the lower ribs, permits the hands to squeeze the ribs to help expel the air from the bases of the lungs. Such exercises purportedly increase voluntary control and air exchange, and may also decrease apprehension, severity, and length of the asthmatic attack. Evidence for other exercises to prevent deformity and to improve posture are not well documented.

Scherr and Frankel (1958, p. 1997) explain the process:

> While performing the abdominal or stomach exercises, the child lies on his back, with knees bent, arms to the side, and completely relaxed. One hand is then placed on the abdomen. He breathes out slowly through the mouth, making an "F" or "S" sound and making the hand sink into the abdomen. He breathes air in quietly through the nose, as abdominal muscles become relaxed and the hand comes up. Exhalation is timed with a stop watch, and improvement is recorded as a gauge of progress. The upper part of the chest does not move. Expiration is long and inspiration is short. Exercises are done three times a day, ten minutes at a time . . .

In reference to the sitting position, these same researchers (Scherr and Frankel 1958, p. 1997) explain: "The child sits in a chair with his back supported against the chair, completely relaxed. The hands are on the lower ribs and the child slowly breathes out with the 'S' sound, tightening the abdominal muscles by making the abdomen go in, and pressing the last air out of the lungs. The abdomen is relaxed as the child breathes in through the nose."

Specific challenges should be used to create interest in the rehabilitation process. For example, place a candle approximately 6 in. from the student's mouth. The child's shoulders must be held in naturally, not "hunched." The student must blow ("bend") the candle flame away from himself without blowing the candle out (breathe in through the nose and out through pursed lips at a ratio of 1:2 sec). Bending the candle flame should be practiced for 5 min at the beginning and end of every adapted physical education class. Subsequently, move the candle 2 in. farther away, thus allowing for progressive strength and development.

Students should also practice blowing to keep a piece of tissue paper or a balloon in the air. Use a stopwatch to check the student's progress each day.

Petty, Hudson, and Neff (1973) suggest that once students learn and practice proper breathing patterns, they should begin a walking program. The program should consist of daily walks; increased levels of distance and duration should be noted on a progress chart.

As the student develops a positive attitude toward exercise and as the program progresses at a rate that does not cause an attack, additional exercises should be introduced.

Aerobic Exercise

Guidelines for prescribing exercises for asthmatics[1] are as follows:

A **warm-up period** is essential to the asthmatic's program. Ghory (1975) finds that warm-up actually causes bronchodilation and improves the breathing process. Programs should begin with 5 min of warm-up that includes (1) mild cardiorespiratory activity such as walking or easy jogging, (2) muscle strengthening exercises such as mild push-ups, sit-ups, and squat thrusts, and (3) flexibility and stretching exercises such as alternating toe touch, side bending, and back arching (Marley 1977). The warm-up should increase body temperature until mild sweating occurs.

Figure 20.3 illustrates warm-up exercises and how they can be used to pace an individual. The metronome can be set at different rates to accommodate various levels of intensity.

Duration—Practice sessions should last 30 to 40 min (an unfit individual may need to begin with sessions of 15 min or less).

Frequency—Four to five times per week.

Intensity—Exercises should start at a low level of intensity and increase gradually in intensity as fitness improves. If interval training is used, the work interval should be at an initial intensity that produces a heart rate of 70 percent of maximum heart rate. Increase the work interval slowly to an intensity of 90 percent of maximum heart rate. The rest interval should be long enough to reduce the heart rate to between 50 and 60 percent of maximum. If using continuous training techniques, work intensity should progress gradually to 85 percent of maximum heart rate.

Mode—Activities and games of the student's choice should be prescribed. For example, one-wall handball or four-square are game possibilities. Ideally, the asthmatic should be involved in swim training as well. Regardless of activity selection, the program must focus on increasing the person's aerobic power. A stationary bicycle or hand ergometer could also be utilized.

Progressive Exercise—Programs should begin with walking. If the student is experiencing EIA regularly, she should start with low-level interval training using work intervals of 10 to 30 sec followed by rest periods of 30 to 90 sec, and progress gradually to high intensity interval training. With suitable medication, either continuous or interval training is generally well tolerated (*The Physician and Sportsmedicine* 1981).

---

1. Modified from Guidelines for Prescribing Exercise for Asthmatics. *The Physician and Sportsmedicine* 9(3):51, March 1981.

Preexercise Medication—Preexercise medication is essential for most asthmatic individuals. Beta-2 agonists or theophylline are the preferred agents to be taken at least 1 hour before exercise.

Medication to Reverse EIA—If EIA occurs during activity, the reaction may be reversed by the appropriate aerosol agent. Examples are the beta-2 medications; two common ones are albuterol and metaproterenol.

Warm-down After Exercise—The student should warm-down at the end of each exercise session. Vigorous work should not stop abruptly. A low level of activity (such as walking) should be continued for approximately 5 min or until the heart rate returns to within 20 beats per min of the resting level.

When beginning progressive exercise training, Marley (1977) suggests that the student work for 5 min, and then rest for 5 min. Work time should increase and rest time decrease as the person gets stronger. Progression for the asthmatic will be slower than for the nonhandicapped student.

Katz (Respiratory Allergy in Athletes 1978, p. 58) discusses the importance for the professional athlete of higher levels of physical fitness in reference to controlling asthmatic attacks: "The endurance of the professional athlete is greater than average, so that more exercise is necessary to produce bronchiospasm."

Vandeweghe (Respiratory Allergy in Athletes 1978, p. 59) states: "An acute attack of bronchiospasm is more likely to occur, in what I would consider the part-time or relatively inactive athlete. . . . Part-time participants or youngsters who are just beginnng sports are more subject to episodes of bronchiospasm . . . mostly because they don't recognize their limits of tolerance and don't always follow medication instructions."

Of all physical activities, swimming is the most efficacious for asthmatics. Studies conclude that fewer asthmatic attacks occur while swimming, even among competitive asthmatic swimmers. Fewer breathing difficulties are apparent in the prone swimming position. (When not in water, however, the same prone position does not facilitate breathing during an attack.) The forced breathing required for the front crawl also has positive benefits. Swimming lends itself to progressive programming because the child will stop when tired and not push to fatigue levels. As muscle strength and cardiorespiratory efficiency improve, the body is more capable of handling the physical stress of activity.

Relaxation Techniques

The asthmatic student should learn **conscious relaxation** techniques, which can assist the individual immediately before or during an asthmatic attack. All individuals, asthmatic or not, can benefit from learning relaxation techniques to alleviate both physical and mental tensions. Relaxation can be achieved by stretching the arms up, over the head, and out to the sides. Yawning and stretching also relieve tightness, pressure, and tension.

Conscious relaxation of excessive physical, mental, or breathing tensions should begin in the supine position. In this position, the body muscles can be relaxed completely. The individual should lie on a firm mat or on the floor. For comfort, the neck can be supported with a firm roll or pillow. Raise the knees slightly with a cushion to relieve pressure on the legs and lower back. The upper legs should turn outward. The arms are on the floor next to, but not touching, the body. Arms can be flexed at the elbows. If possible, the room should be darkened and quiet.

Success of the relaxation program is dependent upon total concentration on the process, and each body part as it is being relaxed, tightened, and relaxed again. To begin, Kelly (1965) suggests that students imagine themselves as bags of granulated salt that dissolve in water and flow away, or loose-jointed puppets with no one holding the strings, or as half-filled sacks of flour resting on an uneven surface. Finally, the student should sink softly into sand and imagine the sound of waves lapping and receding on a beach.

Once total body relaxation occurs, instruct the students to contract isolated muscles or muscle groups. Begin with the eyes and progress downward, so all large muscle groups are stimulated and then relax.

The student must learn to relax a specific muscle group completely. Tell the students to imagine the muscle as a balloon, which loses air slowly until it is completely flat (i.e., relaxed). After thinking *and* feeling consciously that the muscle is relaxed, the muscle should be contracted slowly and smoothly. When full tension occurs, relax the muscle again totally.

The breathing muscles also can be relaxed. In a back-lying position, the child should breathe very deeply through the nose. Count slowly as the child inhales, then double the count for exhalation (through pursed lips). When the child is able to concentrate on exhaling, the diaphragm relaxes as much as possible. Encourage yawning to relax the diaphragm. Release of excess tension in the breathing muscles will increase chest flexibility and have a positive effect on the internal organs. Yoga exercises, as described in Chapter 19, can also be used to help students relax.

Chicago physician Edmund Jacobson emphasizes that students will be successful at muscle relaxation only when they depend entirely on conscious cooperation for muscle control. Encourage students to continue their efforts to increase relaxation so they surpass the point at which muscles seem to be perfectly relaxed. The student should learn to isolate specific tense muscle groups (i.e., respiratory muscles during a bronchospasm) and relax them. Some asthmatic students learn to abort asthmatic attacks completely through conscious relaxation.

Summary

In general, students with respiratory diseases can participate successfully in physical and recreational activities. The child's successful participation depends in part on cooperation between the adapted physical educator and the child's physician.

Most cases of allergy and asthma can be controlled and relieved with the medications now available and a well-planned, progressive exercise program. Many asthmatic children whose condition appeared hopeless several years ago can now be helped to lead a relatively normal life. The role of the adapted physical educator is important to helping the child achieve an active life-style. The educator may have to educate the medical profession about the teacher's role. Many physicians do not realize that the adapted physical educator has the necessary expertise to develop and teach an appropriate individualized, progressive physical education program for students with respiratory conditions.

In planning an individualized exercise program, the teacher must first determine the student's level of physical fitness. General motor skills may be lacking in the child who has been excused repeatedly from physical education activities. These skills must be included in the goals for the individualized education plan.

The educator will find extreme variance from student to student in frequency and intensity of attack. Each student's individualized program must be based in part on past history and in part on present levels of ability. Severely involved students should not be pushed to extremes and must sometimes be restrained from overextending themselves. For some, the program will consist of only the most basic activities introduced in slow progression.

Individuals with allergies or asthma can participate in almost any game or exercise, including physical fitness activities. In past decades, asthmatic youngsters were so coddled that they were barely allowed to walk to school. Now they climb mountains, swim in the Olympics, and engage in everyday activities such as Little League baseball, playground soccer, and back-alley basketball. Former Olympic ice skater Janet Lynn is an asthmatic, as is Bob Gibson, the St. Louis Cardinals' Hall of Fame pitcher. Medical research has determined that exercise actually helps asthmatics. Of importance are warming up and staying in peak physical condition (Berland and Fischer-Papp 1983).

Dr. William Pierson, clinical professor of pediatrics at the University of Washington, states: "The indications are clear to us that these people [asthmatics] can perform at levels comparable to any other athlete. This sends a powerful and positive message to asthmatic athletes and young people everywhere. It says that with proper knowledge, attitude, and good medical management you can be as physically active and competitive as people without asthma and allergies" (The Asthma and Allergy Foundation of America, summer 1984, p. 10).

References

Asthma and Allergy Foundation of America. *Handbook for the Asthmatic.* New York: The Foundation, September 1979.

——. *Allergy in Children.* New York: The Foundation, October 1979.

——. *The Allergy and Asthma Advance* 2(4):12, April 1984.

——. The Big Sneeze. *The Allergy and Asthma Advance* 2(6):9–10, Summer 1984.

——. *Exercise and Asthma.* New York: The Foundation, July 1984.

——. Frontiers of Research: Treating Insect Sting Allergy. *The Allergy and Asthma Advance* 2(1):12, Sept./Oct. 1983.

Belman, J. J., and Wasserman, K. *Respiratory Care* 27(6):724–731, 1982.

Benowitz, E. Finally, Everything Was Worth It, Says Asthma Athlete. *The Allergy and Asthma Advance* 3(4):12, March/April 1985.

Berland, T., and Fischer-Papp, L. *Living With Your Allergies and Asthma.* New York: St. Martin's Press, 1983.

Bierman, C. W., Pierson, W. E., and Shapiro, G. G. Asthma in Childhood. In *Current Therapy 1975*, edited by H. F. Conn. Philadelphia: W. B. Saunders, 1975.

Cavanaugh, J. T. A. Asthma in Childhood. In *Current Diagnosis 4*, edited by H. F. Conn and R. B. Conn, Jr. Philadelphia: W. B. Saunders, 1974.

Cox, J. S. G. Disodium Cromoglycate (Cromolyn Sodium) in Bronchial Asthma. In *Bronchial Asthma Mechanisms and Therapeutics*, edited by E. B. Weiss and M. S. Segal. Boston: Little, Brown, 1976.

Degré, S., Sobolski, J., and Degré-Coustry, C. Controversial Aspects of Physical Training in Patients With COPD. *Practical Cardiology*, January 1979, pp. 37–45.

Druz, W. S., Danon, J., Fishman, H. C., Goldberg, N. B., Moisan, T. C., and Sharp, J. T. Approaches in Assessing Respiratory Disease. *American Review of Respiratory Disease* 119(2):145–159, 1979.

Edwards, R. H. T. The Diaphragm as a Muscle Mechanism Underlying Fatigue. *American Review of Respiratory Disease* 119(2):81–84, 1979.

Feldman, N. T., and McFadden, E. R., Jr. Asthma Therapy Old and New. *Medical Clinics of North America* 61(6):1239–1250, 1977.

Findheisen, D. G. R. The Role of Non-Drug Related Treatment Relying on Sports. *Allergologia et Immunopathologia* (Madrid) 3:145–148, 1975. In W. P. Marley, Asthma and Exercise, A Review. *American Corrective Therapy Journal* 31(4):95–102, 1977.

Fink, J. N. Help Is on the Way for 35 Million With Allergies. *U.S. News and World Report* 96(14):67–68, 9 April 1984.

Fregosi, F. The Population With Chronic Lung Disease: Have We Forgotten Them? *Cardio-Gram* 6(5):5, 1979.

Ghory, J. E. Exercise and Asthma. *Pediatrics* 56:844–846, 1975.

Guidelines for Prescribing Exercise for Asthmatics. *The Physician and Sportsmedicine* 9(3):51, March 1981.

Guyton, A. C. *Physiology of the Human Body*, 5th ed. Philadelphia: W. B. Saunders, 1979.

Haas, A., Castillo, R., and Lustig, F. The Application of Rehabilitation Medicine to Bronchial Asthma. In *Bronchial Asthma Mechanisms and Therapeutics*, edited by E. B. Weiss and M. S. Segal. Boston: Little, Brown, 1976.

Haynes, J. T., and Caplin, I. Hay Fever. In *Current Diagnosis 4*, edited by H. F. Conn and R. B. Conn, Jr. Philadelphia: W. B. Saunders, 1974.

Hendrickson, J. M., and Nielsen, T. T. Effect of Physical Training on Exercise-Induced Bronchoconstriction. *ACTA Paediatrica Scandinavica* 72:31–36, 1983.

Hirsch, S. R. Allergic Rhinitis due to Inhalant Factors. In *Conn's Current Therapy 1984*, edited by R. E. Rakel. Philadelphia: W. B. Saunders, 1984.

Jones, D. E. Exercise Prescription for Asthmatics. Presentation given at AAHPERD annual convention, Anaheim, California, 2 April 1984.

Katz-Smith, L. Personal communication, Division of Allergy, Children's Memorial Hospital, Chicago, Ill., 25 February 1986.

Kelly, E. D. *Adapted and Corrective Physical Education*, 4th ed. New York: Roland Press, 1965.

Leffert, F. Asthma in Children. In *Conn's Current Therapy 1984*, edited by R. E. Rakel. Philadelphia: W. B. Saunders, 1984.

Leith, D. E., Philip, B., Gabel, R., Feldman, H., and Fencl, V. Ventilatory Muscle Training and Ventilatory Control. *American Review of Respiratory Disease* 119(2):99–100, 1979.

Marley, W. P. Asthma and Exercise, A Review. *American Corrective Therapy Journal* 31(4):95–112, 1977.

Marshall, S. G., and Bierman, C. W. Asthma in Children. In *Current Diagnosis 7*, edited by R. B. Conn. Philadelphia: W. B. Saunders, 1985.

McElhenny, T. R., and Peterson, K. H. Physical Fitness for Asthmatic Boys. *Journal of the American Medical Association* 185(2):178–179, 1963.

McFadden, E. A. *Exercise and Asthma.* Park Ridge, Ill.: American College of Chest Physicians, 1981.

Ostrow, J. H. Chronic Obstructive Pulmonary Disease. In *Disability and Rehabilitation Handbook*, edited by R. H. Goldenson. New York: McGraw-Hill, 1978.

Petty, T. L., Hudson, L. D., and Neff, T. A. Methods of Ambulatory Care. *Medical Clinics of North America* 57(3):751–762, 1973.

Puthoff, M. New Dimensions in Physical Activity for Children With Asthma and Other Respiratory Conditions. *Journal of Health, Physical Education and Recreation* 43(7):75–80, 1972.

Respiratory Allergy in Athletes. *The Physician and Sportsmedicine* 6(5):56–65, 1978.

Scherr, M., and Frankel, L. Physical Conditioning Program for Asthmatic Children. *Journal of the American Medical Association* 168(15):1996–2000, 1958.

Sherrill, C. *Adapted Physical Education and Recreation*, 3rd ed. Dubuque, Iowa: Wm. C. Brown, 1986.

Siegel, S. C., Katz, R. M., and Rachelefsky, G. S. Bronchial Asthma. In *Bronchial Asthma Mechanisms and Therapeutics*, edited by E. B. Weiss and M. S. Segal. Boston: Little, Brown, 1976.

Silverman, M., and Anderson, S. D. Standardization of Exercise Tests in Asthmatic Children. *Archives of Disorders in Children* 47(882):165–178, 1972.

Sly, R. M. Exercise-Related Changes in Air-Way Obstuctions: Frequency and Clinical Correlates in Asthmatic Children. *Annals of Allergy* 28(1):34–36, 1970.

———. Exercise and the Asthmatic Child. *Pediatrics Digest* 14:42, 1972.

———. Exercise-Induced Asthma. In *Bronchial Asthma Mechanisms and Therapeutics*, edited by E. B. Weiss and M. S. Segal. Boston: Little, Brown, 1976.

Taplin, P. S., and Creer, T. L. A Procedure for Using Peak Expiratory Flow Rate to Increase the Predictability of Asthma Episodes. *Journal of Asthma Research* 16(1):15–19, 1978.

Thosteson, G. To Your Good Health—Over the Cold and Back to School. *Daily Pantagraph*, December 1979.

Walter, J. B. *An Introduction to the Principles of Disease*, 2nd ed. Philadelphia: W. B. Saunders, 1982.

Wanner, A., and Sackner, M. A. Emphysema and Chronic Bronchitis. In *Current Therapy 1975*, edited by H. F. Conn. Philadelphia: W. B. Saunders, 1975.

Wood, D. W., Krauls, L. P., and Lecks, H. I. Physical Therapy for Children With Intractable Asthma. *Journal of Asthma Research* 7(4):177–182, 1970.

Woods, D. Y. Exercise Rehabilitation in COPD. *Cardio-Gram* 10(1):6, 1982–1983.

CHAPTER 22

Diabetes Mellitus

For more than 4000 years, human beings have recorded facts concerning diabetes mellitus (mell'-a-tus). It is one of the most common diseases today, affecting approximately 4 million people in the United States, of which 10 percent are children (one in 600 school-age children) (Malone 1984). The adapted physical educator can thus expect to come in contact with diabetic youngsters in the public school setting.

Diabetes is a major health problem. It is the direct cause of more than 38,000 deaths per year and a contributing factor in another 260,000 deaths annually. Diabetes mellitus ranks third, after heart disease and cancer, as a leading cause of death in the United States. A baby born today has a one in five chance of becoming diabetic. Furthermore, the incidence of diabetes is increasing at a rate of 6 percent per year. Given that rate of increase, the number of diabetic individuals will double every 15 years.

Physical Education and the Diabetic

A common practice has been to excuse the diabetic child from physical education. This is unnecessary and, in fact, could lead to potentially dangerous physical complications. Appropriate progressive exercise and development of lifetime fitness and sport skills are encouraged and needed by all diabetics. A physical education program and regular exercise may be as important to the child with diabetes as diet and insulin. Engerbretson (1977, p. 18) states: "Rather than being discouraged from participating in physical education activities and athletics, diabetics should be encouraged to take part on a regular basis. Their diabetic control will improve, they will be able to eat a somewhat more normal diet, they will be able to maintain higher levels of physical fitness, and their psychological adjustment to the disease will be more positive."

Although the diabetic individual needs no special school setting, adapted physical educators should have a thorough knowledge of the causes and characteristics of the disease, the effects of exercise programs, and emergency treatment. They must understand why a regular urine test for glucose is necessary, how the child's metabolism changes as a result of physical exercise, and how, when, and why to adjust insulin dosage and diet.

To prevent unexpected diabetic emergencies, the physical educator needs to know if a child is diabetic. The Juvenile Diabetes Foundation (n.d., p. 1) emphasizes that "All teachers, school nurses, principals, lunchroom personnel, playground and hall supervisors, and bus drivers be informed that a student has diabetes." This information must not be withheld, particularly from the physical education teacher or coach. A form (Figure 22.1) is recommended for use in obtaining information from the diabetic child during a personal interview.

Definitions

Generally speaking, **diabetes mellitus** is a chronic metabolic disease that interferes with the body's ability to produce or use insulin or both. The body fails to burn carbohydrate intake properly, so glucose accumulates in the bloodstream. This condition is known as **hyperglycemia,** an overabundance of blood sugar. (**Hypoglycemia** is the condition that occurs when the body has too little blood sugar.)

The name *diabetes mellitus* means literally "sweet urine" and refers to the overabundance of blood sugar in the urine of the uncontrolled diabetic.

When diabetes strikes an adult, it is usually designated **type II,** or **mature-onset diabetes (MOD).** In its early stages, type II diabetes can be controlled with diet and exercise. Occasionally oral drugs are prescribed. When youngsters (up to age 20 years) contract diabetes, it is termed **type I,** or **juvenile-onset diabetes (JOD).** This type is more serious, and the youngsters must have daily insulin injections or they will die.

Date _____

Information to be obtained from parents when conference is held at beginning of school term:

_____   _____

Child's name   Age   Teacher/Counselor

_____   _____

Parent's name   Phone

_____   _____

Alternate person to call in emergency   Phone

_____

Physician's name   Address   Phone

Signs and symptoms the child usually exhibits preceding insulin reaction _____

_____

_____

Time of day reaction most likely to occur _____

Most effective treatment (sweets most readily accepted) _____

_____

Kind of morning or afternoon snack _____

_____

Suggested "treats" for in-school parties _____

_____

FIGURE 22.1.   Diabetes information sheet should be used to gather data from the student or the student's parents.

Although some adults do develop type I and some children develop type II, these cases are comparatively few. Children at high risk for type II diabetes are classified as Mature-Onset Diabetes for Youth (MODY) (Malone 1984), and are usually obese. This form of the disease occurs most frequently among Black teenagers, particularly females. Mexican-American adolescents also are at higher risk for the disease, as are American Indian teenagers (Traisman 1985).

The two types of diabetes reflect differing degrees of insulin deficiency and adipose tissue buildup. The child with type I is generally slender and cannot produce insulin. The individual with type II retains some ability to produce natural insulin but exhibits excess body fat. Goldstein and Podolsky (1978) identify the primary characteristic of type II as obesity. While type II diabetes is more common (90 percent of all diabetes) and its effects on the adult population important, this chapter deals with type I, juvenile onset diabetes, the diabetes that affects school-age individuals.

Type I is often referred to as ketosis-prone diabetes, growth-onset diabetes, insulin-dependent diabetes, insulin-deficient diabetes, or abnormal glucose tolerance (Whitehouse 1978).

Although urine output increases and the urine contains excessive sugar, type I diabetes is not a disease of the kidneys. Diabetes involves carbohydrate metabolism, that is, breakdown and use of carbohydrates. Carbohydrate foods, namely, sugars and starches, are the body's chief source of energy. The digestive system changes carbohydrates into glucose, which can be passed through the stomach and intestine walls into the blood, hence the term "blood sugar." Most blood sugar is carried to the body's cells, including muscle cells, and is burned immediately for heat and energy. Some blood sugar, glycogen, is stored in the liver for future use.

Pancreatic Involvement and the Role of Insulin

Alpha and beta cells are found in the pancreas islets (islands) of Langerhans. Beta cells produce **insulin.** In type I diabetes, the beta cells degenerate by losing their granules. As the disease progresses, they may disappear completely. When this happens, no insulin is produced, and the individual becomes totally dependent on daily injections of manufactured insulin.

When the nondiabetic person digests food, the blood sugar (glucose) level rises, and the beta cells in the pancreas secrete insulin within a few minutes. The insulin in turn causes excess glucose to be transported to cells for energy, or stored as glycogen in the liver, or converted to fat and stored (Guyton 1979). Basically, insulin enables glucose to cross the cell membranes and pass into the cells as nourishment. Without insulin, only one fourth of the needed glucose crosses cell membranes and enters the cells; this is not enough nourishment to live. Essentially, the cells are being starved because insulin is not present to facilitate passage of glucose through the cell walls. If insulin is not administered, the type I diabetic will experience such common symptoms as hunger, nervousness, and perspiration. Next, if cell starvation persists, the individual becomes faint, falls into a coma, and finally, without insulin, dies. Children with type I disease do not have enough beta cells, because these cells are being destroyed, and therefore require daily insulin injections for the rest of their lives.

Insulin also increases the body's supply of glycogen, which is stored in the liver until needed, as when performing continuous exercise.

The Alpha Cell and Glucagon

Alpha cells of the pancreas produce and secrete a hormone called **glucagon** (gloo'-kah-gon). Many glucagon functions do not involve insulin, but some do assist in insulin function. Glucagon raises blood sugar level; insulin reduces it. Both glucagon and insulin increase availability of glucose to the cells. Glucagon changes stored glycogen in the liver to glucose; insulin does this by facilitating transport and entry of glucose into the cells. During heavy exercise, both hormones work in unison to promote glucose use by the muscles (Guyton 1979).

The glucagon process, like the insulin process, regulates blood glucose concentration, but with one difference: the glucagon mechanism keeps blood glucose concentration from falling too low, while insulin keeps it from rising too high. The body activates glucagon during heavy exercise and during starvation, because in both conditions, a decrease in blood glucose occurs.

For the person with type I diabetes, the alpha cells may also be defective. In a study of 14 diabetics and 7 nondiabetic subjects, glucagon levels were measured before and after a period of low blood sugar. The diabetic subjects possessed significantly lower levels of glucagon than did the normal control group. These findings suggest that type I diabetics may have a defect in both beta and alpha cells (Duncan and Oppenheimer 1974).

Causes of Juvenile-Onset Diabetes

Knowledge about the etiology (cause) of insulin-dependent type I diabetes has grown since 1973. Three possible causes are identified by Farquhar (1979): (1) A few viruses are known to destroy pancreatic beta cells. (2) Autoimmunity (i.e., when the body destroys its own tissues) may cause more or less rapid pancreatic islet cell destruction. An autoimmune response can occur in persons who are vulnerable to specific virus action. (3) Certain genetic factors may predispose some children to type I diabetes.

In considering the **virus theory,** Farquhar (1979, p. 575) poses the critical question: "What changes an apparently healthy child into one with JOD (type I) within days or weeks? Rubella and mumps certainly seem to trigger a genetic time-bomb with a delayed action system." Gajdusek (1978) indicates that previously unrecognized microorganisms are responsible for serious diseases of unknown etiology. Research suggests that Coxsackie B virus is associated with destruction of pancreas islet cells. Studies by Rolles et al. (1975) and Cudworth et al. (1977) also conclude that a direct association exists between type I onset and Coxsackie B virus. Extensive research by Mesner and associates (1978) indicates a strong correlation between an offspring's contracting type I diabetes and the mother's having had rubella during pregnancy. Experimental research on the effect of the rubella virus on pregnant rabbits produced destructive changes in fetal pancreatic beta cells.

The **autoimmune theory** is now accepted as one cause of type I diabetes. In a high fraction of those with juvenile onset diabetes, concrete evidence suggests that the body develops an autoimmunity (Goldstein et al. 1970, 1978). The American Diabetes Association (1976, p. 19) defines autoimmunity as follows: "In attacking a living cell, viruses can so change the structure of the cell that the body's defense [immune] system no longer recognizes the cell as part of the body. The cell is then destroyed or rejected like a foreign substance. This rejection of the body of its own cells (in this case beta cells in the pancreas) is called autoimmunity." Additional research has further documented specific destruction of the pancreatic islet cells (Botazzo, Florin-Christensen, and Doniach 1974, Irvine, McCallum, and Gray 1977).

The **genetic** or **hereditary component** also is considered a cause of type I. Falconer (1967) finds a hereditary factor in the history of 70 to 81 percent of young diabetics. The general consensus is that heredity is a major factor in diabetes.

The hereditary, genetic, and diabetic association has been questioned by recent research, which indicates that type I diabetes has little connection with inherited tendencies. MacDonald (1974) compared ancestors of type I patients and a nondiabetic control group. No differences were found. Tattersall and Fajans (1975) studied groups of type I and type II diabetic individuals. They found that only 11 percent of type I patients had a diabetic parent, whereas 85 percent of type II patients had a diabetic parent. In only 6 percent of type I patients was disease found in three generations compared with 46 percent of type II patients who reported a history of diabetes in three generations. Farquhar (1979, p. 572) summarizes: "These studies give further evidence of genetic heterogeneity in diabetes mellitus."

Some association of heredity with type I diabetes seems clear, but the direct relationship remains controversial. The problem stems from a lack of specific molecular-genetic markers that would enable researchers to relate the two factors conclusively. Goldstein and Podolsky (1978, p. 651) summarize the heredity theory: "Data from many diverse sources now indicates that diabetes is a disease complex which in genetic terms is usually multifactorial and heterogeneous."

Strong indications exist that environmental and life-style conditions (overeating and lack of exercise) play a key role in onset of type II diabetes but have little bearing on type I.

Whatever the specific cause of type I, new scientific procedures can now determine if a child is vulnerable to this disease. Those children who are at risk are identified by tissue-typing, because they possess a higher than normal amount of identifiable antigens. (An antigen is a substance that, under appropriate conditions, is capable of forming antibodies.)

Common Characteristics of Type I Diabetes

Youngsters with type I diabetes are generally insulin-dependent from time of diagnosis. When insulin is lacking, blood sugar cannot be changed into glycogen for storage in the liver nor can it be used effectively by muscle cells, so it accumulates in the blood in excessive amounts.

An even greater danger than the body's failure to burn carbohydrates is failure to burn fats. For proper combustion of fat, a certain proportion of carbohydrates must be burned simultaneously. An incorrect combination of fat and glucose results in the incomplete burning of fat particles, which forms toxic acid waste products. These waste products are compounds known as *ketones,* and the chemical condition is called **ketosis,** or **acidoses.** In uncontrolled diabetes, the concentration of ketones becomes very high, and a strong acid effect, known as *ketoacidosis,* occurs. This is an emergency situation, which requires administration of insulin lest the person become comatose and die.

Two different reactions develop when insulin, food intake, and exercise are not in proper balance: (1) when blood sugar becomes too low, **hypoglycemia** occurs, and (2) when blood sugar becomes too high, **hyperglycemia** occurs. Immediate causes, warning signs, and treatments of these two complications are at opposite extremes. It is important for the adapted physical educator to be able to distinguish between the two. (See Table 22.1 for a comparison of symptoms.)

Hypoglycemic reactions (referred to variously as insulin reaction, insulin shock, or low blood sugar) are the most common type of diabetic reactions. When hypoglycemia occurs, the blood sugar drops to too low a level for the body to sustain activity. This condition can arise when the child participates in excessive physical activity without eating extra food. Any delayed meal, limited food intake, or greater than average exercise can cause a hypoglycemic reaction (American Diabetes Association 1976).

TABLE 22.1
COMPARISON OF HYPOGLYCEMIC AND HYPERGLYCEMIC REACTIONS

Warning Signs	Hypoglycemic Reaction (Insulin Reaction)	Hyperglycemic Reaction (Diabetic Coma)
Onset	Sudden	Gradual
Skin	Pale, moist	Flushed, dry
Behavior	Excited, nervous, confused	Drowsy
Breath	Normal	Fruity odor (acetone)
Breathing	Normal to rapid, shallow	Deep, labored
Vomiting	Absent	Present
Tongue	Moist, numb, tingling	Dry
Hunger	Present	Absent
Thirst	Absent	Present
Pain	Headache	Abdominal
Sugar in urine	Absent or slight	Large amounts

Normal bodily functioning requires that chemical processes be kept within restricted limits. The brain and the nervous system burn glucose as their only source of energy. Low blood sugar results in a breakdown of the normal functioning of these systems, producing distinct and progressive symptoms. Typical early sumptoms of hypoglycemia are *paleness* around the mouth and across the bridge of the nose; *perspiration,* particularly of the palms and soles of the feet; *a blank, staring expression;* an *outer trembling* and what diabetics describe as an *inner nervousness;* and at times, *excessive hunger* and a *general sense of weakness.* If hypoglycemia persists, declining function of the central nervous system occurs. This deterioration results in general inability to think clearly. The severely hypoglycemic individual may *not* be able to do the following: remember familiar items such as telephone numbers, perform coordinated movements, or speak or act intelligently.

Continuous physical activity greatly decreases blood sugar level to a degree often not recognized. One problem is that the same exertion that decreases the blood sugar level can be easily misinterpreted as the cause of the symptoms. Sweating, weakness, dull thinking, and poor muscle coordination are wrongly attributed to fatigue from exercise, rather than to low blood sugar level, which is the actual cause of the symptoms. If these symptoms do not diminish after a brief rest period, almost certainly a hypoglycemic reaction is occurring. Reactions as a result of activity usually take place during or soon after exertion, but may develop even hours later in diabetics who are being treated with long-acting insulin (Smelo 1973).

The final phase of hypoglycemia is marked by jerky movements, general inability to move purposefully, and eventual unconsciousness.

Onset of hypoglycemia is usually quite rapid; the reaction *may develop in only minutes.* Engerbretson (1977) states that a few "brittle" diabetics can lapse into unconsciousness almost without warning, but most diabetic individuals know when a reaction is coming on in time to treat themselves or to warn the instructor about their feelings.

Emergency Treatment of Hypoglycemia

Immediate intake of carbohydrates is needed to counteract a hypoglycemic reaction. The child will improve quickly after eating or drinking any form of sugar. The Juvenile Diabetes Foundation suggests the following treatment for an individual having a reaction:

1. Give some form of sugar immediately. (This will rapidly increase amount of sugar in the blood.) Use any of the following: sugar cubes, skim milk or fruit juice (approximately one half cup), pop (one half cup, not diet pop), or candy (equivalent to 6-8 Lifesavers). The child may need to be coaxed to eat.
2. Improvement should be evident within 10 min, then give additional food and have the child resume normal activities.

3. If the child does not improve, call parents, physician, and emergency medical assistance.

If the student becomes unconscious or is unable to take sugar, call the school nurse for assistance. The nurse should have an emergency kit of glucagon and can administer a subcutaneous injection. Regarding this situation, new glucose preparations are available in squeeze bottles, with instructions for inserting the nozzle into the mouth of the unconscious person. The squeeze bottle is marked to show how much to squeeze.

Once a reaction has been treated successfully, its cause should be noted and precautions taken to avoid recurrence. If the reaction resulted from inadequate food intake, this should be discussed with the student. Note that the child's lunch period be scheduled *before* physical education class. If a reaction occurs during the physical education period, extra nourishment should be made available. The fact that the amounts of physical activity are irregular from day to day demands that the child be watched. For example, if one day's activity includes light calisthenics and little strenuous exercise (e.g., demonstration and execution of discus throwing and putting the shot), the student will not need to increase food intake for the day. On another day, however, when the program involves running techniques, the child may need to increase food intake before class, and the instructor may want to have fruit juice on hand. In most cases, recovery from hypoglycemia is rapid once the child ingests the food or liquid.

The student must be told what activities to expect well in advance. This is the teacher's responsibility, and any deviation from the designated program must be taken into consideration.

Emergency Treatment of Hyperglycemia

Hyperglycemic reaction is also called **diabetic coma,** or diabetic acidosis. Diabetic coma is relatively rare, but does occur when a diabetic individual seriously departs from prescribed diet or fails to take insulin. When this imbalance develops, the insulin level becomes too low and excessive sugar builds up in the blood. Without insulin, the cells do not receive adequate amounts of carbohydrates, so the body begins to break down its store of fats. This breakdown is incomplete and results in excessive accumulation of ketones in the blood and urine. This is called ketoacidosis. If insulin is not administered, the child can go into a coma. Immediate treatment is imperative at such time as this occurs.

In contrast to fast-developing hypoglycemia, hyperglycemia progresses slowly over many hours or several days, and the symptoms are more difficult to detect. The reaction is usually characterized by fatigue, sluggishnes, or general lethargy (Seltzer 1977). The student will often experience a frequent need to urinate, and the instructor may become aware that the child is requesting to use the restroom more often than usual. Onset, when specific signs become evident, is usually indicated by deep respiration, known as "air hunger" (Boyd 1971). Engerbretson (1977) states that the most significant sign is the fruity odor of the diabetic's breath. When such an odor is present, ask the student if insulin injections have been missed or delayed, or if urine tests have been positive.

If the child exhibits any of these symptoms or lapses into a coma, immediate treatment is necessary. The student should be rushed to a physician or hospital for proper administration of controlled insulin dosage. If the child is comatose, only a physician or specially trained nurse can inject insulin. This cannot be done by the physical educator.

Control and Treatment of Diabetes

The well-controlled diabetic will exhibit the following characteristics: (1) feeling of physical well-being, (2) normal weight, maintained by a well-balanced diet, (3) generally negative urine tests, and (4) negative blood sugar tests. Ideally students with diabetes are taught by their physicians and parents to understand their condition and how to balance a program of diet, insulin, and exercise. Knox (1975) suggests that diabetic children be taught self-injection of insulin as soon as they reveal capacity to learn, regardless of age. The same applies to self-administration of urine tests for sugar and acetone, recognition and treatment of insulin reactions, and self-adjustment of insulin-dosage. A new kit for self-testing one's blood sugar level is now being used as well. Both hyper- and hypoglycemia can be detected, and the test results indicate one's blood sugar level *at that instant*, which the urine tests cannot do.

There is some confusion regarding the use of oral medications that stimulate production of insulin in the pancreas. Type I children have little, if any, success with this approach, because their beta cells are ineffective and will not produce insulin regardless of stimulation. Oral medication is often beneficial, however, for type II adult diabetics.

Use of Insulin and Exercise

The diabetic student will usually administer a single dose of **long-acting insulin** each morning. This facilitates overall carbohydrate metabolism throughout the day. Additional quantities of more rapid-acting **regular insulin** are given when the blood glucose level rises too high at specific times, such as immediately after meals. Each child should be on an established, individualized treatment routine. Figure 22.2 shows common insulin injection sites.

Because insulin is a protein, it cannot be taken orally because the digestive juices would destroy it before it entered the bloodstream. Insulin therefore must be injected subcutaneously, under the skin but above the muscle tissues. Injection sites should be changed daily (Watkins 1980) to avoid scarring from repeated injections in the same place.

Studies conducted at Yale University by Drs. Philip Felig and Ralph DeFanzo have found that diabetics who exercise regularly are able to maintain lower blood sugar levels and increase effectiveness of available insulin (Ubell 1985).

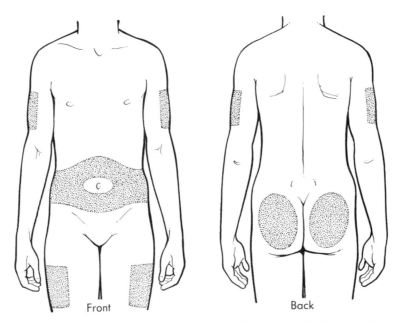

FIGURE 22.2. Shaded areas indicate suitable sites for insulin injections.

Problems arise when the student injects insulin above muscles that are heavily used owing to a difference in absorption rate of working and nonworking muscles. During exercise, hard-working muscles need more fuel (glucose). Insulin, injected directly above a working muscle, defeats that need because it absorbs rapidly into the bloodstream and causes the blood sugar level to drop. Felig and Koivisto (1978) exercised diabetic subjects on a stationary bicycle after insulin injection in the thigh. They found that insulin was absorbed more than twice as fast as it normally would have been. When injections were given in an arm or the abdomen, however, insulin levels of the bicycling subjects remained normal. The investigators conclude that insulin users who plan to exercise should, after checking with their physician, inject themselves at a site where muscles will not be heavily taxed. For individuals who play tennis, basketball, or volleyball, sports in which both leg and arm muscles work hard, injection should be in the abdomen.

The diabetic individual can cope with increased exercise in two ways. If the usual dosage of insulin has already been injected, additional carbohydrates must be taken before and during strenuous exercise to avoid insulin reaction. As a result of exercise, this additional sugar will be used readily by the body. If, however, the student can plan ahead (because the physical educator has forewarned the student) for a period of strenuous activity, *reduction* in the insulin dosage covering a given exercise period can be made in advance. Each person with diabetes must learn by experience just how much dosage should be varied. For a very active person, such as a competitive athlete, the reduction may be almost one half the usual insulin amount.

The following question and answer from "Ask Us" (*Diabetes Forecast* 1977, p. 8) provide specific information:

Question: I have had diabetes for one year and take ten units of Lente [long acting] insulin daily. I'm a very active person and play tennis for at least one or two hours three times a week. I know that insulin burns sugar and exercise burns sugar, but I can't seem to regulate the days I play tennis. After about one hour of activity, I get faint, shaky, and sweaty. Then I must take sugar. Should I give myself less insulin or eat more?

Response: Activity causes an increased need for calories, actually sugar calories or glucose. While you are sitting, your body burns about 75 calories per hour. But while you're playing tennis, your body requires 200 extra calories per hour. Many athletes in your situation take a Coke or other soft drink to provide the additional calories needed for exercise. Decrease the amount of insulin approximately four units. Additional calories will probably not be needed. Usually it is not a good plan to increase food intake and reduce insulin. Do one or the other.

Knox (1975, p. 389) offers the following advice regarding exercise: "When activity is expected to be less than normal, insulin is increased. For greater than normal activity, prior ingestion of carbohydrates is advised. If exercise is strenuous and prolonged, hourly snacks should be taken."

Samsoe (1980–1981, p. 1) describes the benefits of exercise in her account of a diabetic child's experience at summer camp. She states: "With regular exercise, many insulin dependent diabetics have been able to reduce their insulin requirements. This is seen particularly in the summer months when diabetic children go off to camp, increase their caloric expenditure, and require less insulin. As these children return to school in the fall their energy expenditure typically decreases, causing their insulin requirements to usually increase again."

During adolescence, youngsters must be aware of events that lead to an increased need for either insulin or glucose. A common mistake is for students to forget to replenish the candy supply in their purse or jacket. When youngsters are involved in exciting and stimulating activity, they often forget to keep track of time and may skip a needed snack. The instructor should watch for irregular responses when these students are engaged in lengthy activity.

New discoveries in the treatment of diabetics include use of an insulin pump. This small battery-operated machine delivers insulin through a tube inserted under the skin. For persons whose diabetes is difficult to control, this process is an improvement over traditional injections because the pump drips a steady flow of the hormone into the body all day long. A 14-year-old student from Pennsylvania was taking up to six daily injections of regular insulin, but his blood sugar was still uncontrolled. His physician suggested use of an insulin pump. The youngster now states: "I feel a lot better. I hang my pump on my belt, or else I wear a special T-shirt with a hole in the pocket so the tube is less noticeable. Sometimes, when I play sports, the pump gets in the way. But, my friends don't care at all" (Ubell 1985).

Urine Tests to Determine Daily Amounts of Blood Sugar

Students with diabetes must check their urine several times daily to determine whether their blood sugar level is within safe limits. Although slightly bothersome, these checks are absolutely necessary. Specially treated paper that the child dips into a urine sample or directly into the urine stream is used for the test. The tape color changes, indicating amount of sugar in the urine. Urinary glucose testing is another method available. Although testing devices may vary, each diabetic child will require more time for the toilet break (approximately 2 extra minutes). Test should be made before meals.

Students with type I diabetes should perform blood glucose and urine ketone tests before exercise. The glucose level will show whether or not the child needs an extra preexercise snack, and whether the blood glucose level is too high for safe exercising. The ketone test lets the individual know if he has enough insulin available to exercise safely. Ketones in the urine before exercise generally mean that the individual does not have enough insulin available to exercise safely (American Diabetes Association 1985).

Physical Education Activities

Regular physical activity plays a necessary and important role in the physiological and psychological management of a child with type I diabetes. Daily exercise increases cellular uptake of blood sugar, even without insulin. Cunningham and Etkind (1975) found that diabetic children can participate in almost all activities if they maintain a proper balance of insulin and diet. Famous diabetic athletes who have been successful include Ron Santo and Jackie Robinson (baseball), Bobby Clark (hockey), Coly O'Brien (football), and Ham Richardson and Billy Talbert (tennis).

In reference to the appropriateness of exercise for diabetic youngsters, Wentworth and Hoover state (1981, p. 43GE): "Most physicians encourage active participation in exercise, physical education, and extracurricular school sports. Uncomplicated diabetes should never be a reason to exclude a child from activity."

Coping with the psychological aspect of diabetes is especially important in children, because exclusion from normal school activities can become an unbearable situation. Diabetes is not a barrier to a full and happy life-style. Sometimes, however, misunderstanding leads diabetic children to assume that they can never be like other children. Too often, concerned parents and teachers offer excessive amounts of sympathy and not enough understanding. Any chronic disease is psychologically depressing, and depression is heightened when the student is forbidden to participate in physical education and athletic competition. The enjoyment and challenge of physical education is an important force in a child's development, and is especially critical for diabetic children in teaching them to cope with and accept their condition (Engerbretson 1977).

Weight control is often associated with diabetic individuals. Children with type I diabetes are generally underweight and smaller than their peers. (Overweight is more commonly linked with type II.) Arky (1978) emphasizes that youngsters with type I must eat adequate calories to ensure normal growth and maturation. In the past, "diabetic dwarfism" was common among children on restricted diets. The physical education program for these children should therefore include strength development and should emphasize increasing the child's weight and muscular stature. Cunningham and Etkind (1975) state that the performance of diabetic boys is significantly below that of nondiabetic peers with average physical fitness levels. They also indicate that there is no reason to restrict the type I child from strength development activities. An individualized physical education program should therefore include activities that involve large muscle group development.

Activities should also promote cardiorespiratory fitness. Well-trained athletes function with remarkably low concentrations of insulin in their blood. If individuals want to obtain the full benefit of exercise, they must exercise regularly and at a rate that increases oxygen demand significantly. Exercises that have the most beneficial effects involve moving and lifting the entire body, as in controlled and continuous action of aerobic activities.

Some diabetic individuals may possess a very low level of cardiorespiratory fitness and may need to begin their aerobic program by walking. The National Heart, Lung, and Blood Institute has developed a 12-week progressive walking program (Table 22.2). Stretching exercises should be performed before the walking warm-up, and individuals should schedule at least three exercise sessions per week. If the individual finds any one day particularly tiring, then that day's exercise regimen should be repeated before going on to the next session (Krosnick 1984).

Infection is a common problem for diabetics. When blood sugar levels are high, the white blood cells are less able to fight off invading organisms. The feet are particularly susceptible because of general poor circulation in this area. When prescribing walking and running programs for diabetic youngsters, be conscious of new blisters, particularly if the student has new shoes or dirty socks.

Few programmatic differences are needed for diabetic students. If, however, a particular diabetic child has been restricted in the past and has had little opportunity to develop normally, the program must begin slowly and build gradually to higher skill and fitness levels. Do not push or expect the child to become a competitive athlete in a short time. Engerbretson (1977, p. 20) warns: "During this early learning period, it may be necessary for the teacher or coach to make certain allowances and adjustments in the diabetic's program, and to allow the student to work at reduced levels. . . . Perhaps the best procedure . . . is for the students or athletes to be allowed to judge their own capabilities and for the teacher or coach to make no hard and fast rules concerning training, competition, or class performance." The initial introduction to the physical education program should allow the child time to concentrate on adjusting diet and insulin to the new exercise regimen. An increase in the program's intensity should be a cooperative effort of the adapted physical education teacher and the child.

TABLE 22.2
TWELVE-WEEK PROGRESSIVE WALKING PROGRAM

Week	Warm-up (Slow Walking) (min)	Exercise (Brisk Walking) (min)	Cool Down (Slow Walking) (min)	Total Time (min)
1	5	5	5	15
2	5	7	5	17
3	5	9	5	19
4	5	11	5	21
5	5	13	5	23
6	5	15	5	25
7	5	18	5	28
8	5	20	5	30
9	5	23	5	33
10	5	26	5	36
11	5	28	5	38
12	5	30	5	40

SOURCE: Modified from Krosnick, Spring 1984, p. 5.

Diabetic children are, like other youngsters, impatient and overenthusiastic. They may not attend to reaction warning signs and may play well past the danger limit. The child must be encouraged to use good judgment and to take short breaks for snacks or a brief rest. Students and athletes must be taught that they can be of more value to the team by resting for a minute or so to enable their bodies to adjust to the demands of intense physical activity. A prearranged signal from player to coach can indicate the need for a break. An adequate supply of dextrose tablets, hard candy, soft drinks, or fruit juice should be available.

The adapted physical educator should be aware that a diabetic child may need more fluids than other youngsters. This is because higher than normal blood sugar levels draw needed water from the body tissues. The amount of water lost depends on activity level, physical fitness level, and weather conditions. The student should be encouraged to drink plenty of water. A good rule for most situations is to provide water every 15 min when the student is doing strenuous activity. This becomes the responsibility of the teacher (Casey 1984).

Should the diabetic child become sick and vomit, an imbalance may occur involving appropriate amounts of blood sugar and insulin. The child should be excused from strenuous exercise for the rest of the day, and the school nurse and other teachers should be notified to watch for possible adverse reactions.

Summary

Diabetes mellitus is not a contagious disease. Type I, juvenile-onset diabetes, is a lifelong condition that begins in childhood and results from a lack of insulin in the body. Davidson (1985) finds that type I diabetics can attain and sustain near-normal levels of blood sugar if they routinely monitor their blood glucose levels at home and make indicated adjustments in their insulin, diet, and exercise patterns on a daily basis. He states: "There is evidence that these planned programs will prevent the acute complications, and may prevent, delay the appearance of, or even reverse the vascular problems specific to the diabetic state" (p. 744).

Hypoglycemic reactions occur when the blood sugar level is too low. Insulin and exercise both lower blood sugar. Food intake raises blood sugar level. Good control requires that these three factors (insulin, exercise, and food intake) be balanced. Hypoglycemic reactions occur because of (1) too little food or a delayed meal, (2) strenuous exercise not covered by extra food, or (3) too much insulin, given the amount of exercise. A hyperglycemic reaction can occur when there is too much sugar in the blood. Additional insulin is then required (Lodewick 1984). Knowing the warning signs and symptoms of diabetic reactions is key to avoiding possible coma by applying proper and immediate treatment.

The student's prescribed diet will often include snacks to maintain the food and insulin balance. Routine is important; the diabetic child should eat every snack and meal on time. Delay may result in a hypoglycemic reaction.

Urine testing is one of the ways to monitor blood sugar level and control diabetic reactions. Testing must be done several times a day, especially before each meal. Allow the student time to test before lunch and make appropriate arrangements for privacy.

Physical activity is essential to help the diabetic individual control her condition and lead a full existence. Progressive programs should be planned around each child's existing level of physical fitness and motor development. The diabetic youngster need not be excused from physical education. The individualized adapted physical education class may be more appropriate for some youngsters who are significantly below their peers in motor performance.

References

American Diabetes Association. *What You Need to Know About Diabetes.* New York: The Association, 1976.

Arky, R. A. Current Principles of Dietary Therapy of Diabetes Mellitus. *Medical Clinics of North America* 62(4):655–662, 1978.

Ask Us. *Diabetes Forecast* 30(3):8, 1977.

Botazzo, G. F., Florin-Christensen, A., and Doniach, D. Islet Cell Antibodies in Diabetes Mellitus With Autoimmune Polyendocrine Deficiencies. *Lancet* 2:1279–1282, 1974.

Boyd, W. *An Introduction to the Study of Disease.* Philadelphia: Lea & Febiger, 1971.

Casey, J. L. Exercise Caution. *Diabetes '84*, Summer 1984, p. 8.

Cudworth, A. G., White, G. B., Woodrow, J. C., Gamble, D. R., Lendrum, R., and Bloom, A. Actiology of Juvenile-Onset Diabetes. *Lancet* 1:385–388, 1977.

Cunningham, I. N., and Etkind, E. L. Let the Diabetic Play. *JOPER* 46(5):40–42, 1975.

Davidson, J. K. Diabetes Mellitus. In *Current Diagnosis 7*, edited by R. B. Conn. Philadelphia: W. B. Saunders, 1985.

Diabetes '85. American Diabetes Association, Winter 1985, p. 6.

Duncan, T. G., and Oppenheimer, H. E. New Discoveries in Diabetes Reported. *ADA Forecast* 27(5):15–18, 1974.

Engerbretson, D. L. The Diabetic in Physical Education, Recreation, and Athletics. *JOPER* 48(3):18–21, 1977.

Falconer, S. D. The Inheritance of Liability to Diseases With Variable Age of Onset, With Particular Reference to Diabetes Mellitus. *Annals of Human Genetics* 31:1–20, 1967.

Farquhar, J. W. Juvenile Diabetes Mellitus. *Archives of Disease in Childhood* 54(8):569–580, 1979.

Felig, P., and Koivisto, V. A. Exercise and Insulin. *Time*, 27 February 1978, pp. 52–53, 61.

Gajdusek, D. C. *Proceedings of the Working Conference of Preventable Aspects of Genetic Morbidity*. Cairo, Egypt: April 1978.

Goldstein, D. E., Drash, A., and Gibbs, J. Diabetes Mellitus: The Incidence of Circulating Antibodies Against Thyroid, Gastric and Adrenal Tissue. *Journal of Pediatrics* 77:304–306, 1970.

Goldstein, S., and Podolsky, S. The Genetics of Diabetes Mellitus. *Medical Clinics of North America* 62(4):639–654, 1978.

Guyton, A. C. *Physiology of the Human Body*, 5th ed. Philadelphia: W. B. Saunders, 1979.

Irvine, W. J., McCallum, C. J., and Gray, R. S. Pancreatic Islet-Cell Antibodies in Diabetes Mellitus Correlated With the Duration and Type of Diabetes, Coexistent Autoimmune Disease and HLA Type. *Diabetes* 26:138–147, 1977.

Juvenile Diabetes Foundation. *What the Teacher Should Know About the Student With Diabetes*. Downers Grove, Ill.: Juvenile Diabetes Foundation, n.d.

Knox, K. R. Management of the Diabetic Child. In *Current Therapy 1975*, edited by H. F. Conn. Philadelphia: W. B. Saunders, 1975.

Krosnick, A. Walk Your Way to Health. *Diabetes '84*, Spring 1984, p. 5.

Lodewick, P. How to Treat Low Blood Sugar. *Diabetes '84*, Spring 1984, p. 11.

MacDonald, M. J. Equal Incidence of Adult-Onset Diabetes Among Ancestors of Juvenile Diabetes and Nondiabetics. *Diabetologia* 10(3):767–773, 1974.

Malone, J. I. Diabetes Mellitus in Childhood and Adolescence. In *Conn's Current Therapy 1984*, edited by R. E. Rakel. Philadelphia: W. B. Saunders, 1984.

Mesner, M. A., Forrest, J. M., and Bransby, R. D. Rubella Infection and Diabetes Mellitus. *Lancet* 1:57–60, 1978.

Rolles, C. J., Rayner, P. H., and Mackintosh, P. Letter: Aetiology of Juvenile Diabetes. *Lancet* 2:230, 1975.

Samsoe, M. Aerobics for Diabetics. *Cardio-Gram* 8(1):1, Dec. 1980-Jan. 1981.

Seltzer, H. S. Urinary Glucose Tests—A Consumers Guide. *Diabetes Forecast* 30(3):25–27, 1977.

Smelo, L. S. The Recognition and Care of Hypoglycemic Reactions. *ADA Forecast* 26(1):1–6, 1973.

Tattersall, R. B., and Fajans, S. S. A Difference Between the Inheritance of Classical Juvenile-Onset and Maturity-Onset Type Diabetes of Young People. *Diabetes* 24:44–53, 1975.

Traisman, F. S. Type II Diabetes—Not for Adults Only. *Diabetes '85*, Summer 1985, p. 7.

Ubell, E. A Cure for Diabetes? *Health On Parade*, 21 April 1985, p. 12.

Watkins, P. J. Insulin Infusion Systems, Diabetic Control, and Microvascular Complications. *British Medical Journal* 280:350–352, 1980.

Wentworth, S. M., and Hoover, J. The Student With Diabetes. *Today's Education* 156:42–44GE, 1981.

Whitehouse, F. W. The Diagnosis of Diabetes. How to Determine Which Patients to Treat. *Medical Clinics of North America* 62(4):27–37, 1978.

CHAPTER 23

Swimming for the Student With Disabilities

> *I guess I will never forget the time, some years ago, when a little guy with cerebral palsy looked up at me with big blue eyes from where he was resting, propped up in the corner of the pool, and said, "You know something, Louise! This is the only place in the world where I can walk!" . . . It just tore me up! But it was true; for him, with his disability, walking was impossible on land, but the water provided the support, lessened the need for weight bearing and balance, and made it possible for him to have independent mobility. It was the freedom from disability, a time to achieve. Looking from his perspective, there was no question about why he should be in the water.*
>
> (Priest 1982, p. 2)

The most desirable physical education programming includes instruction in swimming. In fact, Public Law 94-142 specifically identifies water skill development as a part of all physical education curricula. Swimming, therefore, should be used to develop the physical and motor needs of the handicapped (AAHPERD 1975).

Goals and Benefits of a Swimming Program for the Handicapped

The primary goal is to teach disabled students to swim or to swim better. In addition, students should learn water safety and that the swimming experience is fun.

Physiological, psychological, and social benefits can be gained from swimming, which provides these benefits for both handicapped and nonhandicapped individuals. Swimming activities give youngsters opportunities and experiences not possible in any other environment. Buoyancy and ease of movement in water occur because of (1) reduced gravity, (2) less weight on joints, (3) less strength needed for movement, and (4) easy attainment of the independent standing position. These contribute to greater participation in basic skills. The physical benefits of swimming include better coordination, more endurance, improved range of motion, strengthened muscles, and effortless muscle performance.

Swimming can be used to develop social acceptance of the handicapped child and is an important way to improve the child's self-image. Handicapped children often possess distorted or negative feelings about themselves. One's self-image, the subjective picture of one's physical appearance, is influenced both by self-observation and by noting the reactions of others. To the handicapped teenager particulary, overt handicaps may be discouraging because they not only limit the motor skill repertoire but may also promote a devalued sense of self. Depressed physical and psychological development may follow. For example, Pagenoff (1984) found that a 14-year-old, spastic cerebral palsied student was exceptionally different from her peers in her approach to many activities. Fearing failure, the youngster refused to perform many activities both in treatment and extracurricularly. Her development of self-esteem and performance skills was therefore limitied. The girl in Pagenoff's study was quoted as saying: "I'm deformed, no one wants me around. I can't do what my friends can." A 2-day-a-week program was planned for the girl for an 8-week-period. To ensure optimum participation and performance, it became necessary to restrict the immediate area surrounding the pool during treatment sessions because the student refused to perform swimming activities when her mother or any outside observers were present. After completing the program, in addition to positive physiological and motor skill improvement, Pagenoff (p. 472) found that: "The most significant changes were noted in self-image. The patient became an active participant in planning the pool sessions. . . . Although body image continued as a concern, the patient began participating in the presence of pool observers and other guests." Steinbrunner (1982) agrees with Pagenoff about the benefits of a swimming program when he states: "There are secondary characteristics which often flow out of good [swimming] programs. One of them is the building of confidence in an individual. . . . I think this is more important in working with special populations than the actual program itself" (p. 28).

Safety Considerations

Some disabled students pose unique problems and challenges directly related to their handicapping condition. These problems affect the student's personal safety and the ability to learn water safety skills. The normal pool hazards are increased because the handicapped youngster often has vision difficulties, balance problems, impaired sense of direction, space, or distance, and may lack muscular control. Any one of these disabilities creates a potentially dangerous situation that should not be overlooked. For example, a child with cerebral palsy may have extreme difficulty walking on a wet, slippery deck.

The American National Red Cross (1977a) lists these suggestions for poolside safety:

1. Individuals with balance difficulties should always be assisted in walking on wet decks and ramps.
2. Wheelchairs should be used whenever possible. Carrying children, even small children, is unsafe on wet, slippery decks.
3. Wheelchairs should be locked in place at poolside before the student is taken out of the chair or returned to it.

Role of the Lifeguard

The adapted aquatics program requires constant student supervision. Lifeguards should be trained to be aware of specific complications that may arise as a result of handicapping conditions. They should be told which children experience seizures and should understand the procedure to be followed if a child has a seizure in the locker room or shower area, on the pool deck, or in the water (American National Red Cross 1974). (Procedures to follow when a seizure occurs are discussed later in this chapter.)

The lifeguard's first responsibility is to ensure each student's safety. The person who is lifeguarding an adapted physical education class must *not* have any other teaching or leadership assignments (Priest 1980). Lawrence and Hackett (1975) warn that lifeguards must be cautioned not to watch games and to remain constantly alert.

To ensure complete communication between swimming teacher and lifeguard, all water policies should be written and understood by all regular and substitute guards. When dealing with handicapped students, nothing should be left to chance. Most problems can be avoided if everyone understands clearly what must be done. This includes procedures for acquiring medical help: who should phone a physician, what physician should be called, what instructions should be given to locate the pool area.

Facilities for the Handicapped Swimmer

Most pools are not suitable for both handicapped and nonhandicapped individuals. Indeed, most pool facilities require adaptations to provide an acceptable program. The American National Red Cross (1977a, p. 110) identifies some of the necessary adaptations as follows: "Generally, specific adaptations are to overcome problems such as architectural barriers, water depth, temperature adjustment, and the ever-present problem of getting some less mobile individuals into the water. It is far better to adapt existing facilities than it is to forego programs for lack of special facilities."

Locker Rooms, Dressing Areas, and Showers

Handicapped students often need assistance and special accommodations to prepare for a swimming class. Physically impaired youngsters must remove braces, which usually requires assistance. The student should be encouraged to assist in this process with minimum help from the instructor. A classroom teacher or the therapist should show the swimming instructor how to remove prosthetic devices.

Blind students may have difficulty with combination locks found on most dressing room lockers. Key locks are more appropriate, and lockers or baskets should be easily located. Special locks are not necessary for all students and should be provided only when a student is spending an inordinate amount of time trying to get into the locker. Opening a lock may be a valuable learning experience but should not shorten swimming time excessively.

When undressing and dressing, students should become as independent as their handicap allows. The American National Red Cross (1977a, p. 98) offers the following advice on dealing with retarded youngsters: "Aides [and teachers] in the dressing room can provide a real service to retarded children and their families by encouraging the children and teaching competence in self-help. The aides should reward, in some way, any act that approximates desired behavior. For example, half a knot tied in a shoelace is better than none. Verbal approval is in itself a reward."

The locker room should be on the same level as the shower room and pool, with no curbs or stairs. Aisles should permit easy movement of wheelchairs. All benches should be securely fastened to the floor in locker room and shower areas. All lockers should be large enough to accommodate braces. Durfee (1977) also suggests that a 3 × 5 ft table be available in the locker room to assist students who cannot bend over easily to pick up an article from the floor.

Priest (1980) strongly suggests that wheelchairs be a permanent apparatus in locker and pool areas. These chairs would not become dirty from daily school activities. They should be the "stripped-down" collapsible kind that can be pushed directly down the pool ramp into the water.

Astroturf or other thick nonskid material should be used on floors and pool decks. Smooth paint and nonskid patches or paint do *not* provide a safe enough walking surface. The shower room should contain safety railings.

Pool Deck

The deck should be wide enough to permit passage of two wheelchairs. The surface must consist of a nonskid material that meets safety standards, that is, a child using crutches or canes will not slip and fall.

The water level should be not more than 12 in. below the pool deck, or more desirably, at the same level as the deck to permit easier entry and exit from the water. This is particularly important for students using pool ladders.

Regardless of water level, all pool edges should have a slightly raised lip to minimize danger of wheelchairs slipping into the water.

Pool Equipment

Getting the students in and out of the water easily and safely is important. Ideally, the pool should have wide, broad steps with hand rails for entering, exiting, resting, and learning. A wheelchair ramp from deck to pool floor should be provided. The ramp should be flush with the pool wall, but out of the way of those swimmers who are not wheelchair-bound. Hand rails should be installed on the ramp sides to enable students on foot or in wheelchairs to pull themselves up the ramp or to control their descent.

Hydraulic or hand-cranked lifts are extremely helpful for lowering or raising students in and out of the water. Manual lifting of students is considered a technical violation of Section 504 of the Rehabilitation Act of 1973, which prohibits lifting or carrying individuals to circumvent requirements to make facilities barrier-free and accessible to all (Bradtke 1979). The intent of this law is not to restrict handicapped students from the water, but to encourage school boards and public pool managers to be aware of and provide appropriate and accessible facilities.

Should a handicapped child be unable to enter the water by hydraulic lift (because of inability to sit in *any* chairlike device), then it is appropriate to lower the child by lifting and handing the child to another individual who is already in the water. To do this, a stable body position must be maintained by the person who is lifting, and proper balance support is required for the person being lifted. Using proper hand positions and firm grips to support the child are also important.

Resting platforms, such as small benches, should be located in the shallow end of the pool. These facilitate teaching and help handicapped students (e.g., double amputees) to grasp the sides of the pool.

Water Temperature

A comfortable pool setting, not loud or noisy, can help relieve any anxiety the child might have. Air temperature and water temperature are also critical. Water temperature will have a decided impact on how the child accepts the situation, and should be carefully controlled. The more severe the child's impairment is, the warmer the water should be.

Authorities disagree about the ideal water temperature. The American National Red Cross (1977a) recommends that the temperature for handicapped swimmers be between 78 and 84 °F (26 and 29 °C). Their publications also state that a higher water temperature may be desirable for some individuals, especially the severely cerebral palsied or persons with specific orthopedic problems. Durfee (1977) states that the ideal temperature is between 88 and 90 °F (31 and 32 °C) in summer and 91 and 93 °F (33 and 34 °C) in winter. Harris (1978) suggests that the water temperature should be between 96 and 100 °F (36 and 38 °C) for individuals with hypertonic, spastic cerebral palsy.

If the water temperature can be regulated to accommodate the activity levels of different groups of students, it should be adjusted to maximum comfort level for each group in turn. Youngsters who cannot move about quickly will need higher water temperatures, shorter periods in the water, or activities that increase participation.

Therapeutic Benefits

Lasko and Knopf (1984) endorse rehabilitation exercises in the water. They use the term **hydrogymnastics** to refer to a medically prescribed therapeutic exercise program performed in the water. In hydrogymnastics, the water is used as a therapeutic modality to habilitate the disabled individual. They state: "Many people prefer Hydrogymnastics because it occurs in warm water (92–93 °F). It is believed that warm water decreases pain and induces relaxation. With this decreased pain, many clients can see noticeable improvements in their range of motion" (p. 176).

General Teaching Techniques

The instructor should be aware of each child's handicap and the important characteristics that each child exhibits, because many students must rely on the instructor for physical support. The educator, therefore, must be continually aware of the child's comfort and safety needs.

For handicapped individuals who need a one-on-one teaching situation, the best results are attained by having an assistant or aide work with each child. Durfee (1977) suggests that the supervising teacher provide specific learning instructions and serve as demonstrator and roving assistant. This allows the teacher to assist many swimmers and aides with suggestions and comments.

Basic Teaching Factors

The American National Red Cross (1977b) identifies three factors that are basic to teaching swimming to disabled persons. The handicapped individual must be able to (1) make the physical and mental adjustment to the water in relationship to the skill being learned, (2) find and maintain good body position for each skill, and (3) practice each skill with adequate teacher correction.

The *first basic factor* recognizes that each child must become totally adjusted to the water. Grosse and McGill (1979) explain that many handicapped individuals have had little or no exposure to swimming pool settings. They state: "Nervousness, excitement, fear, or just concentration can increase muscle tensions, limit further voluntary movements and increase involuntary actions. Therefore, the primary goal in water adjustment is to make the individual comfortable in water" (p. 3). It is thus important that the child's first experience in the swimming pool be both nonthreatening and enjoyable. Durfee (1977, p. 2) stresses that it is important "to teach self-confidence before skills, for once the child is comfortable, mentally and physically, learning is absorbed and retained at a quicker and deeper learning level."

Fear of water is a natural response of many youngsters, both handicapped and nonhandicapped. Each child comes to the experience with preconceived ideas. Handicapped students may not understand the dangers or the potential joys of swimming. If the youngster is openly afraid of the water, the instructor is responsible for helping the child feel relaxed so the student can gain confidence and eventually enjoy playing in the water. Some students may be afraid of the simple task of getting in the pool or of having water splashed in their faces. Newman (1976, p. 5) suggests the following technique when dealing with an extremely frightened child: "Do not be distressed, even if it takes many sessions in the water, talk to him, reassure him, just walk into the pool carrying him while allowing him to cry it out. . . . If a child feels that you like him, he soon loses his reluctance to respond to you. *Never try to reason a child out of his fears.*"

Games and Activities to Overcome Fear of the Water

Lawrence and Hackett (1975, p. 87) discuss using games and activities to move a child into a water learning environment. They state:

Feelings of self-confidence acquired by participation in activities and games are so important to handicapped children that the leader should modify activities in any way that will allow for maximum participation. This may mean abolishing some very traditional rules or ignoring standard team "positions," in order to incorporate all eager participants. The leader will soon discover that most of the well-known games can be modified or even eliminated, while the essence of the games is preserved. The joy on the players' happy faces is far more rewarding and important than strict adherence to rules.

The following games and techniques were developed by Durfee (1977) to overcome students' innate fear of water.

1. Use toys (e.g., boats) to help the children get their minds off initial fears.
2. Gently pull the swimmer into the water from a sitting position on the pool

side by saying, "Humpty Dumpty sat on the wall . . . Humpty Dumpty had a great FALL!" Many rhymes can be used in this fashion.

3. To reduce fear and have fun while getting wet, sing and play "London Bridge" and "This Is the Way We Wash Our Hair."
4. Push floatable objects, such as oranges, apples, grapefruits, ping-pong balls, and plastic milk bottles, in relays and races.
5. Spit water over heads to learn not to swallow and to have fun squirting and blowing water with the mouth.
6. Other suggested activities include:
   a. Throw a sponge at a plastic milk bottle.
   b. Throw small balls into a floating bucket.
   c. Play target toss, increasing the difficulty by slowly moving the target away.
   d. Carry a ping-pong ball in a spoon.
   e. Push a balloon with only the chest, only one hand, only the head.
   f. Carry a piece of paper or a cloth flag without getting it wet.
   g. Carry or balance an object on the head.

Prebeginner Techniques

For some handicapped youngsters, entry into a large pool may be inappropriate until they develop a basic enjoyment of the water. This is often true of severely involved children. Lawrence and Hackett (1975) recommend several alternative methods for introducing prebeginners to the water. They state that a child's first exposure to water can occur in almost any setting and under varied conditions. Children experience water fun by splashing and playing in a wading pool or in a large tub or bucket. Their suggested interactions to facilitate water orientation include the use of tub toys, animals, boats, and soap containers (p. 24):

1. Which is your favorite toy? Why do you like it best?
2. What does your favorite toy do? Show me.
3. Can you show me the smallest toy you have in the tub?
4. Does it float or sink? Let me see.
5. How many of the toys in your tub float? Count them for me.
6. Can you tell me how many of them do not float?
7. What colors are your boats?
8. Make a bridge with your body and see if your boat can float under it.

The American National Red Cross (1977a, pp. 158–159) has some excellent exercise suggestions for prebeginners using sponges:

1. Let it fill with water, squeeze it out, and wipe your face.
2. Let it fill, don't squeeze it out, and wipe your face.
3. Let it fill, place it on top of your head, don't squeeze it.
4. Let it fill, place it on the teacher's head, and squeeze it.

5. Let it fill, place it on your own head, and squeeze it.
6. Play a sponge-toss circle game with the other class members.

Once the prebeginner feels secure in basic water orientation, established levels of advancement should be followed. Figure 23.1 shows skill breakdown progression charts.

The *second basic swimming factor* identified by the Red Cross involves learning how to maintain an efficient body position in the water. The instructor must teach those skills that enable students to learn breath control, prone float, back float, turning over, and changing direction (American National Red Cross 1977a).

Some disabled youngsters have difficulty maintaining a standing or floating position because their handicap causes irregular and unwanted movements. Children with cerebral palsy require special attention, and many handicapped individuals may need some form of **personal flotation device (PFD)**.

PFDs such as rubber tubes, inflatable vests, swimsuits with built-in air pockets, water skiing life jackets, or regular life preservers can be used for effective teaching and learning. These devices enable the student to assume and maintain correct body position. Each child's abilities and disabilities must be analyzed when selecting the appropriate PFD and determining how it will aid the student. Instructors should ask themselves:

1. Can the child stand alone in the water (e.g., muscular dystrophy, spina bifida)?
2. Does the child have extreme balance problems (e.g., ataxic cerebral palsy)?
3. Does the child have uncontrollable flexion movements (e.g., spastic cerebral palsy)?
4. When in supine position, will the child's head submerge due to involuntary hyperextension (e.g., athetoid cerebral palsy)?
5. Does the child have sufficient neck strength to hold up the head (e.g., muscular dystrophy)?

Newman (1976, p. 163) questions the use of PFDs:

Personally, I do not use swim aids, with the exception of swim tubes. . . . I do use kick boards and swim tubes (rubber inner tubes) since they are not fastened on the child's body and are more easily discarded; they are only used for part of a swim lesson. Swim tubes have two uses: (1) For children who will never swim independently, but who can learn to become water safe and actually swim strokes in a tube, to provide him pleasure and a sense of independence; they can also join in swim games and often come up with unique methods of attaining goals; and (2) as a play activity toy during play period, as they are not attached to the body, there is not a feeling of dependence, as new skills are achieved children tend to rely on the tubes less often.

Bradley et al. (1981) warn that PFDs may not give adequate support if used as a life jacket for some handicapped individuals. From their study, they conclude that the PFDs on the market today are not safe for the physically handicapped. They stress that those available for use do not provide correct positioning in the water and are difficult to put on. They suggest that further study be done to develop appropriate PFDs for the physically handicapped.

SUGGESTED SKILL BREAKDOWN BELOW BEGINNER LEVEL

LEVEL I

THE STUDENT WILL:

___ 1. Enter pool via ladder with assistance.
___ 2. Leave pool via ladder with assistance.
___ 3. Sit on deck and enter pool with assistance.
___ 4. Climb on deck from pool with assistance.
___ 5. Bob up and down in water to chin level with support of two arms of instructor.
___ 6. Bob up and down in water to chin level with support of one arm of instructor.
___ 7. Bob up and down in water to nose level with support of one arm of instructor.
___ 8. Bob up and down in water to forehead level with support of two arms of instructor.
___ 9. Bob to top of head with support of one arm of instructor.
___10. Put mouth on surface of water and blow bubbles.
___11. Walk width of pool with support of instructor.
___12. Walk width of pool unassisted.
___13. Run width of pool with support of instructor.
___14. Run in water width of pool without support.
___15. Pick up ring off bottom with foot.
___16. Move arms in crawl movement with aid of instructor on deck of pool.
___17. Do crawl arm movement while standing in water facing side of pool.
___18. Use crawl arm movement while walking across pool in water.
___19. Play catch with plastic balls with instructor in water.
___20. Kick legs while instructor tows student.
___21. Kick legs using kickboard with assistance.

Date completed _____

Student's name _____

Instructor's name _____

LEVEL II

THE STUDENT WILL:

___ 1. Climb down ladder unassisted.
___ 2. Climb up ladder unassisted.
___ 3. Enter pool from deck unassisted.
___ 4. Leave pool from water unassisted.
___ 5. Bob up and down in water without support of instructor, using bobbing progression in Level I.
___ 6. Bob down deep and touch ankles and jump up high in air and maintain balance, using both arms to balance body.
___ 7. Touch bottom of pool.
___ 8. Open eyes underwater and count instructor's submerged fingers.
___ 9. Sit on bottom of pool.
___10. Put face on surface of water and blow bubbles out of *mouth*.
___11. Put face on surface, blow mouth bubbles, roll head to side (one ear underwater), take breath of air, repeat five times.
___12. Hang onto side of pool in prone position and kick legs ten times, using a straight-arm support.
___13. Pick up ring off bottom with hand.
___14. Hold onto side of pool in supine (back) position and kick legs.
___15. Assume prone (front) floating position with two-arm support of instructor. Regain footing.
___16. Jump into pool from crouched position.
___17. Jump into pool from standing position.
___18. Assume back floating position with two-arm support of instructor. Regain footing.
___19. Use kickboard unassisted.

Date completed _____

Student's name _____

Instructor's name _____

FIGURE 23.1. Skill breakdown progression charts. (Excerpt from *Methods in Adapted Aquatics,* copyright © 1977 by The American National Red Cross, reprinted with permission.)

The *third basic swimming factor* cited by the Red Cross involves teaching techniques to develop specific skills. Swimming programs almost always group students by ability classifications such as beginner, advanced beginner, intermediate, and advanced. Both handicapped and nonhandicapped students should be placed in the group that is most compatible with their swimming ability level. This concept reinforces the philosophy of individualized instruction because the child's ability determines placement in the least restrictive environment. Many students with disabilities are able to take advantage of mainstream swimming opportunities.

Helpful teaching points include the following:

1. Most impaired students do not want to be babied or pitied.
2. Ask students about their disabilities, their capabilities, their range of movement, their fears, and their interests.
3. Do not do for students what they can do for themselves.
4. Keep verbal directions short and simple. Remember that constant repetition can be boring. Make practice sessions short and change activities often. Let students use a variety of movement skills, and most important, vary actual skill practice with games and stunts.
5. Teach new skills early in the lesson before fatigue sets in.
6. When teaching young students and mentally handicapped students, remember that demonstration by other children rather than adults is more effective. Many children love competition and will attempt a skill that another child is demonstrating.
7. Look for signals that indicate learning has stopped.
8. Read the medical clearance sheet for each student to ensure that the physician's suggestions are being followed.
9. Reinforce the student continually with constructive feedback and performance corrections.

These teaching methods emphasize success. It is important that students experience success quickly at whatever level of skill they possess. In planning an individual program, consider carefully the skills to be taught. Activities must be planned so the student is reasonably challenged without creating undue pressure to complete the task. Although success is critical, skills to be learned must not be so simple that the student loses interest.

Specific skill progression should be noted and recorded. Figure 23.2 is a typical evaluation sheet. The skills to be learned will vary from student to student. The instructor should record comments for each student.

When dealing with behavioral objectives, Meyer (1985) lists specific tasks to teach a disabled child to enter the water, walk the width of the pool, and exit the pool (Table 23.1).

Putting the face under water usually proves to be difficult for most beginning swimmers. This apprehension should be expected. The two most important concepts to be taught are: (1) water will not hurt the eyes, and (2) a mouthful of water can be spit out.

EVALUATION SHEET

Name _____   Diagnosis _____

Movements indicated _____   Movements contraindicated _____

Skills	Number of Times	Distance	Amount of Time	Manner
Entering pool				
Walking across pool				
Putting face in water				
Blowing bubbles				
Bobbing				
Face float, assisted				
Back float, assisted				
Kicking with board				
Beginner arm motion				
Face float alone				
Back float alone				
Use of life jacket				
Beginner crawl				
Safety skills				

Instructor's comments: Date:

FIGURE 23.2. Evaluation form for specific skill progression. (Excerpt from *Adapted Aquatics,* copyright © 1977, The American National Red Cross, reprinted with permission.)

The old and simple technique of wiping water out of the eyes is very successful with beginners. The youngster should be told to wipe the fingers downward over the eyes to remove water. Some experts suggest that this method teaches students bad habits because one cannot wipe the eyes while swimming. A more effective method involves blinking several times.

Newman (1976, p. 6) suggests that breath control exercises be incorporated in the first swimming lesson. She cautions that "this does not mean that a child will blow bubbles or that he will at that time even put his face in the water. There may be many small steps to climb and problems to solve before he actually learns this skill. Some small children with handicapping conditions cannot even blow a small puff so that the act of blowing must be taught. Small easy-to-blow whistles, noisemakers, candles, and party pop-outs usually motivate a child to attempt to blow. The instructor should not

---

TABLE 23.1

TASK ANALYSIS FOR ENTERING THE POOL, WALKING IN WATER, AND EXITING THE POOL

I. Given a pool, the learner will climb down and up ladder to enter and exit at a point where water is waist deep:
    1. Locates ladder
    2. Turns back to water
    3. Grabs railing
    4. Lowers one leg onto rung
    5. Lowers opposite leg onto rung
    6. Holds rail until firmly on pool bottom
    7. Stands in water
    8. Completes task
II. Given a pool, the learner will slide into the water at a point where water is waist deep:
    1. Locates shallow end of pool
    2. Climbs out of chair, crutches, etc.ª
    3. Sits on edge of pool
    4. Twists body around to stomach
    5. Bends at waist
    6. Grips edge
    7. Lowers body down slowly
    8. Stands on pool bottomª
    9. Holds onto edge
    10. Completes task
III. Given a sensory cue, the learner will walk through chest-deep water the entire width of the pool:
    1. Stands along edge
    2. Steps forward with left foot
    3. Reaches forward with right arm
    4. Steps forward with right foot
    5. Reaches forward with left arm
    6. Looks straight ahead
    7. Completes task

SOURCE: Adapted from Meyer 1985.
ªIf appropriate.

be discouraged if this first step in swim training takes a month or more to accomplish. When blowing practice is consistent, most children learn."

Another teaching suggestion involves the students practicing breath control out of the water. The instructor times the youngsters and encourages them to increase the length of time they can hold their breath (e.g., 5, 10, 15, 20, and 25 sec).

Games that allow the student to become accustomed to putting the head totally under the water are as follows:

1. Have student submerge face only (up to, but not including, the ears) in the water, and identify whether the instructor's submerged fist is open or closed. When the student is able to see clearly underwater, use number of fingers for a more difficult challenge.

2. Tap two metal objects together underwater to encourage the student to listen and think (count) underwater. Breath holding is also practiced in this activity.
3. Have student try to sit on the bottom.
4. Have student attempt a jellyfish float, and also a dead man's float.
5. Have student retrieve objects from the bottom of the pool. This develops associative skills such as breath control, eye opening, eye-hand coordination, movement, and self-confidence.
6. Place a weight in the student's hands (a lifesaving brick is ideal), and have the student go underwater. Later, put the brick underwater and ask the youngster to pick it up.

Meyer (1985) lists specific behavioral objectives for the instructor to follow when teaching children to submerge their heads (Table 23.2).

Patterned Arm and Leg Movements

This technique is designed to teach basic swimming movements to handicapped students who usually do not have the physical or mental capability to understand or accomplish coordinated skills. Difficulty arises when the student is asked to move two or more body parts at the same time. Newman (1976) believes that when a handicapped child uses the large muscles and is told which body parts are being used, the youngster realizes for the first time that he has a right and a left arm, and a right and a left leg.

TABLE 23.2
TASK ANALYSIS FOR PUTTING THE HEAD UNDERWATER

I. Given a sensory cue, the learner will bend forward and submerge the entire head under water for 10 sec:
   1. Takes deep breath
   2. Bends forward
   3. Places entire head in water _____ sec
   4. Places entire head in water _____ sec
   5. Lifts head out of water
   6. Completes task

II. Given a sensory cue, the learner will exhale into the water each time the face is submerged:
   1. Inhales above water
   2. Lowers head to water
   3. Exhales above water
   4. Exhales with lips touching water
   5. Exhales with mouth in water
   6. Exhales with face in water
   7. Completes task

SOURCE: Adapted from Meyer 1985.

He also learns the meaning of directions such as in-out, up-down, back-front, and bend-straight.

Incorporated in this teaching method is the hands-on approach—the instructor moves the student's arms and legs through the basic positions. To assist learning, the instructor should sit on a step in shallow water and hold the student in a back float position, making sure the child's ears are submerged. Newman (1976, p. 10) explains: "All movements should be slow and rhythmic. Do each pattern at least five times. Counting out loud is one way to keep your movements steady. The child should be patterned passively until his own muscles take over. Patterning is especially beneficial for children with coordination problems."

Basic arm and leg strokes should be repeated until the child can successfully complete the skill alone. When a physical handicap restricts the child from accomplishing a correct movement, the instructor should note this irregularity and realize that the child will be attempting certain strokes with a modified movement similar to the original pattern.

Moran and Kalakian (1977) identify a multisensory approach to teaching swimming. They stress that simultaneous use of two or more senses increases the chance that learning will occur, and makes learning more rapid and more permanent. The following techniques and explanations are considered examples of desirable teaching methods to use when teaching swimming to the handicapped:

1. **Assistive:** Guidance of body parts through movements provides kinesthetic (proprioceptive) feedback from the muscles to the brain, allowing the child to feel and sense her body parts as they move. An example of this teaching approach would be the teacher's turning of the child's head as rhythmic breathing is practiced.
2. **Tactile:** Touching of body parts enables the child to sense the part to be moved, such as the arm to be used in stroking or the leg to be kicked. Tactile reinforcement facilitates visual or verbal stimuli or both.
3. **Visual Stimulus:** The eyes are stimulated through demonstrations and simple visual aids, enabling the child to reproduce the movement by imitation. Good demonstrations and simple visual aids are effective instructional methods.
4. **Verbal Stimulus:** The ears are stimulated through the spoken word. Simple and accurate word descriptions of the activity to be performed should be used. Oral instruction should reflect the child's level of understanding.
5. **Abstract Stimulus:** Use of stimuli, such as signals, signs, numbers, and colors, requires the student to receive, interpret, and transfer those stimuli into actions.

Assistive Equipment

A strap with one end tied to a plastic gallon jug and a slipknot on the other end is helpful for strengthening lower extremities. The strap length depends on depth of water. While standing against a support (e.g., wall or railing) in waist-deep water, the swimmer inserts one foot in the slipknot. The swimmer then pulls the jug underwater. The stress exerted against the limb can be regulated by filling or emptying the jug. Thick plastic jugs work best.

Passive range of motion can be achieved in many ways. One way is to place a swim fin on the affected hand, foot, or both, then to move the body so water resistance will push-pull the flipper and limb.

Swim fins or flippers can be used for swimmers with lower extremity anomalies or spasticity to develop a stronger dolphin kick and flutter kick. The fins allow the swimmer above-average speed with minimum effort while strengthening the lower limbs. Diving masks help swimmers to see underwater, a new experience for many. A snorkel may aid swimmers who cannot get their face above water to breathe properly while swimming (Durfee 1977, p. 4).

Techniques for the Student With Mental Disabilities

Mentally handicapped students can usually learn most basic swimming skills if they can *remember* which skill is being taught or reviewed. Words and phrases must be reinforced continually because the child often forgets what was taught only the day before. The instructor's vocabulary should be carefully adjusted to the student's intellectual level. For example, the mildly mentally handicapped will understand and remember better than the moderately mentally handicapped. The child's intellectual level, *not* chronological age, should dictate the terminology used. Most moderately mentally handicapped teenage students function at an I.Q. level equivalent to that of a 6- or 7-year-old nonhandicapped child. Behavioral and learning characteristics of the two groups are the same and include short attention span, an inability to follow detailed explanations, and a tendency to be egocentric.

Adjustments also must be made in selection of teaching techniques. It is important to establish safety rules, repeat them often, and never change them. A structured environment in which students know what to do and what not to do provides a feeling of security. Establish a pattern for poolside procedures such as walk in, sit on deck, and wait for command to enter water.

Some students may exhibit a real fear of the pool environment; others will show none at all. Both groups need careful, clear directions and sound instruction. If a youngster becomes belligerent or uncooperative, the child may not understand what is being taught. The instructor should explain the skill or situation in a positive way that is easily understood.

The severely mentally handicapped student has intellectual characteristics similar to those of a nonhandicapped child under 3 years of age. The severe and profoundly mentally handicapped often possess other handicapping conditions, such as epilepsy or cerebral palsy, and therefore need special considerations when being taught to swim. These youngsters progress more slowly, display longer stages with no apparent development, and are less consistent in using and building on information that appeared to be learned. In teaching these youngsters, the American National Red Cross (1977b) suggests that instructors should (1) use wider limits of time and patience, (2) break learning experiences into smaller units, and (3) provide a stimulating, multisensory, enthusiastic atmosphere.

Skills must be segmented and the teaching approach modified. It is necessary to task-analyze basic skills into the simplest components and develop entirely new progressions to be successful. Motivation should include basic behavior modification techniques, including visual, verbal, tactual, and taste reinforcers.

Most severely or profoundly handicapped students seem to lack a sense of fear and thus require close supervision. The instructor should make very few assumptions about what the students understand because these youngsters lack the ability to remember specific dangers of a swimming pool environment. They commonly jump into deep water and make no effort to move or swim. They may remain underwater and make no effort to come up for air. Close, individualized supervision is imperative (1:1 ratio) for these students.

Water adjustment activities such as those described for prebeginners earlier in this chapter are necessary.

Techniques for the Student With Cerebral Palsy

When teaching the child with cerebral palsy, repetition must be stressed. Newman (1976) suggests that new skills be introduced early in the lesson because children with cerebral palsy tire quickly and chill easily. This is particularly true initially until the youngster develops greater strength and endurance.

Contractures, immobilized joints, and limited range of motion require modifications of normal swimming movements. Proper execution of the stroke is not important. The goal should be for the student to learn the skill in the best way possible and then to strive for greater efficiency of movement. PFDs may be effective for some students, but overdependence on them should be avoided. Many individuals cannot walk without braces or crutches or are wheelchair-bound. Learning to stand and walk in water is possible and can be taught in chest-deep water. Students should be instructed in how to use their hands to make finning, sculling, or winging motions. These same movements are also used to teach supine floating skills.

Severely involved students tend to draw the knees to the stomach, making it difficult to float in either the front or back position. PFDs are recommended for these individuals.

Each student must be assessed to determine ability to control the head in the prone or supine position without involuntary movements. A child who exhibits strong hip flexion or head and neck hyperextension movements must be watched carefully. A common reflex found in cerebral palsied individuals is described in the American National Red Cross literature (1977a, p. 50) as follows: "A prone body position results in an upward thrusting of the head and neck. The supine position results in a hyperextension of the head and neck back into the water." Youngsters with this particular problem require close hands-on supervision by the instructor or aide to prevent submersion when attempting a particular skill. The fear that results from accidental submersion will inhibit the child's desire to continue.

Once the child has made some physical and mental adjustments and has learned to put her head underwater, swimming instruction can begin. The easiest stroke for most cerebral palsied students is the back float position. This requires movement by finning, sculling, or winging the arms, or by modifications of these. The legs are moved by flutter kicking.

Recovery from the back float position is easier for the cerebral palsied person than recovery from the prone position. Instruction to recover from the back float position should therefore be taught first.

Techniques for the Student With Spina Bifida or Traumatic Paralysis

Students with spina bifida or traumatic paralysis often exhibit lack of bladder or bowel control (incontinence) or both and paralysis of the legs.

At one time, these individuals were not allowed to participate in swimming activities. These students, however, gain valuable benefits from aquatic activities. For some, swimming may be the only form of recreation within their capabilities. All phases of swimming are appropriate for these students. From a sanitary point of view (i.e., contamination of pool water), new techniques that control seepage more effectively can correct this concern.

Because of inability to control excretory functions, many disabled people do not wish to participate in swimming programs. Embarrassment and fear of an accident in the pool area have kept many individuals from this activity. The instructor must make a conscious effort to convince students to participate. As a result of spinal cord impairment or damage, proper innervation to the lower body does not occur. These students usually cannot sense when the bladder or bowel needs emptying. They also cannot voluntarily relax the external sphincter muscles that control urination and defecation. In addition, muscle strength, which assists in voiding waste materials, may be lacking. Most spinal cord injured children who cannot control bladder function have, however, usually been taught bowel training and use of a urine collection bag early in life.

Urinary Incontinence

When students are unable to control urination, they often use urine collection bags. For females, a tube (catheter) is inserted directly into the urethra to allow drainage through a flexible tube into a bag. Males commonly use a condom catheter, which connects the condom with a urine collection bag. The bag can be detached from the catheter and clamped off while swimming. All students should empty the bag prior to pool entry to prevent pool contamination.

Fecal Incontinence

Diapers or plastic rubber pants under a child's swimsuit are usually sufficient if bowel incontinence is a problem. Both should fit snugly to ensure sanitation and a neat appearance.

Individuals who are unable to control bowel function often require surgery. An artificial opening, or *stoma*, is made in the abdominal wall to excrete body waste. There are three types of operation, or *ostomy:* an ileostomy, a colostomy, and a ureterostomy. With proper management, the ostomy is only a minor inconvenience to the individual.

Ostomy appliances consist of a plastic disk to which a pouch is attached. These devices are simple, comfortable, nonirritating, inexpensive, inconspicuous, odor free, and leakproof. Attachment to the body is accomplished with contact adhesive cement, double-faced adhesive disks, or karaya gum rings. A belt or waterproof tape is often used to reinforce adhesion. Odor is controlled by special deodorants (Henderson and Mapel 1984).

Questions about bladder or bowel program, collection bags, or catheters should be addressed directly to the student. If the student is too young to understand the procedures or is unable to communicate effectively, the child's parents or a physician should be consulted.

Specific Swimming Suggestions

It is important that each student's balance point be found. Because of each student's distinct handicapping condition, locating the child's balance point aids in developing the proper floating position for that individual. Newman (1976, pp. 39–40) stresses that learning the floating position is necessary because it teaches the child the concept of buoyancy necessary swimming on the back and to safe skill practice. "The ability to float on the back when tired or frightened is of utmost importance. Until the balance point is determined it will be impossible to perform a back stroke, if at all. No two students are alike. One may be paralyzed from the waist down; another may have some use of the legs; one may have legs of different lengths; often the older child has a fused back; plus other differences."

Concerns Related to Students Who Experience Seizures

The swimming pool can be particularly hazardous for individuals who have seizures or a convulsive disorder. Before these students are taught to swim, the following questions must be answered. What type of seizure disorder does the child have? Are the seizures completely controlled by medication? If not, are seizures frequent or do they occur rarely? The child's parents, physician, and medical records should supply answers to these questions.

Generally speaking, the student with infrequent seizures should be allowed to swim if the instructor is aware of the condition and knows simple first aid techniques to employ in the event of a seizure (see Chapter 16 on seizures and convulsive disorders).

The necessary precautions include alerting the lifeguard about specific children who could experience seizures. Seizure-prone youngsters should wear an easily identifiable swimming cap, which is distinctly different from the caps of other swimmers. A buddy system should be used, and the buddy should know what to expect, what to do, and who to call if a seizure occurs.

Because swimming is considered a strenuous activity, it has been suspect of bringing on seizures. This outdated concept is not valid. In fact, physical activity and high levels of physical fitness tend to ward off seizures.

Grand Mal Seizure

During a grand mal seizure, the student will hold the breath momentarily and so will not inhale water. The instructor (or buddy) should roll the child onto his back and tilt the head backward while supporting the back with the forearms. The child should not be removed from the water unless this can be accomplished easily. In fact, the water may provide a soothing atmosphere in which the child's thrashing movements present no danger.

Do *not* use a portable oxygen unit to administer oxygen during a grand mal seizure. Oxygen merely prolongs the seizure.

Swimming Progressions

Table 23.3 outlines a progressive system of swimming instruction.

Summary

Major goals of a swimming program for handicapped students include enjoying water activities, learning how to swim, and improving swimming performance.

A good swimming program should provide periods of training and periods of relaxation for improving and maintaining balance, gait, muscular strength and endurance, power, agility, coordination, and flexibility (Thome 1980). Socialization and emotional well-being also should improve.

TABLE 23.3
SWIMMING INSTRUCTION: A PROGRESSIVE SYSTEM

First Level: Making Mental and Physical Adjustments to Water	Second Level: Maintaining Constant Motivation to Learn and Survive (Drownproofing)	Third Level: Propulsion	Fourth Level: Coordinated Stroking	Fifth Level: Challenging Advanced Skills	Sixth Level: Achievements
1. Talk to swimmer. Let swimmer trust you. Self-confidence is delicate to teach.	1. Assistants and aides provide good one-to-one motivation and decrease need for flotation devices.	1. Prone glide (pushing off bottom or edge with legs or arms to go from point A to point B).	1. Dog paddle (with face submerged).	1. Object recovery (toys, weights, etc.) from varying depths.	1. Earn swimming certificates and cards for achievements. Award Red Cross skill cards to those who qualify (local organizations or camps may issue their own cards).
2. Use safest, easiest method for each person to enter and exit from water.	2. Prone float and recovery.	2. Sculling, finning, and winging: a. Walking. b. Face down. c. On back.	2. Elementary backstroke (works well with hemiplegia).	2. Swimming between instructor's legs (one or many instructors).	2. Present water shows to demonstrate accomplishments before an audience of family and friends (themes are effective if incorporated into show).
3. Face in water: a. Inhale air through mouth. b. Exhale through nose (bubbles release air and keep water out, thus avoiding sinus irritation). c. Hold breath. d. Open eyes underwater (pick up pennies, count instructor's fingers).	3. Gradual depth progression—from steps, to shallow, to deep. 4. Survival float (jellyfish or dead man's float): a. Rhythmic breathing. b. Rhythmic bobbing. 5. Back float (provides best position to survive).	3. Flutter kick. 4. Breaststroke kick—frog kick, modified whip kick. 5. Dolphin kick. 6. Modified kicks.	3. Crawl (with rhythmic breathing). 4. Breaststroke (with rhythmic breathing). 5. Sidestroke (with rhythmic breathing). 6. Modified or combined strokes.	3. Underwater distance swimming. 4. Jumping, diving, or falling from side into water. 5. Use of mask, fins, and snorkel. 6. Disrobing and inflating clothes to survive.	3. Include: a. Individual demonstrations. b. Relay races. c. Underwater races.

SOURCE: Adapted from Durfee 1977, pp. 4–7.

An individualized swimming program needs to follow a written plan like any other activity area. Assessment is the critical first step in planning the program. Each student's physical, intellectual, emotional, and social development determines the specific activities, skills, and strokes to be taught.

Some students will progress as rapidly as their nonhandicapped peers and should be allowed to develop at a rate appropriate for them. Severely handicapped youngsters progress at slower rates, and small accomplishments are satisfying and rewarding.

Instructors must remember that nonhandicapped children control their arms and legs willfully, but physically handicapped youngsters, especially the cerebral palsied and brain damaged, find this difficult. Many handicapped children receive great pleasure and a sense of achievement simply from splashing or moving their arms and legs in the water. Small enjoyable progressions often lead to positive experiences that reinforce future learning. Newman (1976, p. 169) states: "Everything is relative. That which is good for one is bad for another. . . . Just learning to propel and move around the pool in a swim tube is a thrill beyond words for many of these children. Avoid the trap of judging things in terms of your [the teacher's] interests, abilities, and experiences rather than those of the children with whom you work."

Progressions can begin by introducing students to the water through activities involving water-filled buckets, sponges, sprinkling cans, and shallow wading pools. The most important objective is to help the child develop a positive attitude toward water learning. Simple games provide an ideal learning experience. With slight modifications, most land games can be played in the water. These activities, along with water games and stunts, provide stimulating, challenging, and enjoyable opportunities for students.

Critical points for the beginning swimmer include balance, buoyancy, and propulsion (Priest 1980).

When writing the individualized swimming program, progressions for nonhandicapped children can be used as a guide and modified appropriately. Because handicapped children have specific disabling conditions, each program should be designed to complement the individual's unique abilities. Effective instruction requires initiative, imagination, and patience when teaching swimming to the handicapped. Instruction must also be slow, deliberate, progressive, and specific (Cordellos 1976).

The importance of an individualized swimming program is emphasized in the following statement by a severely handicapped student (Kuechler 1978, p. 8):

I used to stand and sit in the wheelchair using the rail in the pool. To learn to swim, I used a life preserver. Then I used an air collar around my neck. Now I swim without the collar, with my hands in the air. I can swim on my back without anything to keep me floating. I kick my legs and use my back to swim. I hold onto the rails and push back and forth with body hands to turn circles, and to swim in a straight line. I swing my left hand over my head to swim. At first I was afraid of the water when I was standing up and sitting down in the wheelchair. I was not afraid when I started using the life preserver. Then I used the collar which I liked so I wouldn't get water in my ears. I was afraid to swim without the collar at first, but not now. Now that I know how to swim, I enjoy the water.

References

AAHPERD. *Physical Education and Recreation for Impaired, Disabled, and Handicapped Individuals . . . Past, Present and Future.* Reston, Va.: AAHPERD, 1975.

American National Red Cross. *Swimming for the Handicapped—A Manual for the Aide.* Washington, D.C.: American National Red Cross, 1974.

———. *Adapted Aquatics.* Garden City, N.Y.: Doubleday & Company, 1977a.

———. *Methods in Adapted Aquatics—A Manual for the Instructor.* Washington, D.C.: American National Red Cross, 1977b.

Bradley, N. J., Fuller, J. L., Pozos, R. S., and Willmers, L. E. PFD's Personal Flotation Devices. A Lifejacket Is a Lifejacket . . . Not Necessarily So, Especially if You're Disabled. *Sports 'N Spokes.* May/June 1981:23–25.

Bradtke, J. S. Adapted Devices for Aquatic Activities. *Practical Pointers* 3(1):4, 1979. Reston, Va.: AAHPERD.

Cordellos, H. C. *Aquatics Recreation for the Blind.* Reston, Va.: AAHPERD, 1976.

Durfee, E. Teaching Persons Who Are Handicapped to Swim. *Occasional Papers of the National Easter Seal Society for Crippled Children and Adults* 25:1–10, 1977.

Grosse, S. J., and McGill, C. D. Independent Swimming for Children With Severe Physical Impairments. *Practical Pointers* 3(2):1–15, 1979. Reston, Va.: AAHPERD.

Harris, F. A. Correction of Muscle Balance in Spasticity. *American Journal of Physical Medicine* 57 (3):123–138, 1978.

Henderson, M., and Mapel, J. R. The Colostomy and Ileostomy. In *Medical Aspects of Developmental Disabilities in Children Birth to Three*, rev. 1st ed. Edited by J. A. Blackman. Rockville, Md.: Aspen Systems Corporation, 1984.

Kuechler, T. I Swim in a Straight Line. *Bethesda Messenger* 69(3):8, 1978.

Lasko, P. M., and Knopf, K. G. *Adapted and Corrective Exercise for the Disabled Adult.* Dubuque, Iowa: Eddie Bowers Publishing, 1984.

Lawrence, C. C., and Hackett, L. C. *Water Learning: A New Adventure.* Palo Alto, Calif.: Peek Publications, 1975.

Meyer, J. R. Assessment of Swimming Skills of Physically Handicapped Students. Lecture presented at Adapted Physical Education Conference, Glen Ellyn, Ill., 2 November 1985.

Moran, J. M., and Kalakian, L. H. *Movement Experiences for the Mentally Retarded or Emotionally Disturbed Child*, 2nd ed. Minneapolis: Burgess Publishing, 1977.

Newman, J. *Swimming for Children With Physical and Sensory Impairments.* Springfield, Ill.: Charles C Thomas, 1976.

Pagenoff, S. A. The Use of Aquatics With Cerebral Palsied Adolescents. *The American Journal of Occupational Therapy* 38(7):469–473, July 1984.

Priest, E. L. *Teaching of Adapted Aquatics.* Lecture presented at summer workshop, Illinois State University, Normal, Ill., July 1980.

Priest, L. *Adapted Aquatics Teaching Methods.* Indianapolis: Council for National Cooperation in Aquatics, 1982.

Steinbrunner, D. The Process of Leadership Development. *Adapted Aquatics—Leadership Development.* Indianapolis: Council for National Cooperation in Aquatics, 1982.

Thome, K. Adapting Aquatic Circuit Training for Special Populations. *Practical Pointers* 4(3):3, 1980. Reston, Va.: AAHPERD.

CHAPTER 24

Opportunity in Sport

Education opens many doors. It must not be perceived as an end in itself, but rather as the means to many ends. When better education provides more means, more doors can be opened.

Physical education is an integral part of the means-to-ends educational philosophy. If physical education were of immediate value only, its impact on people's lives would be vastly diminished.

The primary goal of physical education is to prepare the individual to become and remain physically active throughout life. For many, this means having the opportunity to participate in a variety of sports experiences. Participation may be informal and among friends or organized and formal.

Historically, the opportunity to participate in sport programs has been an option mainly of the nondisabled. Persons with disabilities often did not have the physical education background that develops sport skills and enables a person to follow an active life-style.

With sport opportunities for the disabled emerging and prospering, physical educators must exert leadership to help the trend gather momentum. Timely leadership from concerned professionals is the best assurance that the trend will maintain a proper course.

Sports Participation and Mainstreaming

Sports opportunities for disabled persons should not automatically conjure up images of disabled people in special programs. Public Law 94-142 calls for a physical education program conducted in the least restrictive environment. Physical education is defined in the law as participation in individual and group games and sports, including intramurals and lifetime sports. A reasonable interpretation of the law requires the school to implement mainstreaming in sports, including athletic programs, and in physical education programs.

A primary concern in mainstreaming in sport and athletic programs is whether all participants, both nondisabled and disabled, can experience reasonably safe, successful participation. At first mention, the phrase *safe and successful participation for all* prompts concern primarily for the disabled athlete. Mention of similar concerns for nondisabled athletes results at first in wrinkled brows. Consider, however, the nondisabled athlete who comes in physical contact with a participant wearing an artificial limb. Impact of an artificial limb, depending on configuration and materials, can inflict serious injury to bone and soft tissue. This does not suggest that participants in athletic contests do not sustain injury, but rather that no one should sustain injury resulting from exposure to undue risk.

Section 504 and Access to Opportunities in Sports and Athletics

Section 504 states that no person shall be denied access to a given program purely because that person is disabled. If the disability does not influence participation materially, the person is entitled to participate in a regular program. When disabilities do materially influence participation and when athletic participation is an opportunity afforded the nondisabled, the providing agency must offer substantially equal participation opportunities for those who are disabled. The relevant passage from Section 504 is as follows:

> A recipient may offer to handicapped students . . . athletic activities that are separate and different from those offered to nonhandicapped students only if . . . no qualified handicapped student is denied the opportunity to compete for teams or to participate in courses that are not separate or different (*Federal Register*, Section 84.37, 4 May 1977).

Examples of Access Denial

Alberts (1984) reports that the American Medical Association (AMA) has established medical eligibility guidelines for student athletes. Disorders listed for disqualification from athletic participation were uncontrolled diabetes, jaundice, active tuberculosis, enlarged liver, absence of a paired organ, and sensory impairments. Based on these AMA recommendations, many disabled athletes were denied the right to participate in school athletic programs. Denial on the basis of being disabled is in strict violation of Section 504. Each case must be judged on its unique characteristics. For example, in the federal district court decision of *Grube v. Bethlehem Area School District 550* (1982), the court ruled that a male high school senior who had only one kidney should be able to play on the interscholastic football team. The court decided that the plaintiff had provided enough medical and statistical evidence to indicate that his participation would not be harmful to himself or others.

Historically, persons with mental retardation have often been denied access to sport and athletic programs simply because of their retardation. In certain states, high school leagues or athletic associations have relied on academic eligibility requirements to exclude the mentally retarded from regular program participation. While these exclusions are objectionable on philosophical grounds, they are now considered invalid on legal grounds as well. If, for example, a mentally retarded student posts the fastest yard dash time for the school and if that person's disability does not otherwise affect negatively the quality of anyone's participation in the track program, then the person with mental retardation is entitled to full participation in the regular track program.

When Special Sport Program Participation Is Indicated

Students with disabilities who should not participate in regular sport programs but who can benefit from modified participation are entitled to such opportunities. In addition, Section 504 ensures that special programs must be of the same educational quality as regular programs. To match the quality of regular programming, special programs require acceptable budgets; equitable access to facilities, equipment, and supplies; and quality coaches whose professional preparation and remuneration are comparable to those of coaches for the regular programs. For many reasons (e.g., conflicting educational philosophies, inflation, categorical discriminations), opportunities for students with special needs to participate in special athletic programs will not always evolve voluntarily. Considerable debate and, in some cases, litigation have resulted when disabled student athletes sought athletic experiences.

Selected Examples of Sport and Athletic Opportunities

In recent years, those athletes whose disabilities do not affect their involvement in regular programs are already participating. Some persons with limited lower extremity function have participated in gymnastics and skiing (Figures 24.1 and 24.2). Attesting to successful participation in the regular program are the place kicker in football who is an upper extremity amputee, the woman archer who, shooting from a wheelchair, qualified for and competed in the "regular" U.S. Olympic trials, and the blind wrestler. In the case of these individuals, the ability rather than the disability was the criterion. It would be difficult to quantify the numbers of asthmatics or diabetics whose disabilities, when managed, allow safe, successful participation in regular programs.

For some individuals, placement in regular sport programs is not appropriate. When modified programming is needed, programs must exist or be created to meet those needs.

Perhaps the program most visible to the general public is the **Special Olympics.** This program, supported by the Joseph P. Kennedy Jr. Foundation, exists so that persons with mental retardation can have the opportunity to gain positive experiences through athletics. Although the Kennedy Foundation provides the Special Olympics impetus, the participating individuals and their groups, schools, and agencies whose efforts and support make the Special Olympics work, must be recognized as well. The Special

FIGURE 24.1. Amputee skier has modified poles that function as outriggers. (Photograph courtesy of Courage Center, Golden Valley, Minn.)

FIGURE 24.2. Lower extremity amputee skier wearing prosthesis (left extremity) and skiing on two skis. (Photograph courtesy of Courage Center, Golden Valley, Minn.)

Olympics program encourages athletes, when appropriate, to "graduate" to participation in regular programs.

For many years, students with mental retardation have had the opportunity to participate in Special Olympics programs, but persons who were otherwise disabled did not have similar opportunities. In response to these persons' needs, several modified sport programs and modified sport associations have emerged.

The 1985 **Cerebral Palsy/Les Autres Games** were held at Michigan State University. Approximately 800 athletes from the United States, Canada, and the Netherlands either met or exceeded qualifying standards. Anderson (1986, p. 25) reflects on those games: "National records crumbled during the track and field competitions. Younger, intense, well-trained, highly skilled, and competitive athletes made their presence known. Determination burned in athletes' eyes as they waited at the starting line. Mental and psychological preparedness became just as vital, if not more so, than long months of physical training."

Jeff Jones, 1985 Games Director of the Cerebral Palsy/Les Autres Association, speculates on the impact of the games on future competitions: "The long term ramifications of an event such as this are yet to be seen. Our success at hosting joint disability games was mainly due to the unique structure that already existed within NASCP [National Association of Sports for Cerebral Palsy]. Will future Games include other disability groups? Will we see the time when the Amputee, Spinal Cord Injured, Cerebral Palsy, Les Autres and Blind National Games are all run concurrently at the same location? The precedent has been established. Now only time will tell" (1986, p. 27). Table 24.1 shows the different sport events, competitions by disability, and number of competitors entered in the 1985 Games.

In Minnesota, the **Minnesota Association for Adapted Athletics** now exists. This association was organized to provide modified competitive athletic experiences for students with physical disabilities. Participants, who are in the seventh through twelfth grades, may be ambulatory or in wheelchairs. Disabilities range from muscular dystrophy, cerebral palsy, and congenital abnormalities to spina bifida and quadriplegia. Participation is coeducational and may merit a school athletic letter. Opportunities are offered in adapted floor hockey (Figure 24.3), soccer, whiffleball, and other seasonal sports. For more information about this organization and competitive activities offered, contact the Minnesota Association for Adapted Athletics, % Courage Center, 3915 Golden Valley Road, Golden Valley, MN 55422.

TABLE 24.1

1985 NATIONAL CEREBRAL PALSY/LES AUTRES GAMES—NUMBER OF ENTRIES PER SPORT BY DISABILITY

	CP[a]	LA[b]
Number of athletes	640	104
Field	170	63
Track	148	38
Swimming	128	36
Slalom	29	12
Power lifting	36	10
Cycling	39	6
Cross country	7	0
Bowling	13	6
Boccia	12	4
Target shooting	7	2
Archery	1	1
Table tennis	7	6
Golf	0	3
Basketball	0	3
Soccer	3	0
Wheelchair soccer	3	0
Equestrian	75	44

SOURCE: Modified from Jones, 1986, p. 26.

[a] CP = cerebral palsy.

[b] LA = les autres (the others).

FIGURE 24.3. Wheelchair athlete participating in Minnesota Association for Adapted Athletics floor hockey contest. (Photograph courtesy of Courage Center, Golden Valley, Minn.)

Many adapted sport and athletic opportunities are sponsored by organizations outside the school setting. The **United States Association for Blind Athletes** (USABA) sponsors competitions at the local and national level. At present, no age limits are specified for participation in any USABA-sponsored sport. USABA sports include goalball (Figure 24.4), swimming, wrestling, and track and field. To be eligible for USABA competition, an individual must have no more than 20/200 visual acuity in the better eye after correction, or a visual field arc in the better eye, after correction, of no more than 20 degrees, or both. Participants are classified for competition by degree of visual impairment.

Another sport organization for the partially sighted and blind is the **National Beep Baseball Association** (NBBA). Beep baseball uses an official 16-in. softball that contains a high-pitched audible beeping device. After batting a fair ball pitched by a sighted player, the participant runs to a cone-shaped base that buzzes when the umpire determines that the ball is fair. The batter must arrive at the base before a defensive player fields the batted ball. If the batter prevails, a run is scored for his team. If the ball is cleanly fielded before the batter touches base, the batter is out. Approximately 25 teams are active in national level NBBA competition in the United States and Canada. Outside NBBA auspices, approximately 100 teams play recreationally and competitively in the United States, Canada, and other countries.

FIGURE 24.4. Goalball, one of the sports sanctioned by the U.S. Association for Blind Athletes. (Photograph courtesy of Courage Center, Golden Valley, Minn.)

The **National Wheelchair Basketball Association** (NWBA) has promoted and sponsored wheelchair basketball since shortly after World War II. The NWBA is the oldest, and remains the largest, of all wheelchair sports organizations in the United States. Participation opportunities for both sexes are available in local through national level championship competitions (Figure 24.5).

Some ten years after inception of the NWBA, the **National Wheelchair Athletic Association** (NWAA) was formed. The NWAA also has a long and extensive history of promoting competition among wheelchair athletes. Events sanctioned by the NWAA are staged regionally throughout the country. Regional events provide immediate participation opportunities and, in addition, opportunity to qualify for national competition in track and field, swimming, table tennis, weight lifting, and archery. Each June national competitions are held in which participants vie for national honors and for berths on the U.S. Wheelchair Athletic Team, which competes in the International Stoke-Mandeville Games. These games are staged annually in England except during Olympic years, when the games are traditionally held in the Olympic's host country.

Many participants in NWAA-sanctioned events do not use wheelchairs for daily ambulation. These are persons who cannot participate in a meaningful manner in regular sports events because of a permanent physical disability of the lower extrem-

FIGURE 24.5. National championship women's wheelchair basketball sanctioned by the National Wheelchair Basketball Association. (Photograph courtesy of Courage Center, Golden Valley, Minn.)

ities. The NWAA has implemented a classification system based on spinal cord injury site that enables participants to compete on an equitable basis against athletes with a similar degree of disability. The classification system has undergone modifications periodically that have resulted in an increase in the number of competitive classes. Assignment to a competitive class requires a specially certified judgment by a physical therapist or physician. The classification system can be found in Appendix C.

There are also national wheelchair associations for bowling, tennis, and softball. For more information about sport and athletic opportunities for disabled wheelchair athletes, contact the national office of the Paralyzed Veterans of America, 4330 East West Highway, Suite 300, Washington, DC 20014.

Historically, the NWAA has sponsored athletic opportunities for persons with cerebral palsy. To achieve fairness in competitions, athletes with cerebral palsy do not compete directly against athletes with other disabilities. In addition to NWAA activities for participants with cerebral palsy, sports opportunities also are sponsored by the **National Association of Sports for Cerebral Palsy** (NASCP). For further information, contact the NASCP Sports Coordinator, 66 East 34th Street, New York, NY 10016. In a manner similar in intent to that of NWAA, NASCP has developed its own classification system for sports participants with cerebral palsy. The competitor class to which the participant is assigned reflects both type of cerebral palsy and extent of involvement. Among the unique provisions of the NASCP classification system is that it recognizes the appropriateness of competitors in certain classes standing up. (See Appendix C for classifications of the National Association of Sports for Cerebral Palsy.)

Space does not permit us to mention all of the associations, activities, and sport opportunities available to handicapped athletes. In this chapter, we have merely touched on the many sport and athletic activities for the disabled.

A Final Word About Competition

The thought of athletic competition for persons with disabilities, particularly those whose disabilities are substantial, causes mixed emotions. We perceive competition as being neither good nor bad. As with any competitive experience, the quality of the experience is no better than the participant's readiness for it and the quality of the leadership that provides the experience with direction.

Any individual's athletic endeavor must be judged by the quality of the effort. A second, third, or last place finisher who put forth great effort has achieved more than a first place winner who did not try his hardest. Winning is certainly one of many desirable outcomes of any competitive activity, but it is not the only outcome. Any effort to organize competitive experiences, particularly within the educational setting, should ensure that all second-place winners are not perceived as losers.

When the need to win is viewed in proper perspective, many desirable outcomes are achievable. Competition often means travel, staying overnight, self-reliance, self-discipline, expanded social contacts, and an opportunity to demonstrate ability and excellence to people who are important in the participant's life.

Finally, each athletic opportunity needs to be evaluated on its own merits. The following questions will assist in evaluating such programs:

1. Will the program result in the most good for the greatest number?
2. Does the emphasis on athletics and competition detract from the fulfillment of other, equally important needs?

3. How is winning placed as a priority in evaluating program and individual success?
4. Is there a classification system to equalize opportunities for success? Is the system sensitive to each participant's circumstances?
5. With reference to long-range outcomes, are the skills that receive primary emphasis ones that will have lifelong value?
6. Does the desire to excel in the activities of an athletic organization influence unnecessarily the emphasis of the recipient's physical education program?
7. Are the opportunities for the disabled to participate in sport programs substantially equal to those available to the nondisabled?

Summary

Opportunity in sport is not a new phenomenon for persons with disabilities. Among the early opportunities were those developed in response to the activity interests of veterans who became paralyzed in World War II. Only recently, however, have such opportunities become available to the handicapped under direct school sponsorship. Such opportunities are likely to increase in response to growing public awareness and assertiveness of the handicapped community. Consensus is growing that the school or agency that provides sport programs for the able-bodied but not for the disabled is in direct violation of Section 504 (federal civil rights legislation protecting persons with handicaps from arbitrary discrimination).

Participation guidelines can help the educator to determine when a handicapped student might safely and successfully participate in the regular sport program. Guidelines should also be developed that suggest ways of modifying selected activities so the handicapped athlete's participation neither jeopardizes her own nor anyone else's safety nor compromises the activity's integrity for participants.

Many specific organizations and athletic associations sponsor and promote sport opportunities for the handicapped. For individuals with spinal cord injury or cerebral palsy, classification systems based on handicap and achievement level foster equitable competition among athletes with similar degrees of disability.

A relatively recent trend is the emergence of state high school adapted athletic associations in response to the growing need for formal adapted sports participation opportunities that are under school sponsorship. At present, these associations often are administered apart from the state high school associations or leagues that sponsor athletic activities for nonhandicapped students. In all probability, many state adapted athletic associations will become integral to the state associations that govern athletics for the able-bodied. This absorption process will occur largely owing to recognition that state high school athletic associations, which provide for the able-bodied student, should not deny handicapped students an opportunity to benefit educationally from athletic experiences.

References

Alberts, C. L. Section 504 of the Rehabilitation Act and the Right to Participate in School Athletic Programs. *Educational Considerations* 11(1):23–26, 1984.

Anderson, N. E. An Athlete's Reflection. *Palaestra* 2(2):25–26, 1986.

Grube v. Bethlehem Area School District 550. Federal Supplement 418 (D. Penn. 1982).

Jones, J. The 1985 National Cerebral Palsy/Les Autres Games—A Director's Perspective. *Palaestra* 2(2):21–27, 1986.

Adapted Physical Education in the Future

Recognition of the educational rights of the disabled is becoming a significant issue for society. While much still needs to be done to provide appropriate education for persons with disabilities, much has been accomplished in recent years and times are indeed changing. The field of adapted physical education is in a state of transition and change. The profession's major responsibility is one of active participation in the change process, for any dynamic, viable profession must accept responsibility for initiating trends.

This chapter examines directions that the profession may take in coming years. In some instances, the seeds for change have already been sown and new directional emphases seem imminent.

A New Criterion for Program Effectiveness Must Be Recognized

Stein (1979, p. 6) states that "success and effectiveness of programs, activities, and efforts should be based upon numbers of students screened out of—not screened into—special programs." He suggests that the potential exists for successful integration of 90 to 95 percent of children with handicapping conditions into regular physical education programs and activities. This concept of integration includes a variety of program assignments from part-time placement in a regular program with some special assistance and modifications required to full-time placement in the regular mainstream program without special assistance.

The trend already begun is for more persons with disabilities to receive special education in less restrictive environments. At this time and in the future, educators must be watchful to ensure that children with disabilities are not indiscriminately "dumped" into the mainstream in a misguided effort to implement legal mandates. The quotation that opened this discussion emphasizes **screening.** Screening involves the careful process of identifying individual needs, then modifying instruction so that education occurs as close to the mainstream as possible. This process should emphasize the positive, and shield the student from overprotection.

To remove students with special needs from restrictive settings and place them in mainstream settings requires effective screening and considerable creativity and innovation. Merely rescheduling the child into a mainstream setting is not the challenge or intent of mainstreaming. The challenge is ensuring that the least restrictive alternative is achieved, because special services (but only as needed) can support the learner's special needs.

Effective screening requires the physical educator to play an active part in the screening and placement process. With few exceptions, specially prepared physical educators will administer assessments and make the value judgments that provide the individualized educational program (IEP) committee with data for proper screening and placement. The validity of data otherwise gathered may be questionable owing to the tester's limited comprehension of movement-centered curricula. Screening and placement should be based on objectively gathered and interpreted data. Subjective input, including observational and anecdotal information, can supplement objectively gathered data but should not substitute for the data base. Subjective input should be relied on as a last resort and only after a thorough perusal of available assessment tools fails to produce any that are appropriate for the student.

Guided by these criteria, adapted physical educators should chart a course to ensure that students are not indiscriminately "dumped" into the mainstream or placed in programs categorically by disability. The educator must accentuate the positive by recognizing the student's ability first, and then, through creative effort, finding ways to blunt the impact of the student's disability on the learning process.

Improved Cooperation Among Allied Professionals

Mandates that have influenced the current trends in special education, including adapted physical education, require that allied professionals work together. Today, allied professionals, including the school principal, regular physical educator, adapted physical educator, regular classroom teacher, special education teacher, school nurse, physical therapist, occupational therapist, corrective therapist, and therapeutic recreationalist, work side by side in meetings and individualized planning conferences. More than ever before, their collective expertise is now shared so the child's individual needs can be better understood and fulfilled (Figure 25.1).

As in the past, groups of allied professionals sometimes misperceive or misunderstand each other. Such feelings are often prompted by concern that one group may encroach on another's area of service or expertise. The physical therapist, for example, becomes concerned when she thinks that the adapted physical educator might want to perform physical therapy. The adapted physical educator becomes concerned that the occupational therapist is trying to teach physical education because the therapist was developing a child's manipulative skills through ball handling.

Most professional groups are concerned about *who* provides service in an area of expertise. Such concern is understandable and appropriate. It also is understandable that allied professionals whose missions are similar sometimes disagree about who should provide the service. Such professional issues may never be resolved fully, but through day-to-day contact and team planning for individualized education, allied professionals will discover new avenues of mutual understanding, respect, and trust. This positive trend should continue as teams of cooperative professionals provide the best possible education for each child.

Mainstreaming the Curriculum

In the past when handicapped children were placed in special classes according to disability, the logical outcome was that preservice and in-service teachers learned adaptive subject matter and teaching methods in special classes that dealt with one specific disability.

Today, handicapped children are no longer categorically isolated, but are assessed individually and placed according to developmental level and unique needs. This impetus for appropriate placement in or near the mainstream requires that teachers in mainstream settings be prepared to serve effectively children who have a wide variety of special needs.

Achieving better service in or near the mainstream means that preparation for special education and adapted physical education must become part of the regular

FIGURE 25.1. Cooperation is needed among professionals if a handicapped child's needs are to be met.

teacher curriculum. Stein (1977) suggests that if we are to mainstream children effectively, we must consider the logic of mainstreaming the curriculum that prepares teachers. This means that subject matter and adaptations should be integrated throughout the teacher curriculum, as opposed to being taught in special classes that unintentionally emphasize children's differences and disabilities. Teaching methods classes at the undergraduate level should be modified to include adapted components (e.g., How and when might a child with paraplegia owing to spinal cord injury be integrated effectively into a unit on movement education? How might a teacher identify or accommodate a learner with a hearing handicap?). Biomechanics classes should focus on the application of movement principles to persons with disabilities (e.g., What are the most efficient ways to get in and out of a wheelchair? What mechanical principles influence the efficiency of crutch or cane walking? How do prostheses affect balance?). Exercise physiology classes should focus on development and maintenance of fitness. Test and measurement classes should include units on special physical fitness and motor proficiency batteries. Classes in motor development should emphasize that the stages of human development are universal, irrespective of disability, and that the impact of a disability is on rate and potential for development, not on type or stage of development. In most instances, additional time in the total major should not be required to address adapted course material, but material now addressed in specific adapted courses could be offered instead in courses for all majors. The importance of adapted physical education will not diminish as the subject matter is absorbed into the mainstream of teacher preparation. On the contrary, its importance mandates that material be removed from a segregated context to facilitate a widespread understanding of how and when regular settings can be modified to meet special needs.

When this trend gathers momentum, college and university professors of adapted physical education will work with students who have elected an adapted emphasis, and will also serve as consultants for colleagues who are mainstreaming the curriculum for preservice and in-service teachers.

Evolving Responsibilities of Adapted and Regular Physical Education Teachers

As teacher preparation programs are broadened to include adapted curricula, teachers in regular settings who have completed these programs will be better able to modify settings to meet the unique needs of special students. When minor to moderate accommodations are necessary for safe and successful participation, the regular physical educator should be able to make these changes so the students can participate actively with able-bodied peers. In some instances, aides or special education assistants may be needed, but the regular physical education teacher will emerge as the primary physical education provider for most students with special needs.

Because many mildly and moderately handicapped students now enter the regular physical education setting, the adapted physical educator will have more time to spend with students whose special physical education needs are substantial. In many instances, the student's handicapping condition may be severe enough to require small group or one-on-one interaction. As the adapted physical educator's attention is focused on serving the severely handicapped, the educator often will serve as consultant to other health care professionals, and some of the educator's efforts will be perceived as therapeutic.

New Opportunities in Sports

Laws protecting the handicapped from arbitrary discrimination will result in more participation by handicapped students (when appropriate) on regular sport teams. When handicapping conditions prevent participation on the regular team and when team opportunities are available for the nonhandicapped, the providing agency is legally obligated to offer comparable opportunities to the disabled. Should teacher or coaching leadership in the latter programs constitute additional responsibility, the providing agency will compensate the teacher or coach in a manner comparable to compensation for coaching regular teams. To offer less would be in conflict with Section 504.

The Adapted Physical Educator as Resource Person

In response to commitments to recognize and tap the learning potential of children with special needs, many new roles are emerging for the adapted physical education specialist. While these roles may not require the specialist to teach directly, each role will positively affect how future adapted physical education will be taught.

Among the adapted physical educator's emerging roles, Stein (1979, pp. 10–11) cites these as representative. In addition to traditional teaching roles, the adapted physical education specialist will serve as consultant and resource person to regular physical educators, special education personnel, and elementary school classroom teachers. Increasingly, according to Stein, the resource specialist (consultant) in adapted physical education will do the following:

"Demonstrate and/or team teach for/with teachers and other personnel who need this type of assistance." In this capacity, the specialist works directly with the regular teacher in the motor development setting. The specialist will suggest and demonstrate ways to accommodate effectively students with special needs so they can participate safely and successfully in regular program activities. For example, the specialist may suggest ways to integrate an orthopedically handicapped student into a regular softball setting without compromising the activity's integrity for able-bodied participants. The disabled participant could bat from a tee, be granted additional strikes, ambulate shorter distances to be considered safe, or do all three. In the field, the disabled participant might tally an "out" against the opposition by cleanly fielding the ball, without error, before it stops rolling. For effective integration, these suggestions would be implemented periodically as needed in consort with the specialist. Between the specialist's visits, the regular teacher would implement the specialist's modifications.

"Conduct in-service training programs and activities for other school personnel." Periodically, the adapted physical education specialist should share new information or techniques with colleagues in other specialty areas. The specialist should attend adaptive conferences and continue to search out and evaluate the latest ideas, resources, and teaching aids for her colleagues.

"Help teachers obtain and make adapted devices and equipment for use with individual children." Often, children with special needs can participate in regular settings if equipment is modified to accommodate the child. A blind child can bowl with sighted peers if a guide rail is provided. The student who cannot hold a regular bowling ball can use a commercially available one with a retractable handle. A walker can be fitted with wheels so a child with neurological impairment or low motor skills can learn to roller skate. A croquet mallet or floor hockey stick can be affixed to one crutch of a crutch ambulator. A wheelchair can be equipped with a wedge seat, pommel, and chest belt to prevent extensor contractures from causing the student to slip out of the chair. Paddles or rackets can be taped onto hands that cannot manipulate striking implements. These are only a few of the ways in which the adapted specialist can assist the child's regular teacher to accommodate the child with special needs effectively.

"Identify assessment and evaluative instruments (and) batteries . . . as requested by school personnel." As more assessment instruments become available and as the assessment process becomes a more precise art and science, someone must remain abreast of these resources. The adapted specialist who understands disability and motor development should select appropriate instruments and construct meaningful test batteries for specific individuals. The specialist should also interpret results and recommend appropriate physical education services. When adapted specialists perform these services, they will become an integral part of staffings and individualized planning committees that write the physical and motor development portions of the child's IEP.

"Assist in task analysis for breaking down skill progressions and sequences so that they are most appropriate, applicable, and usable to individual students." Task analysis is the process by which individual motor skills are broken down into component parts. Through this process, the specific developmental stages through which the learner passes can be identified. Having identified the student's developmental stage in a particular skill, the teacher can then help the student to achieve the next stage.

Identification of the developmental stages in skill acquisition serves three important purposes: It promotes better understanding of the skill's acquisition, it serves as a basis for evaluation, and it functions as a curriculum by designating specifically what remains to be achieved.

As the significance of the task analysis approach to motor skill development is recognized, the adapted physical educator will be asked to identify developmental stages and to write performance criteria (objectives) so the child's achievements can be monitored.

"Be available for and take the initiative to provide public information, public relations, public education programs and activities." In the adapted physical education area, the specialist should become the advocate for parents of children with special needs, for the children, and for the teachers. Specialists will be called on to make presentations to parent, civic, and community groups and they will communicate often with individual parents. They also will prepare budgets and make presentations to the school board to request program support, and they may prepare grant proposals to ensure that monies from the state department of education are channeled to local districts to support adapted physical education efforts. In many instances, the specialist is the person who makes sure that the significance, accomplishments, and needs of the adapted program become part of the school and community consciousness.

These are a few of the foreseeable trends in adapted physical education. The forces that will affect special education, including adapted physical education, are many and complex and cannot always be predicted accurately. In the midst of trend setting and change, however, the adapted physical educator must accept the opportunity and obligation to act as a prime mover.

David Beaver, editor of *Palaestra: The Forum of Sport and Physical Education for the Disabled*, identifies programmatic directions of the future when he states:

"There remains a great deal to be accomplished in the years ahead. Especially, if we are to encourage those students with a disability to become fit, to increase their neuromuscular skills, to enhance their self esteem through increased meaningful physical activity while further encouraging their acceptance within the realm of their able-bodied peers. Physical education, therefore, has much to offer the individual with a disability in all such categories and must be maintained . . ." (1986, p. 6).

Summary

Forecasting the future is risky because there are many uncontrollable and unanticipated variables. Only time can test the validity of the predictions made in this chapter.

At present, nothing suggests that special education will remain *status quo.* Indeed, special services, including physical education, will continue to become more sophisticated as a result of recent legislation and the public's growing awareness.

In the future, almost all physical educators will be expected to be responsive to persons with special physical education needs, and mainstream physical education teachers will have increased responsibility for adapted physical education. As this shift in responsibility occurs, adapted physical education specialists will function primarily as facilitators and resource persons, whose direct teaching duties involve mainly the severely handicapped.

The number and variety of sport opportunities available to students with special needs will increase to be more nearly equal to those opportunities presently available to the able-bodied. The sports field already has created significant opportunities for disabled athletes.

The future of adapted physical education is bright and challenging. Professional opportunities for those willing to accept the challenge are growing. While the foregoing pages might suggest that adapted physical education has come of age, many challenges remain still.

References

Beaver, D. P. The Free Appropriate Public Education of All Handicapped Children. *Palaestra* 2(2):6–7, 1986.

Stein, J. U. Presentation delivered at Higher Education Leadership Conference in Developmental/ Adaptive Physical Education, Eden Prairie, Minn., December 1977.

———. The Mission and the Mandate: Physical Education, the Not So Sleeping Giant. *Education Unlimited,* June 1979.

Desirable Body Weights for Boys and Girls

Boys[a]
(Weight Expressed in Pounds)

Ht. (in.)	5 Yr	6 Yr	7 Yr	8 Yr	9 Yr	10 Yr	11 Yr	12 Yr	13 Yr	14 Yr	15 Yr	16 Yr	17 Yr	18 Yr	19 Yr	Ht. (in.)
38	34	34														38
39	35	35														39
40	36	36														40
41	38	38	38													41
42	39	39	39	39												42
43	41	41	41	41												43
44	44	44	44	44												44
45	46	46	46	46	46											45
46	47	48	48	48	48											46
47	49	50	50	50	50	50										47
48		52	53	53	53	53										48
49		55	55	55	55	55	55									49
50		57	58	58	58	58	58	58								50
51			61	61	61	61	61	61								51
52			63	64	64	64	64	64	64							52
53			66	67	67	67	67	68	68							53
54				70	70	70	70	71	71	72						54
55				72	72	73	73	74	74	74						55
56				75	76	77	77	77	78	78	80					56
57					79	80	81	81	82	83	83					57
58					83	84	84	85	85	86	87					58
59						87	88	89	89	90	90	90				59
60						91	92	92	93	94	95	96				60
61							95	96	97	99	100	103	106			61
62							100	101	102	103	104	107	111	116		62
63							105	106	107	108	110	113	118	123	127	63
64								109	111	113	115	117	121	126	130	64
65								114	117	118	120	122	127	131	134	65
66									119	122	125	128	132	136	139	66
67									124	128	130	134	136	139	142	67
68										134	134	137	141	143	147	68
69										137	139	143	146	149	152	69
70										143	144	145	148	151	155	70
71										148	150	151	152	154	159	71
72											153	155	156	158	163	72
73											157	160	162	164	167	73
74											160	164	168	170	171	74

[a]The following percentages of net weight have been added for clothing (shoes and sweaters not included): 35 to 64 pounds: 3.5 percent; 64 pounds and over: 2.0 percent.

Girls[a]
(Weight Expressed in Pounds)

Ht. (in.)	5 Yr	6 Yr	7 Yr	8 Yr	9 Yr	10 Yr	11 Yr	12 Yr	13 Yr	14 Yr	15 Yr	16 Yr	17 Yr	18 Yr	Ht. (in.)
38	33	33													38
39	34	34													39
40	36	36	36												40
41	37	37	37												41
42	39	39	39												42
43	41	41	41	41											43
44	42	42	42	42											44
45	45	45	45	45	45										45
46	47	47	47	48	48										46
47	49	50	50	50	50	50									47
48		52	52	52	52	53									48
49		54	54	55	55	56	56								49
50		56	56	57	58	59	61	62							50
51			59	60	61	61	63	65							51
52			63	64	64	64	65	67							52
53			66	67	67	68	68	69	71						53
54				69	70	70	71	71	73						54
55				72	74	74	74	75	77	78					55
56					76	78	78	79	81	83					56
57					80	82	82	82	84	88	92				57
58						84	86	86	88	93	96	101			58
59						87	90	90	92	96	100	103	104		59
60						91	95	95	97	101	105	108	109	111	60
61							99	100	101	105	108	112	113	116	61
62							104	105	106	109	113	115	117	118	62
63								110	110	112	116	117	119	120	63
64								114	115	117	119	120	122	123	64
65								118	120	121	122	123	125	126	65
66									124	124	125	128	129	130	66
67									128	130	131	133	133	135	67
68									131	133	135	136	138	138	68
69										135	137	138	140	142	69
70										136	138	140	142	144	70
71										138	140	142	144	145	71

[b]The following percentages of net weight have been added for clothing (shoes and sweaters not included): 35 to 65 pounds: 3.0 percent; 66 to 82 pounds: 2.5 percent; 83 pounds and over: 2 percent.

Walk-Jog-Run Pace Chart

Pace	Speed mph	Time for Various Distances (Min:Sec)					
		55 yd	110 yd	220 yd	440 yd	880 yd	1 mi
Slow walk	3	:38	1:15	2:30	5:00	10:00	20:00
Moderate walk	4	:28	:56	1:52	3:45	7:30	15:00
Fast walk	4.5	:25	:50	1:40	3:20	6:40	13:20
Slow jog	5	:22	:45	1:30	3:00	6:00	12:00
Moderate jog	6	:19	:38	1:15	2:30	5:00	10:00
Fast jog	7	:17	:33	1:05	2:09	4:17	8:34
Slow run	8	:15	:29	:57	1:54	3:47	7:34
Moderate run	9	:13	:25	:50	1:40	3:20	6:40
Fast run	10	:11	:22	:45	1:30	3:00	6:00

SOURCE: Used with permission: President's Council on Physical Fitness and Sports. Jogging/Running Guidelines. GPO number 907-798, (n. d.), p. 6.
NOTE: Use this chart to help anyone follow the basic jogging program provided here or any other exercise program that involves walking, jogging, or running. If the distance is known, timing over the distance will determine speed.

Competitive Classifications by Disability[1]

The classification system currently utilized for competition in sports for the disabled is the result of years of careful study and adaptation. The classifications are based upon the type of the disability, the degree of disability, and the functionality of the disability.

Amputee Classifications

The system is based on acquired and congenital amputations.

Abbreviations

AK = Above or through knee joint.
BK = Below knee, but through or above talocrural joint.
AE = Above or through elbow joint.
BE = Below elbow, but through or above wrist joint.

---

1. SOURCE: Competitive Classifications by Disability. *Palaestra* 1(2):56–57, Winter 1985. Used with permission.

Classification Code

Class A1 = Double AK
Class A2 = Single AK
Class A3 = Double BK
Class A4 = Single BK
Class A5 = Double AE
Class A6 = Single AE
Class A7 = Double BE
Class A8 = Single BE
Class A9 = Combined lower plus upper limb amputations.

Blind Classifications

B1

No light perception at all in either eye up to light perception, but inability to recognize objects or contours in any direction and at any distance.

B2

Ability to recognize objects or contours up to a visual acuity of 2/60 and/or a limitation of field of vision of 5 degrees.

B3

2/60 to 6/60 vision and/or field of vision between 5 and 20 degrees.

Cerebral Palsy Classifications

Class I

Severe involvement in all four limbs. Limited trunk control, unable to grasp a softball. Poor functional strength in upper extremities, necessitating the use of an electric wheelchair.

Class II

Severe to moderate quadriplegic, normally able to propel wheelchair with legs or if able, propels wheelchair very slowly with arms. Poor functional strength and severe control problems in the upper extremities.

Class III

Moderate quadriplegic, fair functional strength and moderate control problems in upper extremities and torso. Uses wheelchair.

Class IV

Lower limbs have moderate to severe involvement. Good functional strength and minimal control problems in the upper extremities and torso. Uses wheelchair.

Class V

Good functional strength and minimal control problems in upper extremities. May walk with or without aids, but for ambulatory support.

Class VI

Moderate to severe quadriplegic. Ambulates without walking aids, less coordination balance problems when running or throwing.

Class VII

Moderate to minimal hemiplegic. Good functional ability in nonaffected side. Walks-runs with a limp.

Class VIII

Minimally affected hemiplegic. May have minimal coordination problems. Able to run and jump freely. Has good balance.

Les Autres Classifications

L1

Wheelchair bound. Reduced functions of muscle strength and/or spasticity in throwing arm. Poor sitting balance.

L2

Wheelchair bound with normal function in throwing arm and poor to moderate sitting balance. Or reduced function in throwing arm, but good sitting balance.

L3

Wheelchair bound with normal arm function and good sitting balance.

L4

Ambulant with or without crutches and braces; or problems with the balance together with reduced function in throwing arms.

Note

An athlete is allowed to use orthosis or crutches if he so wishes. The throw can be done from a standstill or moving position in L4 and L5.

L5

Ambulant with normal arm function in throwing arm. Reduced function in lower extremities or balance problem.

L6

Ambulant with normal upper extremity function in throwing arm and minimal trunk or lower extremity disability. A participant in this class must be able to demonstrate a locomotor disability which clearly gives him/her a disadvantage in throwing events compared to able-bodied sports men/women.

Spinally Paralyzed Classifications

To compete in the wheelchair sports, athletes must have significant permanent neuromuscular-skeletal disability (spinal cord disorder, polio, amputation, etc.).

Class 1A

All cervical lesions with complete or incomplete quadriplegia who have involvement of both hands, weakness of triceps (up to and including grade 3 on testing scale) and with severe weakness of the trunk and lower extremities interfering significantly with trunk balance and the ability to walk.

Class 1B

All cervical lesions with complete or incomplete quadriplegia who have involvement of upper extremities but less than 1A with preservation of normal or good triceps (4 or 5 on testing scale) and with a generalized weakness of the trunk and lower extremities interfering significantly with trunk balance and the ability to walk.

Class 1C

All cervical lesions with complete or incomplete quadriplegia who have involvement of upper extremities but less than 1A with preservation of normal or good triceps (4 or 5 on testing scale) and normal or good finger flexion and extension (grasp and release) but without intrinsic hand function and with a generalized weakness of the trunk and lower extremities interfering significantly with trunk balance and ability to walk.

Class II

Complete or incomplete paraplegia below T1 down to and including T5 or comparable disability with total abdominal paralysis or poor abdominal muscle strength (0-2 on testing scale) and no useful trunk sitting balance.

Class III

Complete or incomplete paraplegia or comparable disability below T5 down to and including T10 with upper abdominal and spinal extensor musculature sufficient to provide some element of trunk sitting balance but not normal.

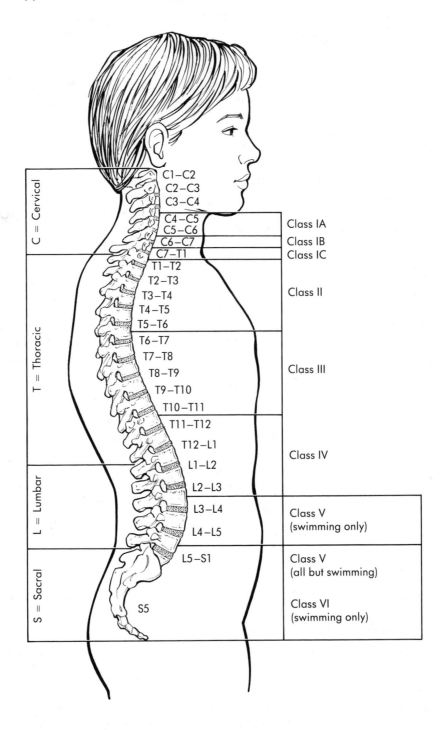

C = Cervical	C1–C2	
	C2–C3	
	C3–C4	
	C4–C5	Class IA
	C5–C6	
	C6–C7	Class IB
	C7–T1	Class IC
T = Thoracic	T1–T2	
	T2–T3	
	T3–T4	Class II
	T4–T5	
	T5–T6	
	T6–T7	
	T7–T8	
	T8–T9	Class III
	T9–T10	
	T10–T11	
	T11–T12	
	T12–L1	
	L1–L2	Class IV
	L2–L3	
L = Lumbar	L3–L4	Class V (swimming only)
	L4–L5	
S = Sacral	L5–S1	Class V (all but swimming)
	S5	Class VI (swimming only)

Class IV

Complete or incomplete paraplegia or comparable disability below T10 down to and including L2 without quadriceps or very weak quadriceps with a value up to and including 2 on the testing scale and gluteal paralysis.

Class V

Complete or incomplete paraplegia or comparable disability below L2 with quadriceps in grades 3-5.

Swimming Events Only

Class V

Complete or incomplete paraplegia or comparable disability below L2 with quadriceps in grades 3-5 and with up to and including 39 points on the point scale.

Class VI

Complete or incomplete paraplegia or comparable disability below L2 and with 40 points and above on the point scale.

Swimming Point Scale

Each of the muscle groups in the lower extremities (legs) is rated according to power on a scale of 1 through 5. There are 10 muscle groups in each leg or 20 in all. Therefore, a 1 rating on all 20 muscle groups would score 20 points. A 5 rating on all 20 muscle groups would score 100 points. Athletes can score anywhere along the point scale from 20 to 100.

Glossary

Acuity   Sharpness or clarity as related to seeing, hearing, or touching.

Acute   Disease or condition having a quick onset and of short duration.

Adam's position   Postural position used to determine if the condition of scoliosis is structural or functional. The child bends forward at the waist and allows the arms to hang in a natural downward position.

Adapted physical education   Modification of traditional physical education activities to allow students with handicapping conditions or low levels of physical or motor ability to participate safely, successfully, and with satisfaction.

Adventitious (acquired) deafness   Severe reduction in hearing as a result of illness or trauma after one is born with normal hearing.

Allergen   A substance that causes an allergic reaction (same as antigen).

Allergic rhinitis   Inflammation of the membrane of the nose caused by allergens and resulting in the common condition of hay fever.

Allergy   Hypersensitivity to substances that are inhaled, ingested, injected, or absorbed.

Amblyopia   A reduction in vision that is not correctable by glasses or contact lens and that is not caused by obvious structural or pathological eye defects.

Amelia   Absence of a limb or limbs at birth.

Amniocentesis   Process of removing amniotic fluid from the pregnant woman for the purpose of genetic analysis. The technique is used to detect birth defects.

Anemia   Condition in which the red blood cells do not have enough hemoglobin, thus creating a loss of energy and decreased ability to sustain effort.

Anorexia nervosa   An obsession with thinness, obtained from starving to become extremely thin. The individual, usually female, eats very little and continues to lose weight in spite of being dangerously underweight.

Anoxia   Insufficient amount of oxygen.

Antigen   A substance that produces an allergic reaction (same as allergen).

Aphasia   Difficulty in using or comprehending spoken language.

Apraxia   Difficulty or inability to perform skills that require purposeful motor or movement tasks.

Arthritis   Inflammation of and pain in the joints.

640

Arthrogryposis   A congenital condition characterized by rigid and curved joints; joints fixed in flexed position.

Asthma   A condition caused by violent contraction of the bronchial tubes because of allergies, exercise, or other irritations, and resulting in wheezing, coughing, and breathing difficulties.

Astigmatism   A curvature defect of the eye that impedes the focusing of rays from a luminous point at a single point on the retina but instead spreads the rays out as a line.

Asymmetrical tonic neck reflex   An infant reflex, which occurs when the head is turned, and causes extension of the arm on the face side and flexion of the arm on the skull side (called "fencer thrust").

Ataxia   Clinical term for the type of cerebral palsy characterized by defective muscular coordination, often involving balance difficulties that result from damage to the cerebellum, pons, or medulla.

Athetosis   Clinical term for the type of cerebral palsy characterized by slow, wormlike movements, and involving a continual change of position of the fingers, toes, hands, arms, and head.

Atonia   Lack of muscle control often found in cerebral palsied and Down syndrome infants ("floppy baby" syndrome).

Audiologist   A specialist who measures hearing ability.

Aura   A warning sensation (e.g., vertigo, noises, flashes of light, burning, or numbing) that precedes a convulsive seizure.

Autism   A disorder usually diagnosed before the child reaches 4 years of age and generally characterized by extreme withdrawal, language impairment, refusal to speak, obsessive demand to keep the environment stable, and monotonous repetition of motor actions.

Behavioral objectives   Statements of conditions, actions, and criteria that have not been mastered by the student. These objectives are directly related to long-term or annual goals.

Behavior modification   A systematic approach using methods designed to alter observable behaviors, including increasing, decreasing, extending, restricting, and maintaining behaviors.

Bilateral   Pertaining to or affecting both sides of the body.

Binocular   Using both eyes to see an object, thus fusing two images into one.

Blind   Cannot see a bright light from 3 ft away.

Blindness   Legal definition: acuity of 20/200 or less in the better eye with corrective lens, or restriction of the width of the visual field to an angle no greater than 20 degrees.

Body image   Ideas and feelings that individuals have about their bodies and the relationship of their body parts.

Body righting   Primitive infant reflex that enables segmental rotation of the trunk and hips when the head is turned.

Borderline mentally handicapped   Those individuals who possess an IQ of 70 to 85. They are not considered legally handicapped.

Bronchospasm   Spasmodic contraction of smooth muscle surrounding the bronchial tubes caused by allergic reaction; directly related to an asthmatic attack.

Bulimia   An obsession with thinness, obtained from vomiting and using laxatives to remove food from the body before it is digested. Often called binge and purge behavior.

Cataract   A condition in which the normally clear eye becomes cloudy or opaque.

Catheter   A tube inserted in the bladder through the urethra to allow urine to drain from the body.

Central deafness   An abnormality of the central nervous system that prevents one from hearing, although the hearing apparatus is functionally normal.

Cephalocaudal development   Gross motor development beginning with the head and progressing down the axial skeleton to the feet.

Cerebral palsy   A condition characterized by lack of control of voluntary body movement and caused by damage to the brain. The condition is nonprogressive, and occurs in infancy and childhood.

Chondromalacia patella   Abnormal softness of the cartilage of the kneecap.

Chromosomes   Small rod-shaped or v-shaped bodies that appear in the nucleus of a cell during cell division and contain the genes, or hereditary factors, of the cell. Humans normally have 46 chromosomes comprised of 22 pairs of autosomes and 2 sex chromosomes. A common chromosome abnormality is Down syndrome.

Chronic   A condition having gradual onset and long duration.

Cleft palate   A birth defect resulting in an opening in the front portion of the roof of the mouth.

Cochlea   A spiral tube, resembling a snail shell, located in the inner ear. It transmits sounds to the cochlear nerve.

Colostomy   A surgical opening in the intestine, which allows fecal matter to pass into an external collection bag.

Conductive hearing loss   Loss of function of the organs of the ear to transmit sound to the inner ear. Most conditions are greatly improved by use of a hearing aid.

Congenital   Present at birth.

Contracture   Abnormal shortening of a muscle owing to extreme lack of use or paralysis; commonly results from spastic cerebral palsy, cerebral vascular accident (stroke), or spinal cord injury (paraplegia).

Corrective therapy   In cooperation with a physician, a corrective therapist applies principles, tools, techniques, and psychology of medically oriented physical education to assist individuals with various physical and mental conditions to accomplish prescribed treatment objectives in rehabilitation or habilitation programs.

Coxa plana   A degeneration of the head of the femur (commonly called Legg-Calve-Perthes disease).

Criterion-referenced test   Measures a student's performance compared with a preestablished, behaviorally stated criterion. These tests are particularly useful in evaluating special populations to which available norms are not applicable.

Cystic fibrosis   An inherited condition that is generally fatal in childhood; characterized by over-production of mucus, which causes progressive lung damage, and by impaired absorption of fat and protein. Youngsters become less able to exercise and have frequent respiratory symptoms such as coughing and wheezing.

Deaf   No measurable hearing (90 dB loss).

Developmental approach   Matching instruction to ability, as measured by developmental milestones.

Developmental period   The time when structural growth begins and ends, from birth to approximately 18 to 20 years.

Diabetes mellitus   A disorder of the pancreas characterized by inadequate production of insulin, which leads to high levels of sugar in the blood. Two basic types of diabetes mellitus are identified: juvenile onset (type I) and mature onset (type II).

Diplopia   Double vision, or the seeing of two images, when the eyes are focused on one object.

Directionality   Feeling or perception of direction in space.

Direct service   Instructional opportunities provided for students with handicapping conditions by certified teachers. Physical education is a direct service. Recreation and physical or occupational therapy are not direct services.

Discrimination   The intellectual ability to determine variations in sensory stimuli.

Disinhibition   A problem of staying on task, with random shifts in paying attention and daydreaming.

Distractibility   Objects or situations that cause a student to lose concentration. Some common distractions are extraneous noises, bright colors, toys or equipment other than those the student is working with, other students or instructors, and especially, new adults.

Dorsiflexion   Bending the foot upward.

Down syndrome   A condition resulting from a chromosomal abnormality. Characteristics commonly include mental retardation (IQ between 20 and 55); abnormal shortness of hands, feet, trunk, arms, and legs; hyperflexibility; and frequently, congenital heart defects.

Duchenne muscular dystrophy   A condition that destroys voluntary muscle fiber, which is replaced by fat and connective tissue. Inherited by males, the condition usually causes death before age 25. Also called pseudohypertrophic muscular dystrophy.

Ductus arteriosus   A fetal artery between the aorta and the pulmonary artery fails to close, resulting in an abnormal mixing of oxygenated and unoxygenated blood in the newborn.

Dwarfism   A hereditary, congenital disturbance of growth and maturation, which causes inadequate bone formation and results in abnormally shortened limbs, normal trunk, small face, and lordosis.

Dyslexia   Neurological dysfunction usually causing a serious reading problem.

Dysrhythmia   A lack of ability to achieve and maintain rhythmic performance.

Educable mentally handicapped (EMH)   *See* Mildly mentally handicapped.

Effusion   Filling of a body part with fluids.

Electrocardiograph   An instrument used to record heart rates; also called ECG and EKG.

Encephalitis   An acute viral infection causing high body temperatures and severe inflammation of the brain. A common cause of mental retardation, cerebral palsy, and convulsive disorders.

Epilepsy   An involuntary increase in electrical impulses in the brain, which results in seizures; caused by damage to the brain or by inherited factors. Epilepsy is now more appropriately called *seizure disorder* or *convulsive disorder.*

Equilibrium reactions   The innate ability to maintain an upright position when the center of gravity is moved suddenly out of its base of support.

Etiology   The study or understanding of the cause of a disease or condition.

Extinction   A behavior management technique involving removal of reinforcers that previously followed the behavior. The technique may also involve removal of the individual from the activity or area.

Extrinsic   Coming from the outside.

Factors   Chemical agents that cause blood to coagulate. Factor VII or IX is usually missing in a male who has hemophilia.

Fading   The process of gradually removing assistance when helping a student perform a task or learn a skill.

Flaccid (flak-sid) paralysis   Condition characterized by extreme weakness or absence of muscle tone.

Genu recurvatum   Hyperextension of the knee, causing improper posture.

Genu valgum   Knock-knee.

Genu varum   Bowleg.

Glaucoma   An increase of fluid pressure inside the eyeball causing decreased vision and potential blindness.

Goal   An annual or long-term observable behavior (e.g., to improve explosive leg power to the 30th percentile).

Goal ball   A highly competitive game played by blind participants using a sound-emitting, air-filled ball.

Grand mal   A form of convulsive seizure that includes a tonic phase (stiffening), a clonic phase (violent, whole body contractions), and a recovery phase (postictal). The individual remembers or feels nothing during the seizure.

Heart murmur   Sound made by backward flow of blood through defective heart valves.

Hemiplegia   Paralysis of one side of the body as occurs in a cerebral vascular accident (stroke), or affecting one side of the body as in cerebral palsy.

Hemophilia   Inherited condition affecting males only and characterized by the absence of blood coagulation factor VII or IX, thus causing the blood not to coagulate.

Hydrocephalus   A condition that develops when spinal fluid accumulates in cerebral ventricles. If not immediately and continuously drained (i.e., shunted), fluid accumulation can produce enlargement of the infant's skull and possible brain damage.

Hyperactivity   A condition in children in which they always seem to be in motion. Sitting or standing still for any length of time is difficult or impossible. Such children routinely interfere with other children.

Hyperglycemia   Abnormally high level of blood sugar, commonly associated with diabetes mellitus and indicating a need for insulin.

Hyperopia   Farsightedness, usually correctable with glasses or contact lenses.

Hyperreactivity   Allergic response to an external or internal allergen.

Hypertrophy   Increased size or enlargement of a body part or organ.

Hyperventilation Abnormally prolonged, rapid, and deep breathing, frequently used as a test procedure in the medical diagnosis of petit mal seizures.

Hypoxia Insufficient amount of oxygen, also called anoxia.

Idiopathic Denoting a disease or condition of unknown cause.

Individualized educational program (IEP) A program specially designed to meet the educational needs (including physical and motor needs) of a specific child.

Innate response system Natural, primitive reflexes that the human infant possesses at or shortly after birth.

Insulin Hormone produced in the beta cells of the islets of Langerhans in the pancreas. Insulin allows glucose to pass through cell membranes. Without insulin, the cells do not receive appropriate amounts of glucose and cease to function.

Intrinsic Coming from inside the body.

Isometric exercise Muscle contraction without movement of body parts, often used in rehabilitation when movement is not indicated but muscle strength is desired. Also called muscle setting.

Isotonic exercise Muscle contraction with body part movement through a range of motion.

Kinesthesis Awareness of body position in space as indicated by proprioceptors found in muscles, joints, and tendons.

Kyphosis Increased thoracic curve (also called humpback).

Laterality An internal awareness of both sides of the body.

Least restrictive environment The best possible learning environment for an individual with handicapping conditions, preferably an environment shared with the nonhandicapped.

Legg-Calve-Perthes disease *See* Coxa plana.

Lordosis An increase in the forward curvature of the lumbar region of the spine (also called swayback), and often causing lower back pain.

Mainstreaming Placement of students with handicapping conditions in traditional classes with nonhandicapped students.

Manual communication A technique, including fingerspelling and sign language, used by hearing impaired individuals.

Meningitis (bacterial) A highly contagious disease affecting the covering of the spinal cord (meninges), and often leading to permanent spinal cord damage.

Meningocele A protrusion of the covering of the spinal cord (i.e., meninges) through an abnormal opening in the vertebra. The spinal cord does not protrude outward, and physical impairment is slight.

Mental age Level of mental development measured by standardized IQ tests.

Mental retardation Significantly below average general intellectual functioning (less than 70 IQ) existing concurrently with deficits in adaptive behavior, all manifested during the developmental period.

Mildly mentally handicapped (EMH) Individuals with IQ between 50 and 70, who also exhibit maladaptive behavior. Includes approximately 89 percent of all mentally handicapped individuals.

Mobility training Specialized approach to teaching blind individuals travel techniques. Use of the long cane is often emphasized.

Modeling Demonstration of a task, skill, or desirable behavior for the benefit of another student.

Moderately mentally handicapped (TMH) IQ between 35 and 50. Includes approximately 6 percent of all mentally handicapped individuals. Approximately 40 percent of all TMH students are Down syndrome children.

Mononucleosis An acute infectious disease caused in 90 percent of cases by the Epstein-Barr virus, and characterized by fever, malaise, sore throat, and liver dysfunction. Enlargement of the spleen can occur.

Monoplegia Neurological involvement of one limb, common in cerebral palsy.

Moro reflex Protective opening and closing of an infant's arms and legs when a loud noise is heard. Also called "startle reflex."

Muscle setting Tensing of a muscle without movement of body parts. Often used when a limb is isolated in a plaster cast.

Muscle testing A subjective technique used by physical therapists to evaluate muscle strength and performance.

Muscular dystrophy An inherited disease characterized by loss of muscle fiber. The most common and destructive type is Duchenne, or pseudohypertrophic muscular dystrophy. (*See also* Duchenne muscular dystrophy.)

Myelomeningocele The most serious type of spina bifida in which the spinal cord protrudes into a sac on the surface of the back, thus causing paralysis or lower extremity impairment. Bowel and bladder control are affected.

Myopia Nearsightedness.

Neonatal Time period between birth and 1 month.

Neurosis A psychological disorder that can include anxiety, obsessions, phobias, or hysteria.

Normalization Providing opportunities for individuals with handicapping conditions to be involved directly with nonhandicapped peers; can include activities of everyday life that are consistent with the norms and patterns of mainstream society.

Nystagmus Uncontrollable rhythmic jerking of the eyeballs when turned sharply sideways.

Obesity An increase in body weight beyond the limitation of skeletal and physical requirement; a result of an excessive accumulation of adipose tissue (fat) in the body.

Orthopedics Branch of surgery including the practice of straightening deformed or injured body parts by use of braces or exoskeletal devices.

Otitis media Chronic inflammation of the middle ear, which can lead to balance or coordination problems.

Parachute reflex A small child's automatic protective extension of the arms when he falls suddenly forward or to the side. This reflex is often delayed in children with cerebral palsy.

Paraplegia Paralysis or involvement of the legs and lower trunk caused by brain damage or spinal cord injury, commonly in the lumbar region.

Perception A process involving the reception of sensory input and converting the information in the brain to data for use or memory storage.

Perseveration An undesirable behavior characterized by persistent repetion of a meaningless, irrelevant, or inappropriate word, phrase, or movement.

Petit (pet tee) mal A mild form of seizure characterized by sudden, brief blackouts of consciousness (hardly more than a few seconds long) followed by immediate recovery. Also called absence seizures, this type of seizure occurs mostly in childhood and adolescence.

Phobia Any persistent abnormal dread or fear.

Polyarticular rheumatoid arthritis An arthritic development affecting all or most of the body joints.

Positive reinforcer A reward given when appropriate behavior is observed.

Positive supporting reaction Neonatal reflex that causes the legs to extend and the feet to point downward when the young child is bounced on the feet.

Profoundly mentally retarded IQ between 1 and 20. Includes less than 2 percent of all mentally handicapped individuals. Of that 2 percent, most have other serious handicapping conditions, including seizures.

Prognosis Prediction of the probable outcome of a disease or condition.

Prosthesis An artificial appliance or limb.

Protective extensor thrust *See* Parachute reflex.

Pseudohypertrophy An increase in size of a body part without true muscle hypertrophy. Commonly observed in the calf muscles of a boy with Duchenne muscular dystrophy.

Psychogenic deafness No sound is heard, although the hearing organs are normal; often the result of an emotional response.

Psychomotor seizures A seizure classification characterized by inappropriate actions, irrelevant speech, and random ambulation.

Quadriplegia Paralysis or involvement of both arms and both legs.

Rehabilitation Act of 1973, Section 504 Civil rights legislation for the handicapped, which states that benefits or services cannot be denied to individuals with handicapping conditions. Accessibility to public buildings and programs is ensured.

Reinforcement Following a desired behavior, the instructor responds positively so the behavior is likely to recur.

Related services Special services that are needed to fulfill a handicapped student's educational, physical, emotional, or social needs. Physical, occupational, and speech therapy are examples of related services.

Retardation *See* Mental retardation.

Rheumatic heart disease A viral infection that, if uncontrolled, could cause heart valve damage.

Rheumatoid arthritis A condition characterized by inflammation of the joints, usually accompanied by deformity of the hands and fingers.

Rhinitis The common cold, including inflammation of the nasal passages and mucous membranes.

Righting reflexes Automatic or involuntary reactions of an infant or small child to regain original position when suddenly moved or pushed.

Rigidity Classification of cerebral palsy involving extreme difficulty when attempting limb movement.

Rubella (German measles) In children, a mild viral infection lasting 3 to 4 days. In pregnant women during the first trimester, the infection is serious and produces fetal abnormalities including defects of the heart, eyes, brain, bone, and ears.

Schizophrenia Abnormal personality accompanied by less than adequate contact with reality.

Scoliosis Lateral deviation of the spine in the shape of an "S," reverse "S," "C," or reverse "C." Deviation can be caused either by functional or structural problems. Functional deviations can be corrected by physician prescribed programs implemented by a physical educator.

Section 504 *See* Rehabilitation Act of 1973.

Sensory input All information received by the body through the senses, that is, seeing, hearing, kinesthesis, and vestibular and tactual input.

Sensory-motor response A combination of sensory input, brain integration and interpretation, and motor output. Feedback completes the total perceptual-motor act.

Severely mentally handicapped IQ between 20 and 35. Includes less than 4 percent of all mentally handicapped individuals. The severely mentally handicapped are considered dependent; they function at a mental age of 3 to 5 years.

Shaping Reinforcement of small progressive steps that lead to a desired learner behavior.

Short-term instructional objectives Statements of observable criteria used to meet annual or long-term goals, always incorporated in an individualized educational program (IEP).

Sickle-cell anemia A severe inherited form of anemia, occurring mainly among Blacks and characterized by fragile, sickle-shaped red blood cells. Sickle cell "trait," a much milder condition, occurs when only one parent passes on the sickle-cell gene to the child.

Somatotype A particular type of body composition (i.e., ectomorph, mesomorph, or endomorph).

Spastic Cerebral palsy classification characterized by hard, jerky, uncontrolled movements. An increased stretch reflex is present and muscle contractures are common. The greatest percentage of individuals with CP fall into this classification.

Spatial relations Identification of objects in space as they relate to the body.

Spina bifida A congenital opening in the vertebral column, with the protrusion of the meninges. If the meninges do not protrude, the type is called occulta.

Strabismus A condition characterized by the eyes not being directed simultaneously to the same object as a result of an imbalance of the muscles of the eyeball. Crossed or deviated eyes are examples.

Symmetrical tonic neck reflex An infant reflex in which the arms flex when the head is hyperflexed; also, when the head is hyperextended, the legs will flex. The locomotor process of creeping becomes extremely difficult when this reflex persists beyond the normal time frame of infancy. Cerebral palsied children often have this difficulty.

Tactile Pertaining to touch.

Talipes equinus Walking on the toes or front portion of the foot.

Talipes valgus Walking on the inside of the foot.

Talipes varus Walking on the outside of the foot.

Tetrology of Fallot (fal-oh) Congenital heart defect involving four different defects.

Time out A behavior modification technique of excluding or removing a child from an activity, or denying the opportunity to participate for a specific period of time.

Tinnitus A ringing or roaring sound in the ears.

Total communication A communication technique used by the hearing impaired, which includes signing, fingerspelling, speech reading, and speaking.

Trainable mentally handicapped (TMH) *See* Moderately mentally handicapped.

von Willebrandt's disease A congenital bleeding disease inherited as an autosomal dominant trait, characterized by a prolonged bleeding time, and resulting from a deficiency of coagulation Factor VIII.

Index